Presented To:

Lisa Hughes

For making the Golden West 2009 ISP Conference such a great event.

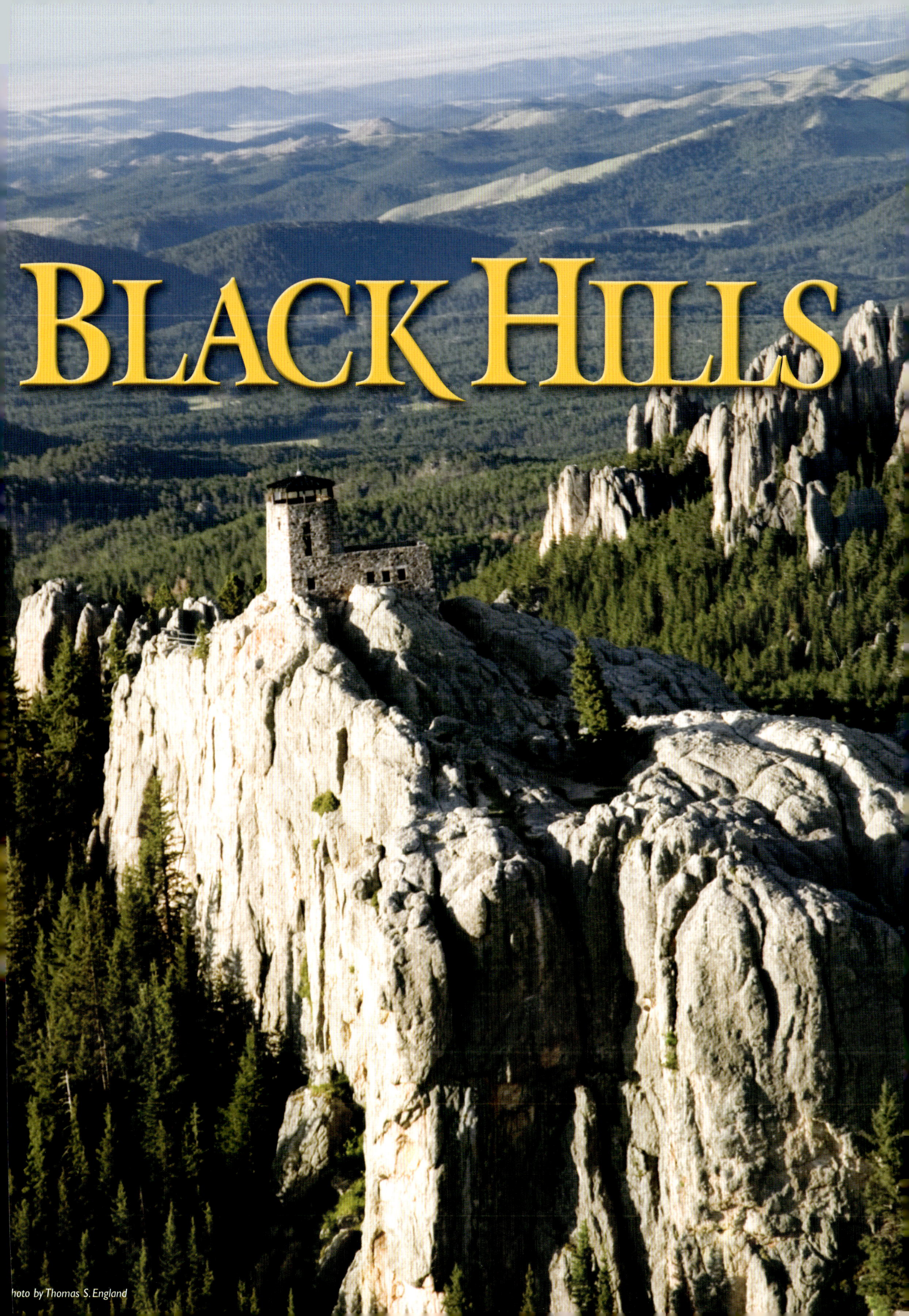

hoto by Thomas S. England

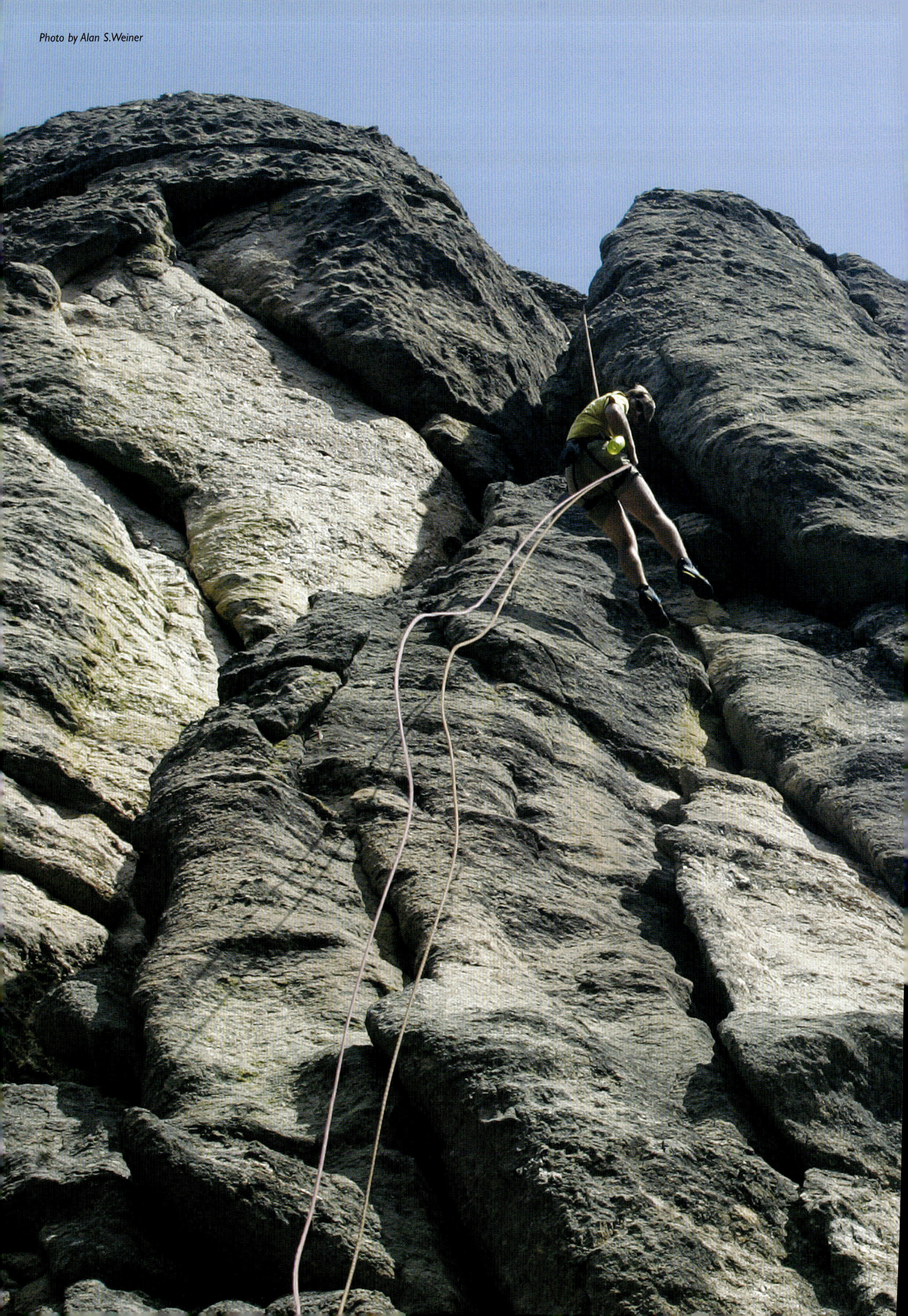

Photo by Alan S.Weiner

Black Hills

Beyond All Expectations.

A Photographic Journey

Photo by Eric Francis

BLACK HILLS

Beyond All Expectations.

Editor .... Rob Levin
Publisher .... Barry Levin
Associate Publisher .... Bob Sadoski
Chamber of Commerce Liaison .... Jim McKeon
Senior Project Director .... Renée Peyton
Project Director .... Cheryl Sadler
Photo Editor .... Jill Dible
Project Coordinator .... Muriel Diguette
Writers .... Kimberly DeMeza, Rena Distasio,
.... Grace Hawthorne, Regina Roths
Copy Editor .... Bob Land
Book Design .... Compòz Design, LLC
Jacket Design .... Kevin Smith
Prepress .... Vickie Berdanis
Photographers .... Thomas S. England, Eric Francis,
.... Doug Henderson, Dennis Keim,
.... Rodger Slott, Johnny Sundby,
.... Alan Weiner, Joleen Zoller

Printed and bound in Korea

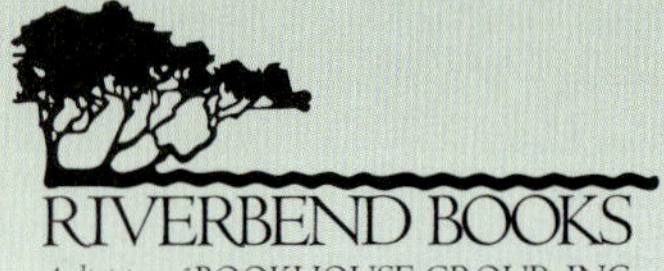

RIVERBEND BOOKS
A division of BOOKHOUSE GROUP, INC.

Published by Riverbend Books
an Imprint of Bookhouse Group, Inc.
818 Marietta Street, NW
Atlanta, Georgia 30318
www.riverbendbooks.net
404.885.9515

ISBN: 1-883987-26-1

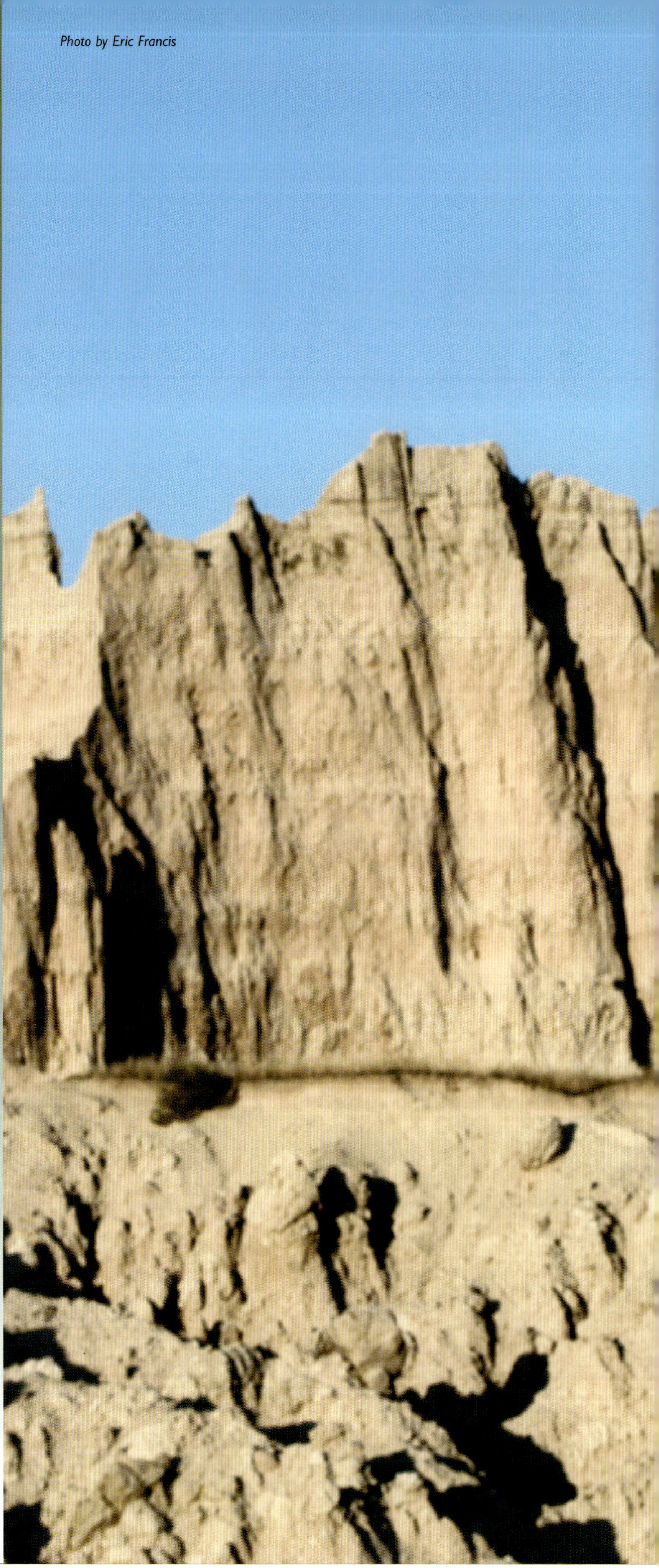

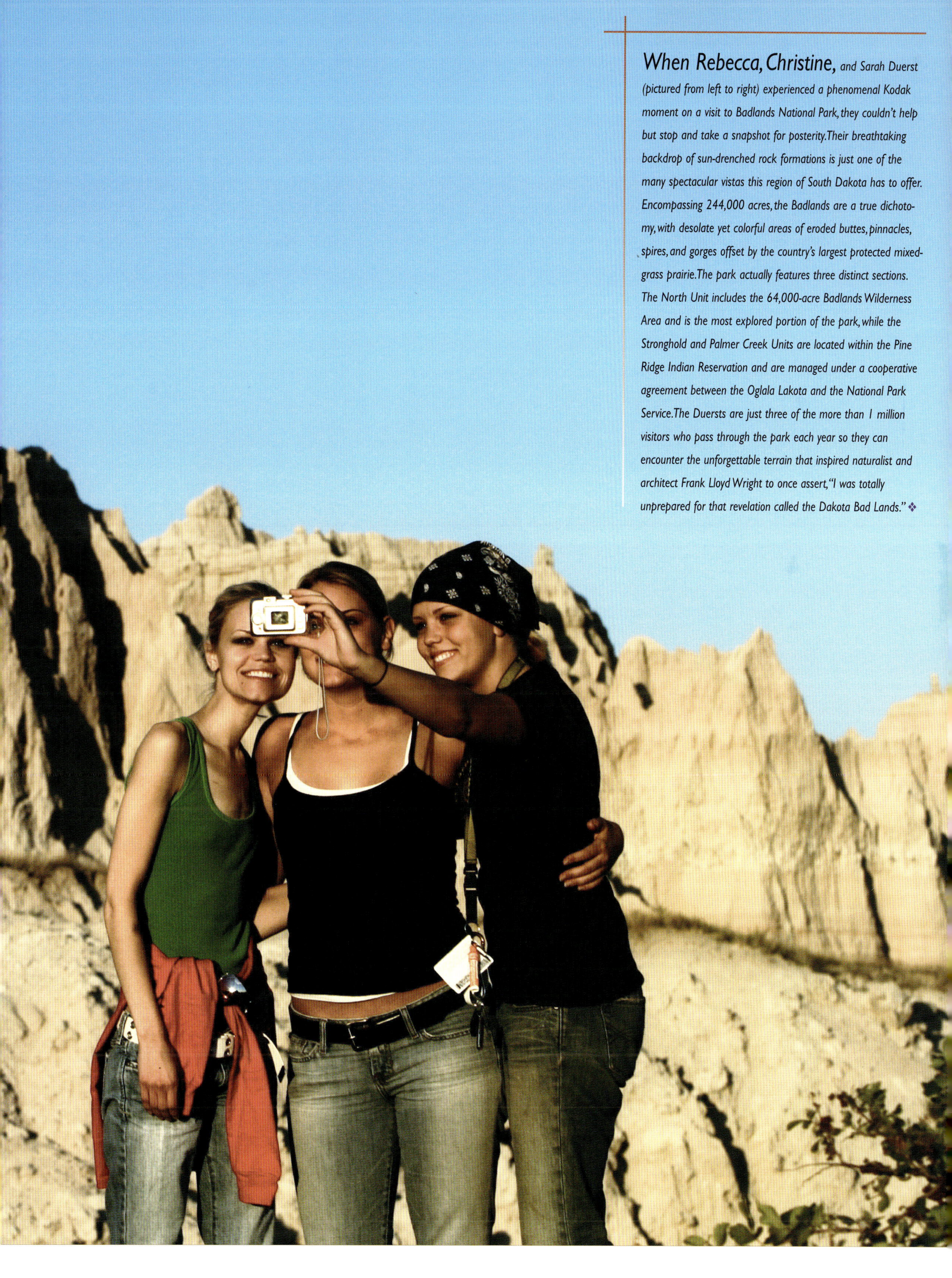

When Rebecca, Christine, *and Sarah Duerst (pictured from left to right) experienced a phenomenal Kodak moment on a visit to Badlands National Park, they couldn't help but stop and take a snapshot for posterity. Their breathtaking backdrop of sun-drenched rock formations is just one of the many spectacular vistas this region of South Dakota has to offer. Encompassing 244,000 acres, the Badlands are a true dichotomy, with desolate yet colorful areas of eroded buttes, pinnacles, spires, and gorges offset by the country's largest protected mixed-grass prairie. The park actually features three distinct sections. The North Unit includes the 64,000-acre Badlands Wilderness Area and is the most explored portion of the park, while the Stronghold and Palmer Creek Units are located within the Pine Ridge Indian Reservation and are managed under a cooperative agreement between the Oglala Lakota and the National Park Service. The Duersts are just three of the more than 1 million visitors who pass through the park each year so they can encounter the unforgettable terrain that inspired naturalist and architect Frank Lloyd Wright to once assert, "I was totally unprepared for that revelation called the Dakota Bad Lands."* ❖

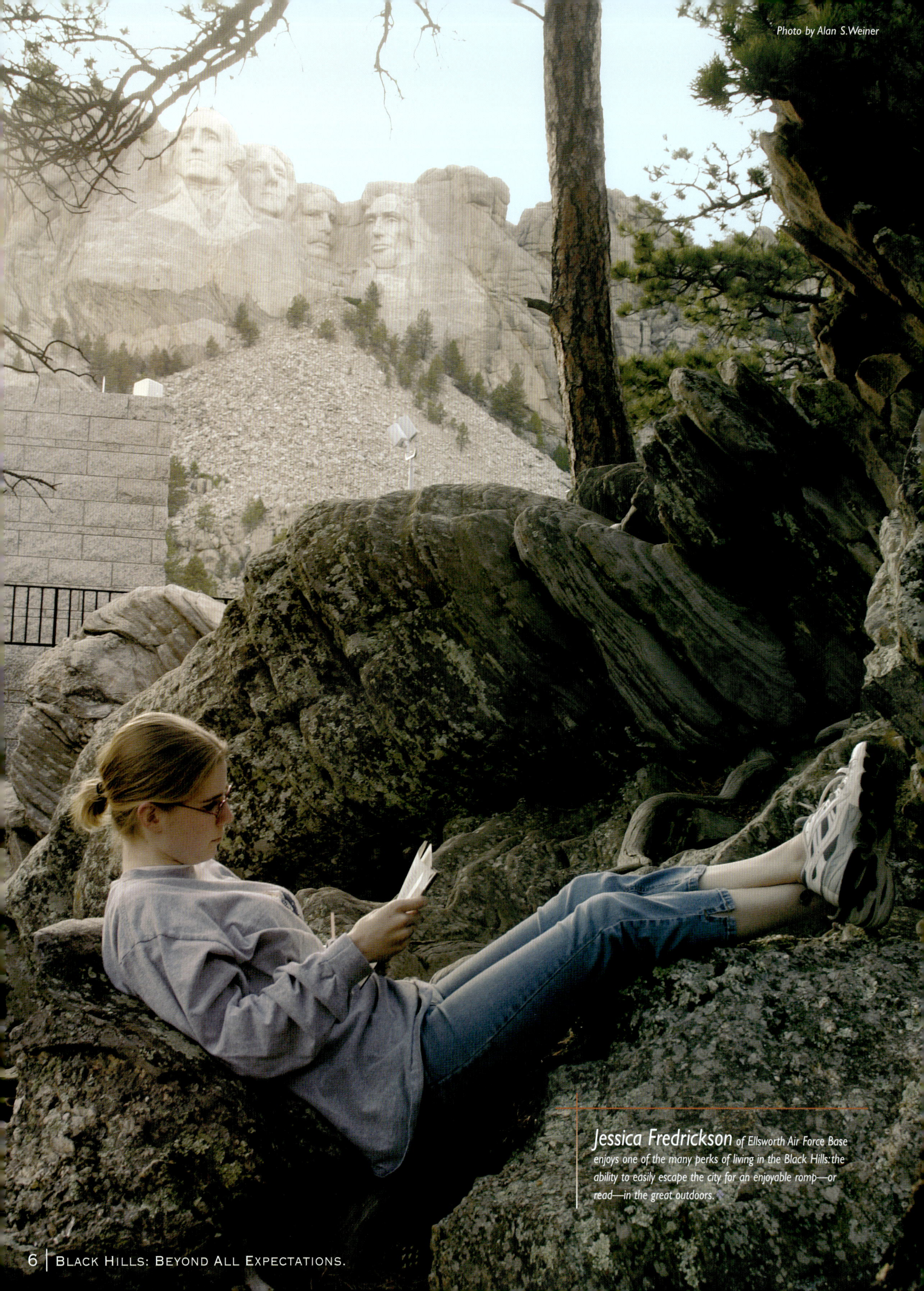

Jessica Fredrickson *of Ellsworth Air Force Base enjoys one of the many perks of living in the Black Hills: the ability to easily escape the city for an enjoyable romp—or read—in the great outdoors.*

Contents

Photo by Dennis Keim

They say Spearfish is Naturally

Inviting. With the Black Hills as its backyard and wildlife as neighbors, Spearfish attracts outdoor enthusiasts, as well as people looking for an informal and comfortable lifestyle. A leisurely drive through Spearfish and surrounding areas reveals many treats for the eyes. The natural scenery of the Black Hills National Forest, Spearfish Canyon, or the three mountains that surround the city is breathtaking, and some residents' proud display of what it means to live in America is heartwarming. ❖

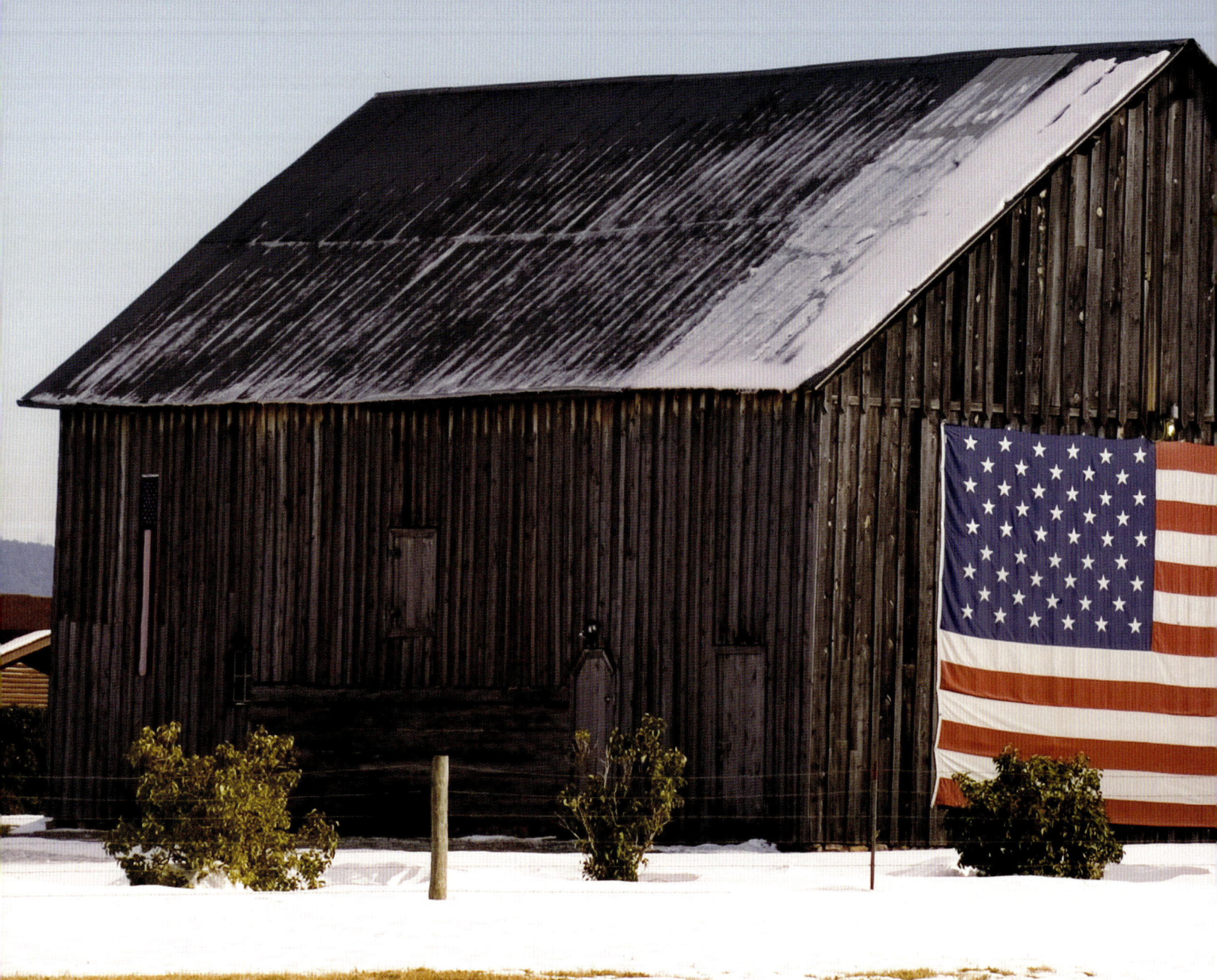

FOREWORD

Welcome to the Black Hills of South Dakota, a place so high, wide, and handsome that it invariably attracts millions of visitors and thousands of new residents each and every year.

This is a place *Beyond All Expectations.*—where men carve mountains and people are free to dream big dreams. With more than a million acres of creek-carved canyons, mountain meadows, and towering ponderosa pine forests, coupled with the highest concentration of parks, monuments, and memorials in America, you'll discover an emerald oasis surrounded by a vast sea of prairie.

This is where the West begins. From the dark depths of Wind and Jewel Caves to the four faces of freedom high atop Mount Rushmore National Memorial, the Black Hills are home to a diverse array of free-roaming wildlife, outstanding adventures, and friendly residents who know their neighbors and still understand the warmth of western hospitality.

A mountain oasis approximately 110 miles long by 40 miles wide, the Black Hills hold a wealth of visitor accommodations, restaurants, shopping, and attractions rivaling any destination in the world. Play in our parks, climb our pine-clad cliffs, visit our museums, fish our lakes and streams, ride our bike paths, and enjoy the myriad of recreational opportunities that await you in this place we call "Real. America. Up Close."

Quality of life and commerce go hand-in-hand here in a place blessed with abundant natural resources, great airline service, cutting-edge technologies, exceptional educational institutions, and people who take pride in their collective past while striving for the promise of tomorrow.

As you review this wonderful work, come to know those individuals, businesses, and communities that have flourished in the shadows of these ancient mountains. Gain a greater understanding of the beauty of the Black Hills and the indomitable spirit of those who inhabit this region. From the stark moonscape of the Badlands to the highest reaches of Crazy Horse Memorial, celebrate with us what it's like to live, work, play, and pray in a land like no other—a land known as the Black Hills.

Jim McKeon
President, Rapid City Area Chamber of Commerce

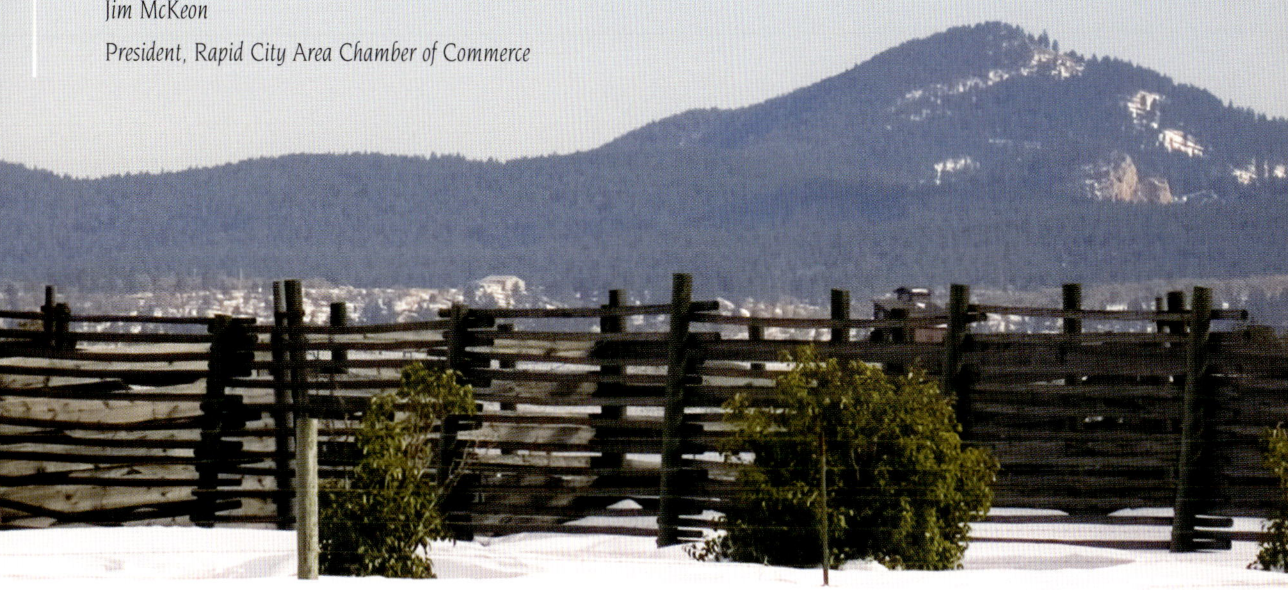

Heritage Sponsors

We proudly note our Heritage Sponsors who have stepped up to support both Riverbend publications about the Black Hills region.

Bangs, McCullen, Butler, Foye, & Simmons, L.L.P.

Behavior Management Systems

Black Hills Corporation–Black Hills Power

Black Hills Orthopedic & Spine Center, P.C.

Black Hills Regional Eye Institute

Black Hills Workshop

Dean Kurtz Construction

Holiday Inn Rushmore Plaza Hotel & Conference Center

National American University

Pete Lien & Sons, Inc.

Radiology Associates, Prof. LLC

Radisson Hotel Rapid City/Mt. Rushmore

Regional Health

South Dakota School of Mines and Technology

The Hotel Alex Johnson

Wells Fargo Bank

West River Electric

Western Dakota Technical Institute

Westjet Air Center

Wyss Associates, Inc.

Photo by Alan S.Weiner

In the Black Hills, the heartland of America, patriotism is a bona fide state of mind, as demonstrated by the proud waving of the red, white, and blue at the annual Black Hills Roundup PRCA Rodeo. With its storied history as part of the Old West, this region is the epitome of the American spirit in its sense of adventure, advancement, and exploration. Once the hunting grounds for numerous American Indian tribes, the Black Hills became a hotbed of activity when European settlers began moving west in the hopes of finding gold and other riches among the land's abundant resources. Throughout the centuries, the Black Hills were the backdrop for battles, struggles, hardships, and eventually prosperity. Today, the area's residents look to the future with great optimism but never forget the tales of the people who made the region what it is today—a thriving locale that has played an integral role in the development of this great country. ❖

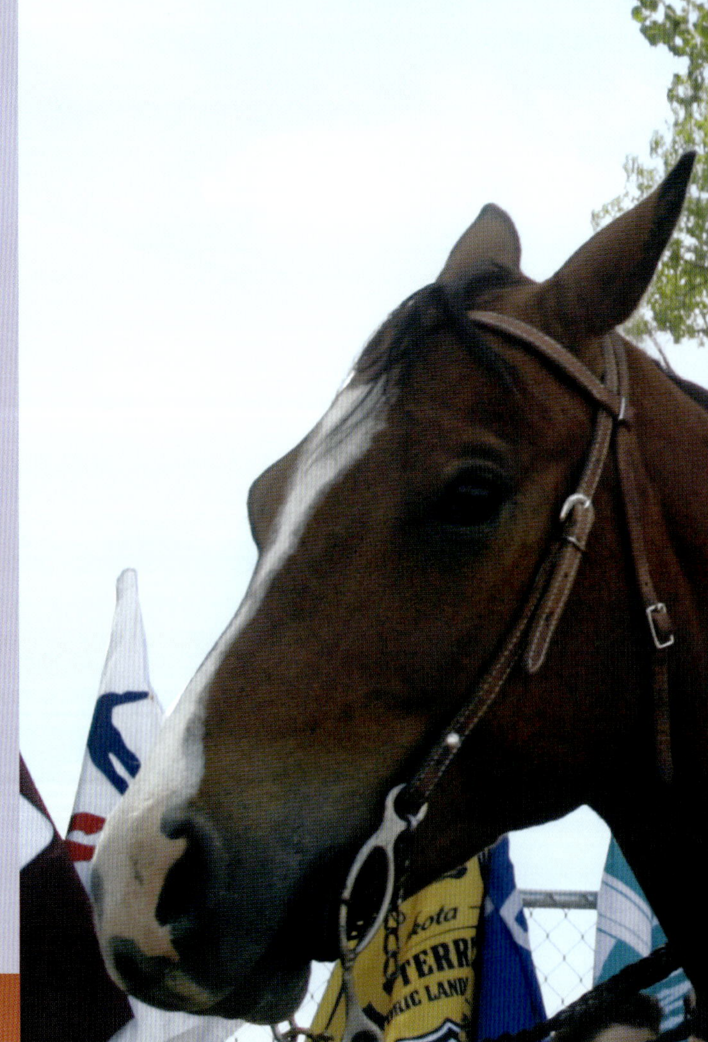

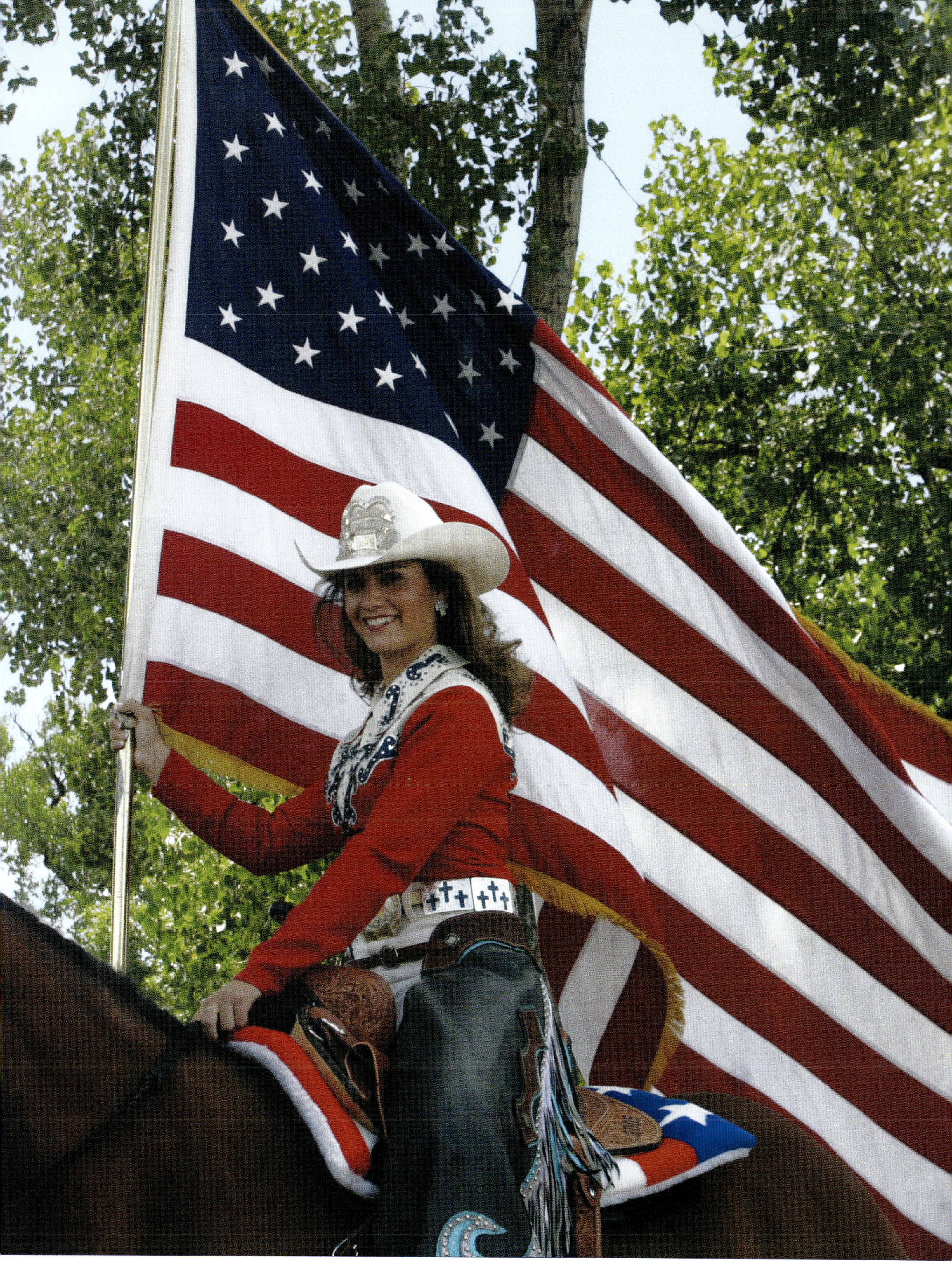

BLACK HILLS

Beyond All Expectations.

would not have been possible without the support of the following sponsors:

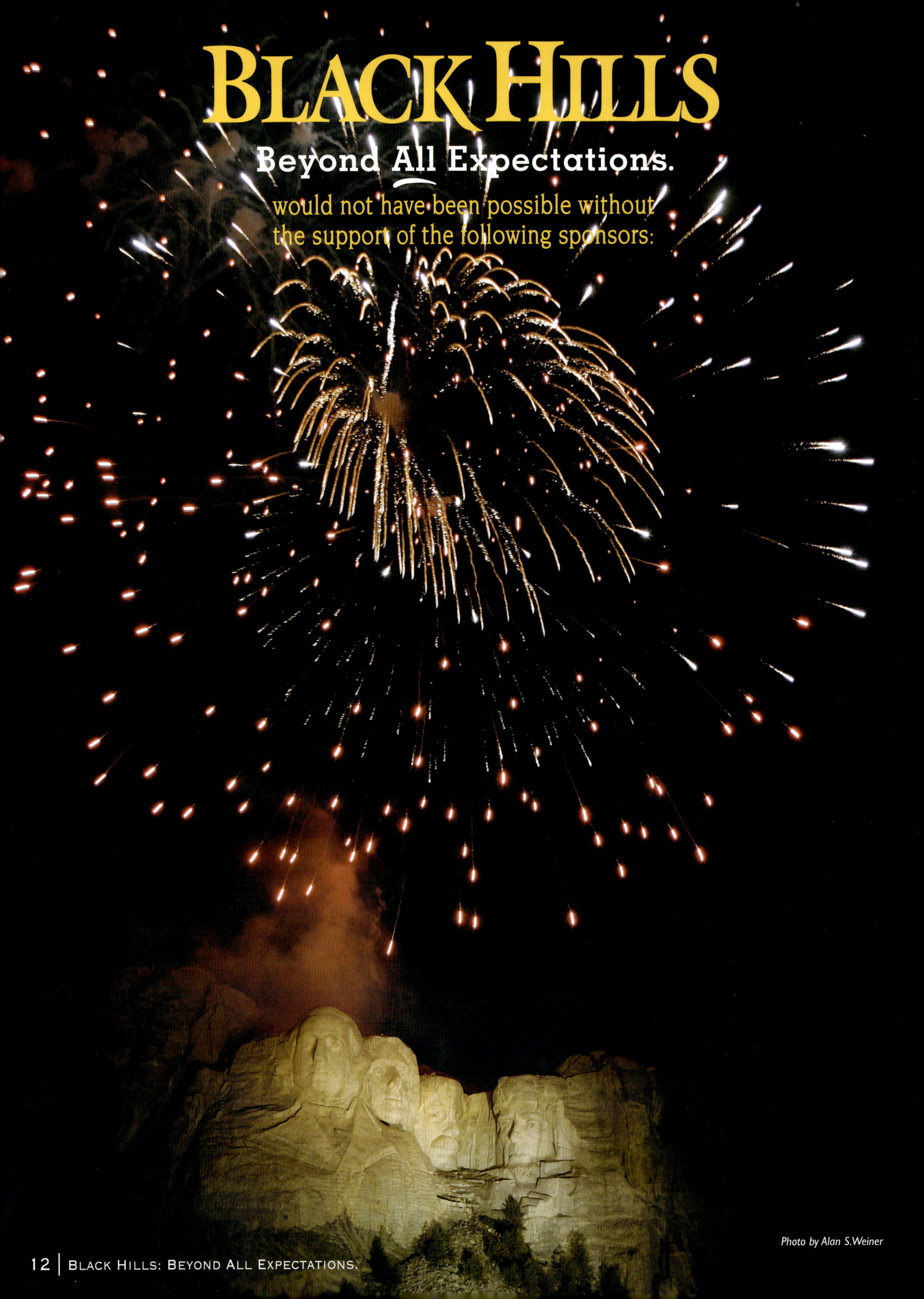

Photo by Alan S.Weiner

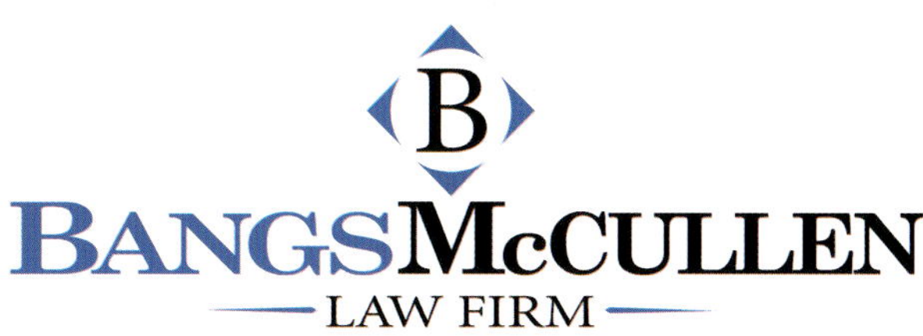

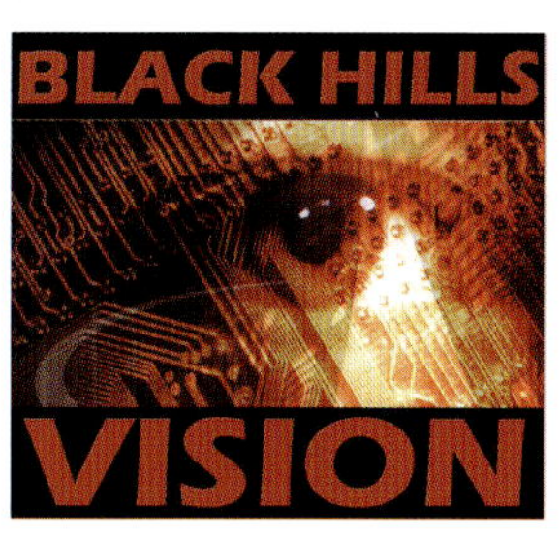

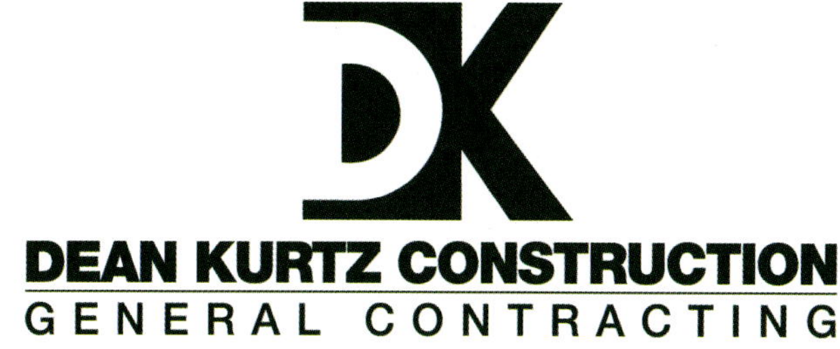

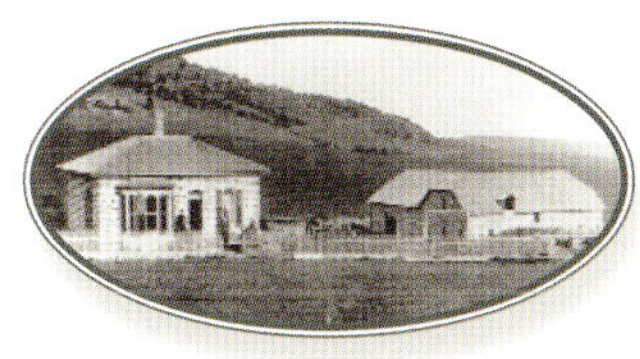

FRAWLEY RANCHES, INC.
A NATIONAL HISTORIC LANDMARK

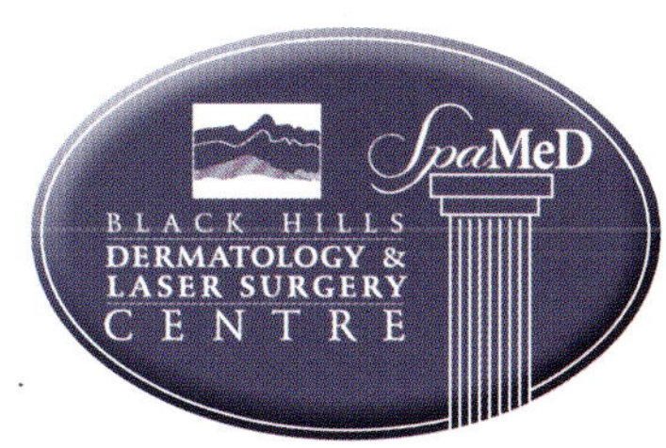

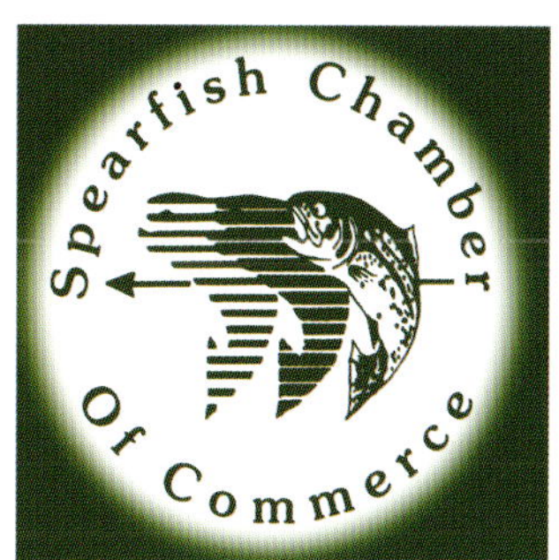

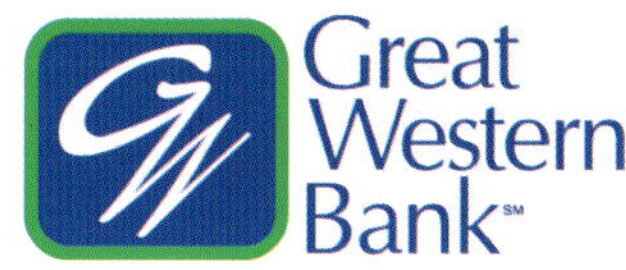

Great People. Great Locations. Great Bank.

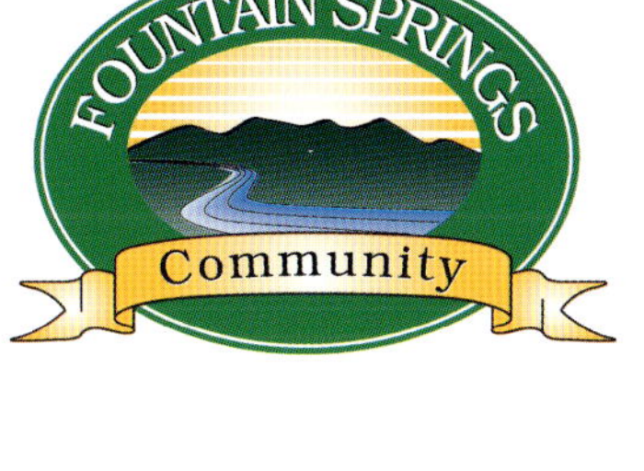

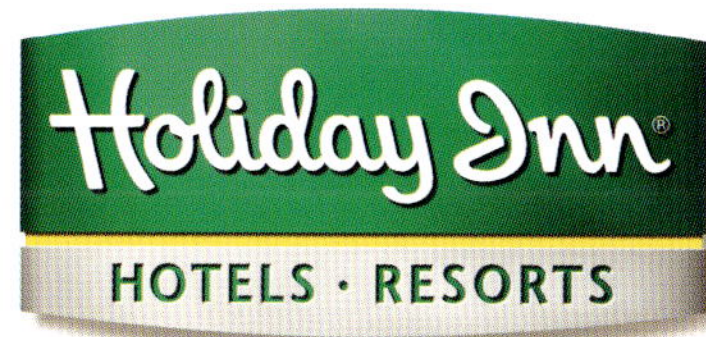

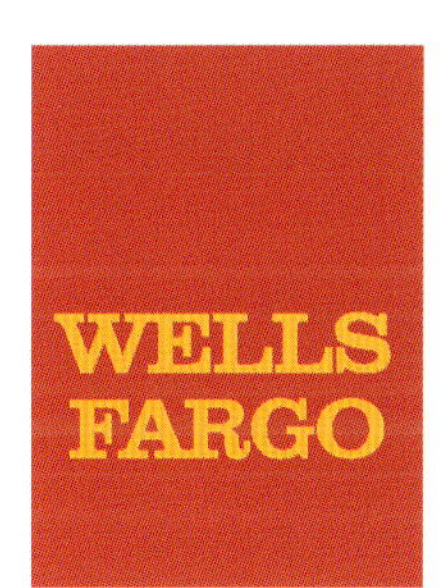

The Next Stage®

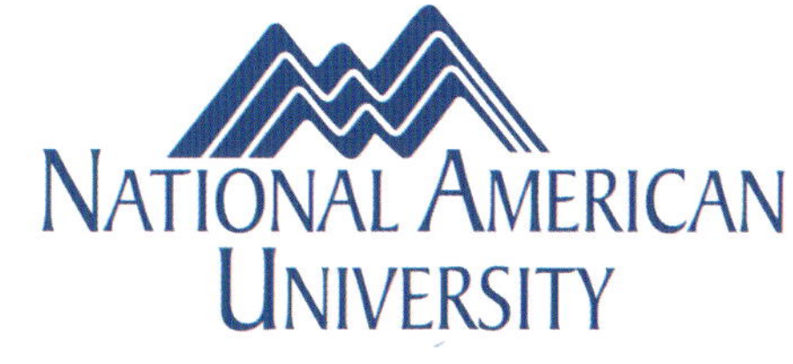

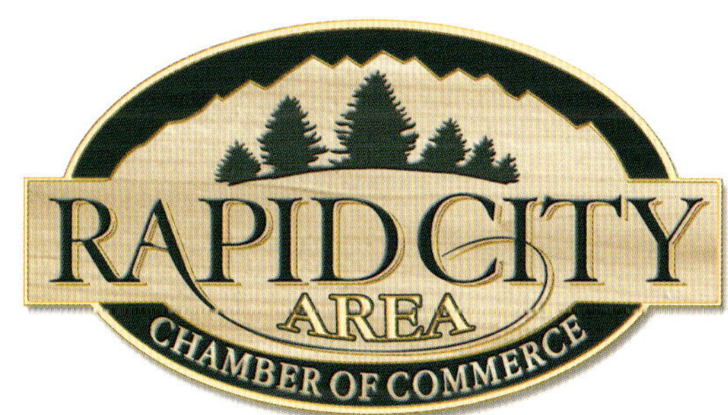

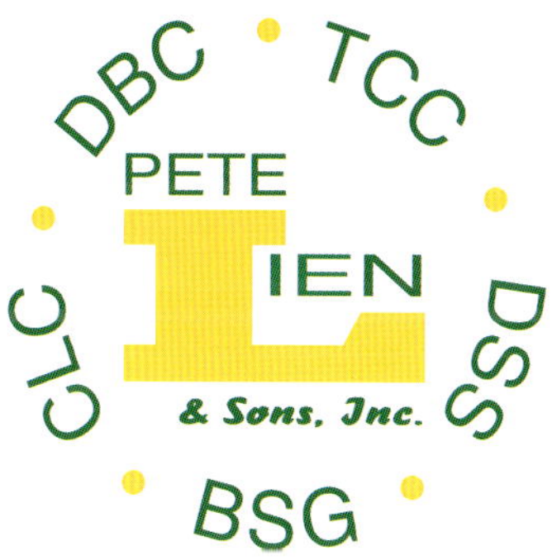

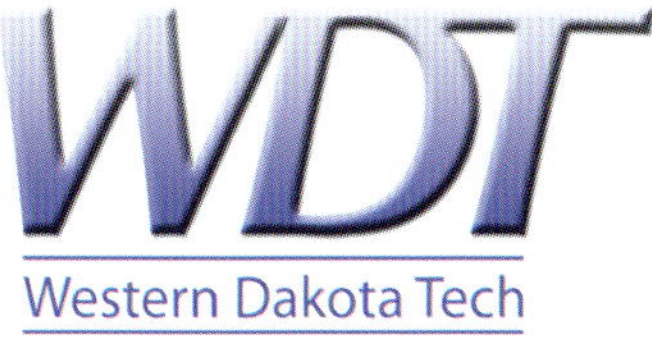

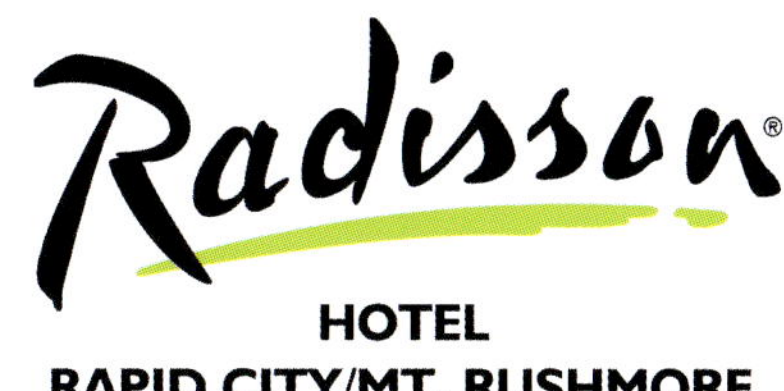

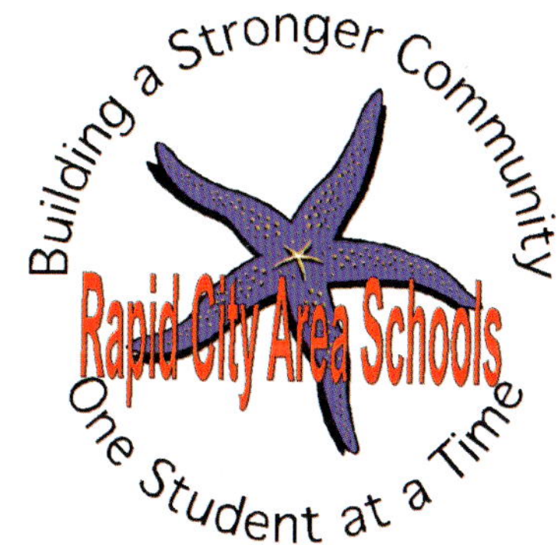

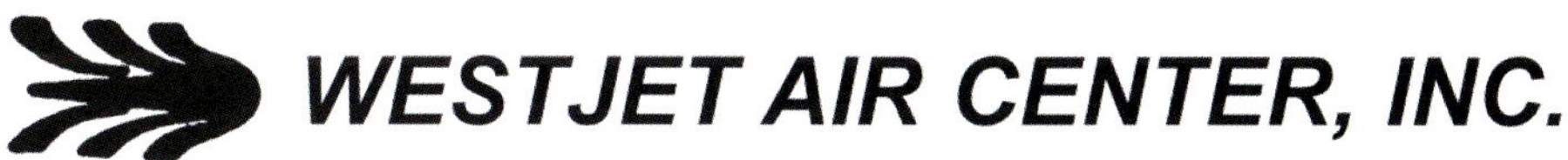

Bangs, McCullen, Butler, Foye, & Simmons, L.L.P. • Black Hills Dermatology & Laser Surgery Centre • Black Hills Vision • Dean Kurtz Construction • Elkhorn Ridge at Frawley Ranches LLC • Fountain Springs Community • Great Western Bank • Holiday Inn Rushmore Plaza Hotel & Conference • National American University • Pete Lien & Sons, Inc. • Radisson Hotel - Rapid City / Mt. Rushmore • Rapid City Area Chamber of Commerce • Rapid City Area School District • Spearfish Chamber of Commerce • Wells Fargo Bank • Western Dakota Technical Institute • Westjet Air Center

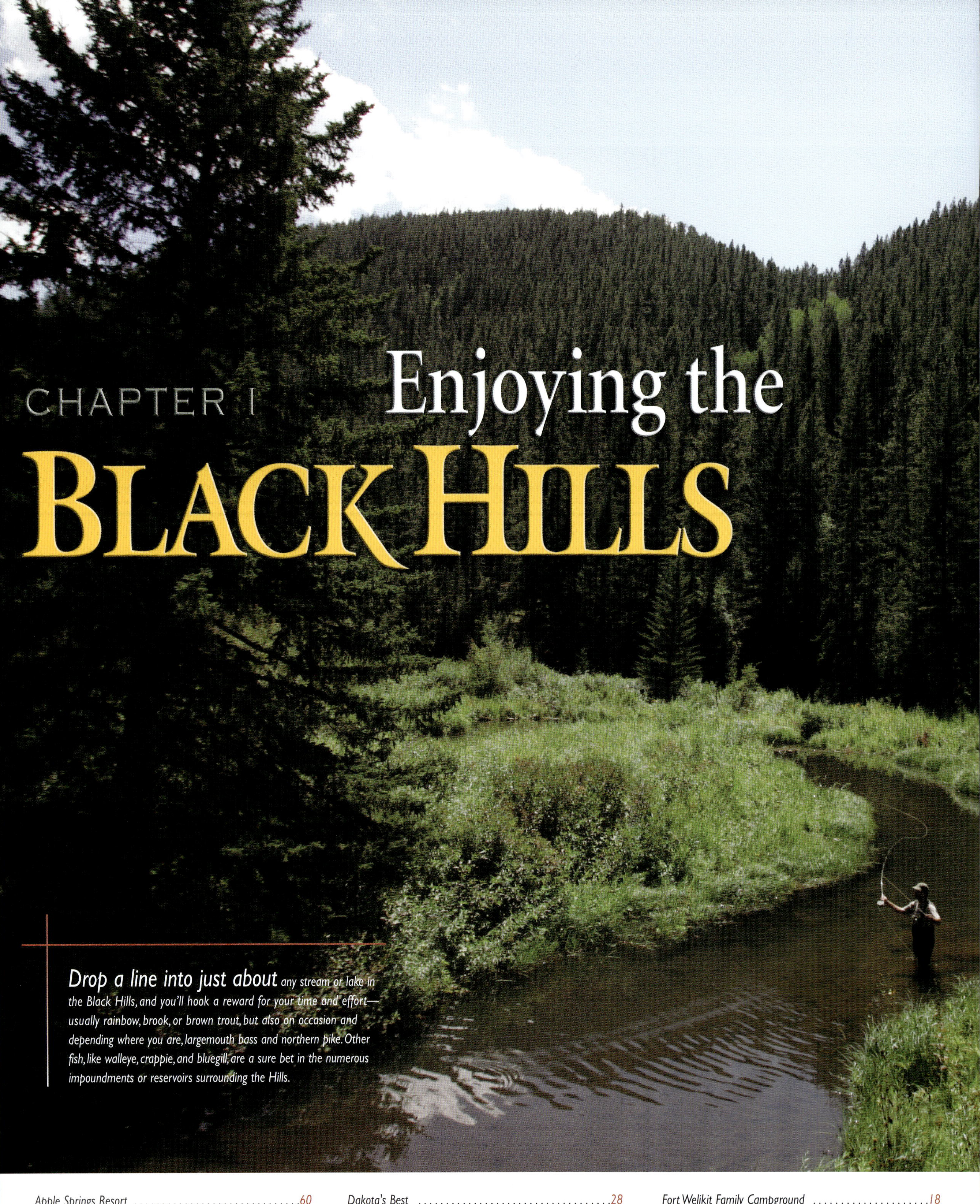

CHAPTER I

Enjoying the BLACK HILLS

Drop a line into just about *any stream or lake in the Black Hills, and you'll hook a reward for your time and effort—usually rainbow, brook, or brown trout, but also on occasion and depending where you are, largemouth bass and northern pike. Other fish, like walleye, crappie, and bluegill, are a sure bet in the numerous impoundments or reservoirs surrounding the Hills.*

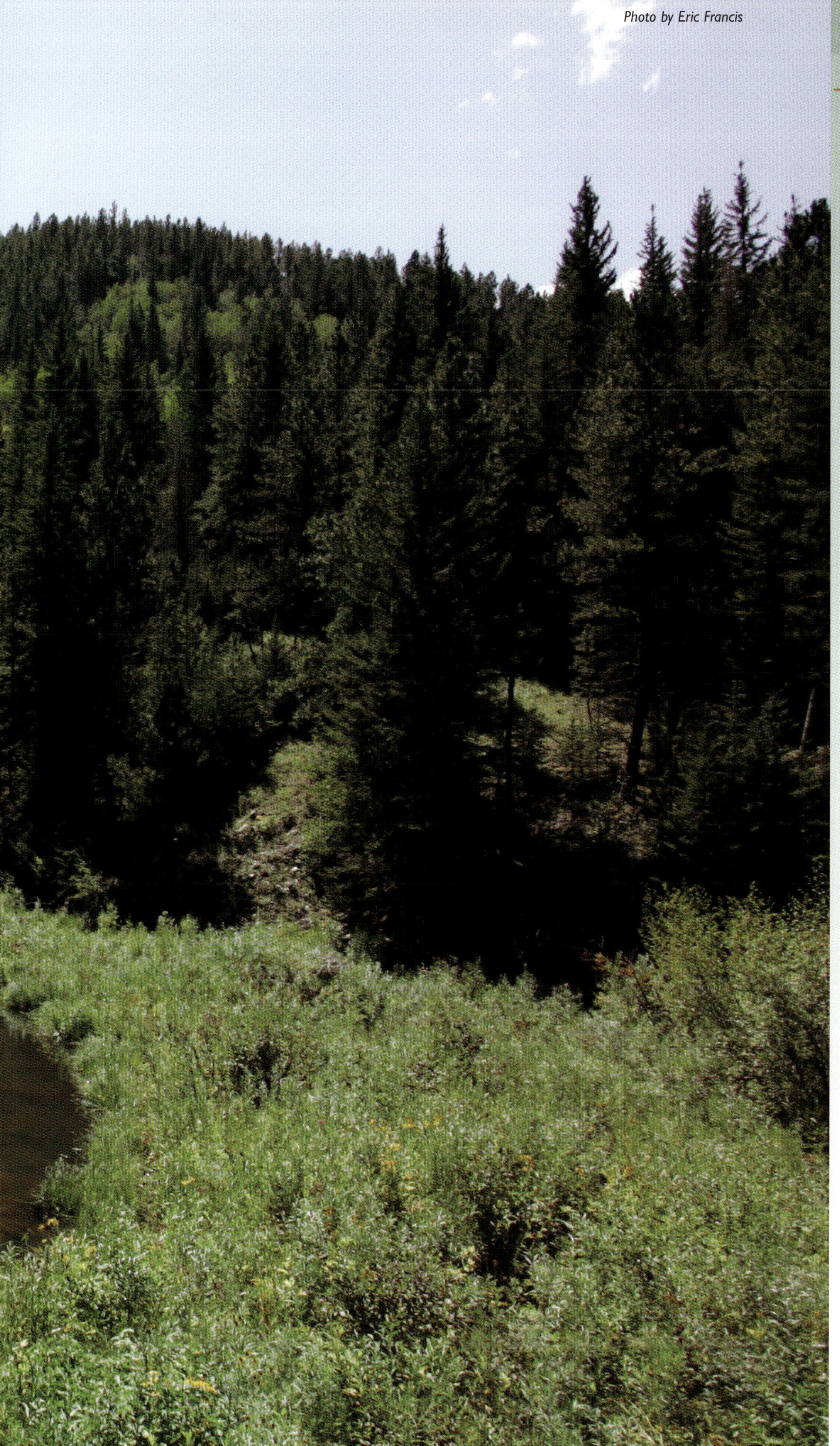

Photo by Eric Francis

Enjoying the Black Hills

If your idea of a good time includes clinging to the face of a granite spire, hiking a seven-thousand-foot peak, skiing a set of moguls, or putting a challenging green, then the Black Hills is your place. Even the sightseeing is larger than life, from the awesome rock formations of Badlands National Park to the breathtaking vision of Mount Rushmore and Crazy Horse. A trip to the Museum of Geology at the South Dakota Schools of Mines and Technology reveals giants of another kind—the fossil skeletons of prehistoric marine reptiles. And where else but in the Black Hills could a tiny town like Sturgis effortlessly host the largest motorcycle rally of its kind in the world?

Then there's the thrill that comes with a firsthand glimpse into the Old West, preserved in towns like Deadwood and Lead and in the countless museums devoted to the era's history and culture.

The area's Native Peoples are also honored and celebrated, with interpretive exhibits at Tatanka and the Indian Museum of North America. Visitors are even welcome at local pow wows and at October's Buffalo Roundup in Custer State Park.

As for the great indoors, the Black Hills is likewise filled with surprises, including professional theatrical companies, Rapid City's top-notch symphony, elegant art galleries, fine shops, and delicious meals at noted restaurants.

Indoors or out, big or small, life in the Black Hills is nothing less than an adventure.❖

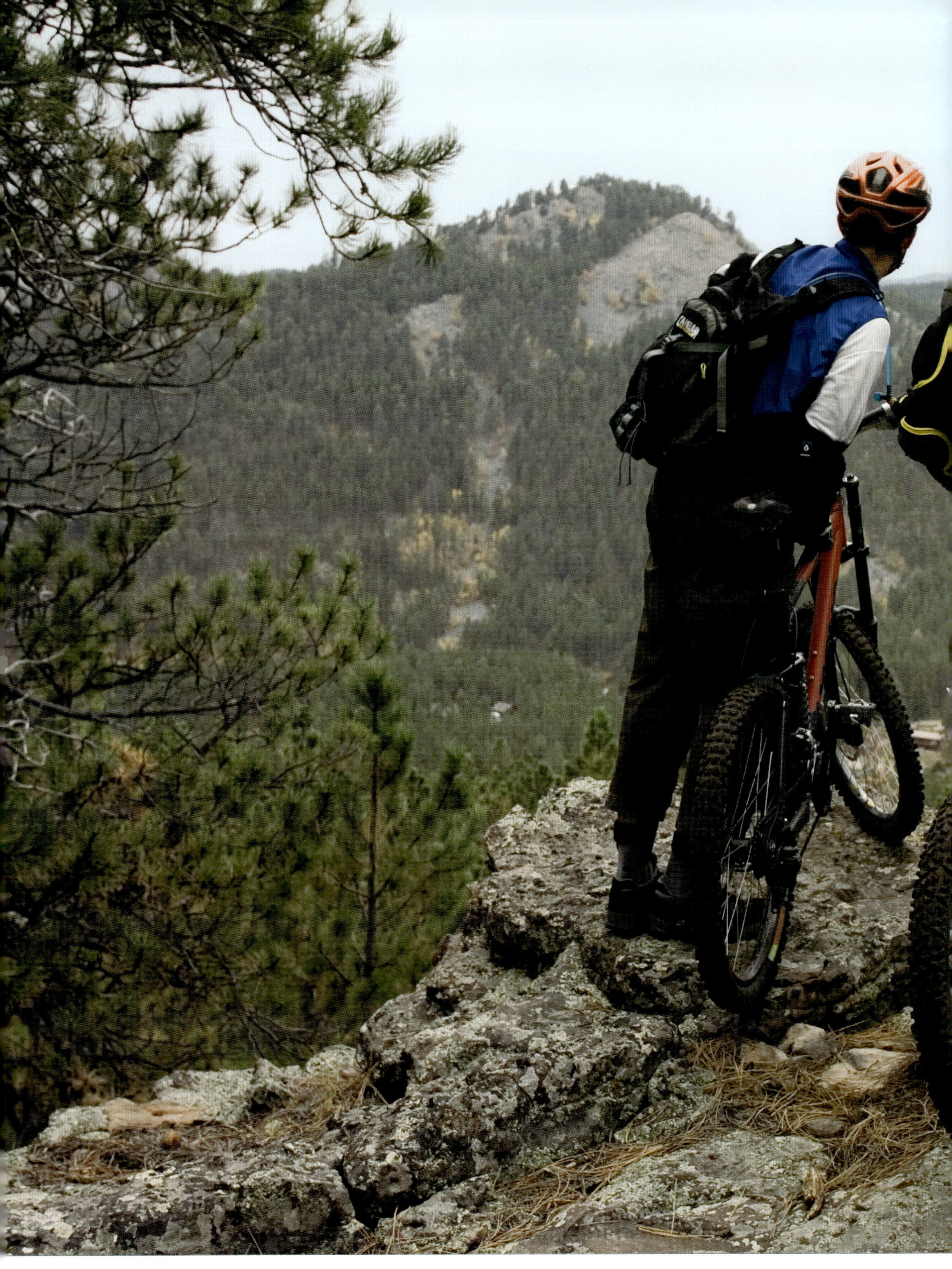

Photo by Dennis Keim

What's a skier to do when there's not enough snow to ski? Become a mountain biker, of course. The Black Hills National Forest features over five thousand square miles of forest crisscrossed with bikeable trails that are available year-round. "We have an open forest policy here," said biker Brent Kertzman. "That means we can ride on any road or trail, rather than just in designated areas." In recent years, more and more mountain bikers have discovered the natural wonders of the area. Custer, a friendly town of about two thousand people, is a good jumping-off point for a Black Hills biking adventure. The city is located just south of the geological center of the Black Hills and provides spectacular views in every direction for bikers like Mikel Cronin and Duane Martenson. ❖

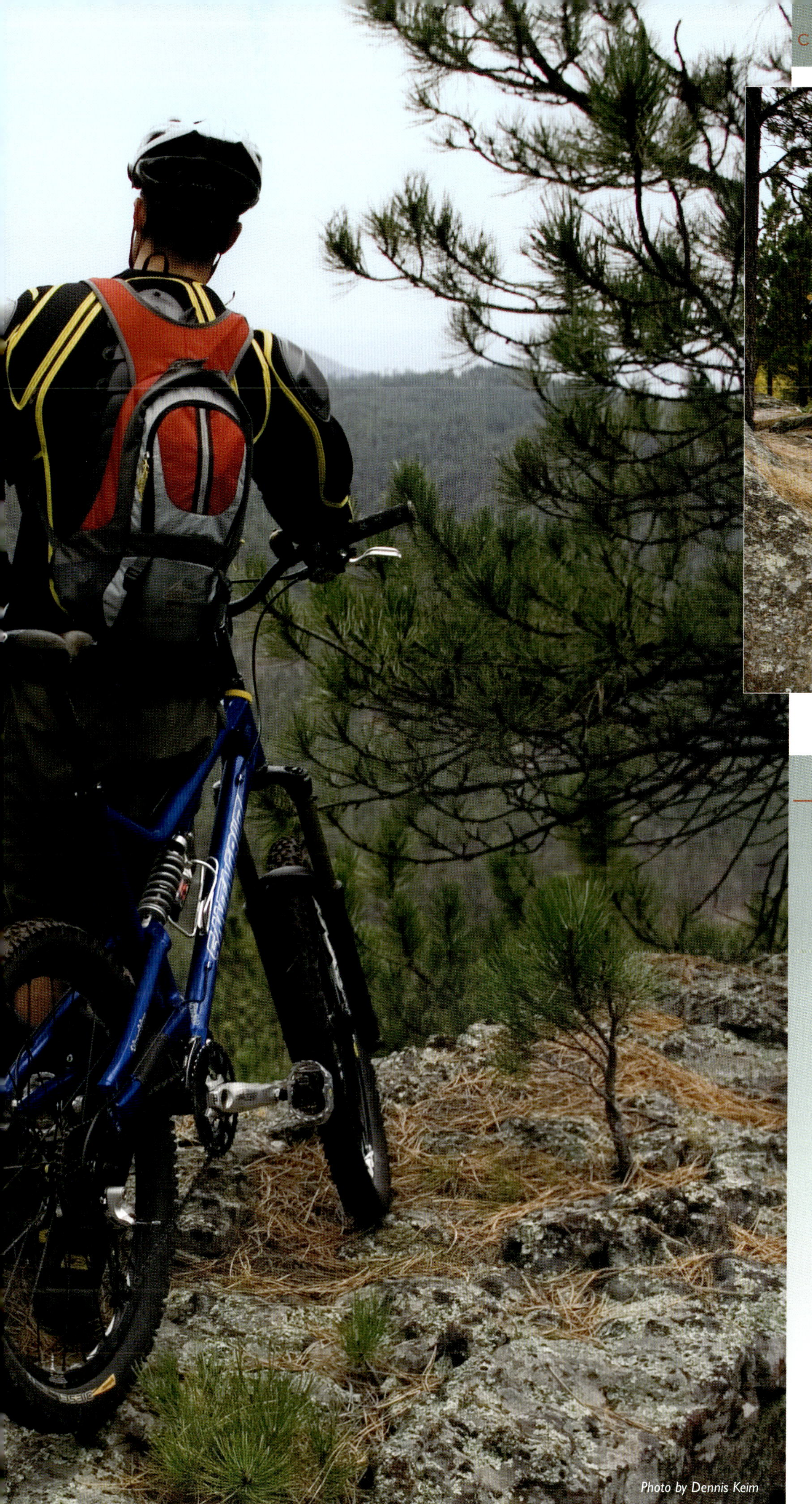

Photo by Dennis Keim

Fort Welikit Family Campground Great Weekend Get-Away

"I always thought it would be fun to live in some great spot and have people pay to stay in my backyard," said Paul LeClair, owner of Fort Welikit Family Campground. He got his wish, and what a backyard he has! The campground is located on Sylvan Lake Road, about a mile northeast of Custer, surrounded by tall evergreens and the splendor of the mystical Black Hills.

For families traveling in the area or anyone looking to get away from it all, this is the place. Visitors can enjoy tent or tipi camping under the stars or park their RV in a long, pull-thru site, enjoy cable TV, and check email on the free Wi-Fi. They can also fly into the Rapid City Airport, where a shuttle will pick them up. Once at the site, they can rent a minivan, go touring on a mountain bike or moped, stay in a tipi, or sleep in one of the on-site camper trailers. There is even a thirty-five-foot Airstream "Cabin" complete with everything including cable TV. "Folks can visit our Web site (www.BlackHillsrv.com) before they leave home and choose from a variety of vacation packages. We'll help book airline reservations and line up a variety of guided tours to local attractions, including an evening tour featuring dinner at the Sylvan Lake Lodge, then on to Mount Rushmore for the lighting ceremony," said Mr. LeClair.

However you get there, playing in Paul LeClair's backyard is guaranteed to be a fun experience, creating lifelong memories for you and your family. ❖

Visitors can enjoy tent or tipi camping under the stars or park their RV in a long, pull-thru site.

Photo by Alan S.Weiner

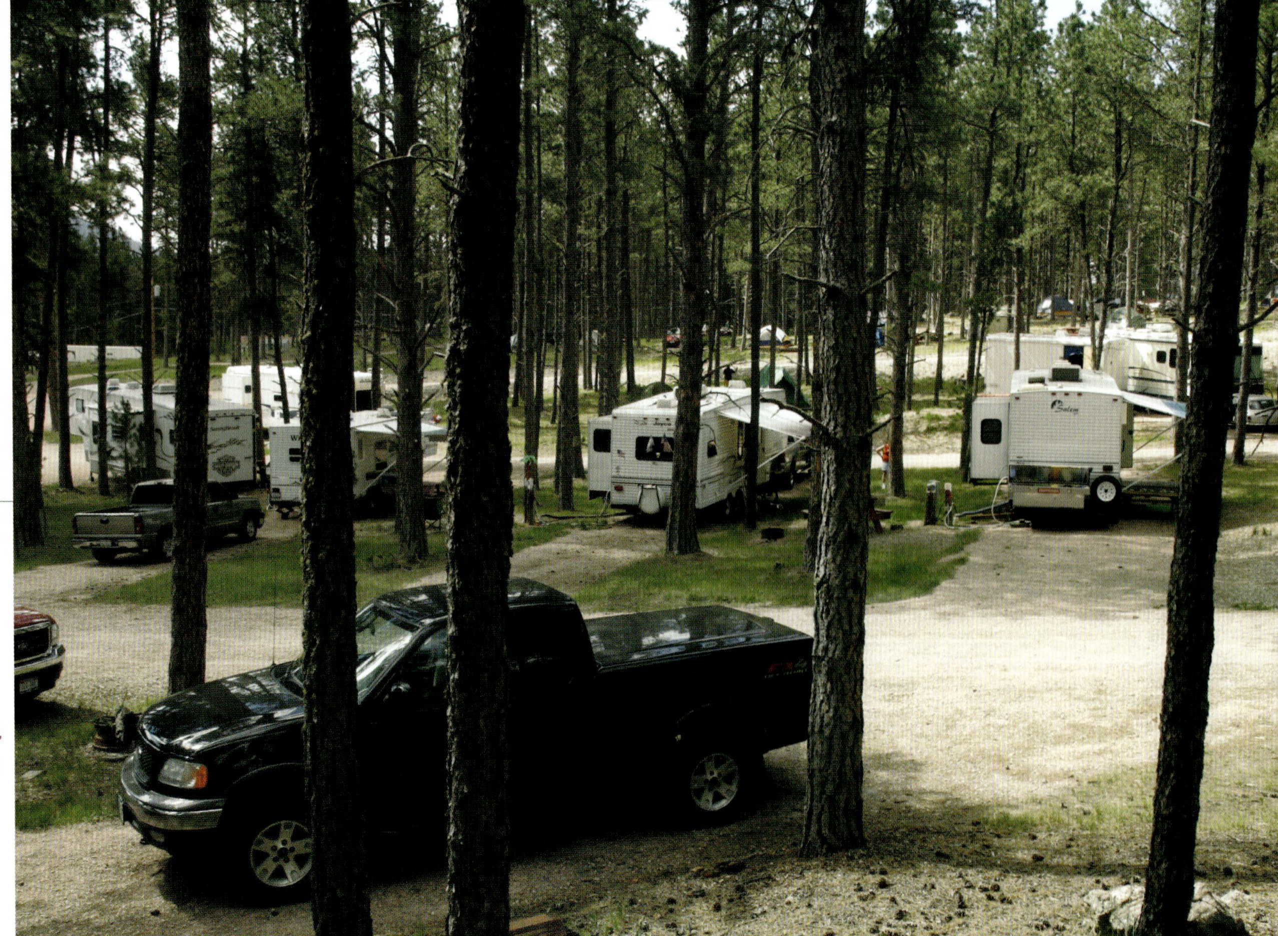

It is estimated that there are 100 billion stars in our galaxy. If you want to check that for accuracy, the Fort Welikit Family Campground is a good place to start counting. With extra-long, pull-thru hook-up sites nestled in a quiet pine forest, it is the perfect spot for a relaxing vacation.

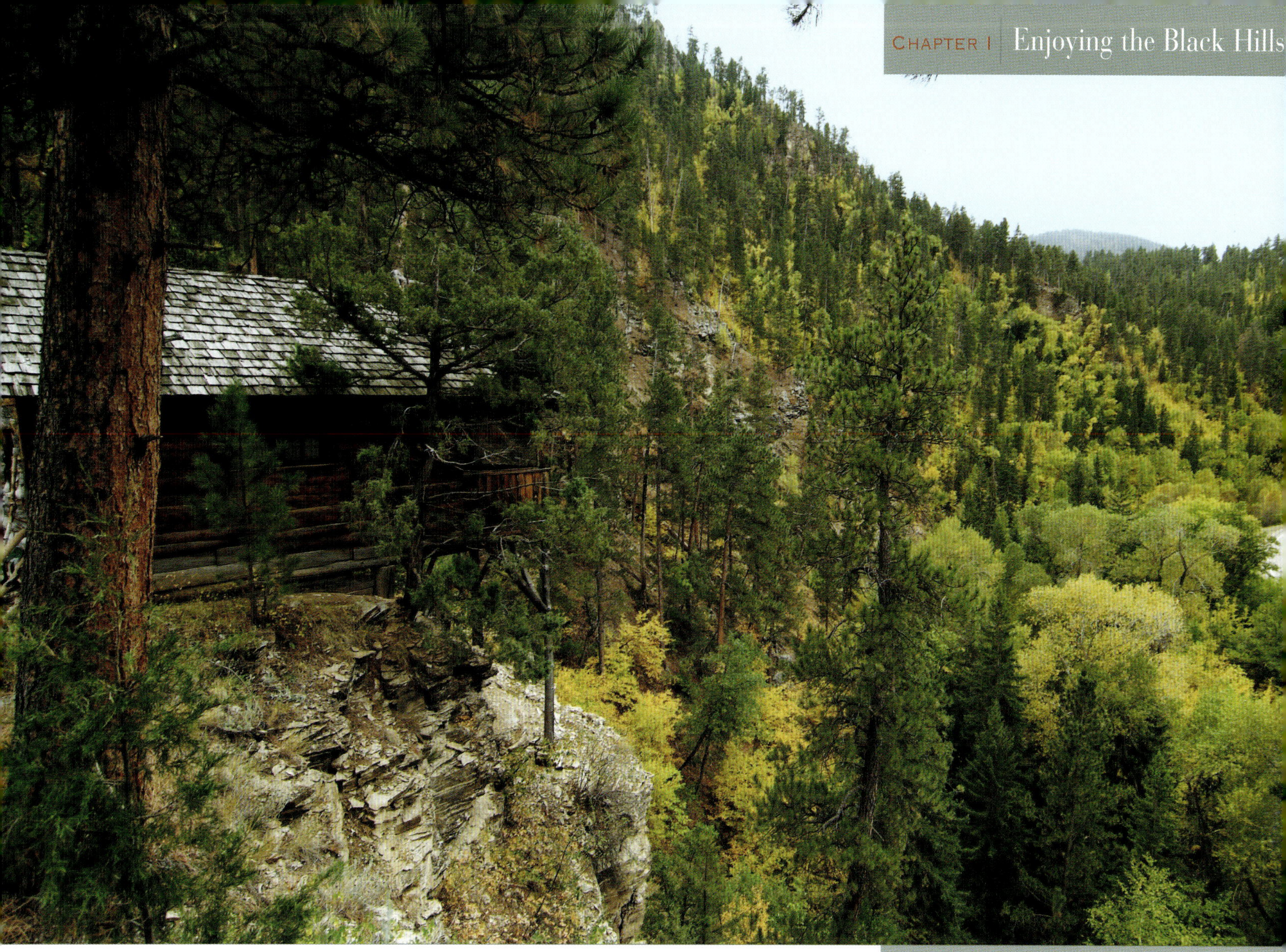

Photo by Doug Henderson

Breathtaking...

Before Spearfish Canyon

became protected as a State and National Forest Scenic Byway, a few hearty souls attempted to live along its steep banks. Formed 30 to 60 million years ago when the waters of a great sea began to subside and erode the softer rock, Spearfish is roughly twenty miles long and one mile wide. Evergreens such as ponderosa and spruce pine trees give the area a lush look no matter what time of year, while aspen, birch, and oak put on a remarkable display of turning colors in the fall. Wildlife is abundant as well and includes whitetail and mule deer, mountain goats, and bobcat, in addition to smaller creatures like raccoons, porcupine, and squirrels. Whether hiking its trails or kicking back and admiring its beauty, Spearfish Canyon attracts many visitors to its impressive landscape. ❖

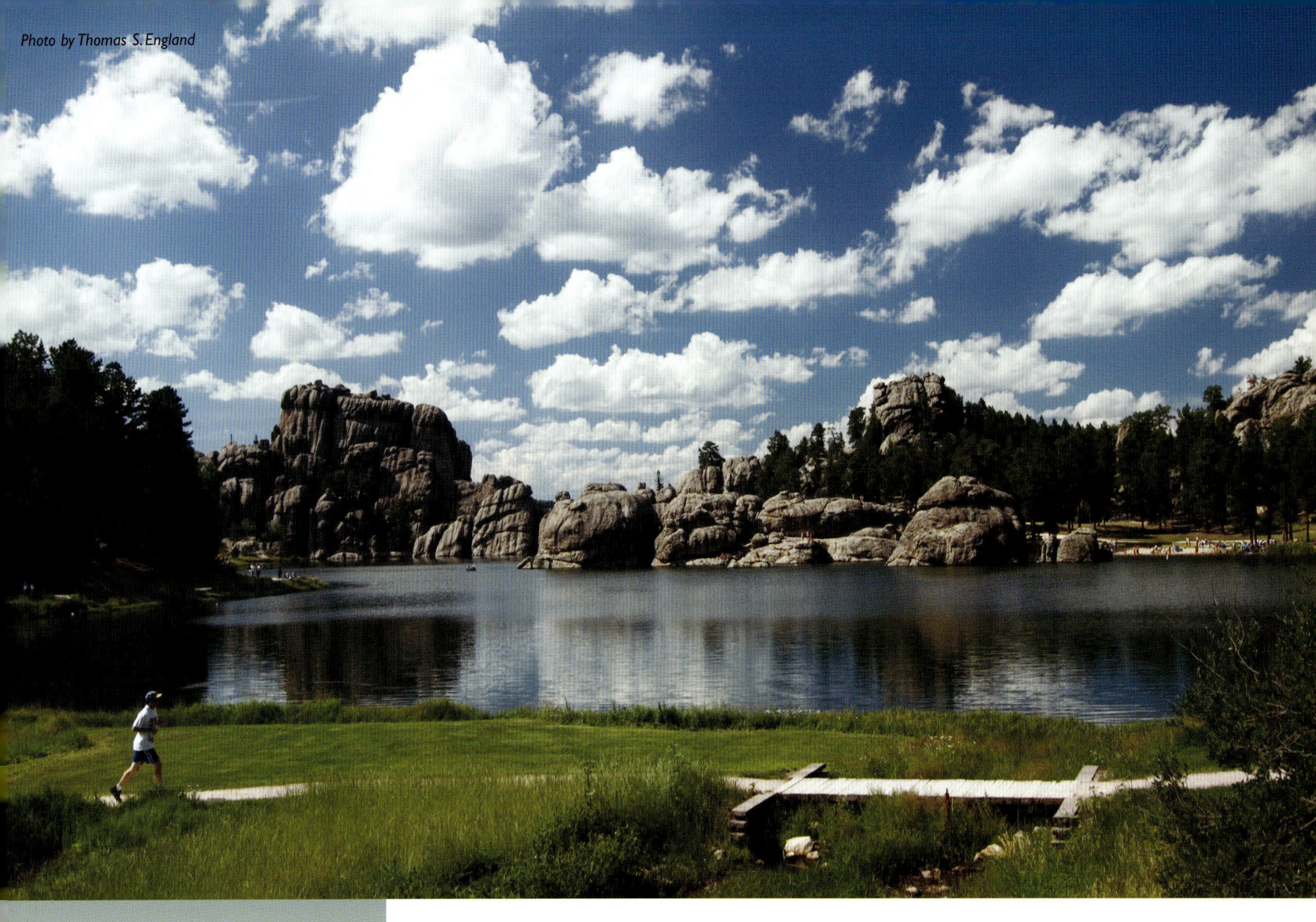
Photo by Thomas S. England

It doesn't matter if you run, jog, or amble, the one-mile loop trail around the Sylvan Lake shore provides plenty of wonderful scenery while you work your legs or stretch them out after a ride through Custer State Park. Sylvan Lake is located at the entrance, with ample parking and a convenience store with water, snacks, and South Dakotan arts, crafts, and mementos. If your visit lingers into the evening, head up the hill to nearby Sylvan Lake Resort and have a delicious dinner in its Lakota Dining Room restaurant. ❖

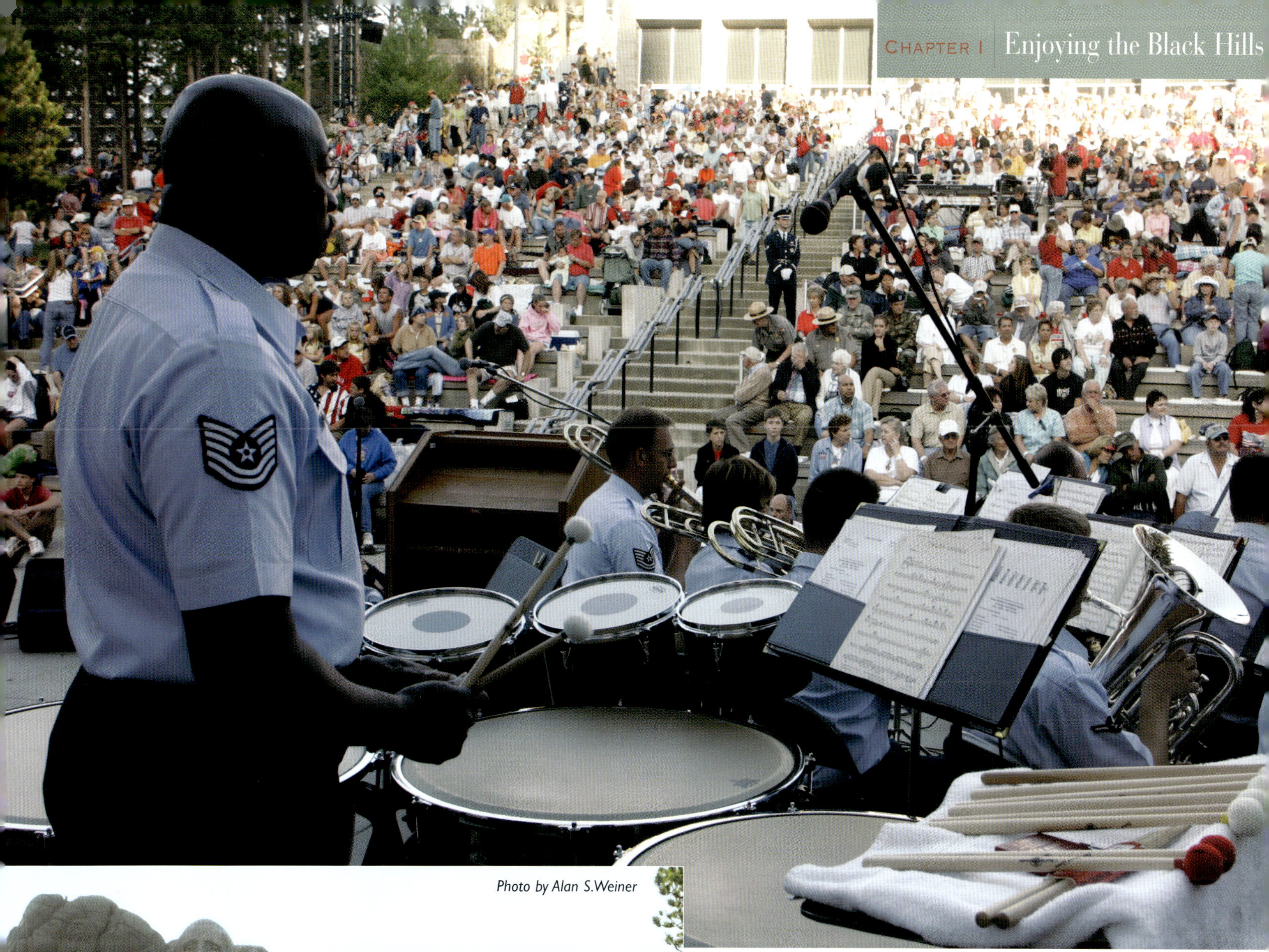

Photo by Alan S.Weiner

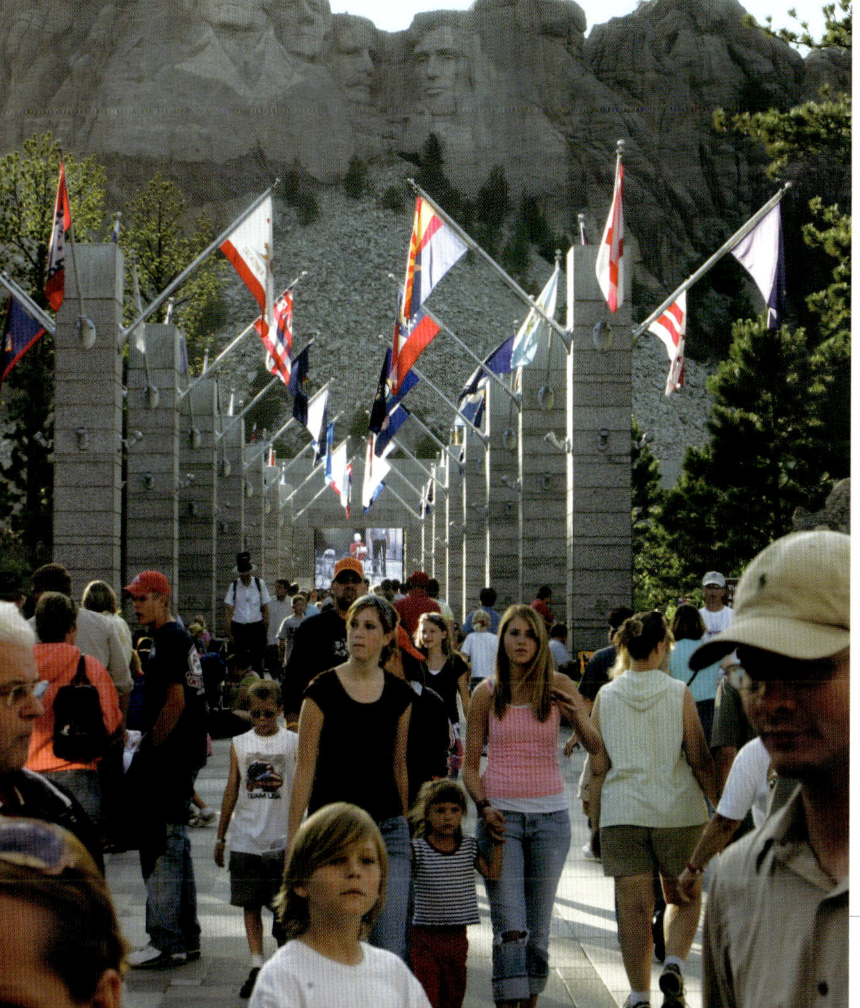

Photo by Alan S.Weiner

Independence Day takes on an extra-special meaning when celebrated in the shadow of our most beloved presidents. Each year, South Dakota honors our nation's birth with two days of activities and festivities at the memorial, including a spectacular fireworks display the evening of July 3. Recently, the thirty-minute spectacular was ushered in by a B-1 bomber flyover from Ellsworth Air Force Base and accompanied by a patriotic musical tribute. The festivities continued on July 4, culminating in an evening performance by the Air National Guard Band of the Central States, a showing of the film Freedom—America's Lasting Legacy, and illumination of the sculpture. ❖

Radisson Hotel Offers the Ultimate Guest Experience

Spend even one night at the Radisson Hotel Rapid City/Mt. Rushmore, and it is immediately apparent that this is no ordinary hotel. One of the city's premier venues for business and pleasure travelers, the Radisson embodies the energy and skill of a dynamic staff, working together to create the ultimate guest experience.

Located in downtown Rapid City, the Radisson reflects in its architecture and decorative artwork the region's spectacular natural beauty. Upon entering the hotel, guests are greeted by a beautiful marble floor which leads to the lobby's own impressive walkway, a masterpiece of inlay work crafted from over six thousand precision-cut pieces of more than seventy-five various stones from around the world.

Behind the front desk, another composite mural complements the floor art. This one features various Black Hills imagery created with fifty-six hundred pieces of marble, granite, limestone, ceramic, and bronze. Like the lobby walkway, nationally known artist Harry Aalto created this work as an homage to the heritage and natural scenery of the Black Hills. His vision continues throughout the hotel's décor, in various wall murals, floor patterns, and tabletop designs.

The hotel distinguishes itself by its philosophy of providing choices so that guests can stay their own way. Greeting each guest is a staff that exemplifies genuine South

The hotel distinguishes itself by its philosophy of providing choices so that guests can stay their own way.

Photo by Alan S.Weiner

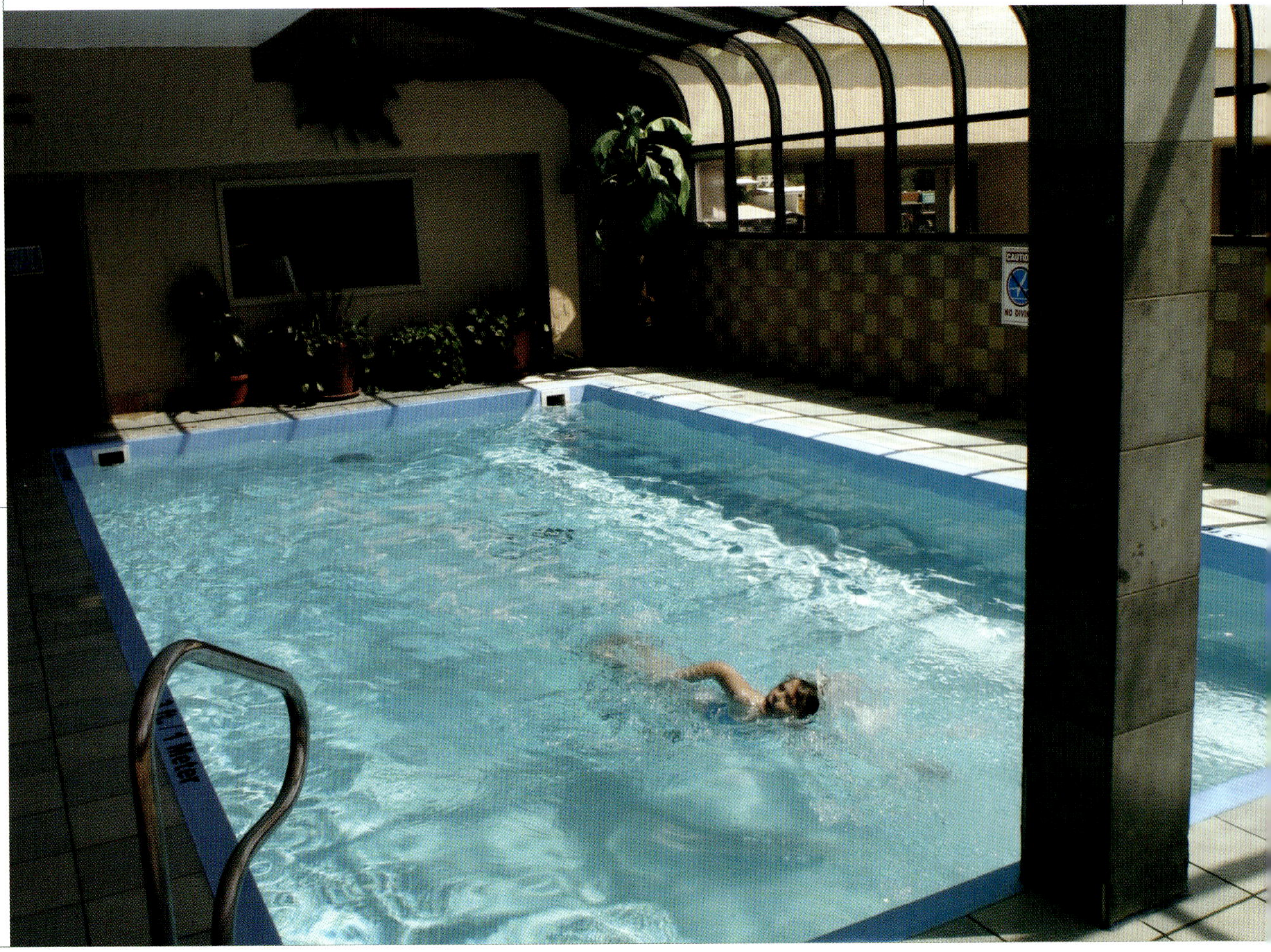

Like everything else in the Radisson, the indoor heated pool is as beautiful as it is functional. Brightly colored porcelain fish created by Harry Aalto and his Creative Edge Corporation line the deck, while the glass enclosure provides striking views of the city.

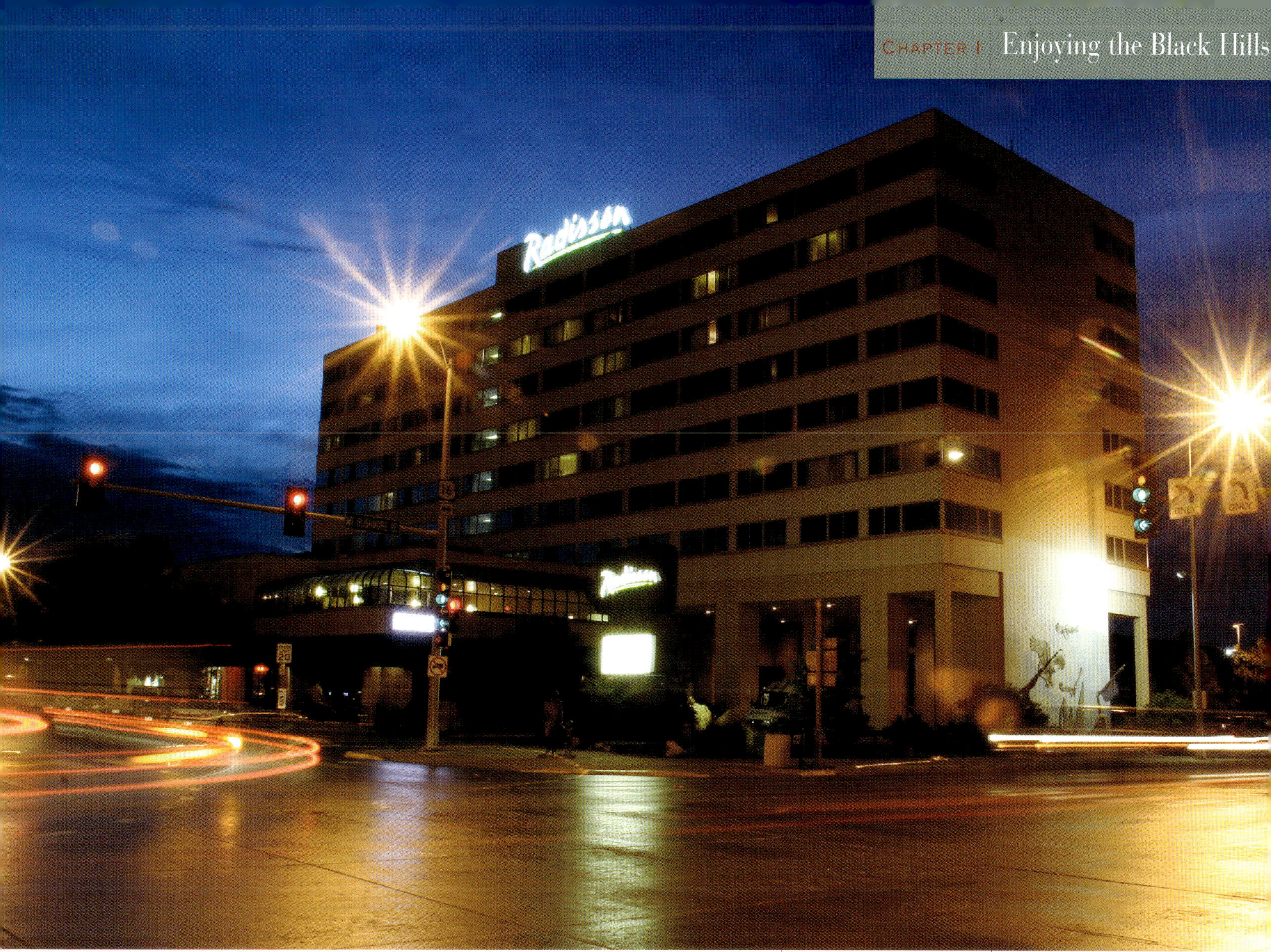

Photo by Alan S. Weiner

A recognized landmark of the Rapid City skyline, the Radisson Hotel reflects the beauty of the region and the warmth of its people. Carefully re-created natural landscaping is found throughout the grounds, while the interior is filled with Black Hills–inspired artworks.
A skilled and friendly staff ensures guests enjoy nothing less than the best in service and amenities.

Dakota hospitality and takes pride in its "Yes, I can!" attitude, backed by an unconditional guarantee of quality service.

Unique to South Dakota, the Radisson Hotel keeps pace with some of the leading trends in luxury hotels. Whether a guest is staying for business or pleasure, the hotel is equipped to meet every need. Spacious rooms and suites feature the only Sleep Number beds in South Dakota, each outfitted with crisp deluxe linens and nonallergenic down comforters. Also included are on-demand movies, oversize desks, complimentary dedicated and wireless high-speed Internet, voice mail with remote access, coffee makers, and hair dryers. For the business traveler there are a host of special touches that make the Radisson feel like a home away from home, including a business center, a postal center, and the Dakota's Best gift shop featuring locally produced foodstuffs, deli fare, and gourmet coffee from Dry Creek Coffee Company.

Guests seeking to unwind after a long day can relax with a specialty cocktail at the Martini Bar or a brew and a bite at the Irish-style Dublin Square pub. Or they can release some endorphins at the hotel's fully equipped fitness center and indoor heated pool overlooking the city.

In addition to catering to travelers, the Radisson is an ideal venue for special events of all kinds, from weddings to conferences to business meetings. Six conference rooms ranging in size from five hundred to twenty-three hundred square feet can be outfitted by the hotel's certified Meeting Solutions professionals to serve a variety of needs.

continued on page 24

continued from page 23

Through a partnership with European culinary talent, the hotel brings to Rapid City a restaurant that shines among the best in the nation. The Enigma Restaurant is a true asset to Rapid City and is known for its selection of aperitifs, specialty drinks, fine wines, and creative cuisine.

Karim and Batool Merali, managing partners of the Radisson Hotel Rapid City/Mt. Rushmore, have a deep pride of ownership, a strong commitment to the people of the community, and a kinship to the land. This commitment shines in every aspect of their business and community relations. For instance, through the Radisson International's "Partnering with the Arts" program, in 1998 the Meralis secured a ten-thousand-dollar grant as a contribution to fund-raising efforts for the local Crazy Horse

Photo by Alan S.Weiner

Whether for cocktails, a pre-dinner drink, or a late-night aperitif, the Martini Bar inside the hotel's Enigma Restaurant is the perfect spot to enjoy good times. The bar also includes a well-stocked wine cellar featuring the best of local, national, and international vintages.

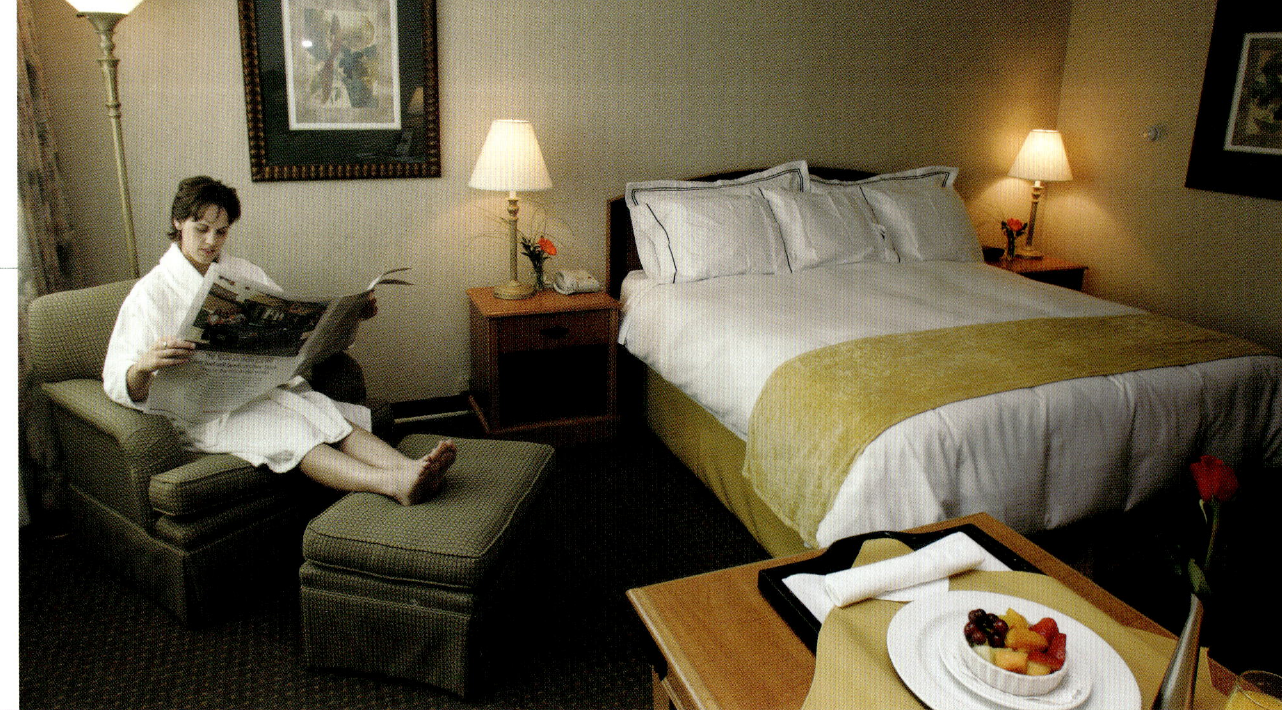

The Radisson spares no expense when it comes to the comfort of its guests. The Sleep Number beds by Select Comfort are dressed with a high-percale thread count deluxe linen package wrapped in a nonallergenic down comforter, making your sleep experience at the Radisson the most comfortable ever, or your money back!

Photo by Alan S.Weiner

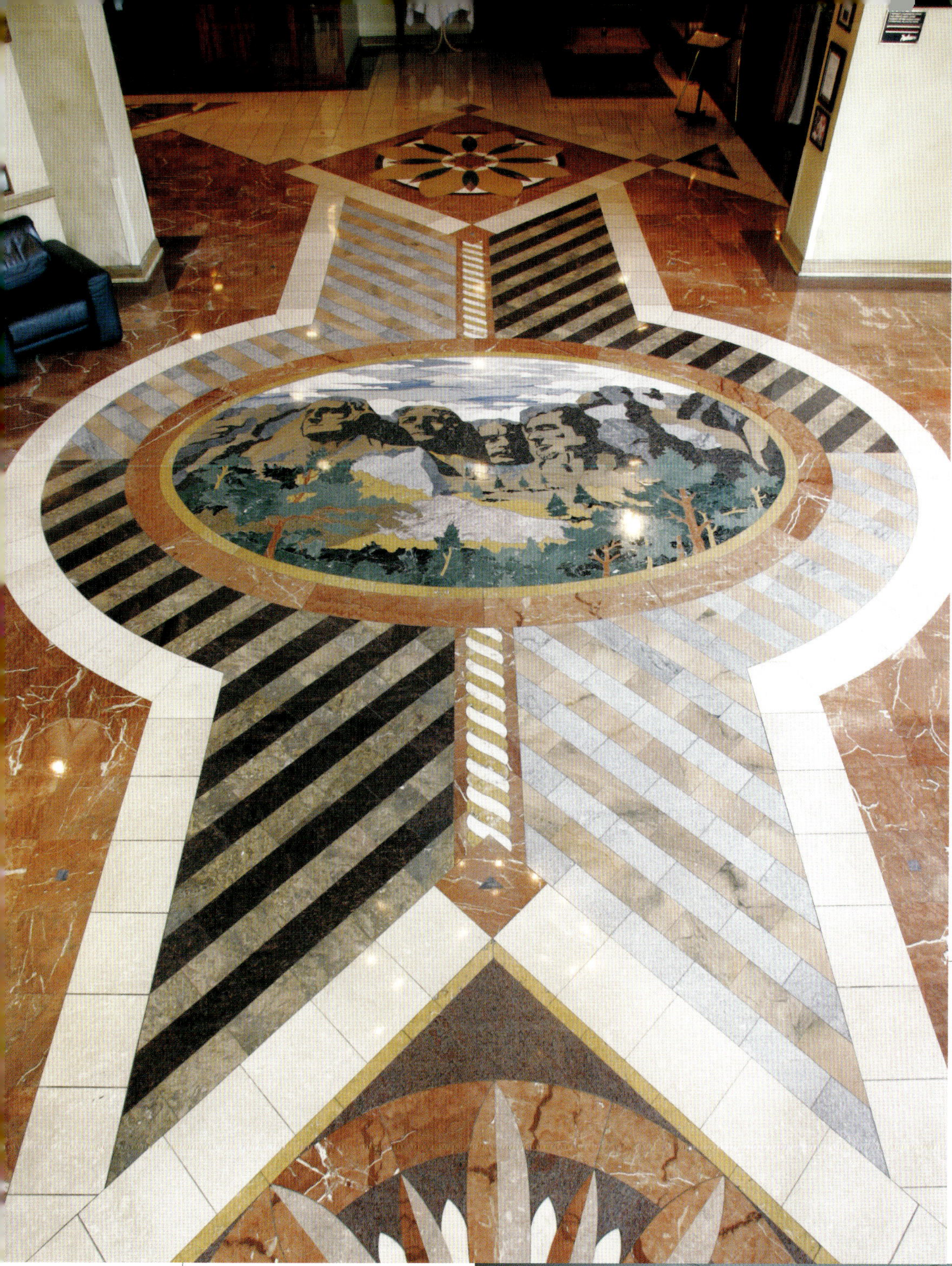

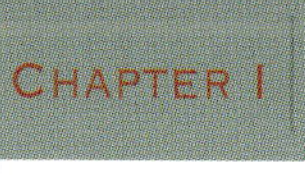

Memorial's new Orientation Center. Only four of these grants are awarded quarterly to Radisson hotels worldwide. To help promote tourism to the area, that same year the Meralis also contributed thirty thousand dollars toward securing a September 1998 broadcast of the *Live with Regis and Kathy Lee* television show from Mount Rushmore.

From a deep-rooted sense of responsibility to customer service to appealing art and design at every turn, the Radisson Hotel Rapid City/Mt. Rushmore is a unique state-of-the-art hotel, combining sophisticated amenities with genuine friendliness and ambience. ❖

An intricate, sixty-foot-long floor mural of Mount Rushmore greets visitors as they enter the lobby. One of many works of world-class art contained within the hotel, the Harry Aalto mural was created from over six thousand precision-cut pieces of more than seventy-five various stones from around the world.

Photo by Alan S.Weiner

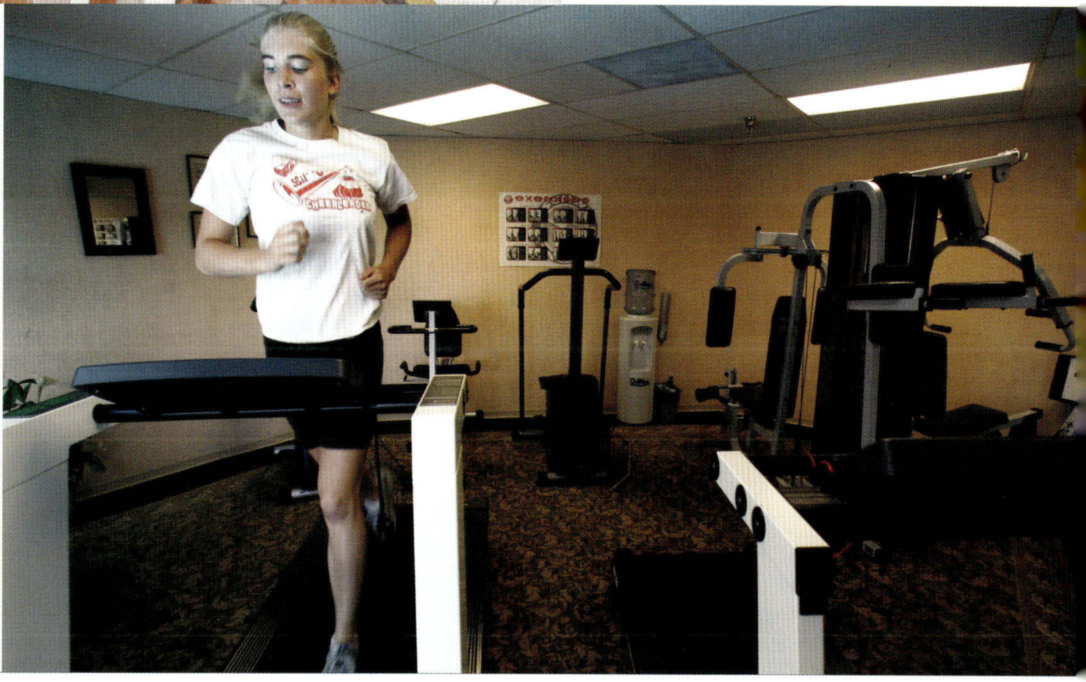

With its full-service fitness room containing the latest in workout equipment, the Radisson allows guests to stay in shape while on the road.

Photo by Alan S.Weiner

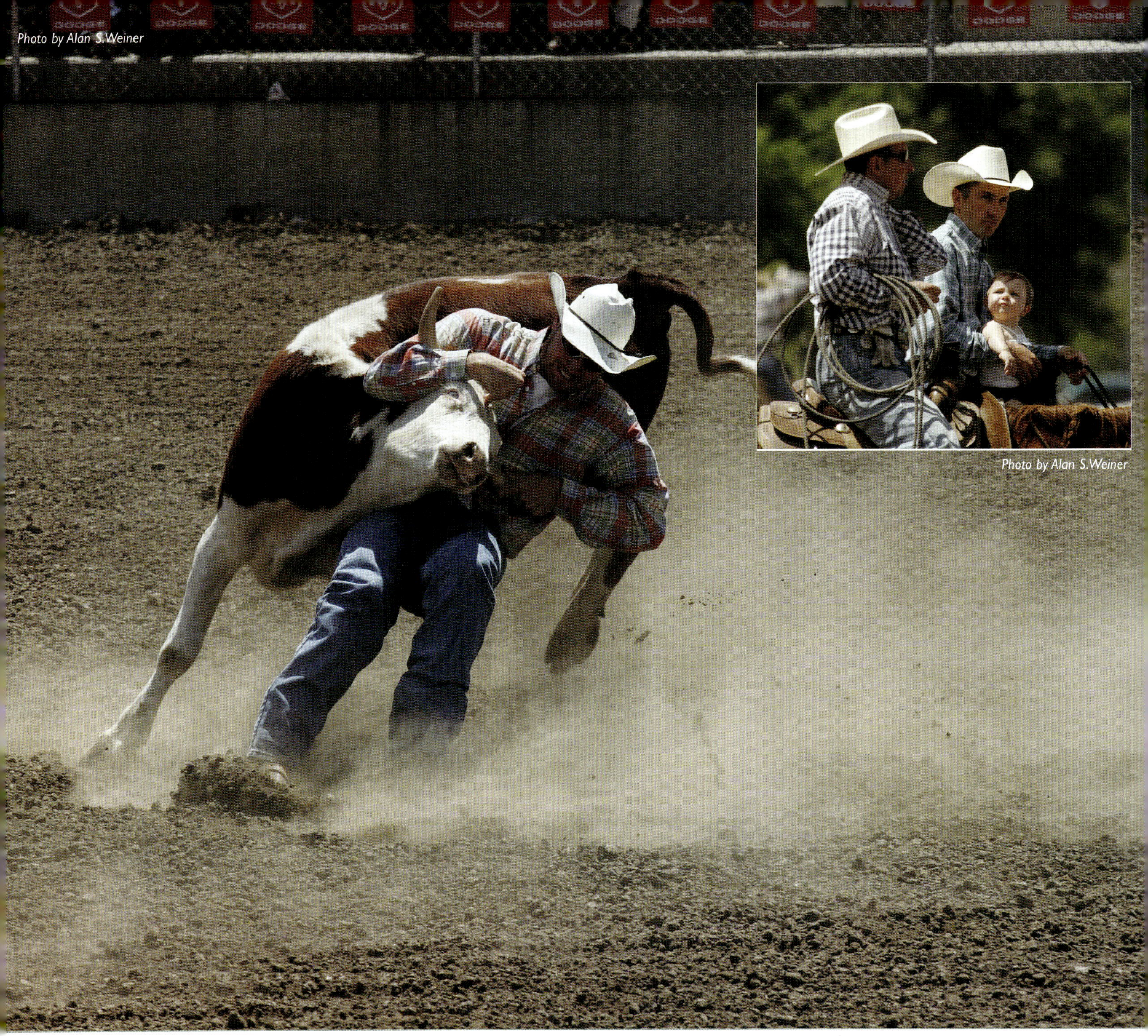

Photo by Alan S.Weiner

Photo by Alan S.Weiner

Photo by Alan S.Weiner

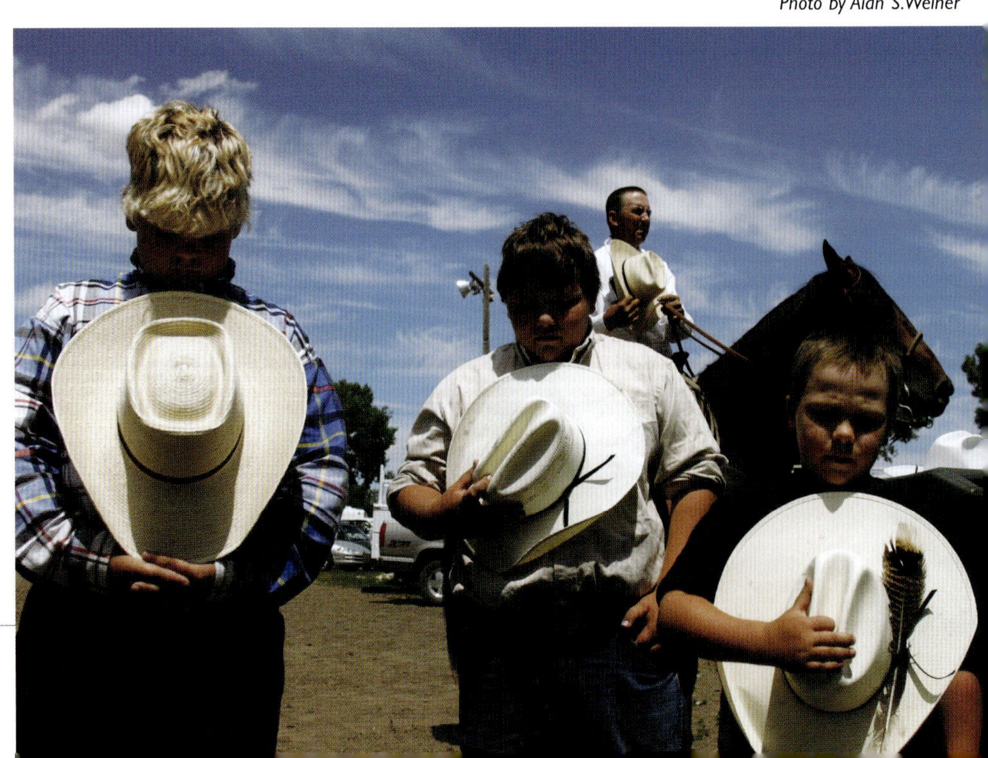

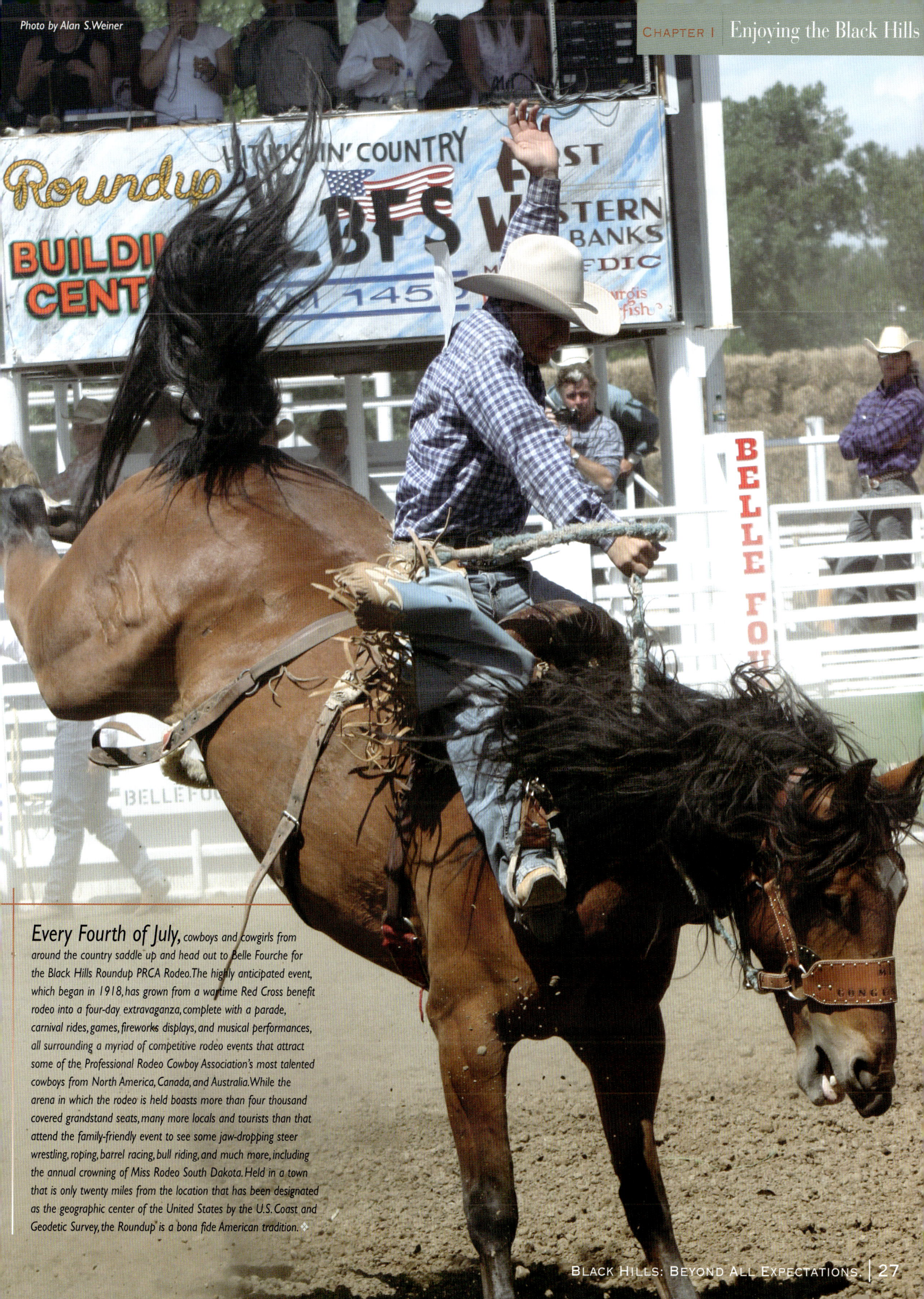

Photo by Alan S. Weiner

Every Fourth of July, cowboys and cowgirls from around the country saddle up and head out to Belle Fourche for the Black Hills Roundup PRCA Rodeo. The highly anticipated event, which began in 1918, has grown from a wartime Red Cross benefit rodeo into a four-day extravaganza, complete with a parade, carnival rides, games, fireworks displays, and musical performances, all surrounding a myriad of competitive rodeo events that attract some of the Professional Rodeo Cowboy Association's most talented cowboys from North America, Canada, and Australia. While the arena in which the rodeo is held boasts more than four thousand covered grandstand seats, many more locals and tourists than that attend the family-friendly event to see some jaw-dropping steer wrestling, roping, barrel racing, bull riding, and much more, including the annual crowning of Miss Rodeo South Dakota. Held in a town that is only twenty miles from the location that has been designated as the geographic center of the United States by the U.S. Coast and Geodetic Survey, the Roundup is a bona fide American tradition.

Dakota's Best Is a One-Stop-Shop for South Dakota Products

Half the fun of travel is searching out the treasures we can take home with us as reminders of our experiences. In Rapid City, Dakota's Best provides travelers with tangible memories of their time in the Black Hills.

Established in 2004 and located in the Radisson Hotel, Dakota's Best encompasses several businesses under one roof. Dakota's Best specializes in manufacturing and distributing South Dakota–made products—"Everything Under the Dakota Sun."

Dakota's Best includes a line of locally produced specialty foodstuffs such as beef, buffalo, wild turkey, and pheasant jerky and sausage; nuts and cheeses; coffee and Native American tea; Lakota popcorn; Sioux Fry Bread; specialty rubs and seasonings; and sauces, salsas, mustards, and jellies. The shop even offers a wide selection of wines from all ten of South Dakota's vineyards.

Dakota's Best provides travelers with tangible memories of their time in the Black Hills.

For locals and travelers alike, the Brown Bag Deli inside the gift shop has become a great place to pick up a quick snack or sweet, including freshly made deli sandwiches, pizzas, nachos, Cheesecake Factory cheesecakes, Honey Roasted Sunflower Seed ice

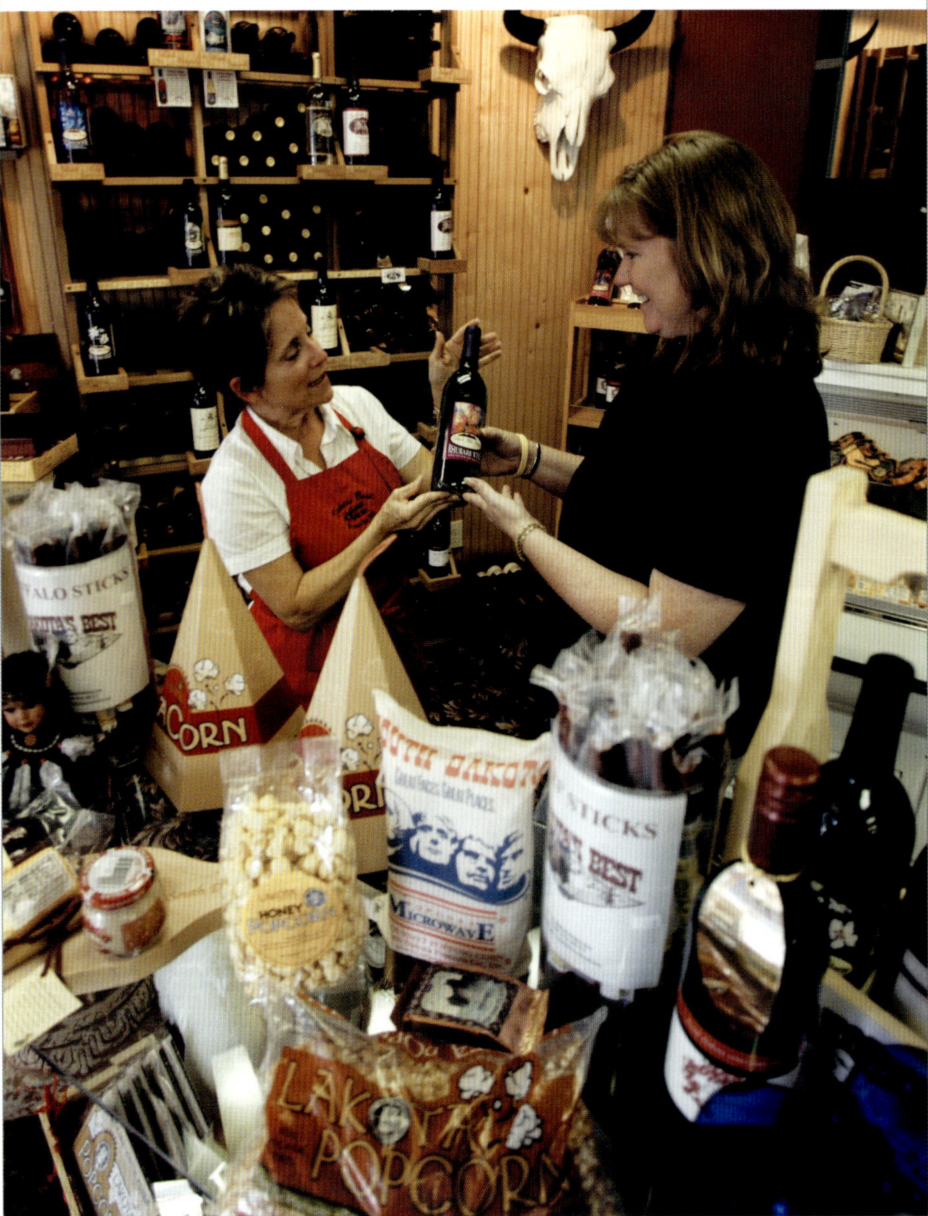

In support of South Dakota's small but thriving wine industry, all the wines carried by Dakota's Best come from vineyards located within the state. Here, one of the shop's knowledgeable salespeople suggests a bottle of rhubarb wine, produced by the Black Hills Winery in Spearfish.

Photo by Eric Francis

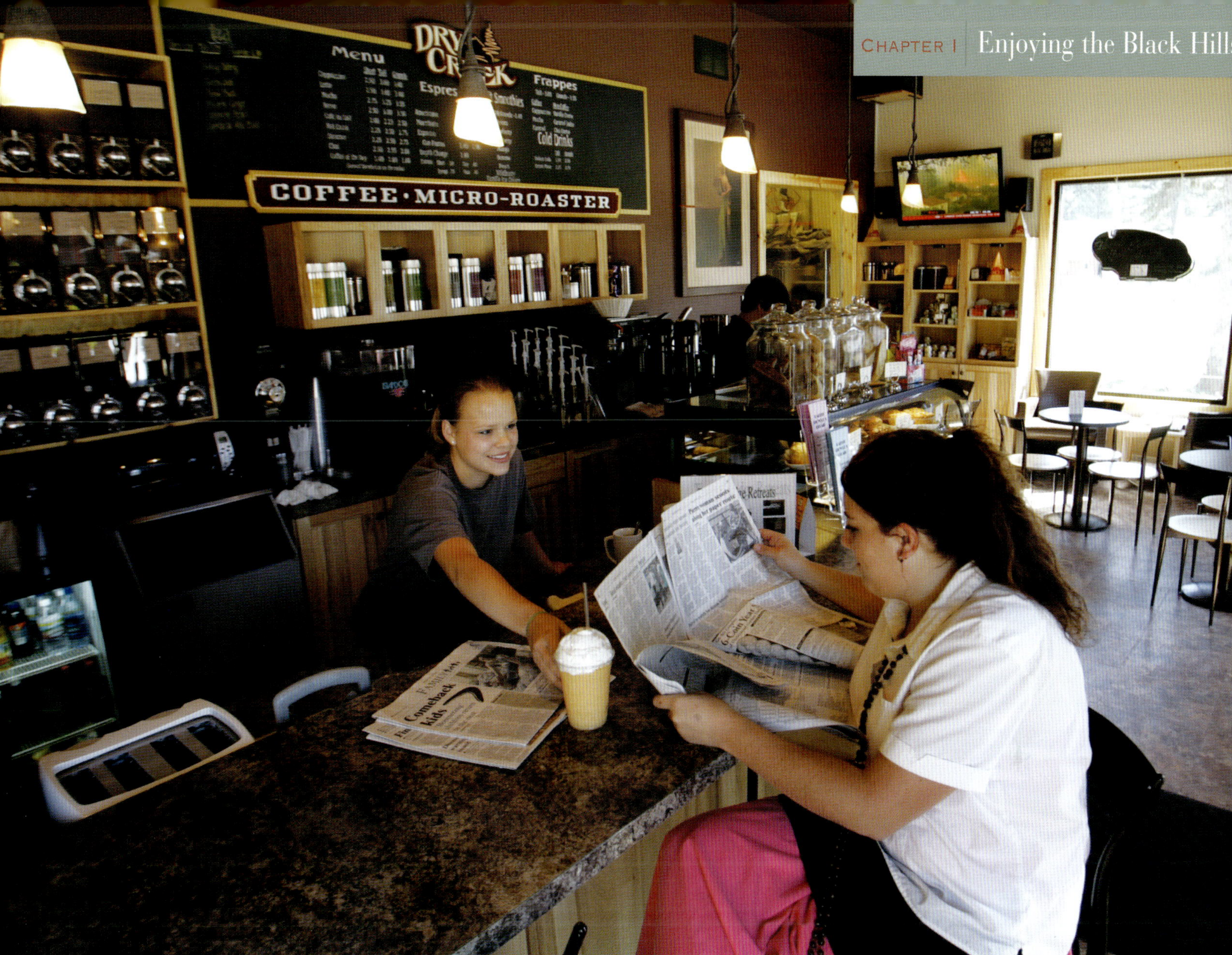

Photo by Eric Francis

Dry Creek Coffee was established in Hill City in 2003 to offer its customers gourmet coffee without the gourmet price. Now, Dakota's Best customers can sample the company's unique blend of Arabica beans, chosen from growers across the globe, but roasted and ground on-premises for the freshest flavor.

cream (created exclusively for Dakota's Best), and Starbucks coffee.

In September 2005, Dakota's Best merged with the Dry Creek Coffee Company, which was established in 2003 initially as a wholesale coffee roaster. Due to demand, a year later, the company expanded into a retail coffee shop, selling specialty coffees, coffee drinks, bagels, and assorted pastries. Dry Creek Coffee Company is located in the small tourist destination city of Hill City, only minutes away from Mount Rushmore.

Also located on-site at Dakota's Best in the Radisson is a business center with high-speed Internet service, computer terminals, and a shipping center that provides U.S. Postal Service, FedEx, and SpeeDee delivery services.

Given the growing desire among consumers nationwide for quality home-grown products as well as the company's record of success, Dakota's Best's owners now intend to expand their reach. In March 2006, Dakota Gateway opens in the First Western Bank Gateway building with a full-service coffee shop serving soups and sandwiches for lunch. Goals for the next few years include enhancing existing production capacity, adding additional South Dakota–made products to its line, and expanding the company's sales efforts.

For Radisson guests who can't carry their goodies home, Dakota's Best gladly ships purchases anywhere in the United States. Locals and visitors who want to share Dakota's Best can order standard or customized gift boxes. These make perfect individual as well as corporate gifts, and the shop even provides custom corporate labeling for that extra personal touch.

Ideally situated in the Radisson Hotel, Dakota's Best is poised to become the one-stop shop for unique and delicious locally made South Dakota products. With the goal to eventually expand beyond the state's borders, no doubt the rest of the country will also soon be experiencing Dakota's Best. ❖

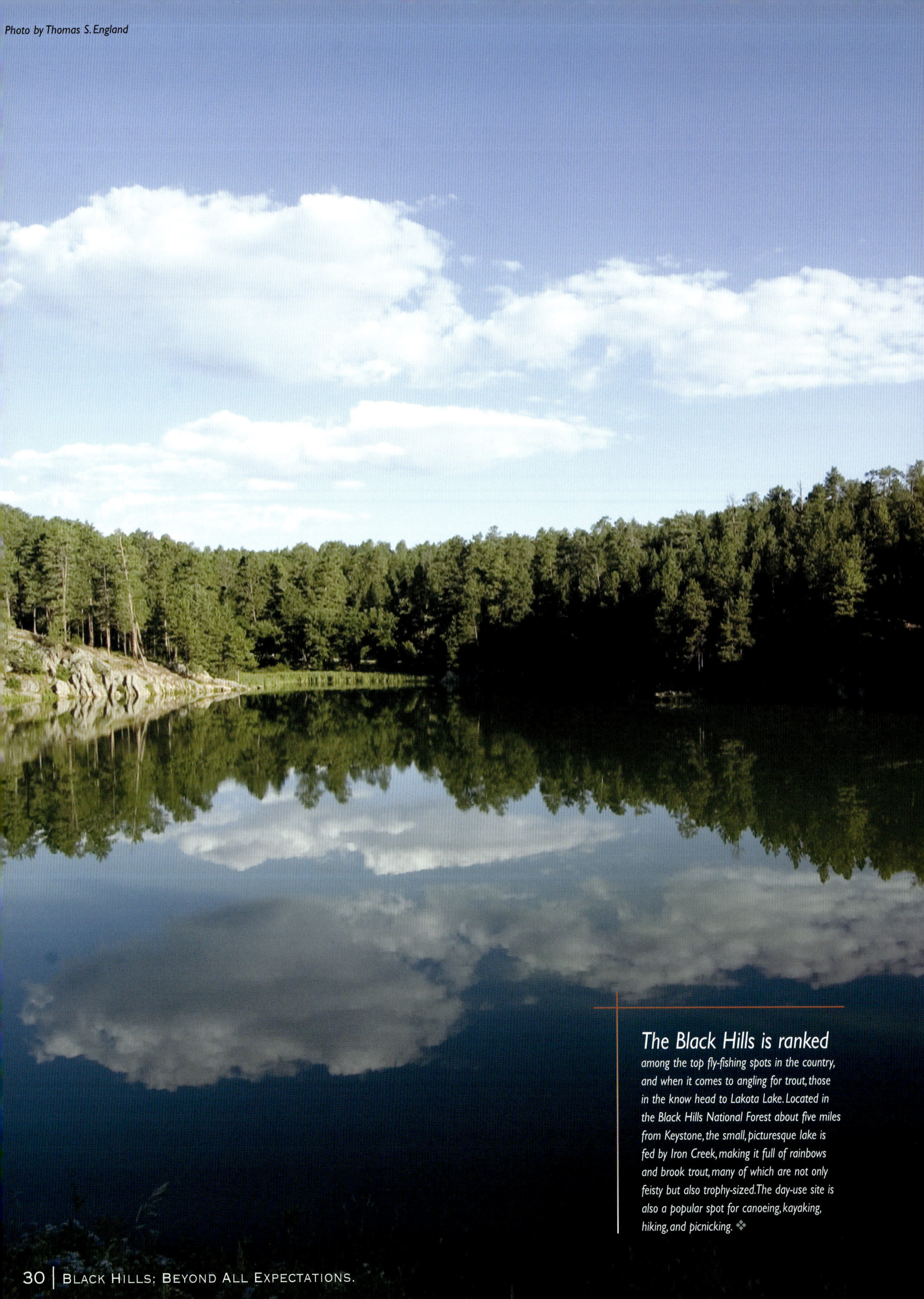

Photo by Thomas S. England

The Black Hills is ranked

among the top fly-fishing spots in the country, and when it comes to angling for trout, those in the know head to Lakota Lake. Located in the Black Hills National Forest about five miles from Keystone, the small, picturesque lake is fed by Iron Creek, making it full of rainbows and brook trout, many of which are not only feisty but also trophy-sized. The day-use site is also a popular spot for canoeing, kayaking, hiking, and picnicking. ❖

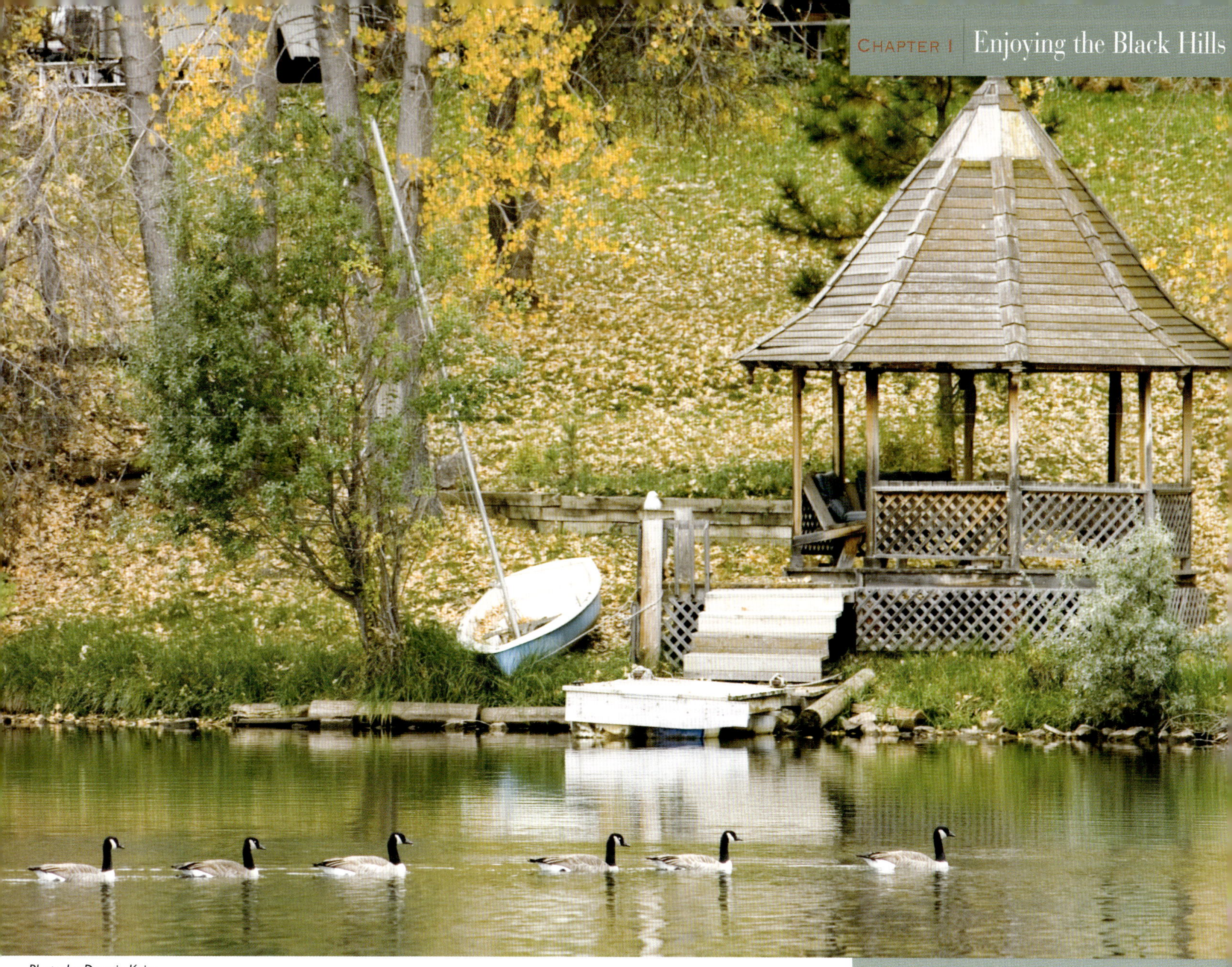

Photo by Dennis Keim

Photo by Thomas S. England

▲ **More than fifteen hundred** acres of parklands are maintained by Rapid City. From picnics to walks, to a game of tennis or horseshoes, or simply a chance to watch a flock of geese float on the lake, there's an array of opportunities to relax outdoors. The twenty-nine-acre Canyon Lake Park (above) is a wooded oasis open year-round. ❖

◄ **Why did the turkey hen** and her chicks cross the road? Why, to see more of the beautiful Black Hills, of course. It's not unusual to see wild turkey, deer, and elk within the area's forests. ❖

Rushmore Plaza Offers Small-Town Charm with Big-City Service

There are big-city hotels with the expected A-plus atmosphere and amenities, and there are small-town hotels that strive to reach that level. But in Rapid City, there is the Rushmore Plaza Holiday Inn Hotel & Convention Center—the hotel with small-town charm wrapped around big-city service.

"I hear guests comment all the time that they would expect this type of hotel in the big city, but not necessarily in a city the size of Rapid City," says David Eisenbraun, general manager. It's no wonder. All 205 of the Rushmore Plaza Holiday Inn Hotel's guest rooms surround an eight-story atrium, lush with greenery and featuring an unexpected sixty-foot waterfall as a focal point. It's easy for people to forget they are in a hotel, much less a city, yet the Rushmore Plaza is situated downtown—minutes from the mall and airport, and less than a half-hour away from attractions in the Black Hills.

"Service isn't just our standard; it's a way of life."

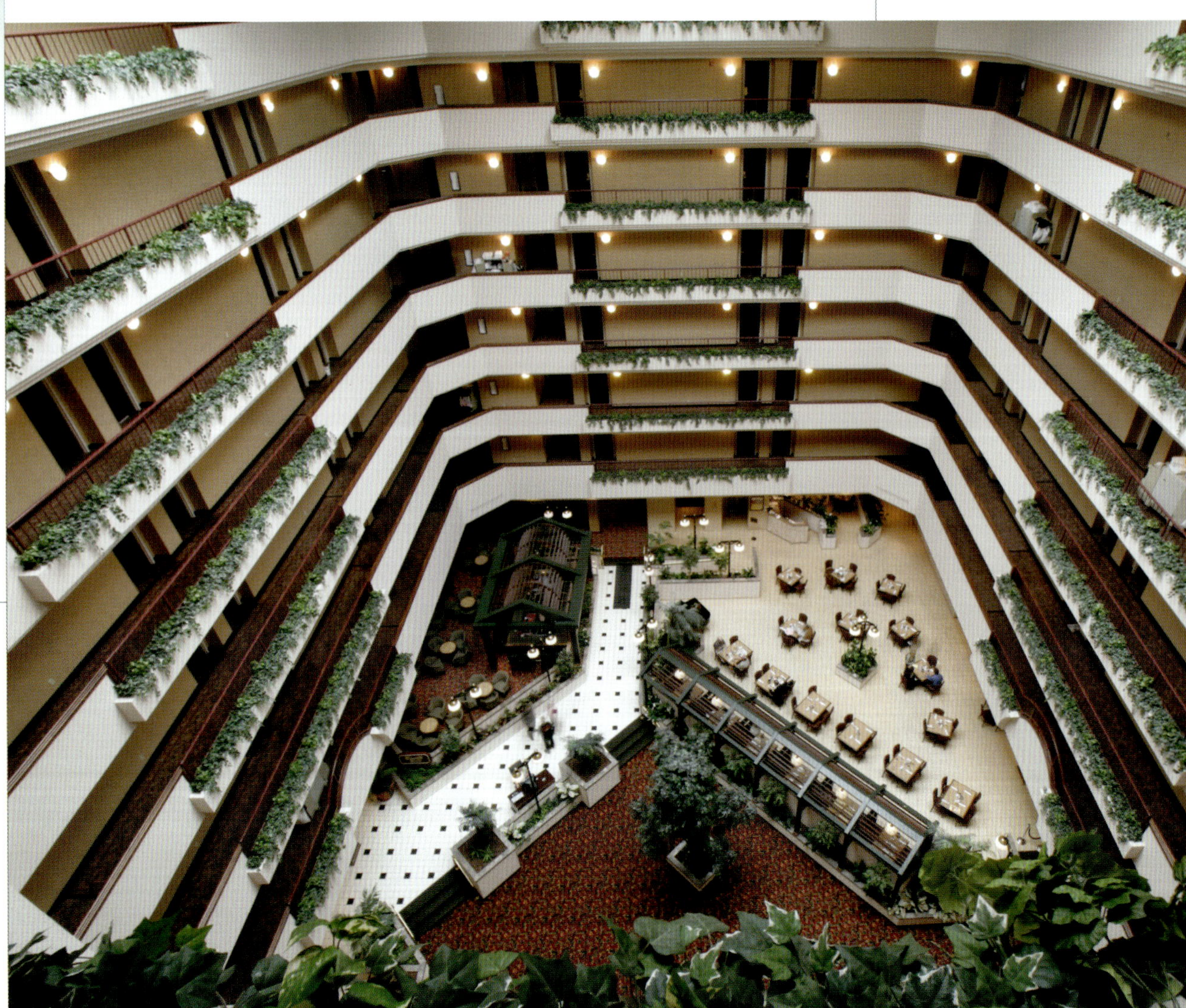

All 205 rooms look out on this impressive eight-story atrium, filled with tropical plants, a sixty-foot waterfall, and glass elevators

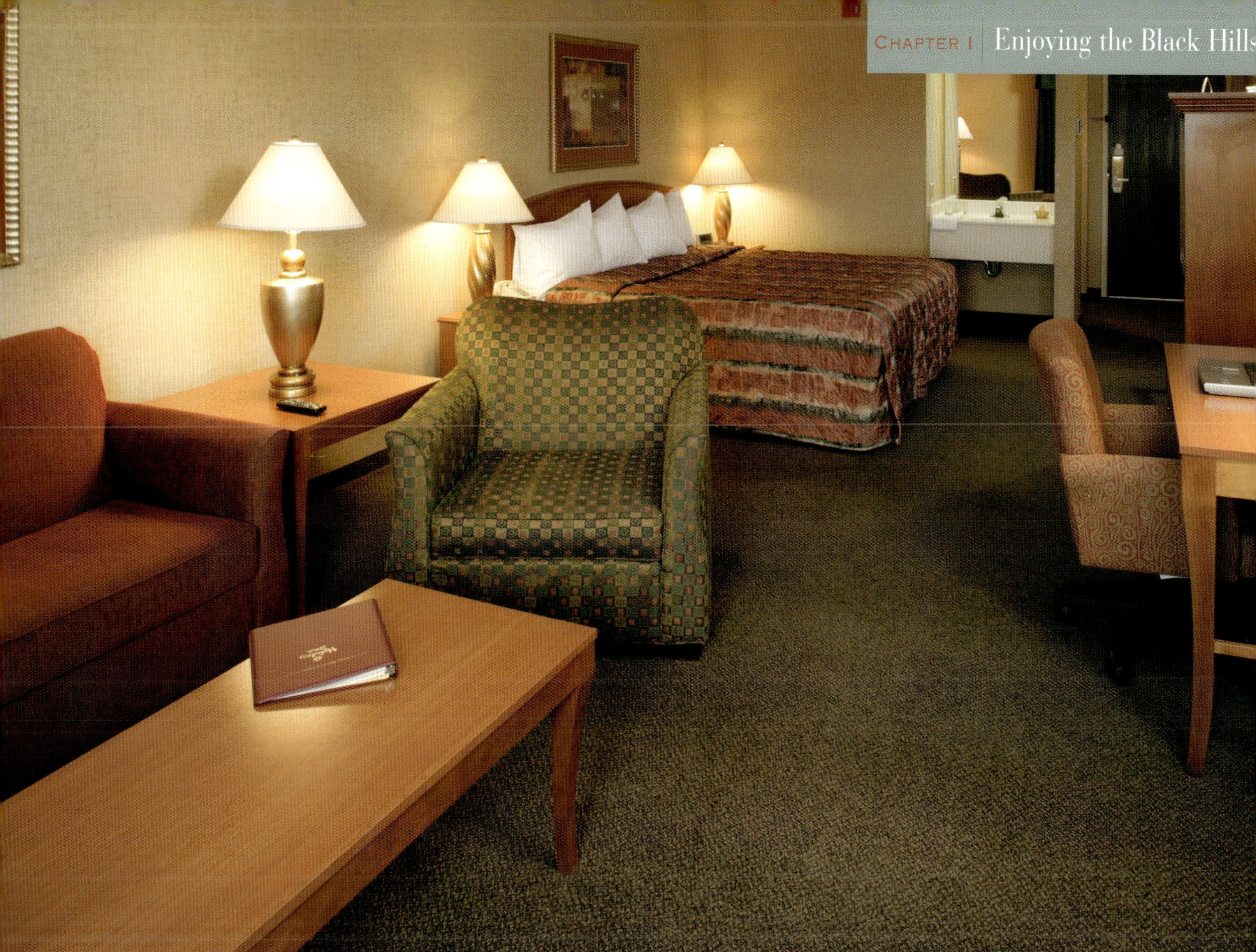

The king executive suites feature amenities designed with comfort, convenience, and productivity in mind.

Recently remodeled and under new local ownership, the hotel offers four room options: standard, king, mini suite, and large suite. The suites are popular with families, as they offer living space separate from the bedroom. All rooms feature standard amenities for comfort, convenience, and productivity, including satellite/cable television, high-speed Internet access, two-line telephone, work desk, coffee/tea maker, and in-room video checkout.

In addition, as a full-service hotel, the Rushmore Plaza Holiday Inn offers a fitness facility, sauna, indoor swimming pool and whirlpool, guest laundry room, and lounge. Its restaurant, Tiffany Grille, is nestled amid the foliage of the serene atrium and serves a delicious breakfast buffet, lunch, and dinner.

The hotel's award-winning chef also presides over a white-glove banquet service for business and convention events. With more than 14,000 square feet of flexible meeting space, the Rushmore Plaza Holiday Inn Hotel & Convention Center can accommodate everything from small meetings to large events, including receptions for up to eight hundred people. All the latest audiovisual equipment is available to produce efficient and effective presentations. If more space is needed, the adjacent Rushmore Plaza Civic Center provides an additional 150,000 square feet.

Continued on page 34

Continued from page 33

The ambience, however, is just one of the reasons this hotel property leaves a lasting impression on guests. Customer service is another. For the staff at the Rushmore Plaza—many of them longtime employees—going the extra mile is simply ingrained in their midwestern personalities. "Service isn't just our standard; it's a way of life," says Eisenbraun. "Anytime people are on the road, they're looking to feel like they are home, and to feel like people care about them and their needs. Our employees go out of their way to make sure the customer is satisfied." Consequently, it's not unusual to find an employee who will leave the hotel to pick something up for a guest—and always with a smile. "I hear people remark all the time about how the staff is so friendly," he says. "Everyone, not just one employee, always says 'Hello' and asks guests if they need anything. That's what makes this hotel stand out." ❖

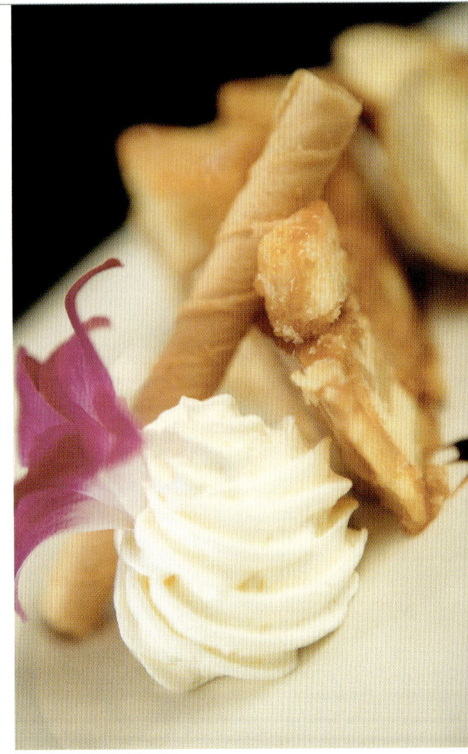

The Rushmore Plaza's award-winning chef creates a delicious variety of entrees and desserts.

With an indoor pool, any time is pool time at the Rushmore Plaza. Guests can also work up a sweat in the fitness center, or relax in the sauna or one of two hot tubs.

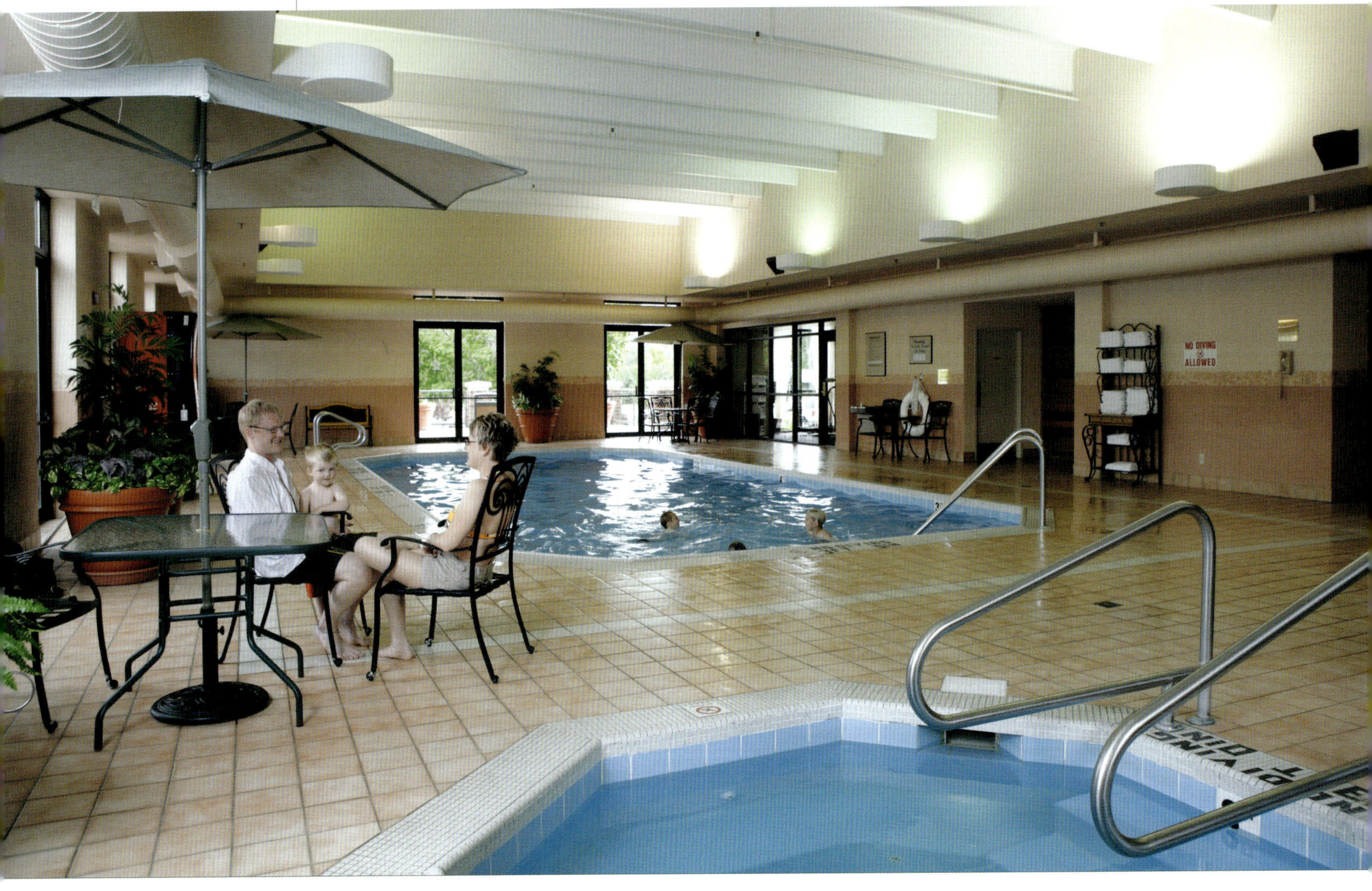

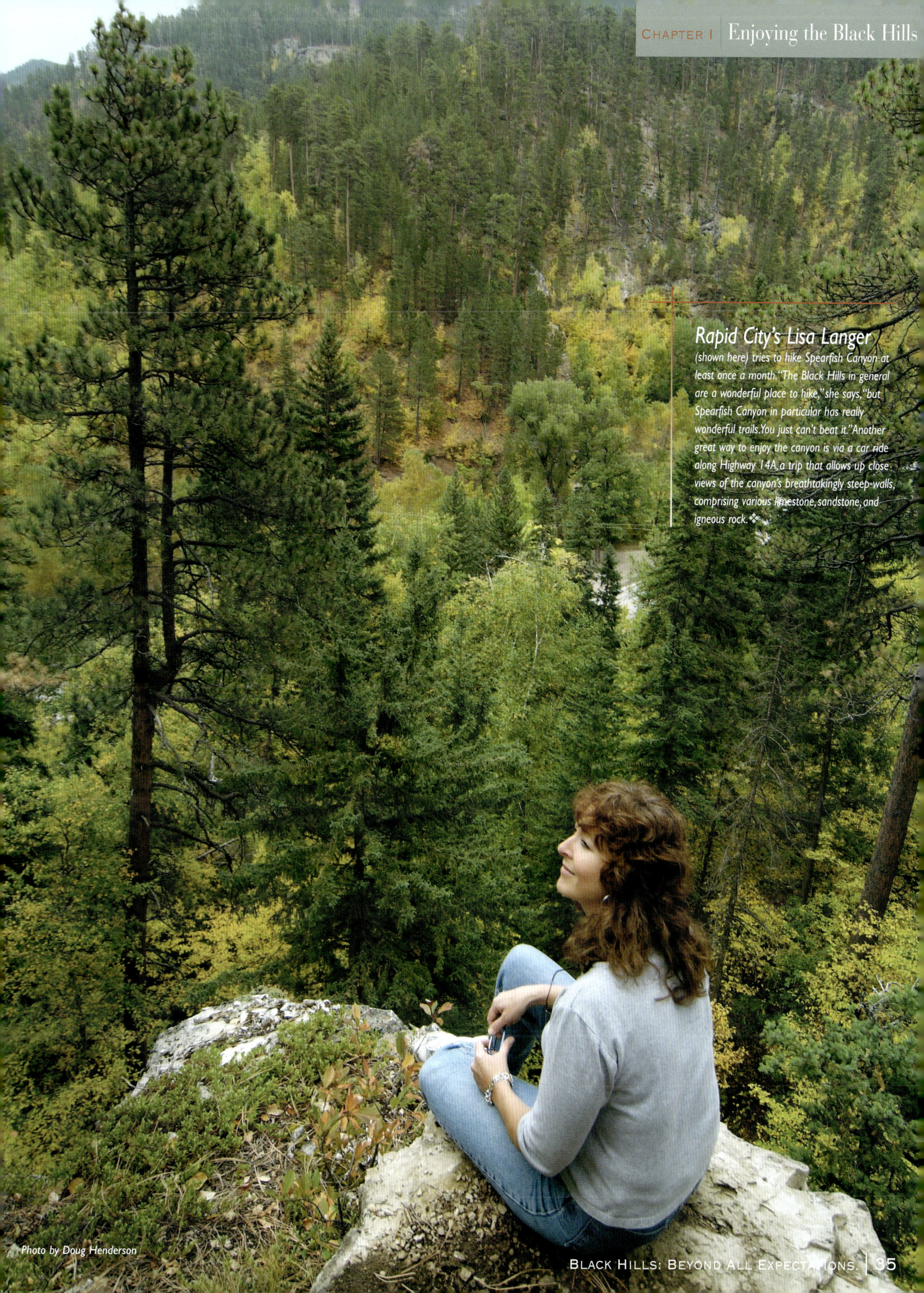

Rapid City's Lisa Langer (shown here) tries to hike Spearfish Canyon at least once a month. "The Black Hills in general are a wonderful place to hike," she says, "but Spearfish Canyon in particular has really wonderful trails. You just can't beat it." Another great way to enjoy the canyon is via a car ride along Highway 14A, a trip that allows up close views of the canyon's breathtakingly steep walls, comprising various limestone, sandstone, and igneous rock.

Photo by Doug Henderson

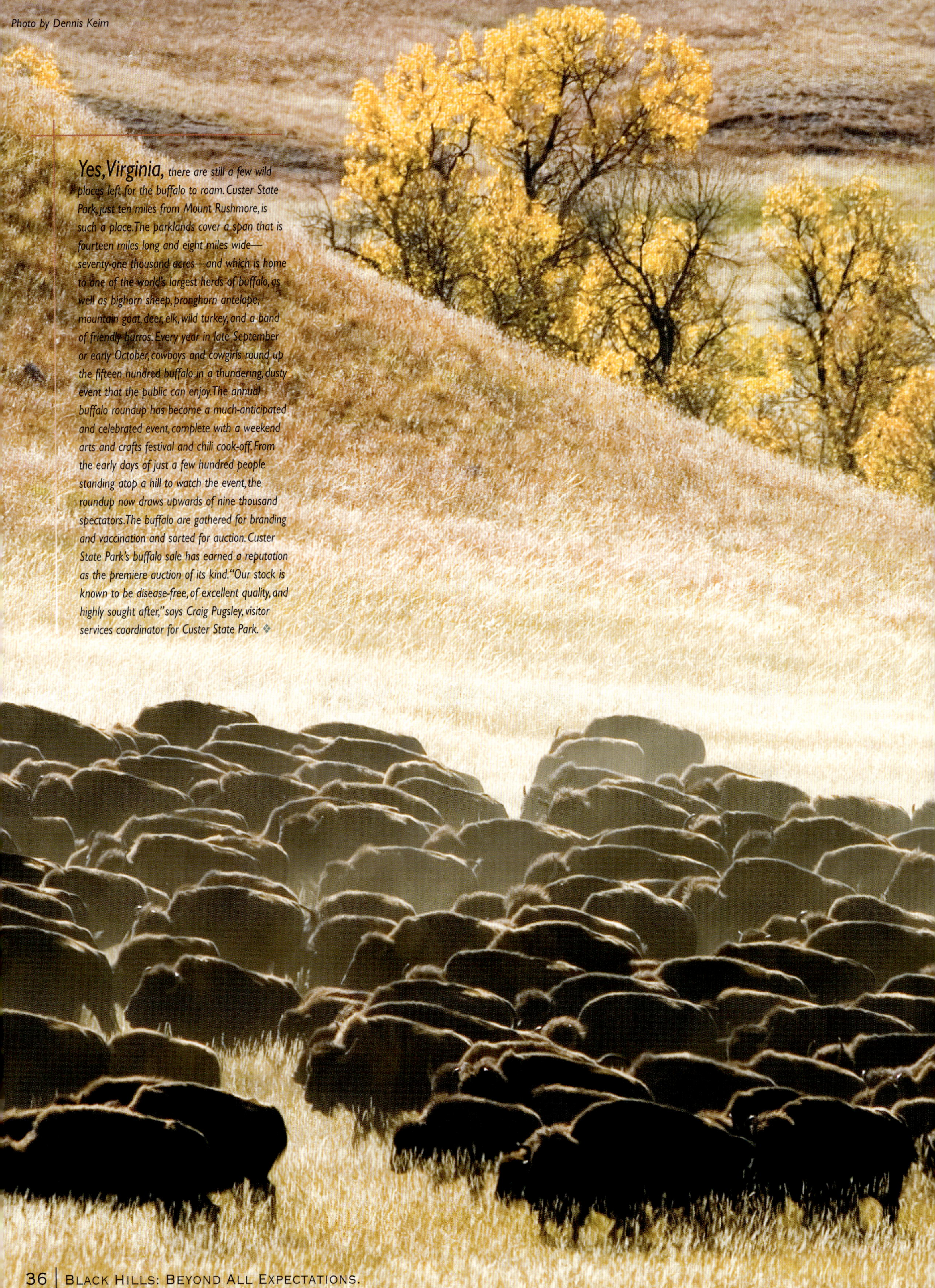

Photo by Dennis Keim

Yes, Virginia, there are still a few wild places left for the buffalo to roam. Custer State Park, just ten miles from Mount Rushmore, is such a place. The parklands cover a span that is fourteen miles long and eight miles wide—seventy-one thousand acres—and which is home to one of the world's largest herds of buffalo, as well as bighorn sheep, pronghorn antelope, mountain goat, deer, elk, wild turkey, and a band of friendly burros. Every year in late September or early October, cowboys and cowgirls round up the fifteen hundred buffalo in a thundering, dusty event that the public can enjoy. The annual buffalo roundup has become a much-anticipated and celebrated event, complete with a weekend arts and crafts festival and chili cook-off. From the early days of just a few hundred people standing atop a hill to watch the event, the roundup now draws upwards of nine thousand spectators. The buffalo are gathered for branding and vaccination and sorted for auction. Custer State Park's buffalo sale has earned a reputation as the premiere auction of its kind. "Our stock is known to be disease-free, of excellent quality, and highly sought after," says Craig Pugsley, visitor services coordinator for Custer State Park. ❖

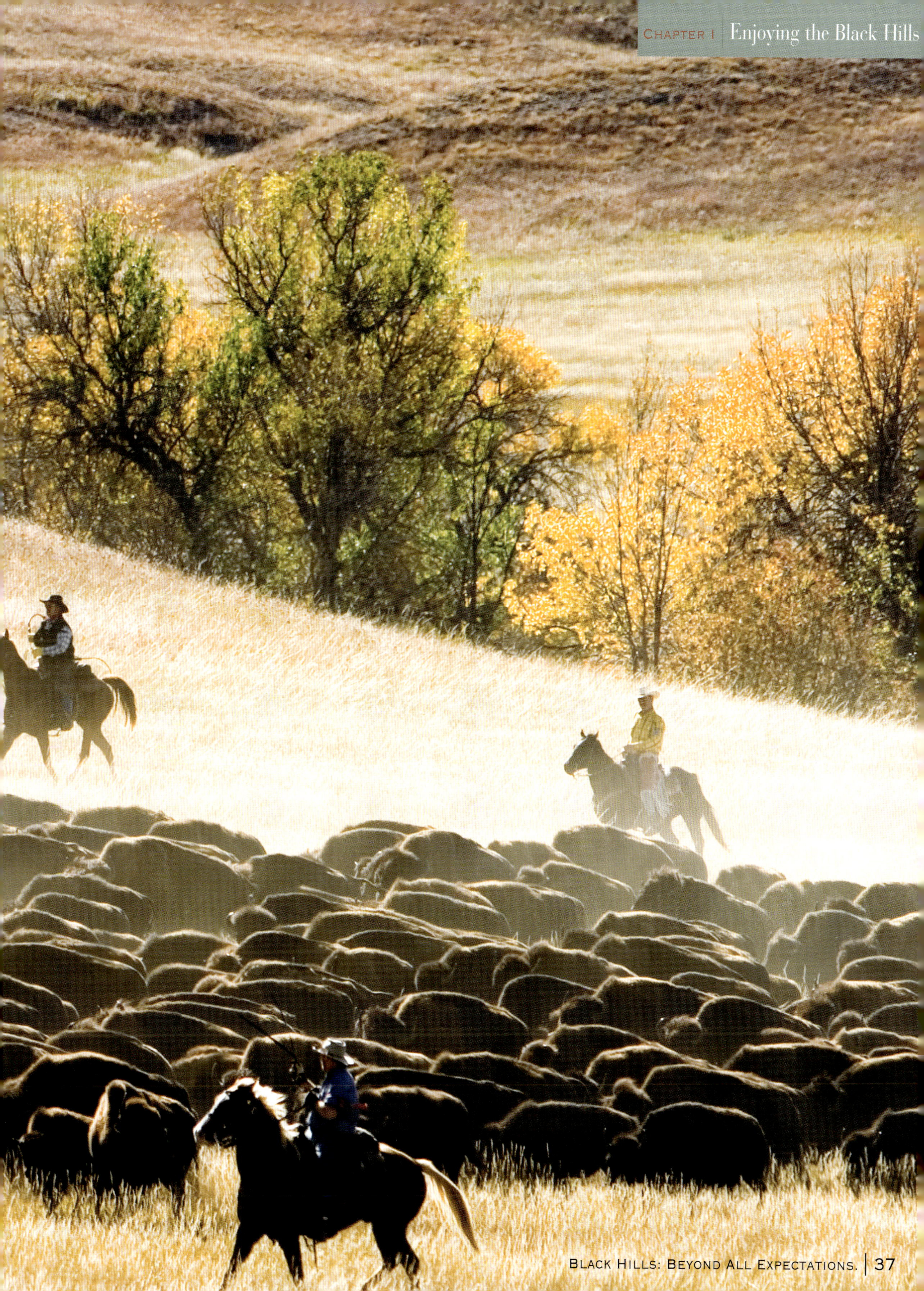

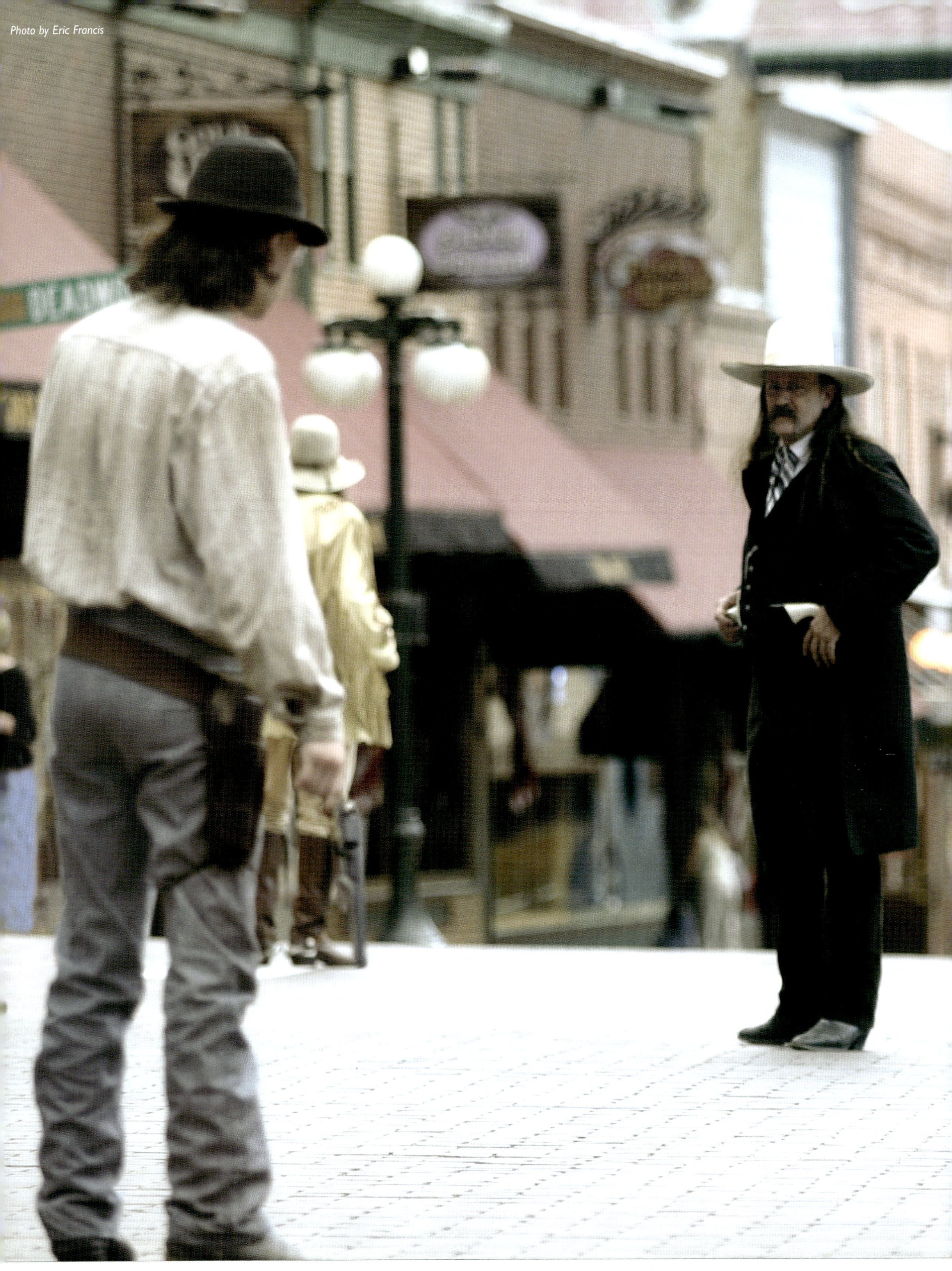

Photo by Eric Francis

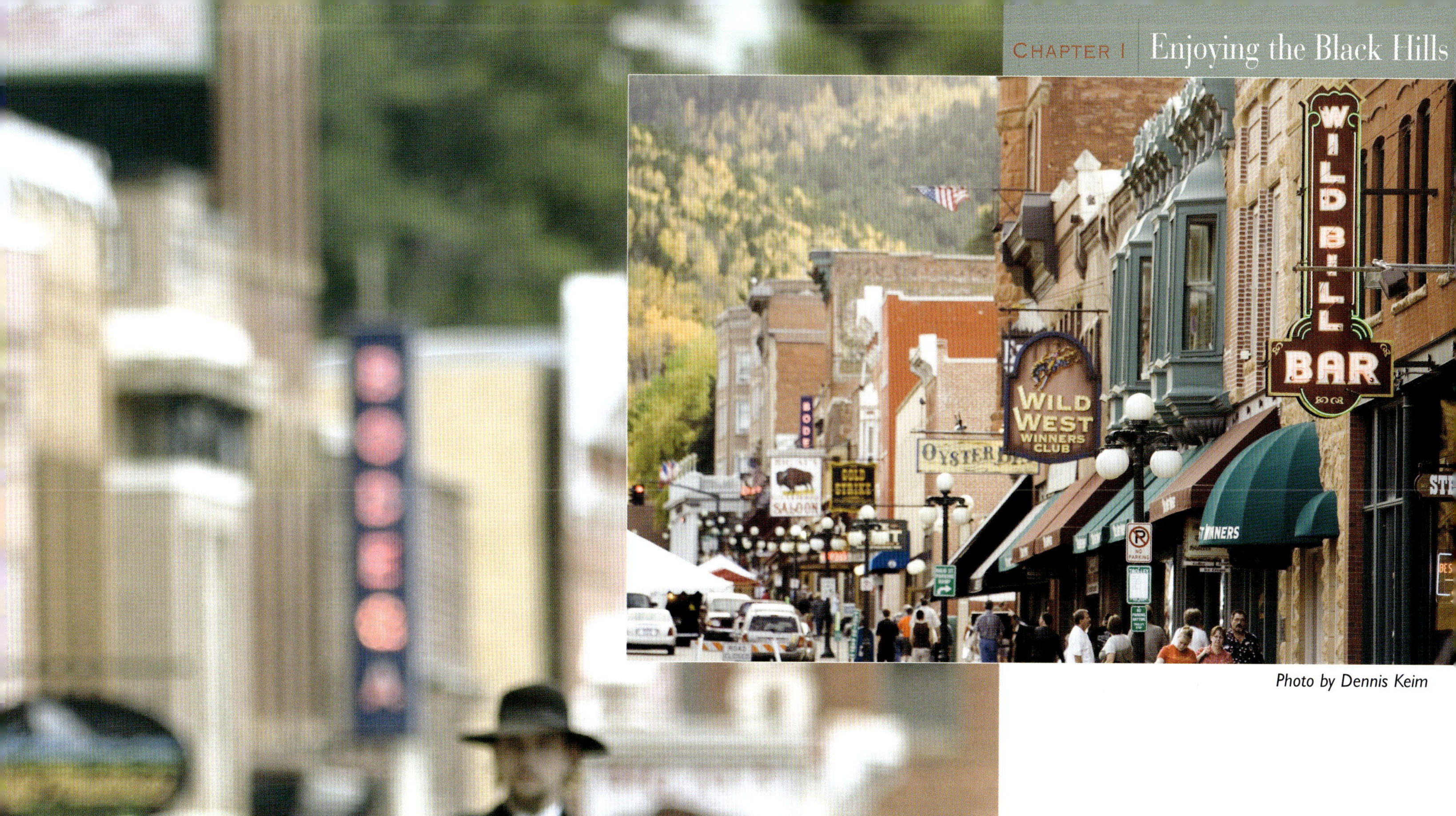

Photo by Dennis Keim

DEADWOOD...
The WILD West

Contemporary cars may have replaced historic stagecoaches on the streets of Deadwood, but taking a trip down the strip is like stepping back in time to 1876, when an irresistible gold rush transpired in the Black Hills and attracted notorious characters like Wild Bill Hickok, Wyatt Earp, and Calamity Jane. Thanks to its colorful past, ripe with saloon brawls that turned into gunfights and gold prospectors hitting it rich on a daily basis, the entire city of Deadwood is now listed on the National Register of Historic Places. Over the years, the once-thriving town, which had become a prosperous trading center for the region, fell into a state of disrepair, its old dilapidated buildings showing the telltale signs of age and neglect. However, when low-wage gambling was legalized in 1989, Deadwood experienced an incredible resurgence. Today, the fully restored town boasts more than eighty gaming halls that tempt the luck of visitors from around the country, many of whom get the chance to witness a thrilling gunfight reenactment right on the city streets. There are historic hotels and saloons, as well as museums and attractions galore. Now, Deadwood is far from dead. It's alive and well, with its history intact and a flourishing future ahead of it. ❖

Breathtaking Views and Championship Golf

Amid the beauty and serenity of the Black Hills is The Estates and Golf Club at Red Rock, a unique residential community that offers luxurious living and an exceptional quality of life.

Tucked among towering pines, rock outcroppings, and sloping hillsides, and overlooking the area's lush meadows rich with year-round wildlife, The Estates at Red Rock blend the beauty and serenity of country life with the convenience and amenities of the city.

Life at The Estates at Red Rock means choosing from an array of custom homes and home sites, each offering breathtaking views of the magnificent Black Hills. From intimate half-acre spreads to expansive three-acre sites to easy and convenient townhomes, every home is a personal experience at the estates.

The Estates at Red Rock are enveloped by the Golf Club at Red Rock, an eighteen-hole public course featured in *The New York Times* article "Great Plains, Great Golf," and rated by *Golfweek Magazine* as number-one in the state and among the top-ten new public golf courses in the nation for 2005. *Golf Magazine*'s architectural critic called the Golf Club at Red Rock "perhaps the best ground-hugging golf course laid out on a mountain

The Estates at Red Rock are enveloped by the Golf Club at Red Rock, an eighteen-hole public course.

Photo by Alan S.Weiner

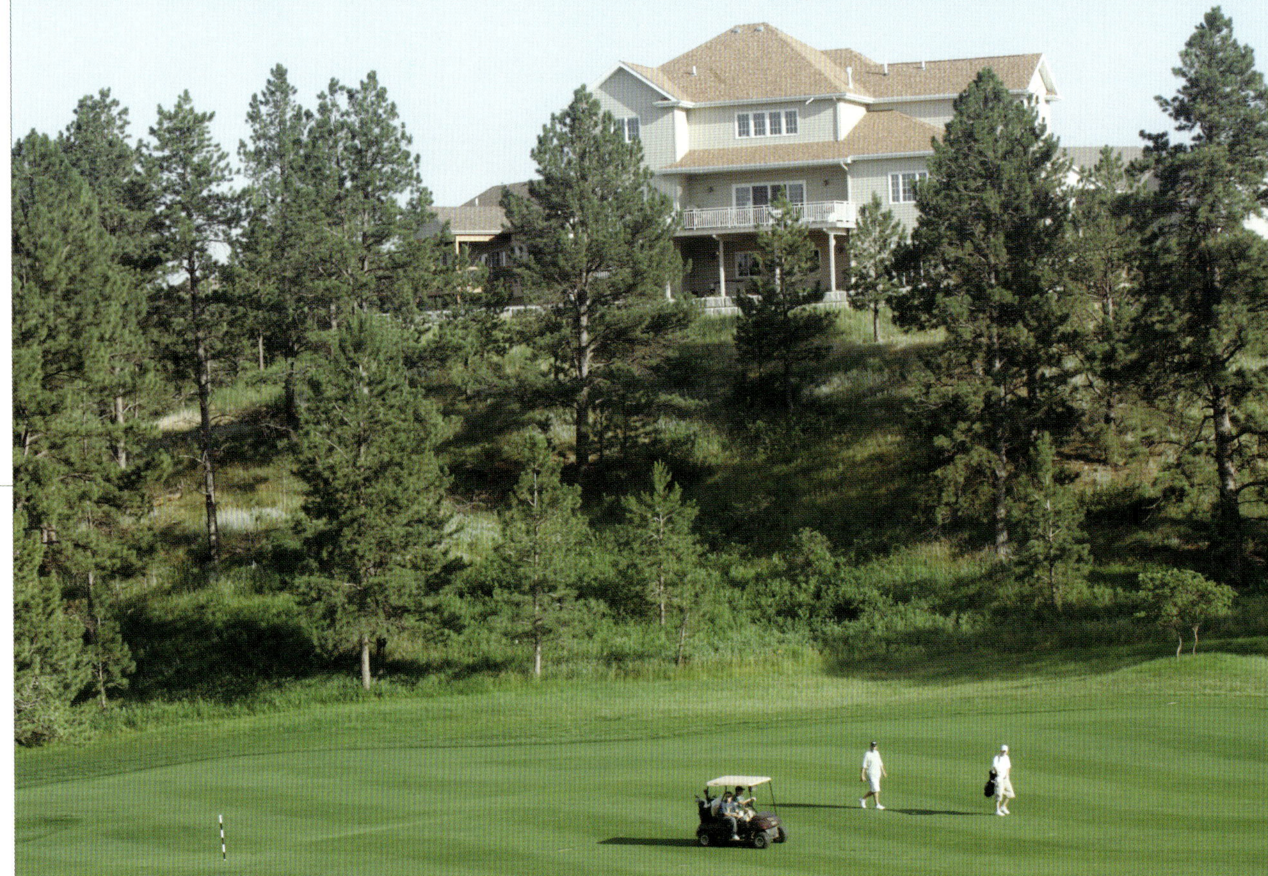

The Estates at Red Rock feature magnificent custom homes and home sites that overlook the golf course and offer panoramic views of the area's natural beauty.

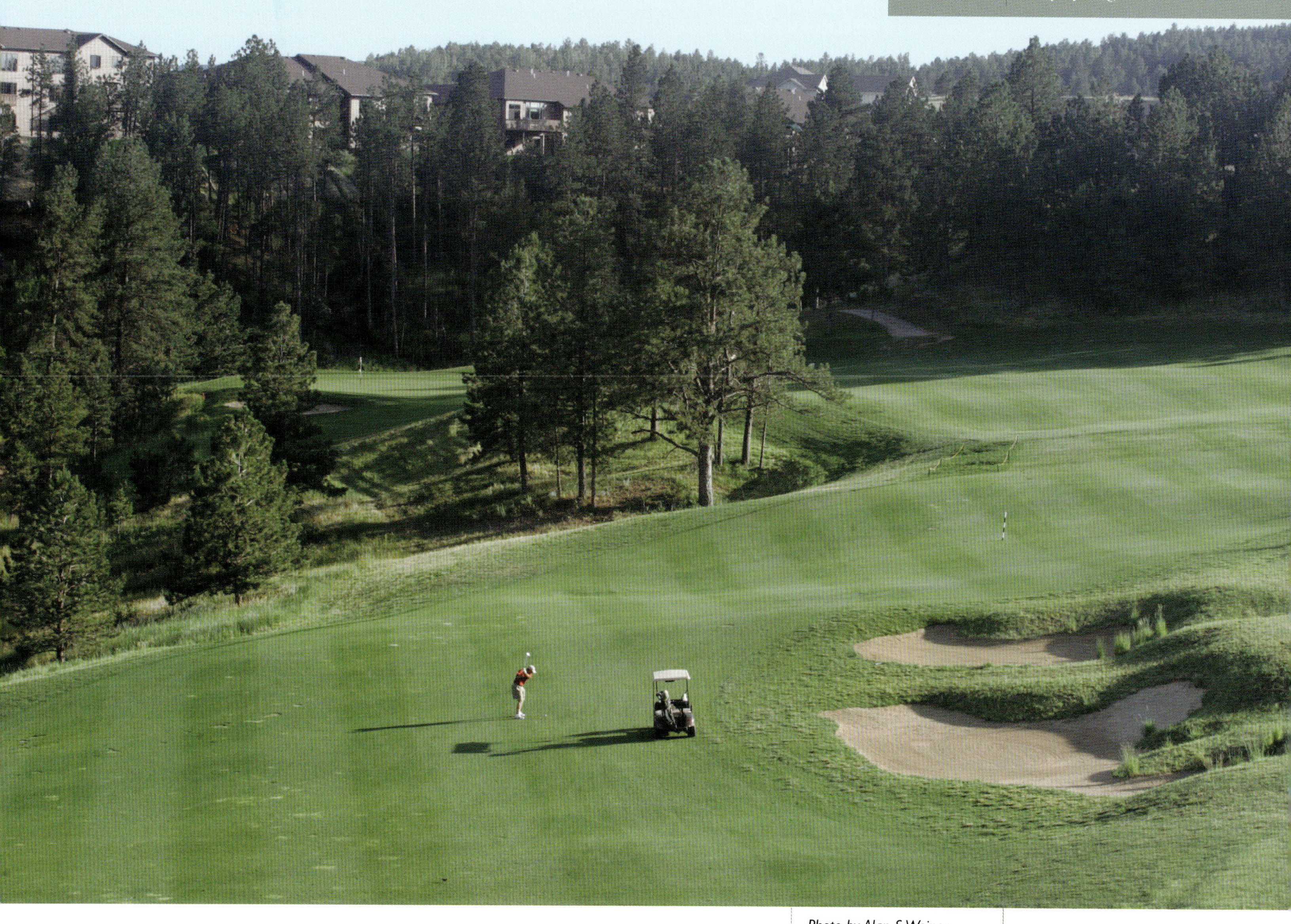

Photo by Alan S.Weiner

Routed through the spectacular Black Hills terrain, the Golf Club at Red Rock is eighteen holes of challenge with rolling fairways, dramatic elevation changes, and USGA-specification greens.

slope since Coore and Chrenshaw's Plantation Course at Kapalua."

Noted as both challenging and fun, the course features rolling fairways, dramatic elevation changes, links-style bunkers, and United States Golf Association–regulation greens. The par 72 course, with a minimum of four tee placements per hole, is a full seventy-one hundred yards of challenge for players of all skill levels. Each hole is distinctive in nature and will leave the golfer with many memories of their round.

All the greens are approachable and offer a variety of choices depending on the shot that is selected. There are classic risk-reward opportunities, and how the golfer feels on a particular day will greatly determine shot selection.

Bounded by native fescue grasses and tall ponderosa pines, the course is both a calming and an exhilarating experience for the demanding professional or the casual player.

Built in 2003, the course has already proven to be a popular spot for tournaments and gatherings. Whether joining in a small competition against another course, participating in a members-only tournament, or catering a company-wide activity, the Golf Club at Red Rock has the staff and amenities to make any event a success.

At The Estates and Golf Club at Red Rock, life is about enjoying all the beautiful and pleasurable lifestyle that the Black Hills has to offer. ❖

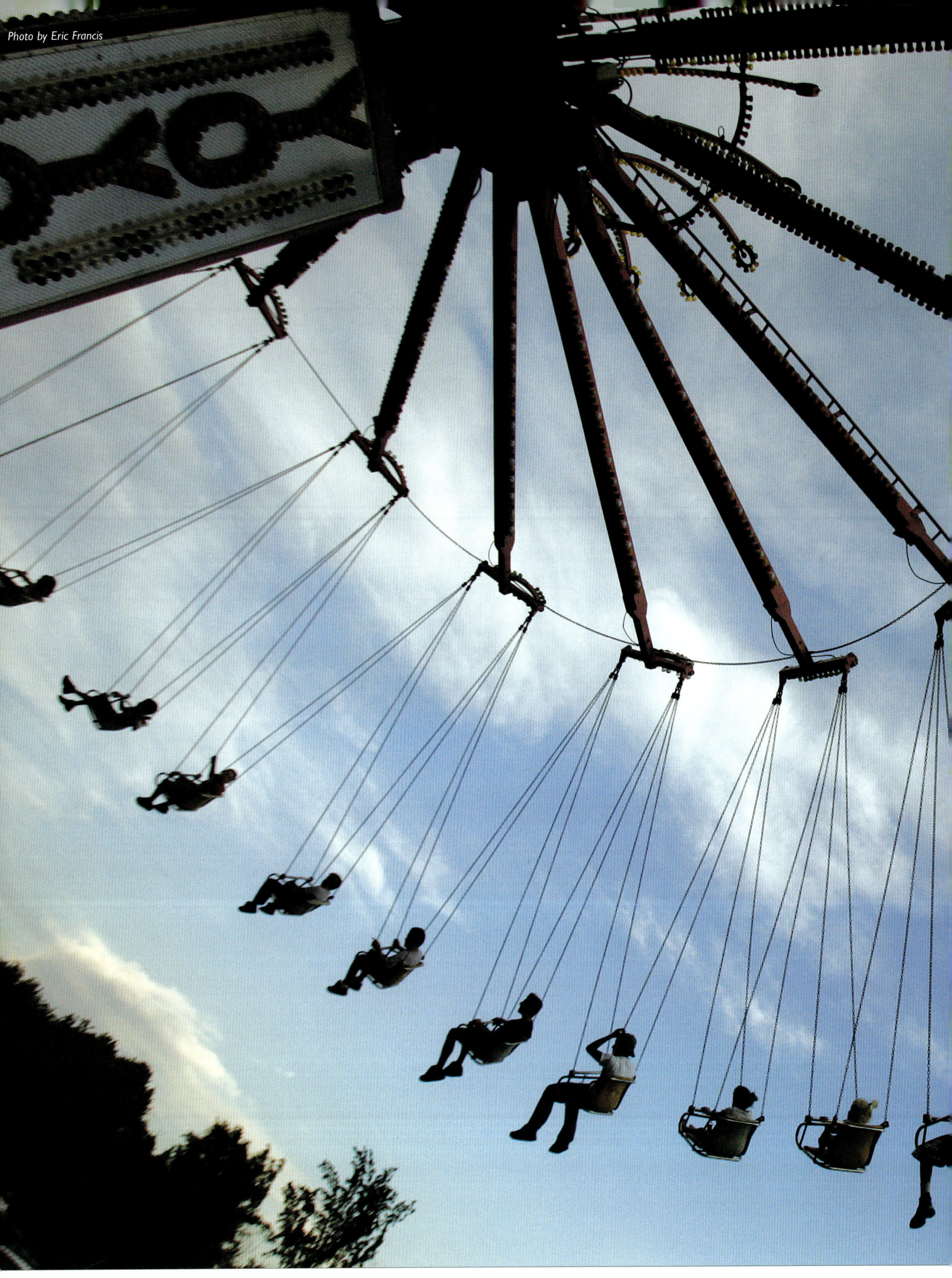

Photo by Eric Francis

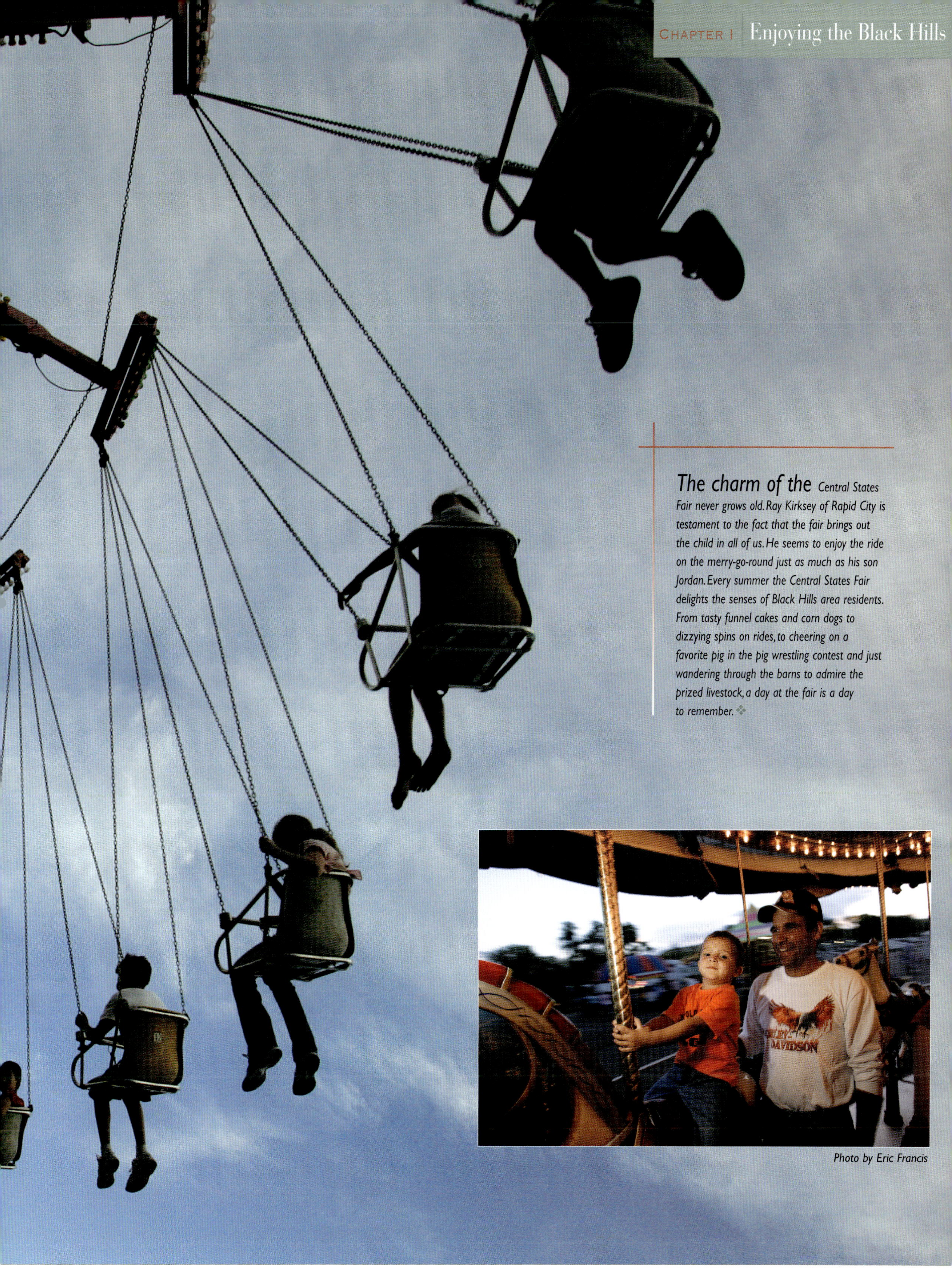

The charm of the Central States Fair never grows old. Ray Kirksey of Rapid City is testament to the fact that the fair brings out the child in all of us. He seems to enjoy the ride on the merry-go-round just as much as his son Jordan. Every summer the Central States Fair delights the senses of Black Hills area residents. From tasty funnel cakes and corn dogs to dizzying spins on rides, to cheering on a favorite pig in the pig wrestling contest and just wandering through the barns to admire the prized livestock, a day at the fair is a day to remember.

Photo by Eric Francis

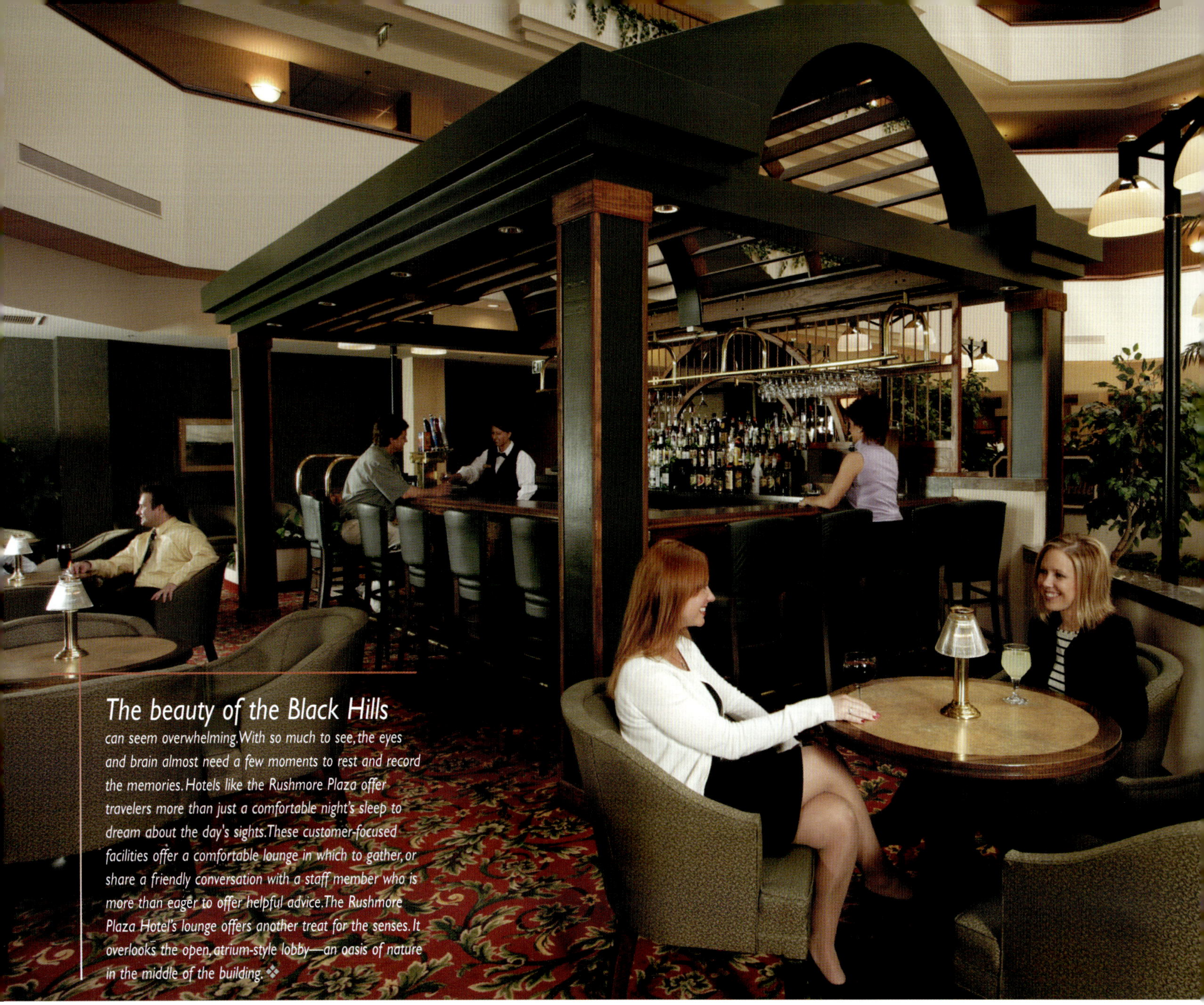

The beauty of the Black Hills

can seem overwhelming. With so much to see, the eyes and brain almost need a few moments to rest and record the memories. Hotels like the Rushmore Plaza offer travelers more than just a comfortable night's sleep to dream about the day's sights. These customer-focused facilities offer a comfortable lounge in which to gather, or share a friendly conversation with a staff member who is more than eager to offer helpful advice. The Rushmore Plaza Hotel's lounge offers another treat for the senses. It overlooks the open, atrium-style lobby—an oasis of nature in the middle of the building. ❖

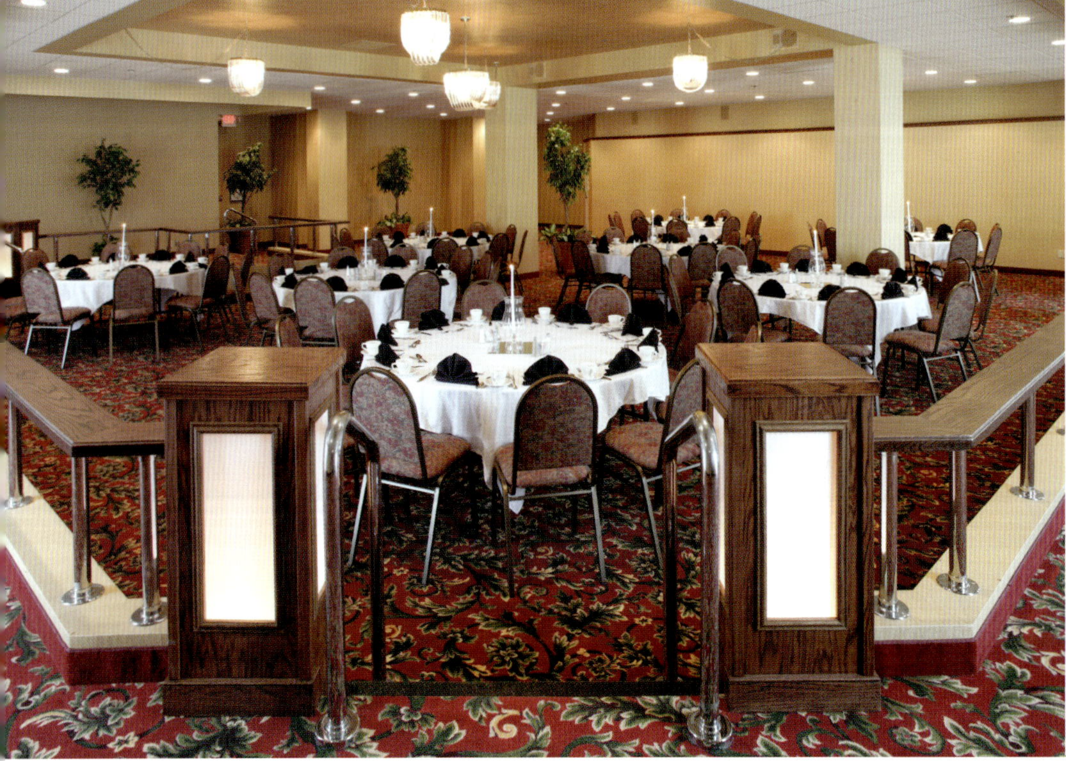

While Rapid City is the

home base for many individuals and families visiting the Black Hills' attractions, the city is also popular with businesses for conventions and trade shows. The Rushmore Plaza Holiday Inn Hotel is a "big city hotel" brimming with small-town service and amenities, such as the banquet and meeting facilities, complete with white-glove banquet service, and top-of-the-line audiovisual equipment. The hotel offers fourteen thousand square feet of meeting space, and can accommodate up to eight hundred people, reception-style. ❖

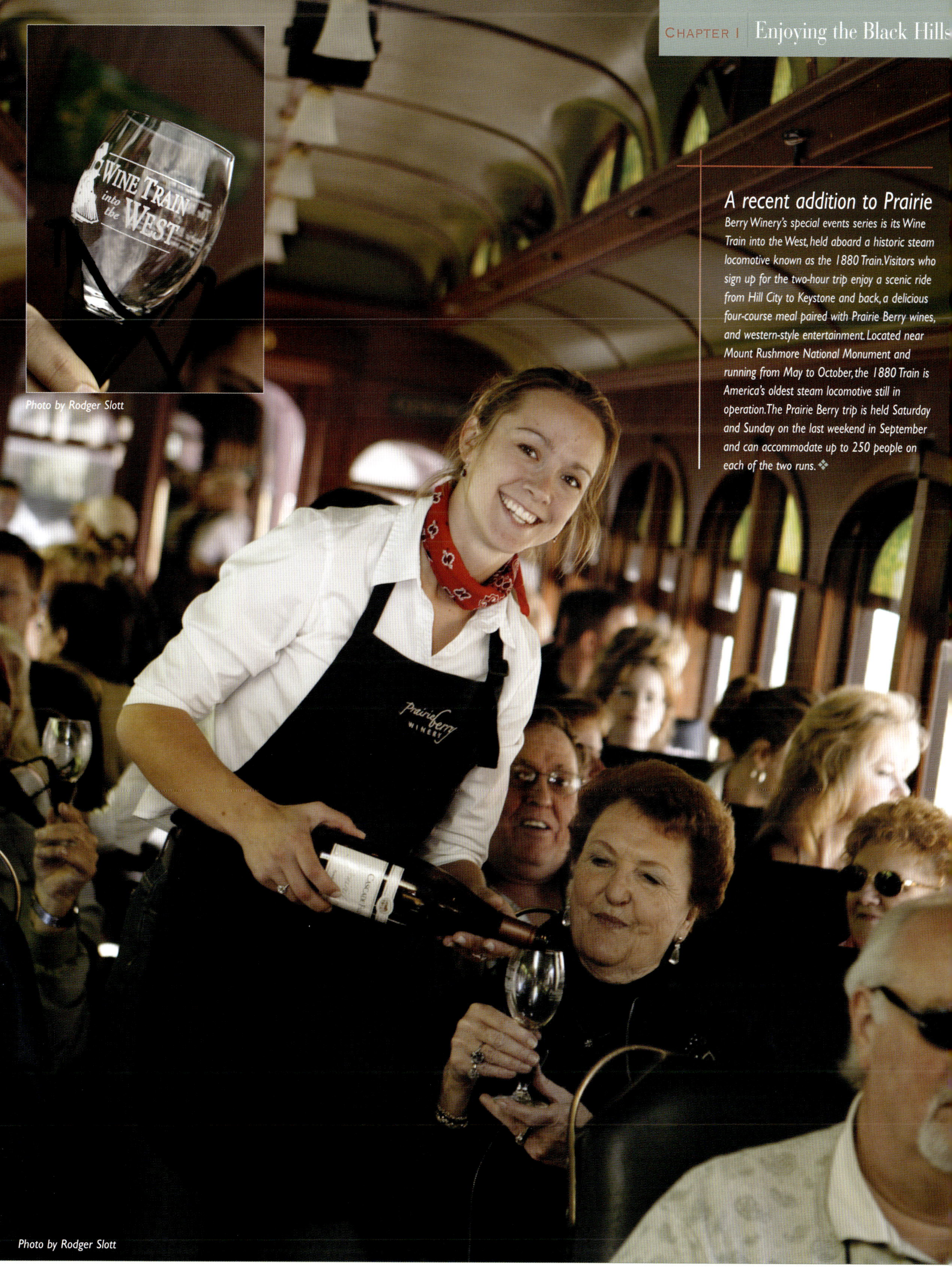

Photo by Rodger Slott

A recent addition to Prairie Berry Winery's special events series is its Wine Train into the West, held aboard a historic steam locomotive known as the 1880 Train. Visitors who sign up for the two-hour trip enjoy a scenic ride from Hill City to Keystone and back, a delicious four-course meal paired with Prairie Berry wines, and western-style entertainment. Located near Mount Rushmore National Monument and running from May to October, the 1880 Train is America's oldest steam locomotive still in operation. The Prairie Berry trip is held Saturday and Sunday on the last weekend in September and can accommodate up to 250 people on each of the two runs. ❖

Photo by Rodger Slott

Spearfish—A Naturally Inviting Town

Spearfish is a town so rich with attributes that it has been described in many different ways. However, the label that says it best is the very reason people choose to visit here, and also the reason people choose to stay: Spearfish is, above all, "Naturally Inviting."

Surrounded by mountains, this pleasantly informal yet micropolitan city is one of the fastest growing in the Midwest. "We have many people moving here from larger areas, and they're bringing a nice mix of varying tastes and experiences," says Lisa Langer, Executive Director of the Spearfish Area Chamber of Commerce. "Yet although we're growing, we've retained this lovely hometown feel." In the lower valley, remnants of the market stands and greenhouses from the farms of the early years punctuate the drive into town. Spearfish Creek, a blue-ribbon trout stream, meanders through the

> "Yet although we're growing, we've retained this lovely hometown feel."

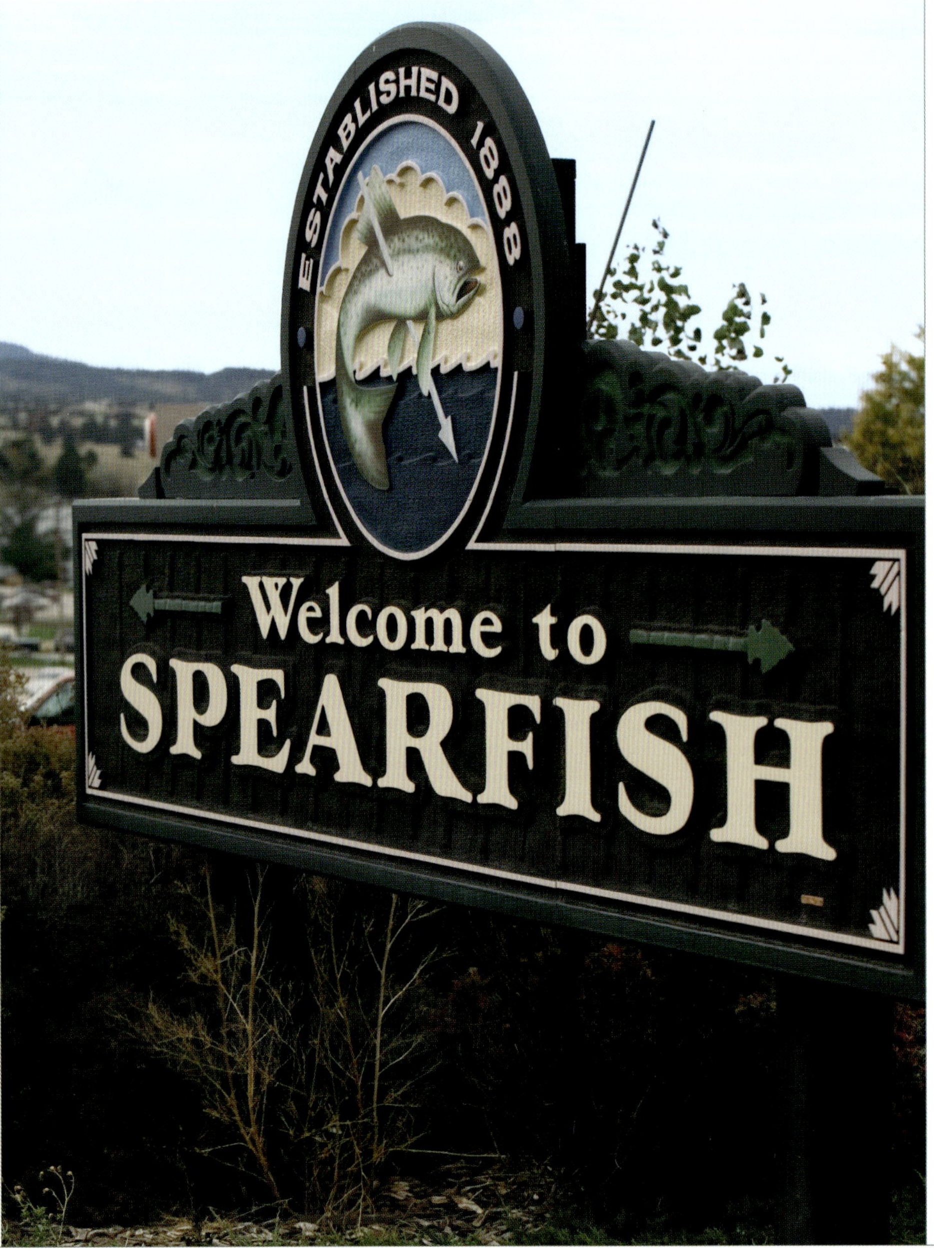

In its early days as a farming community Spearfish drew people from the surrounding Black Hills for food. Today, Spearfish maintains its comfortable ambience, and as a commercial hub, it continues to attract people for retail.

Photo by Dennis Keim

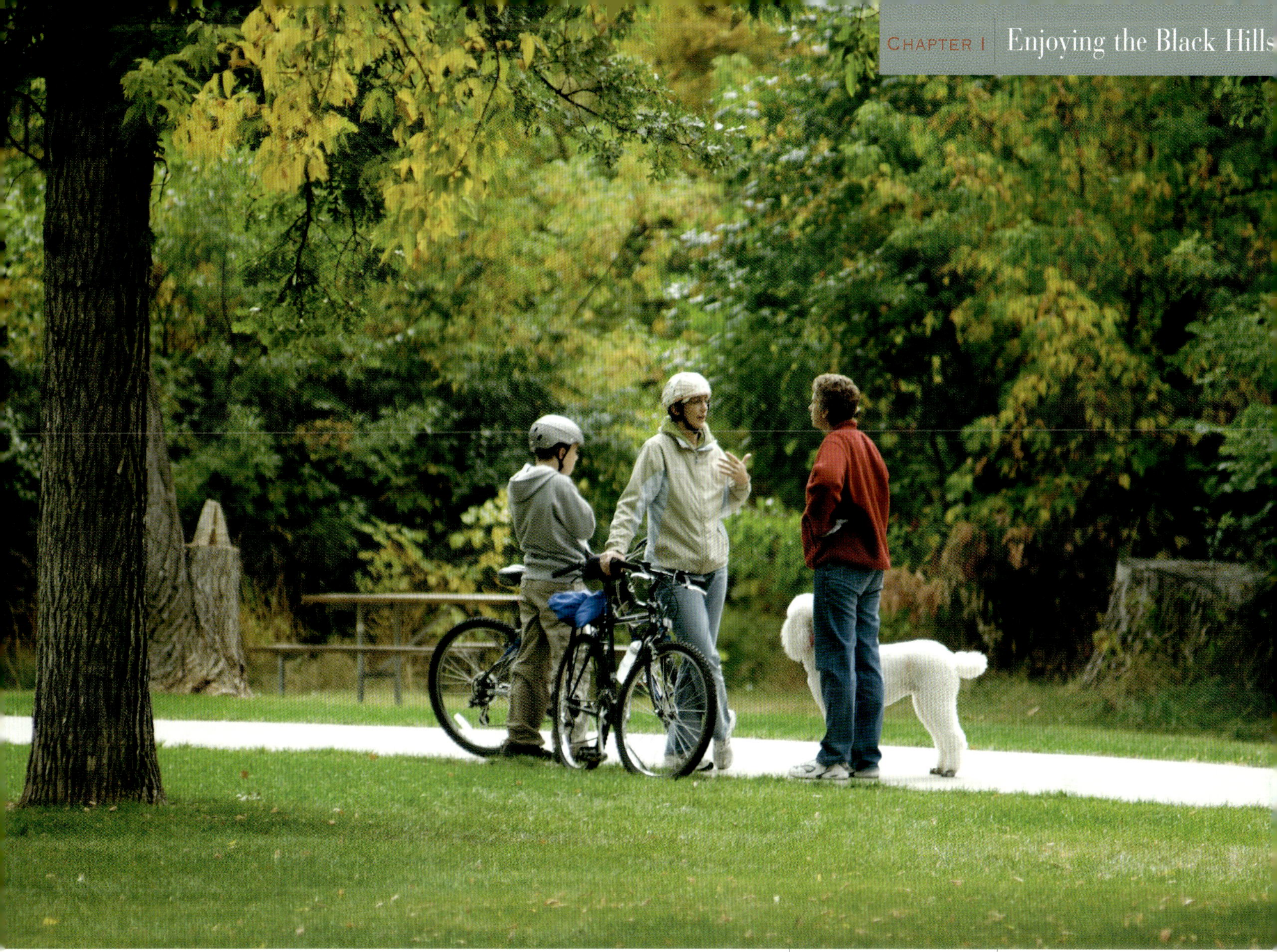

Photo by Doug Henderson

Bikers and walkers enjoy conversation along the Spearfish city bike path. This three-mile path is adjacent to Spearfish Creek and runs through over half a dozen community parks.

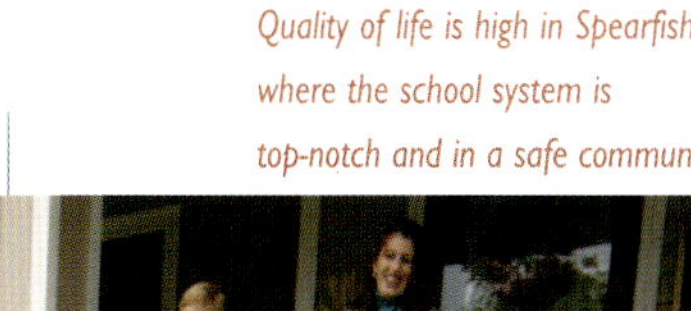

Quality of life is high in Spearfish, where the school system is top-notch and in a safe community.

Photo by Doug Henderson

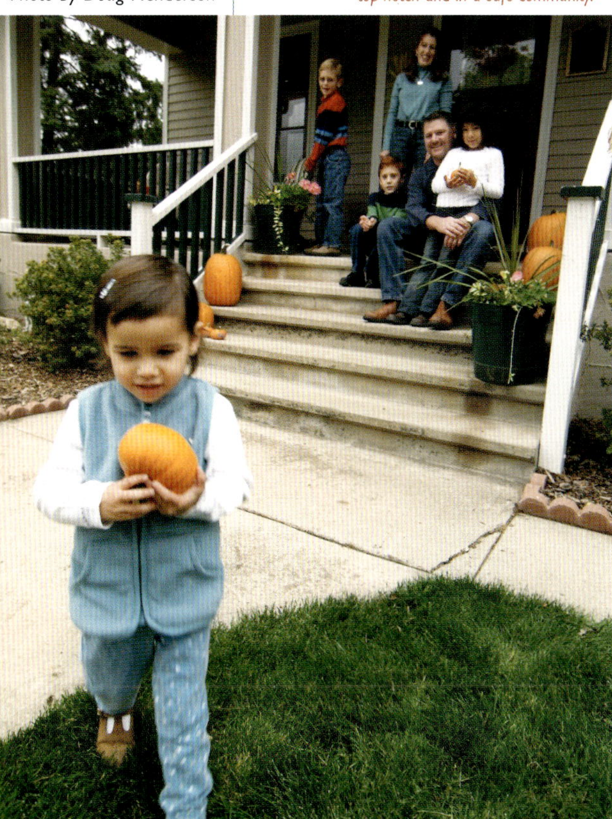

community, flanked by a walking and biking path. The city has many well-maintained parks, including pocket parks tucked into previously unused space. "The city and the Chamber work hand in hand to make this an environment where people want to shop and spend time," she says.

For a community of its size, Spearfish boasts a diverse economy with roots in education, health care, tourism, mining, and timber. Add a highly educated workforce, easy access to major transportation routes, a low cost of living, an excellent tax environment, as well as abundant natural resources, and it's easy to see why Spearfish is so inviting to businesses and individuals alike. "This business community is very cooperative," adds Langer. "That's the Black Hills philosophy: what's good for one is good for all."

Camping trips over the years in the Black Hills introduced Mitch Moe and his family to Spearfish. The lure of nature, the charm of the residents, and the overall quality of life convinced this residential contractor to relocate

Continued on page 48

Continued from page 47

here from Minnesota. "As a business owner, customer service attracts me. Common courtesy is alive and well in Spearfish. You see it from business to business," explains Moe. "That caught my eye, as well as the recreational aspects of the area." Thrice named one of America's fifty best outdoor sports towns, Spearfish attracts outdoor enthusiasts of all types. From snowmobiling to skiing, fly-fishing to hunting, hiking to mountain biking, or motor biking, there are countless ways to take in the beauty of the area. In addition, the geographic location of Spearfish creates a moderate climate with occasional warm banana-belt breezes in winter, and with sunshine year-round.

With near-perfect weather and a healthy business climate giving way to opportunities to work hard, play hard, and live well, many say Spearfish is as close to Utopia as one can get. Calvin Dardis, a resident of Spearfish for three decades, sums it up. "I do a lot of traveling, but I always can't wait to get home," he says. "This little area is just like a secret—and it's home to me." ❖

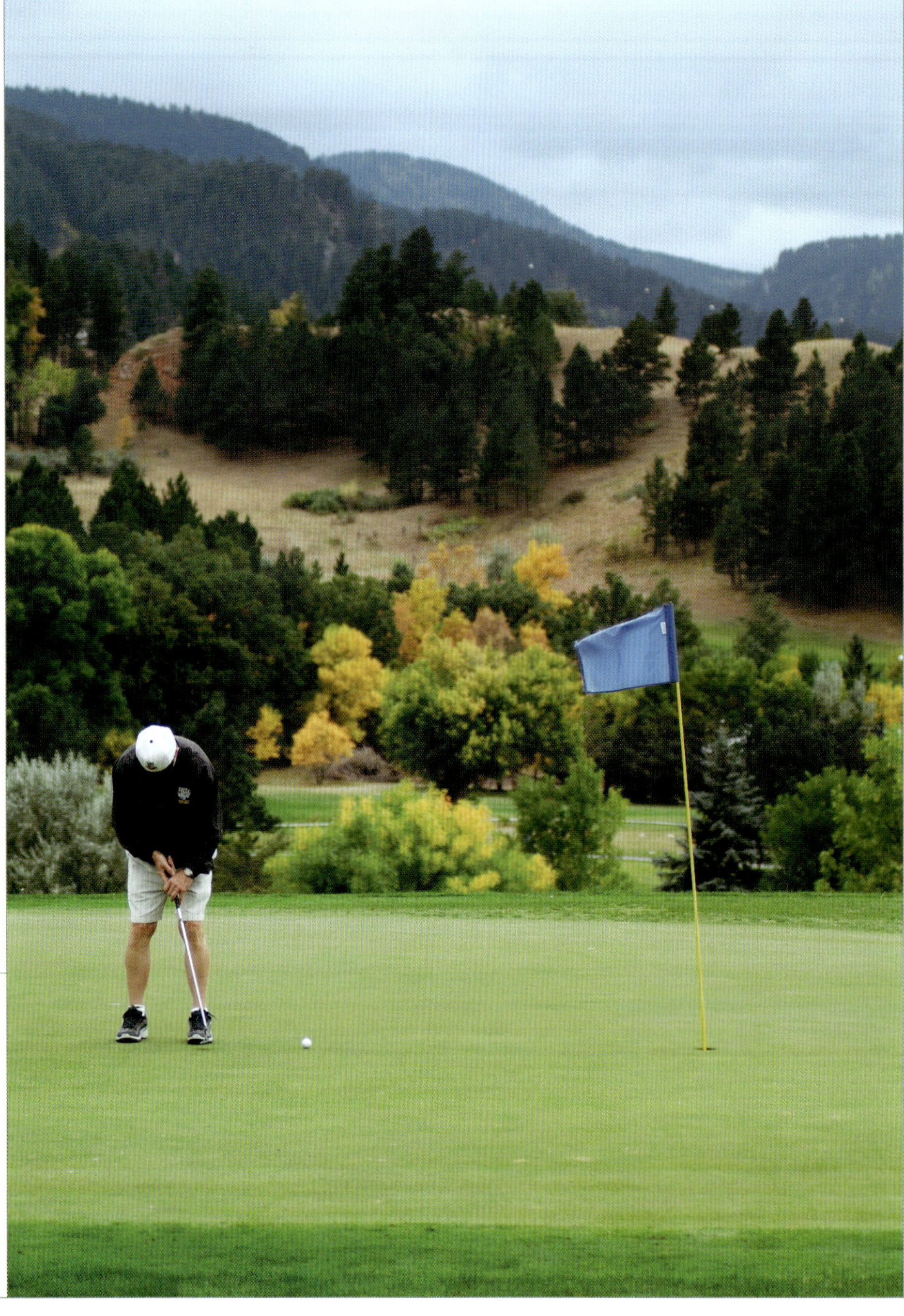

With nearly 350 sunny days, golfing is enjoyed almost year-round in Spearfish.

Photo by Doug Henderson

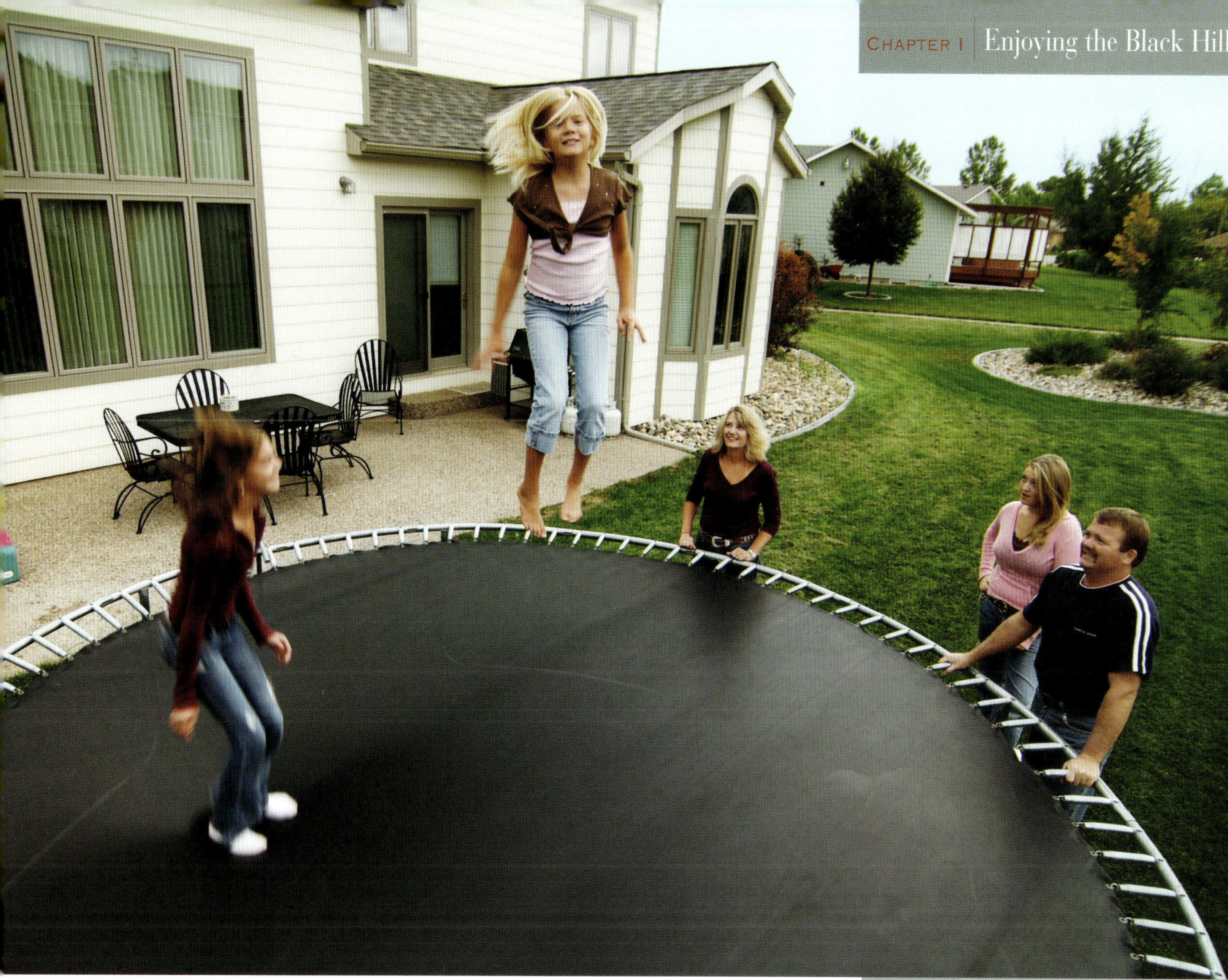

Photo by Doug Henderson

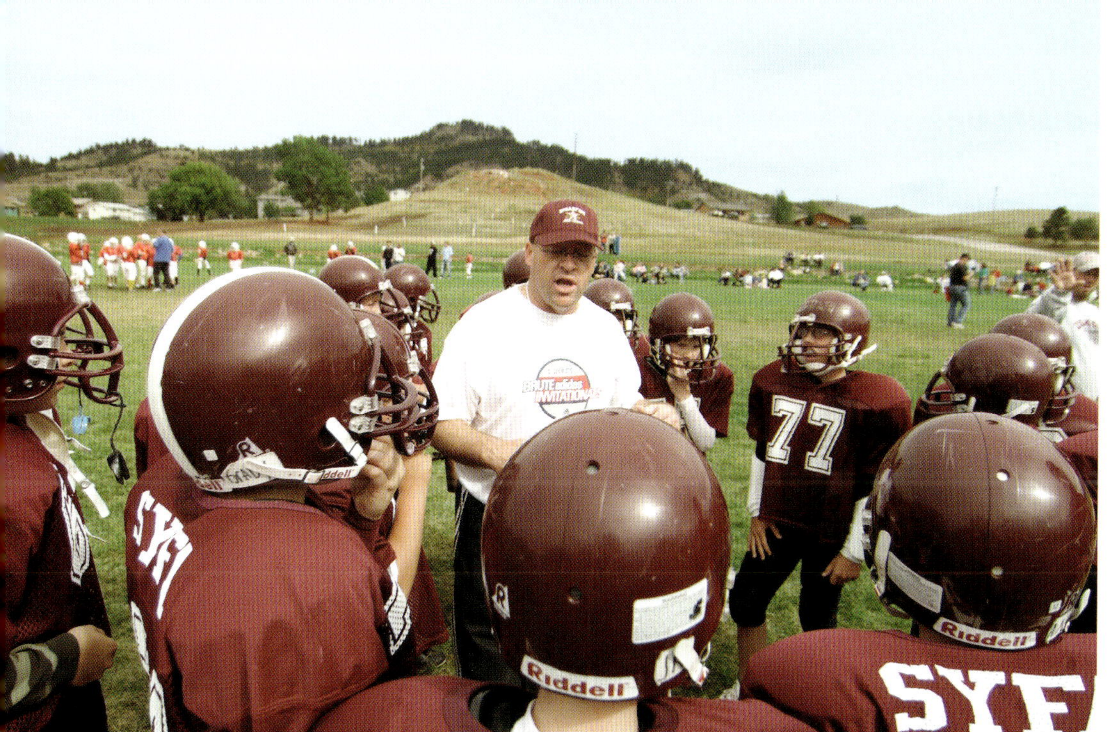

Photo by Doug Henderson

▲ *Safe, affordable, and aesthetically pleasing residential neighborhoods make Spearfish a great place to raise a family and to invest in real estate. Reflecting South Dakota's overall low cost of living, the National Association of Realtors reports that for the last quarter of 2005, the average home price in Spearfish was around $92,000, compared to the national average of around $215,000. Yet, the city continues to grow as a center for economic and educational development.* ❖

◀ *Knowing that today's kids grow up to be tomorrow's leaders, many Spearfish residents volunteer their spare time toward various youth activities. Here, the town's chief of police, Pat Rotert, coaches a local youth football team. It's time well spent, as coaching allows Rotert not only the chance to get out and have some fun, but also to serve as a positive role model.* ❖

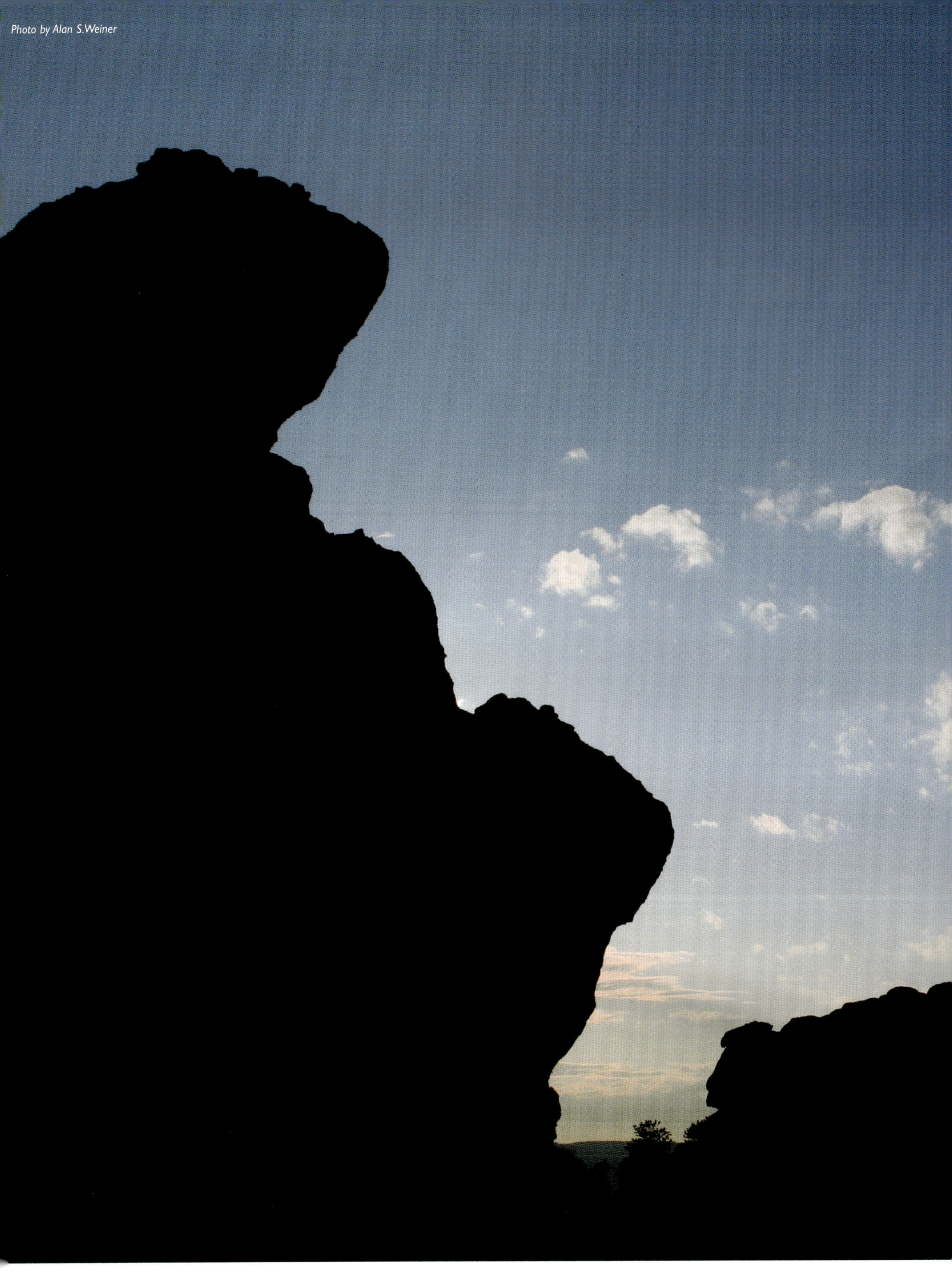
Photo by Alan S.Weiner

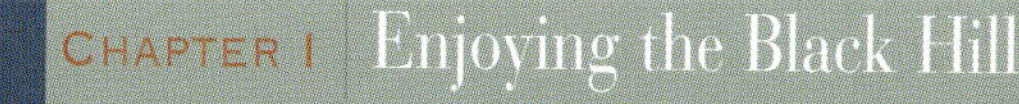

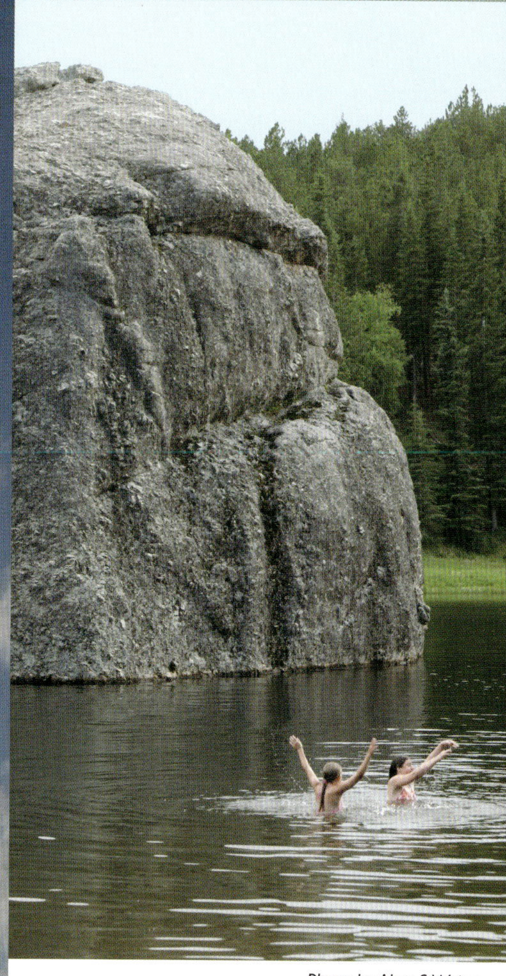

Photo by Alan S.Weiner

When outdoor enthusiasts

want to revel in the Black Hills' natural magnificence, they head to Custer State Park, located just twenty miles south of Rapid City. Encompassing seventy-one thousand acres of rustic splendor, the park offers a host of outstanding recreational opportunities, from driving along Wildlife Loop Road to get a view of the one of the world's largest free-ranging herds of bison, comprising more than fifteen hundred animals, to rock climbing some of the most challenging granite formations in the country and hiking up to the 7,242-foot summit of Harney Peak, the highest point in the United States east of the Rocky Mountains. Sylvan Lake, known as the crown jewel of the park, provides visitors with the chance to go fishing, swimming, diving, and boating in a body of water so clear and pristine that it looks like Mother Nature herself placed a mirror among the picturesque vistas. Biking, horseback riding, and much more are available throughout the area, which also boasts four spectacular resorts and the popular Black Hills Playhouse. ❖

Perhaps no other bar in the world is as famous as Saloon No. 10 in Deadwood. For it was here on August 2, 1876, that one of the American West's most notorious figures, Wild Bill Hickok, was shot dead. By turns an army scout, lawman, gold prospector, and professional gambler, it was Wild Bill's passion for cards that would prove his downfall. On the night of his death, Hickok broke his rule never to sit down at a card table with his back to the door. That allowed Jack McCall, drunk and fuming over a grudge that remains unclear to this day, to sneak up behind Hickok and shoot him in the back of the head. Today, Saloon No. 10 continues to thrive as an entertainment center, offering blackjack, poker, and slots downstairs, and a top-notch dining experience upstairs. During the summer months, it is also the site for four daily reenactments of the shooting and McCall's subsequent capture. Local theatrical group Deadwood Alive! reenacts the murder trial at the Deadwood Theatre in the Masonic temple on Main Street. ❖

Photo by Eric Francis

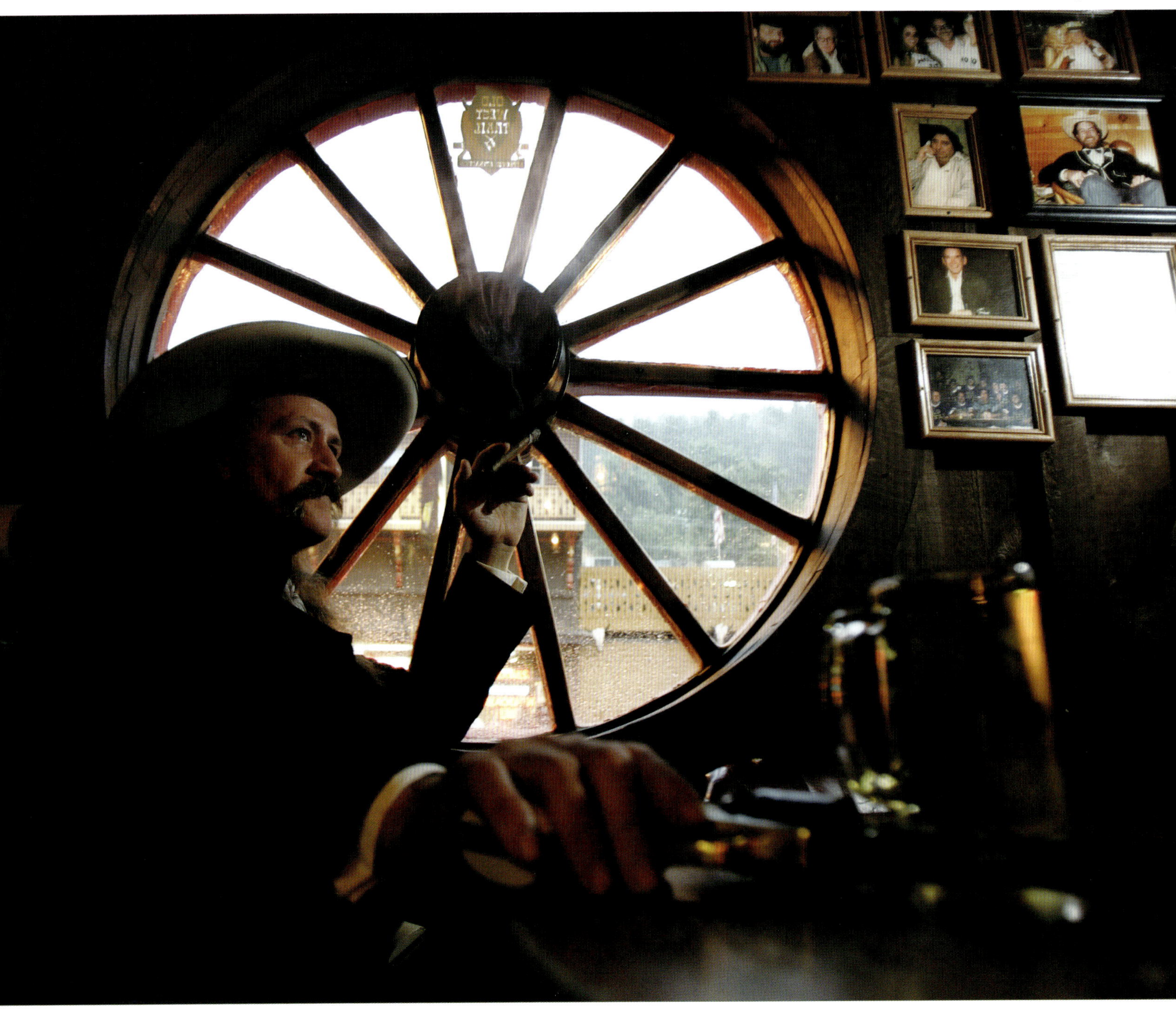

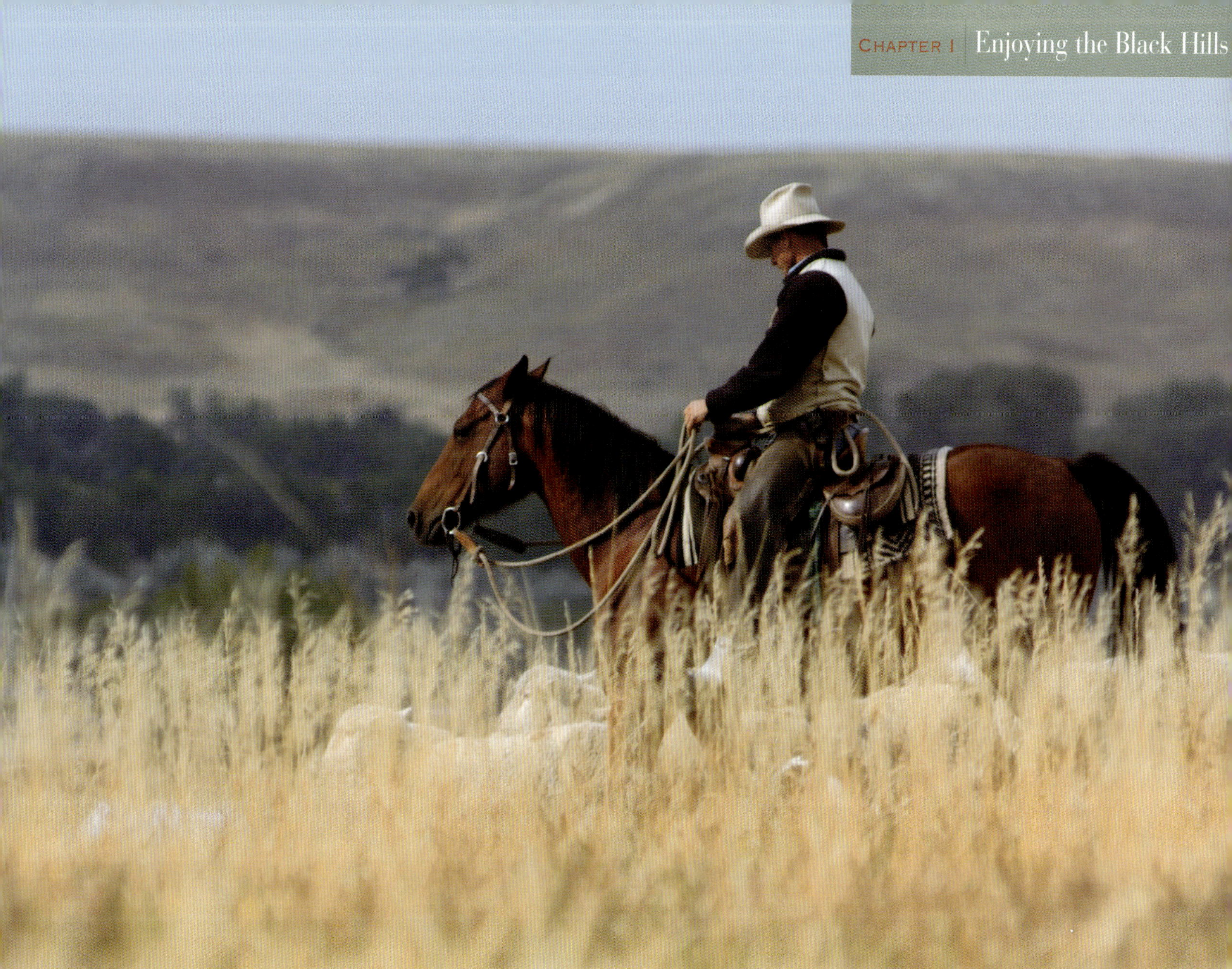

Photo by Doug Henderson

It's one of the most enduring images of the West: a lone cowhand atop his horse, keeping a watchful eye on the herd. And while cattle may be king, sheep also played—and still play—an important role in the development of South Dakota. The Black Hills are no exception. Sheep first appeared in the area around 1870, held by large companies who loaned their animals out to farmers and smaller ranchers to raise. Sheep are still an important part of the Black Hills economy and are raised for both their meat and their wool. In fact, the nation's largest shipping point for fine wool is located at Belle Fourche, located about ten miles north of Spearfish. ❖

Embracing History—Building the Future

Steeped in the history of the American West, the Black Hills region offers many opportunities to learn about life in a bygone era. One of those opportunities is available at Elkhorn Ridge at Frawley Ranches, a unique master-planned community development located in one of the state's most beautiful and historic spots. Here, investors and guests can experience a part of pioneer history and in so doing help preserve that history for future generations.

Encompassing over 4,500 acres of terrain in the scenic Centennial Valley, Frawley Ranches has been in the same family since its founding in 1876. Today the property is one of only two National Historic Sites in South Dakota (the town of Deadwood is the other) and is also one of the few historic ranches in the country whose nineteenth-century buildings, tools, furnishings, and memorabilia have been preserved virtually intact.

"We make every effort to make your visit with us a top-notch experience."

But managing such vast holdings is an expensive undertaking. In order to ensure the long-term preservation of his family's legacy, in 1998 ranch owner Hank Frawley formed a partnership with real estate developers Daryll Propp and Mike Kreke. Together, they outlined a development plan designed to benefit the local community and preserve the Frawley Ranch as a historic and cultural landmark.

"The maintenance of the ranch and its structures is a continual process," says Propp. "By developing a portion of it, we will create a revenue stream which will enable proper support of the entire ranch."

Photo by Thomas S. England

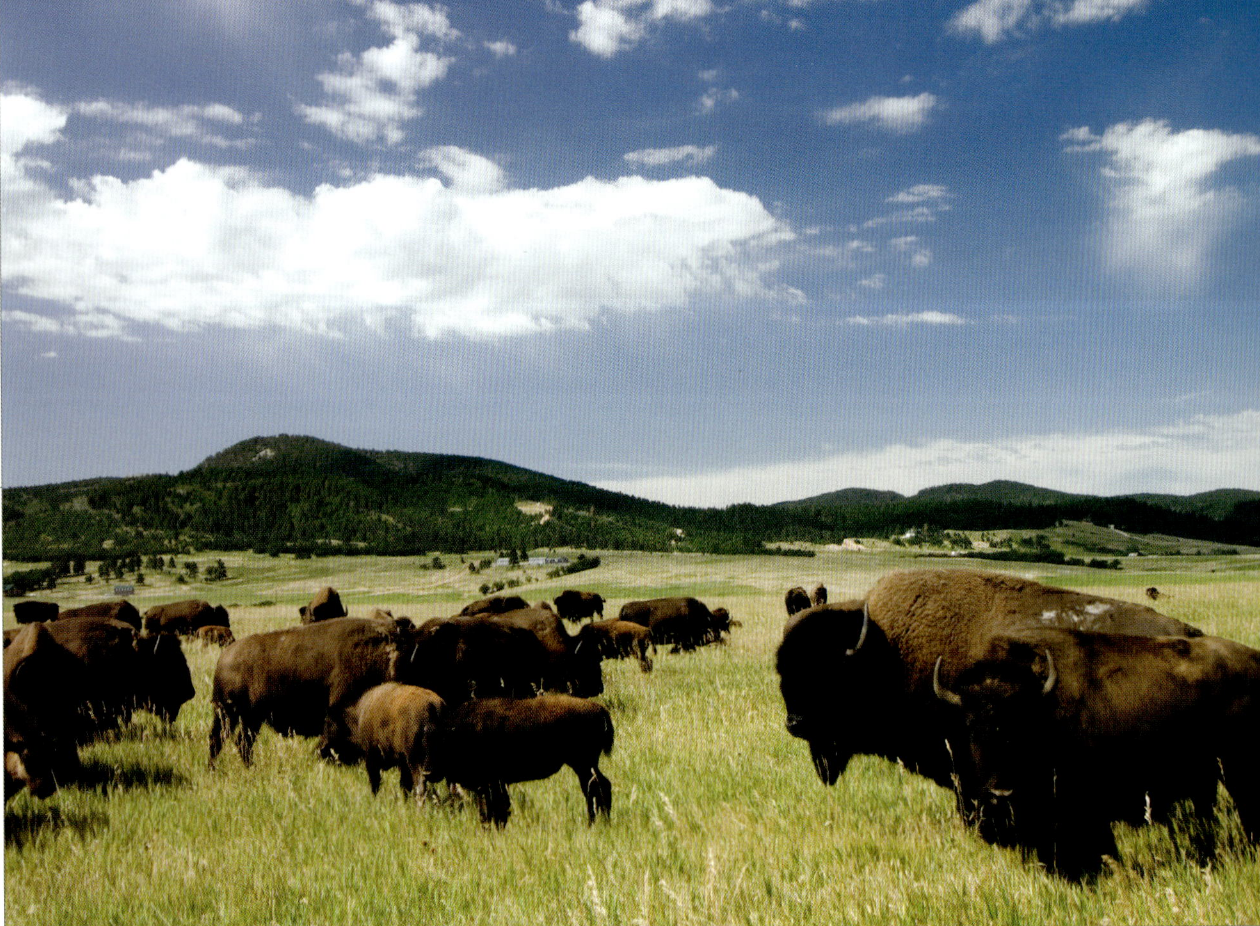

In its management and preservation of the property's eighty-head herd of buffalo, five wild mustangs, and four wild burros, Frawley Ranches preserves a vital part of the Black Hills' natural history. The animals have over two thousand acres on which they can freely roam.

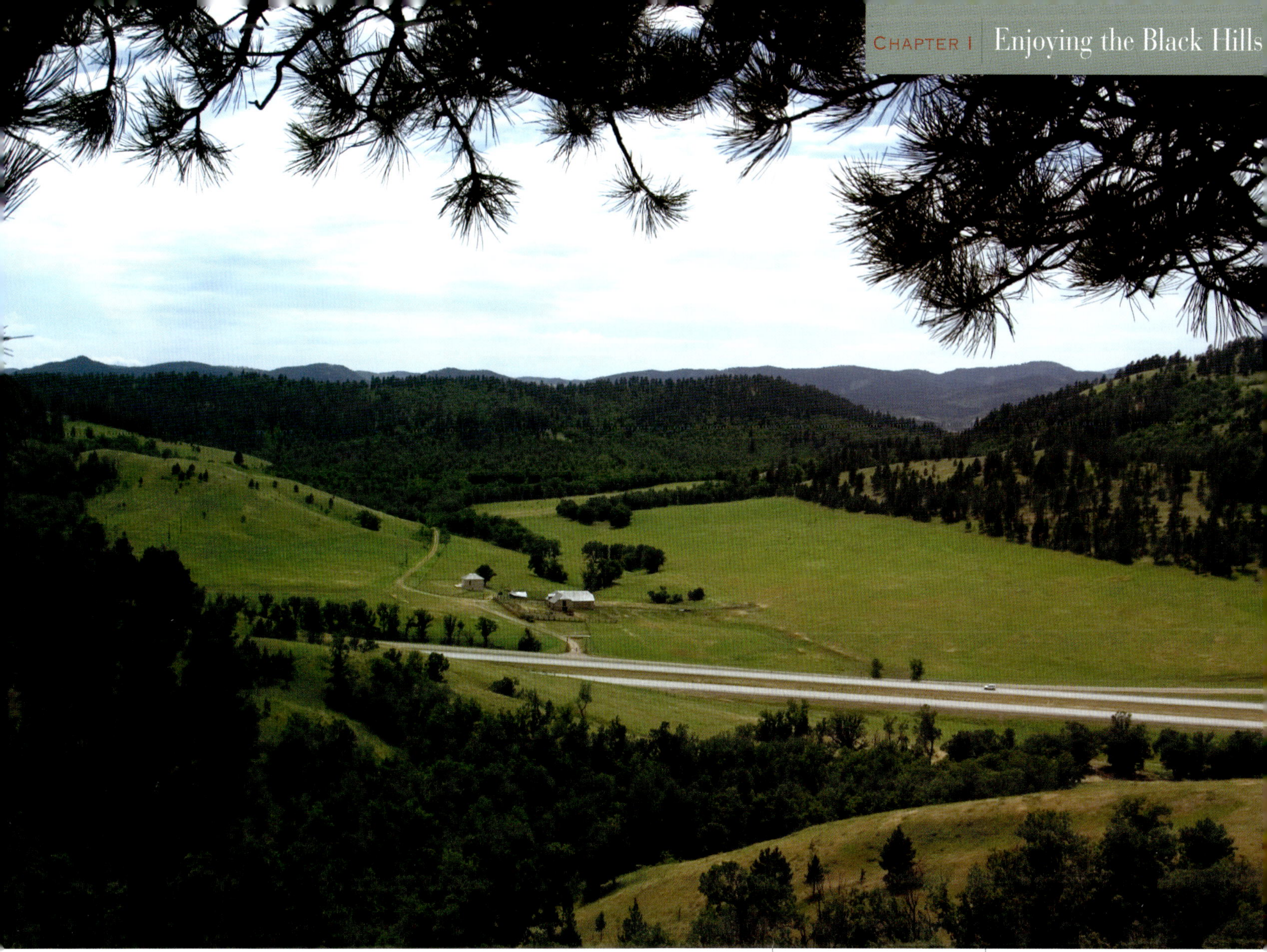

Photo by Thomas S. England

A view of the Frawley Ranches encompassing the lovely Centennial Valley and the Black Hills in the far background. The ranch's developments are ideally situated to offer residents and tenants easy access to the best the region has to offer.

The development portion of the ranch is ideally situated at the junction of U.S. Highway 85 and Interstate 90. The 1,000-acre Elkhorn Ridge at Frawley Ranches is in Spearfish and located thirty-five minutes west of Rapid City. It is also within easy driving distance to a wealth of nearby attractions, including Deadwood, Sturgis, Mount Rushmore, Crazy Horse, Custer State Park, and Devil's Tower in western Wyoming.

Elkhorn Ridge at Frawley Ranches' Master Plan is designed to provide managed growth for the area's business, recreational, and residential needs. "The

Continued on page 56

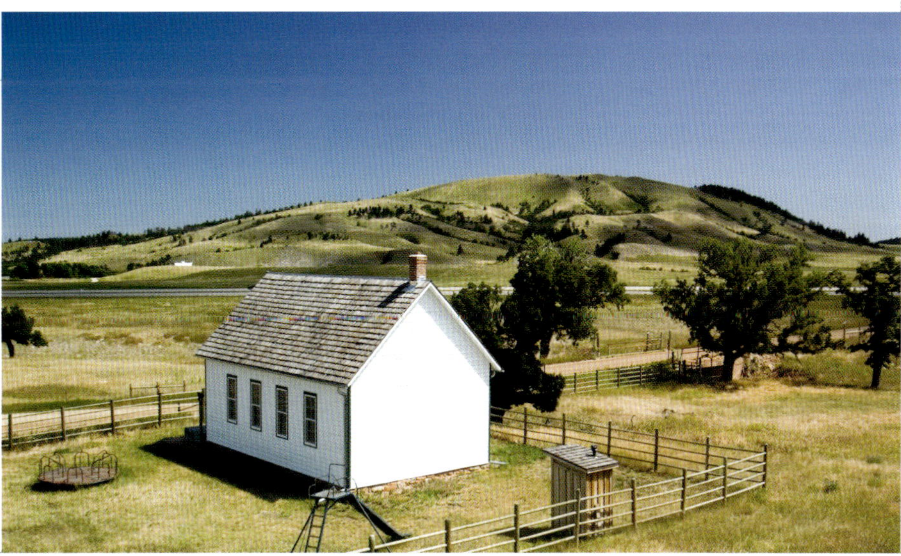

Development of a small part of the ranch ensures its long-term preservation, including many of the nineteenth-century buildings that still stand on the property. The Centennial School House is a reminder of the settlers' will to make better lives for themselves and their children through hard work and education.

Photo by Thomas S. England

Continued from page 55

development will open employment opportunities within the community and improve the local options for shopping, dining, and recreation," says Propp. "We also want to promote the area as an exciting tourist destination. The historic aspect of the ranch offers a vast early history of the settlers' life in the American West and many educational opportunities for visitor and locals alike."

The first part of the development is the 75-acre upscale Elkhorn Ridge RV Park and Campground, opening in May 2006 with 373 level RV sites, 34 cabins, and 30 campsites. Additional amenities include paved road access, water, sewer, power and Internet hookup, swimming pool, showers, and laundry facilities. In the initial stages are plans for a four-hundred-room hotel complex; a gas station, convenience store, and visitor information center; an office park and retail center; and an eighteen-hole championship golf course. An 1880-style railroad is also in consideration.

For area residents seeking affordable and accessible housing with panoramic views, Elkhorn Ridge at Frawley Ranches has set aside 170 acres for seven hundred home sites, some of which will have golf course frontage. They will include single-family detached units and townhome/condominium units. Architectural covenants ensure that all development maintains the historic ambience of the property.

Frawley Ranches remains very much a working ranch. As the third generation of his family to work the land, Hank Frawley oversees all operations, and even works the combines come hay-harvesting time.

Photo by Thomas S. England

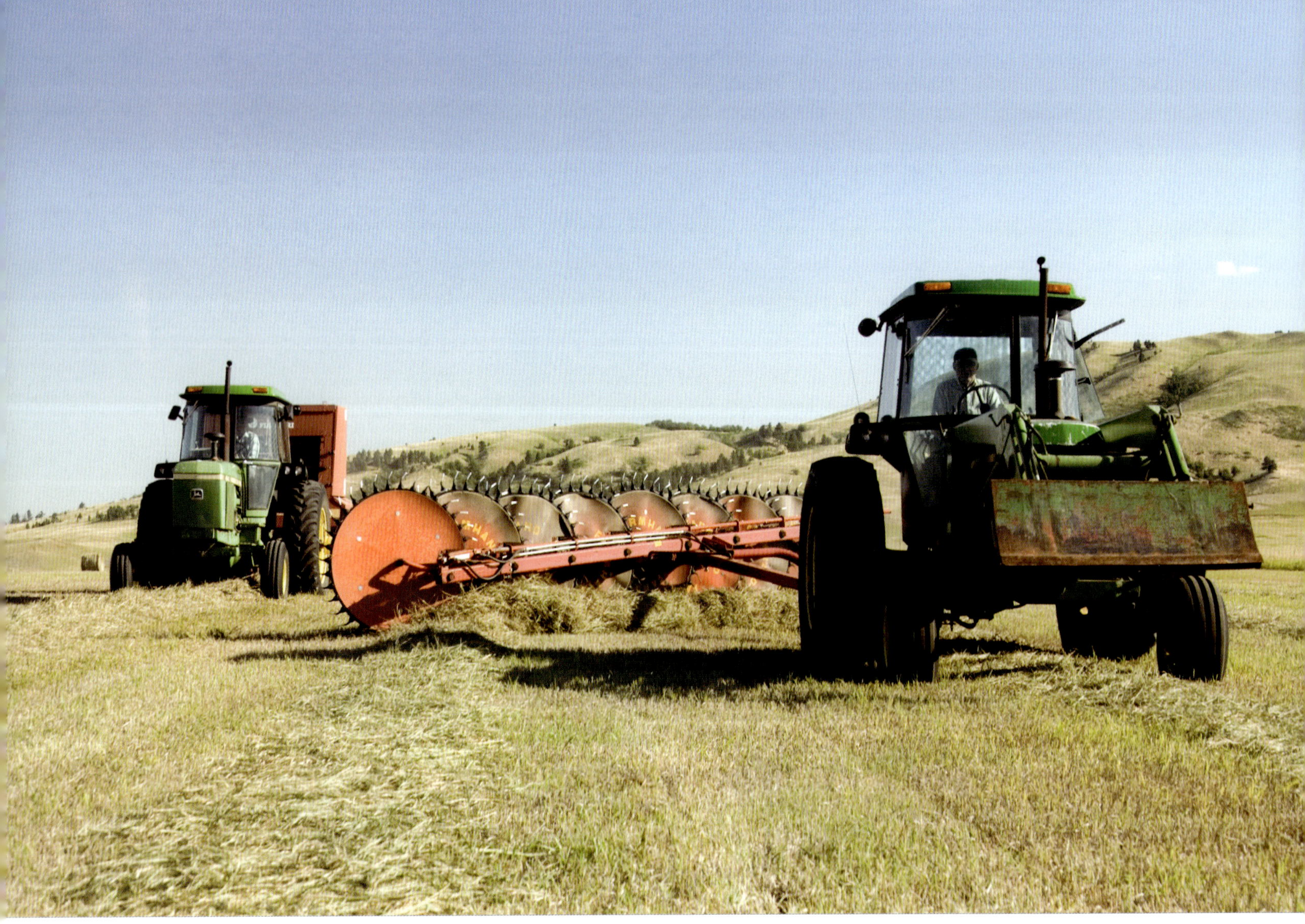

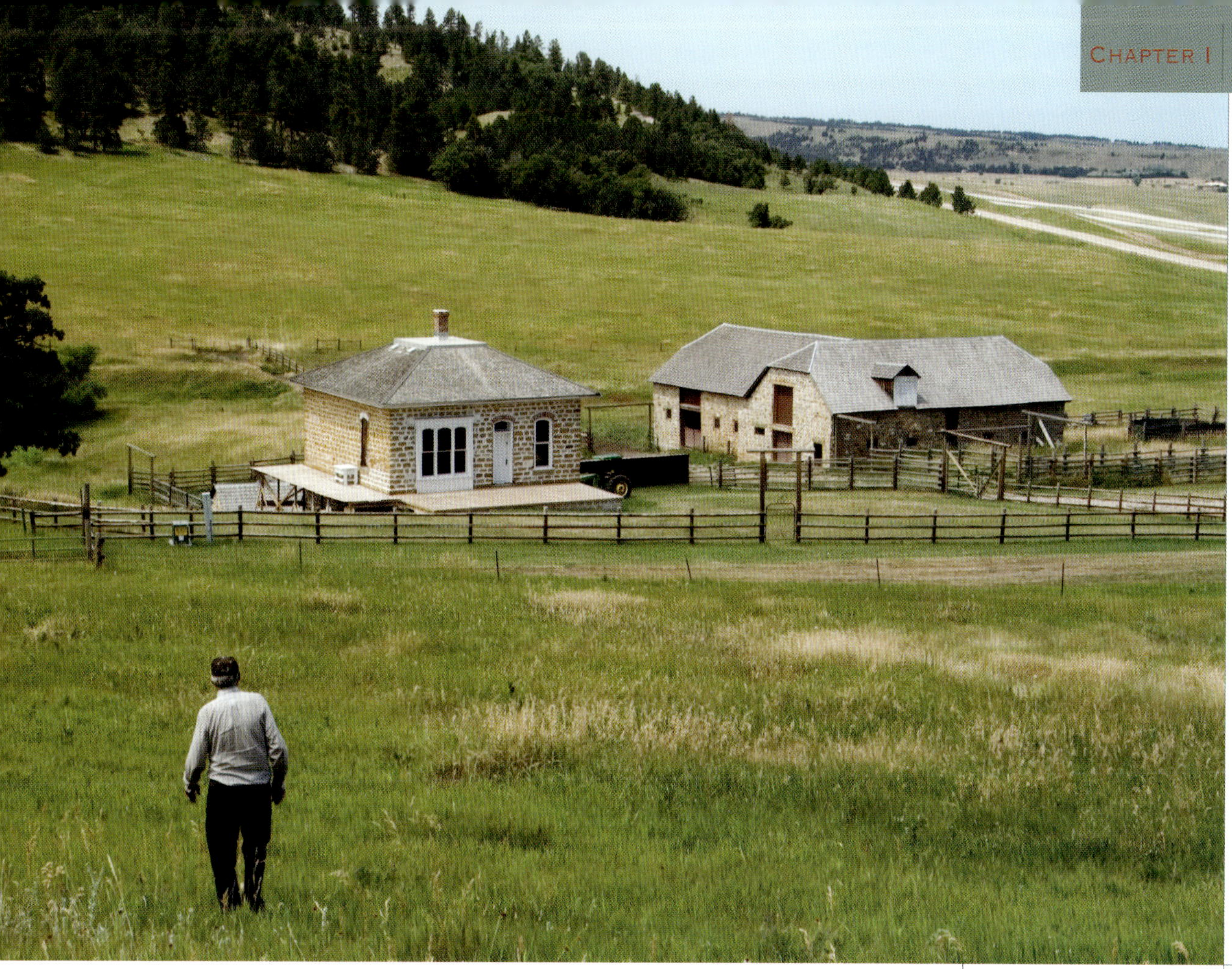

Established on the ranch in 1877, the Anderson Dairy Farm once provided milk for settlers in the area. Today it is being revitalized as another of the ranch's enterprises: a 100-million-gallon-a-year water bottling operation, thanks to the abundance and purity of the site's natural spring.

Photo by Thomas S. England

The partnership is also planning a separate residential development in the wooded hills overlooking the Centennial Valley. When completed, Frawley Ranches Estates will offer seventy-two covenant-controlled home sites ranging in size from 2 to 8 acres. And in 2001, South Dakota health officials tested and approved the water at the historic Anderson Dairy Ranch spring; the Frawley Ranch partnership will begin to bottle and make available to consumers up to 100 million gallons of spring water per year.

Adding to the attractiveness of the development is the ranch itself, the vast majority of which will remain open space. That means plenty of room to roam for the ranch's herds of wild horses, burros, and buffalo. Likewise the partnership has teamed up with the Deadwood Historic Preservation Commission to maintain the ranch's many historic structures, including numerous old houses, dugout homesteads, a one-room schoolhouse, a thirty-thousand-square-foot courtyard barn, and the Anderson Dairy Ranch Homestead and Barn.

There are few places left in this country where one can experience life as it was in the Old West. Frawley Ranches is one of those places. By embracing history in order to build the future, the partnership of Frawley, Propp, and Kreke is making a positive impact on the local economy while at the same time ensuring for generations to come the preservation of one of our country's great unspoiled treasures. ❖

Located on the ranch, the Burton Dugout is a finely preserved example of a common form of housing built by settlers on the American Plains. Whether made of sod, wood, or stone, dugouts such as this provided residents with a cozy, easy-to-maintain home that also offered protection from the elements in both winter and summer.

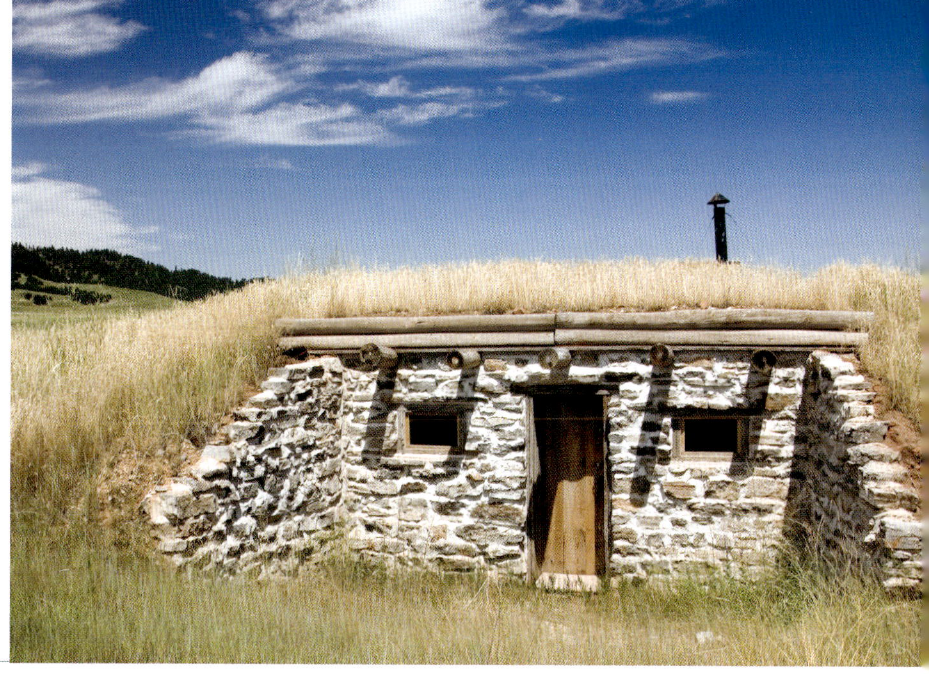

Photo by Thomas S. England

Photo by Alan S.Weiner

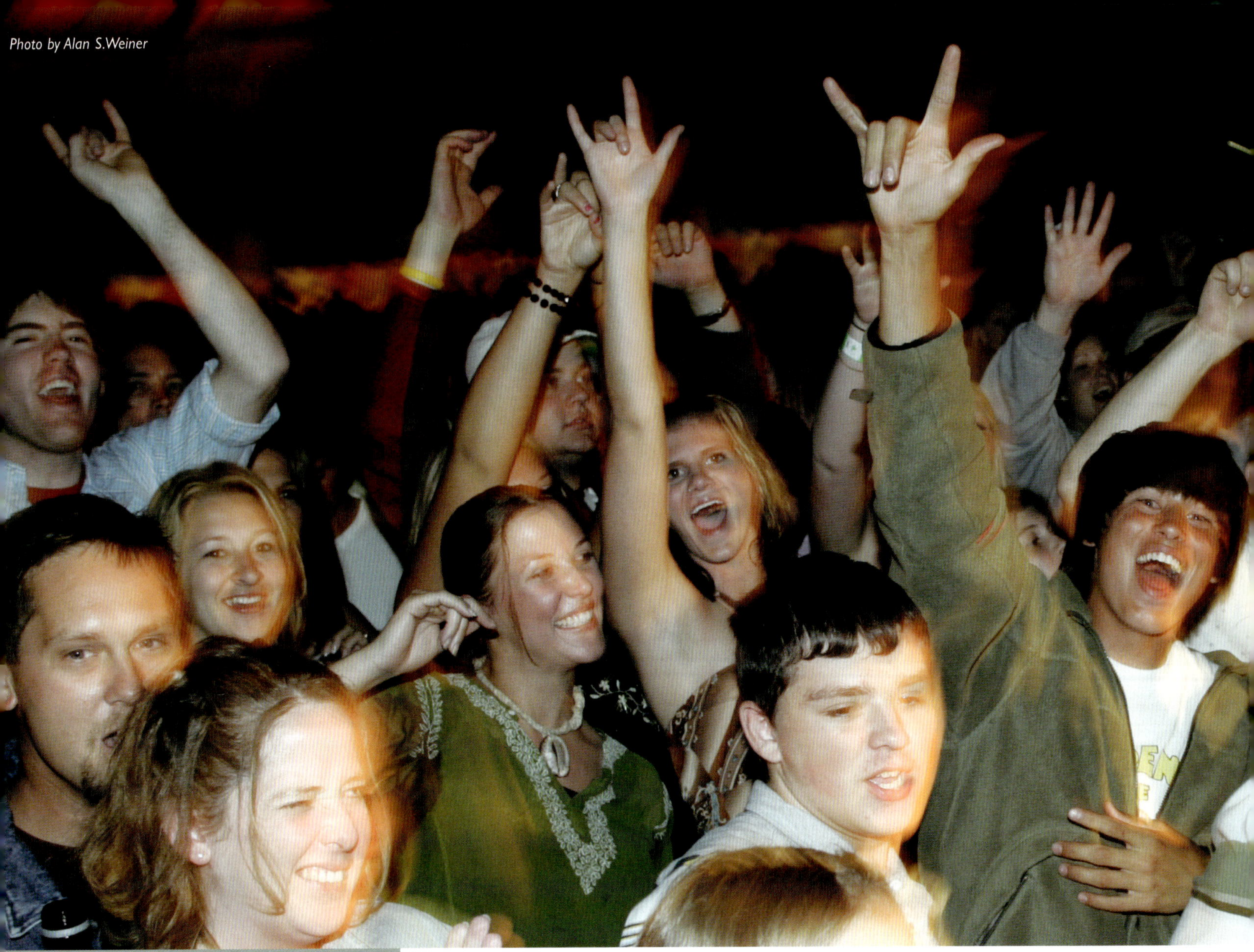

If you like music—any kind of music—then the Heritage Festival is the place for you. This event, which is more about a heritage of fun than anything historic, has a wide variety of arts and crafts booths, a children's pow wow, and plenty of activities to keep everyone happy. However, it is the music that really draws the estimated seventy thousand fans over the July 4 weekend. In addition to South Dakota fans, folks come from Nebraska and Wyoming as well. From the Beatles to reggae, soft rock, blues, fiddlers, rap, jazz, and new world, it's all there. Visitors may hear Ecuadoran musicians performing traditional music from the Andes Mountains, followed by blues and rock music from the Rosebud Indian Reservation, or Highland bagpipes and drummers. "The festival has been going on for about twenty years in Memorial Park downtown, and it's definitely something folks look forward to," said Matt Reed, who has volunteered at the event for the past ten years. ❖

Photo by Alan S.Weiner

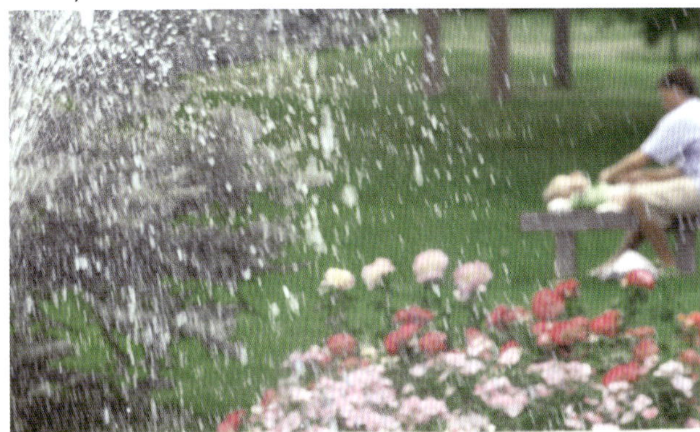

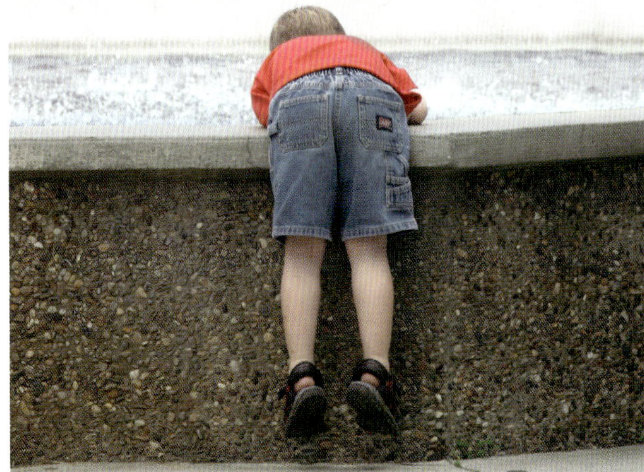

Photo by Alan S.Weiner

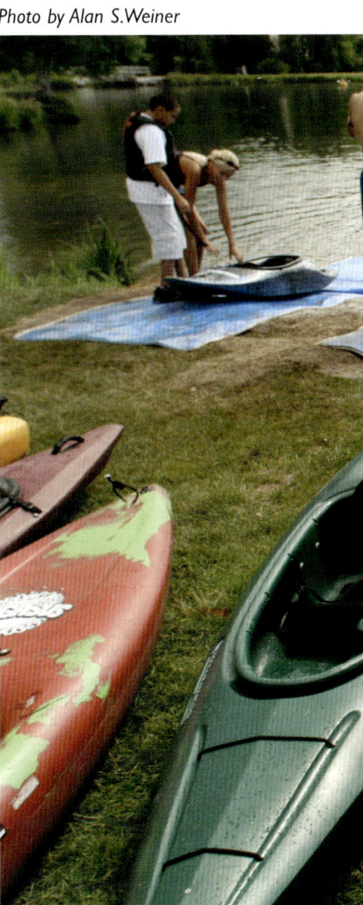

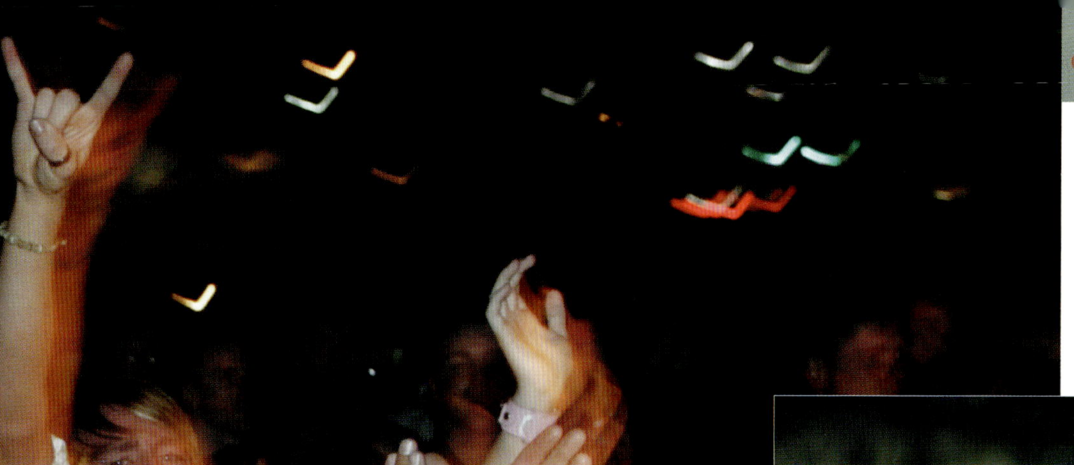

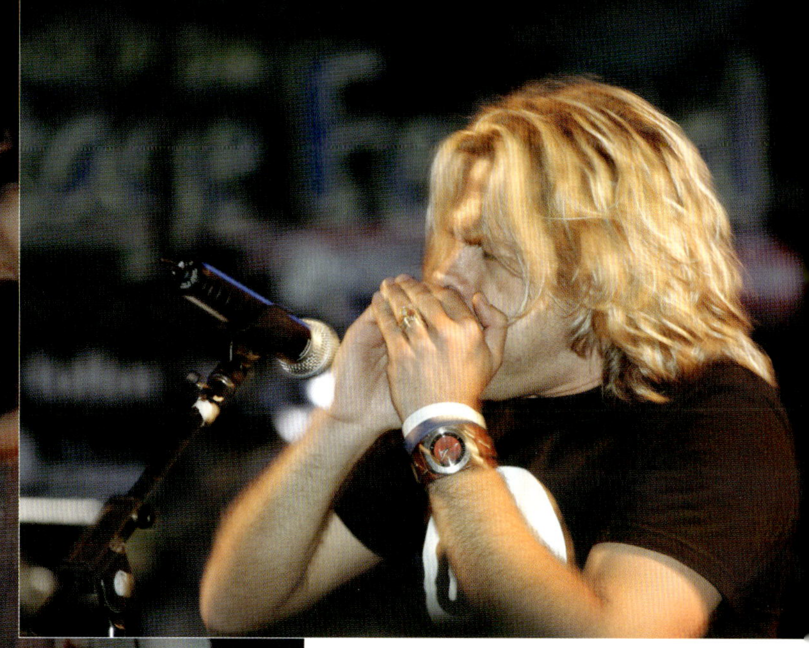

Photo by Alan S.Weiner

Photo by Alan S.Weiner

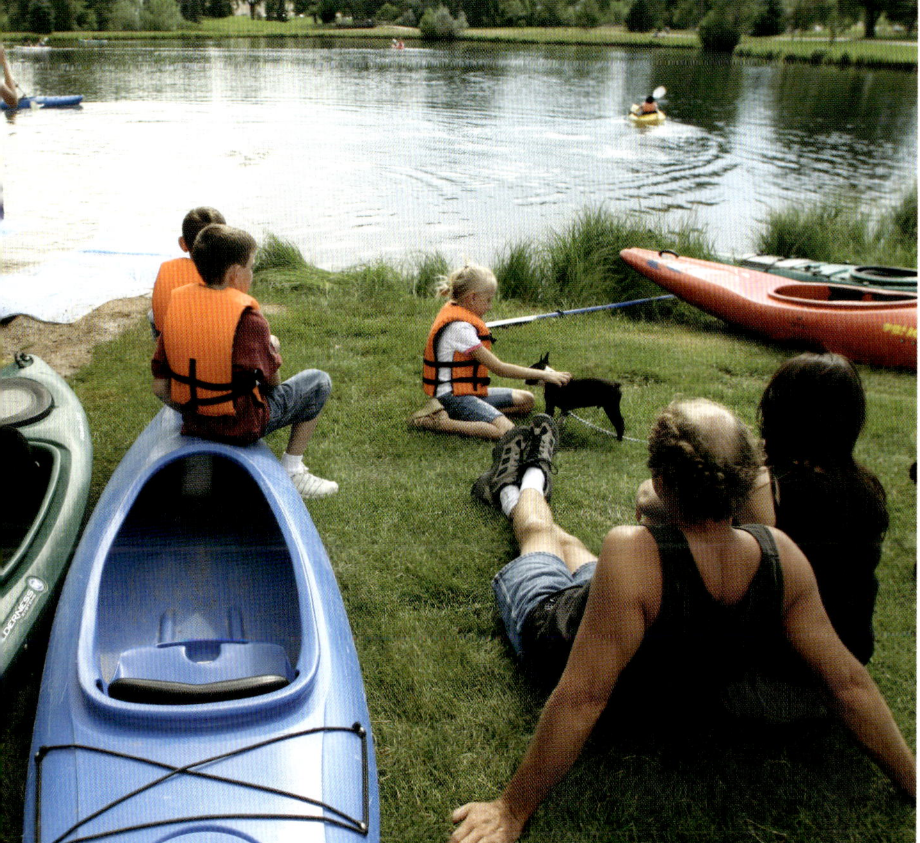

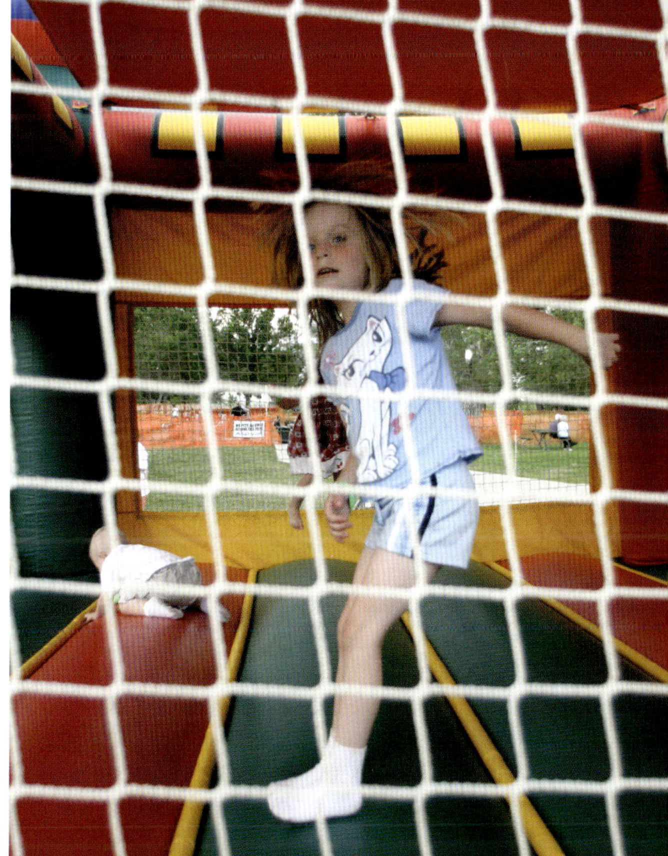

Apple Springs Resort Offers Something for Everybody

Apple Springs Resort is the kind of place where life slows to a more peaceful pace. Nestled in the arms of Boulder Canyon in the beautiful Black Hills, the residential resort community is a combination of vacation homes, single-family dwellings, and luxurious resort accommodations designed for today's country living.

"Our goal is to preserve the pristine beauty of the area and incorporate aspects of the local flavor and history as the framework for the community," explains local entrepreneur Mark Simpson, who, with his brother Dave, cofounded the project, which broke ground in 2005. "The property contains buildings that existed as the original 1920s-era homestead. The farmhouse, schoolhouse, and several outbuildings are surrounded by a twenty-five-acre farm meadow. Ultimately, apple orchards, vineyards, and botanical gardens will be woven throughout the landscape," he says. The site calls for new country-style rental cottages and vacation home building lots, as well as a resort-style lodge. A challenging golf course complete with clubhouse, driving range, and practice facilities will be a fabulous source of recreation as well as a backdrop for many home sites.

When the nearly six-hundred-acre development is complete, Simpson believes Apple Springs will propel the Black Hills area to the forefront in the minds of vacationers, as well as area residents and businesses. "Apple Springs is uniquely suited for a residential resort community similar to concepts that have been done with great success in Colorado, Montana, and Wyoming," says Simpson. "It will be a unique Hills experience that honors the history and beauty of this area."❖

"Our goal is to preserve the pristine beauty of the area and incorporate aspects of the local flavor and history as the framework for the community."

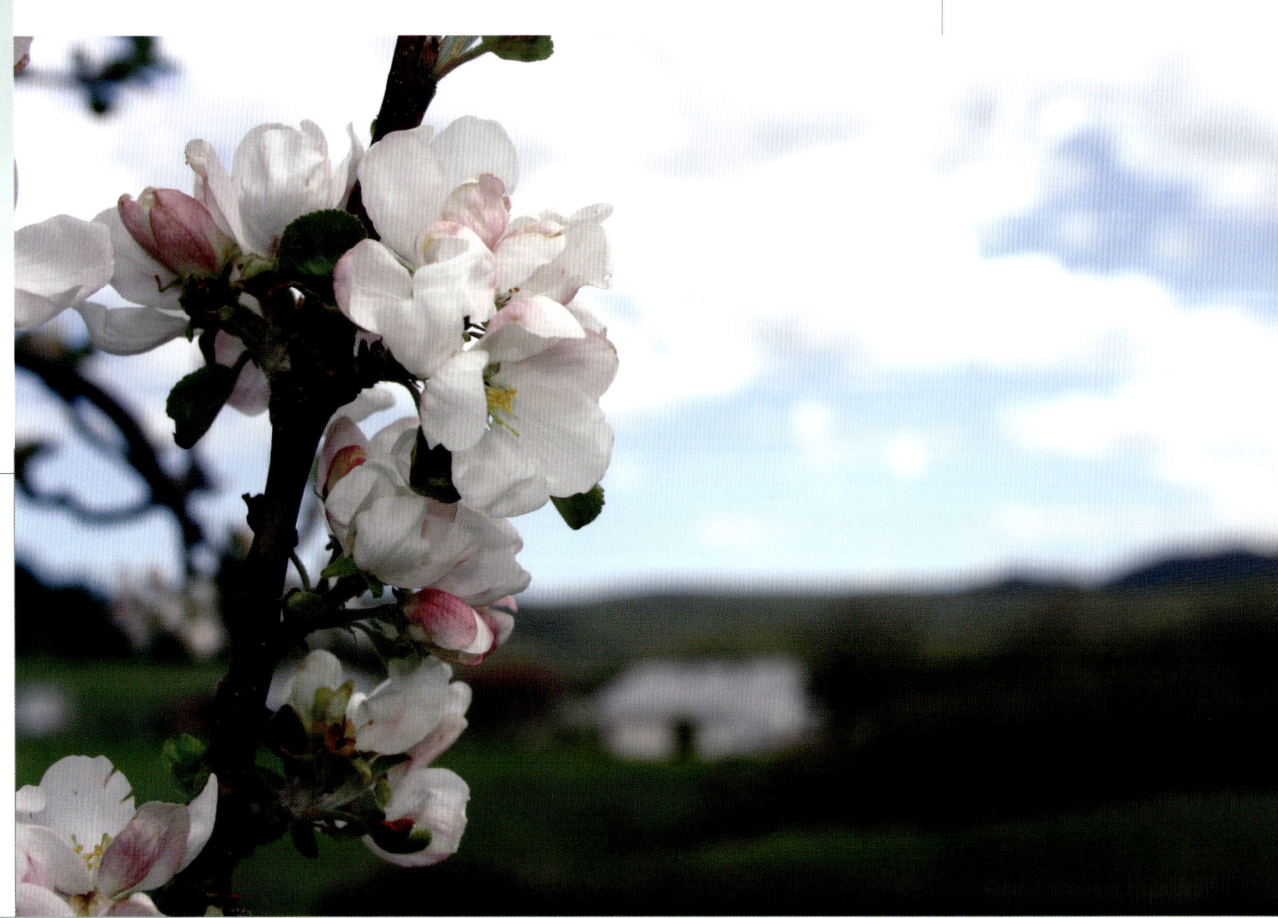

Photo by Thomas S. England

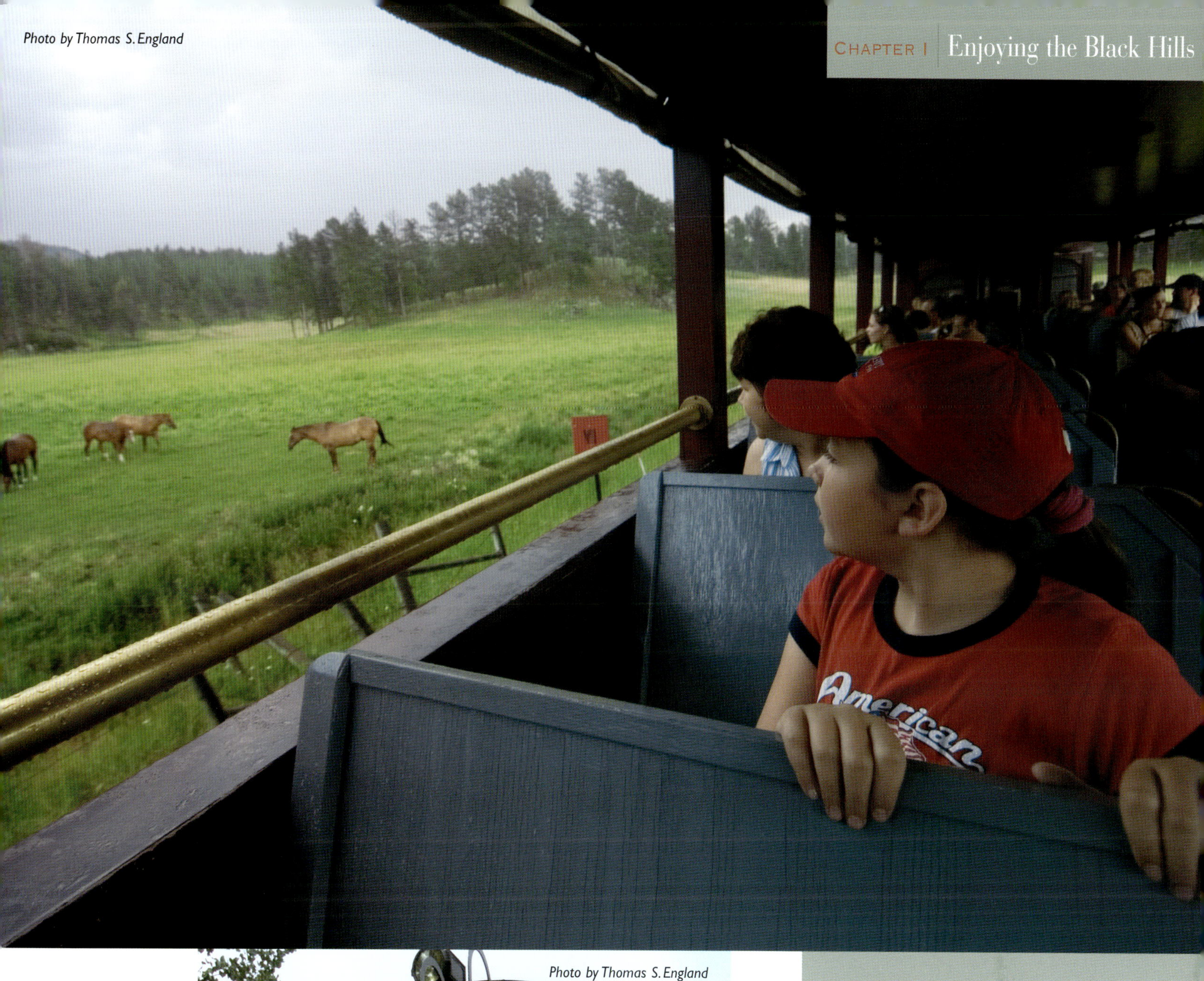

Photo by Thomas S. England

All aboard! It's time to take a trip back in time via the 1880 Train, a vintage steam locomotive that traverses the scenic hills between Hill City and Keystone and gives riders like Stephanie Schroeder a unique glimpse of the American West. The Black Hills Central Railroad 1880 Train actually operates three restored Baldwin steam locomotives—the No. 7, the No. 104, and the No. 110—run by experienced crew members, such as conductor Ed Spargur, pictured here as he awaits the whine of the whistle indicating this train's departure. The locomotives follow the original route of the CB&Q Railroad during their two-hour excursions, which provide sweeping views of the southern Black Hills' breathtaking terrain and most notable natural attractions, including Harney Peak, the tallest peak in North America east of the Rocky Mountains. And while the views are spectacular, visitors are just as captivated. ❖

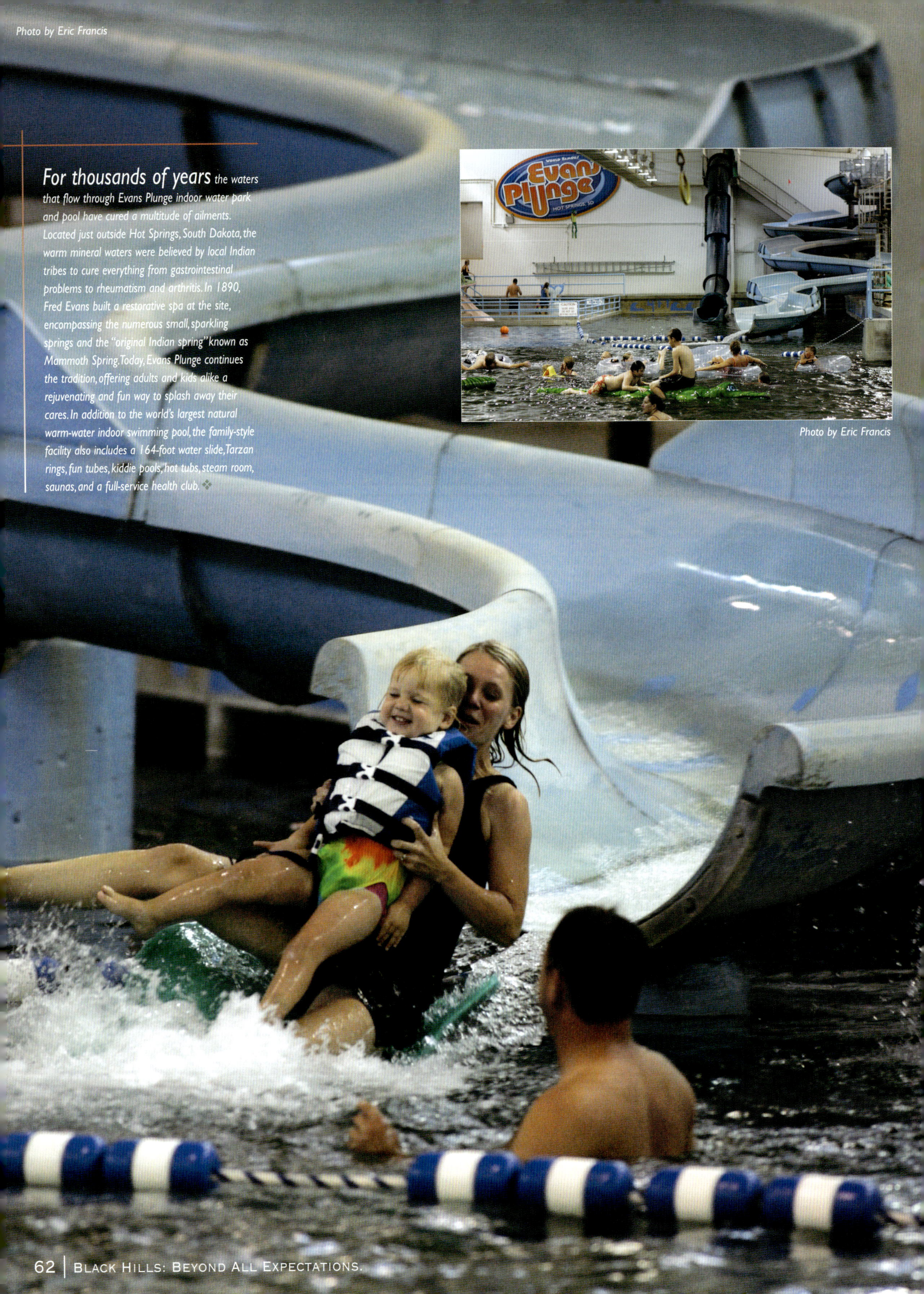

Photo by Eric Francis

For thousands of years the waters that flow through Evans Plunge indoor water park and pool have cured a multitude of ailments. Located just outside Hot Springs, South Dakota, the warm mineral waters were believed by local Indian tribes to cure everything from gastrointestinal problems to rheumatism and arthritis. In 1890, Fred Evans built a restorative spa at the site, encompassing the numerous small, sparkling springs and the "original Indian spring" known as Mammoth Spring. Today, Evans Plunge continues the tradition, offering adults and kids alike a rejuvenating and fun way to splash away their cares. In addition to the world's largest natural warm-water indoor swimming pool, the family-style facility also includes a 164-foot water slide, Tarzan rings, fun tubes, kiddie pools, hot tubs, steam room, saunas, and a full-service health club.

Photo by Eric Francis

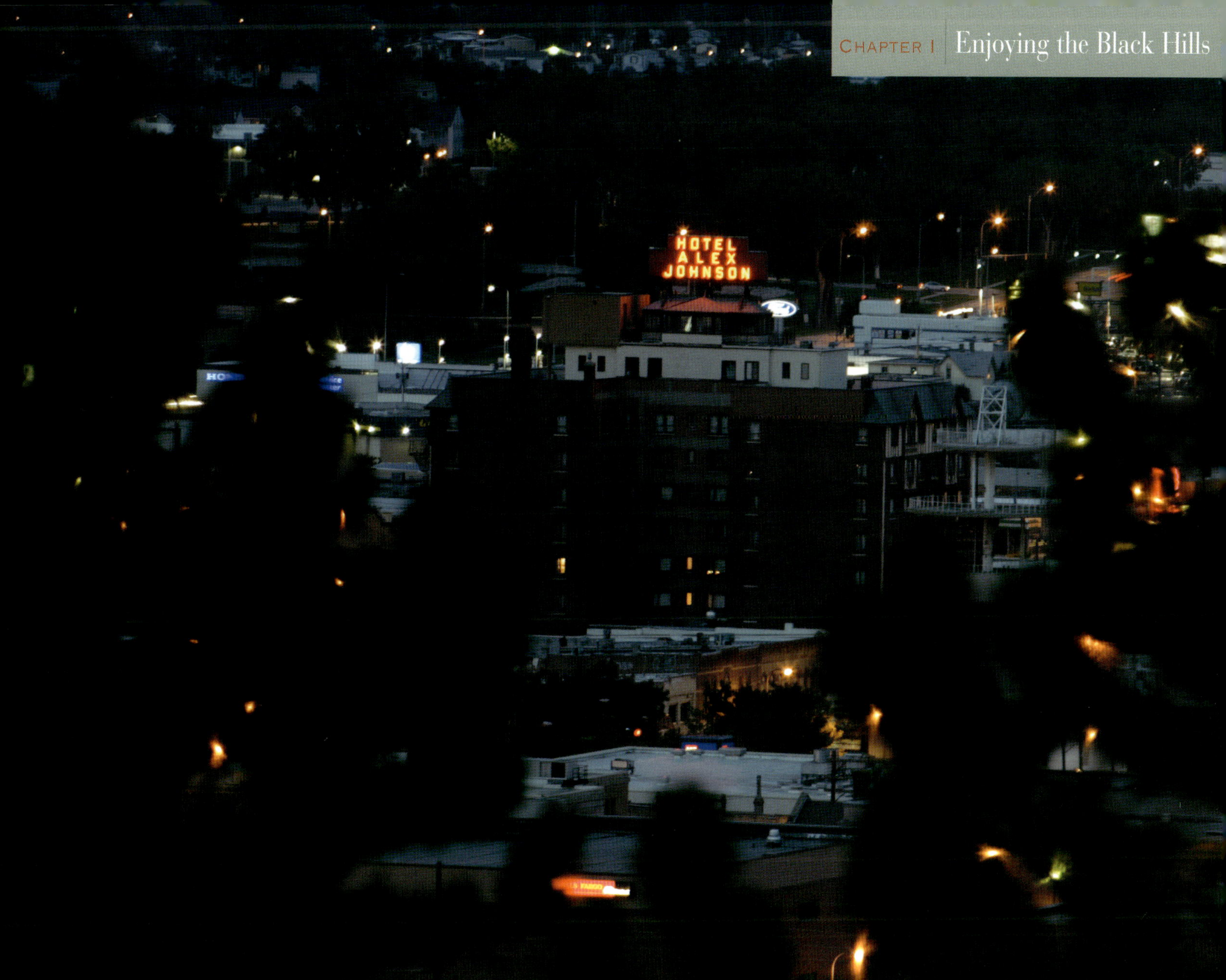

Photo by Eric Francis

The 143-room historic Hotel Alex Johnson is in the heart of downtown Rapid City. Listed on the National Register of Historic Places, the hotel was constructed by Chicago-Northwestern Railroad executive Alex Carlton Johnson with the intent to be "The Showplace of the West." Throughout the years, guests, ranging from Hollywood stars to everyday folk, have enjoyed the hotel's proximity to the Black Hills, natural and manmade attractions. ❖

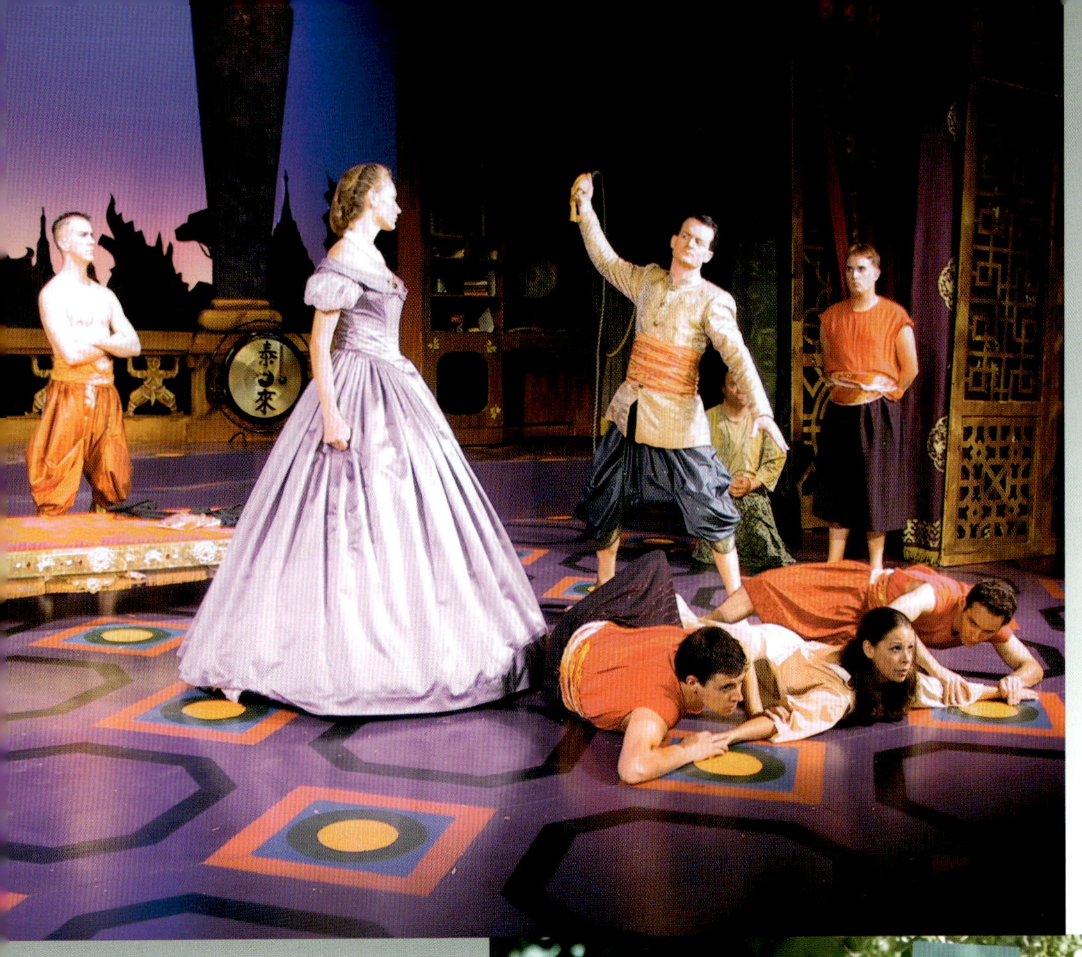

The performances are equal to those produced at any major metropolitan playhouse, but the location is something entirely unique. When University of South Dakota drama professor Doc Lee established the Black Hills Playhouse in 1945, he envisioned a theatrical company that could practice its craft in an atmosphere of total creative freedom. So instead of the middle of the city, Lee established his company in the middle of the Black Hills, first performing in tents, then in the facilities of a 1930s job relief camp. When the playhouse moved into its own building in 1955, it remained in its rural setting. Located in Custer State Park about a half hour's drive from Rapid City, the Black Hills Playhouse continues its sixty-plus-year tradition of bringing high-quality live performances to appreciative audiences. Theatrical professionals from around the world come to participate in the half-dozen summer season productions that include such classics as The King and I (shown here from the 2005 season), The Pirates of Penzance, A Chorus Line, and Play It Again, Sam, to name just a few. ❖

Not many people know that Cinderella, Dr. Seuss, Winnie the Pooh, Tin Man, Dorothy, Toto, the Cowardly Lion, Humpty Dumpty, Pinocchio, and lots of other characters live in Rapid City. Of course, anyone who has visited Storybook Island is in on the secret. In August 1959, the Rapid City Rotary Club created a charitable, nonprofit corporation, Storybook Island, Inc., to open and operate a free children's park. With the exception of the 1972 flood, the park has been open from Memorial Day to Labor Day each year since then. In addition to the animated and real-life scenes from nursery rhymes and fairytales, the park includes a kiddy train and petting zoo. The Storybook Island Children's Theater is one of the largest theaters of its kind in a five-state area. In addition to quality theatre they also offer educational programming through the Summer Theatre Camp. Storybook Island is managed by a board of directors, with members from Rapid City Rotary and Rushmore Rotary, and hundreds of community volunteers. ❖

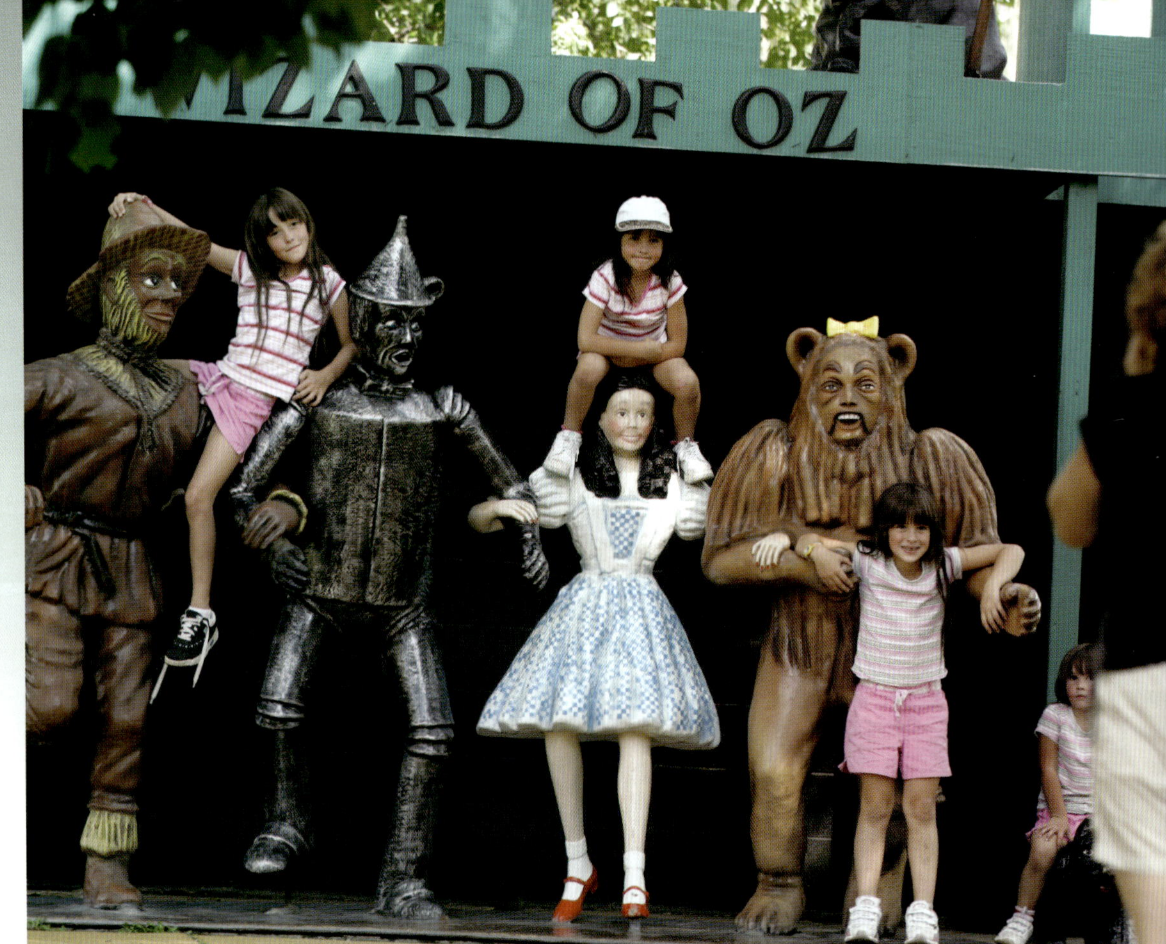

Photo by Eric Francis

It's SHOW TIME!

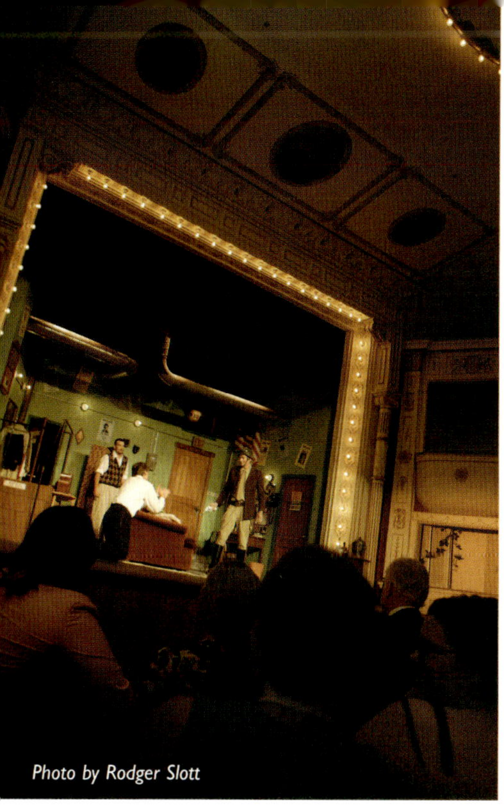
Photo by Rodger Slott

When it was founded in 1933, the Black Hills Symphony Orchestra was a small group of string players who gave occasional concerts. Today, the orchestra, under the direction of conductor Jack Knowles, employs approximately eighty musicians and has both a pops and a classical concert season plus a number of educational outreach programs. One of the most popular programs is the Young Artists Competition held each January. It features top instrumental high school players from grades 10 through 12. First prize is six hundred dollars and the opportunity for the winner to be a guest soloist and to perform his or her audition piece with the symphony in concert. The event is organized by the Symphony Board of Directors and is supported by the Symphony League and a host of other volunteers. The competition has gained such a local following that the advertising posters have become collectors' items. The 2006 winner was cellist Tiffany Bell. ❖

▲ **Like any building** that has been around for over one hundred years, the Matthews Opera House has gone through a number of identities. Thomas Newton Matthews first opened it as a grand, three-hundred-seat opera house in December 1906. Nine years later, the son, Thomas W. Matthews, removed the permanent seats so the auditorium could double as a dance hall. Next came silent movies, and the building was renamed the Princess Theater. In 1930 it was closed and in the following years was used as a shooting gallery. Finally the Spearfish Downtown Association formed the non-profit Matthews Opera House Society and raised approximately $250,000 for repairs and restoration. Today the stately old building it is again the showplace it was meant to be. ❖

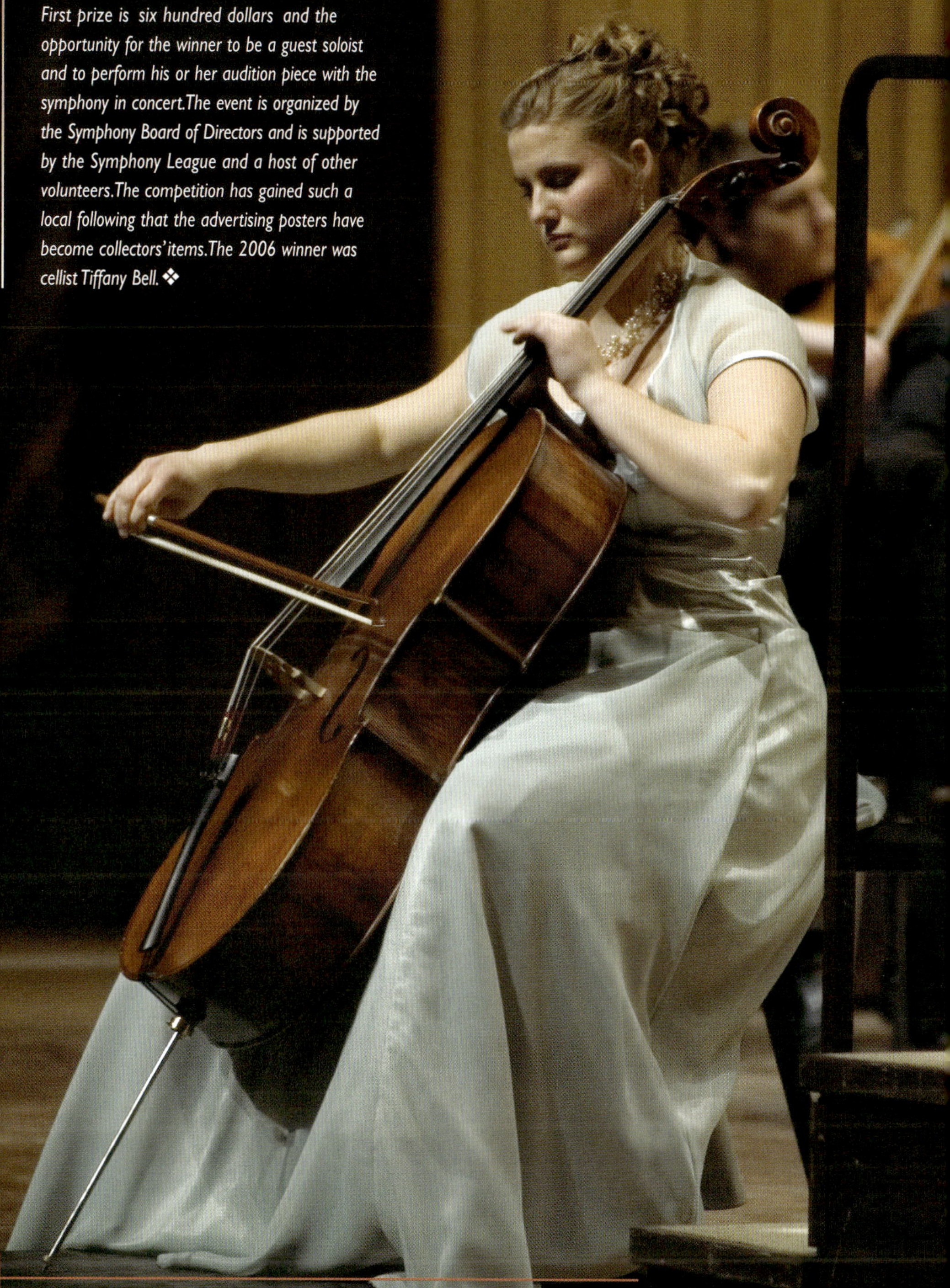

◄ **The 1912 Elks Theatre** in downtown Rapid City originally showcased musical performances and vaudeville acts. When moving pictures became popular, the theatre was transformed into a movie palace. In the late '20s, it was one of the hottest spots in town because it was one of the first locations to show "talkies." Over the years, Rapid City grew and changed around the movie house, which closed its doors in 1989 but reopened after an extensive renovation in 1992. Now, the two silver screens within the theatre entertain audiences with the latest films. ❖

Photo by Joleen Zoller

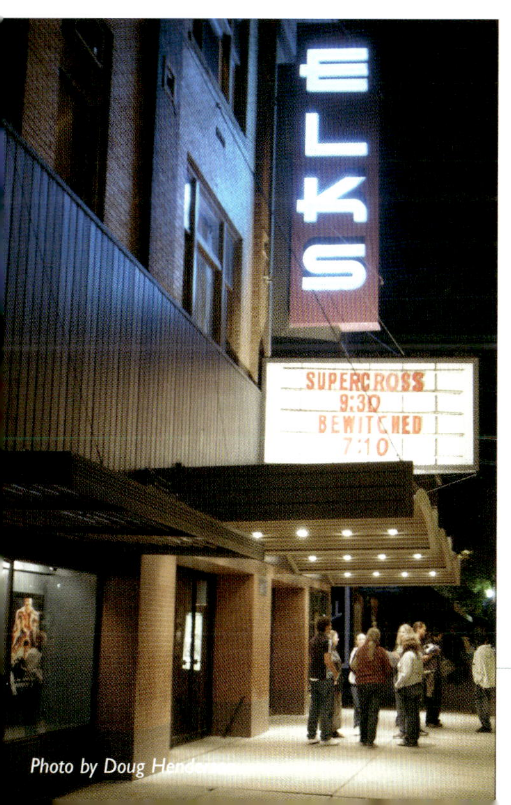

Photo by Doug Hend

Custer Resort Company: A Vacation Experience of a Lifetime

Since 1978, Custer Resort Company has helped provide visitors to the Black Hills with the vacation experience of a lifetime. As an authorized concessionaire of South Dakota's Department of Game Fish & Parks, the privately owned and operated company manages the operations of four scenic Custer State Park resorts: Sylvan Lake Lodge & Resort, Blue Bell Lodge & Resort, Legion Lake Resort, and the historic State Game Lodge & Resort.

For many visitors, these facilities serve as summer vacation headquarters from which to explore the seventy-three-thousand-acre Custer State Park, its two scenic highways, awesome natural beauty, and abundant outdoor adventure activities. But for others, the resorts are a destination in and of themselves, proving that where you stay can be just as inspiring as what you see and do.

Creating memorable stays is what Custer Resort Company is all about. Says founder and president Phil Lampert, "We manage every operation that goes into making these resorts full-service facilities—from the lodging to the restaurants, the gift shops, and convenience stores to the outdoor activities."

From the May to October resort season, Lampert's company employs over 350 personnel, making it not only South Dakota's largest seasonal employer, but also one of

Creating memorable stays is what Custer Resort Company is all about.

Photo by Thomas S. England

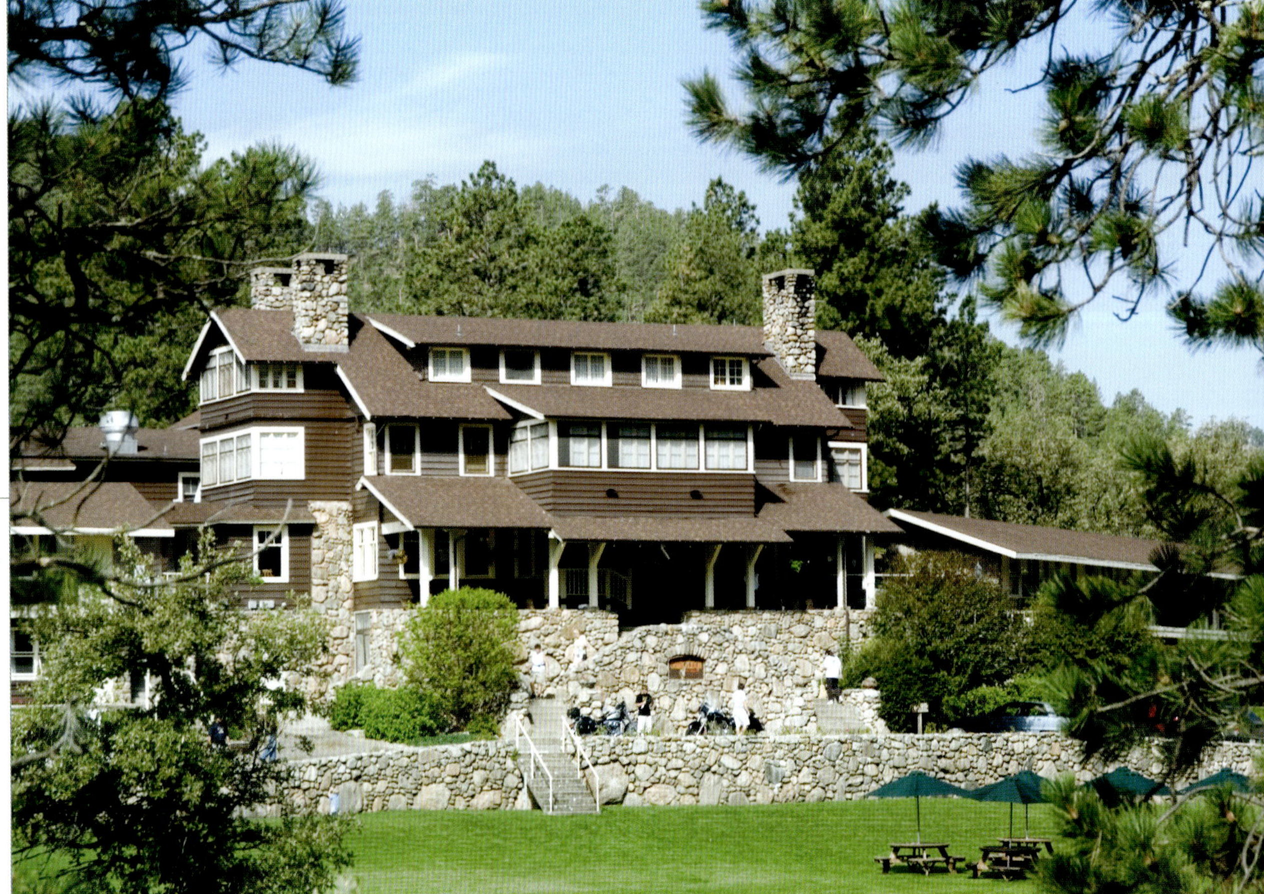

Built in 1920 and listed on the National Register of Historic Places, the State Game Lodge and Resort exemplifies the wilderness lodge experience. Located in a picturesque mountain valley at the eastern edge of Custer State Park, the resort offers guests stately, cozy accommodations, fine western-style dining, and access to an array of outdoor activities.

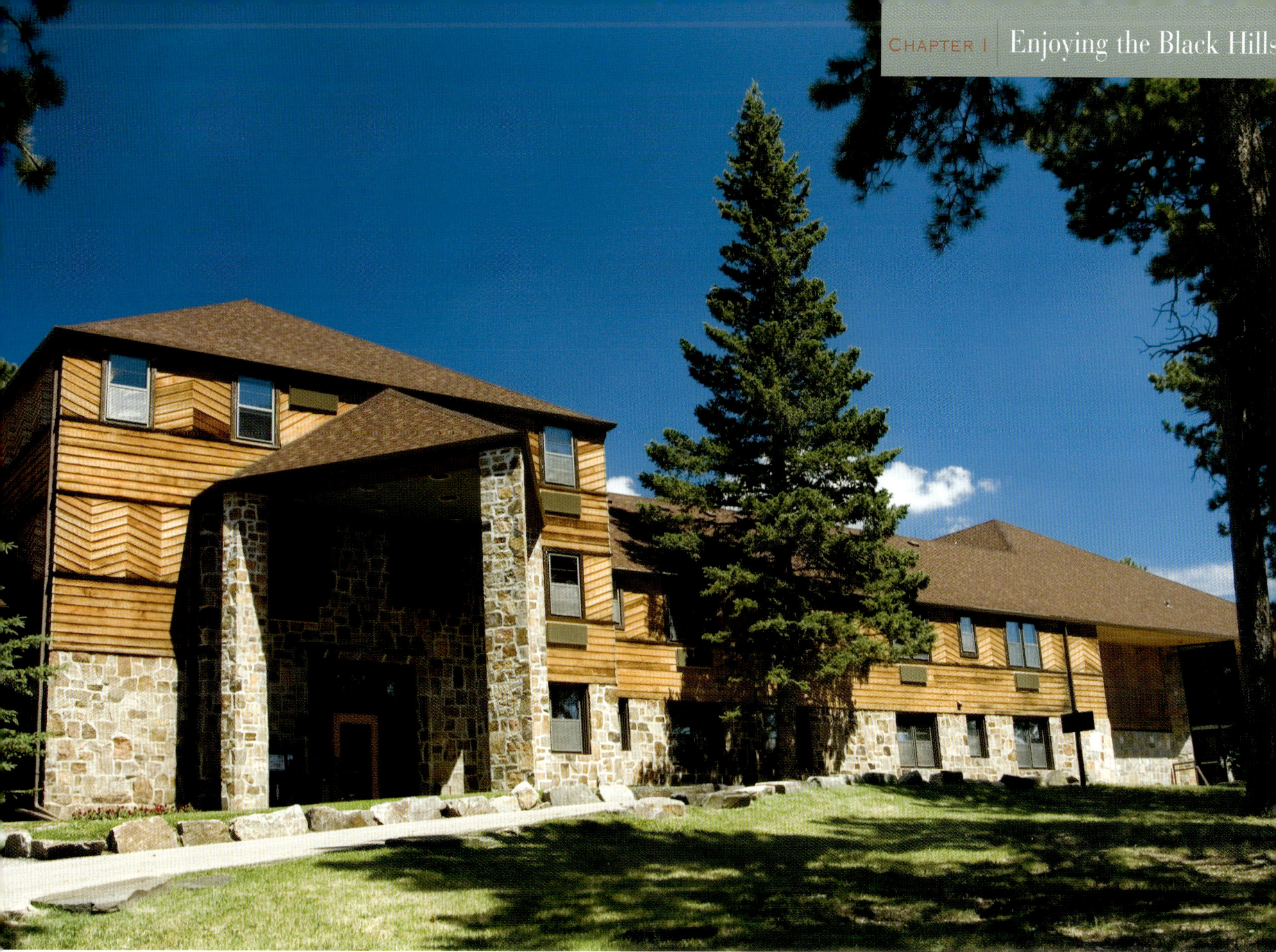

Photo by Thomas S. England

Located where Needles Highway terminates at the entrance to Custer State Park, the Sylvan Lake Resort makes a perfect base from which to explore the area. Not only is the resort situated a short walk from Sylvan Lake for swimming, fishing, and boating, it is close to numerous hiking trails and world-class rock climbing.

its busiest. With a combined total of 188 rooms, the resorts accommodate thousands of visitors each summer. But the park itself attracts visitors in the millions, and many of them also stop by the lodges to sightsee, dine, and sign up for resort-based outdoor adventures, such as the State Game Lodge and Resort's popular Buffalo Safari jeep tours.

Each resort is located in a different section of the park, and each offers guests a distinctive variation on the wilderness lodge experience, from the nostalgic elegance of the State Game Lodge & Resort, which served as a summer retreat for both Calvin Coolidge and Dwight D. Eisenhower, to the scenic Sylvan Lake Lodge & Resort with its proximity to world-class hiking, biking, fishing, and climbing. Elsewhere, Blue Bell Lodge & Resort attracts guests with its laid-back Old West ambience, complete with chuck-wagon cookouts, hayrides, and horseback riding, while Legion Lake Resort's secluded cabins are favorites with families seeking immediate access to boating and fishing.

All of them successfully balance the needs of modern-day and nature-loving travelers. Says Lampert, "When we first started managing the resorts, there were no televisions or phones in many of the rooms. While we still provide that kind of secluded experience, we're also doing it along with modern amenities like high-speed Internet and fine dining. So I like to say we're rustic but also luxurious." This balance, he believes, is what makes both the resorts and Custer State Park as a whole so appealing. "We are on par with any national park in the United States, and I believe it's because we can provide so much to see and do while remaining unspoiled. We're not over-commercialized or congested, and that makes us unique." ❖

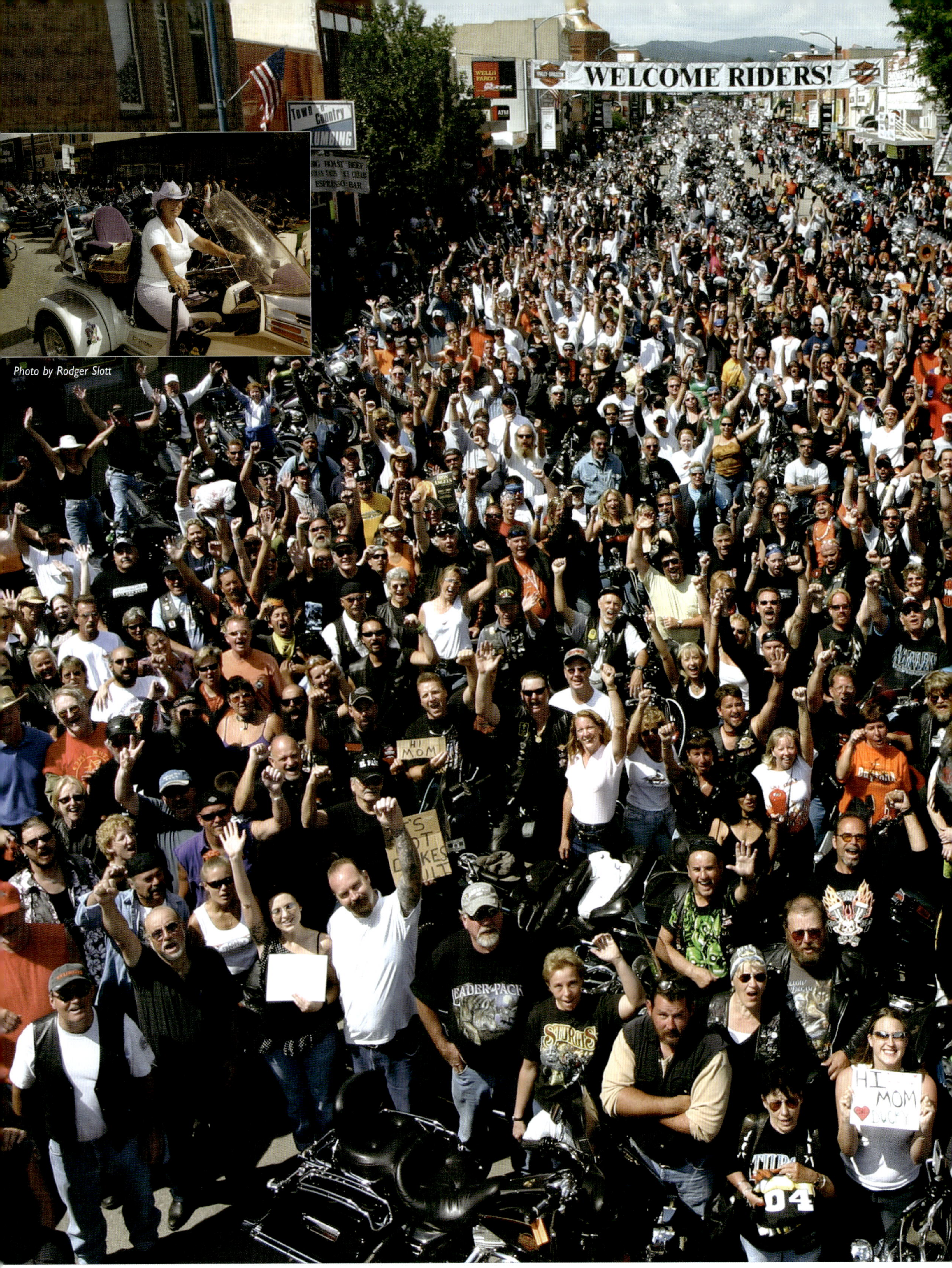

Photo by Rodger Slott

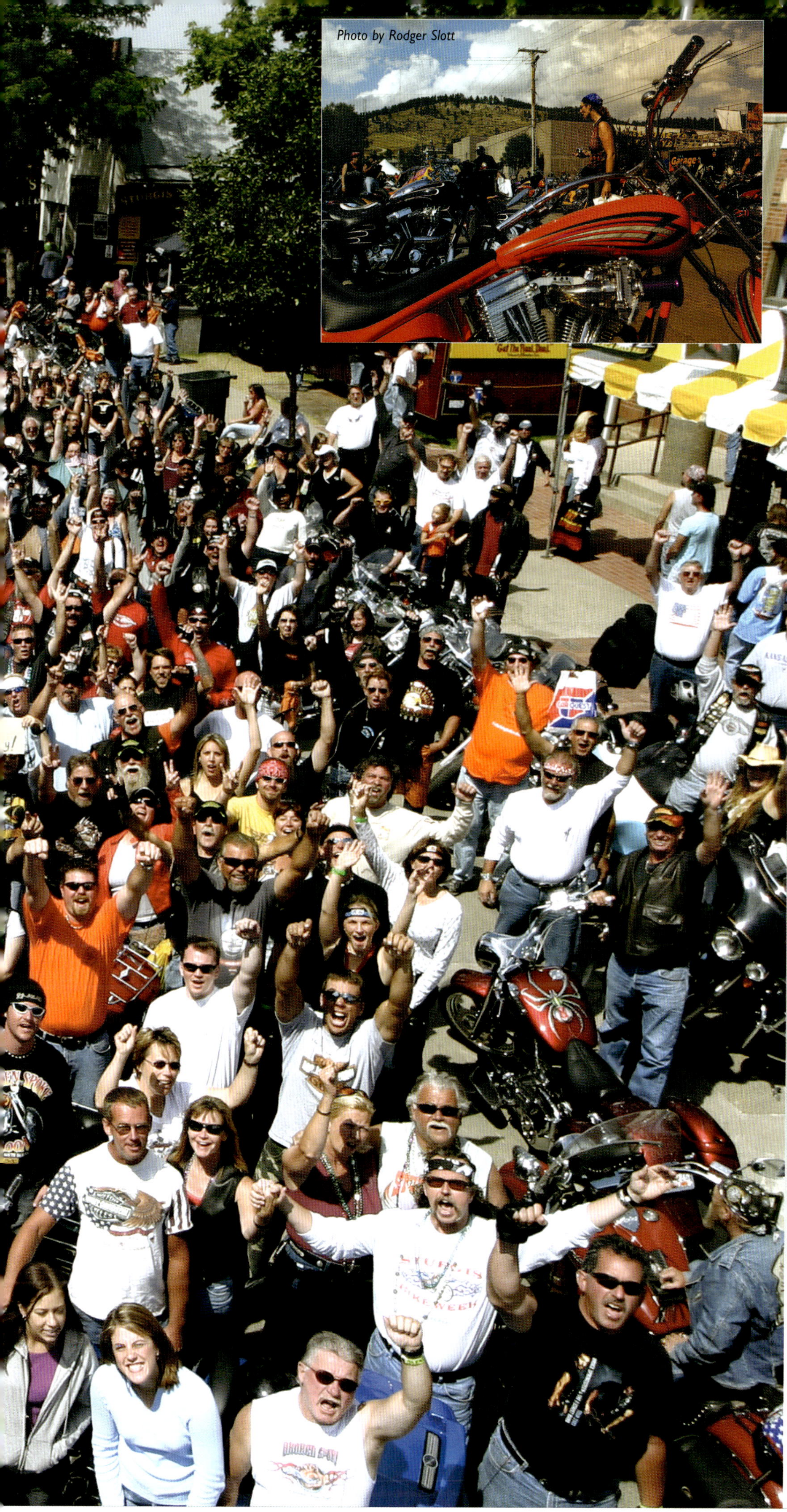

Photo by Rodger Slott

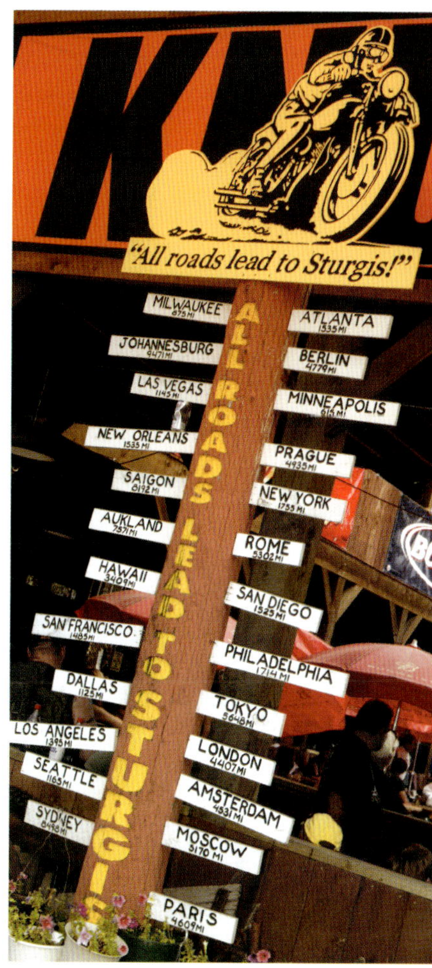

Photo by Rodger Slott

Whether you ride a Harley or a Honda, a sleek chopper or a hunky trike, the Sturgis Motorcycle Rally welcomes you as part of one big family. Established as a weekend event in 1938 by founding members of the local Jackpine Gypsies Motorcycle Club, the rally has grown to become the largest and most popular event of its kind. Each year during the first full week of August, motorcycle lovers and riders from around the world converge at Sturgis to race, visit with bike and accessory vendors, tour the area, and just hang out with like-minded folk. And not all of them ride in, either. Some fly in—with their bikes—from as far away as Australia. For these folks, WestJet Air, Rapid City Regional Airport's premier fixed-base operator, provides hangar space for participants to house their bikes during the rally. Like dozens of other area individuals, communities, and businesses, WestJet Air regards the rally as a cooperative event that benefits the entire Black Hills region. ❖

Hotel Alex Johnson: Showcase of the West

If you could page through the seven decades of guest ledgers from the Hotel Alex Johnson, you'd be impressed. Five presidents; a multitude of movie stars, musicians, and artists; as well as more nondescript but equally important people have enjoyed the comforts of this historic hotel. But perhaps what is most impressive is the fact that this grand hotel has prospered since 1928—successfully mixing the famous with the everyday folks, preserving tradition while providing modern amenities, and all the while proudly showcasing its city and its stunning surrounding Black Hills.

Railroad executive Alex Carlton Johnson built the hotel, which he called "The Showplace of the West" to accommodate travelers visiting the Black Hills area. An admirer of Native Americans, Johnson also dedicated the hotel as a tribute to the Lakota Indian Nation by embellishing the structure and décor with symbols of Indian culture.

"We've remained independent, which has allowed us to be more receptive to the needs of our individual travelers."

As a unique coincidence, construction on the hotel began one day before work started on nearby Mount Rushmore. While it took more than twenty years to complete Mount Rushmore, the Hotel Alex Johnson received the first guests just shy of one year, including Gutzon Borglum, the mountain's famous sculptor. Year after year, decade after decade, when people came to Rapid City, they chose the "million-dollar" Hotel Alex Johnson as much for its unique charm as for its accommodations. The Alex boasts visits by five U.S. presidents, as well as foreign dignitaries and entertainment luminaries including Jimmy Stewart, James Mason, Alfred Hitchcock, Marty Stuart, Viggo Mortenson, and Jay Leno.

Photo by Eric Francis

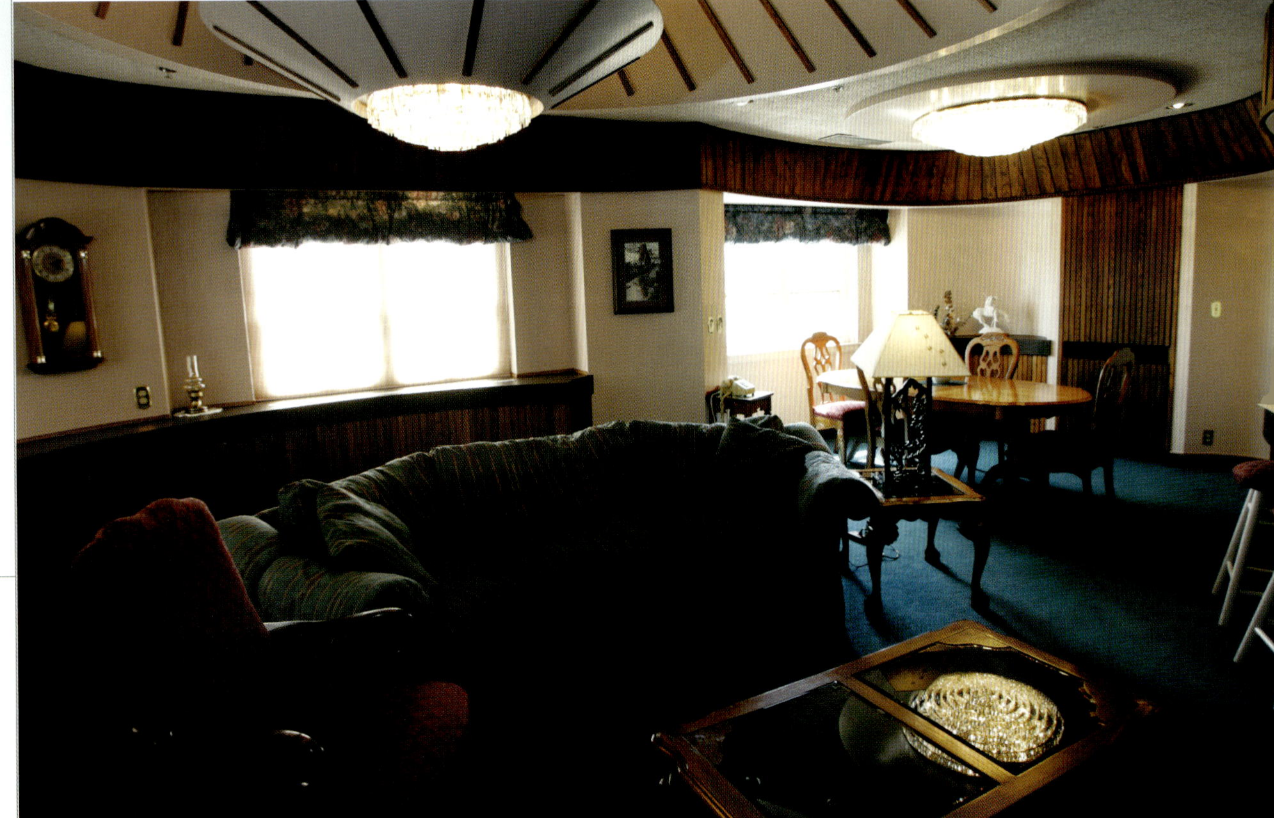

The interior living area of the Presidential Suite highlights unique lighting and wall features.

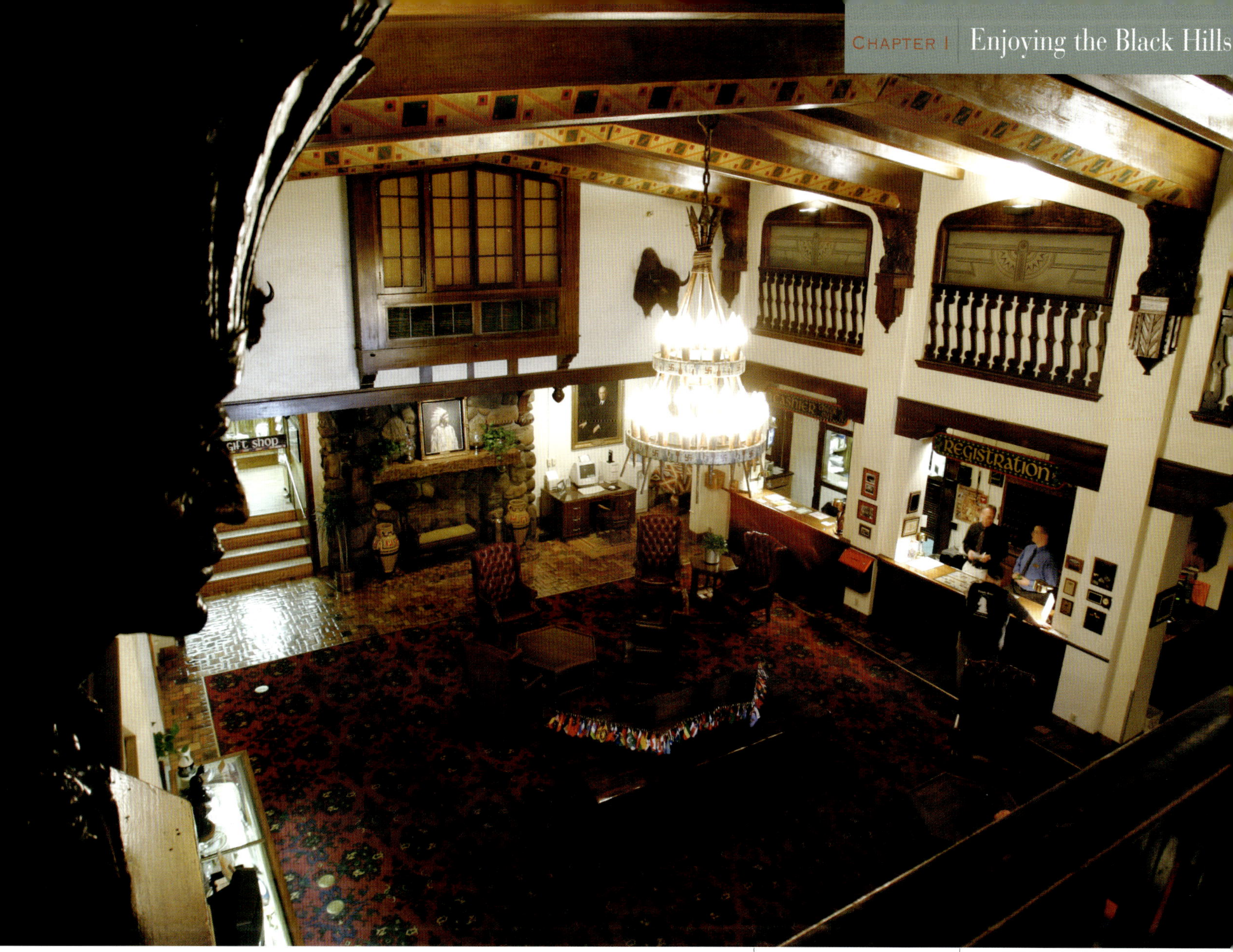

Photo by Eric Francis

View of the lobby from the mezzanine.

"As stand-alone properties, railroad hotels survived on their own reputation—providing the best in lodging and dining services," says Jim Didier, owner. "We've remained independent, which has allowed us to be more receptive to the needs of our individual travelers." Instead of the typical themes found in corporate or franchise properties, the Hotel Alex Johnson's rooms feature the original replicas of the early 1920s furniture that was custom built for the hotel. Every room is different, making it even more enticing for guests to return another year. While the hotel originally featured 200 rooms, there are now 143 rooms, made larger and more comfortable, including a presidential suite, a bridal suite, and several family parlors (two rooms that share a bathroom). Other renovations and upgrades, like high-speed Wi-Fi Internet, blend the best elements of the past, present, and future.

A stay here is far more than lodging, however. It's a holiday for the senses. It's an opportunity to surprise the palate with native dishes like walleye and buffalo, creatively prepared by award-winning chef Dennis Olivier. It's also an eye-opening exploration of the heritage of the Midwest and its native people, as the lobby is graced by original Indian figurines and century-old headdresses. Clearly, the Hotel Alex Johnson remains the Showcase of the West. "We've always been a viable part of this community, showcasing downtown Rapid City as well as the Black Hills," says Didier. "That's why this hotel was started, and that's why we've continued that tradition." ❖

Photo by Eric Francis

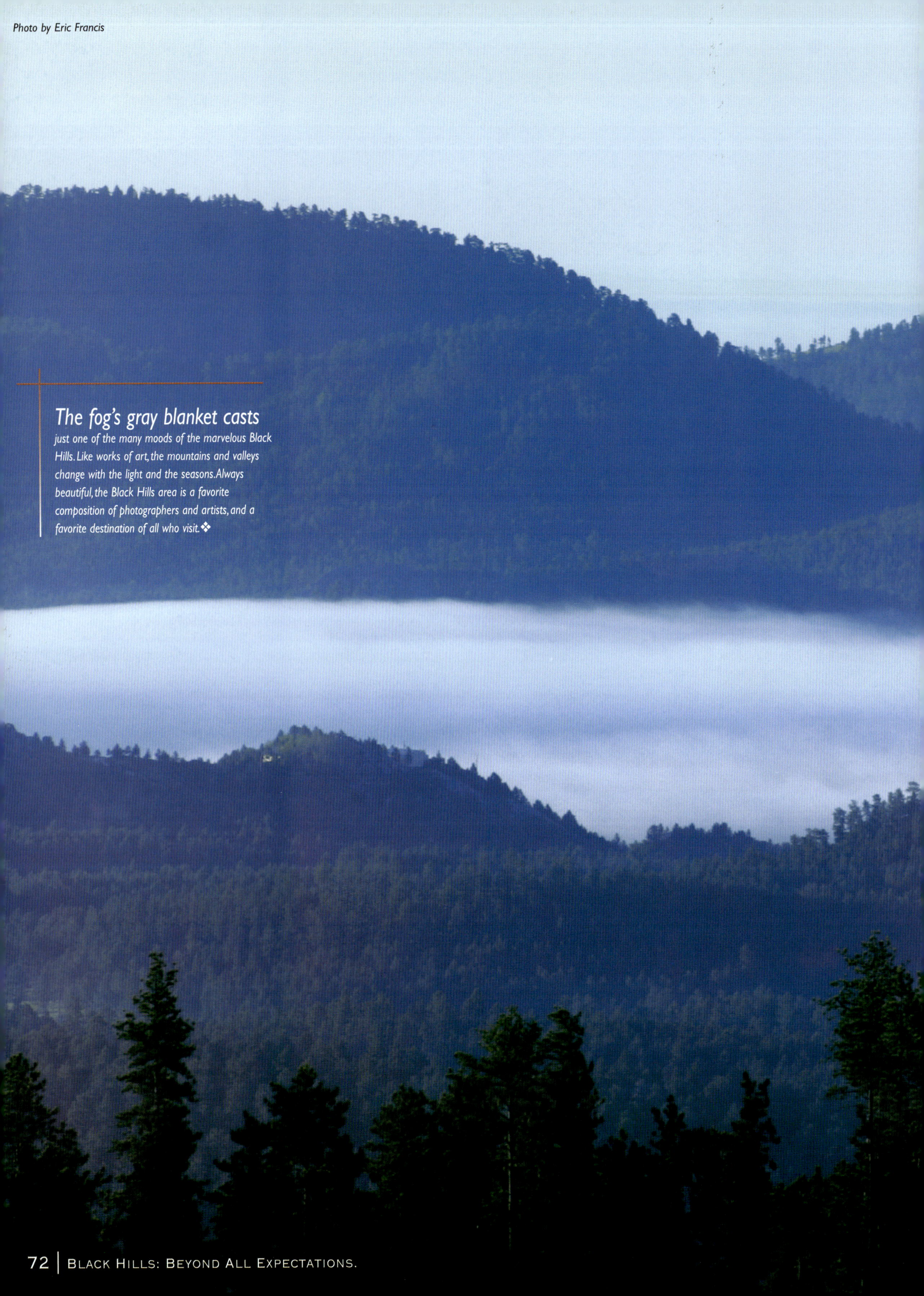

The fog's gray blanket casts just one of the many moods of the marvelous Black Hills. Like works of art, the mountains and valleys change with the light and the seasons. Always beautiful, the Black Hills area is a favorite composition of photographers and artists, and a favorite destination of all who visit. ❖

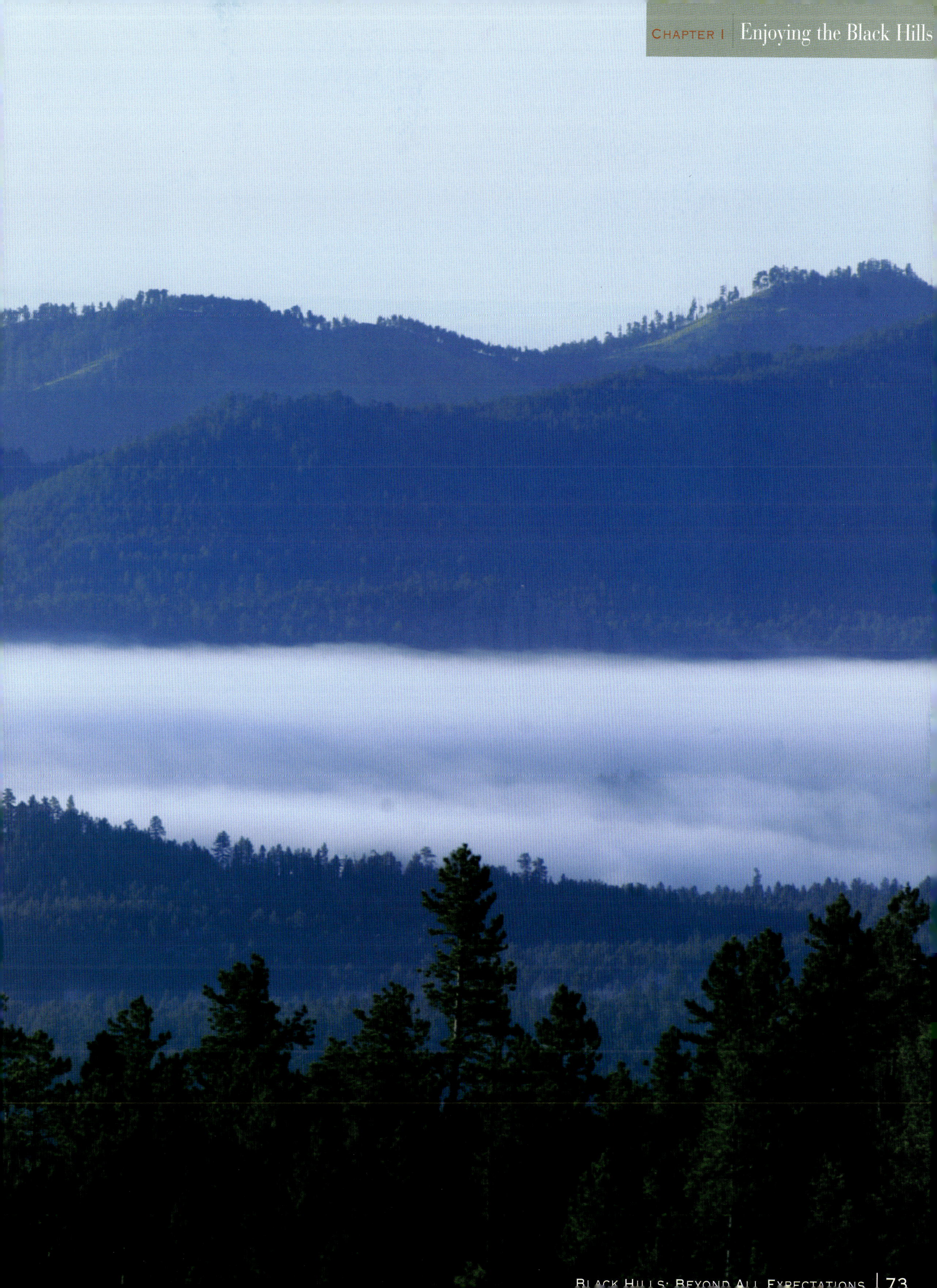

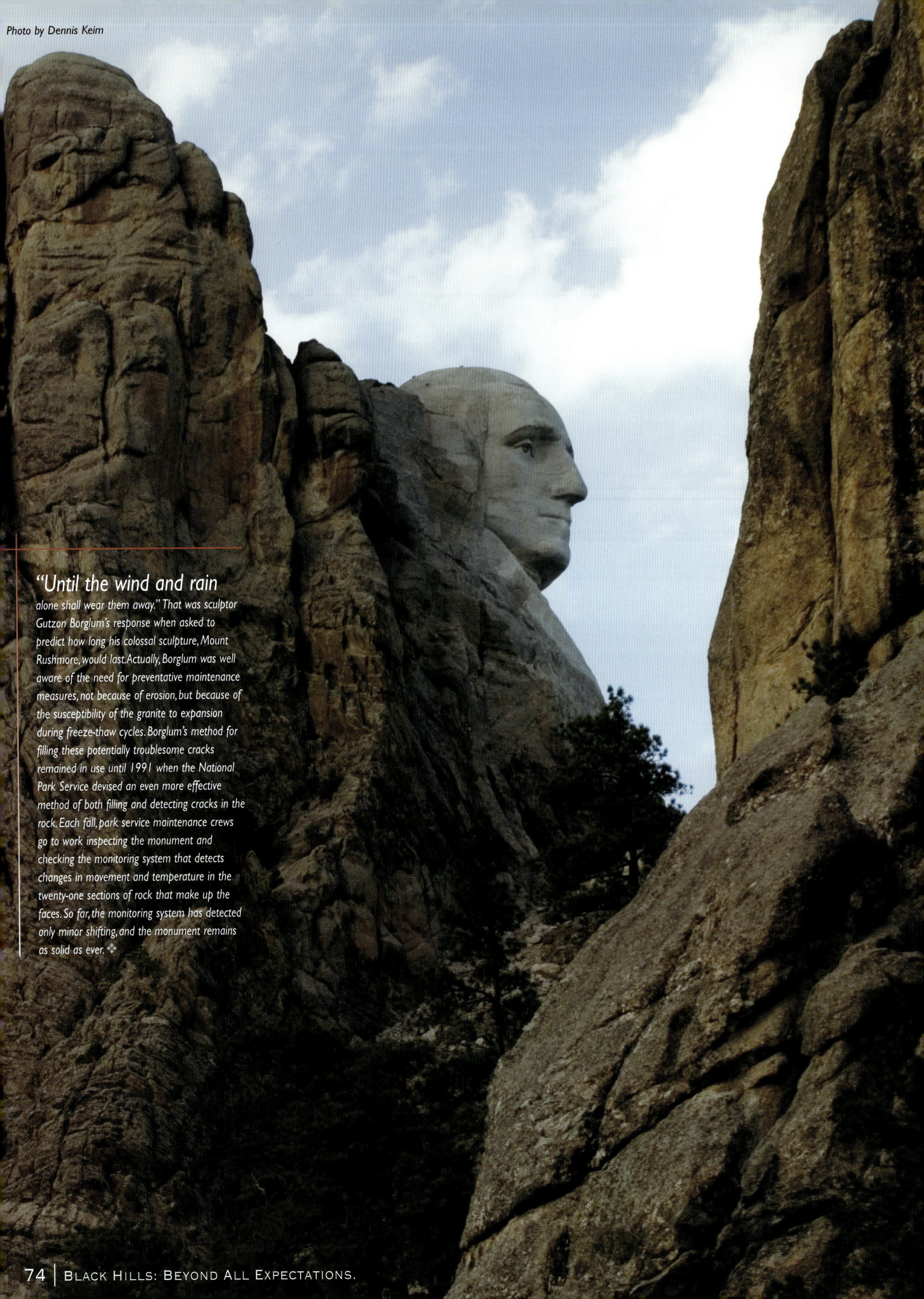

Photo by Dennis Keim

"Until the wind and rain alone shall wear them away." That was sculptor Gutzon Borglum's response when asked to predict how long his colossal sculpture, Mount Rushmore, would last. Actually, Borglum was well aware of the need for preventative maintenance measures, not because of erosion, but because of the susceptibility of the granite to expansion during freeze-thaw cycles. Borglum's method for filling these potentially troublesome cracks remained in use until 1991 when the National Park Service devised an even more effective method of both filling and detecting cracks in the rock. Each fall, park service maintenance crews go to work inspecting the monument and checking the monitoring system that detects changes in movement and temperature in the twenty-one sections of rock that make up the faces. So far, the monitoring system has detected only minor shifting, and the monument remains as solid as ever. ❖

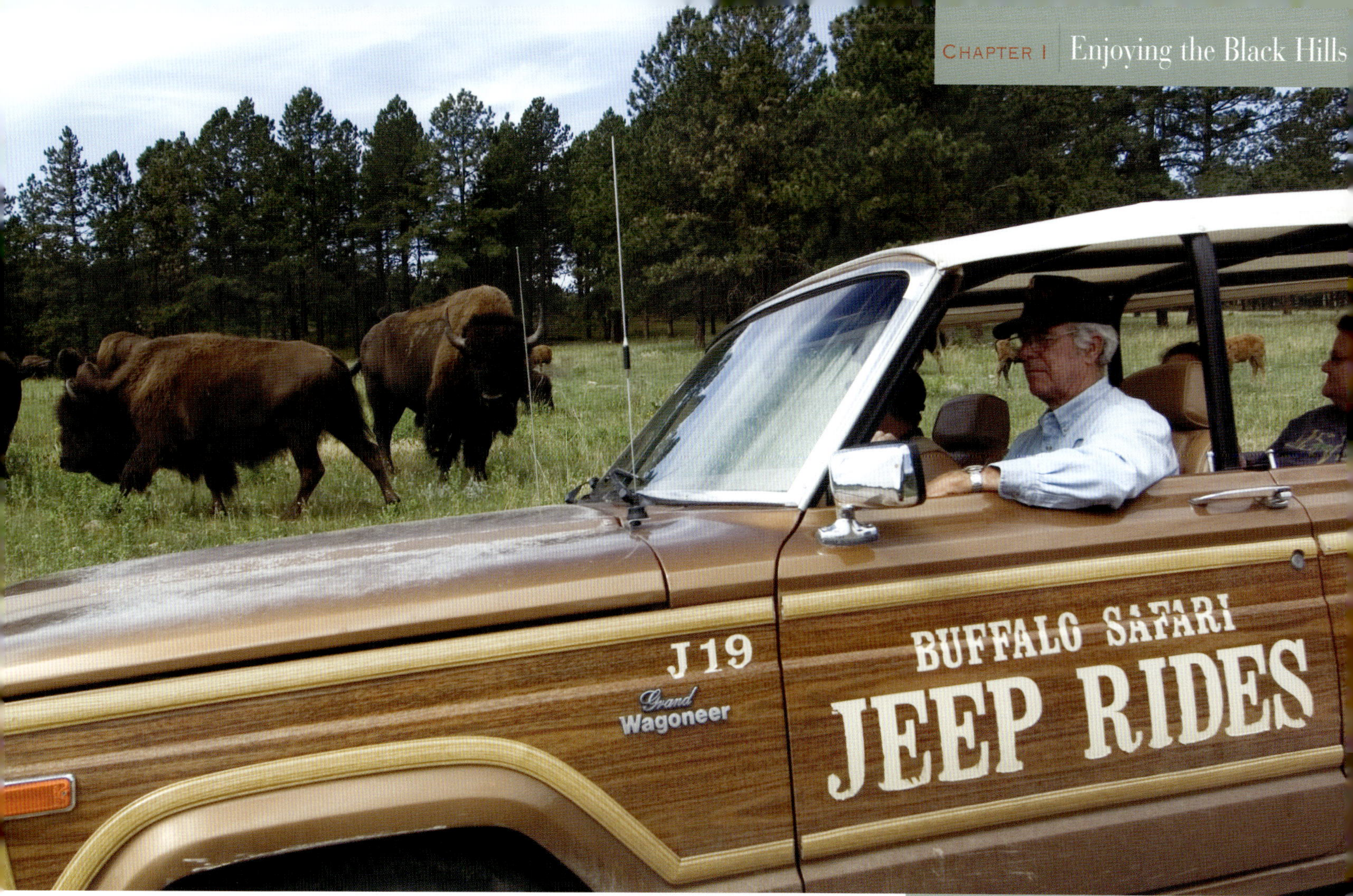

Photo by Thomas S. England

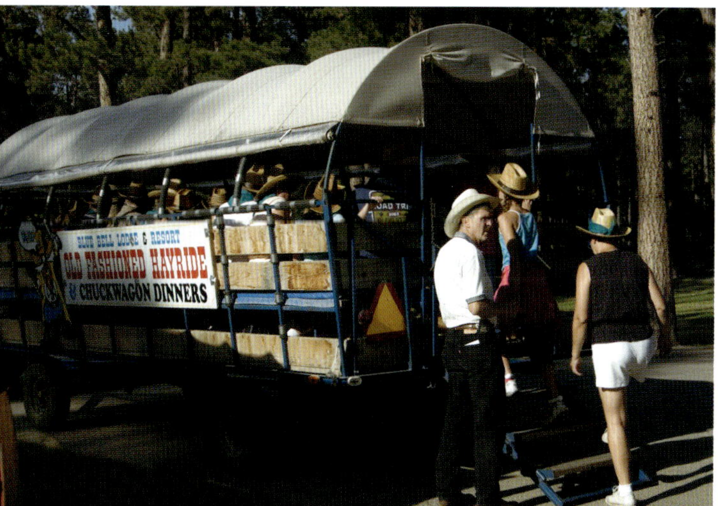

Photo by Thomas S. England

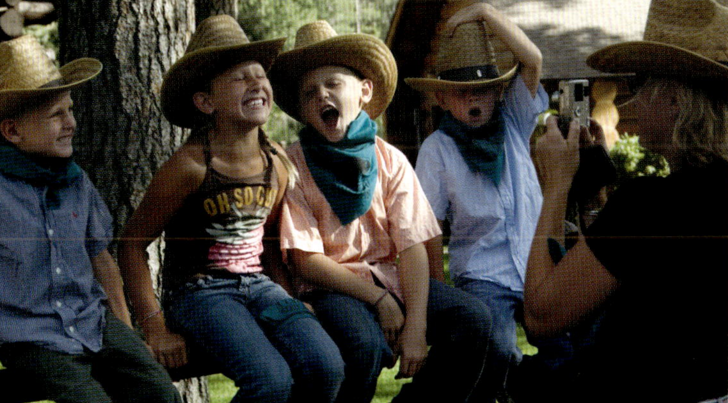

Photo by Thomas S. England

▲**One of the best ways to** experience Custer State Park is by booking a tour with Buffalo Safari Jeep Rides. Originating at the State Game Lodge and Resort, the two-hour drive winds its way through an eighteen-mile, on- and off-road loop through the park's scenic back-country. Driver/guides offer excellent information about the park's history, geography, flora, and fauna, while visitors get an up-close and personal view of the area's abundant native wildlife, including antelope, elk, turkey, bobcat, and, of course, buffalo. Tours are available seven days a week, morning to late afternoon, from just after Mother's Day to the first of October. ❖

◀**Yahoo!** Get your cowboy hat and bandanna at Blue Bell Lodge's Hayride Chuck Wagon Cookout. Just one of several western-themed activities offered by the lodge, the fun begins with a hay wagon ride through scenic backroads to a secluded mountain meadow canyon and ends with an old-fashioned chuck wagon dinner and country music sing-a-long. For even more adventure, saddle up and head out for an all-day trail ride, led by seasoned cowboys. A Custer Resort Company operation located at the southern end of Custer State Park, Blue Bell Lodge offers guests ranch-style amenities in a comfortable, unassuming environment that's perfect for family vacations and get-togethers. ❖

Hill City Offers Visitors Cozy, Small-Town Atmosphere

Nestled in the center of the beautiful pine-covered Black Hills is a living, breathing mountain community that is remarkable in many ways. "Hill City is a wonderful discovery," says Mike Verchio, executive director of the Hill City Area Chamber of Commerce. "It's a place where spectacular scenery and some of the best parks and attractions in America mingle with a century-old tradition of hard work and friendly western hospitality. It's truly the heart of the hills."

Hill City's history is as rich as the gold veins that run through its soil. Founded in February 1876, less than two years after George Armstrong Custer found gold along Spring Creek, Hill City was a booming town of miners, merchants, and muleskinners. But when gold was discovered further north in Deadwood Gulch, Hill City's population moved almost overnight. The town quickly turned from wild mining town to sleepy hamlet—that is, until tin was discovered in 1883. This cycle of mining booms and busts continued for decades, but even after the last mine closed for good, Hill City survived.

Hill City's history is as rich as the gold veins that run through its soil.

Today, visitors to Hill City can spend a relaxed day just sauntering down the town's sidewalks, stepping into colorful shops, art galleries, museums, brew pubs, candy stores, and outstanding restaurants. Just beyond Hill City lies a recreational playground of outdoor activities, including Mount Rushmore, Crazy Horse, Custer State Park, Wind Cave, and the Mickelson Trail. ❖

Photo by Doug Henderson

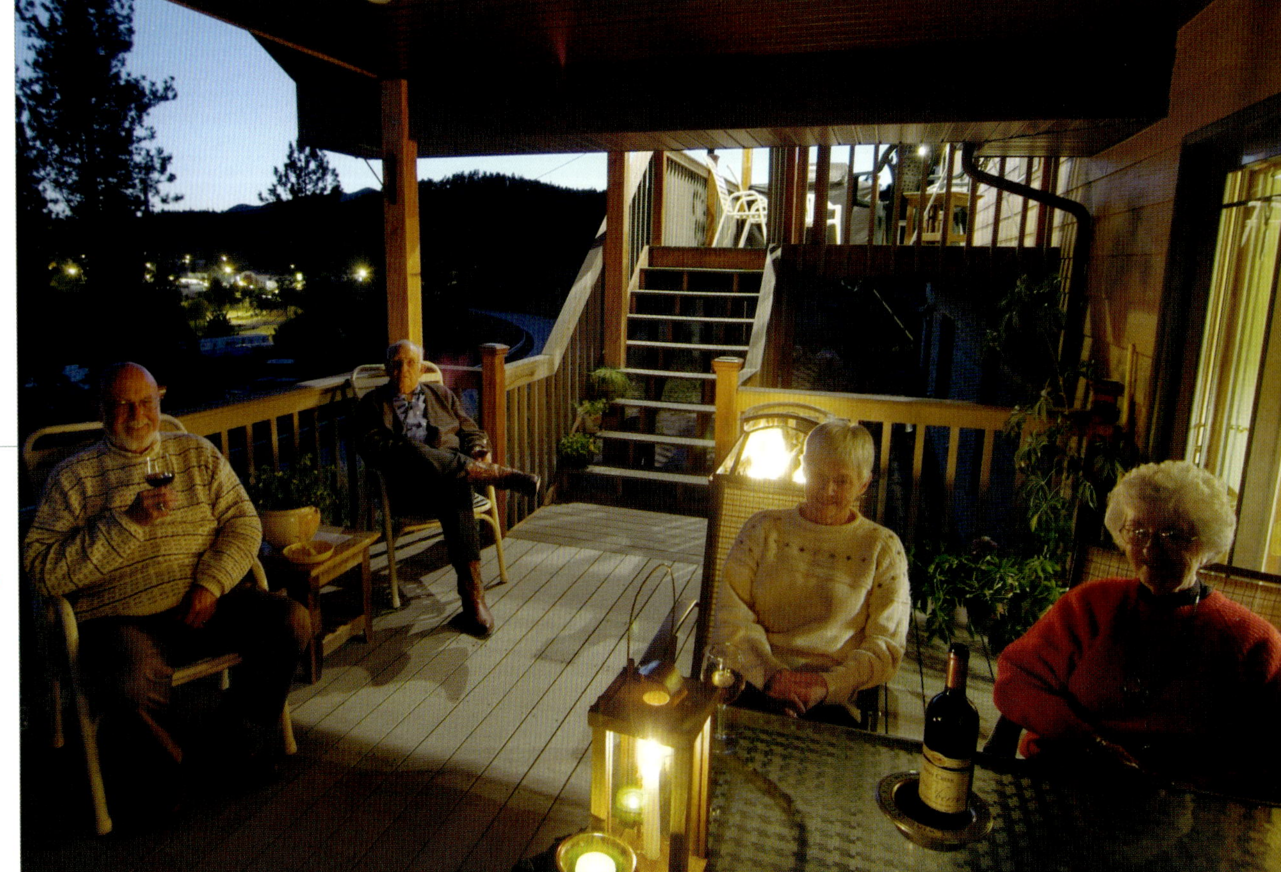

Everything about Hill City says "cozy small-town atmosphere." From dinner on the deck overlooking Main Street to enjoying warm days and cool evenings, Hill City's laid-back lifestyle and close-to-nature beauty are irresistible.

Take me out to the BALLGAME!

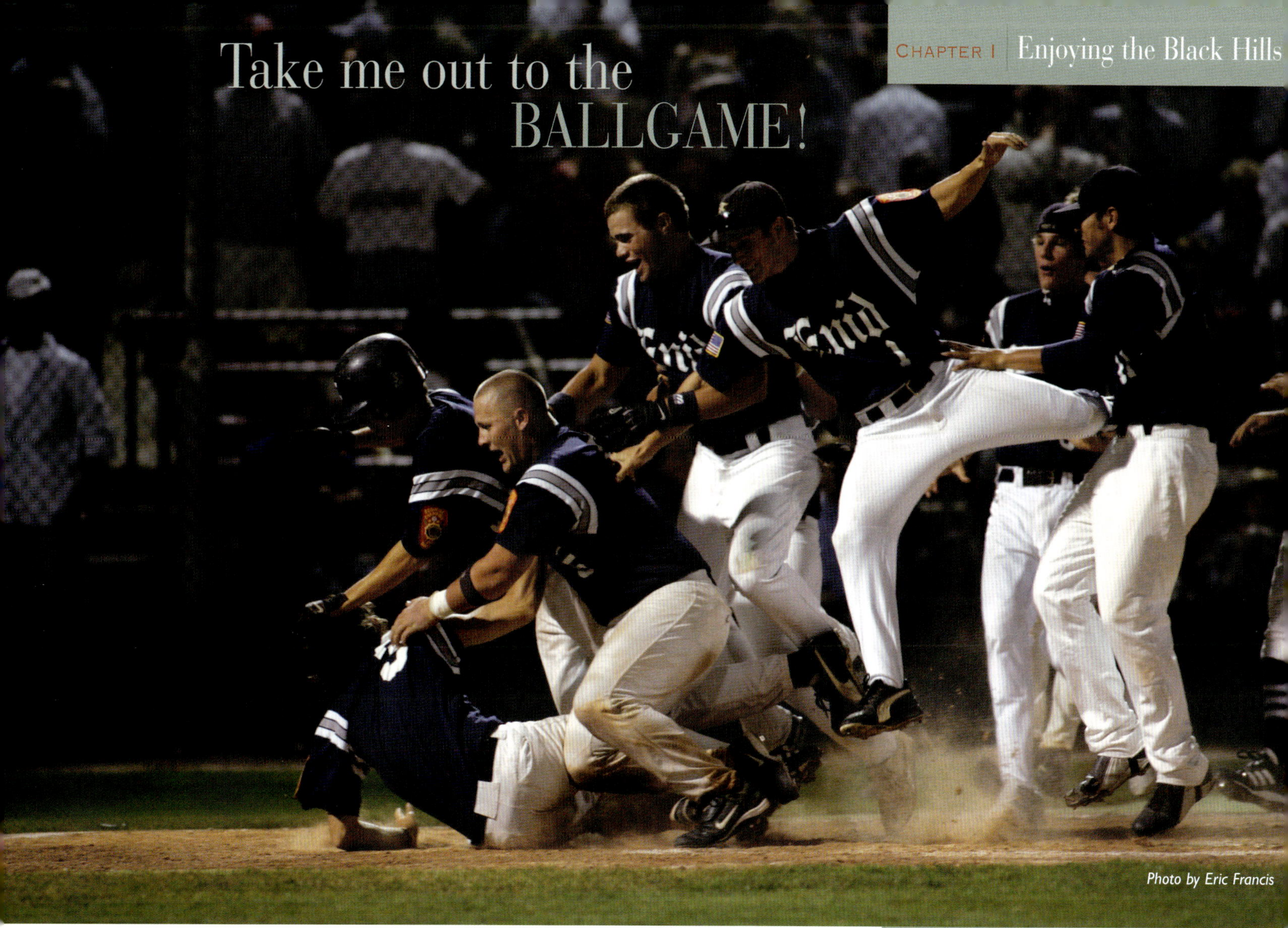

Photo by Eric Francis

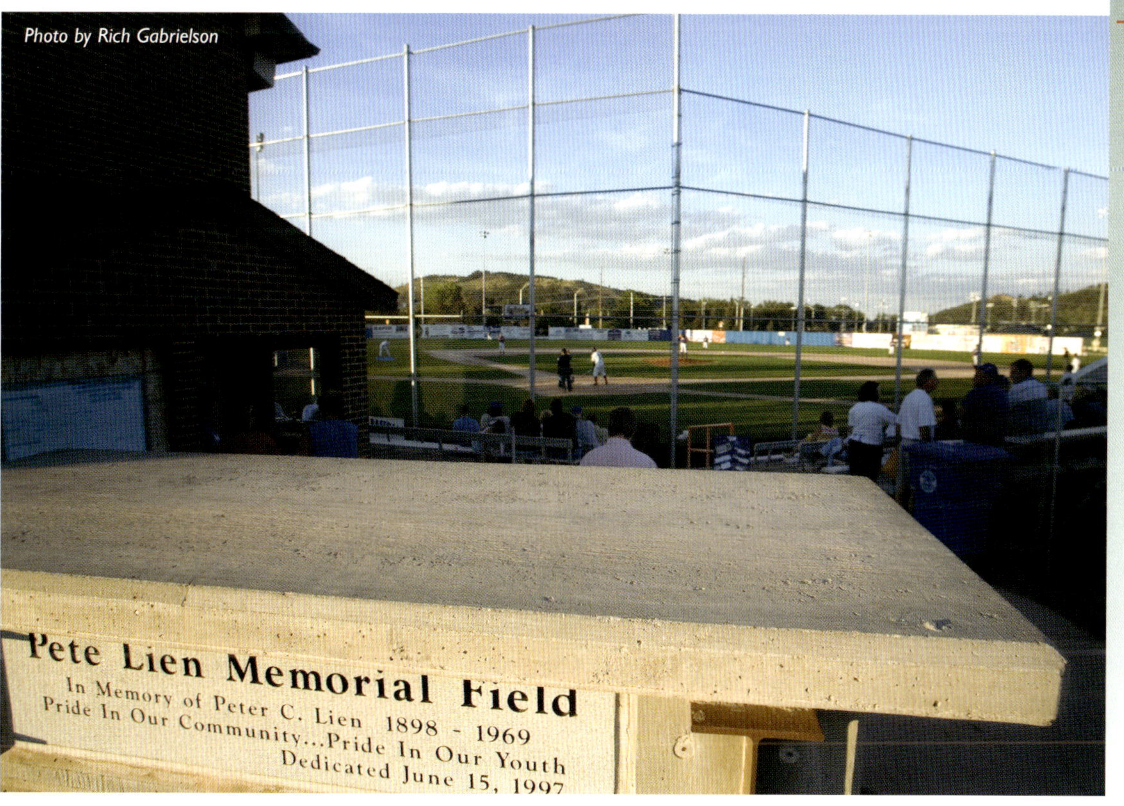

Photo by Rich Gabrielson

Rapid City is indeed a baseball town. For more than forty years, the Rapid City American Legion has sponsored Post 22 Baseball. In 2005 they were Central Plains Regional Champs and went to the American Legion World Series, which coincidentally was played at Fitzgerald Stadium in Rapid City. "Different cities bid, and we were just lucky enough to get the bid, and to have a team playing," said Kevin Heater, cochairman of the five-day event. Approximately twenty-eight thousand fans turned out to cheer their teams. "Volunteers take care of everything," said Heater. Unfortunately, Post 22 did not win, but the players still benefited from the experience. "We have about seventy kids involved in the total program, and they usually stay from four to five years," said coach Dave Ploof, who has been with the program since it started. Parents and volunteers spearheaded a fund-raising campaign to open a new half-million-dollar indoor training facility connected to Fitzgerald Stadium. Another facility spawned by the love of baseball is Pete Lien Memorial Field. The late Pete Calmer Lien, cofounder of the mining and processing company Pete Lien & Sons, loved the game and felt strongly that every child should have an opportunity to learn to play. "Baseball teaches a lot about life in the form of teamwork," he said. In his honor, Pete Lien & Sons, Inc., donated cash plus rock, sand, gravel, lime, block, and steel—the materials the business still mines and manufactures—to build the field.. ❖

Roosevelt Park Ice Arena

proclaims itself the "coolest place in town," and judging from the programs offered and the number of people taking advantage of them, they're right. Developed under the administration of Mayor Jim Shaw, the $4 million complex, which opened on Christmas Day 2001, offers a variety of programs and classes. There is hockey instruction for all ages. For those starting out with no skating experience, there is a Learn to Skate program which is a supplement to the Learn to Play Hockey program. Participants can take part in youth and adult hockey development programs, advanced programs, and the Rapid City Adult Hockey League. If you like your ice skating a little more on the artistic side, there is a full schedule of figure skating classes from the International Skating Institute. The ISI is recognized as the leading provider of classes for the recreational skater, and they promote skating as a lifetime sport for all ages, abilities, and interests. All Roosevelt Park Ice Arena instructors are ISI-certified. ❖

The coolest place in town!

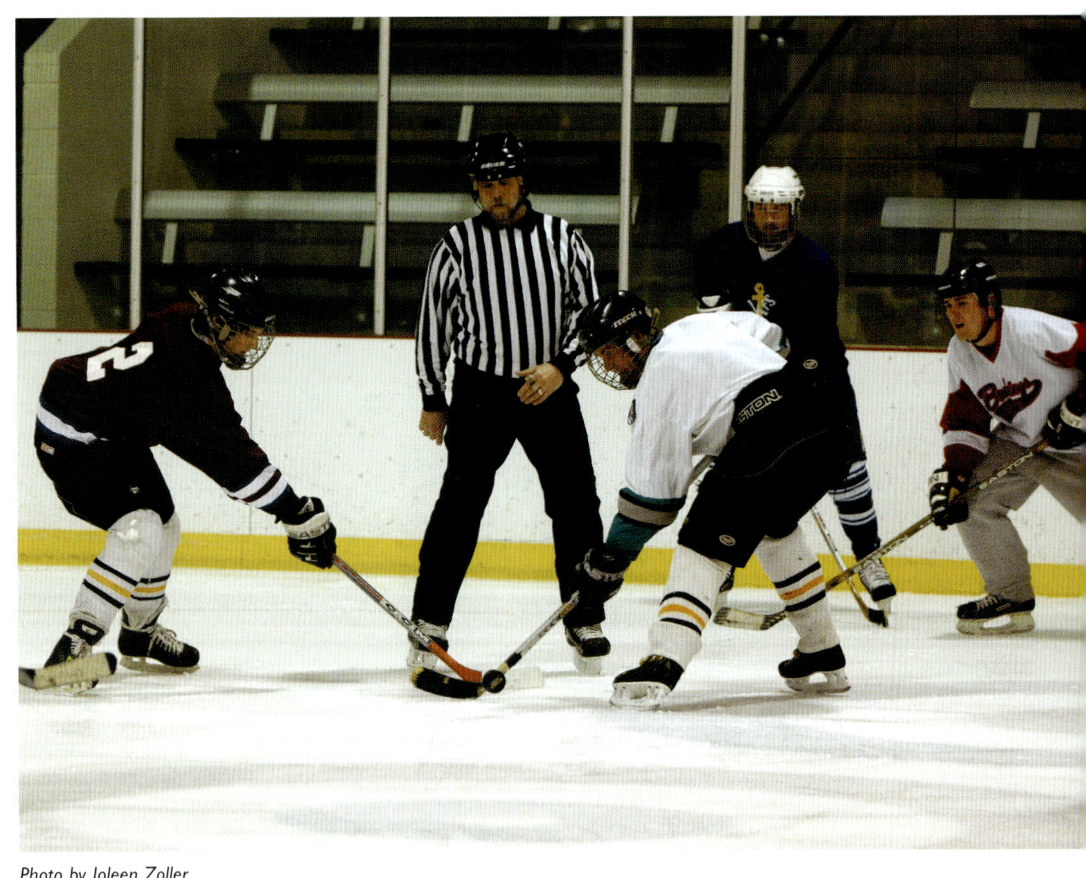

Photo by Joleen Zoller

It's about community

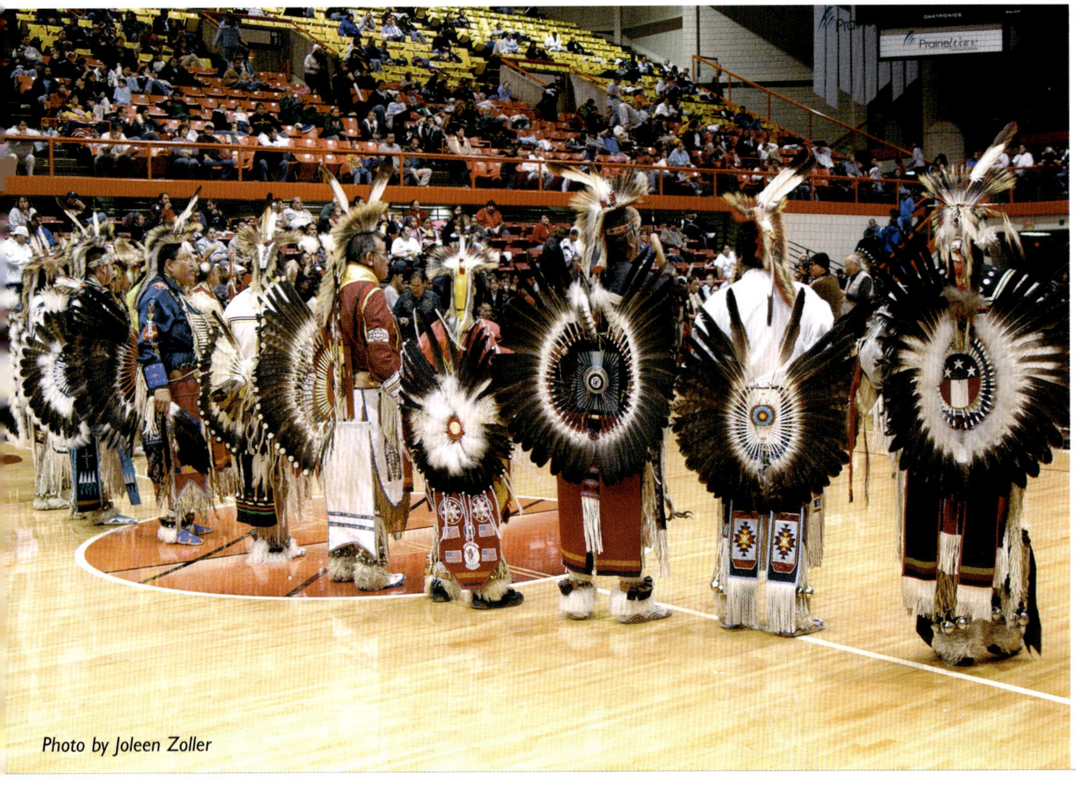

Photo by Joleen Zoller

It's all about basketball,

but then again it isn't. The Lakota Nation Invitational has been around since 1977. It does draw boys and girls basketball teams from all nine South Dakota reservations and as many as five thousand spectators, but as Bryan Brewer, founder and longtime coordinator, is quick to explain, "It's not just about basketball. There's wrestling, a knowledge bowl, hand games, an art show, and Lakota language bowl tournaments. It's a mix of athletes and academic standouts giving their all for their favorite sport, game, or art." Winners in all the competitions receive championship jackets like those awarded to basketball tournament players. More than fourteen hundred students from thirty-five schools participate in the four-day event, which is one of the premier gatherings of athletes, scholars, and tribal officials in the nation. It has become a special feature in Sports Illustrated. *"I can't get enough copies to go around," Brewer said. In addition to sports, tribal elders hold meetings to discuss historical trauma, health, education, Missouri River control and management, environmental concerns, law enforcement, and treaty issues. "Sure, it's about basketball," said Brewer, "but it's also about community."* ❖

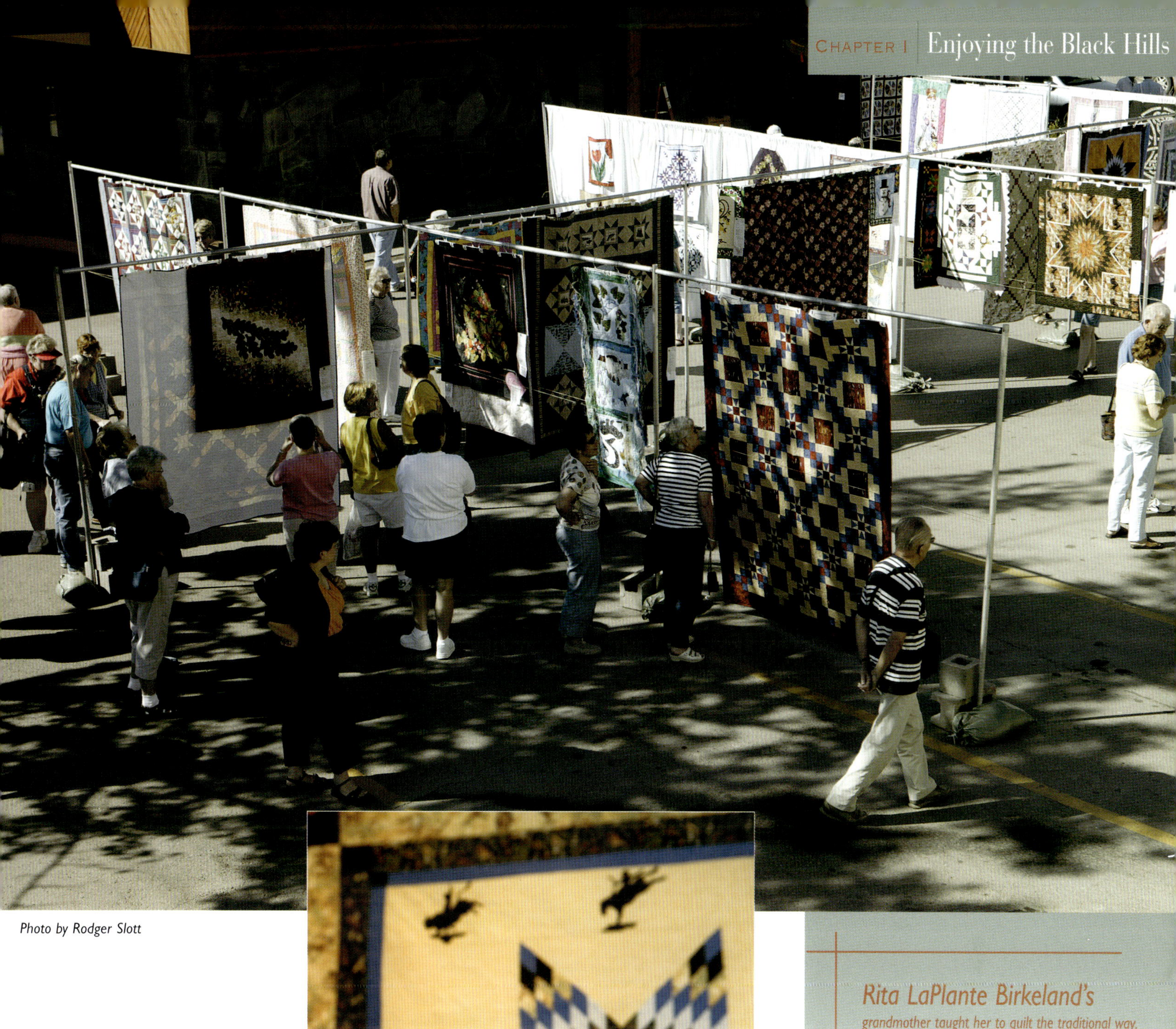

Photo by Rodger Slott

Photo by Rodger Slott

Rita LaPlante Birkeland's

grandmother taught her to quilt the traditional way. "The Indian women of the past cut one diamond at a time for their star quilts," explains Rita, a Native American who has lived in South Dakota all her life. Today Rita, and the other women who comprise the Prairie Strippers Quilt Guild in the little town of Dupree, create beautiful and unique quilts using the more popular and modern "strip" method, cutting several strips of fabric at a time. Being able to produce her artful creations more efficiently was a plus when she was called on to make three quilts at one time for her triplet grandchildren. While Rita always gives her quilts as gifts to friends or family, she was honored when asked to show seven quilts in the Warriors Work Art Gallery at the Native American Quilt Show, one of the events of the Hill City Outdoor Quilt Show. Hill City's colorful cascade of quilts is a must-see, according to the American Business Association. Hundreds of quilts—from those that can be worn as clothing, to quilts that warm the soul on a cold winter's night, and those that warm a home or business's room as artwork—line the streets, each beckoning to tell its own story. ❖

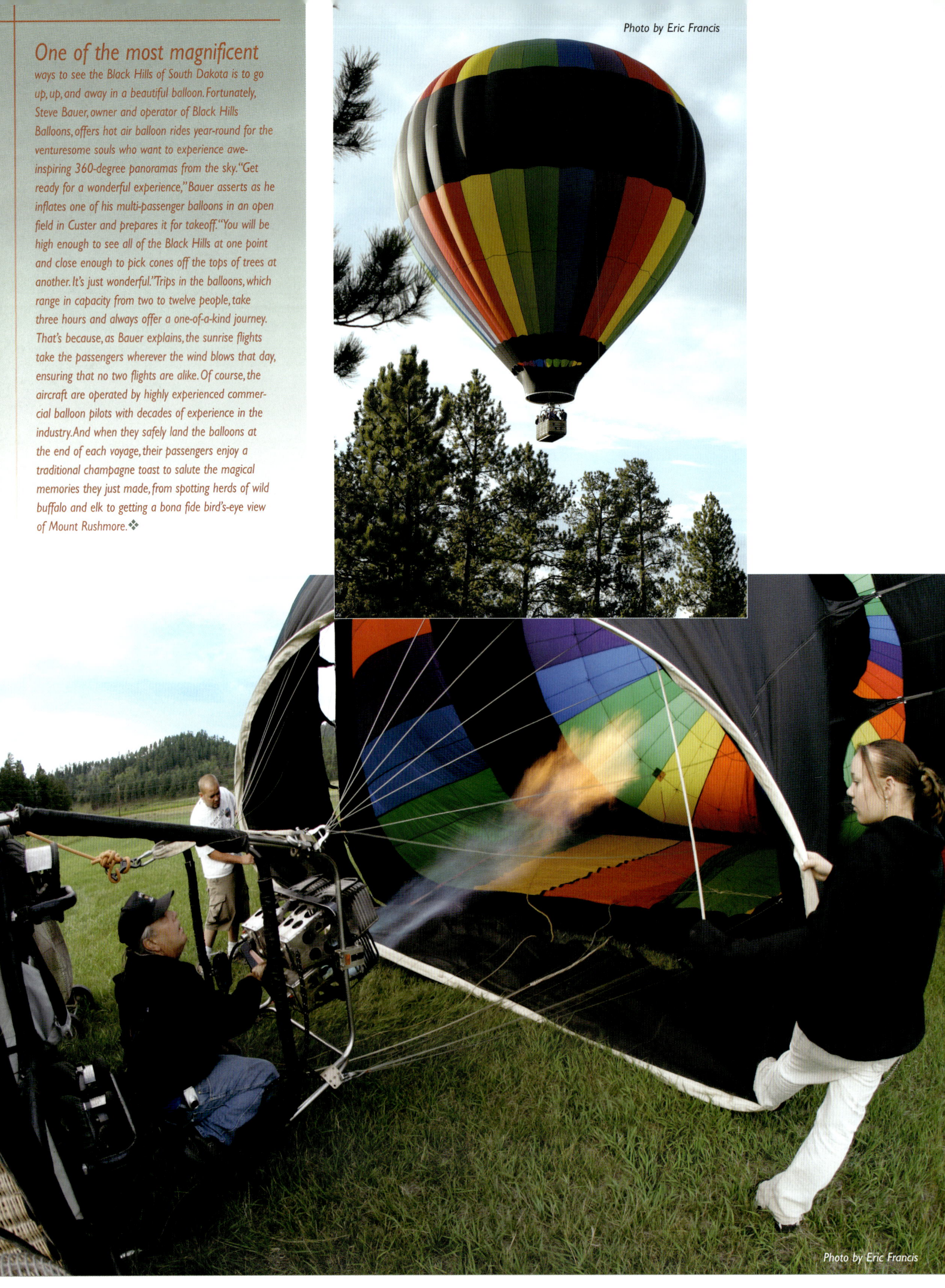

One of the most magnificent ways to see the Black Hills of South Dakota is to go up, up, and away in a beautiful balloon. Fortunately, Steve Bauer, owner and operator of Black Hills Balloons, offers hot air balloon rides year-round for the venturesome souls who want to experience awe-inspiring 360-degree panoramas from the sky. "Get ready for a wonderful experience," Bauer asserts as he inflates one of his multi-passenger balloons in an open field in Custer and prepares it for takeoff. "You will be high enough to see all of the Black Hills at one point and close enough to pick cones off the tops of trees at another. It's just wonderful." Trips in the balloons, which range in capacity from two to twelve people, take three hours and always offer a one-of-a-kind journey. That's because, as Bauer explains, the sunrise flights take the passengers wherever the wind blows that day, ensuring that no two flights are alike. Of course, the aircraft are operated by highly experienced commercial balloon pilots with decades of experience in the industry. And when they safely land the balloons at the end of each voyage, their passengers enjoy a traditional champagne toast to salute the magical memories they just made, from spotting herds of wild buffalo and elk to getting a bona fide bird's-eye view of Mount Rushmore. ❖

Photo by Eric Francis

Photo by Eric Francis

Photo by Eric Francis

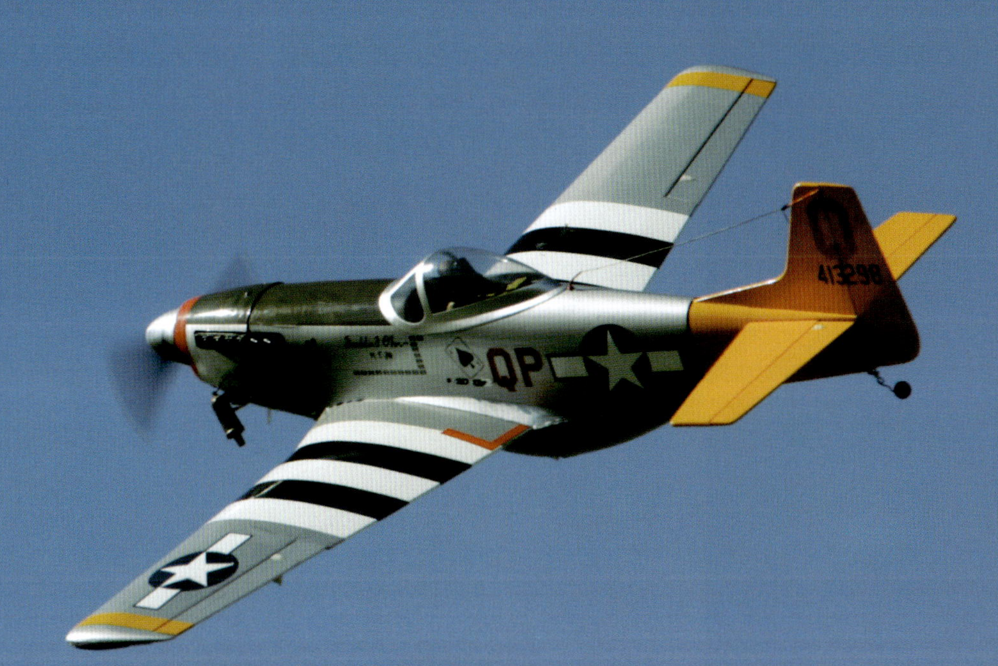

Birds aren't the only things

that soar free above the plains outside Rapid City. Each month, the thirty or so members of Rapid City Propbusters meet to fly their radio-controlled model planes and engage in a bit of friendly flying competition. "Mostly, though, we just get together to have fun and enjoy the camaraderie of people who all love aviation," says member Jim Tiller. An aviation enthusiast and onetime pilot, Tiller says of his hobby, "I can do more flying with the small ones than with the big ones. Our planes can also do anything full-sized airplanes can do." Sometimes even more. The club has members whose planes can hover and perform acrobatics not possible with regular aircraft. Rapid City Propbusters flies twelve months out of the year, even in January, when it ushers in the New Year with its annual Frost Your Buns chili and flying get-together on January 1. The club also has a flight demo team that puts on shows and demonstrations at local festivals and events. ❖

Photo by Eric Francis

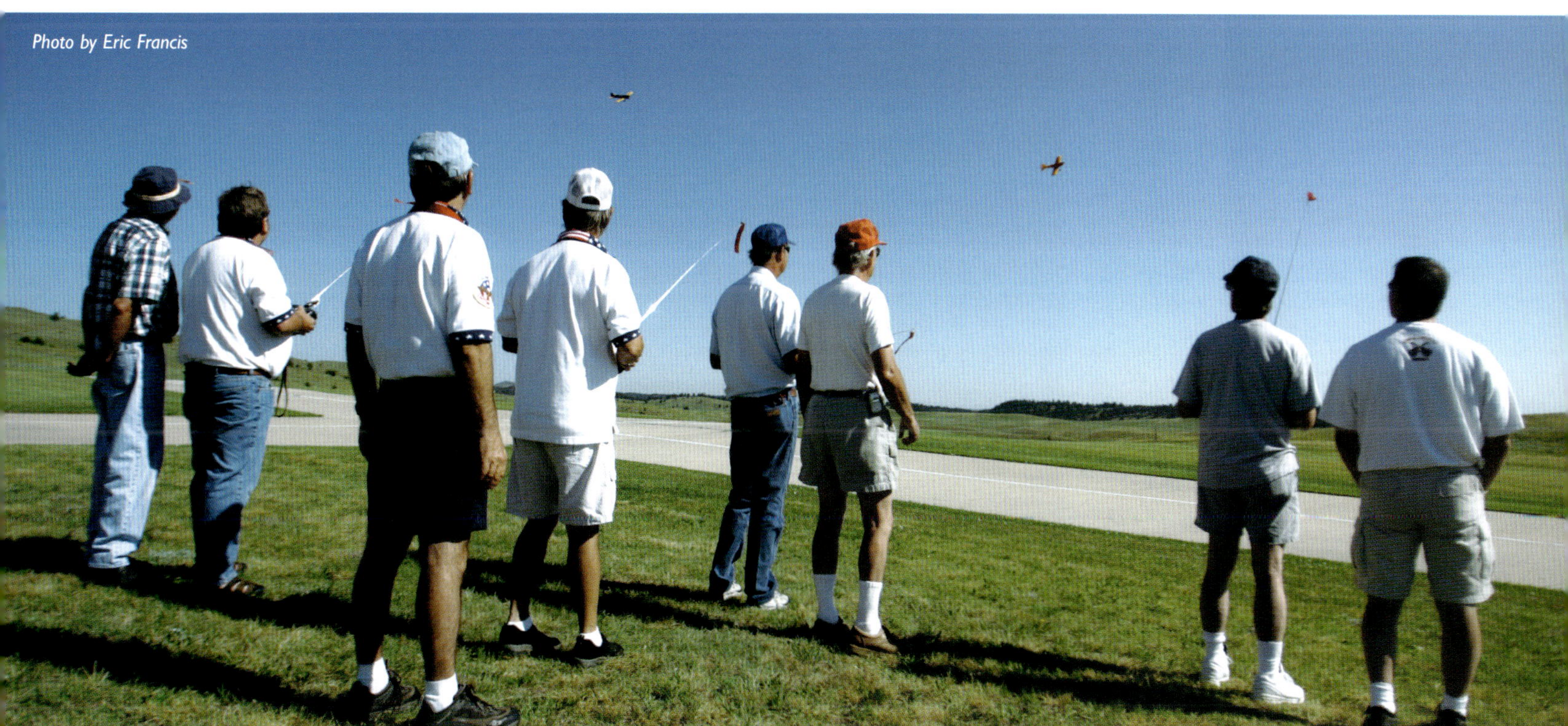

Photo by Eric Francis

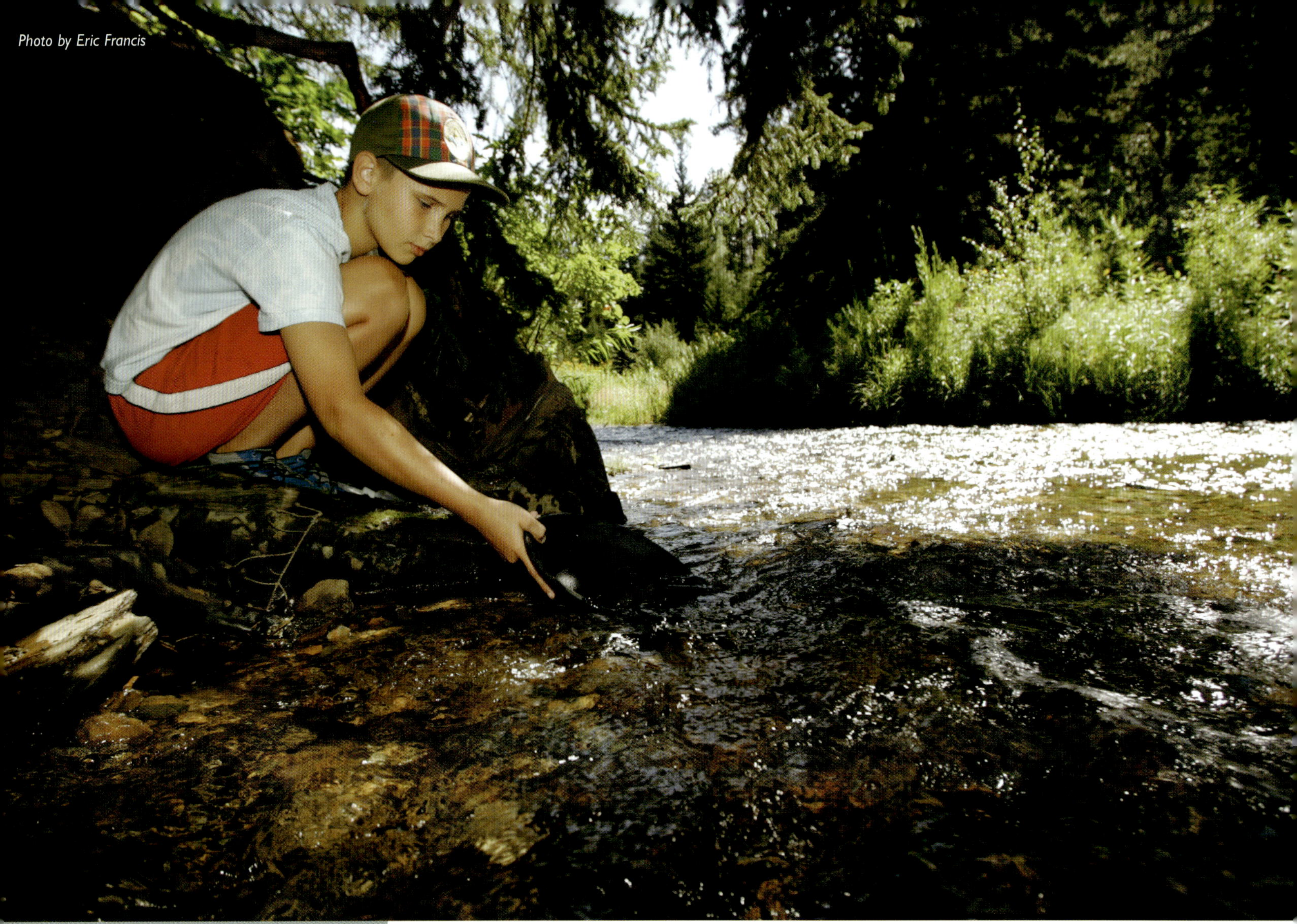

Yes, there's gold in them thar hills! Sure, it's not enough to make you rich, but it is enough to bring together the members of the Black Hills Prospecting Club for a day of fun in the great outdoors. Founded in 2000, club members meet about once a month at a local Black Hills claim to prospect for gold and share a potluck lunch. According to the club's membership coordinator Ken Durbin, it's not unusual to find gold. But the size of the find, well, that's another matter. "I've seen finds of a gram to two grams, but that was after about six hours of twenty-person output," Durbin says, laughing. "Usually where these claims end up is on our dressers and shelves." The main goal is to have fun with friends and family and honor the area's gold prospecting heritage. ❖

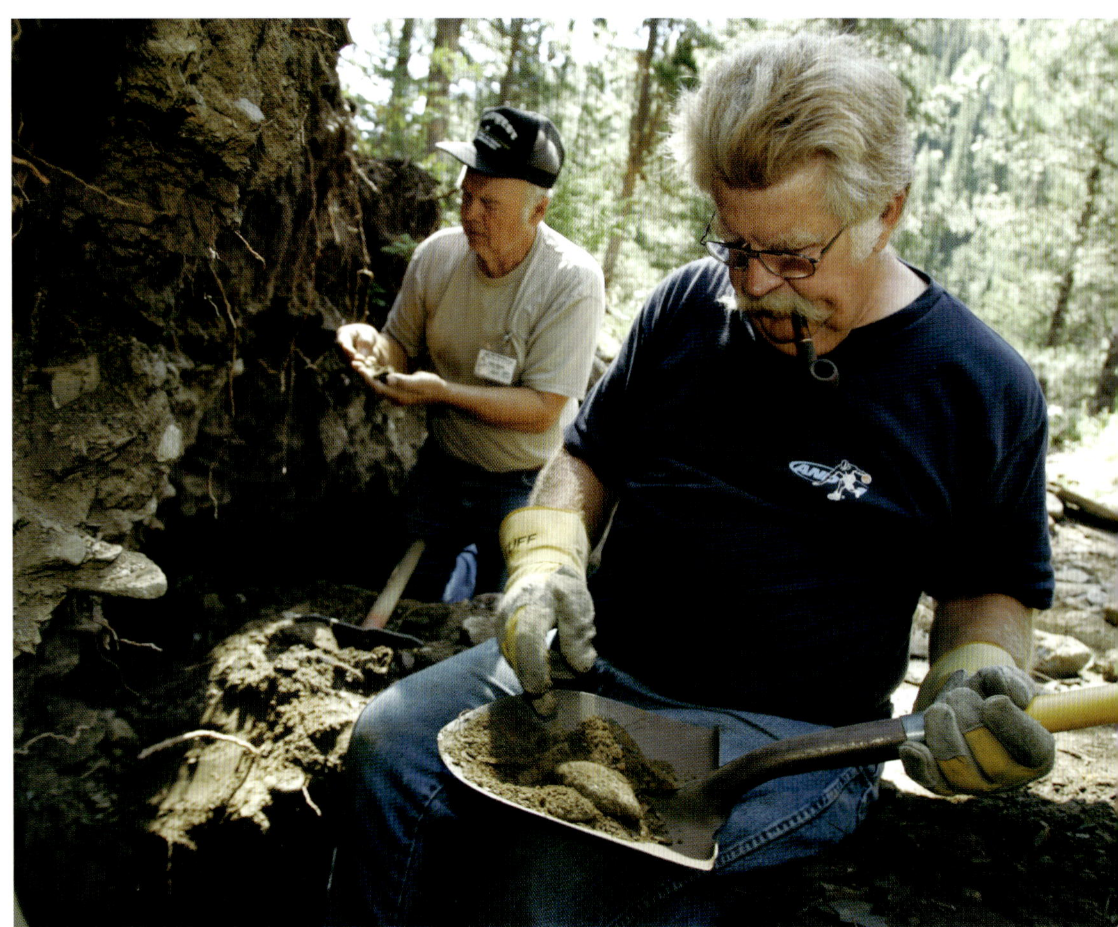

Photo by Eric Francis

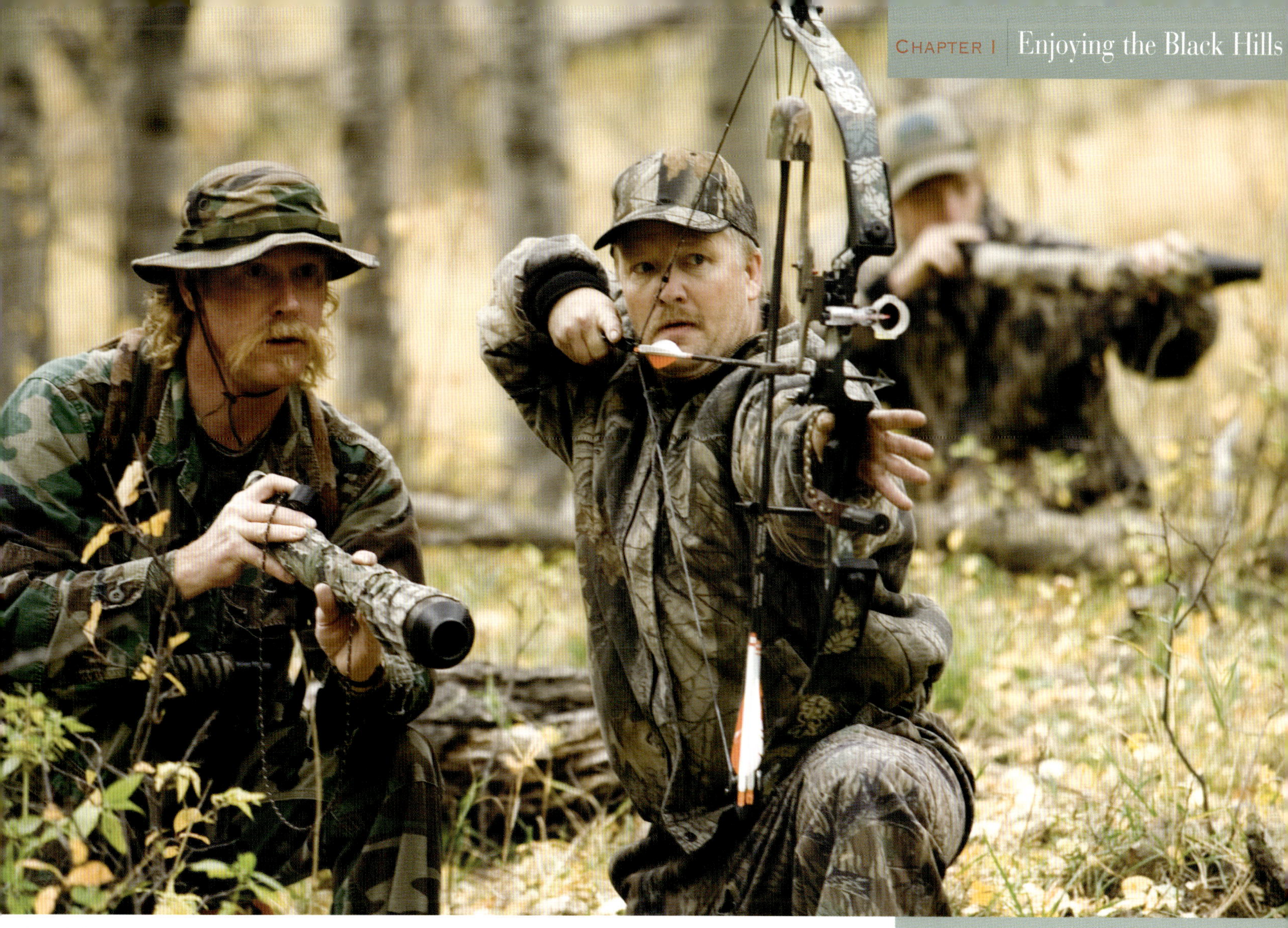

Photo by Dennis Keim

In the early days, elk ranged over from the eastern prairies to the western Black Hills. By 1889, when South Dakota gained statehood, there were no elk to be found. However, that has changed. In the early 1900s efforts began to reestablish elk in the state. Today's herd consists of more than two thousand Rocky Mountain elk. The herds are carefully managed by the Division of Wildlife, and only South Dakota residents are eligible to received an elk hunting license. Recent changes have increased the elk license numbers, some elk season dates, and modified a few elk unit boundaries. On crisp days, both private hunting parties and commercial guided groups take to the field. It is not unusual for guides Mitchell and his son Zachariah McLain to take a hunter like Ronnie Johnston to an area where they see one hundred to two hundred head within a two-day trip. In an interesting combination of historic weaponry and modern technology, hunters can apply for bow-hunting licenses through the Internet at the South Dakota Game, Fish and Parks Web site. But even with a license, don't forget that hunters need to get permission to hunt on private land in South Dakota.❖

Rushmore Plaza Civic Center—An Entertainment Hub

Few businesses try to be all things to all people, but for the Rushmore Plaza Civic Center, that's exactly the mission. The versatile facility is the region's premier entertainment center, drawing more than a million people annually from a three-hundred-mile radius around Rapid City. "We consider ourselves the place where memories are made," says Brian Maliske, general manager. "We draw from North Dakota, Montana, Wyoming, and Nebraska, as well as South Dakota, and therefore it's important that we provide an event to remember."

"We consider ourselves the place where memories are made," says Brian Maliske, general manager.

Situated in the heart of downtown, the Rushmore Plaza Civic Center offers much under its one large roof, and outside its walls there's easy access to retail, area attractions, and the natural beauty of the Black Hills. The hub of the Civic Center is the Arena, which features seating for 10,000 fans of basketball, concerts, rodeos, ice shows, and just about any other entertainment event that draws a crowd. For the fine arts crowd, the Civic Center's Theatre seats up to 1,779 people in ultimate comfort amidst a beautiful, acoustically tuned atmosphere. The third component, the Convention Center, provides 150,000 square feet of convention space, with spacious halls that can be subdivided to accommodate any size meeting or exhibition. "I'm not aware of any other facilities within this region that offer all we do under one roof," adds Maliske. ❖

Photo by Dennis Keim

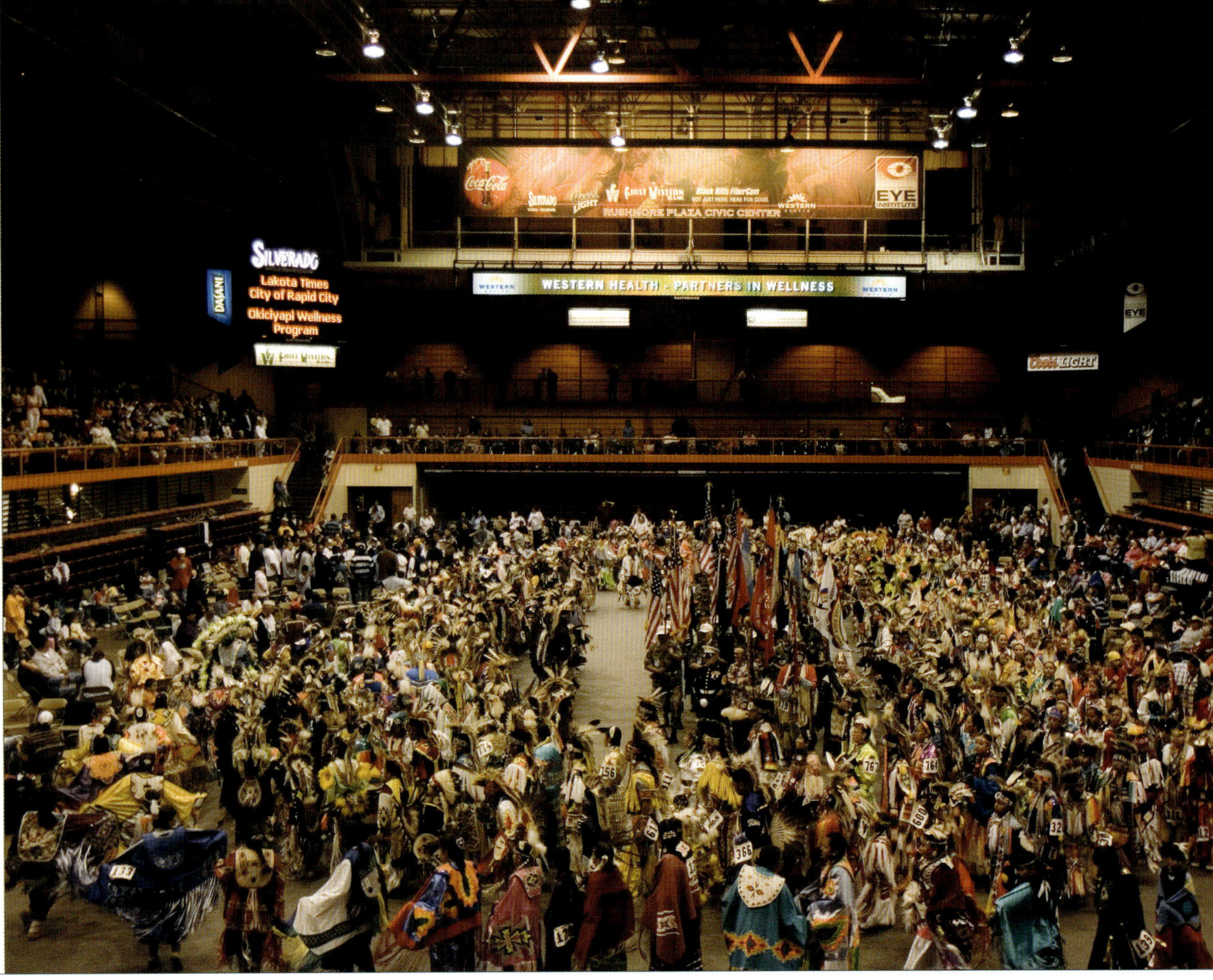

Every year the He Sapa Wacipi, or Black Hills Pow Wow, draws crowds to see dancers and singers representing American Indian tribes across the country compete for top prizes. The main goal for the annual event always remains the same: to provide a forum for the gathering of extended families. The Black Hills Pow Wow is just one of many events held at the Civic Center, which has earned a reputation for creating many memories for all.

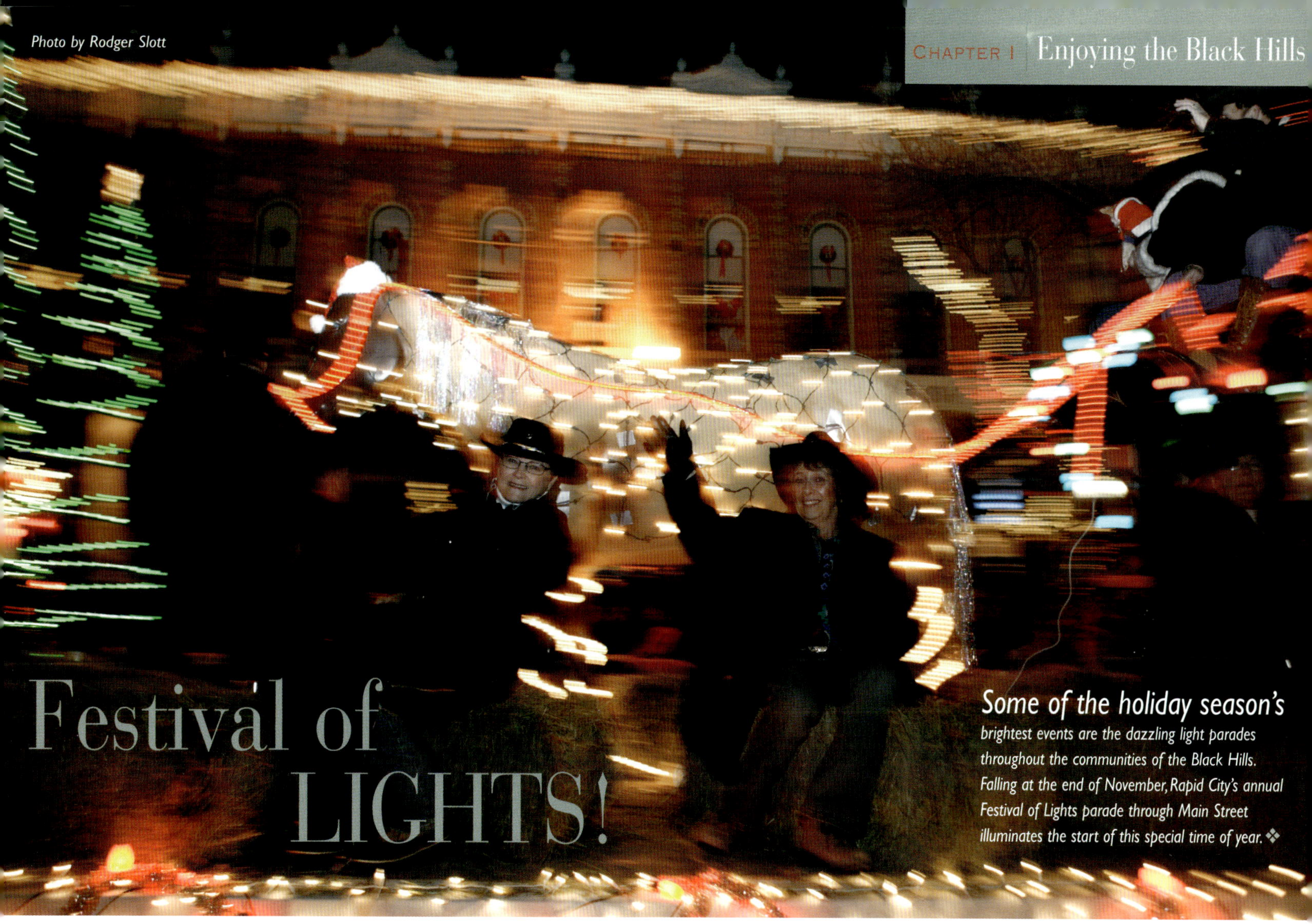

Photo by Rodger Slott

Festival of LIGHTS!

Some of the holiday season's brightest events are the dazzling light parades throughout the communities of the Black Hills. Falling at the end of November, Rapid City's annual Festival of Lights parade through Main Street illuminates the start of this special time of year. ❖

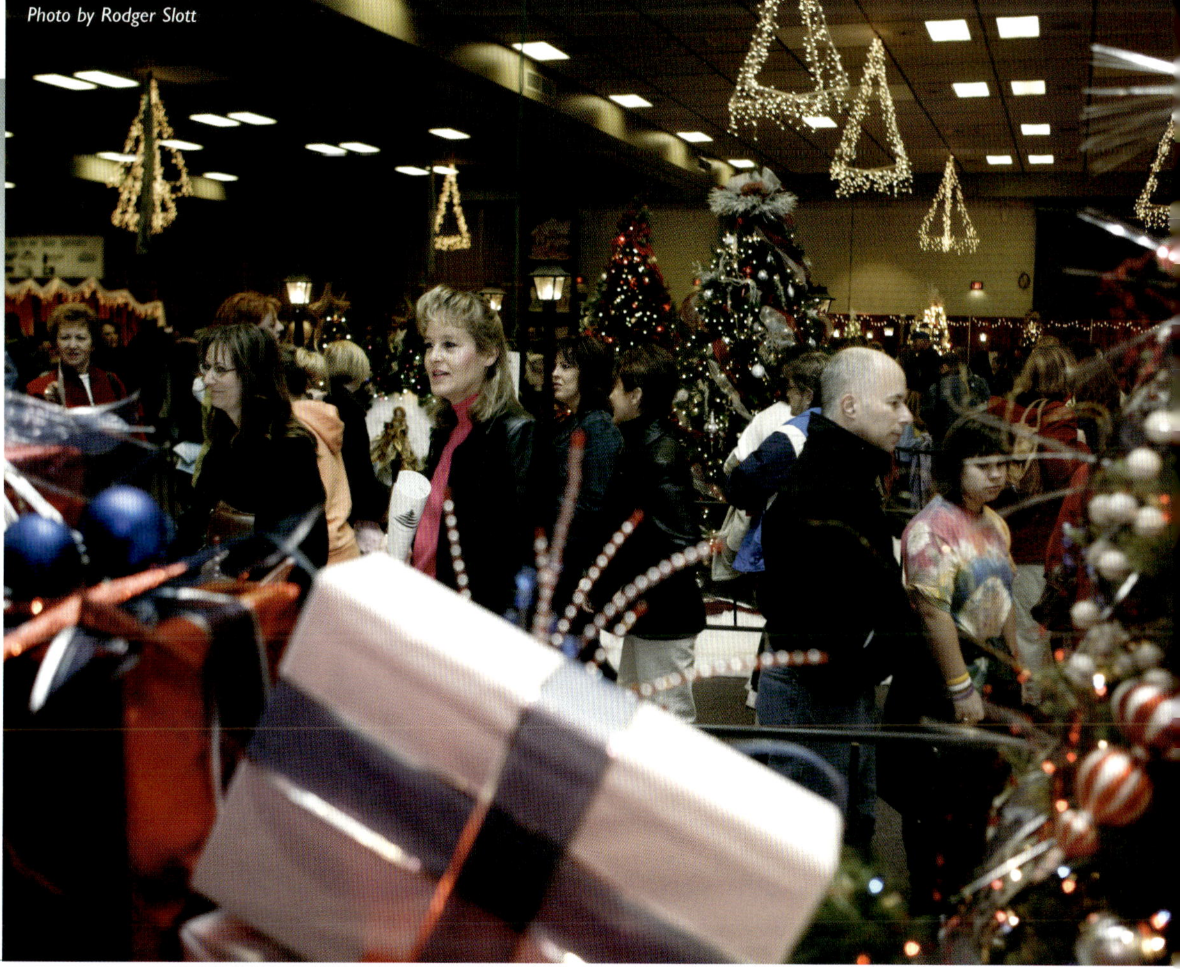

Photo by Rodger Slott

The Festival of Trees is Behavior Management Systems' only fund-raiser. Held the weekend before Thanksgiving, it is the premier kickoff event for the holiday season. ❖

Photo by Thomas S. England

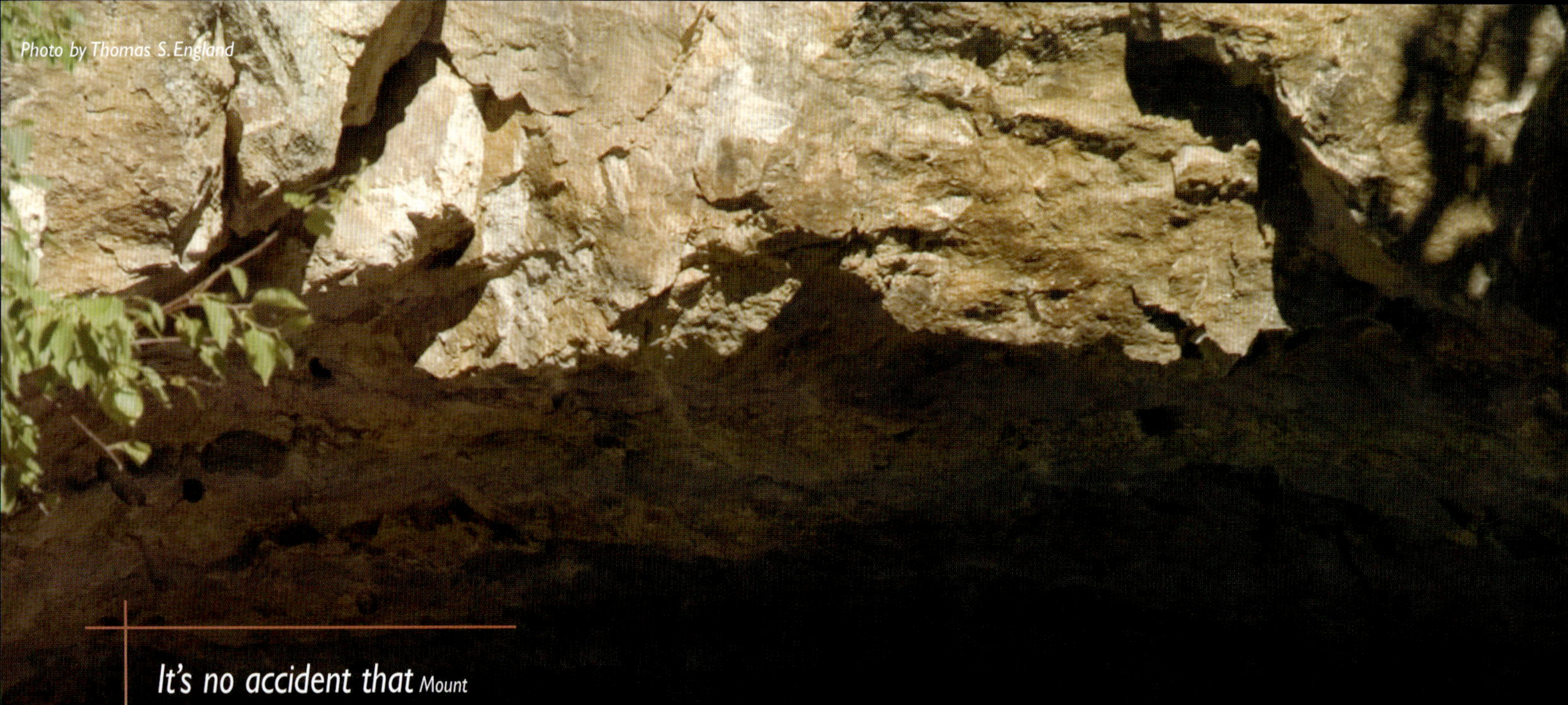

It's no accident that Mount Rushmore is so perfectly framed through the tunnels along Iron Mountain Road. The road's creator, conservationist and South Dakota Senator Peter Norbeck, was also instrumental in passing the legislation authorizing the monumental carving. Iron Mountain Road was therefore designed not only to link Custer State Park to Mount Rushmore, but also to showcase the sculpture's magnificence, no matter the direction—hence, the road's serpentine twists, hairpin curves, and pigtail bridges, which also have the added advantage of encouraging motorists to slow down and enjoy the views. ❖

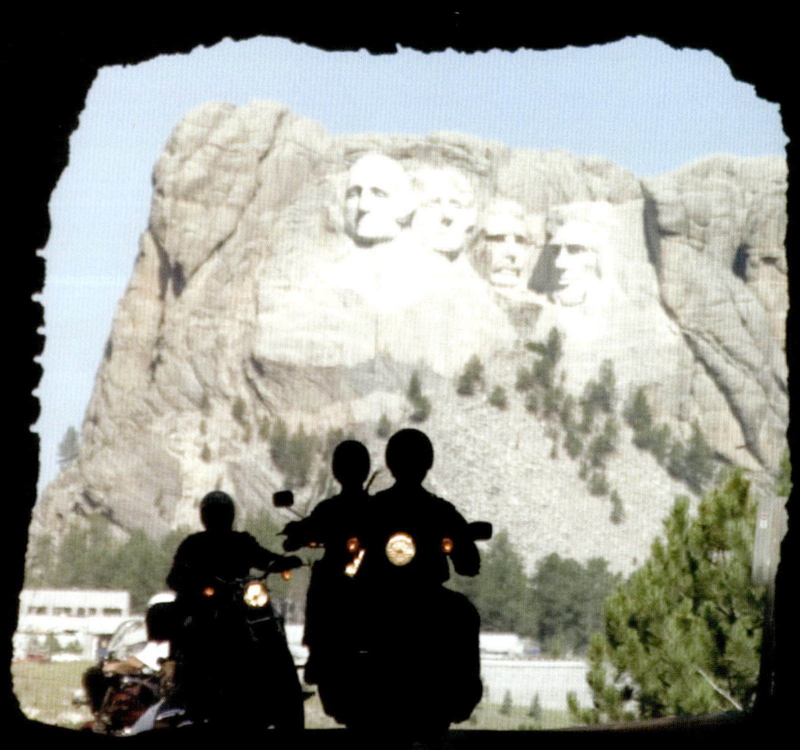

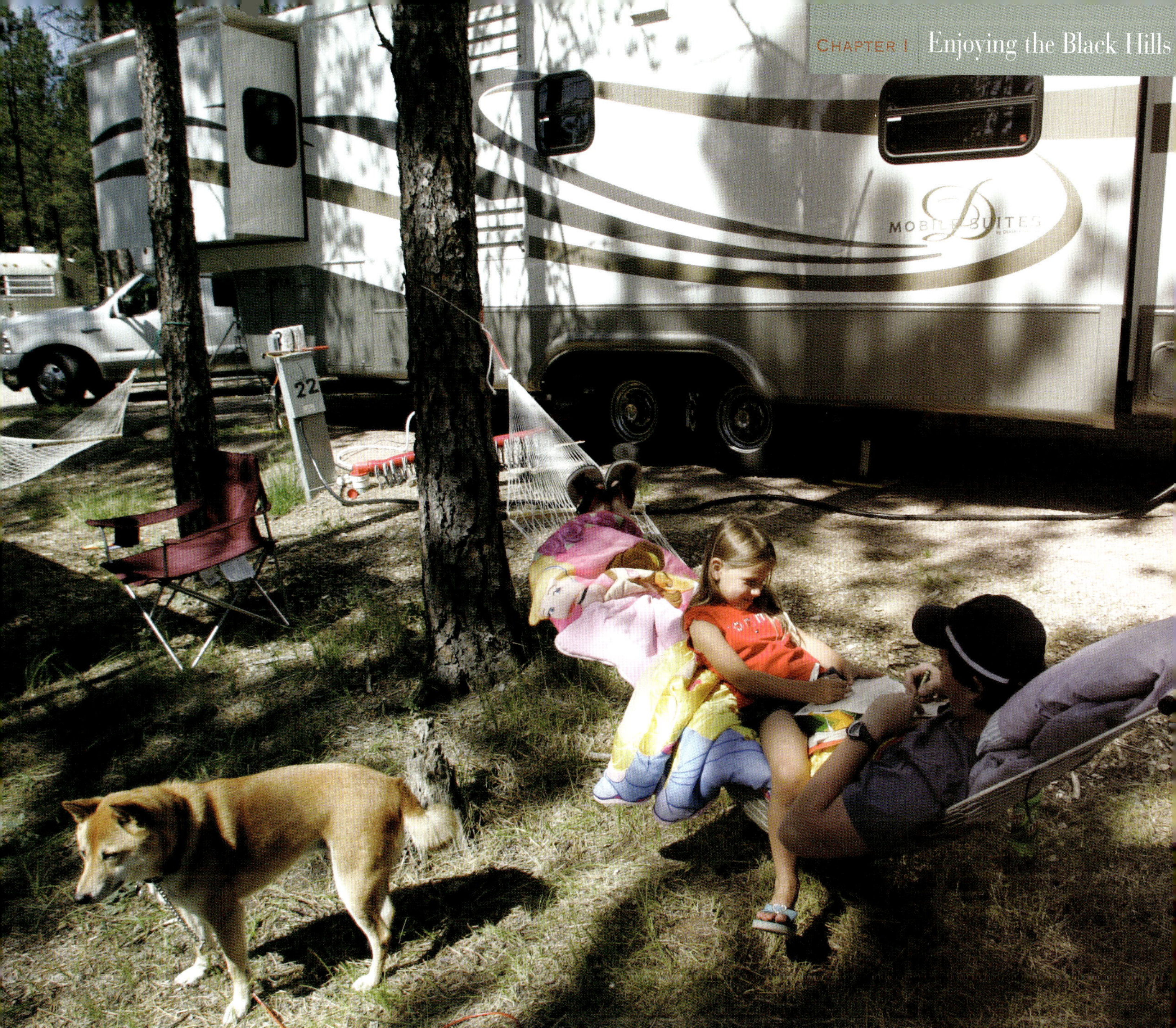

Photo by Alan S.Weiner

The Black Hills region was named by the Lakota people because the thick forest of pine and spruce looked black from a distance. Depending on the direction you travel from Rapid City, you might see wild horses or bison roaming the land or you might be lucky enough to see work in progress on the Crazy Horse Memorial, which will stand 563 feet high and 641 feet long when it is finished. You could visit the 'Shrine of Democracy,' Mount Rushmore, or go to Badlands National Park, with its sharp ridges and steep canyons carved by wind and water. Then again, you might choose one of the four other national parks in the area. You could go caving, or rock climbing, or hiking, or fishing, or ...you could follow the example of Dawn Mattern and her niece, Taryn Abede, and just while away some time in a comfortable hammock in the shade of pine trees at a convenient camp site like this one at Fort Welikit. ❖

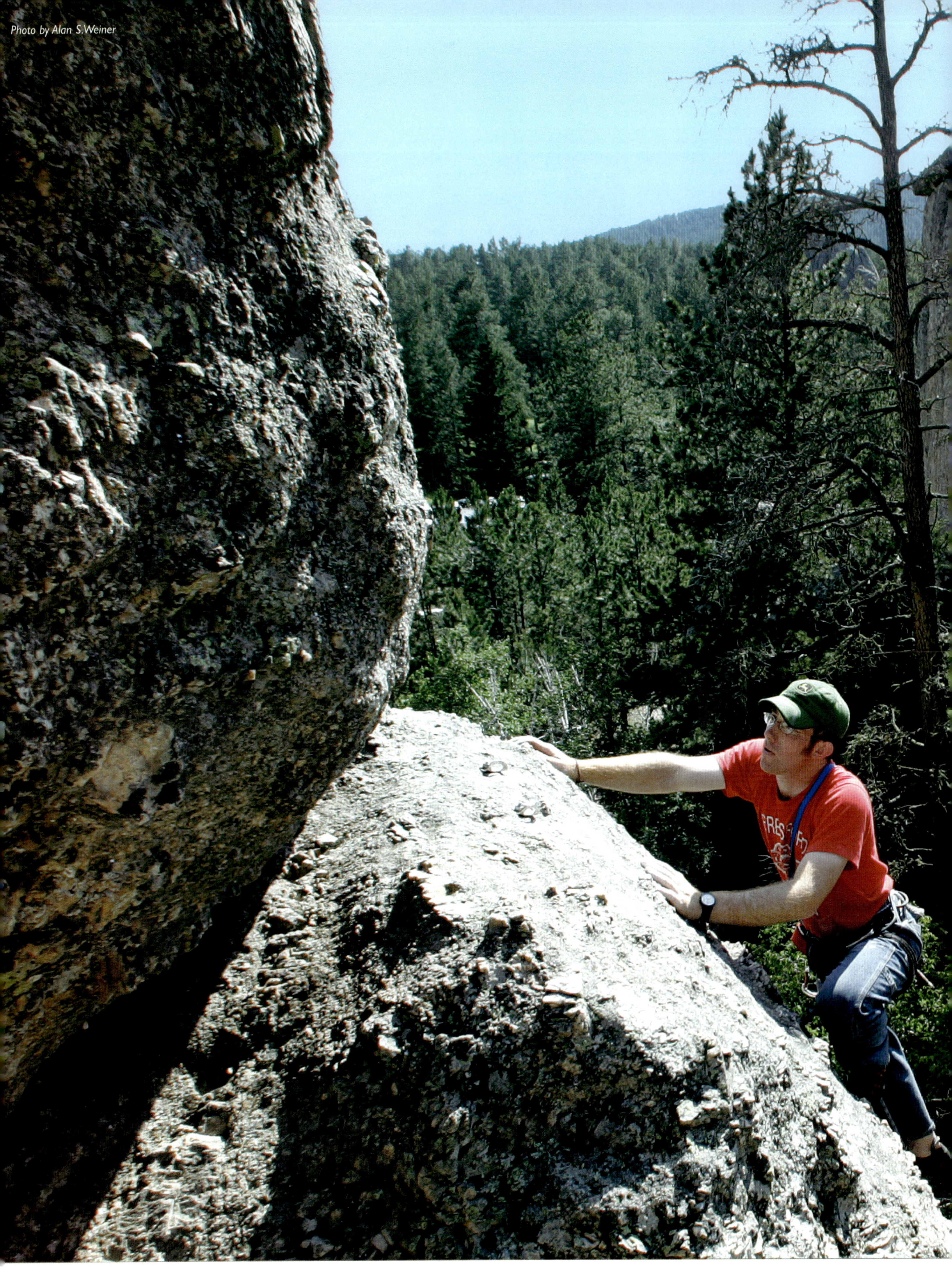
Photo by Alan S. Weiner

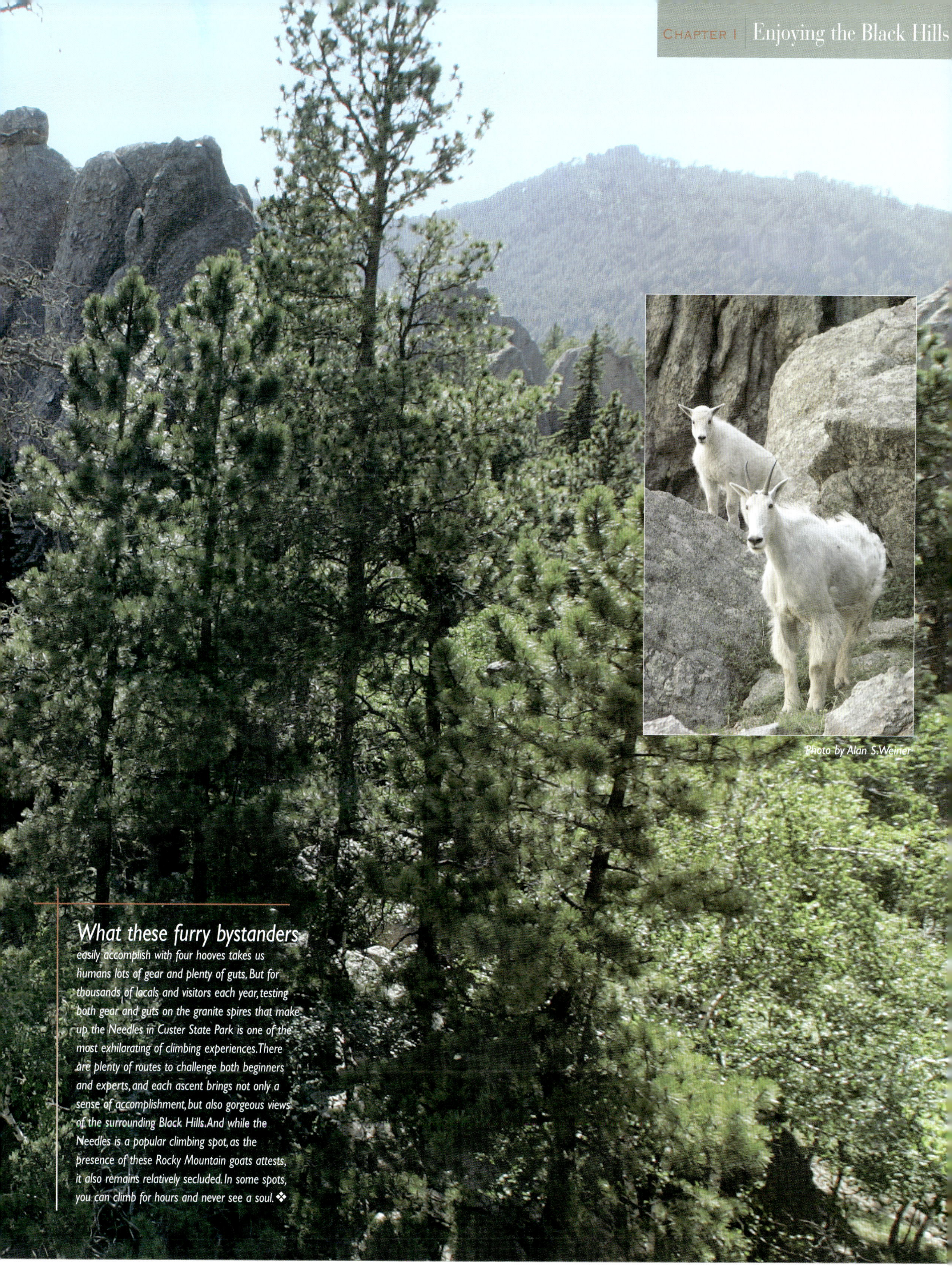

Photo by Alan S. Weiner

What these furry bystanders easily accomplish with four hooves takes us humans lots of gear and plenty of guts. But for thousands of locals and visitors each year, testing both gear and guts on the granite spires that make up the Needles in Custer State Park is one of the most exhilarating of climbing experiences. There are plenty of routes to challenge both beginners and experts, and each ascent brings not only a sense of accomplishment, but also gorgeous views of the surrounding Black Hills. And while the Needles is a popular climbing spot, as the presence of these Rocky Mountain goats attests, it also remains relatively secluded. In some spots, you can climb for hours and never see a soul. ❖

A Splashin' Good Time!

When the weekend rolls around, there's nothing like a nice evening out, complete with dinner and a movie. But in Rapid City, moviegoers typically have to wait at least an hour after eating before settling in for a good a flick. At least, the ones seen here do. That's because they are participating in one of the area's most unique recreational opportunities: the Saturday Night "Dive-In." Presented by the Aquatics division of the Rapid City Parks and Recreation Department and held at the Rapid City Swim Center monthly throughout the year, this one-of-a-kind experience certainly puts a new spin on an old favorite. Decked out in their finest swimwear and toting their own rafts, attendees young and old head down to Waterloo Street—whether it's summery or snowy outside—so they can be treated to a wide array of family-friendly movies like Madagascar and Robots. When the movie projector is fired up at 8:30 PM, after forty-five minutes of unstructured water play for little ones, the only sounds that fill the room are the gentle lapping of water on the sides of the pool and the hearty laughter of families sharing a truly special night. ❖

Photo by Johnny Sundby

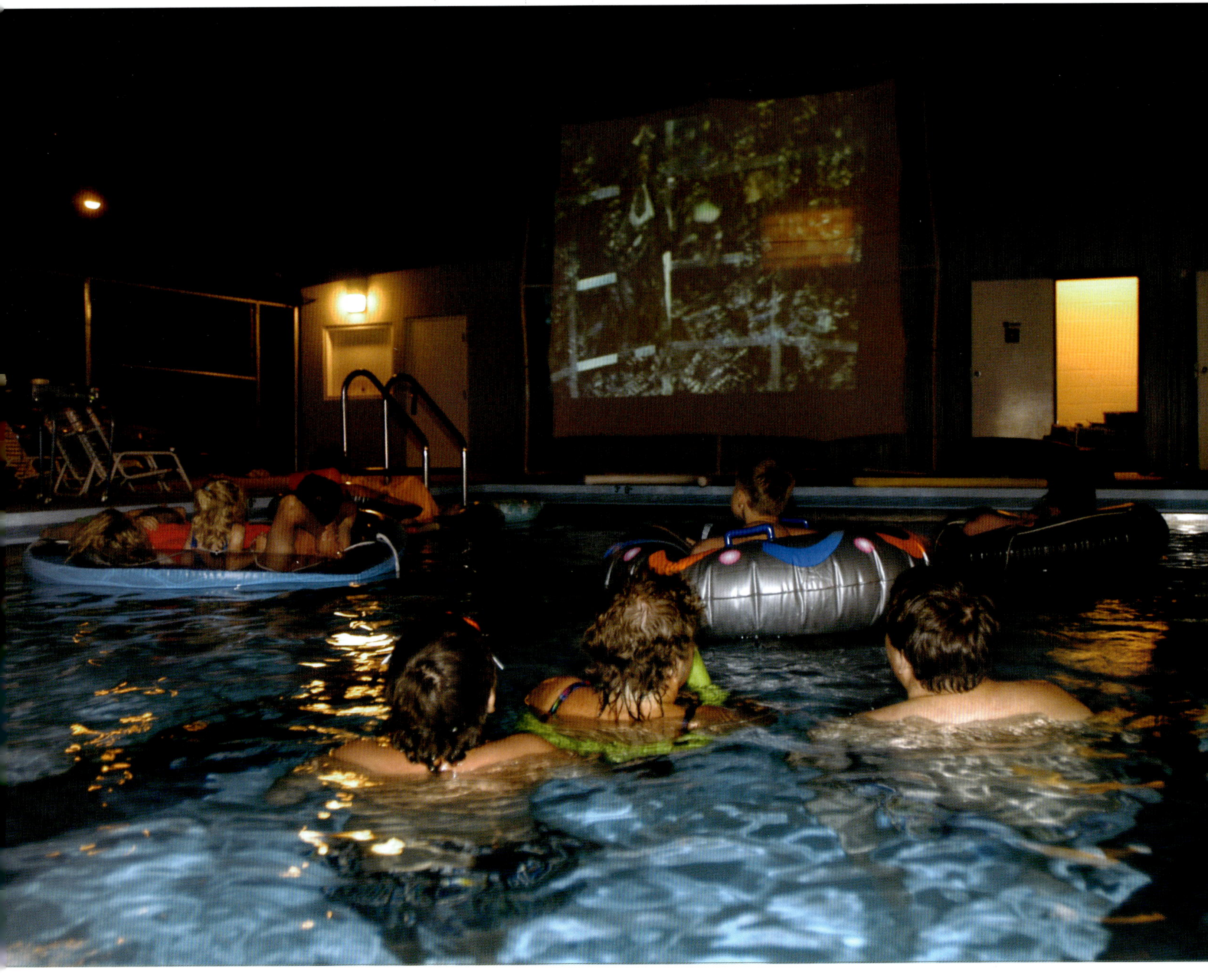

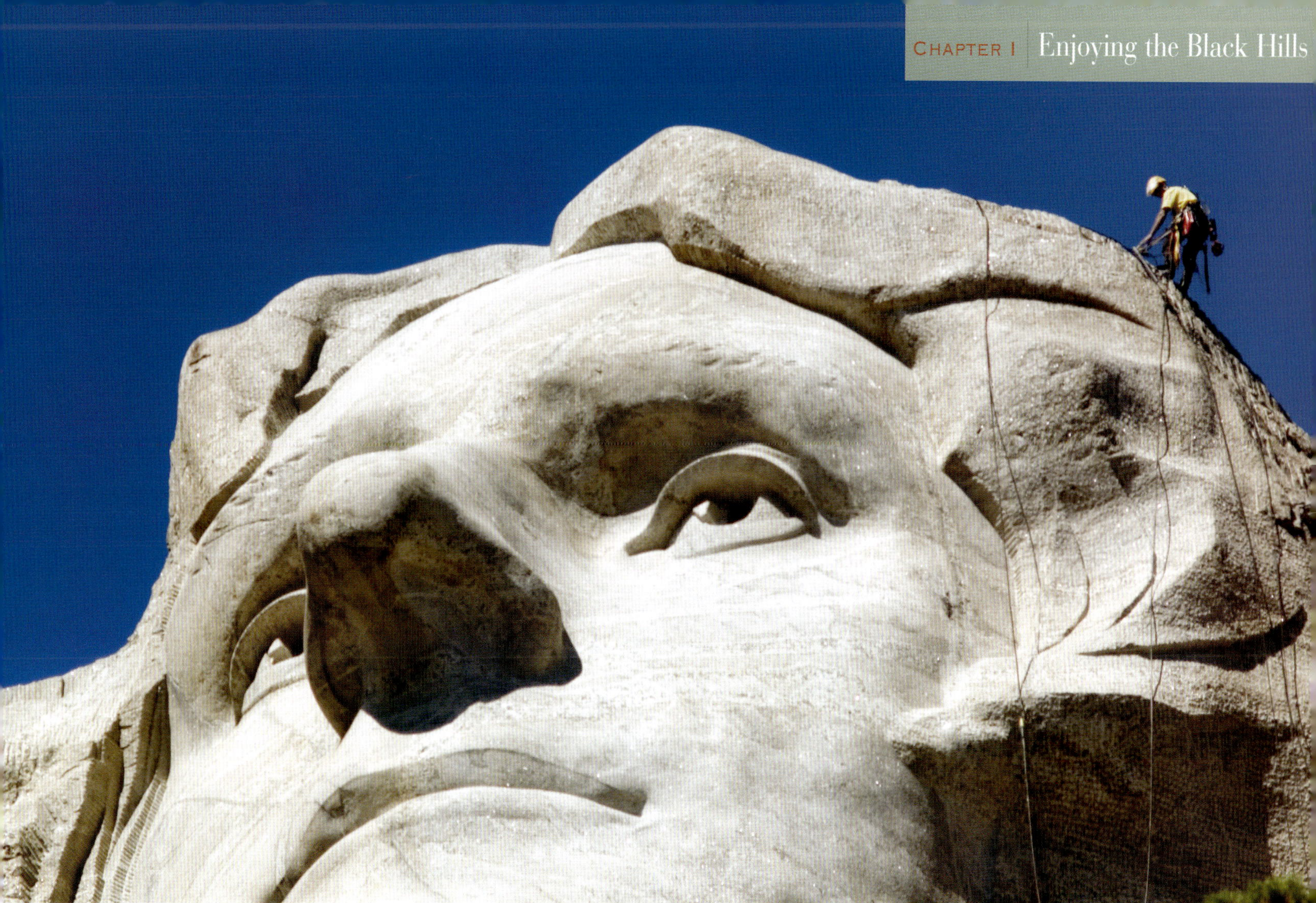

Photo by Thomas S. England

Talk about pressure. *Pressure washing, that is. In July 2005, the National Park Service teamed up with Kärcher USA, the world's largest manufacturer of pressure washers, to give Mount Rushmore a much-needed facelift. As part of a culture-sponsoring project, Kärcher, a wholly owned subsidiary of Germany-based Alfred Kärcher GmbH & Co. KG, donated the use of five diesel-powered Kärcher hot water pressure washers to remove decades worth of dirt, algae, moss, and lichens from the faces of George Washington, Thomas Jefferson, Theodore Roosevelt, and Abraham Lincoln. It was the first time in the monument's sixty-five-year history that this type of meticulous cleaning has taken place. While crews regularly scale the mountain to fill in the granite's cracks with silicone sealant, the lichens, or slow-growing plants, that grow in the crevices still pose a threat by causing bio-corrosion, which produces an acid that can damage the monument over time. During the five-week project, six National Park Service rangers and one volunteer from the Crazy Horse Memorial worked with Kärcher's technicians to spray the faces from top to bottom with streams of pressurized two-hundred-degree water and restore them to mint condition. And this is not the first major venture Kärcher has undertaken. Since the mid-1980s, the company has performed more than eighty similar cleaning projects, tackling the base of the Statue of Liberty in New York, the Colonnades of St. Peter's Square in Rome, the Brandenburg Gate in Berlin, and the Colossi of Memnon in Egypt.* ❖

Photo by Alan S.Weiner

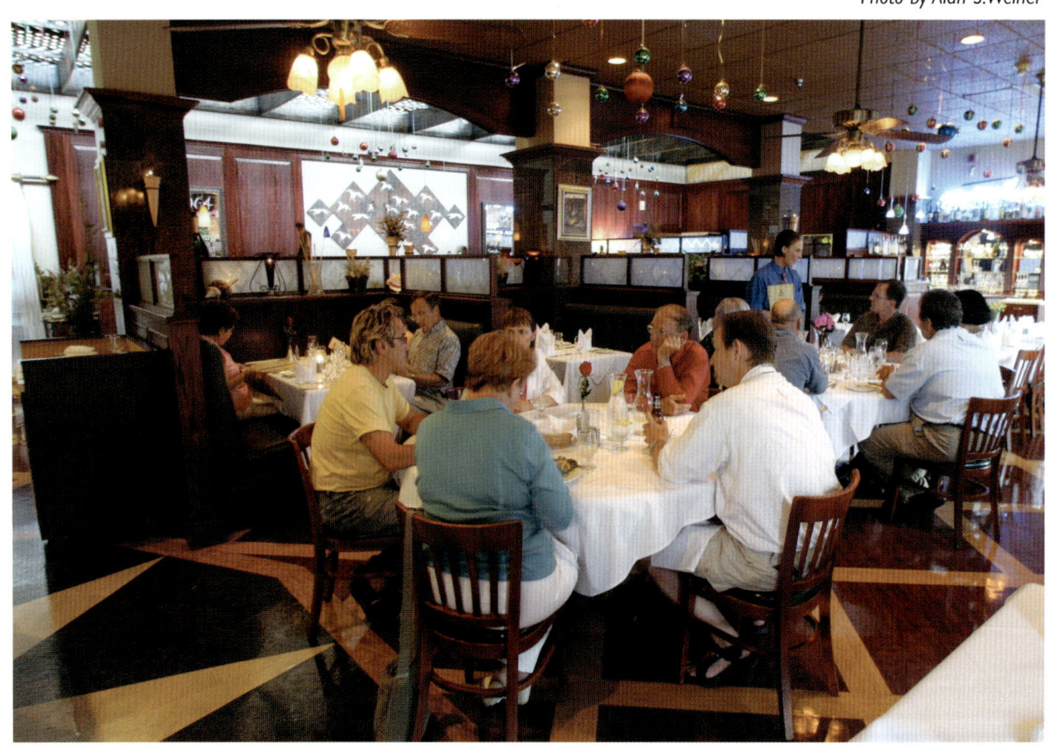

Dinner at the Enigma Restaurant is not just a meal; it's a culinary event. Located inside the Radisson Hotel Rapid City, this elegant eatery is distinguished by top-tier service and its two head chefs' inspired creations—traditional European fare coupled with fresh regional ingredients. The menu features a wide selection of French, Italian, and Greek dishes; luscious homemade desserts; and an internationally flavored wine list. Or let the chefs create something special as part of their popular five-course Mystery Dinners, available nightly by advanced reservation. ❖

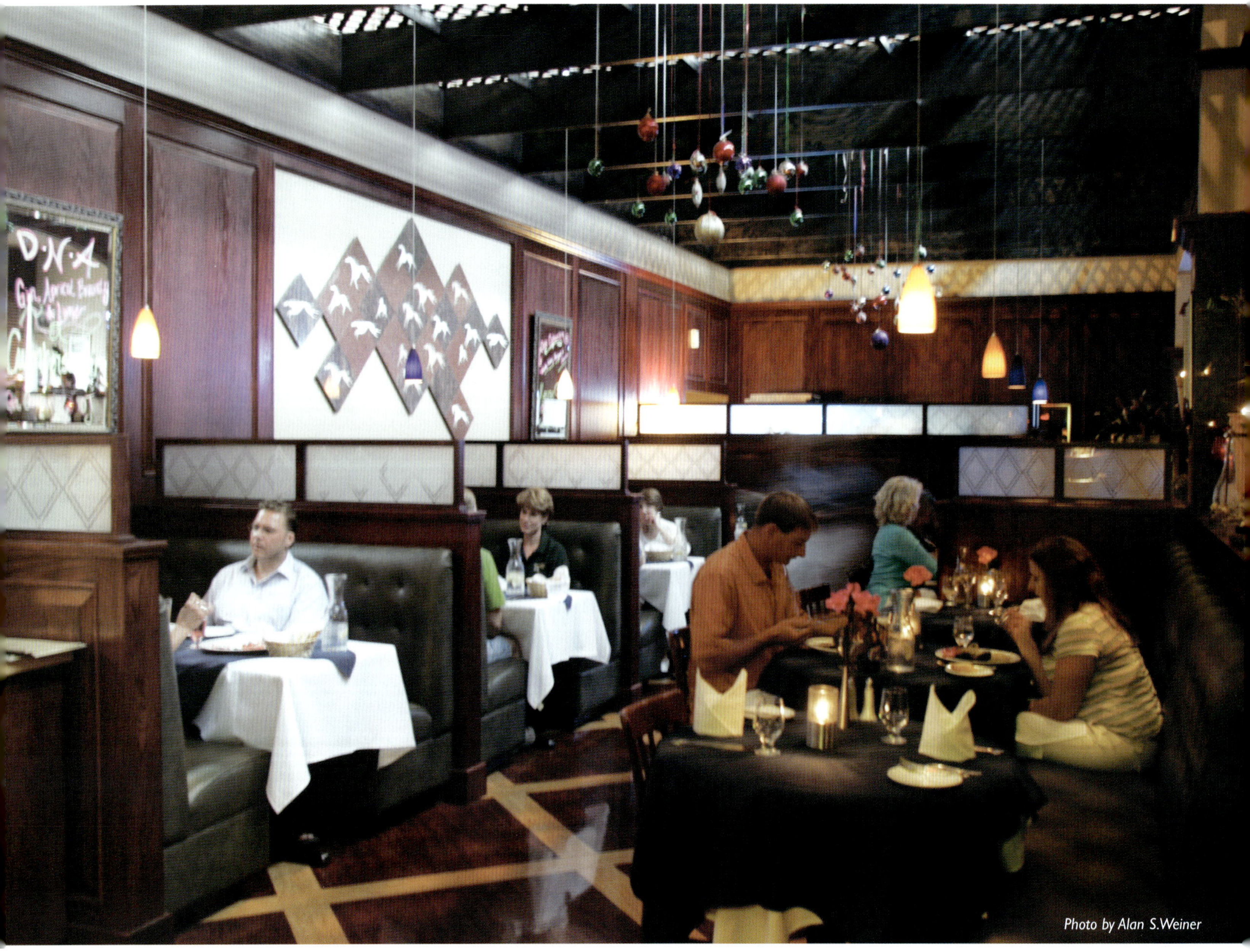

Photo by Alan S.Weiner

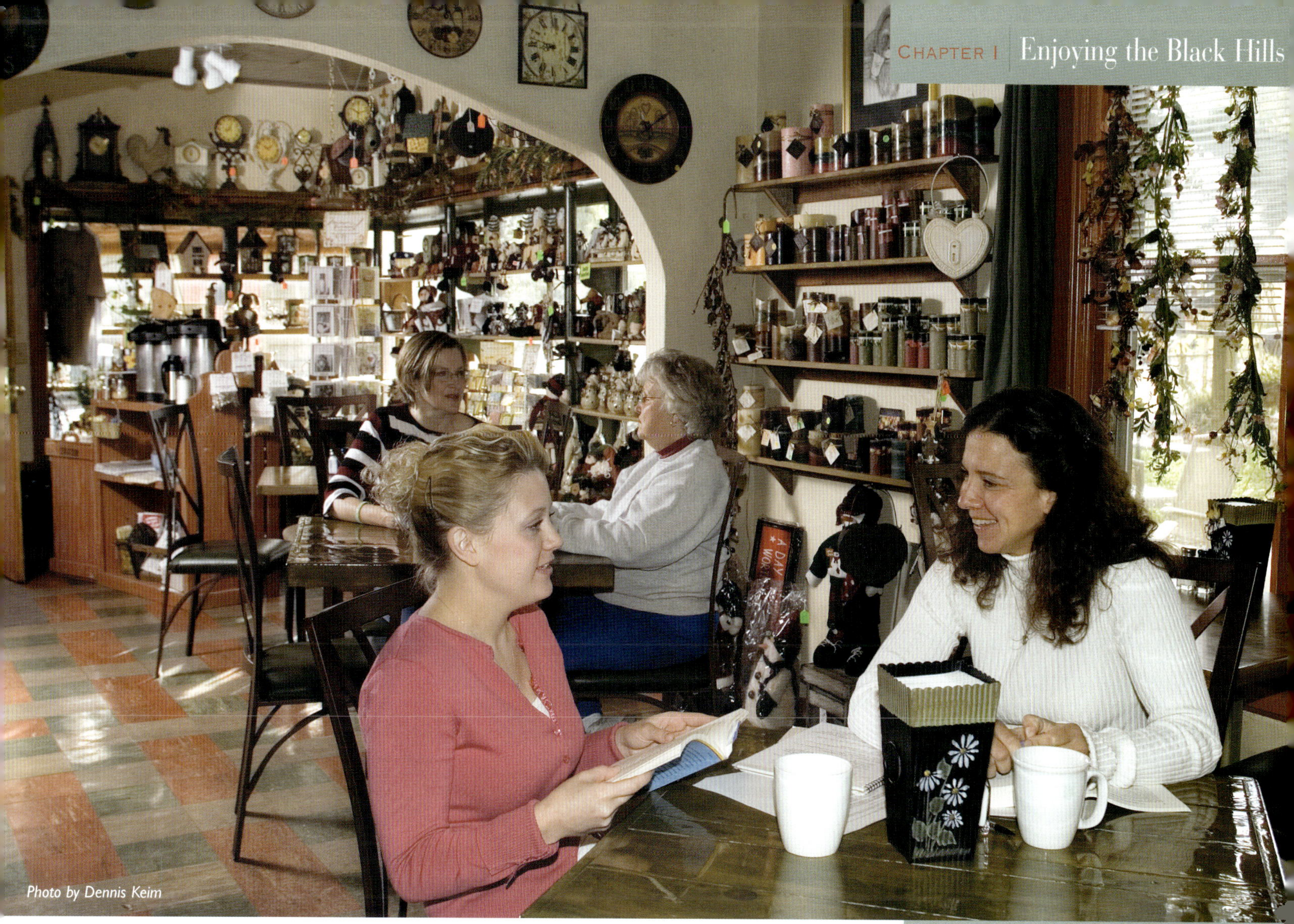

Photo by Dennis Keim

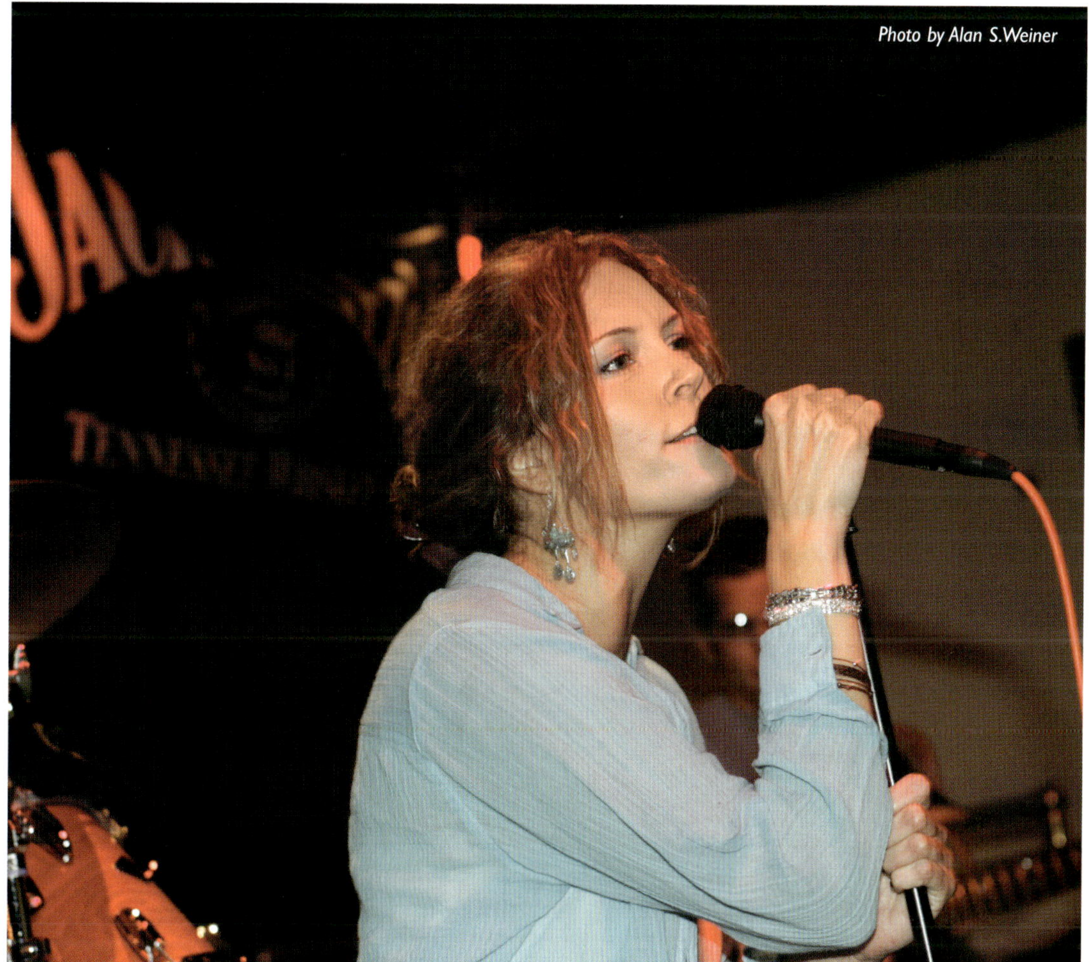

Photo by Alan S.Weiner

▲ **Many Spearfish** entrepreneurs have converted older residences into shops, creating a relaxed cosmopolitan feel. Two Pines Lodge Espresso & Gift Shop on Main Street features quality coffees and foods in an eclectic atmosphere. ❖

◀ **A friendly town** whose people like to work hard and play hard, Rapid City is filled with many lively pubs and dining spots. One of them is Dublin Square, a favorite with locals as well as travelers. Located inside the Radisson Hotel Rapid City at the site of the former Filly's Pub, Dublin Square is modeled after the Irish pubs that so impressed owner Ray Graff during his trips to Ireland. The pub is distinguished by its amiable, relaxed atmosphere; traditional food like fish and chips, Irish meatloaf, and shepherd's pie; a piano bar; and live music on the weekends. And, of course, plenty of Guinness beer, poured the old-fashioned way: slowly and with love. The only thing missing? Irritating cigarette and cigar smoke. Dublin Square is the first and only nonsmoking bar in all of Rapid City. ❖

Rapid City Offers Residents Unmatched Quality of Life

"I could have located my company's high-tech equipment anywhere in the world. I came to Rapid City because of the perseverance and enthusiasm of the mayor, the governor and his office, South Dakota Tech, and private citizens who sold me on the advantages of this area."

That statement, from the founder of Zyvex—a company specializing in cutting-edge manipulation and testing tools for nanoscale research, development, and production—is exactly what the leaders of Rapid City like to hear.

"For 125 years we relied on natural resources," said mayor of Rapid City Jim Shaw. "Gold mining, timber, and farming and ranching were the mainstays, along with more recent additions of the military and tourism. These industries are still important, but now we're making a concerted effort to take control of our destiny by focusing on building a high-tech corridor throughout the Hills."

> "We're making a concerted effort to take control of our destiny by focusing on building a high-tech corridor throughout the Hills."

The quality of life certainly recommends it. The protection of the Black Hills means Rapid City is sheltered from much of the severe weather. "During winter, we get several periods of what we call 'mini springtime,' when the temperature warms up and folks enjoy being outside," Shaw said. And there is a lot to enjoy: golf, biking, rock-hounding, hiking, camping, fishing, horseback riding, wildlife photography, mountain climbing, and a variety of snow and water sports.

Photo by Joleen Zoller

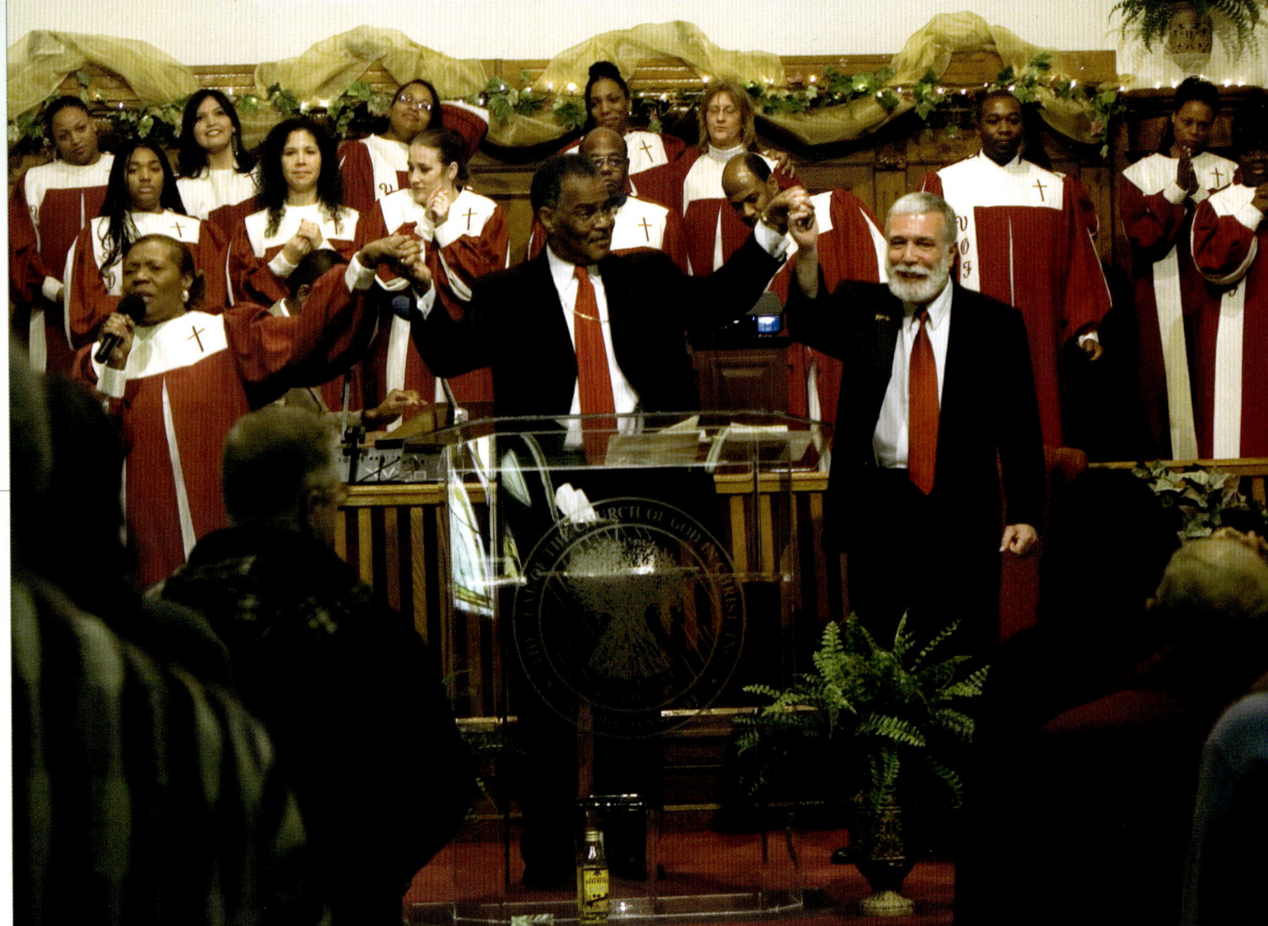

Mayor Jim Shaw joins Mrs. Lorenzo Kelly, Bishop Lorenzo Kelly, and the Voices of Faith choir at the Faith Temple Church of God in Christ for the celebration of Martin Luther King Jr. Day. As the featured speaker at the special noontime service, Mayor Shaw described his Undoing Racism initiative for Rapid City. In the spirit of the day, various other events throughout the area brought people of different cultures and backgrounds together.

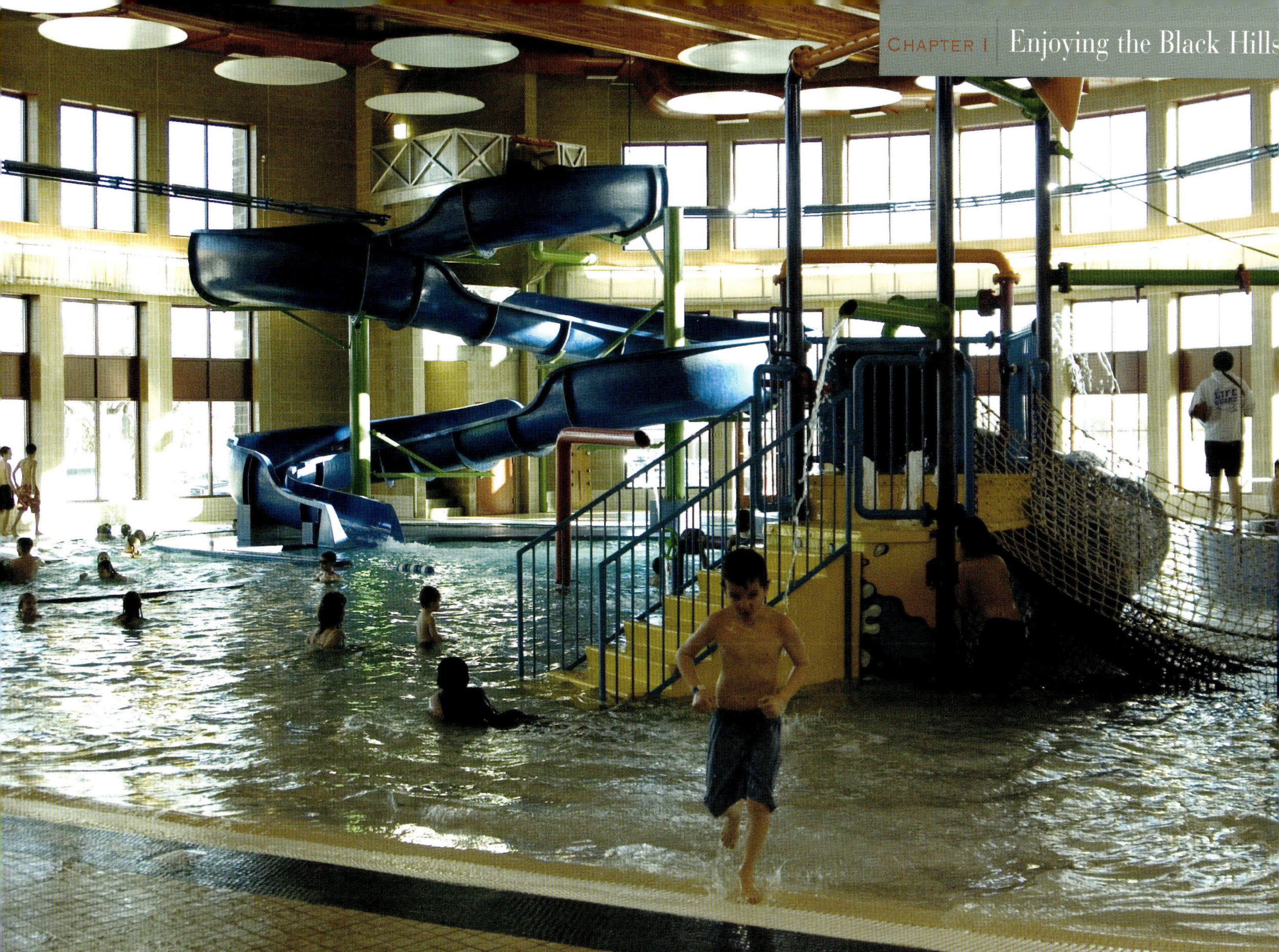

Photo by Joleen Zoller

Thousands of individuals and families enjoy the Rapid City Indoor Swim Center at Roosevelt Park. In addition to the fun play-and-splash area, there is a competition-size pool for swim meets as well as family use.

Then there are the indoor activities. The Rushmore Plaza Civic Center hosts year-round events, including several unique to the area. Each fall the He Sapa Wacipi (Black Hills Pow Wow) draws thousands of visitors. This colorful event involves five hundred Native American dancers and twenty drum groups, representing fifty-six tribes from seventeen states and Canada.

Another major event is the Lakota Nation Invitational, one of the premier basketball tournaments and gatherings of athletes, scholars, and tribal officials in the nation. It brings in an estimated $5 million, according to the Rapid City Chamber of Commerce.

In late January, the Civic Center is host to the Black Hills Stock Show and Rodeo, which is consistently ranked as one of the top-five such events in the country.

The indoor Swim Center and Ice Arena, and numerous national concerts and shows make up a year-round calendar of fun.

"In all our activities, we think of ourselves as an inclusive city," Shaw said.

With an eye to the future, Rapid City established the Vision 2012 Program in 1992, the twentieth anniversary of the devastating flood of 1972, which killed 238 people and destroyed thousands of homes and businesses. Out of that, however, came new life represented by the beautiful 754-acre green way—which is actually a flood plain—that runs through the entire town.

Based on the extraordinary regeneration following the flood, the city voted to extend a half-cent sales tax and use the proceeds for community-oriented projects in the next twenty years. In addition to wooing high-tech companies, here are just a few of the plans

Continued on page 96

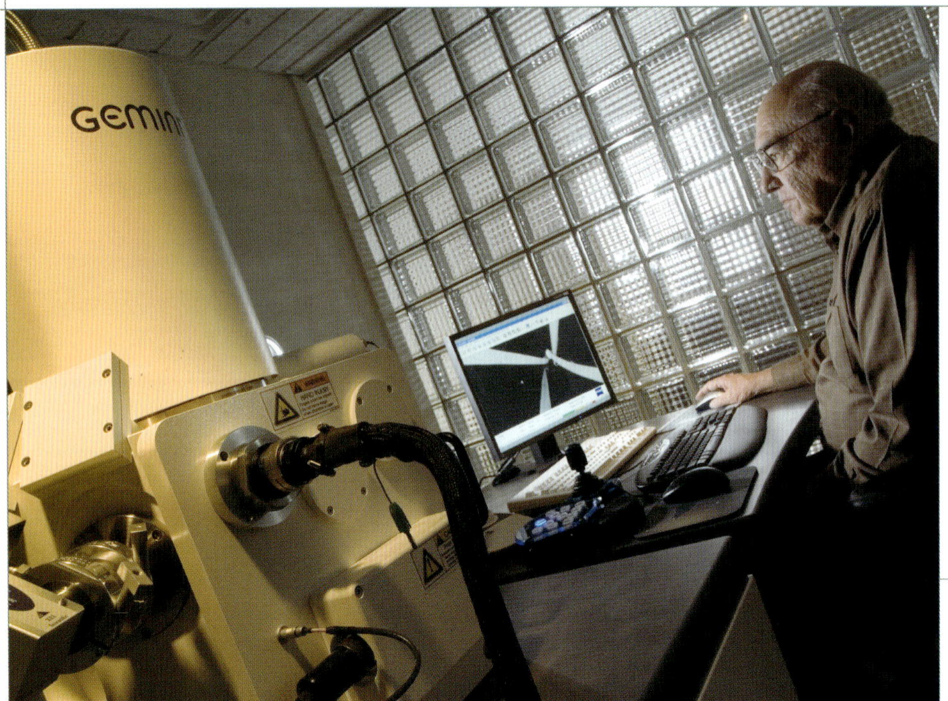

Located at the South Dakota School of Mines and Technology, the Center for Accelerated Applications at the Nanoscale (CAAN)—a Governor's 2010 Center—is focused on the evolving field of nanotechnology. Viewed by many as the next industrial revolution, nanotechnology offers the potential for the development of entirely new materials and processes, starting at the molecular level. CAAN is poised to be a pivotal part of this exciting new field through basic and applied research leading to marketable applications for commercial products and processes.

Photo by Dennis Keim

Continued from page 95

for Vision 2012: $6.5 million for more fine arts facilities, a $15 million arena addition to the Civic Center, a new twenty-five-field soccer complex, and an outdoor Pow Wow grounds to showcase Native American events, arts, and products to create a Santa Fe of the North.

So keep an eye on the area. Exciting things are happening that will continue to showcase Rapid City's reputation as the Star of the West. ❖

Photo by Johnny Sundby

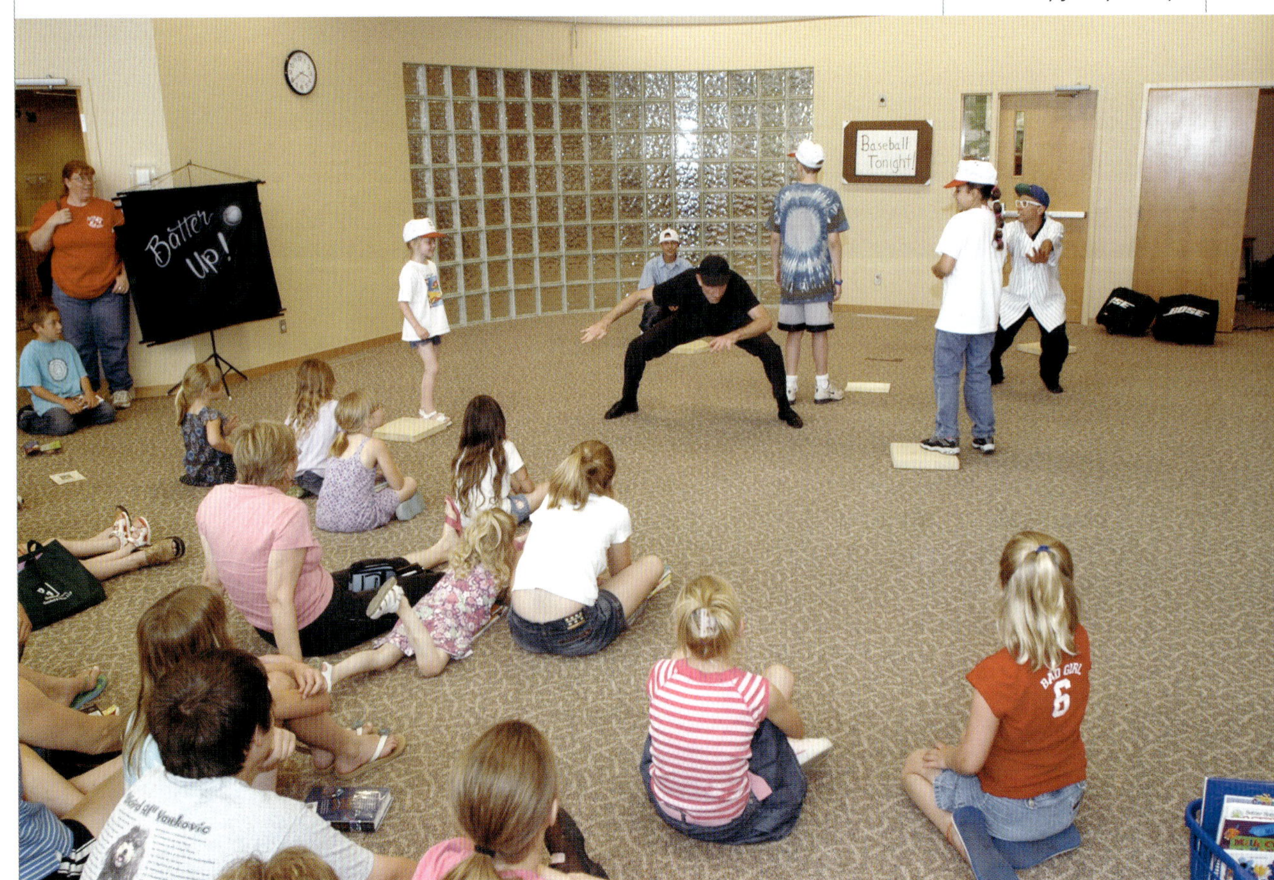

The expanded Rapid City Public Library has everything a modern library should have ... plus a few surprises. It has books, of course, more than 140,000 of them. It also has computers, computer classes, a wireless lab, and sixteen laptops, which are taken out into the community to make people aware of what is available for their use. The library has programs for visitors of all ages, including activities like the mime class led by Dennis Schaller of the Silent Echoes Mime Theatre; Dennis was part of the summer reading program. There are other interesting programs—like Discovery Days, where kids may bring their instruments and make CDs or perhaps take apart old computers to see how they work. For patrons' convenience, the library has a drive-through window for picking up or dropping off books. Now for the surprises: On the first floor, there is an aquarium with types of fish found in local waters, and on the second floor, there is an aviary filled with several dozen colorful song birds. The aquarium was a gift, and the aviary was supplied by the Friends of the Library.

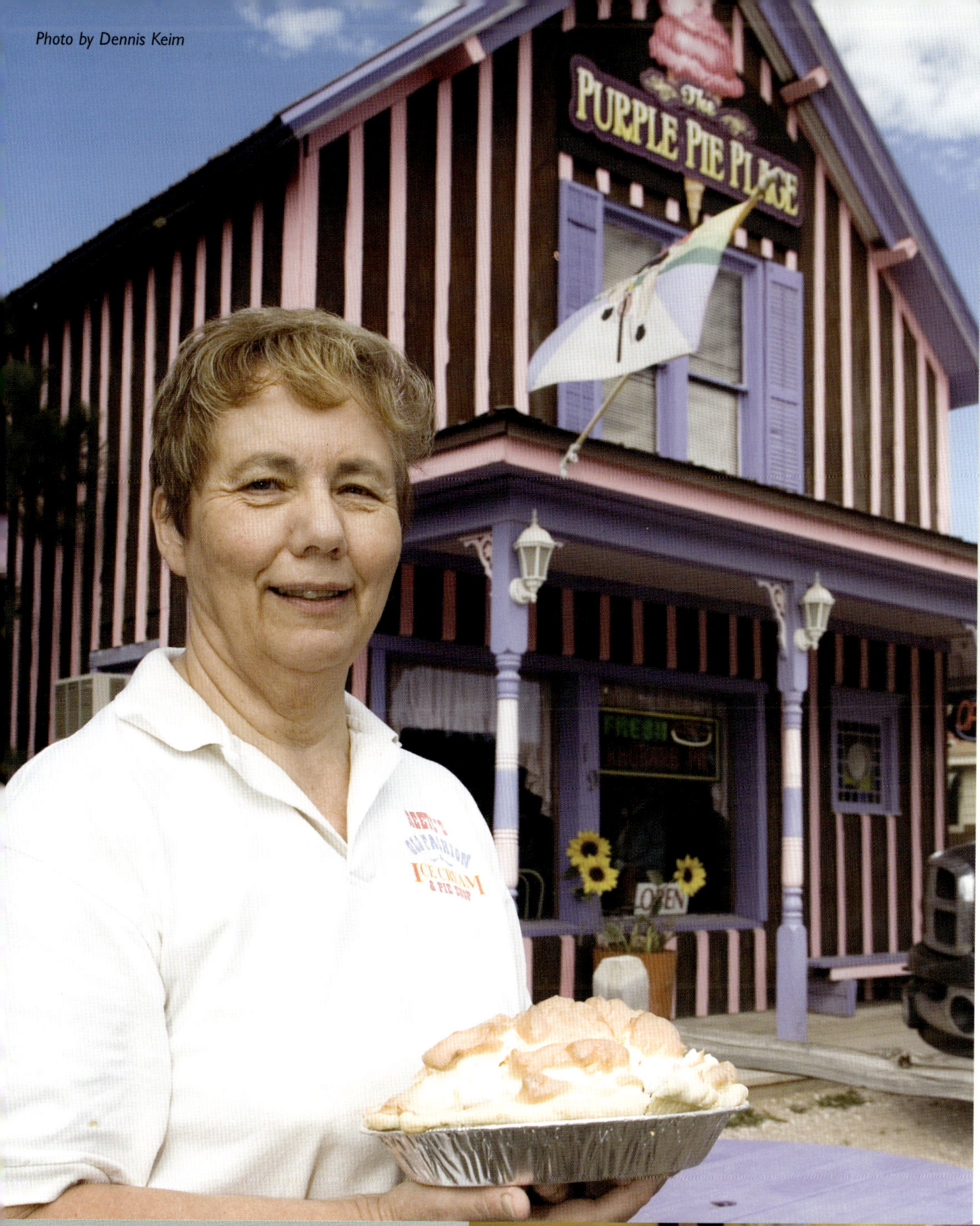

Photo by Dennis Keim

Originally built in the early 1890s as a private home, the establishment now known as Reetz's Old Fashion Ice Cream & Pie Shop is one of the oldest residences in Custer City. It's also one of the most colorful. Nicknamed the Purple Pie Place, Reetz's was renovated into an ice cream parlor by Daryl and Carol Whitmore in 1984 and purchased by frequent customers Terry and Arle Reetz in 1998. "We thought it would be a fun business," says Arle, shown here with one of her spectacular lemon meringue pies. Terry and Arle expanded the business to include sixteen flavors of ice cream, twelve different pies, and a restaurant serving homemade soup, sandwiches, and salads. Although the pies reign supreme—in 2005, Reetz's produced 6,325 over a five-month period—Arle says customers also love their fun and friendly atmosphere. "We are a family business, so it's a great place for our customers to come relax and have fun. We've made some awesome friendships just talking and making sure people get the best service available." ❖

Photo by Thomas S. England

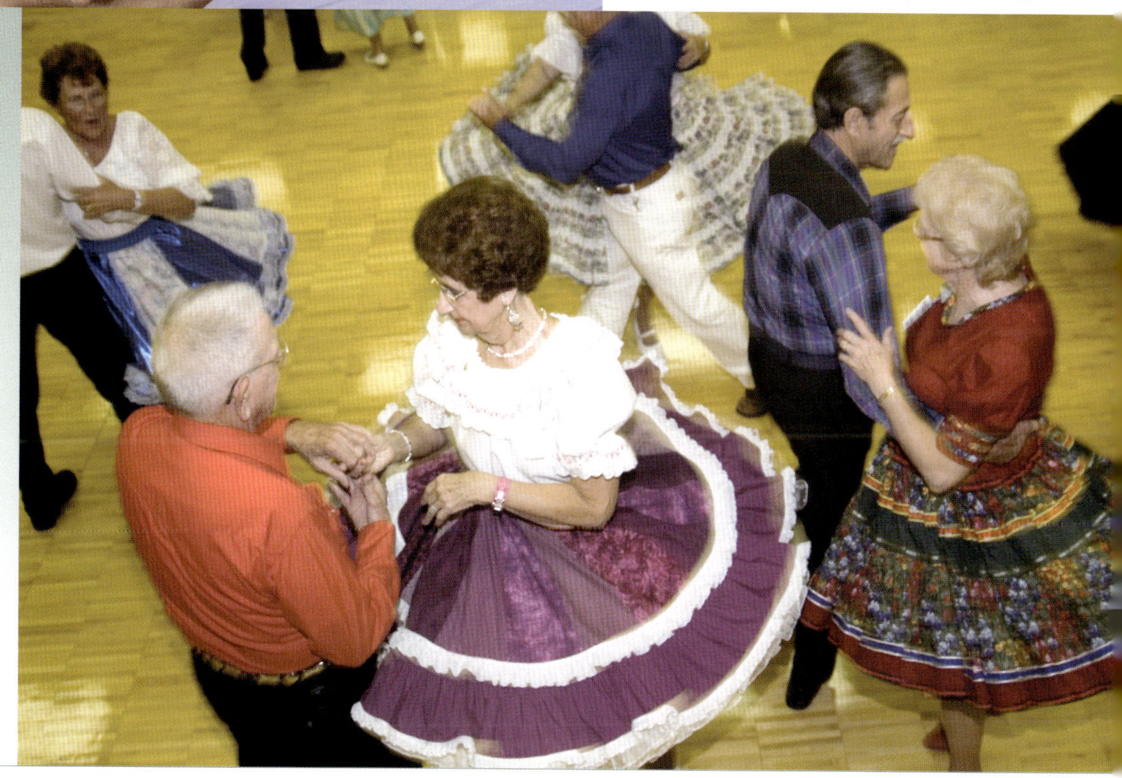

Violet Haraldson's partner spins her round and round during the 2005 Black Hills Festival at the Rushmore Plaza Civic Center. The festival, sponsored and organized by the Black Hills Square & Round Dance Association, brings together more than eighty hoofers from around the region each year to celebrate the traditional social dance that they enjoy so much. In fact, many of these avid dancers congregate on various days each month to do-si-do and promenade with their respective dance clubs, like Buckles & Bows, the Custer Gold Busters, the Dakota Diamonds, and Levis and Lace, among others. Each of these groups is a member of the Black Hills Square & Round Dance Association, which was established to promote square, folk, and round dancing and help its member groups coordinate and participate in monthly dances, promotions, parades, and special events. And when all of the groups gather for an event like the Black Hills Festival, their shindig is anything but square. ❖

Each year nearly 4 million vehicles pass the Interstate 90/U.S. Highway 85 interchange between Rapid City and Spearfish. The Elkhorn Ridge RV Park offers those travelers a scenic and convenient spot at which to rest, relax, and refuel before once again hitting the road. Opened in May 2006 as a development project of Frawley Ranches, Inc., the seventy-five-acre park includes 375 RV sites, 34 cabins, and 30 camping sites, all equipped with water, sewer, Internet access, power hookups, and shower and laundry facilities.. ❖

Preservation...

Photo by Dennis Keim

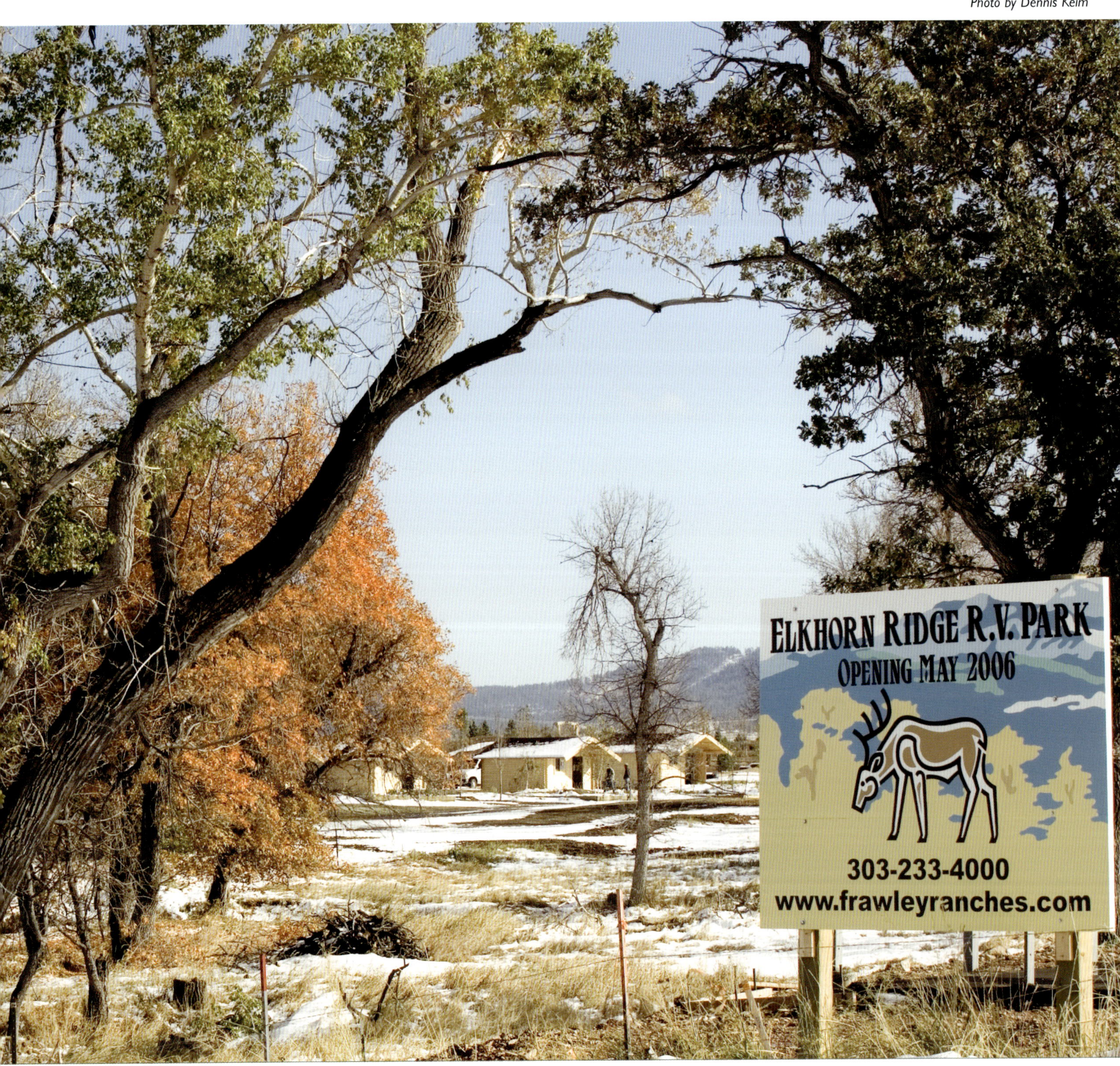

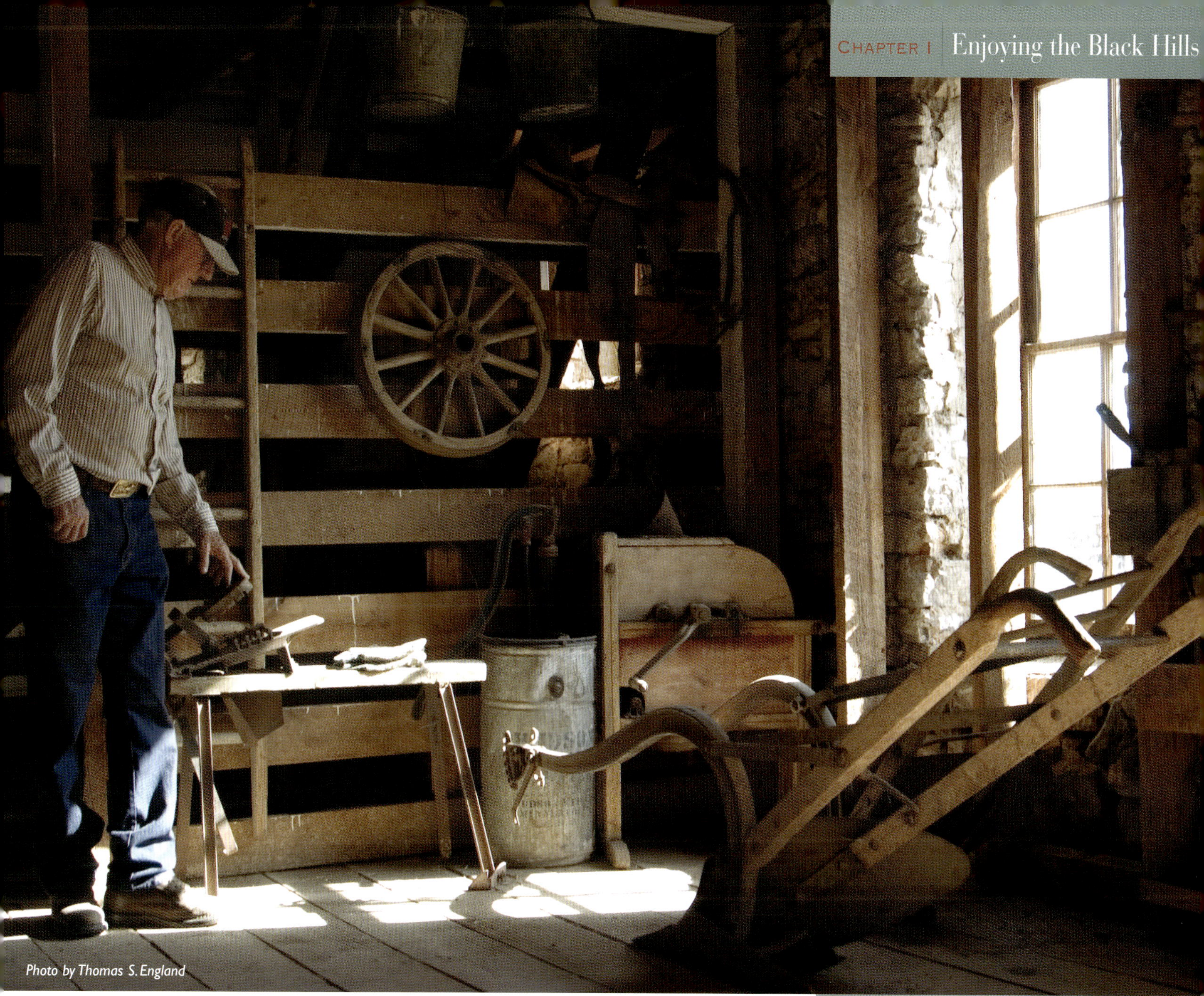

Photo by Thomas S. England

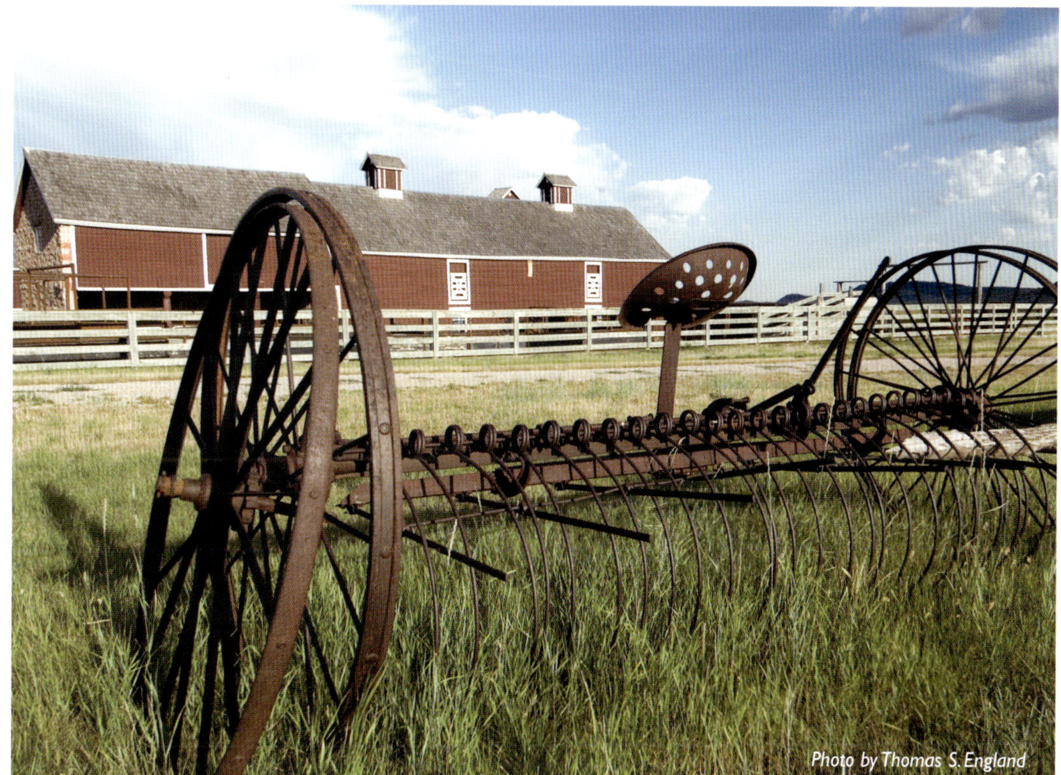

Photo by Thomas S. England

Owned and operated by the same family since 1876, the forty-five-hundred-acre Frawley Ranch has become a model of how responsible development can help preserve a vital historical site. Under the management company of Frawley Ranches, Inc., owner Hank Frawley and real estate developers Daryll Propp and Mike Kreke have created a plan that allows for a quarter of the ranch to be developed into residential and mixed-use sites, while preserving the remaining thirty-five hundred acres under a conservation easement. A National Historic Site, the ranch features forests, rolling hills, and prairie with roaming herds of wild buffalo, horses, and burros. Also on-site are many historic nineteenth-century buildings, farm equipment, implements, and household items. These buildings and items are being preserved through a restoration partnership between Frawley Ranches, Inc., and the Deadwood Historic Preservation Commission. Eventually, the site will be open to the public, offering visitors a rare glimpse into Old West life. ❖

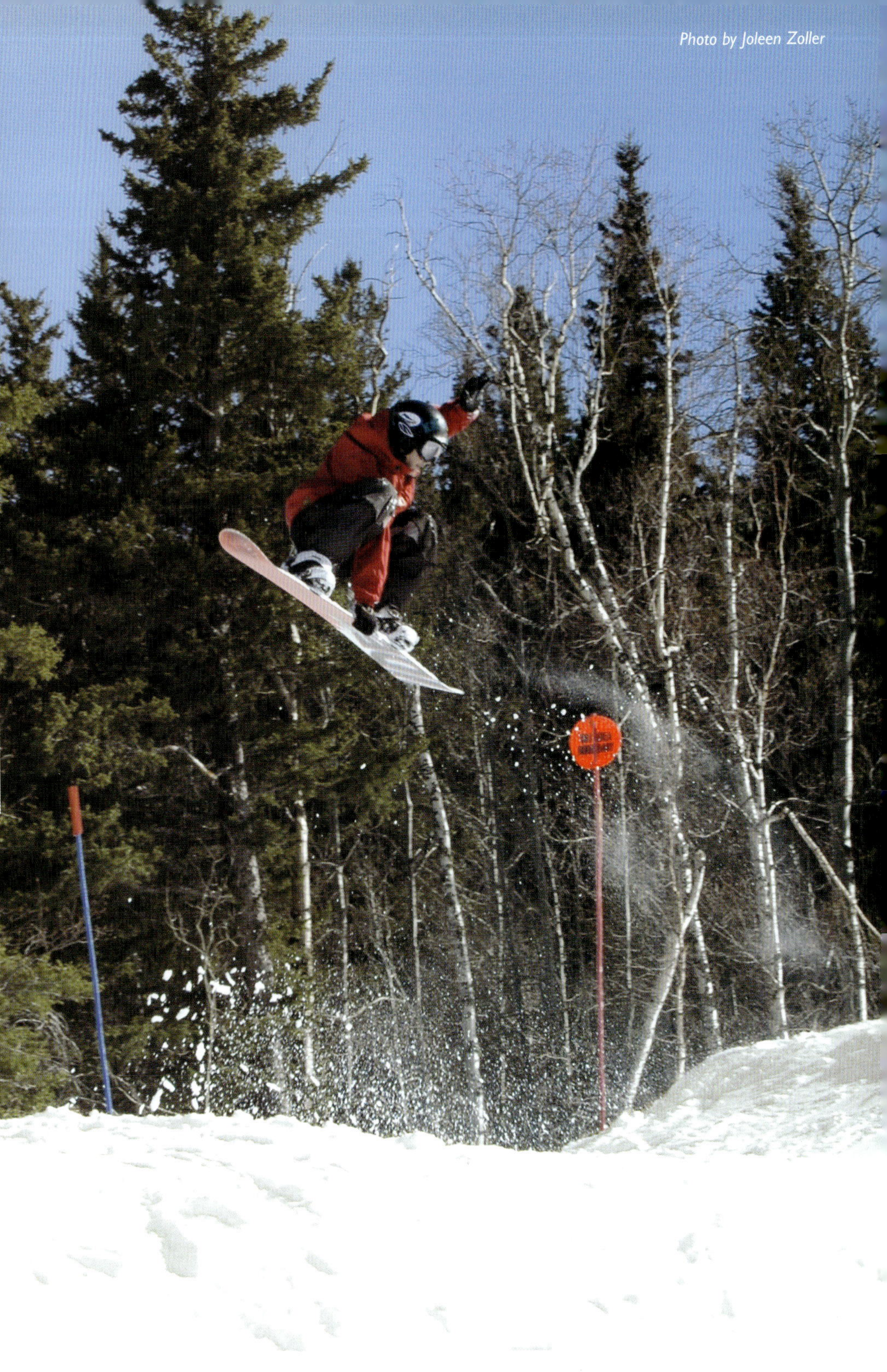

Photo by Joleen Zoller

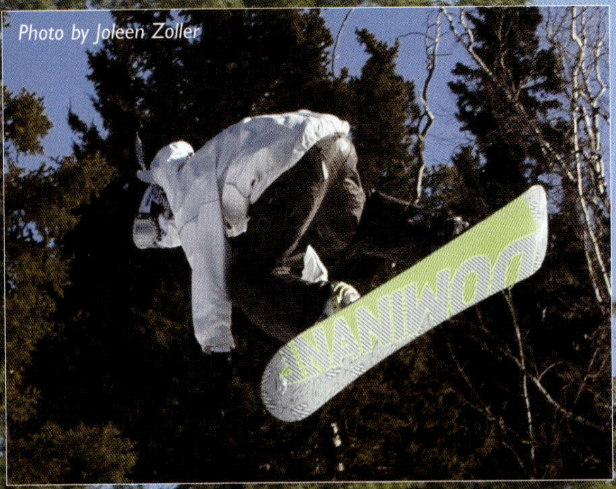

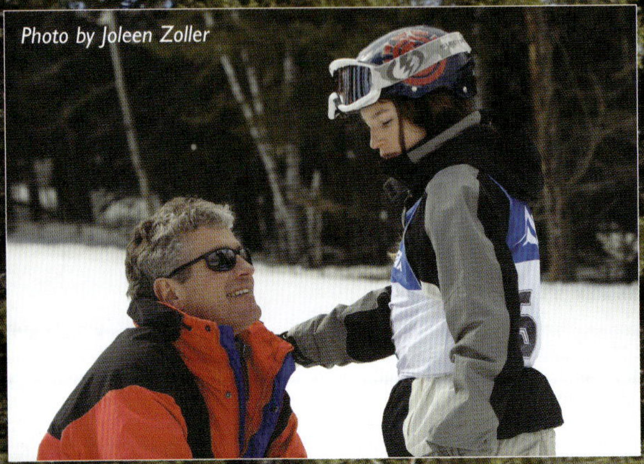

Photo by Joleen Zoller

Photo by Joleen Zoller

It began in 1936 as a recreational area for the Bald Mountain Ski Club—a half dozen members with a towrope and a thirst for winter fun. Today, the Terry Peak Ski Resort offers thousands of skiers and snowboarders the most exciting downhill action of any in the Black Hills. Located about an hour northwest of Rapid City and only minutes from Lead and Deadwood, the 450-acre ski resort features thirty trails, a half pipe with twelve-foot walls, a freestyle terrain park, and four chairlifts. For après-ski fun, relax at the Stewart Day Lodge, with its restaurant, bar, and a three-thousand-square-foot sundeck. ❖

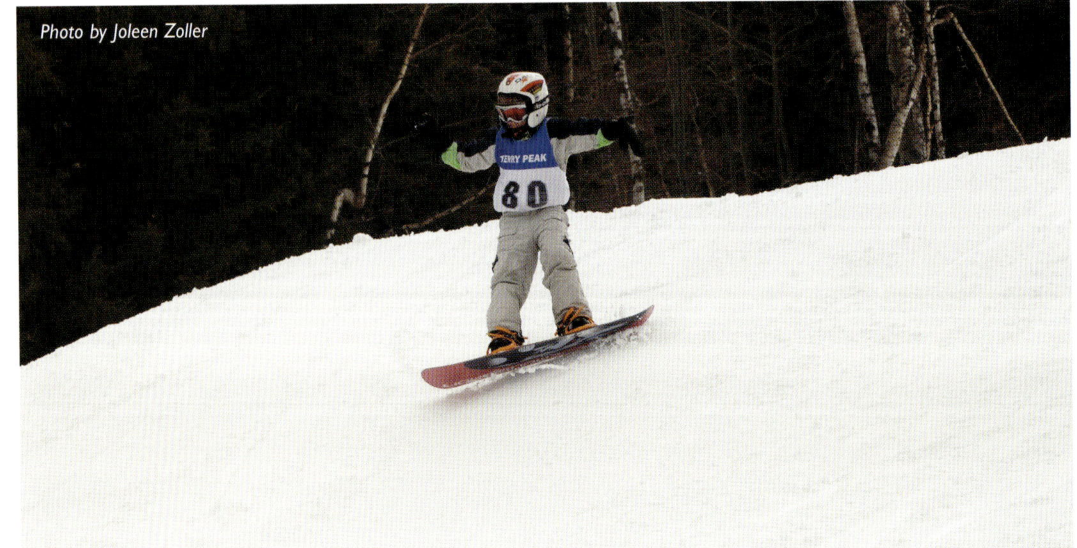

Photo by Joleen Zoller

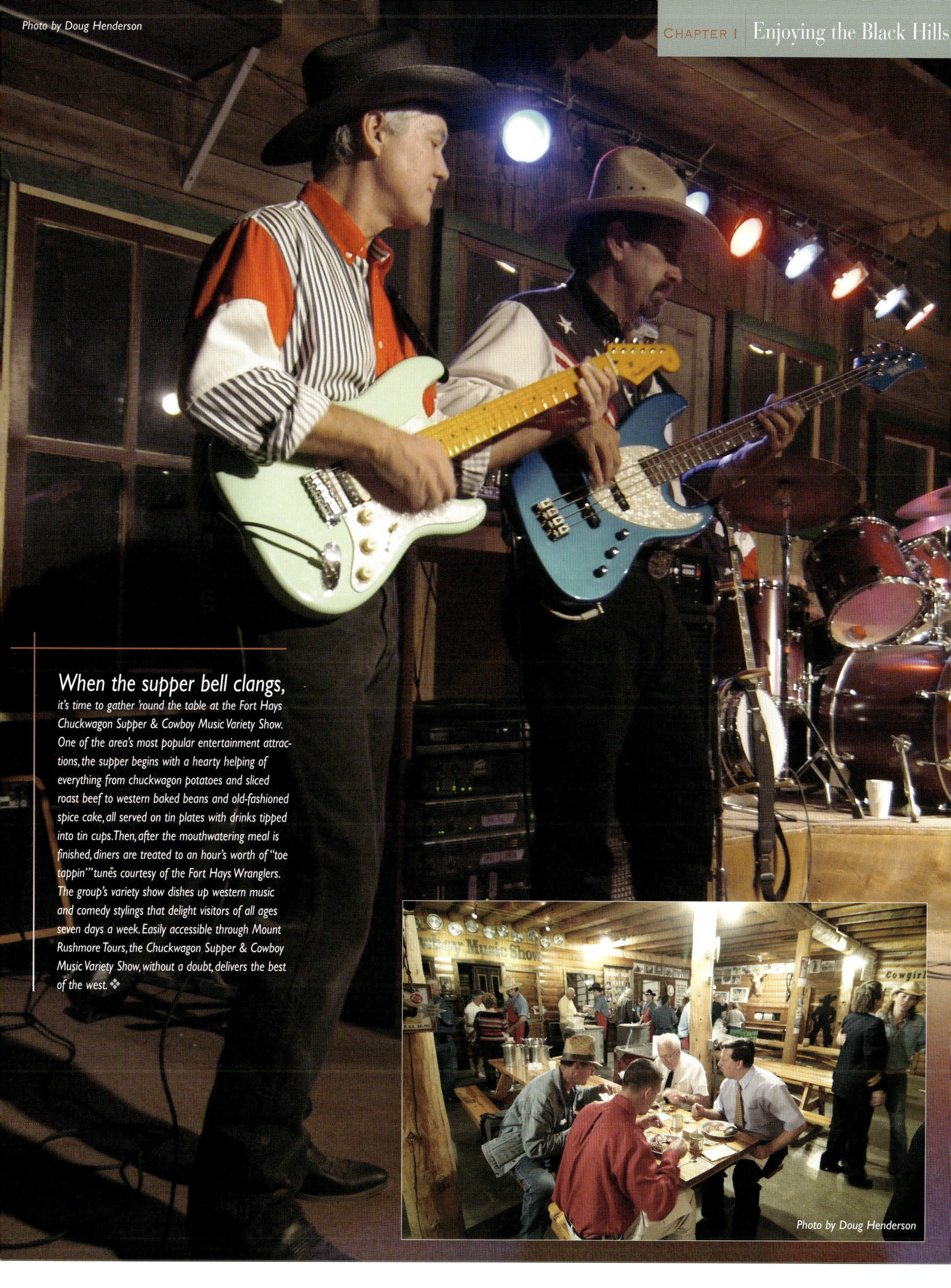

Photo by Doug Henderson

When the supper bell clangs, *it's time to gather 'round the table at the Fort Hays Chuckwagon Supper & Cowboy Music Variety Show. One of the area's most popular entertainment attractions, the supper begins with a hearty helping of everything from chuckwagon potatoes and sliced roast beef to western baked beans and old-fashioned spice cake, all served on tin plates with drinks tipped into tin cups. Then, after the mouthwatering meal is finished, diners are treated to an hour's worth of "toe tappin'" tunes courtesy of the Fort Hays Wranglers. The group's variety show dishes up western music and comedy stylings that delight visitors of all ages seven days a week. Easily accessible through Mount Rushmore Tours, the Chuckwagon Supper & Cowboy Music Variety Show, without a doubt, delivers the best of the west.* ❖

Photo by Doug Henderson

Photo by Dennis Keim

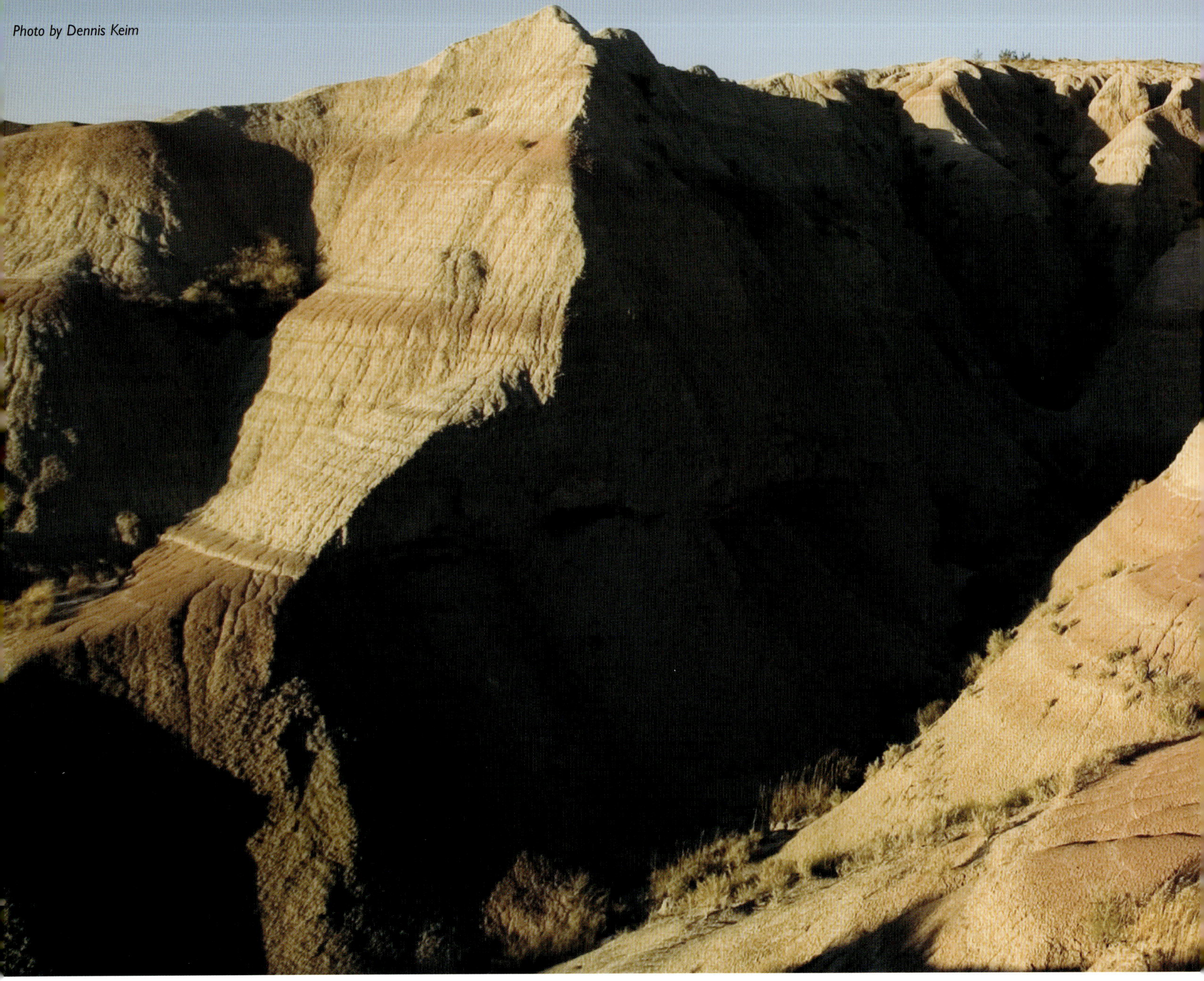

Photo by Doug Henderson

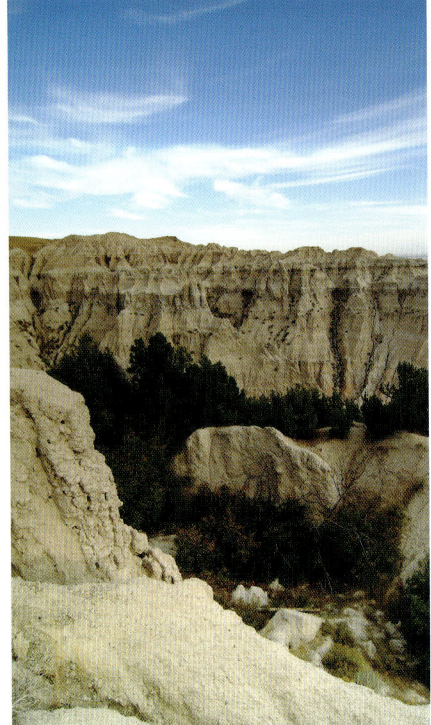

Photo by Doug Henderson

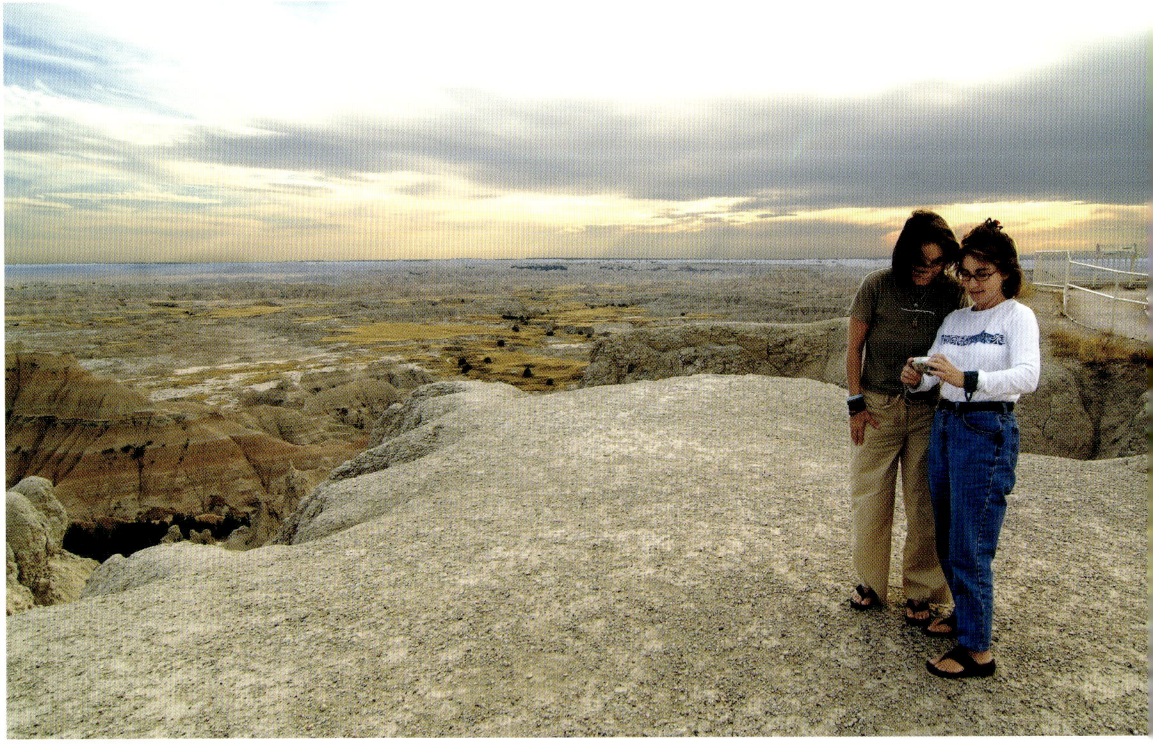

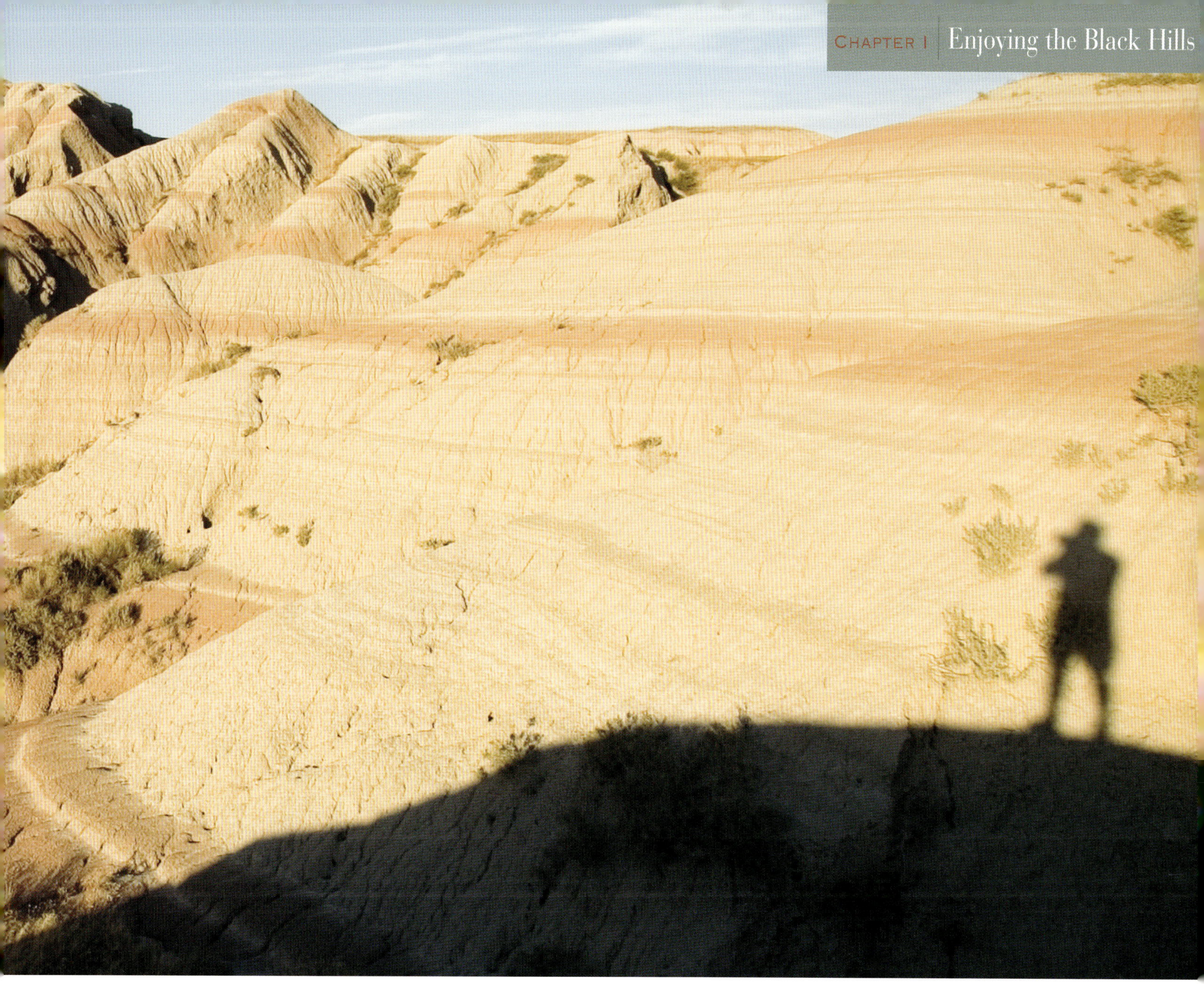

Photo by Dennis Keim

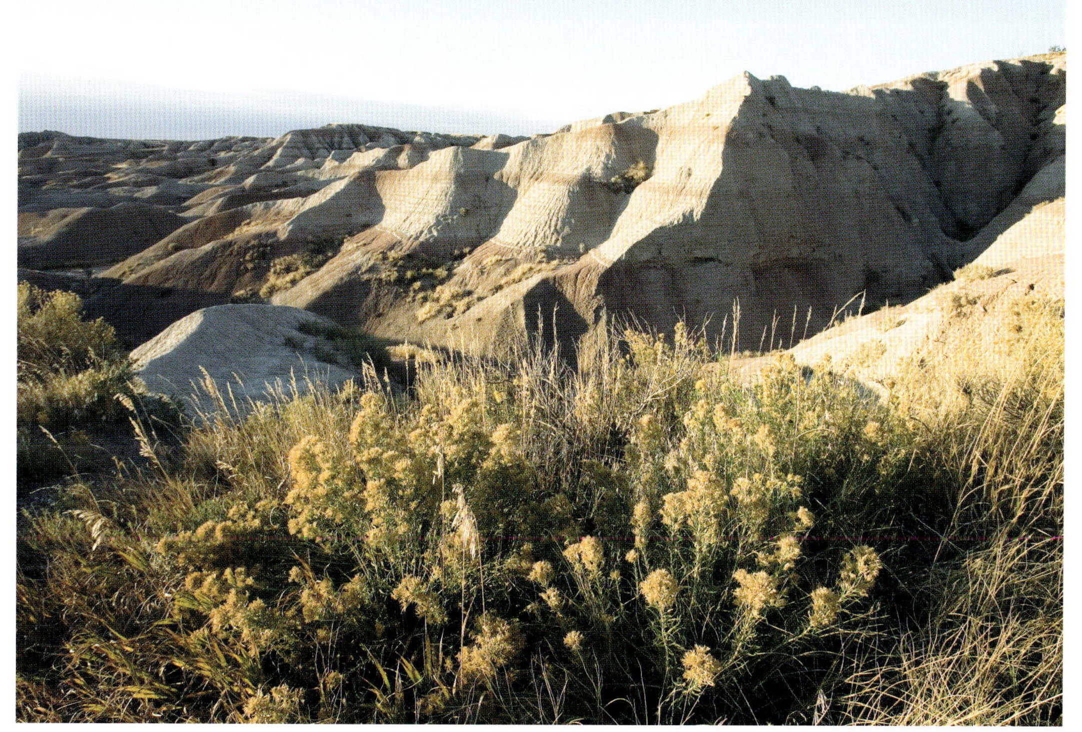

It appears endlessly vast and lonesome, but the landscape preserved as the Badlands National Park contains evidence of human occupation that goes back eleven thousand years. Long before that, other life forms flourished as well—as far back as 23 to 35 million years ago, evidenced by the park's abundant deposits of Oligocene-epoch fossil beds. Established as a national park in 1978 to preserve the area's scenic and scientific value, the Badlands National Park encompasses over 244,000 acres of towering rock formations, eroded buttes, and the largest protected mixed-grass prairie in the United States, site of the reintroduction of the endangered black-footed ferret. Humans still occupy the area, too. Located about a ninety-minute drive east of Rapid City, the park offers visitors a series of ranger-led walks and interpretive programs, and abundant self-guided backcountry hiking. ❖

Photo by Alan S.Weiner

CHAPTER II Building the BLACK HILLS

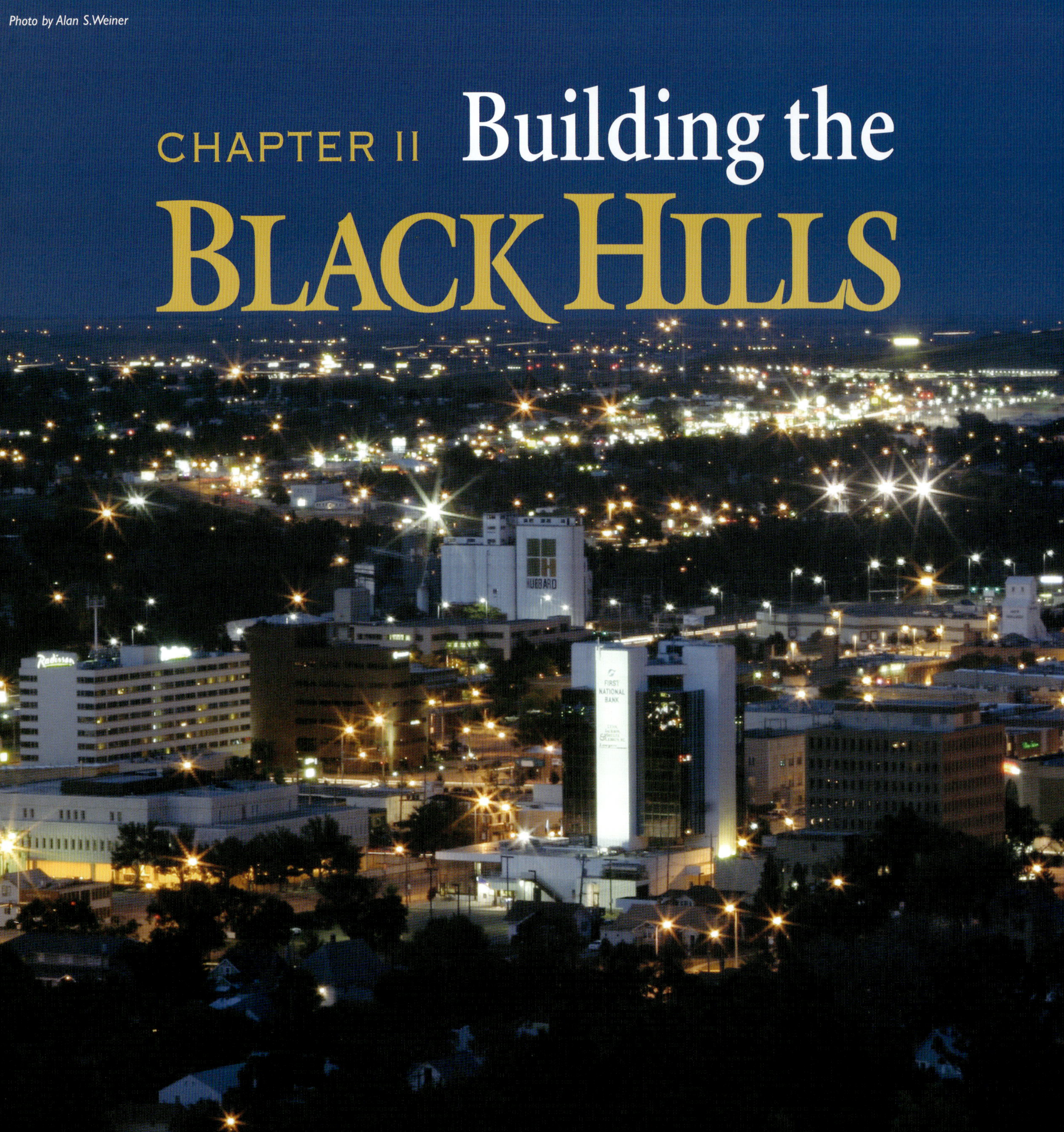

Those who followed the way west in the mid-1800s and ended their journey in southwestern South Dakota found a land filled with opportunities as expansive as the region's landscape.

Gold. Cattle. Mining. These industries helped build the Black Hills in the early years. In some of the rough-and-tumble towns, fortunes could be made as quick as a bullet from a six-shooter. That was part of the draw. If the frontier symbolized anything, it was the opportunity to go head-to-head with Lady Luck.

Along with the speculators also came individuals and families who braved the odds to raise livestock, plant crops, and establish family businesses. That spirit continues to this day, in the people that South Dakota Governor Mike Rounds calls "mountain carvers" for their ability to set and stick to long-range goals.

Some of today's carvers include Elkhorn Ridge at Frawley Ranches, an innovative property development company; Rapid City's Black Hills Business Development Center; and Black Hills Vision, a regional economic development initiative.

High in quality of life, low in cost and crime, cities like Rapid City, Sturgis, and Spearfish are attracting businesses that appreciate cooperative relationships with state and local governments, generous economic incentives, a close sense of community, and an educated, resourceful workforce. With all that and more going for it, it's clear that business is still booming in the Black Hills. ❖

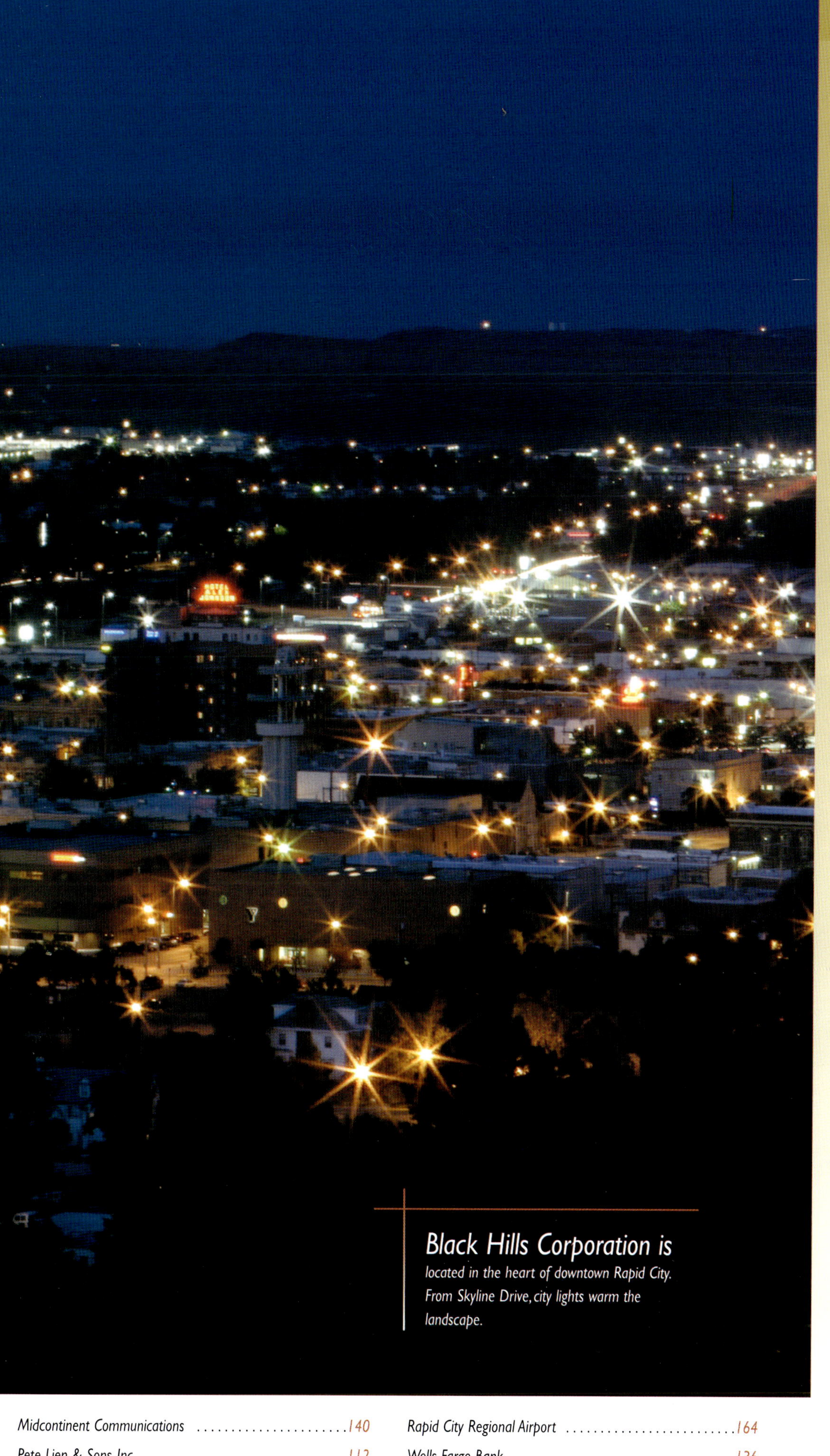

Black Hills Corporation is located in the heart of downtown Rapid City. From Skyline Drive, city lights warm the landscape.

Black Hills Workshop: Providing Opportunities

"Having this job means I can have my own apartment, go shopping, or go to the movies, and I get to interact with lots of people every day," said Natalie Molitor, a receptionist at Black Hills Workshop Concourse Enterprises.

Her coworker Joey Bsharah added, "Working here has helped me be more sociable. I know I have to take responsibility to get to work on time and be ready to do my job. I'm living with my family now, but I'm working to live fully independent. That's what I want."

The Black Hills Workshop and Training Center is a community rehabilitation program for adults with disabilities. Employment allows them to explore opportunities and make choices. Since its inception in 1958, the workshop has provided employment for hundreds of individuals with disabilities.

"We are a value-added provider for government and industry. We specialize in subcontract assembly, packaging, mailing, and many other services," said Dorothy Rosby, community relations director. "Our goals are to expand our business partnerships in the manufacturing industry, to increase the number of job opportunities for the individuals we serve, and to continue to deliver products and services of exceptional quality to our customers."

Plant manager for Sanmina-SCI James Larson says, "We've used BHW as a subcontractor for almost twenty years, and they provide a good, flexible workforce for us. We always get what we need, and we get it done right, neat, and on time." ❖

> "We always get what we need, and we get it done right, neat, and on time."

Photo by Thomas S. England

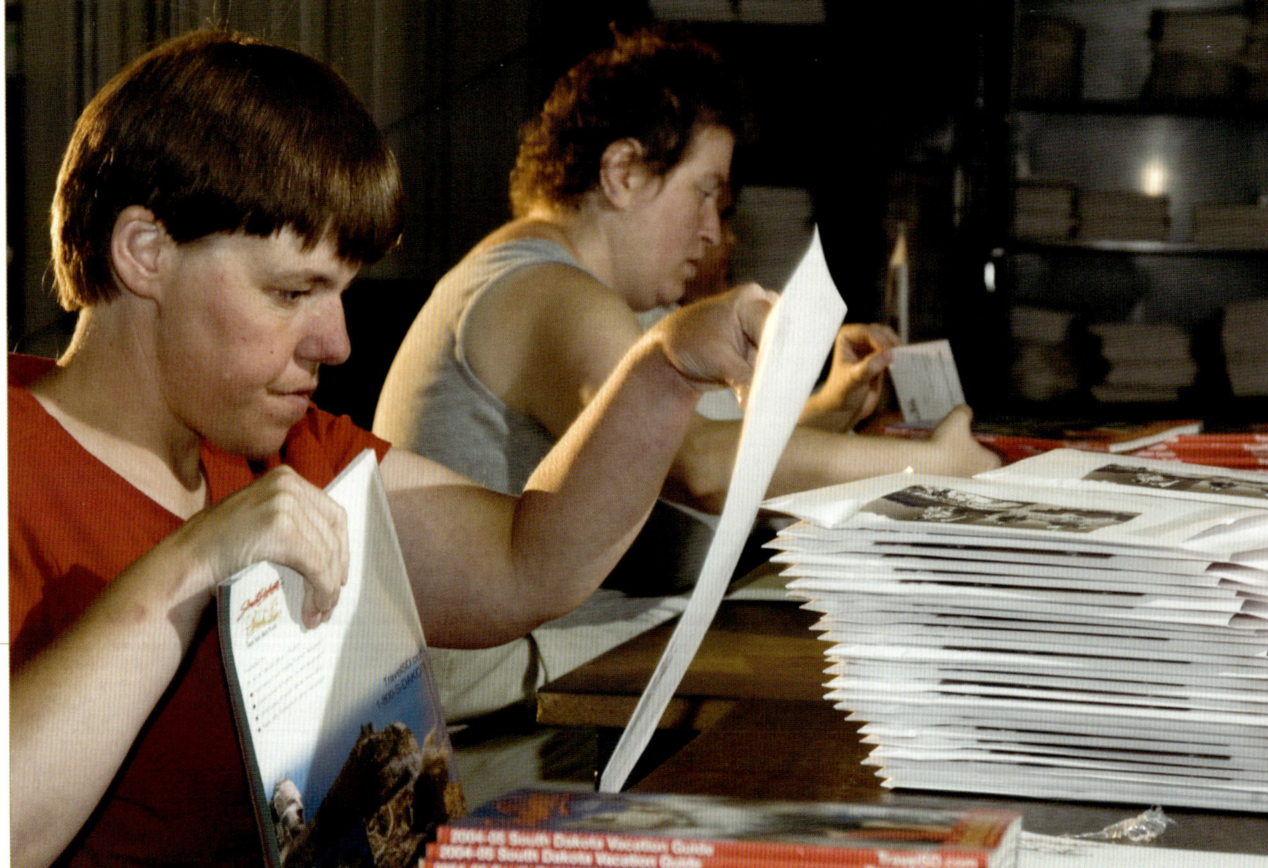

Lisa Lawler and Windy Criss collate promotional packages for the South Dakota Department of Tourism.

Photo by Thomas S. England

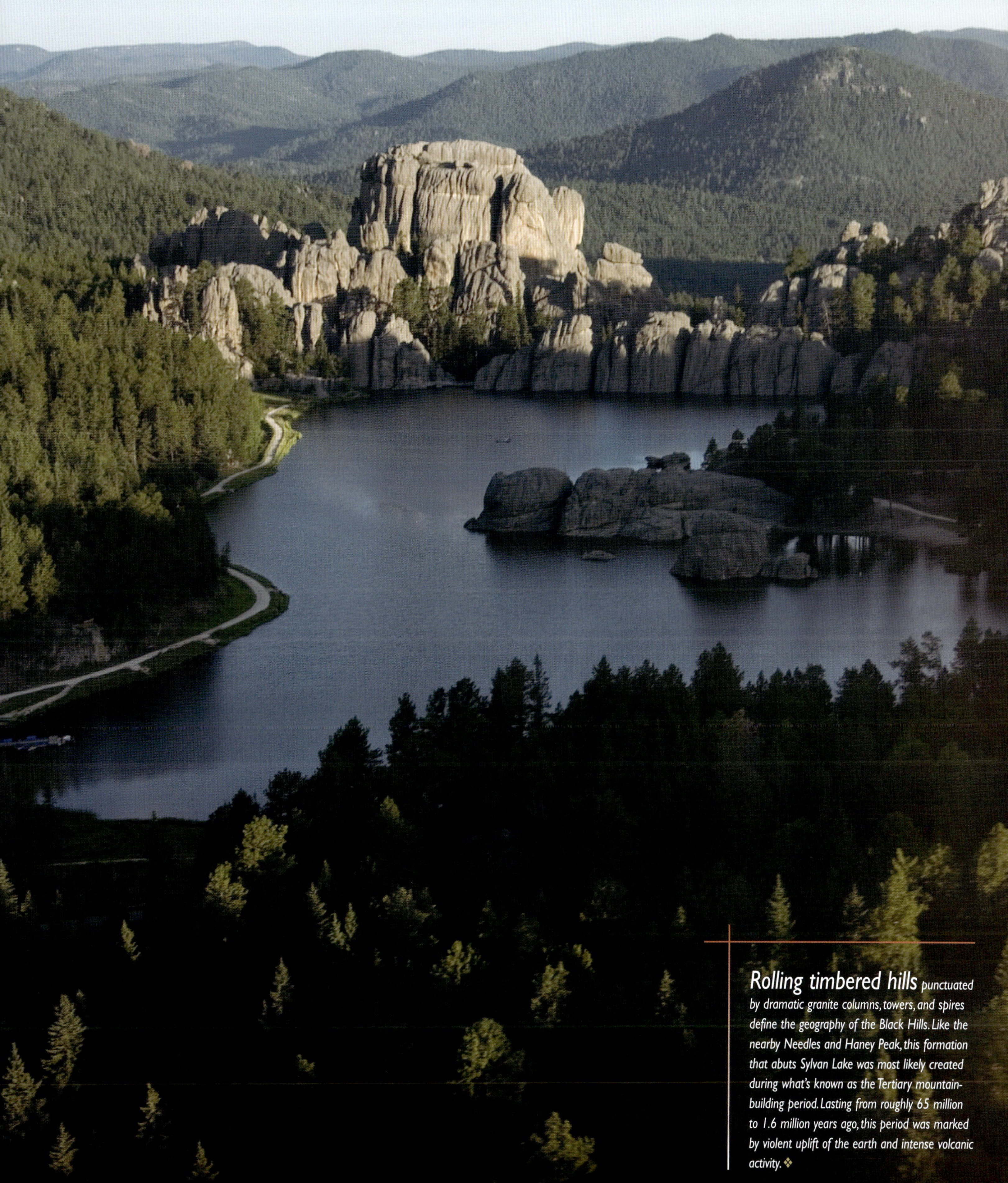

Rolling timbered hills *punctuated by dramatic granite columns, towers, and spires define the geography of the Black Hills. Like the nearby Needles and Haney Peak, this formation that abuts Sylvan Lake was most likely created during what's known as the Tertiary mountain-building period. Lasting from roughly 65 million to 1.6 million years ago, this period was marked by violent uplift of the earth and intense volcanic activity.* ❖

Great Western Bank Molds Products and Services to Fit Customer Needs

During the first ten months of 1930, at the outset of the Great Depression, 744 banks in this country failed. Conventional wisdom would surely have said it was not a good time to start a bank. However, a group of independent-minded South Dakotans disagreed. They saw a need for the services a local bank could provide to the customers and communities in their area, so in 1935, with five full-time employees and total assets of $300,571, Great Western Bank opened its doors. They have been open ever since.

Today, Great Western Bank has twenty-seven locations throughout South Dakota and northeastern Nebraska, including seven in the Black Hills. Their combined assets have grown to over $1 billion. What has not changed is the independent-minded way they do business.

"Because of our commitment and involvement in the local communities, we understand what customers in those areas need," said group president Lloyd Sohl. "We don't mold the customers to fit our products; we mold our products and services to fit our customers. For instance, take a little thing like banking hours. We have six in-store locations, and our branches in those stores are open until 7:00 p.m. This results in our providing the longest banking hours of any financial institution in the area. In addition, these banks accommodate electronic transactions at any time of the day or night."

A further example of molding services to situations is the relationship Great Western Bank has developed with the tourist industry. "Their work is seasonal, so we make every effort to schedule loan payments during the height of the tourist season when cash flow is more readily available," explained Sohl.

"Because of our commitment and involvement in the local communities, we understand what customers in those areas need."

Photo by Thomas S. England

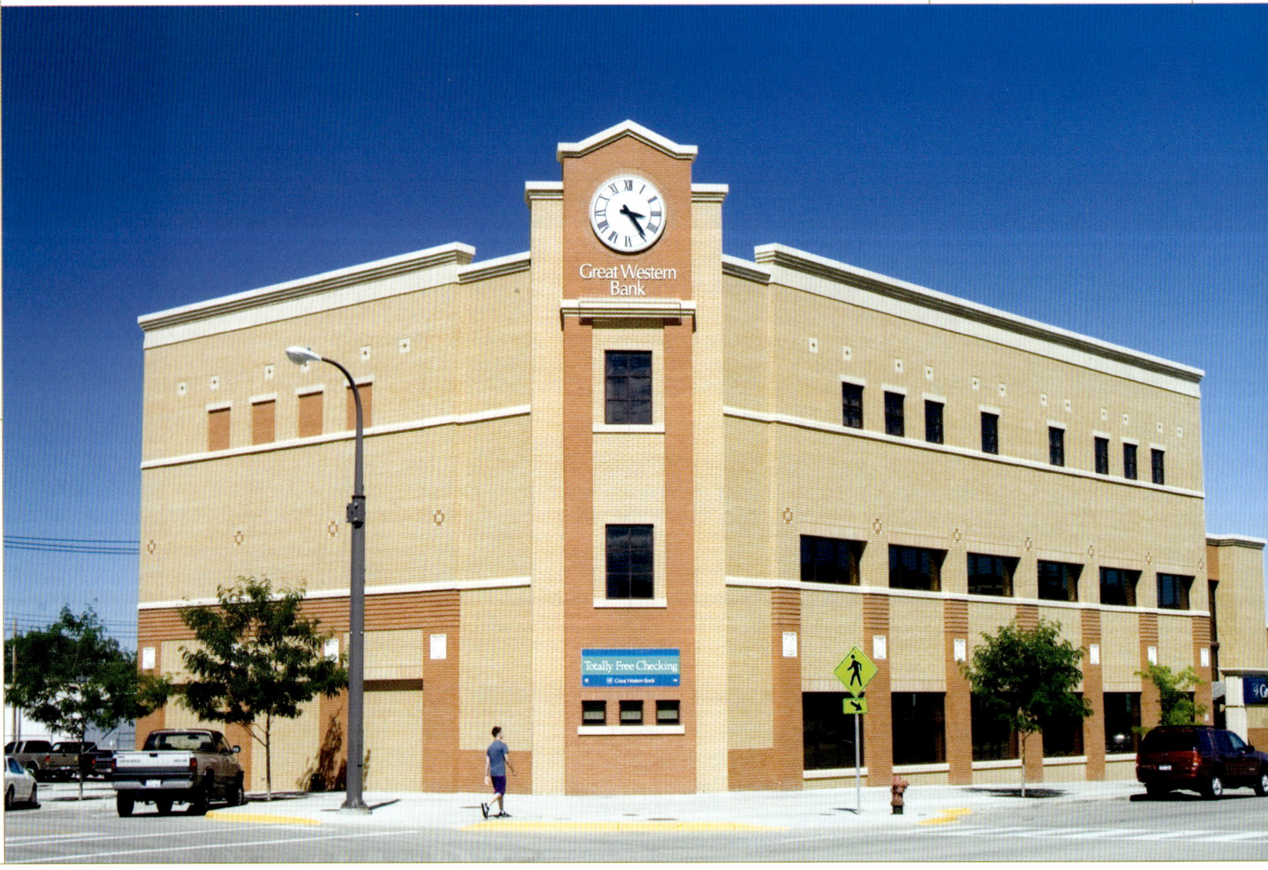

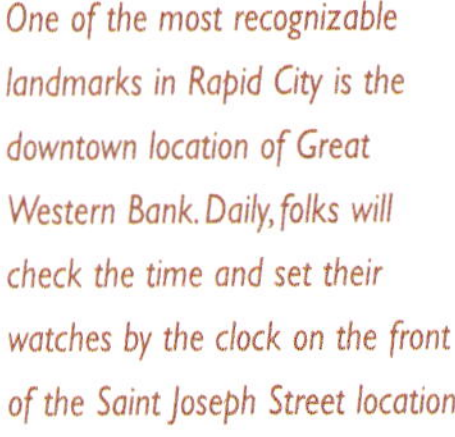

One of the most recognizable landmarks in Rapid City is the downtown location of Great Western Bank. Daily, folks will check the time and set their watches by the clock on the front of the Saint Joseph Street location.

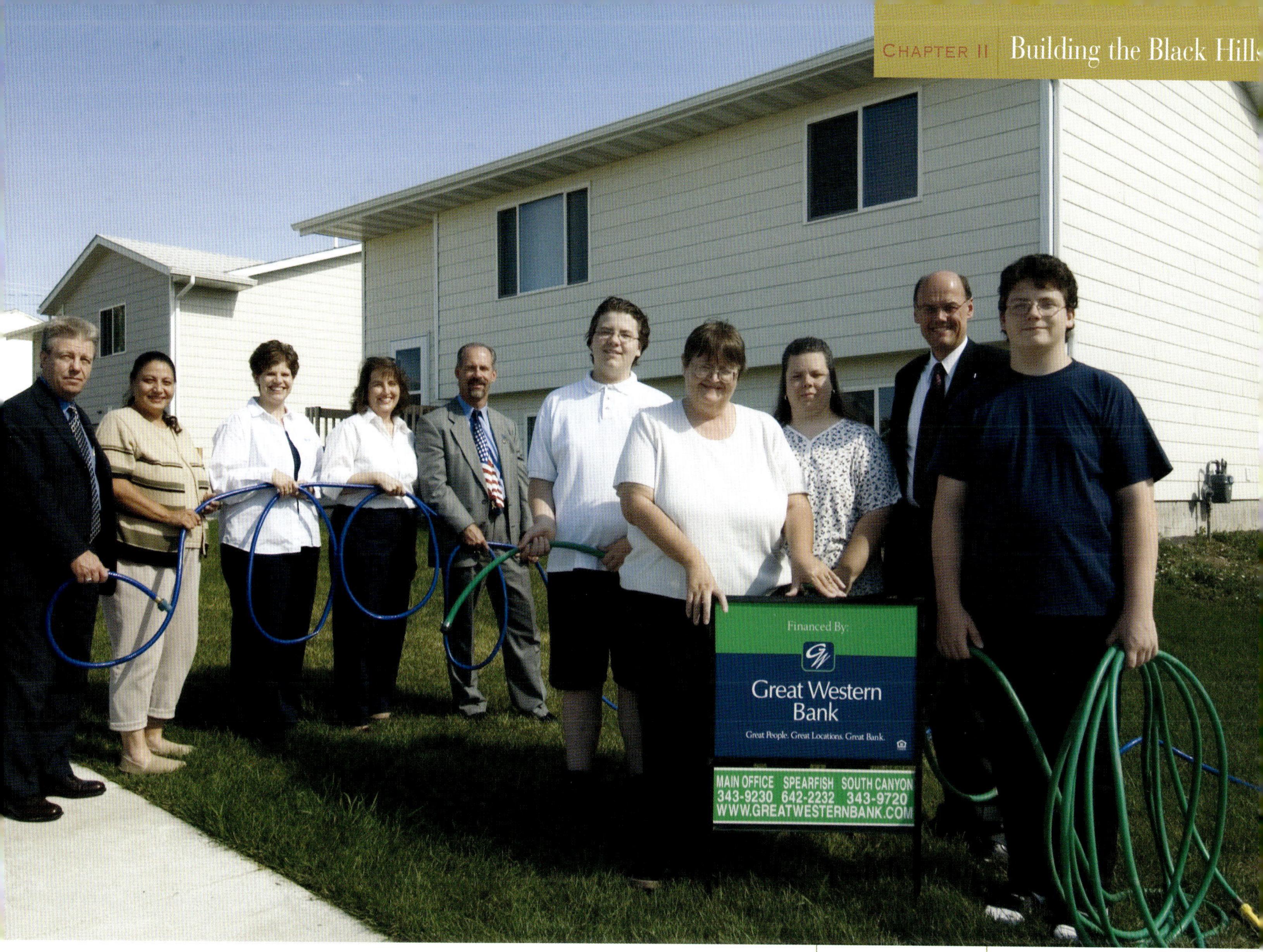

Photo by Thomas S. England

Banks frequently work with customers to secure home loans, but how often do bank employees turn out to lay sod for the new homeowner? Considering the healthy lawn, perhaps that accounts for the obvious pride of the Great Western Bank employees, the homeowners, and the representatives of the Teton Coalition.

Another business segment that benefits from Great Western Bank's customer-first attitude is real estate. "We make sure our loan officers are empowered to make decisions without having to go through a committee. Loan requests don't need to be sent out of town for underwriting and determination for loan approval. That shortens the turnaround time."

Great Western Bank further promotes home ownership in the Rapid City area through its unique relationship with the Teton Coalition. Founded by the Center for Community Change and dedicated to providing affordable housing for low-income families, the Teton Coalition has assisted 650 families in becoming homeowners since 1993.

Continued on page 110

Photo by Thomas S. England

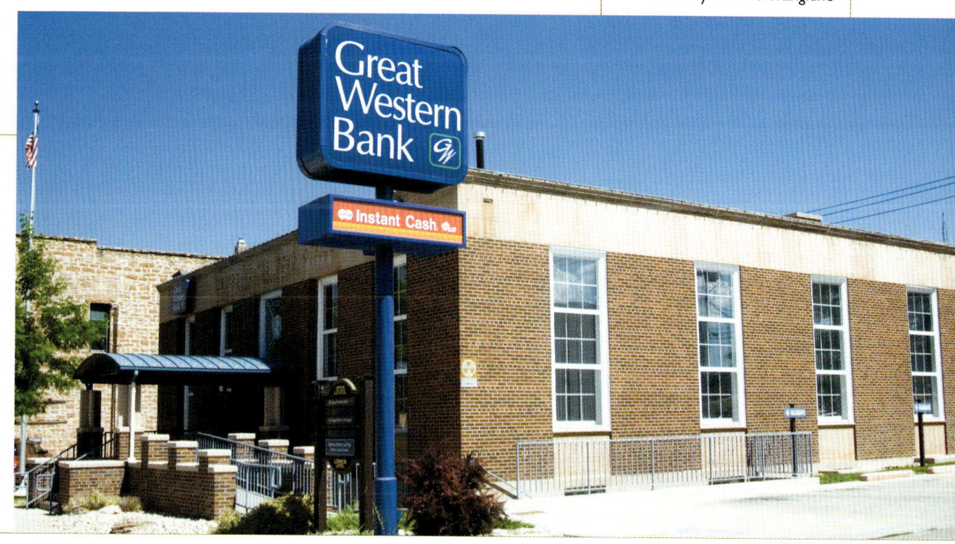

In the Black Hills, distances become relative. Although the Spearfish location of Great Western Bank, pictured on the right, is 50 miles west of Rapid City and 450 miles away from the bank's main office, the services offered are the same in all their locations. "When we say we cover the state, we really do," said Lloyd Sohl, group president.

Continued from page 109

Great Western Bank is always looking for ways to assist their community. The bank maintains a long-term depositing and loan relationship with Dakota Craft, Inc., a local family-owned business that uses state-of-the-art manufacturing facilities to provide building components for residential and commercial projects to a multistate customer base. Great Western Bank's hometown convenience, regional strength, and stability make these services possible. "Supporting businesses means supporting good-paying jobs, and that increases the quality of life for all of us here in the Black Hills," Sohl added.

Great Western Bank is moving to support small rural communities at a time when many businesses are moving out of these areas. From Sioux Falls with a population of 141,000, to Rosholt with its population of 419, Great Western Bank is there doing what they have always done: going against conventional wisdom to provide customers and communities with the financial products and services they need and doing it with an unusual degree of success. ❖

This truckload of floor trusses manufactured by Dakota Craft might be destined for either a residential or a commercial installation.There are many variables in supplying building components,but one constant is the ongoing business relationship between Alan and Shannon Thornburg of Dakota Craft and Lloyd Sohl (center), representing Great Western Bank.

Photo by Eric Francis

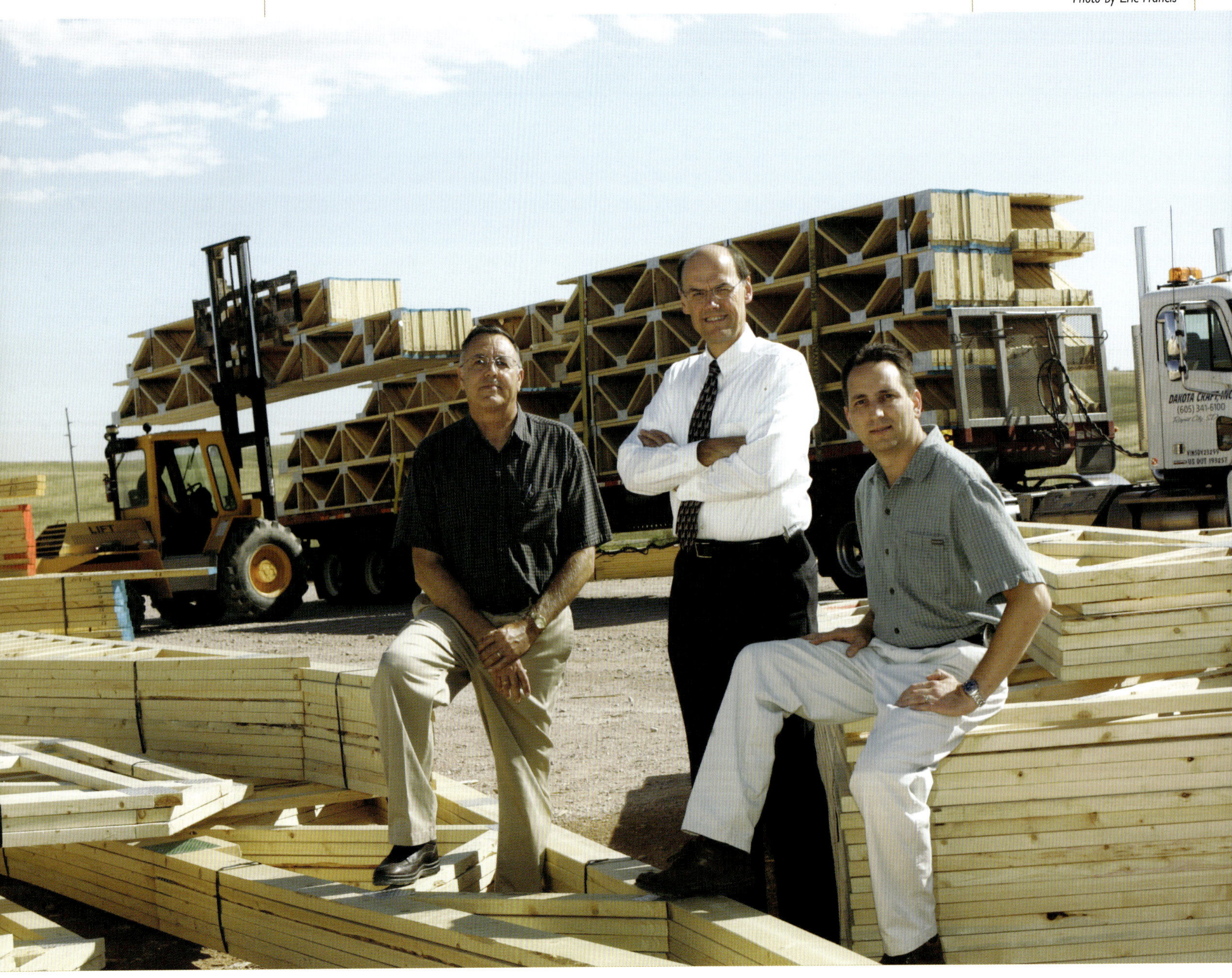

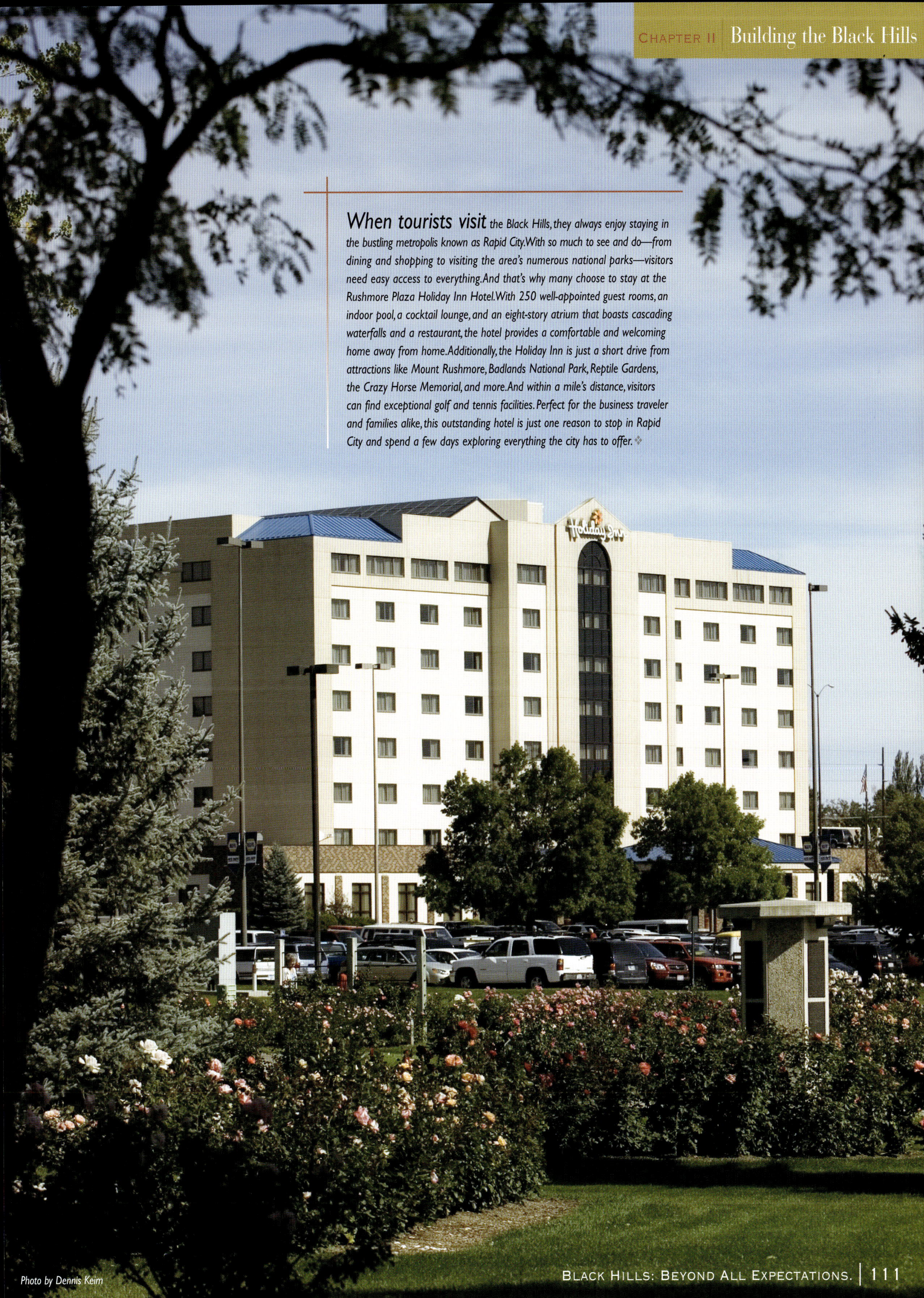

When tourists visit the Black Hills, they always enjoy staying in the bustling metropolis known as Rapid City. With so much to see and do—from dining and shopping to visiting the area's numerous national parks—visitors need easy access to everything. And that's why many choose to stay at the Rushmore Plaza Holiday Inn Hotel. With 250 well-appointed guest rooms, an indoor pool, a cocktail lounge, and an eight-story atrium that boasts cascading waterfalls and a restaurant, the hotel provides a comfortable and welcoming home away from home. Additionally, the Holiday Inn is just a short drive from attractions like Mount Rushmore, Badlands National Park, Reptile Gardens, the Crazy Horse Memorial, and more. And within a mile's distance, visitors can find exceptional golf and tennis facilities. Perfect for the business traveler and families alike, this outstanding hotel is just one reason to stop in Rapid City and spend a few days exploring everything the city has to offer.

Photo by Dennis Keim

Pete Lien & Sons Believes in Giving Back

To understand one of the region's leading mining and processing companies today—Pete Lien & Sons, Inc.—you have to look not only to the past, but also to the future. The success of this now third-generation family-owned business is a result of unwavering principles of honoring the past and planning for the future—a delicate balance at best, but particularly vital in this industry.

Founded in 1944 by Pete Lien Sr. and sons Chuck and Bruce, the company's inveterate history as a stable employer, a good steward of the land, and philanthropic partner to the community speaks to the Christian values passed on from one generation to the next. "Our father, Chuck, gave each of his nine children a pendant with the Bible passage Isaiah 51, 'Look to the rock from which you were hewn, and to the quarry from which you were digged,'" explains LaRece Lien, controller. "That reminds us to look to the past, take pride in the gifts and lessons we've been given, and pass these on to others. It's also appropriate to our industry."

"We try to do whatever is right, as opposed to what will make the most money."

According to five Lien siblings who are working in the family business, Chuck Lien began such lessons early on. While each may note a favorite that holds particular personal meaning, all point to the "Nine Liens Partnership" established by their father as the vehicle that taught them the most about free enterprise and working together. By doing so, Chuck planted the seeds of succession that would grow in the business culture that he, his brother, and his father carefully cultivated. Perhaps that's the underlying reason that Pete Lien & Sons, Inc., has beaten the national odds of family-owned businesses and prospered well into the third generation.

Photo by Rich Gabrielson

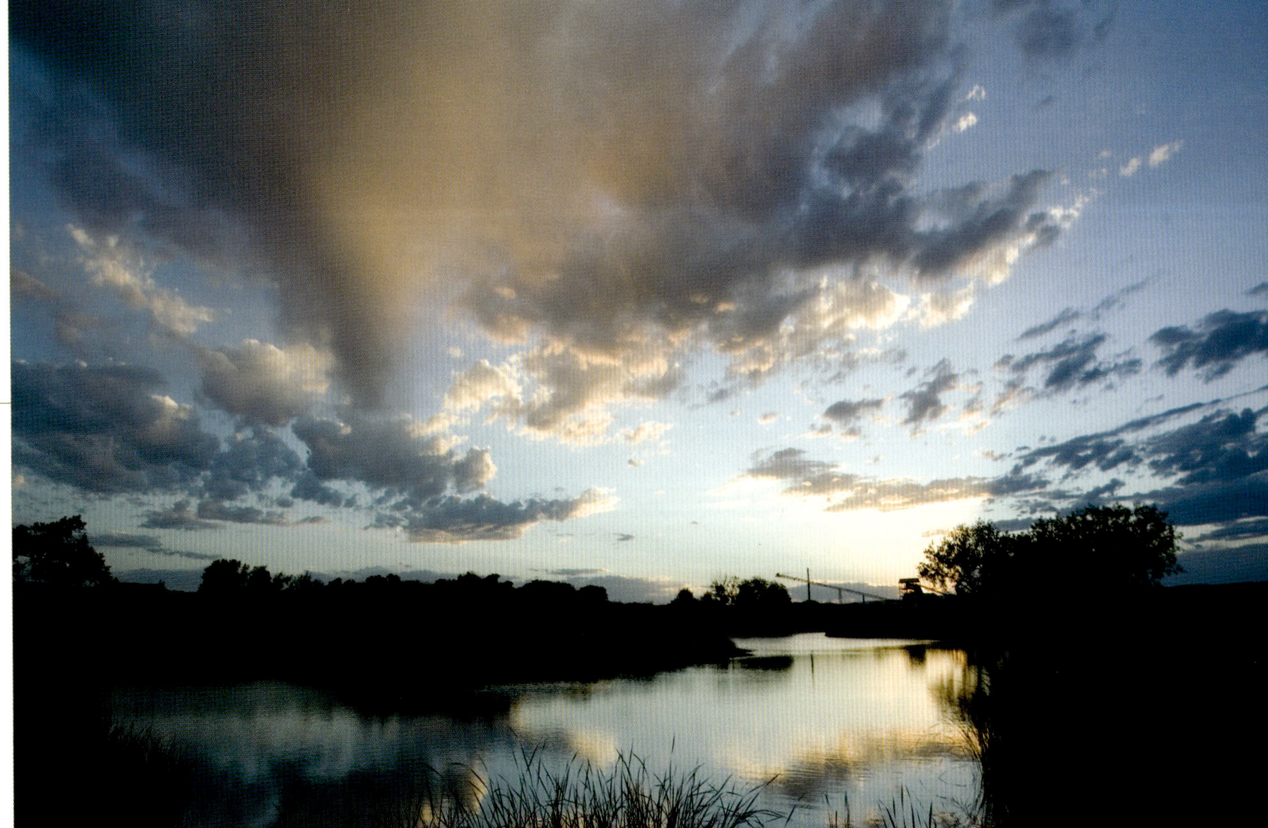

Committed to leaving the land in as good, if not better, condition than before mining, Pete Lien & Sons is renowned for its efforts toward reclaiming the land. Pete Lien, president, received the National Stone, Sand and Gravel Association's 2003 Environmental Steward Award, a coveted national honor recognizing the best efforts to care for the environment.

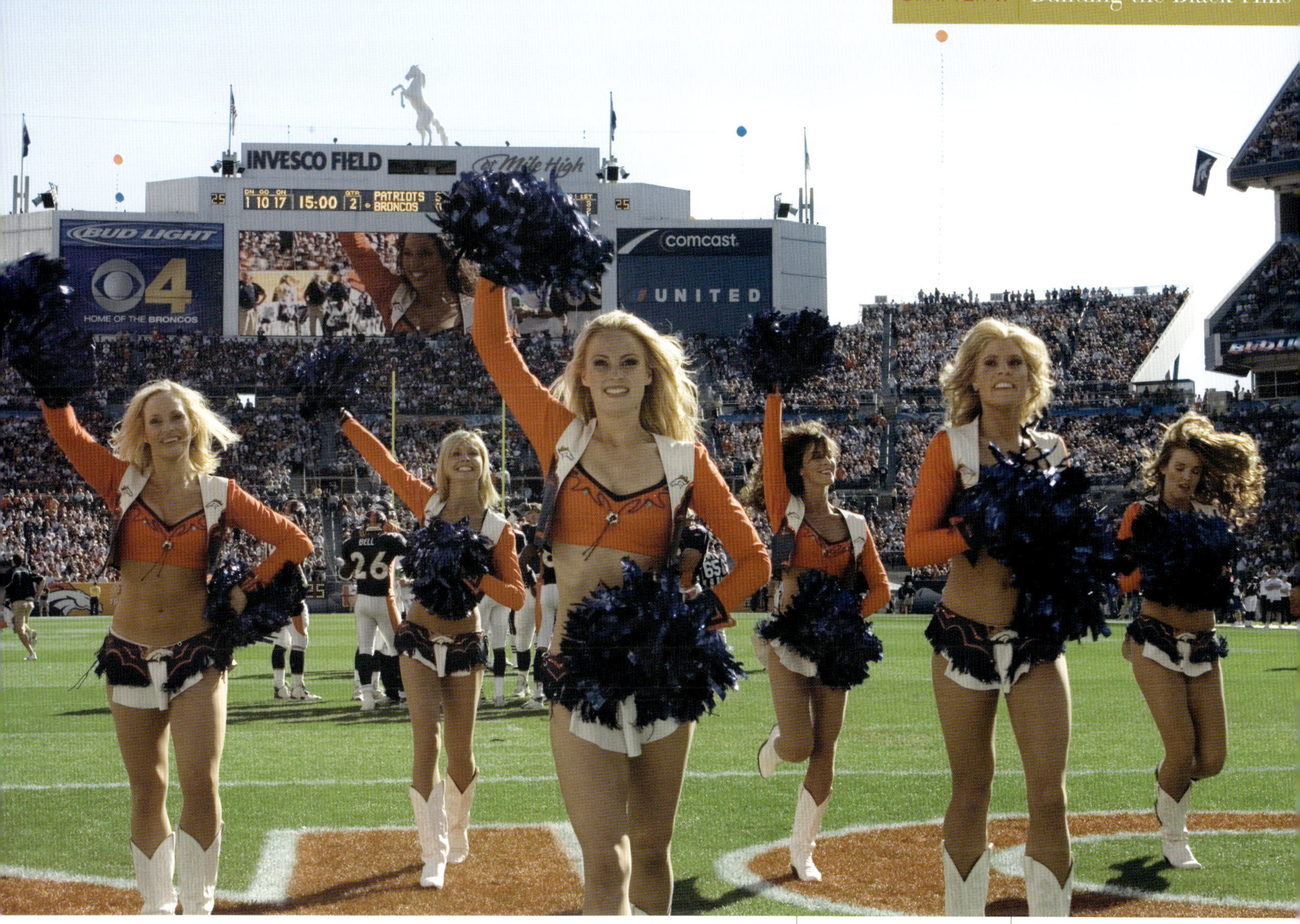

Photo by Rich Gabrielson

With the most talented fabricators in the region, Dakota Steel & Supply built the structural steel for the huge scoreboards at Invesco Field at Mile High Stadium, home to the Denver Broncos.

From sales of just sixteen thousand dollars in the founding year of 1944 to sales topping more than $100 million today, the mining and manufacturing companies of Pete Lien & Sons extract natural products, process the byproducts, and produce materials that touch nearly every sector of everyday life. "We build communities," says Sam Lien Brannan, vice president of corporate development. Pete Lien & Sons' products helped build Ellsworth Air Force Base, and in 1972 the company's products helped rebuild a community after a disastrous flood. Today, nearly every new bank building in Rapid City is built with fabricated steel from Pete Lien & Sons, and the company produces enough gypsum each day to concrete a mile of four-lane highway. In addition, the block and concrete divisions produce more than ten thousand different sizes, shapes, and colors of masonry block.

The byproducts of limestone, one of the key minerals mined in a four-state area, also have vital agricultural and environmental applications. For example, sales of high-calcium pulverized limestone feed more than 250,000 head of cattle, 30,000 turkeys and chickens, 10,000 hogs, and 1.8 million cats and dogs daily. Lime also treats water, waste, air, and solids, removing unwanted substances—clarifying and purifying the water and air—as well as allowing safe disposal of solids and waste.

While the companies under the umbrella of Pete Lien & Sons—Birdsall Sand & Gravel, Colorado Lien Company, Dakota Block Company, Dakota Steel & Supply, Trans Colorado Concrete, and Wyoming Lime Producers—are in the business of enhancing natural resources to valued products, the value of the land is always foremost. "We'd better be doing as we're going," explains Pete Lien, president. "The questions

Continued on page 114

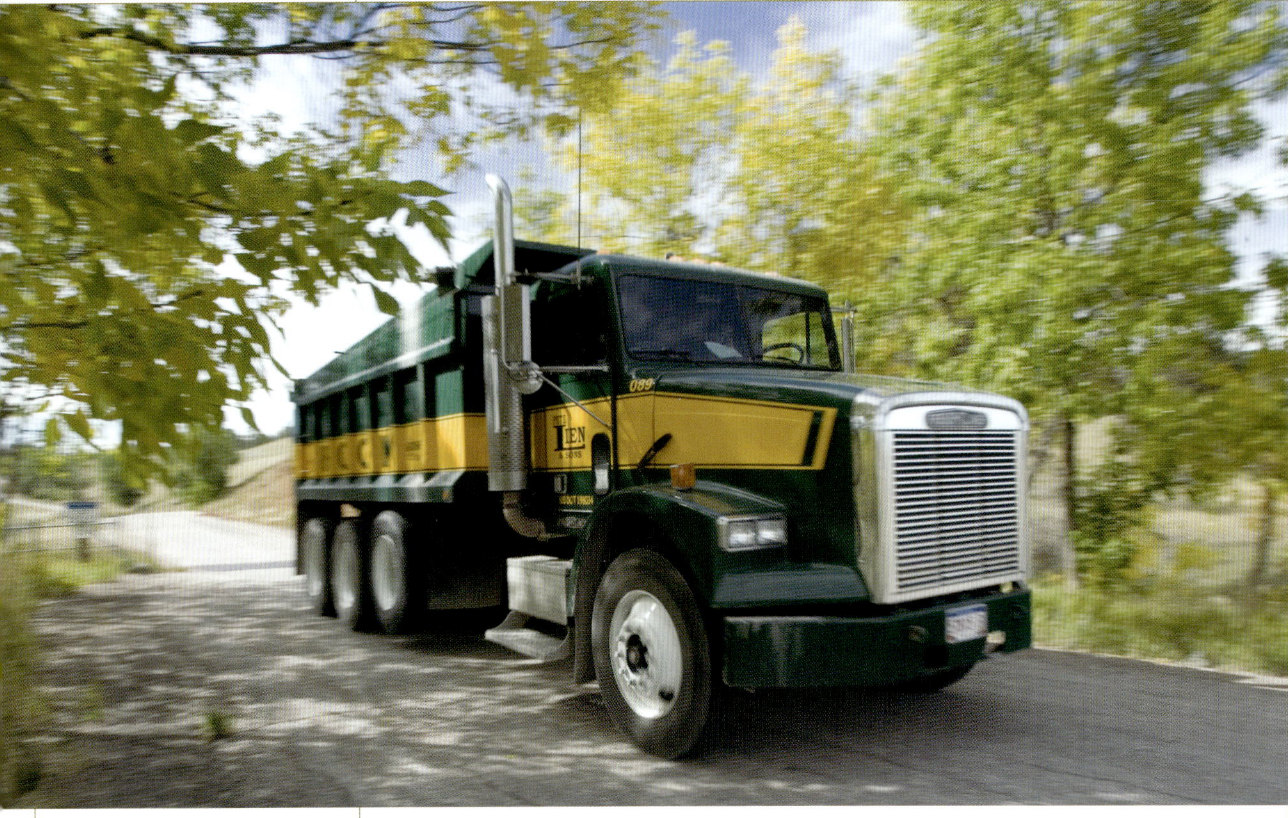

Green and yellow were chosen as the company colors for the strong farming heritage of the Lien family. Green symbolizes life and growth; yellow, the harvest and prosperity.

Photo by Rich Gabrielson

Continued from page 113

we always ask are, 'How do we leave the land? What's going to be a better use?'" With a proven track record of reclamation, it's no wonder Pete Lien & Sons receives numerous awards for land stewardship.

All the Liens believe in good stewardship for the company, for the land, and for the community. "Not only must the business succeed, but the community must succeed as well," says Chris Lien, president of Birdsall Sand & Gravel. "We try to do whatever is

Photo by Rich Gabrielson

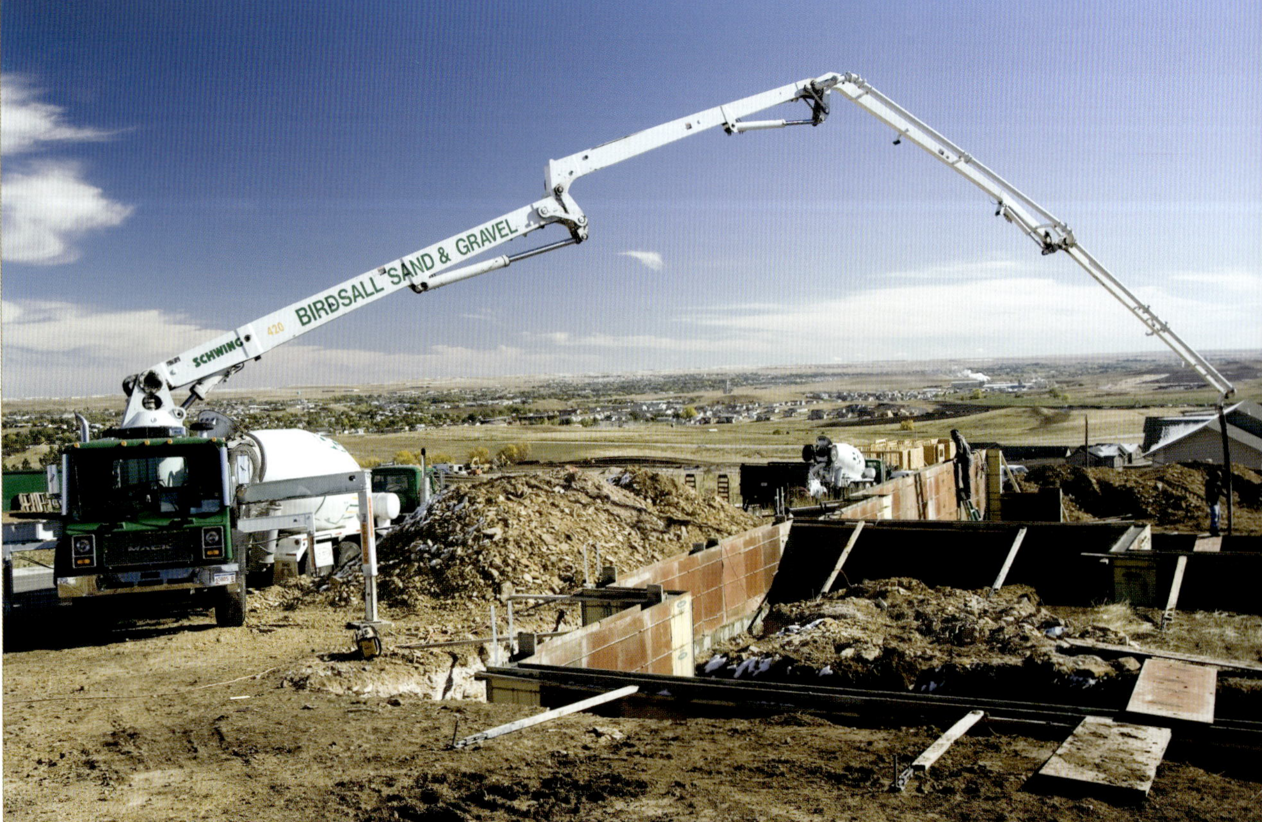

Birdsall Sand & Gravel—one of the Pete Lien & Sons companies—has been the leader in construction material supplies for the Black Hills for more than sixty years.

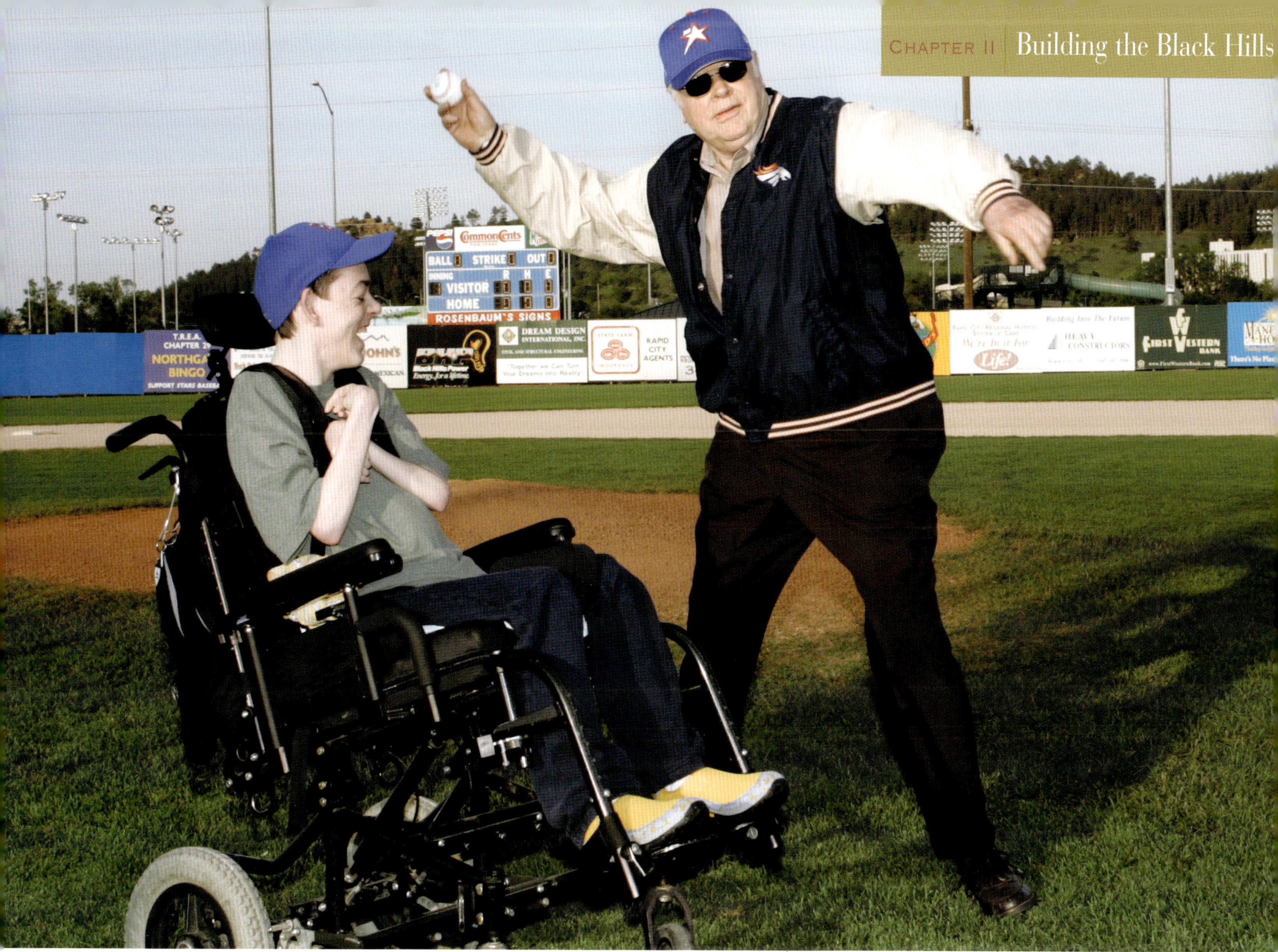

Photo by Rich Gabrielson

right, as opposed to what will make the most money." In other words, profit is also measured in goodwill: how the company treats employees, customers, suppliers, and the community. "To whom much is given, much is expected," echoes Suzy Lien Gabrielson, chief financial officer, who also chairs the corporate donations committee, which gives more than a quarter-million dollars annually to community organizations. "Giving back has always been a big part of Pete Lien & Sons." ❖

The mission of the founders for over sixty years is H.E.L.P.—to Have fun, to be Ethical, to stay Legal, and to make a Profit. Chuck Lien and his grandson Jake enjoy the fun by throwing the opening pitch for a game at Pete Lien Memorial Baseball Field.

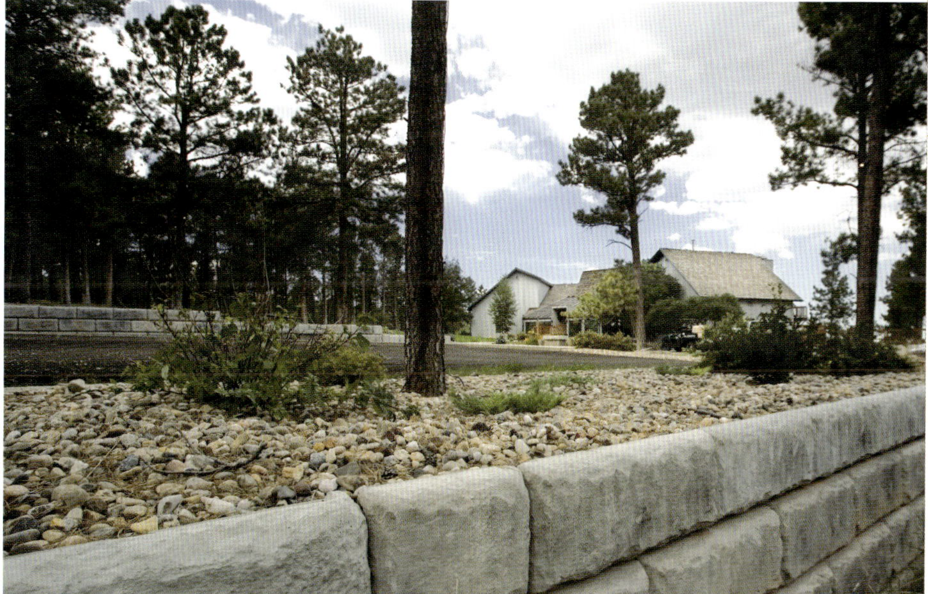

Natural and environmentally sensitive products, such as gravel and recycled material formed into this strong retaining wall product, replace the need for water-intensive grasses and minimize time needed for care and maintenance.

Photo by Rich Gabrielson

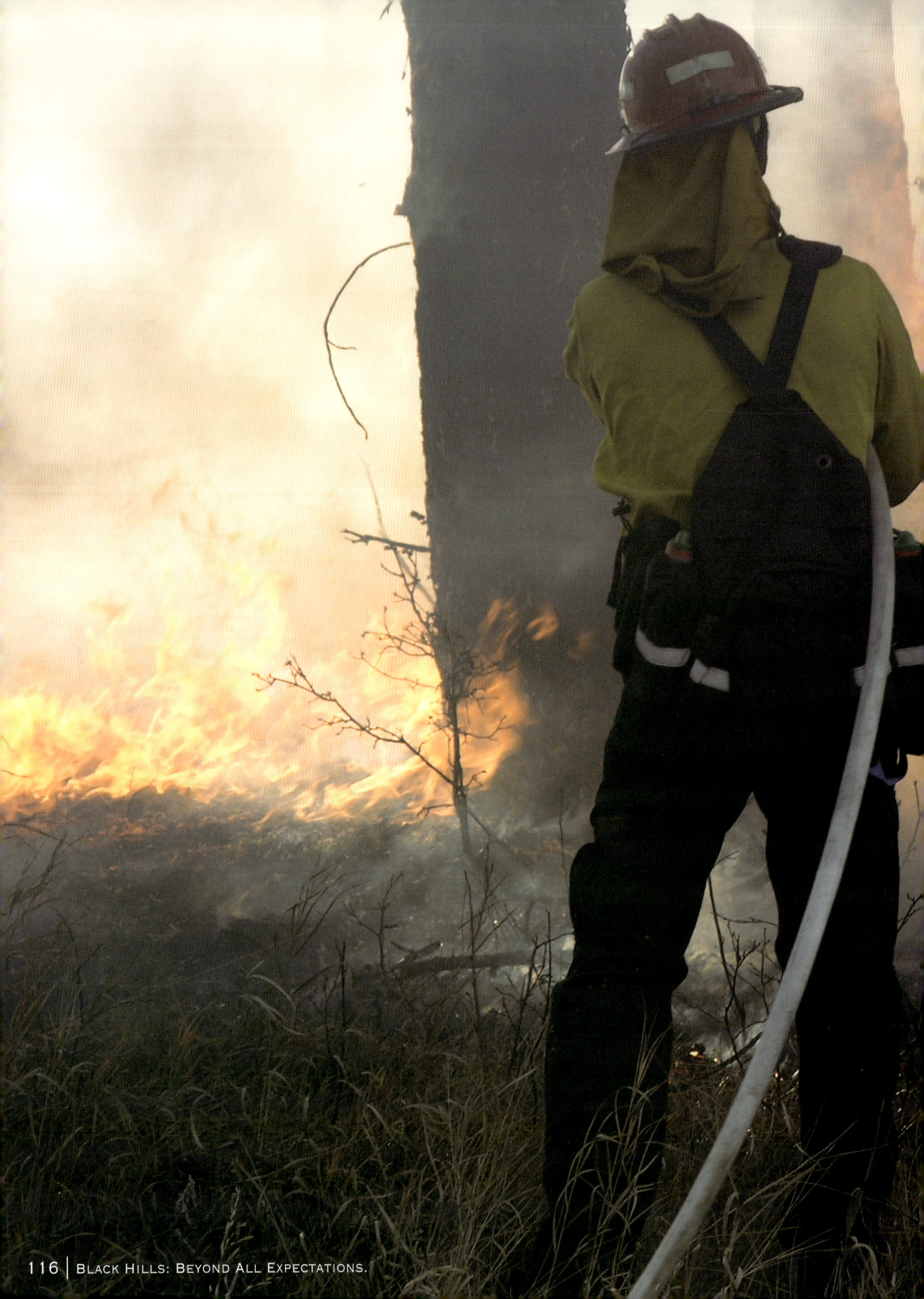

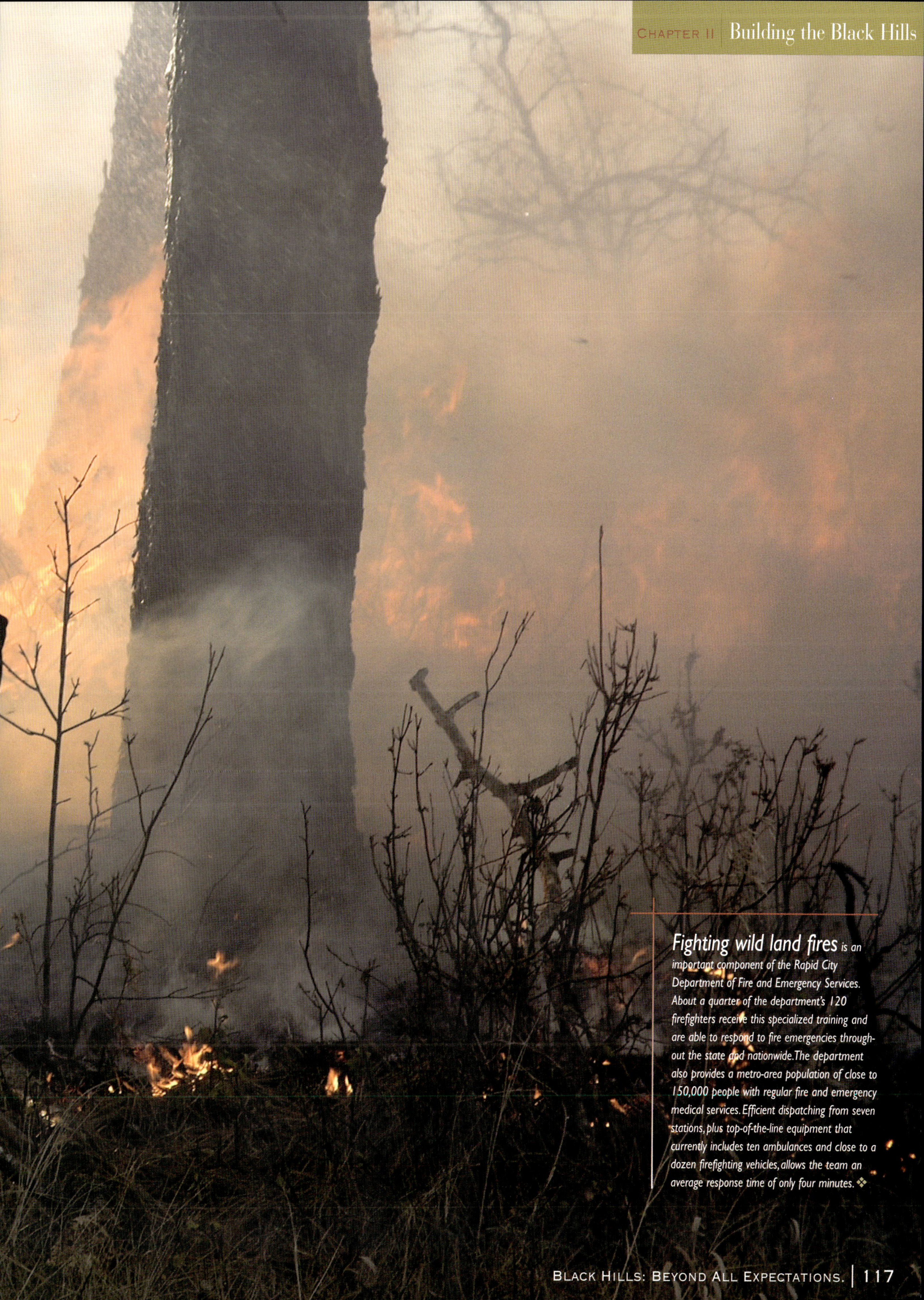

Fighting wild land fires *is an important component of the Rapid City Department of Fire and Emergency Services. About a quarter of the department's 120 firefighters receive this specialized training and are able to respond to fire emergencies throughout the state and nationwide. The department also provides a metro-area population of close to 150,000 people with regular fire and emergency medical services. Efficient dispatching from seven stations, plus top-of-the-line equipment that currently includes ten ambulances and close to a dozen firefighting vehicles, allows the team an average response time of only four minutes.* ❖

Cement Is Big Business in South Dakota

GCC Dacotah, Inc.'s cement plant dominates the skyline of northwestern Rapid City. The company's product—a million tons of cement produced annually—is the basic component of concrete, the most universally used building material for construction projects of South Dakota and the surrounding states. Roads, sidewalks, bridges, buildings, precast beams, concrete pipe, airport runways, and even oil wells all depend on concrete.

"GCC Dacotah's goal is to be the cement supplier of choice in this region of the U.S.," explains Steve Zellmer, president. "Our plant, which has been in operation since 1924, operates 24 hours a day, 365 days a year. We are proud to be a member of the Rapid City business community." The cement produced at the Rapid City plant is shipped 60 percent by rail and 40 percent by truck to distribution terminals in Sioux Falls, Brookings, and Watertown, South Dakota; Moorcroft and Casper, Wyoming; and Denver and Irondale, Colorado. All of the raw materials used in manufacturing cement—limestone, sand, shale, and iron ore—are quarried and produced locally.

"GCC Dacotah's goal is to be the cement supplier of choice in this region of the U.S."

GCC Dacotah employs more than two hundred people and is a subsidiary of parent company GCC, which operates a cement plant in Albuquerque, New Mexico; three plants in Mexico; and a coal mine in Durango, Colorado. ❖

Photo by Eric Francis

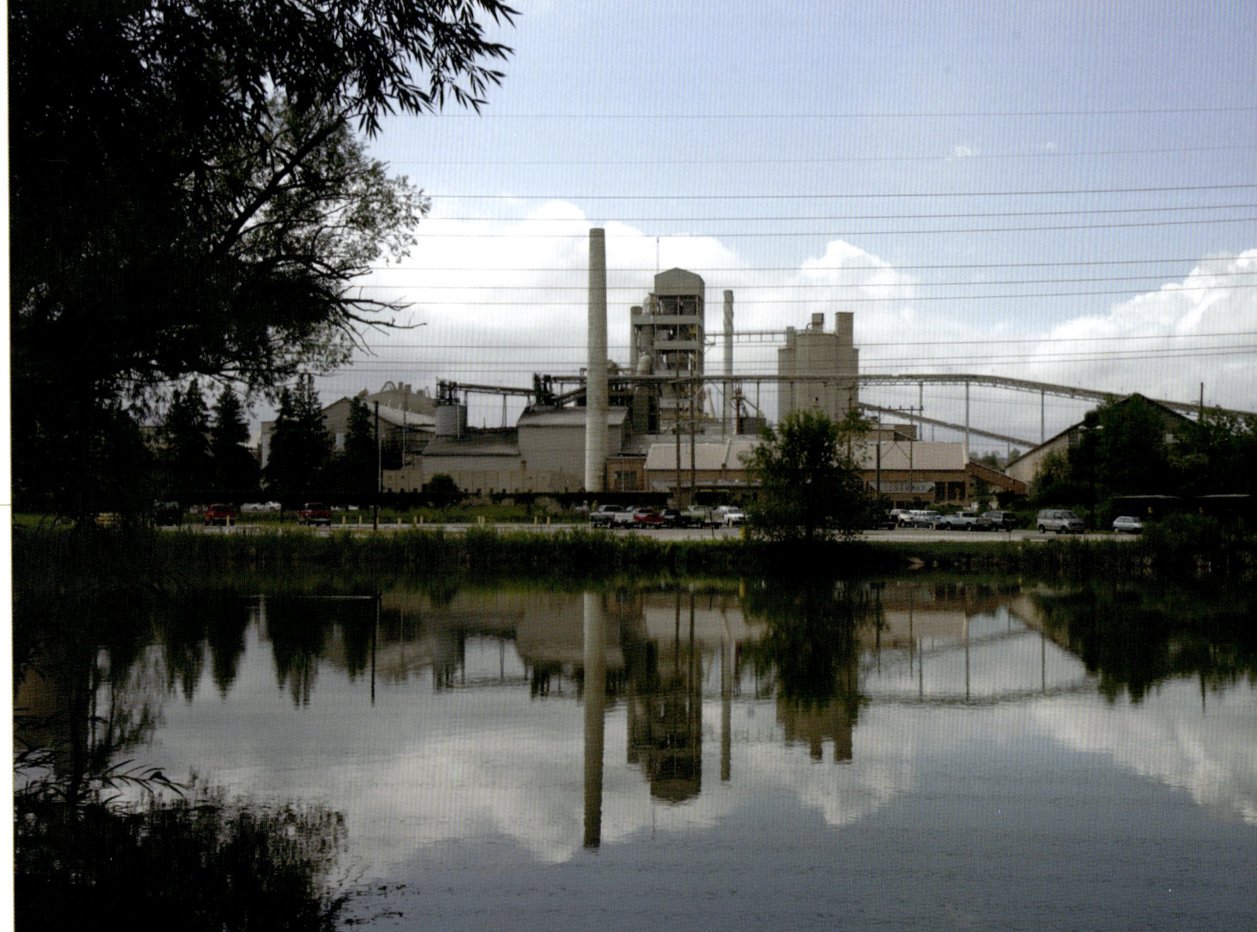

More than a million tons of the most universally used building material—cement—is produced annually at GCC Dacotah's Rapid City manufacturing facility.

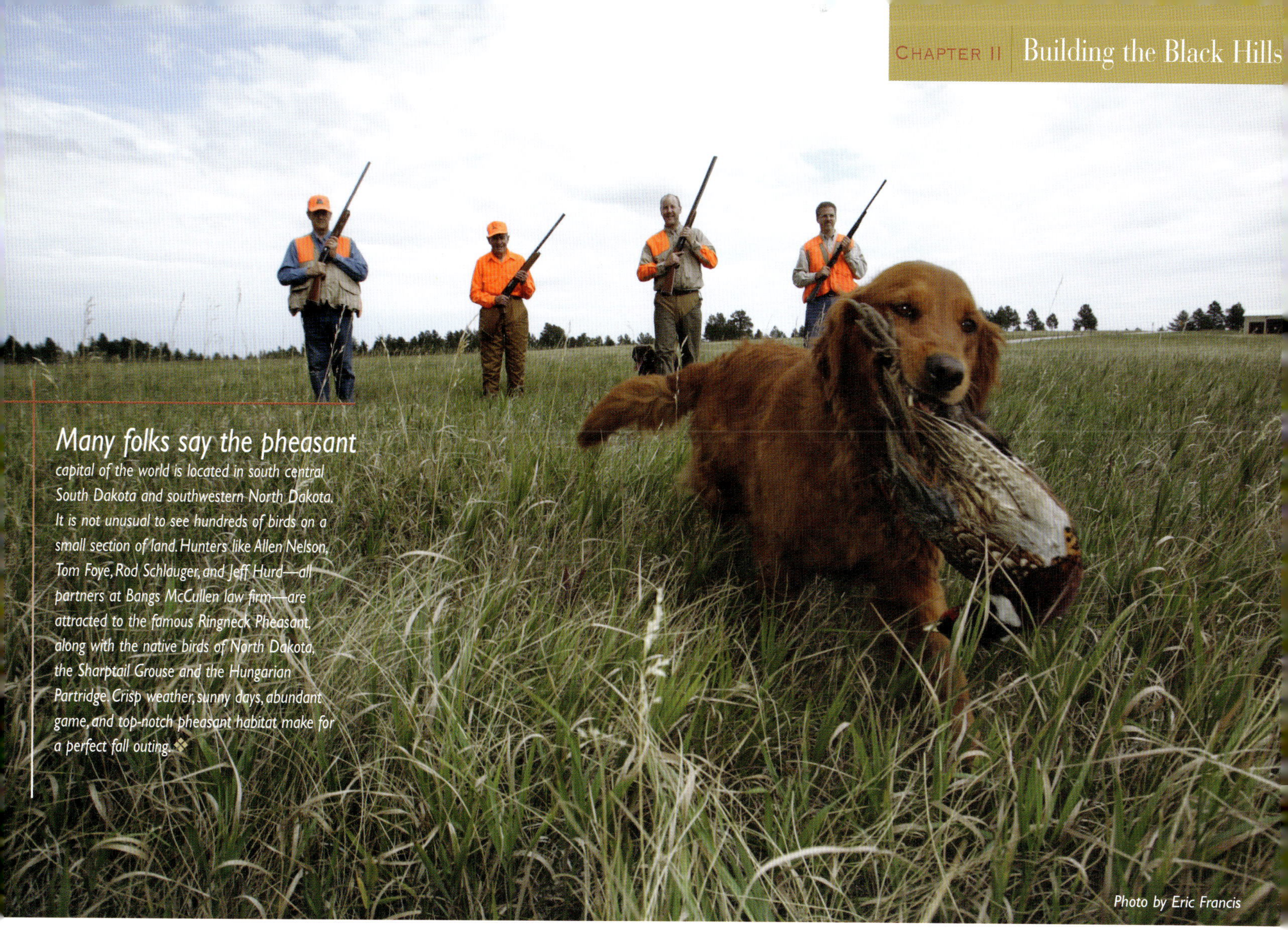

Many folks say the pheasant capital of the world is located in south central South Dakota and southwestern North Dakota. It is not unusual to see hundreds of birds on a small section of land. Hunters like Allen Nelson, Tom Foye, Rod Schlauger, and Jeff Hurd—all partners at Bangs McCullen law firm—are attracted to the famous Ringneck Pheasant, along with the native birds of North Dakota, the Sharptail Grouse and the Hungarian Partridge. Crisp weather, sunny days, abundant game, and top-notch pheasant habitat make for a perfect fall outing. ❖

Photo by Eric Francis

The Black Hills are some of the oldest mountains in North America. Because Black Hills National Forest takes up 1.2 million acres or about one-third of the state, this public land is—for the most part—unspoiled. To take advantage of the beauty of the area, outdoor recreation of all kinds abounds. Biking, golfing, fishing, horseback riding, hiking, camping, mountain climbing, and many more activities draw tourists and local residents alike. The Parks Division maintains approximately fifteen hundred acres of parkland in Rapid City, and Canyon Lake Park is one of the most popular, with an array of water sports and picnic facilities. Local builder Dean Kurtz Construction was engaged to create a picnic facility to fit on a knob in Canyon Lake. Through the imaginative use of concrete, they matched the natural color of the red stone found along the lake and created a facility that blends in perfectly with the surrounding landscape ... a perfect marriage of form and function. ❖

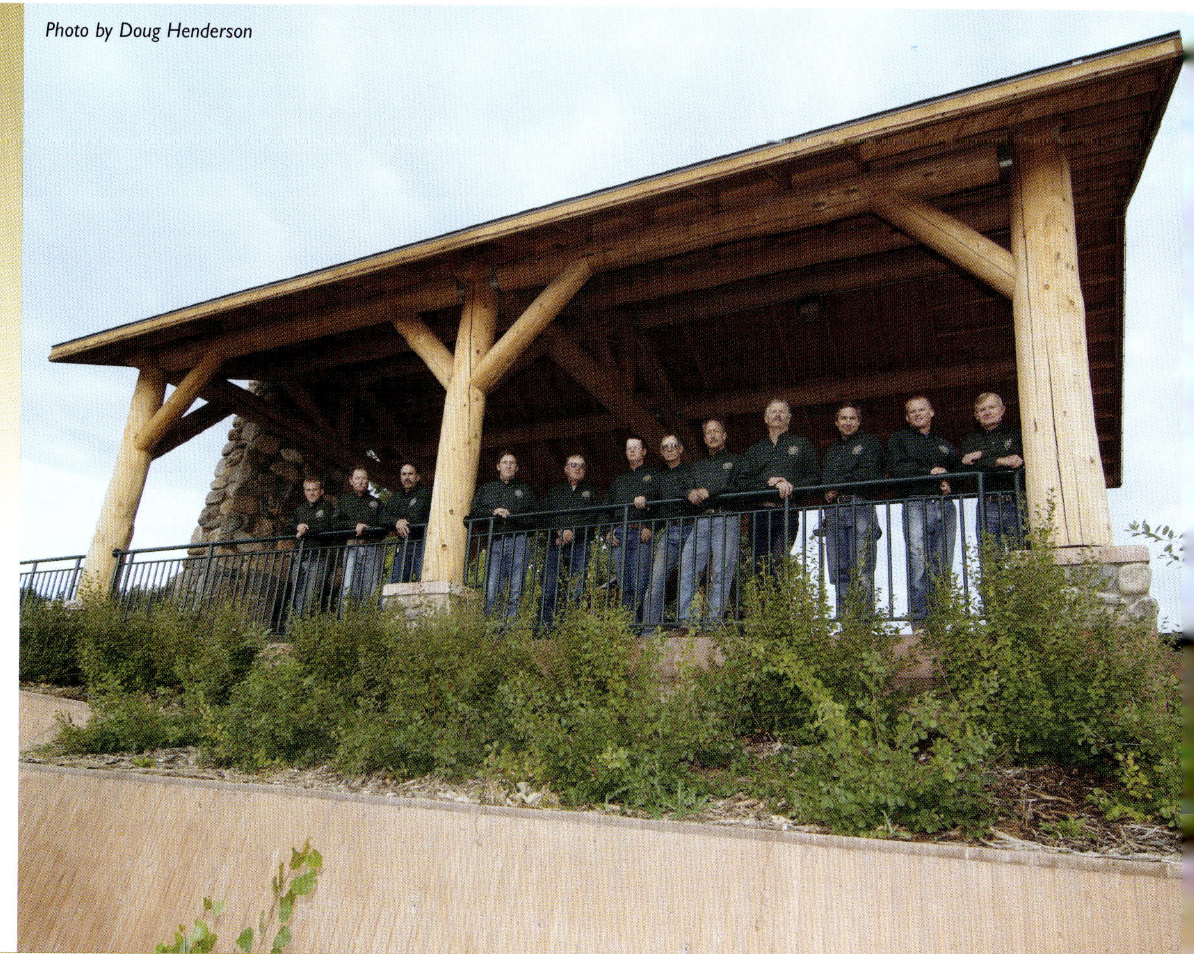
Photo by Doug Henderson

GPGN Scores High on Ethics and Results

Ask any professional at the law firm of Gunderson, Palmer, Goodsell & Nelson, LLP what they consider their firm's distinguishing quality, and they'll tell you without hesitation that it's the ability to listen.

"Senior attorneys will ask again and again, 'Are you really listening to the client?'" says the firm's legal administrator, Mike Gibson. "We are 100 percent client-focused, no question."

"We are 100 percent client-focused, no question."

Since its establishment in Rapid City in 1975, GPGN has used that focus to meet the business, financial, and legal objectives of clients throughout the Black Hills. The firm's relative youth, coupled with a hard-working, progressive outlook, appeals to clients who seek not just attorneys, but partners who continually anticipate needs and produce results. "We don't sit back on our laurels," says Gibson. "Our client orientation has expanded our services and, as a result, necessitates continual growth."

As a full-service law firm, GPGN's twenty-one attorneys and thirty support staff work together as a team both in and out of the courtroom. Clients depend on the firm to protect them against legal challenges ranging from administrative law to workers' compensation, and to serve as savvy litigators should any matter go to court. In either case, clients can rest assured that GPGN's attorneys will provide successful results while maintaining the highest ethical standards in the practice of law.

Photo by Doug Henderson

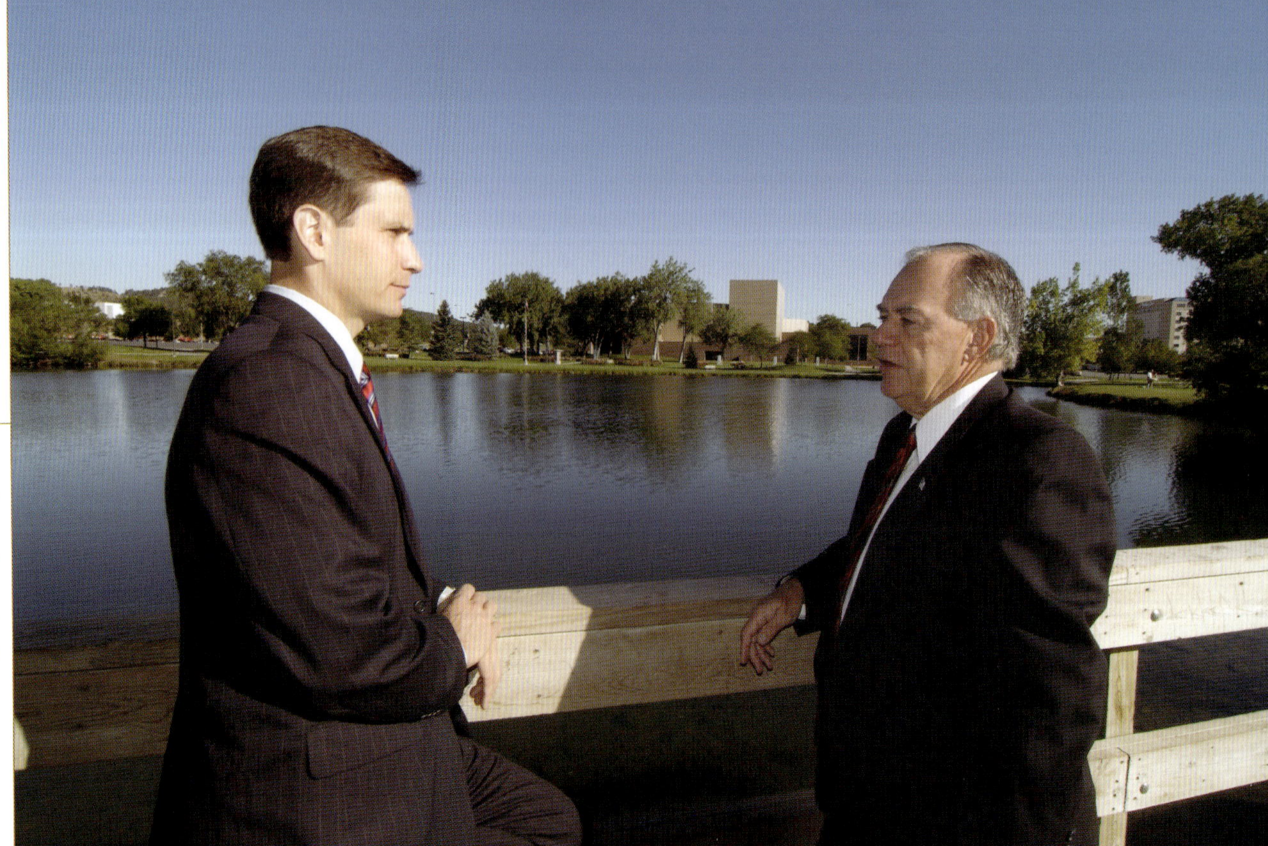

At GPGN Law, community involvement is not an obligation; it's a privilege. Staff and professionals both donate their time and money to a variety of programs. Here, attorney and Rapid City Chamber of Commerce board member David Lust (left) discusses community affairs with Chamber president Jim McKeon.

In the realm of complex civil litigation, the firm has years of demonstrated experience in class actions, insurance defense, personal injury, product liability, and medical malpractice. Likewise, its experience in business organization, real estate, and probate/trust administration allows the firm to confidently guide its business clients through all phases of growth, from mergers and acquisitions, recapitalizations, and antitrust issues to estate planning and business succession.

Attorney credentials include membership in the Pennington County, South Dakota, and American Bar Associations, as well as in the Harmonie Group, a nationwide network of leading law firms that provides GPGN clients with access to proficient legal counsel in all fifty states. The firm's attorneys are also regularly featured in *The Best Lawyers in America*, the U.S. legal profession's preeminent referral guide.

As devoted to the Black Hills community as to its clients, GPGN lends its leadership talent to a variety of local and regional causes and organizations. The firm boasts board involvement in the Girl Scouts, Junior Achievement, Rapid City Area Chamber of Commerce, the Rapid City Arts Council, and the Northern Plains Eye Foundation, to name a few. Likewise, GPGN attorneys volunteer time and as trainers for Teen Court and as legal advisors to Youth and Family Services.

At thirty-plus years young, Gunderson, Palmer, Goodsell & Nelson is one of Rapid City's most progressive law firms, offering clients effective legal solutions from an innovative and focused team of professionals and support staff. Couple this ability to capably and ethically serve clients at a variety of levels with a demonstrated concern for the community at large, and you have what is undoubtedly one of the region's standout legal firms. ❖

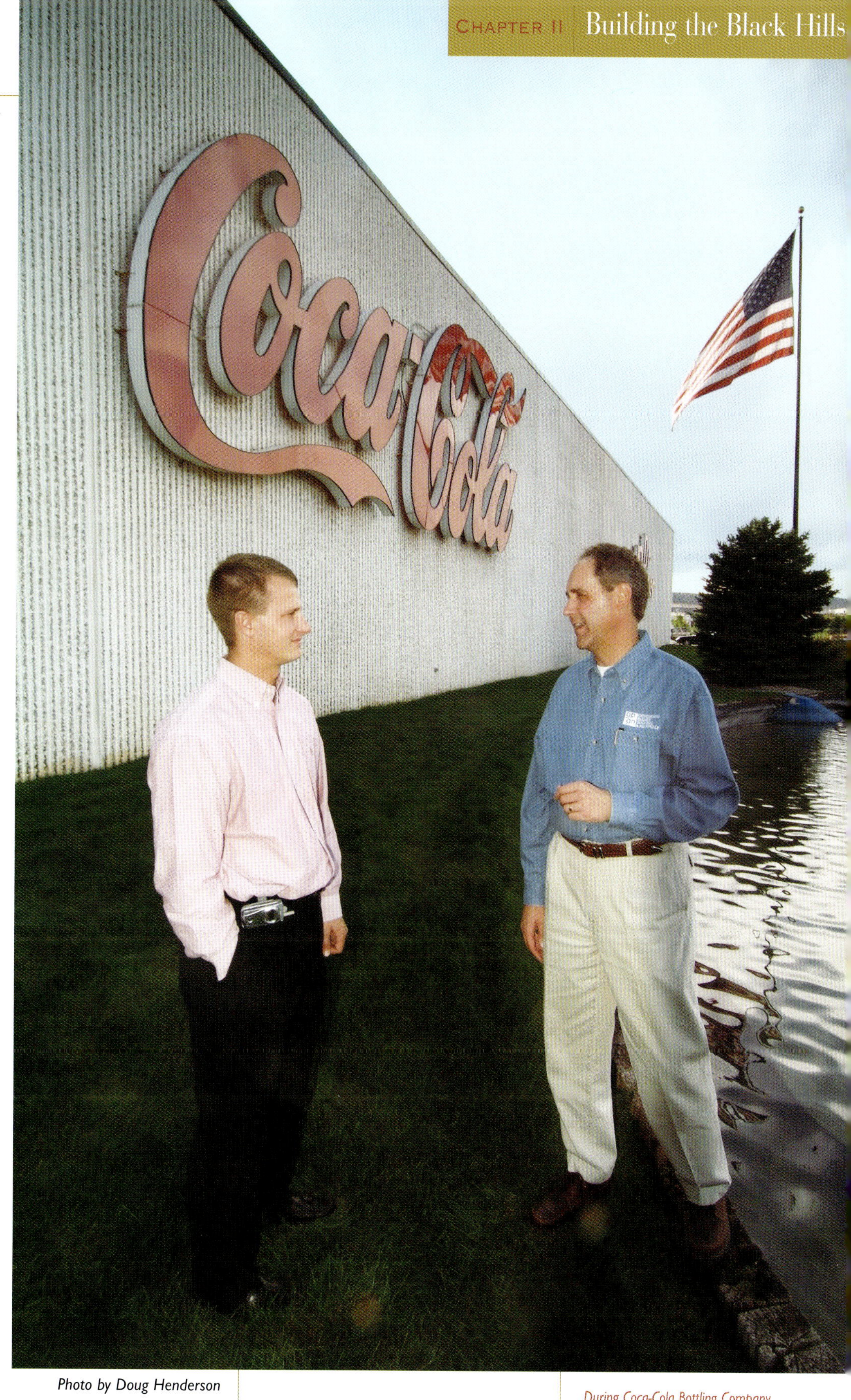

Photo by Doug Henderson

During Coca-Cola Bottling Company High Country's expansion, GPGN Law attorney Patrick Goetzinger (right) frequently consulted with the bottling company's president and COO, Trevor Messinger. The law firm assists in guiding companies such as Coca-Cola Bottling through complex business matters, including expansions, mergers, acquisitions, and divestitures.

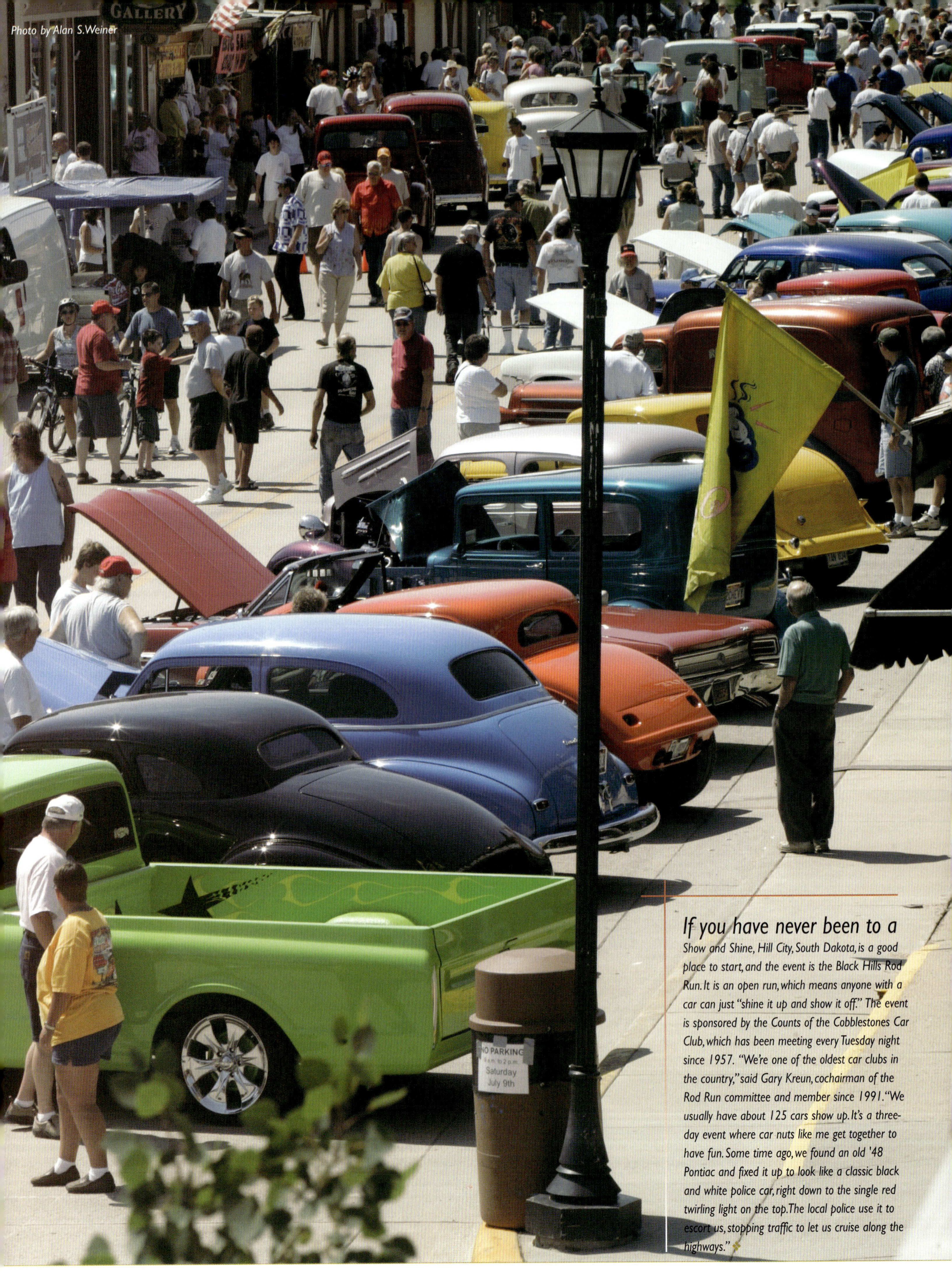

Photo by Alan S. Weiner

If you have never been to a

Show and Shine, Hill City, South Dakota, is a good place to start, and the event is the Black Hills Rod Run. It is an open run, which means anyone with a car can just "shine it up and show it off." The event is sponsored by the Counts of the Cobblestones Car Club, which has been meeting every Tuesday night since 1957. "We're one of the oldest car clubs in the country," said Gary Kreun, cochairman of the Rod Run committee and member since 1991. "We usually have about 125 cars show up. It's a three-day event where car nuts like me get together to have fun. Some time ago, we found an old '48 Pontiac and fixed it up to look like a classic black and white police car, right down to the single red twirling light on the top. The local police use it to escort us, stopping traffic to let us cruise along the highways."

Photo Eric Francis

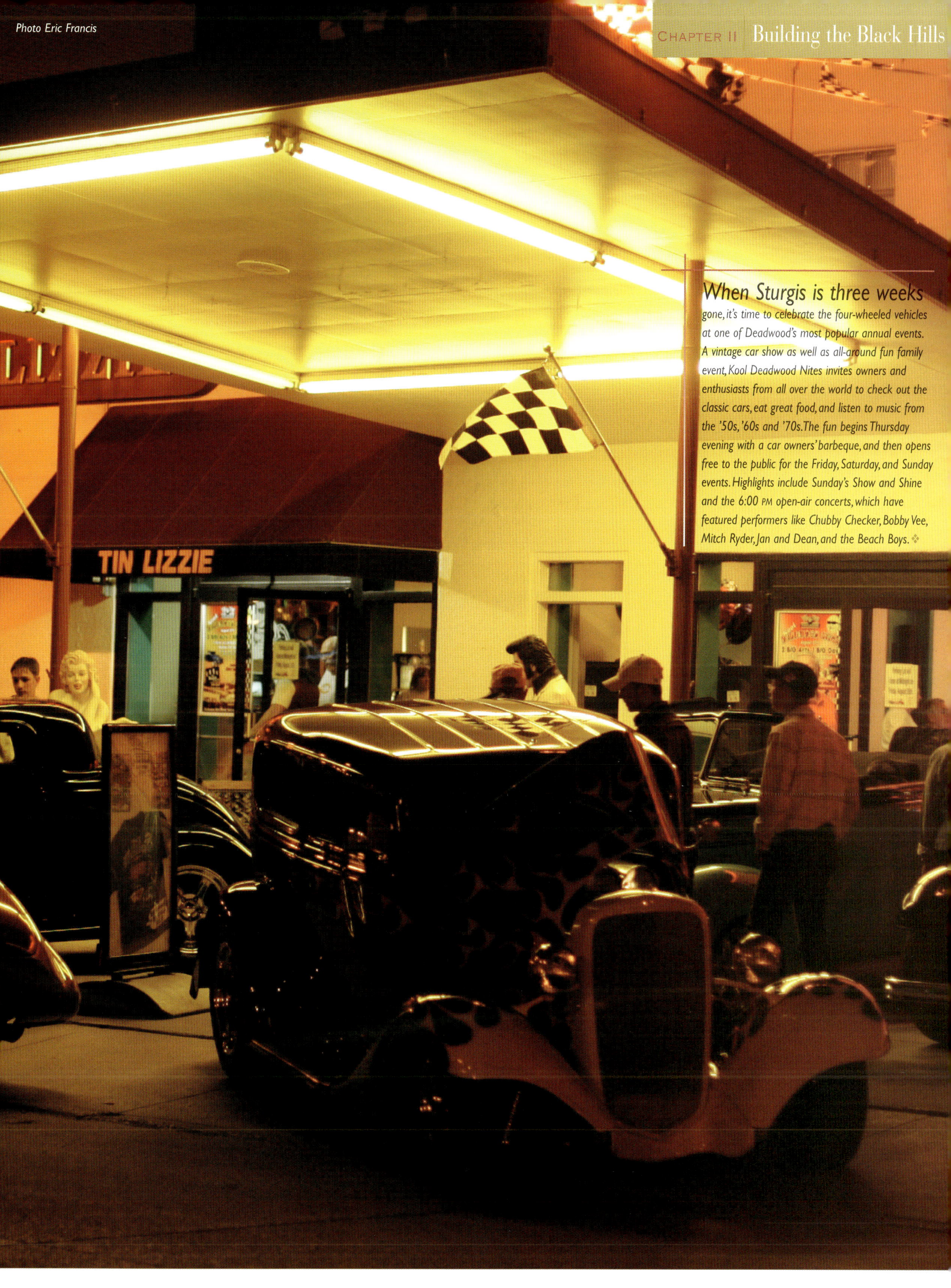

When Sturgis is three weeks gone, it's time to celebrate the four-wheeled vehicles at one of Deadwood's most popular annual events. A vintage car show as well as all-around fun family event, Kool Deadwood Nites invites owners and enthusiasts from all over the world to check out the classic cars, eat great food, and listen to music from the '50s, '60s and '70s. The fun begins Thursday evening with a car owners' barbeque, and then opens free to the public for the Friday, Saturday, and Sunday events. Highlights include Sunday's Show and Shine and the 6:00 PM open-air concerts, which have featured performers like Chubby Checker, Bobby Vee, Mitch Ryder, Jan and Dean, and the Beach Boys.

PrairieWave Communications Sets Pace in Technology

PrairieWave Communications believes service and communications are inseparable. "We know the importance of listening to our customers," says Craig A. Anderson, CEO and chairman. "They want a pleasant, no-hassle phone, cable, and Internet experience. They want relevant technology made easy. They want reasonable charges for excellent services. That's how we do business, and that's why so many customers trust us for their communications needs."

Founded in 1902 as the Hurley Telephone Company, PrairieWave Communications set the pace in this last century for advanced communications service in South Dakota: the first all-buried phone system, the first telephone company to expand into cable TV, the first independent long distance provider, the first hybrid fiber/coaxial cable network, the first in the region to provide no-charge, on-net long distance calling, the first to offer spam and virus filter, and the first to launch Video On Demand service.

> "We're not just a phone, cable, and Internet company. We're a complete communications provider."

With the 2005 purchase of another communications leader—Black Hills FiberCom—PrairieWave Communications strengthens its position as one of the largest and most successful facilities-based broadband providers in the region. "'Facilities-based' means we use our own phone, cable, and Internet lines instead of renting access from other companies. This allows us to offer lower prices and maintain all-important quality control over the technology that supplies our services to our customers," Anderson explains. "In summary, we're not just a phone, cable, and Internet company. We're a complete communications provider." ❖

Photo by Doug Henderson

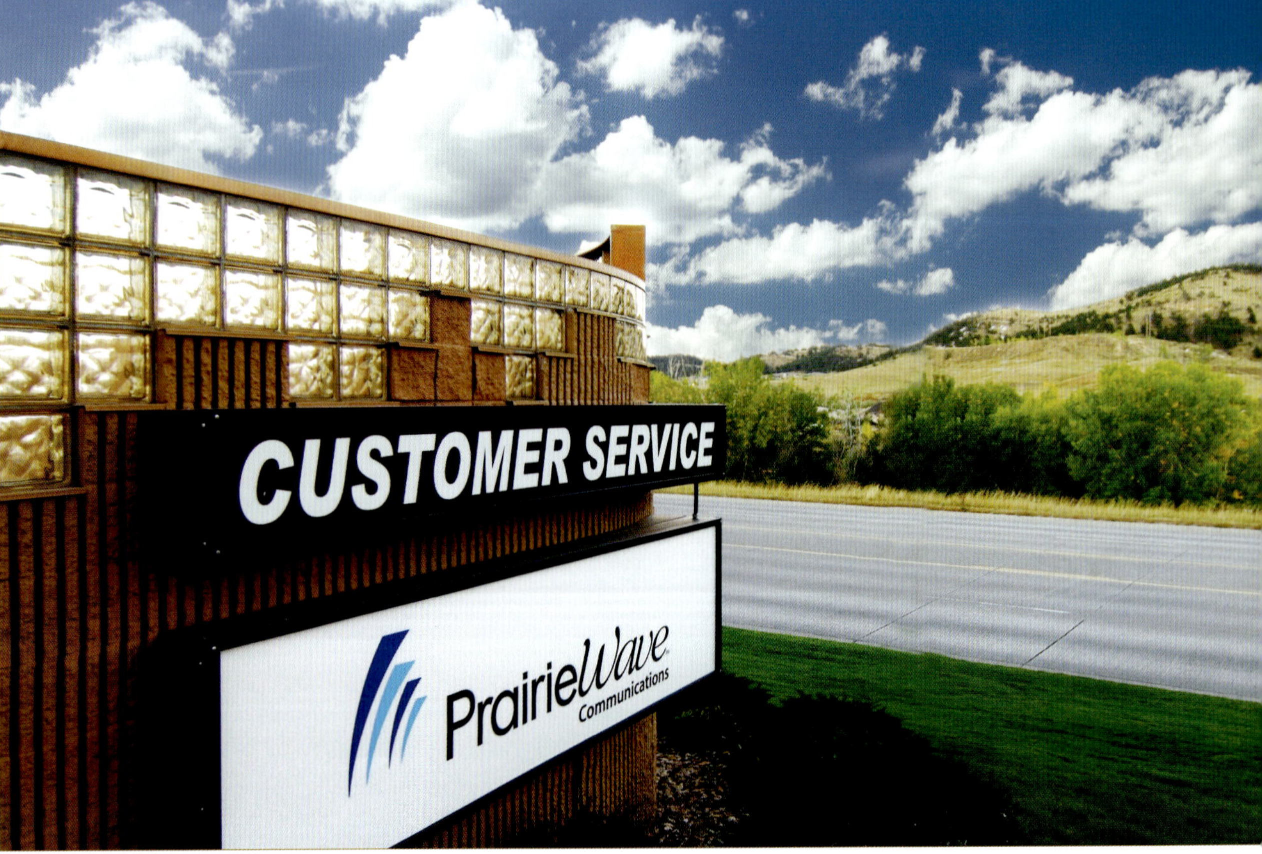

PrairieWave's customer service office in Rapid City is one way the company stays focused on a local presence. By providing reasonably priced advanced communications services to homes and businesses, PrairieWave supports economic development and strives to enhance quality of life.

FREE Ice Water!

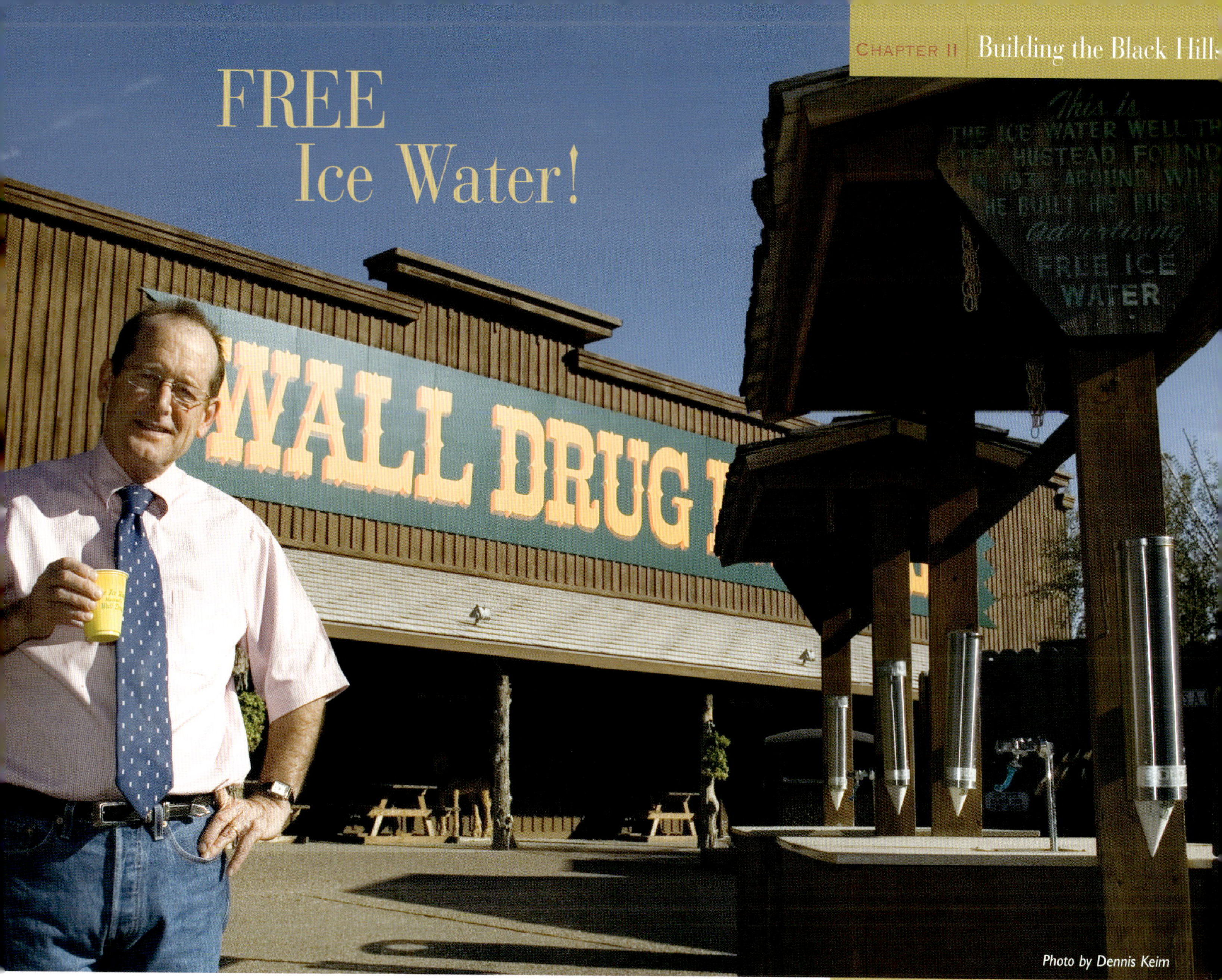

Photo by Dennis Keim

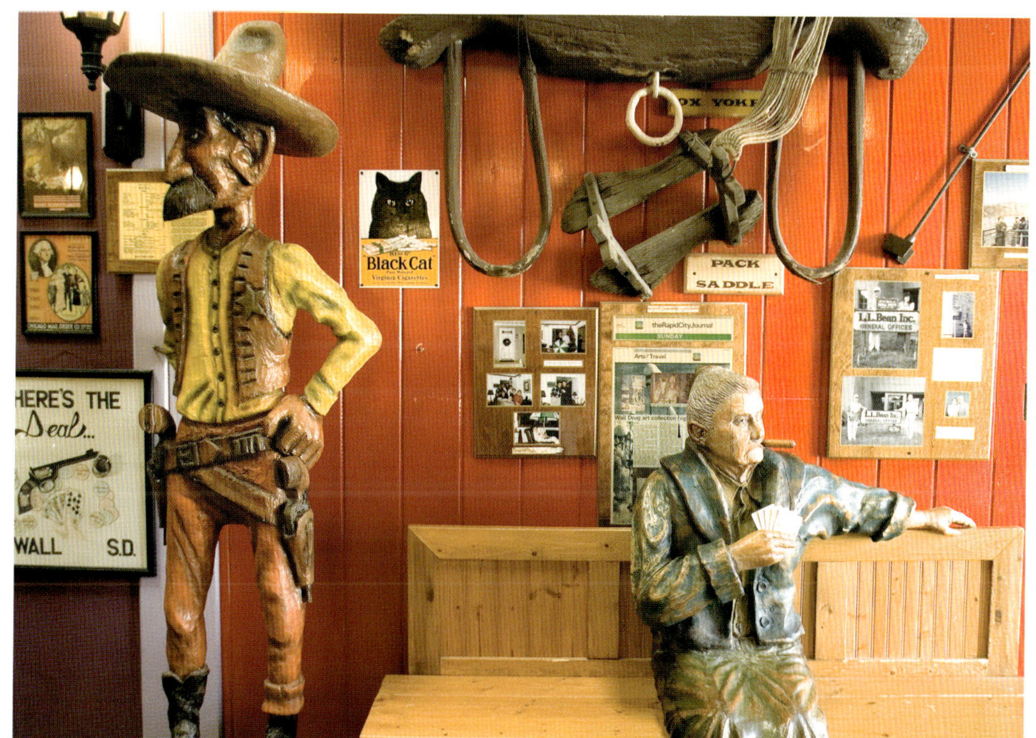

Photo by Dennis Keim

In 1931 Ted and Dorothy Hustead purchased a small drugstore in the town of Wall, located at the edge of the Dakota Badlands. It was the height of the Depression, and everyone thought they were crazy. Indeed, five years later, the Wall Drug Store was languishing. Then Dorothy got an idea. She told her husband, "It's 106 degrees outside. Why don't we advertise free ice water?" Sure enough, it worked. Travelers headed to area attractions stopped for the free water, but ended up purchasing other things. Today grandson Teddy Hustead (shown) oversees the business, which has become an attraction in and of itself, with a restaurant, gift shops, pharmacy museum, and what Hustead calls one of the best private collections of western art in the country. Of course, the ice water is still free. That's because Hustead is dedicated to preserving his grandparents' legacy of perseverance and customer service, saying, "I'm challenged every day to be a good steward for this business for a potential fourth generation." ❖

"Approachable" Law Firm Takes Relationships Seriously

"Approachable" is not a word generally associated with law firms, but for Bangs, McCullen, Butler, Foye & Simmons, it is the perfect description. Clients who enter the building are frequently met by an attorney coming down the hall, greeted with a pleasant, "Can I help you?" or "Come with me, and I'll take you there," followed by a friendly conversation about some local event.

"Although there are some elements of 'old school' about us, we never lose sight of the fact that we're in a service industry," said Jeff Hurd, partner. "The outcome of our representation is important, of course, but we have to deliver quality service in a manner that makes people feel comfortable and at ease."

"Although there are some elements of 'old school' about us, we never lose sight of the fact that we're in a service industry."

Another aspect of their accessibility is the firm's team approach. "Our clients are introduced not only to the attorneys who will be working with them, but also to the receptionists, secretaries, runners, and paralegals, because everyone is part of the team," said Allen Nelson, managing partner.

However, do not be misled by the relaxed atmosphere. Bangs McCullen has a long and proud history of providing authoritative legal counsel for individuals and businesses throughout South Dakota, Wyoming, Nebraska, North Dakota, Minnesota, and Iowa. What began as a one-person firm in the 1800s has grown into one of the most recognized and respected law firms in the area.

Photo by Eric Francis

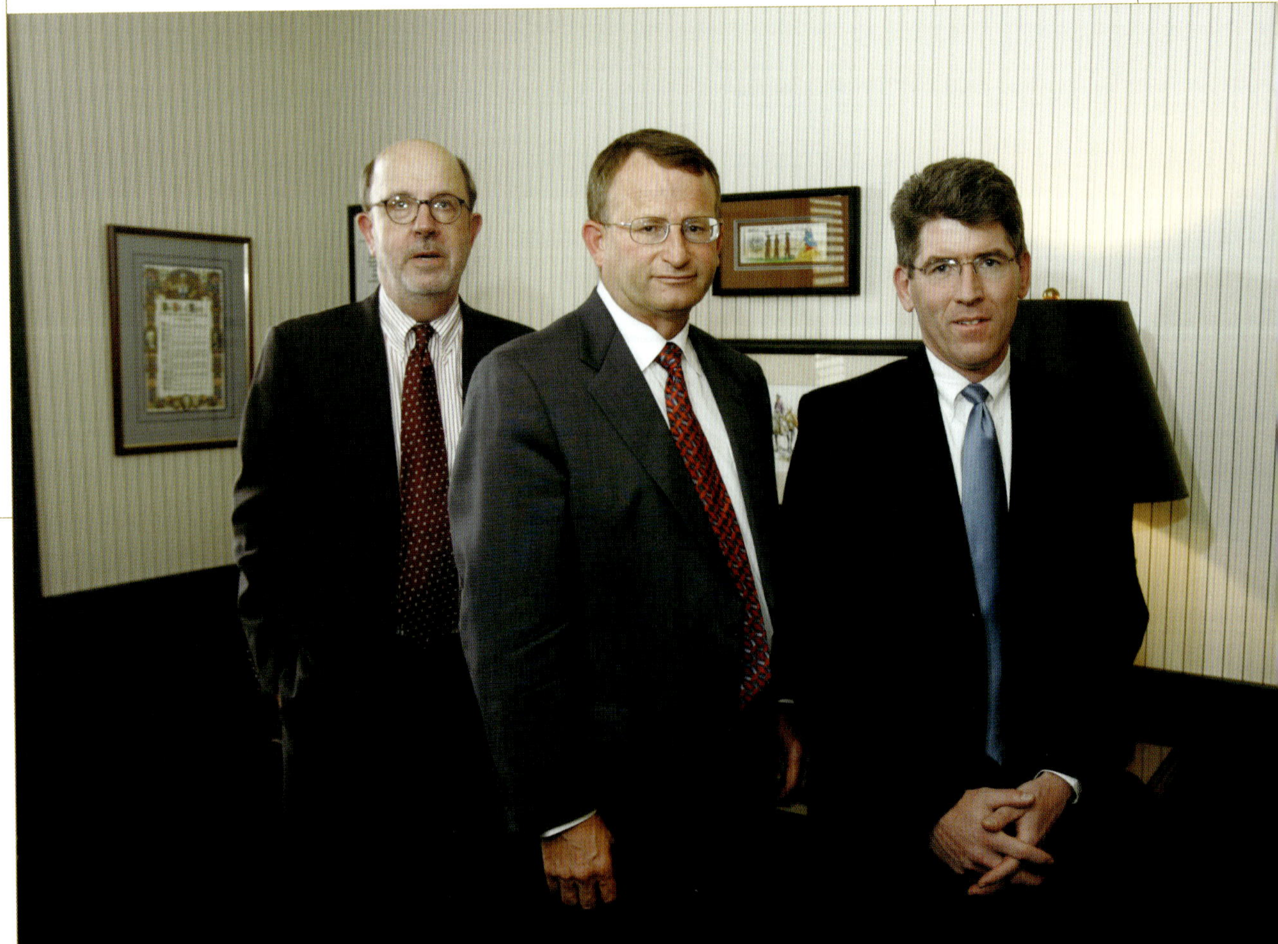

Since the 1800s, the law firm of Bangs McCullen has been providing legal counsel throughout South Dakota, Wyoming, Nebraska, North Dakota, Minnesota, and Iowa. Partners Chuck Riter, Terry Hofer, and Dan Duffy work together to carry on that tradition.

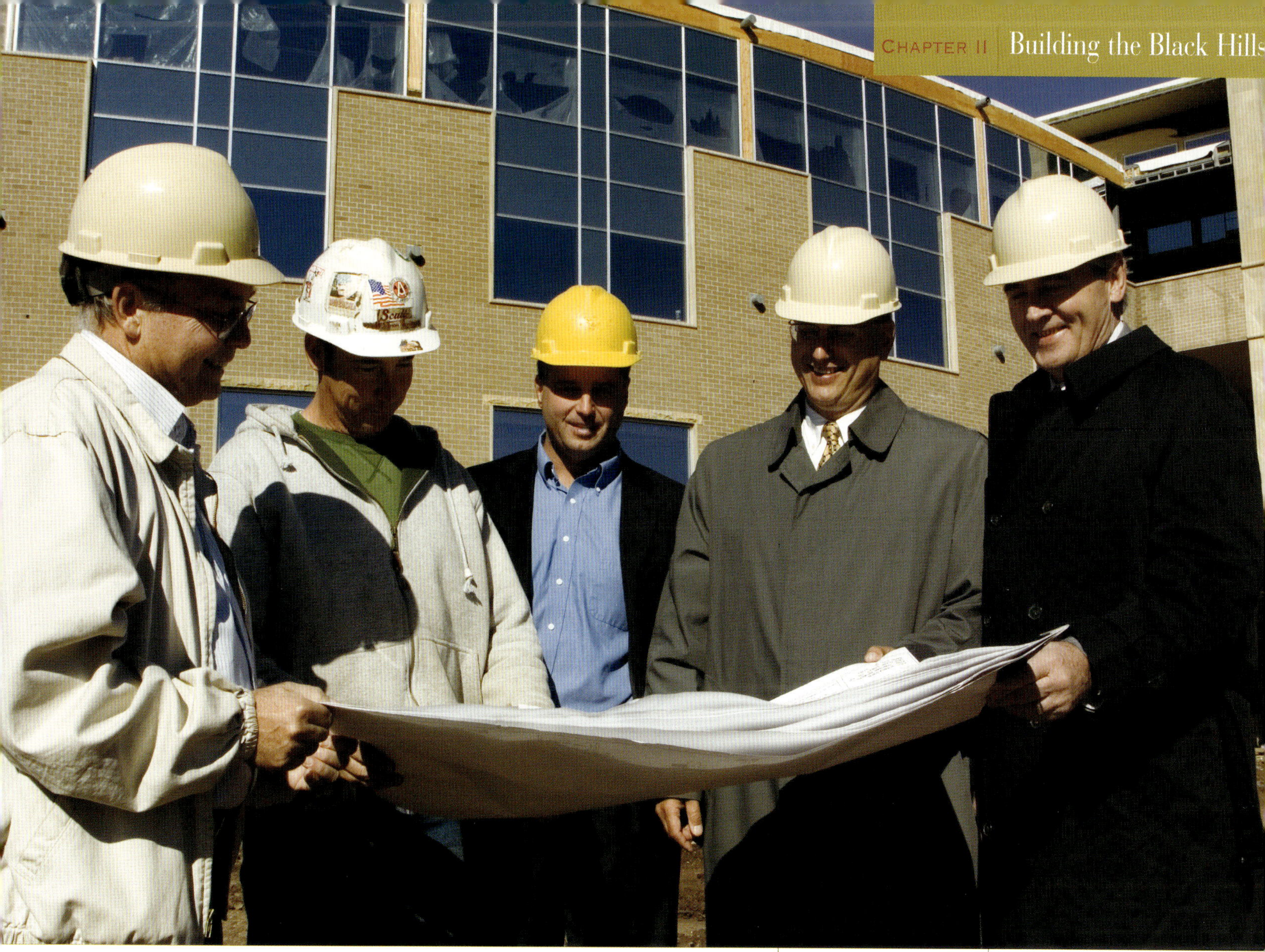

Photo by Dennis Keim

Dan Carlson (second from left), the foreman on the project, shows blueprints to four partners from Bangs McCullen. The firm will occupy the fourth floor in the new building, which is the first thing people see when they come into Rapid City via Exit 57 off Interstate 90. However, it is the expanse of windows—which were in very short supply in the firm's previous location—that is of real interest to Mike Hickey, Steve Nolan, John Raforth, and Jim Hurley.

The firm is structured to serve two distinct but overlapping areas of practice: planning and counseling for businesses, estates, trusts, and tax issues, and litigating a broad range of disputes. Bangs McCullen can accurately be described as a full-service firm, able to handle all kinds of legal issues with specialized knowledge in federal, state, and local tax law; estate planning and administration; trust work; and health-care, construction, and business litigation.

Bangs McCullen also has in-house technology to process large numbers of documents in a way that makes information accessible and easy to refer to during case preparation. The significance of this becomes clear when you realize that some cases may involve as many as one hundred thousand pages of documents.

Another asset is stability. Many of the partners have known each other since law school; one friendship even goes back to the second grade. The advantage to clients is that businesses and individuals often establish a relationship with attorneys in the firm that lasts for decades.

The firm is always looking for new ways to meet their clients' needs. Several years ago they opened a branch in Sioux Falls, extending their services to the eastern part of the state. More recently they moved into a new building, which provided much-needed centralized storage, more functional workspace, modern décor, additional parking, and windows. "Our former space was connected on both sides so only the offices on the ends of the building had windows. Of course, we love the new space, but our clients seem to like the new look, too," said Greg Erlandson, partner.

Whether it is a friendly greeting, specialized knowledge, the team approach, stability, technology, or even brighter office space, it takes many strengths and a lot of hard work behind the scenes to consistently go above and beyond for their clients by practicing Law @ The Next Level. ❖

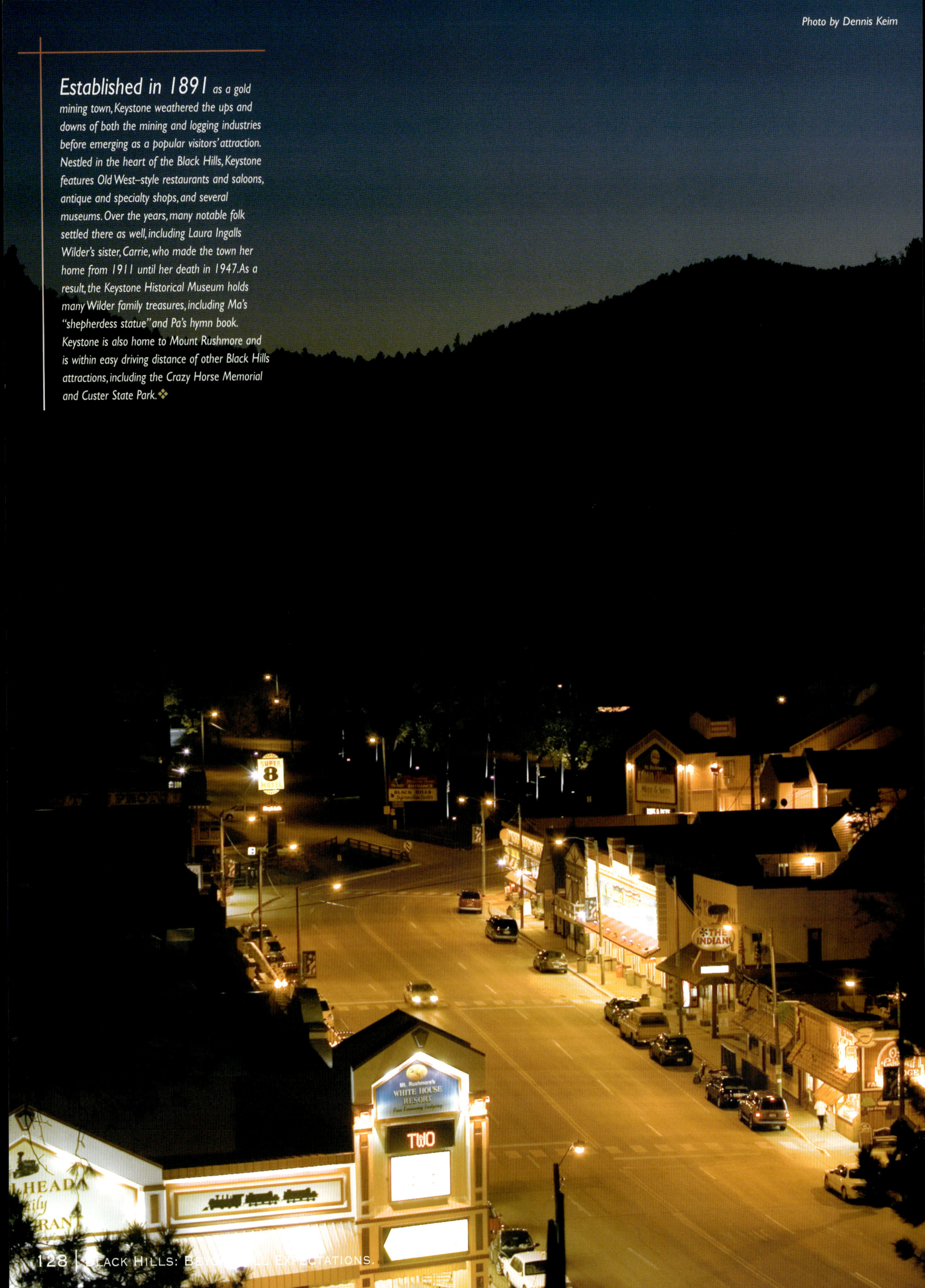

Photo by Dennis Keim

Established in 1891 as a gold mining town, Keystone weathered the ups and downs of both the mining and logging industries before emerging as a popular visitors' attraction. Nestled in the heart of the Black Hills, Keystone features Old West–style restaurants and saloons, antique and specialty shops, and several museums. Over the years, many notable folk settled there as well, including Laura Ingalls Wilder's sister, Carrie, who made the town her home from 1911 until her death in 1947. As a result, the Keystone Historical Museum holds many Wilder family treasures, including Ma's "shepherdess statue" and Pa's hymn book. Keystone is also home to Mount Rushmore and is within easy driving distance of other Black Hills attractions, including the Crazy Horse Memorial and Custer State Park. ❖

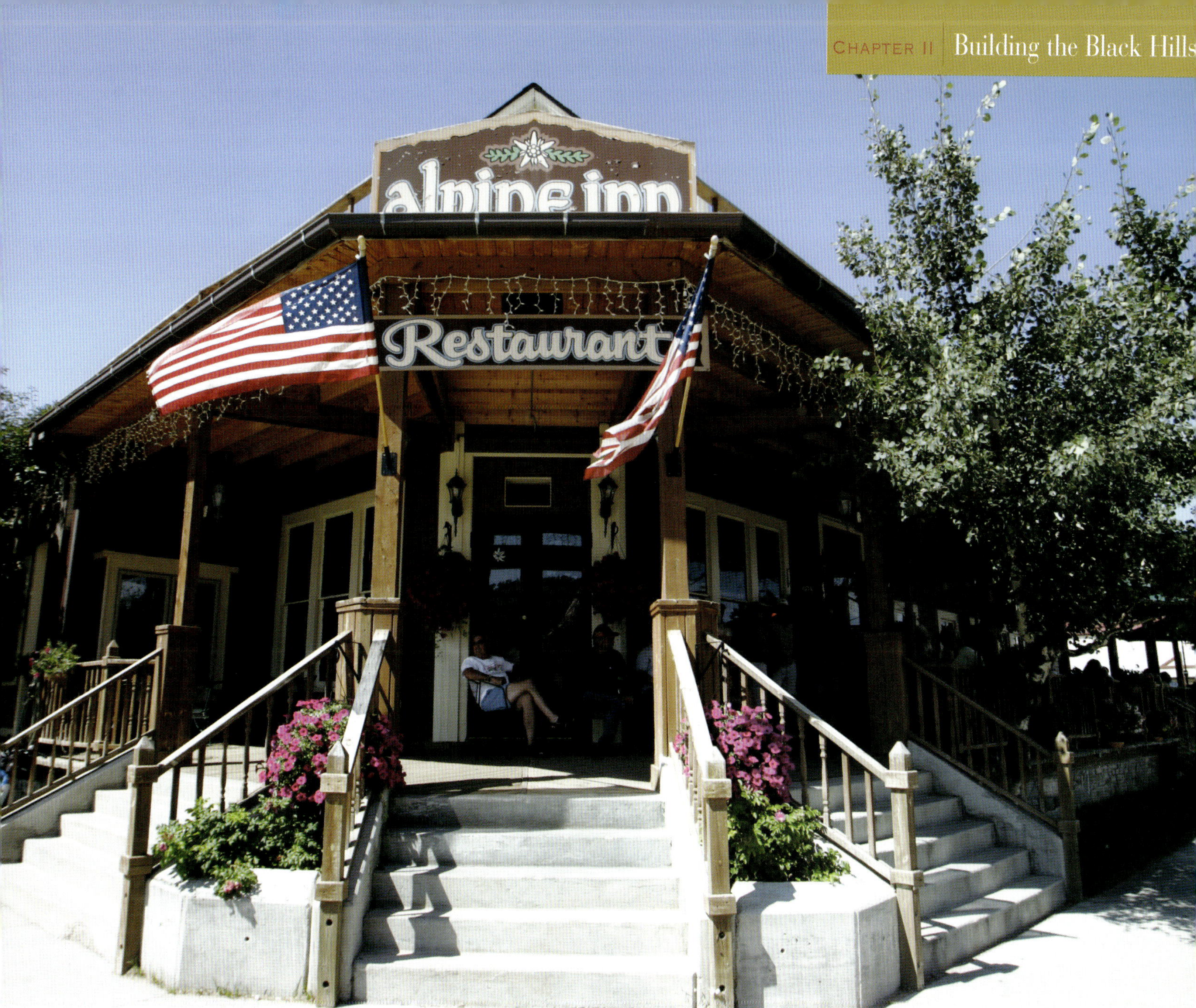

Photo by Eric Francis

When Richard A. Dybuig and Kevin Brende (pictured left to right) want to feast upon "the best filet mignon in the world," they know exactly where to go: the Alpine Inn Restaurant in Hill City. For years, this popular local institution, located on Main Street in the historic Harney Peak Hotel, has served up American cuisine with a European twist. In fact, the restaurant is famous for its German-inspired lunch menu, as well as its succulent steak, which is the only entrée offered at dinnertime. Of course, patrons don't seem to mind the evening's concise carte du jour, especially since it is complemented by a list of thirty homemade pastries and delectable desserts. And after diners partake of the restaurant's fabulous fare, they can stroll out to the veranda to enjoy the nice weather and great conversation—the perfect end to a perfect dining experience. ❖

HiQual Manufacturing Revolutionized the Livestock Industry

If the livestock industry is synonymous with hard work, then HiQual Manufacturing is synonymous with hard-working equipment for the livestock industry. Since 1978, the company has produced livestock handling equipment that stands for safety, quality, innovation, and value.

"HiQual equipment is time tested, cowboy tough, and cattleman approved," says Brian Chleborad, president. "Listening to our end user has allowed us to continually bring innovative new products to the marketplace, which have revolutionized the way we take care of all our four-legged friends." HiQual continues to incorporate the knowledge and expertise of local ranchers and animal health specialists into the design of new products. HiQual's lines include equipment for the equine as well as the cattle market, from shelters and stalls to fencing and feed equipment. HiQual's complete line of cattle products also includes squeeze chutes, working systems, and calving products. Both lines feature several innovative and patented products exclusive to the HiQual name.

> "HiQual equipment is time tested, cowboy tough, and cattleman approved," says Brian Chleborad, president.

The company took innovation beyond the product lines with the institution of HiQual University in 1997. Guided by its commitment to personal development and company growth for its dealers as well as the company, HiQual provides a weeklong training program at its Rapid City facility for more than one hundred of its dealer representatives each year. ❖

Photo by Doug Henderson

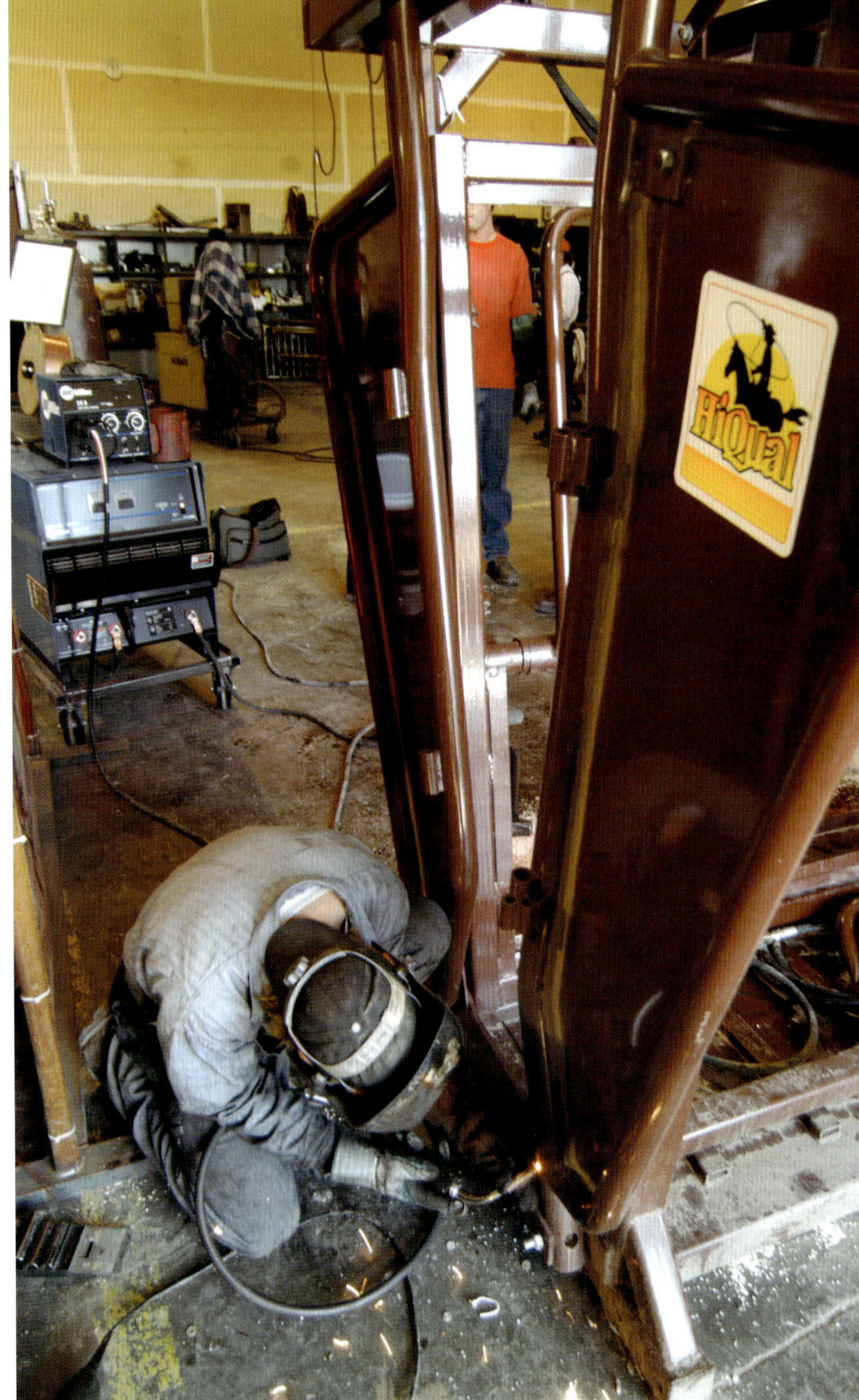

Meticulous workmanship goes into every HiQual product. Here a HiQual employee puts the finishing touches on a piece of livestock equipment.

Created in 1997, the Black Hills Air Service Task Force has become a key player in promoting the region as a premier vacation destination. This organization comprises numerous businesses, chambers of commerce, and convention and visitors' bureaus, as well as the South Dakota Department of Tourism and Black Hills Visions. With a primary goal of increasing inbound air traffic, the task force supports the growth of incumbent air carriers and works to cultivate additional air service to the area. It maintains relationships with all of the airlines serving Rapid City Regional Airport and partners with the airlines in their vacation programs. The Air Services task force also conducts travel agent education programs for agents throughout the country and undertakes marketing campaigns in key national markets. ❖

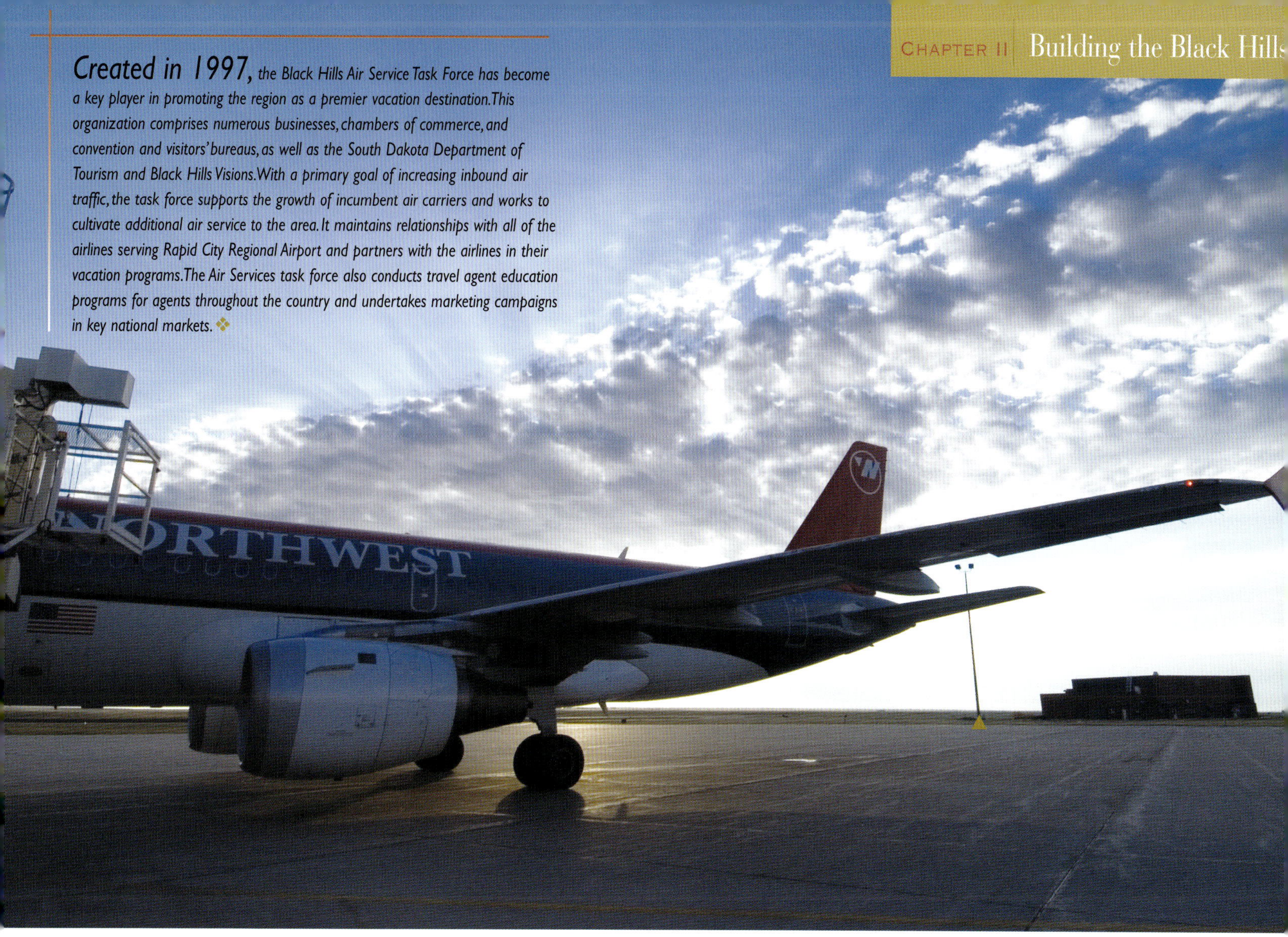

Photo by Thomas S. England

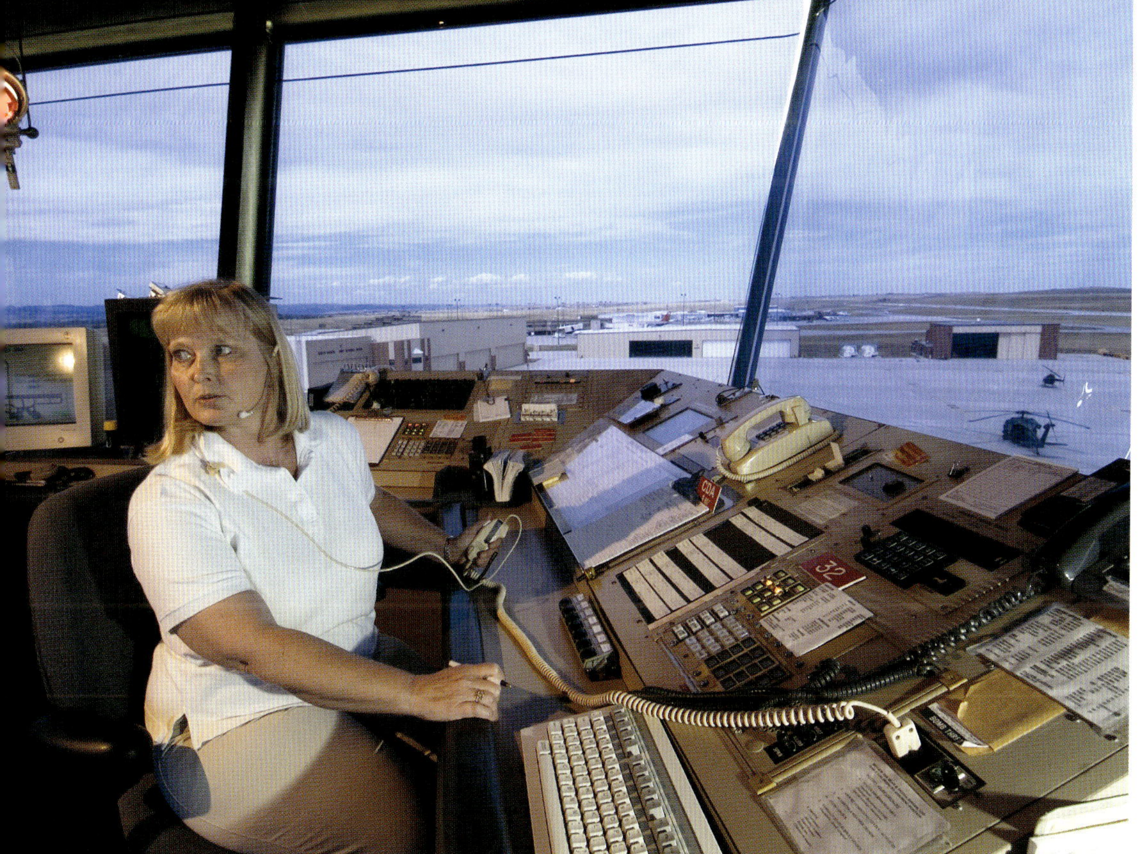

Photo by Thomas S. England

Safely guiding over sixty thousand yearly takeoffs and landings is just one of the duties of the Rapid City Regional Airport's air traffic controllers. Because Ellsworth Air Force Base is only seven miles away, these controllers also keep the skies safe for additional aircraft, not only passenger jets and small private planes, but also supersonic B-1 bombers. In addition to the safety provided by the controllers' skills, Rapid City Regional Airport was the recent recipient of the FAA's Airport Safety Award, given out only to those airports that exceed the government's stringent airfield safety standards, both on the ground and in the air. Rapid City Regional Airport also exceeds on a daily basis all of the FAA's standards for airfield safety—a result of the airport's continual focus on excellence in airfield operations every single day. ❖

West River Electric Offers Many Benefits to the Community

As one of the region's fastest-growing electric cooperatives, West River Electric offers over thirteen thousand meters the best possible service at reasonable prices, while also providing businesses in western South Dakota with programs to help them run more efficiently and competitively.

Established in 1939, West River Electric has grown into the second-largest electric cooperative in South Dakota. Its highly trained staff include line workers, technicians, administrators, and consultants, each dedicated to ensuring continual services. Located in Wall and Rapid City, West River's physical plant consists of over twenty-five hundred miles of line in western South Dakota, with a distribution system covering a six-county, forty-five-hundred-square-mile area.

Both members and nonmembers benefit from West River's educational and safety services.

Like a credit union or food cooperative, West River Electric's customers are also its owners. Each year at the company's annual meeting, member-owners elect the company's

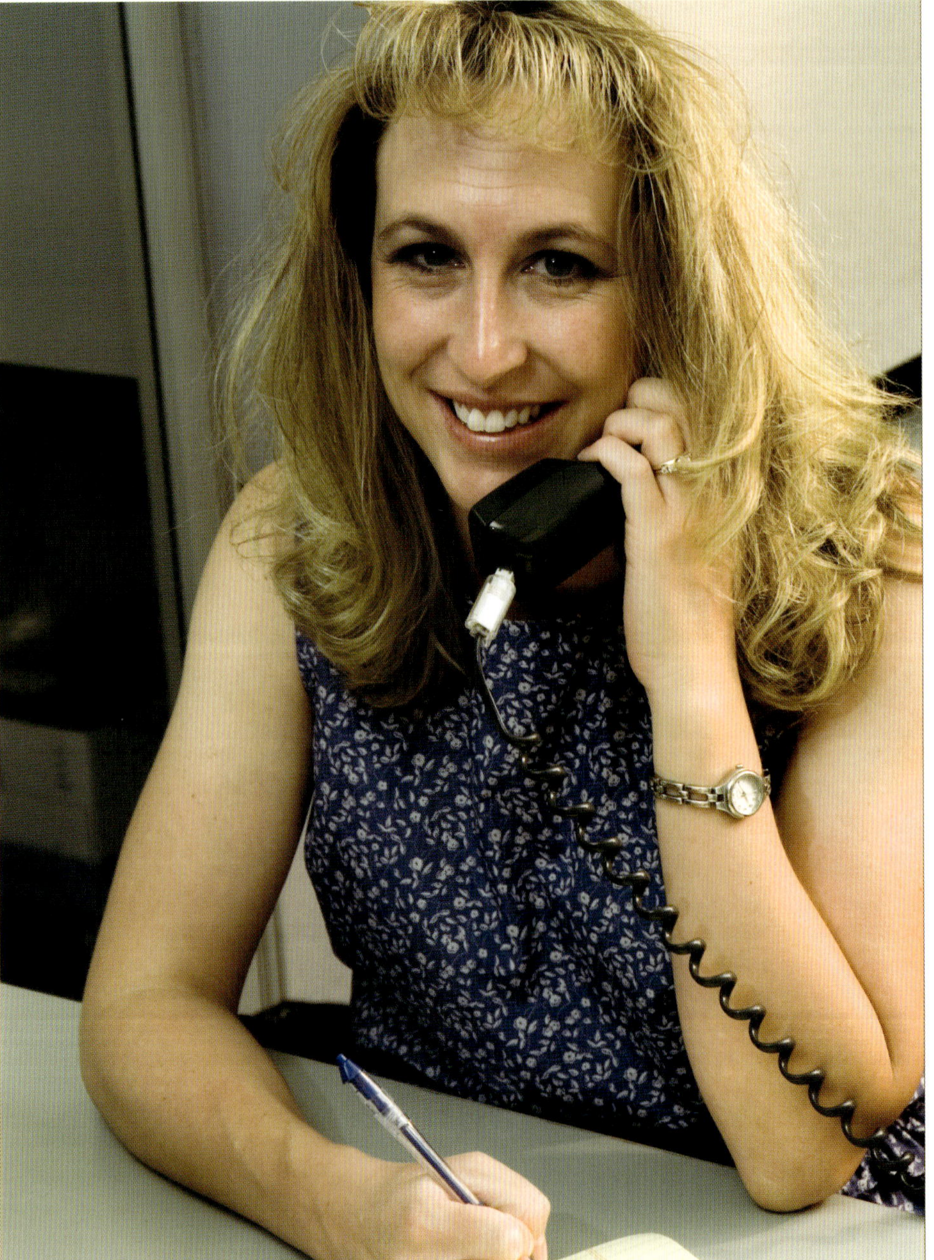

Customer service representative Tracea Ladner assists a customer over the phone. Representatives can be contacted by phone, fax, or email during normal business hours and via a separate number that's open 24/7 for outages and other emergencies.

Photo by Thomas S. England

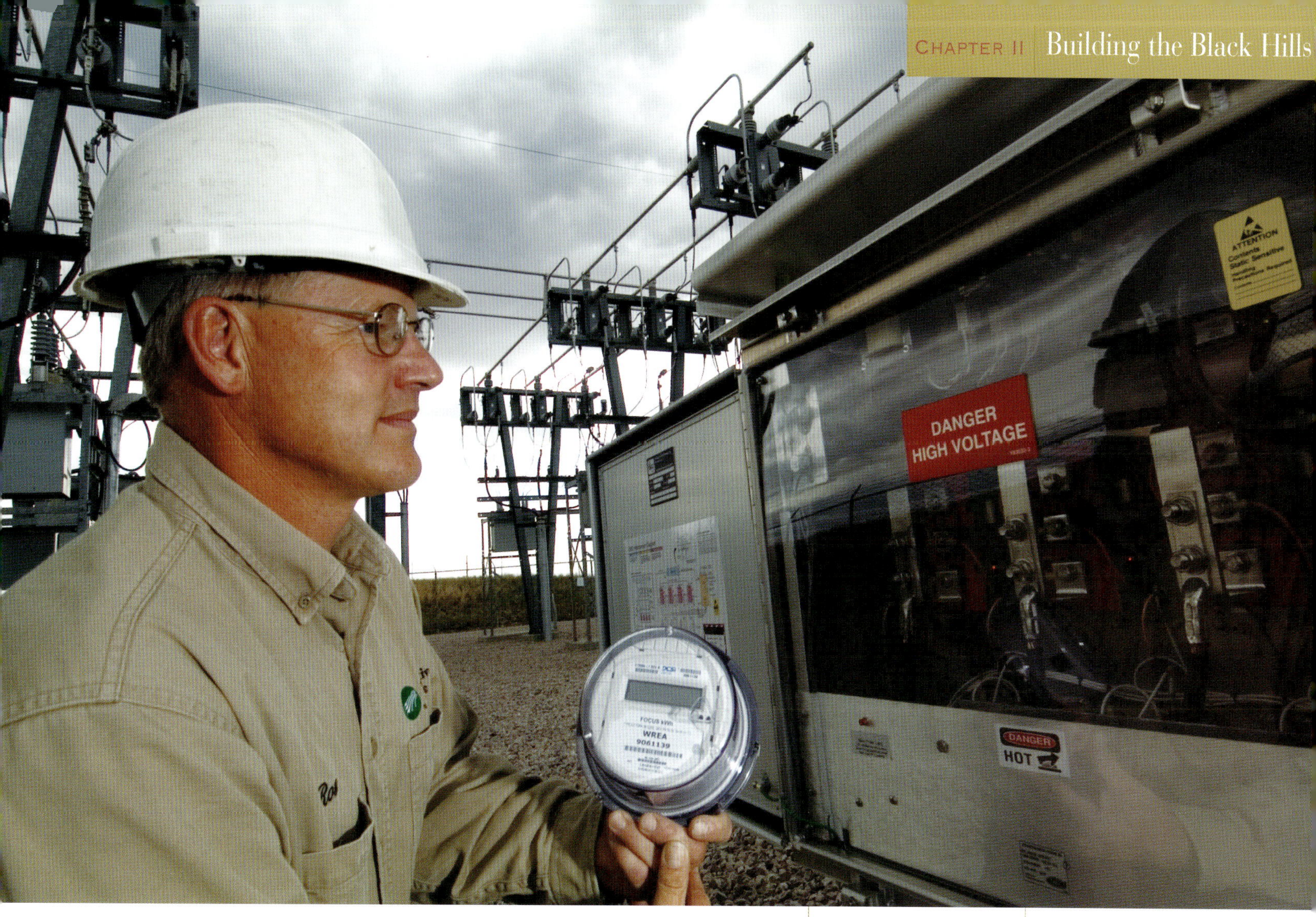

Photo by Thomas S. England

To ensure accurate and timely billings, metering foreman, Ross Johnson continually monitors the outbound modulations units, which provide signals for West River's state-of-the-art metering system, known as TWACS (Two Way Automatic Communication System).

governing nine-member board of directors, which meets monthly to set policies. Furthermore, as a non-profit, consumer-owned organization, West River returns to its members in the form of capital credits any remaining revenue after meeting all expenses.

Both members and nonmembers benefit from West River's educational and safety services, including surge protection systems to guard against damage from electrical blips, electrical safety demonstrations for local schools, and free advice for homeowners on energy-saving measures and heating system installations.

The cooperative is also committed to promoting economic opportunity and growth in the region. West River invests both time and resources in helping to create jobs throughout its service territory and the Black Hills region. Creating growth in western South Dakota and the Black Hills economy creates opportunities for better jobs and quality of life for area residents.

Since its inception, West River Electric has been an active participant in the Black Hills Vision Project. Black Hills Vision began as a regional economic fund-raiser, but has since evolved into a catalyst for expansion of technology-based economic development for the region. A primary focus of Black Hills Vision has been to promote higher-paying jobs and wealth creation through technology-based industries.

Representatives of West River Electric are also actively involved in the Rapid City Area Economic Development Partnership, and the Rapid City Economic Development Foundation, both of which have been working for over a decade at creating jobs and opportunities in the region. West River is proud to be a part of these economic development efforts.

The cooperative also invests its resources in future leaders. Since 1990 and in conjunction with Basin Electric Power Cooperative, West River Electric has awarded scholarships to college and vocational/technical-bound high school seniors across the company's service area. These scholarships provide economic incentives for students to continue their education, with the hope that recipients will remain in or return to the community and apply their skills and knowledge at home.

Whether providing efficient, reasonably priced electrical services, educational and safety programs, or incentives for economic development, West River Electric continues to help grow the community and region. ❖

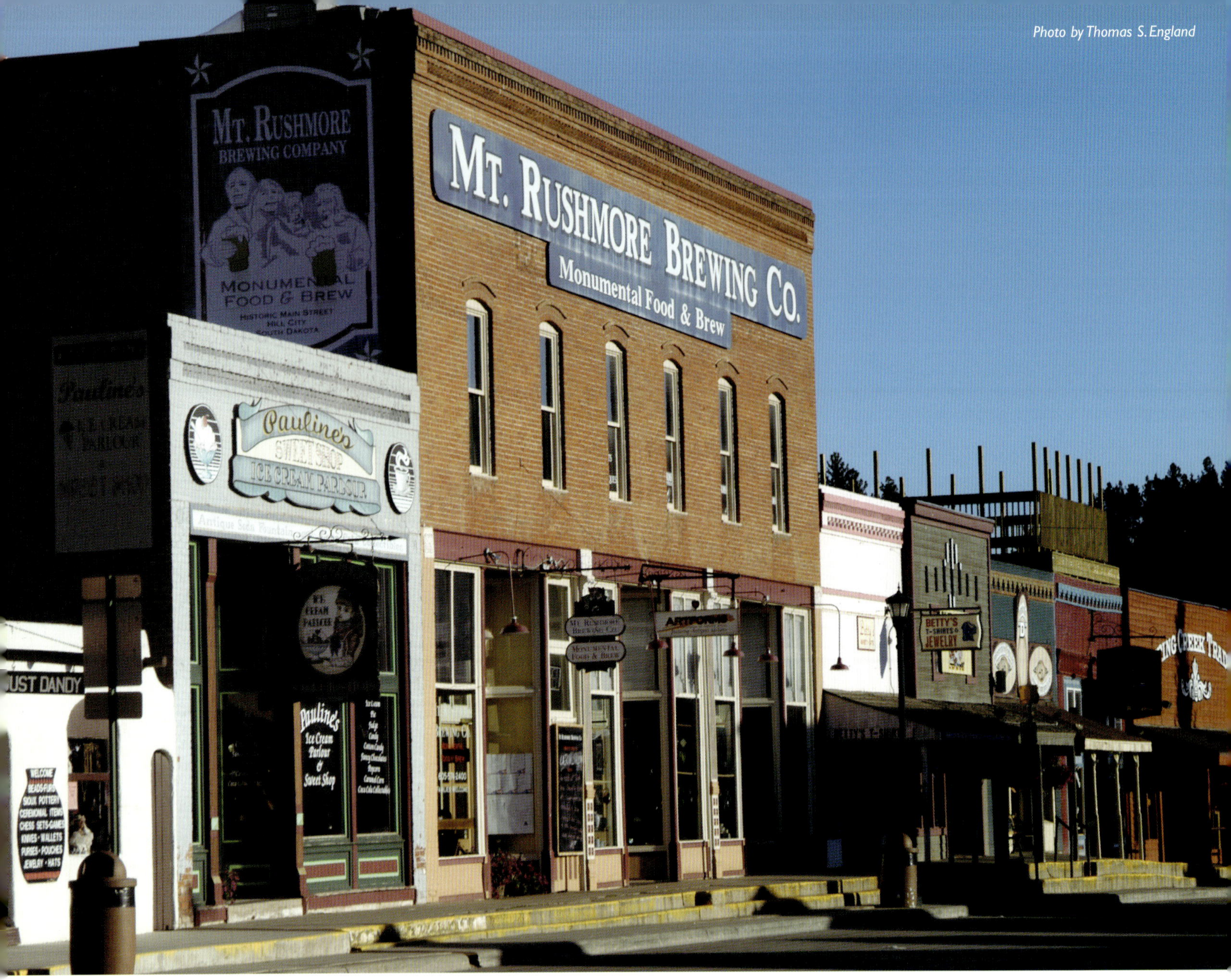

Photo by Thomas S. England

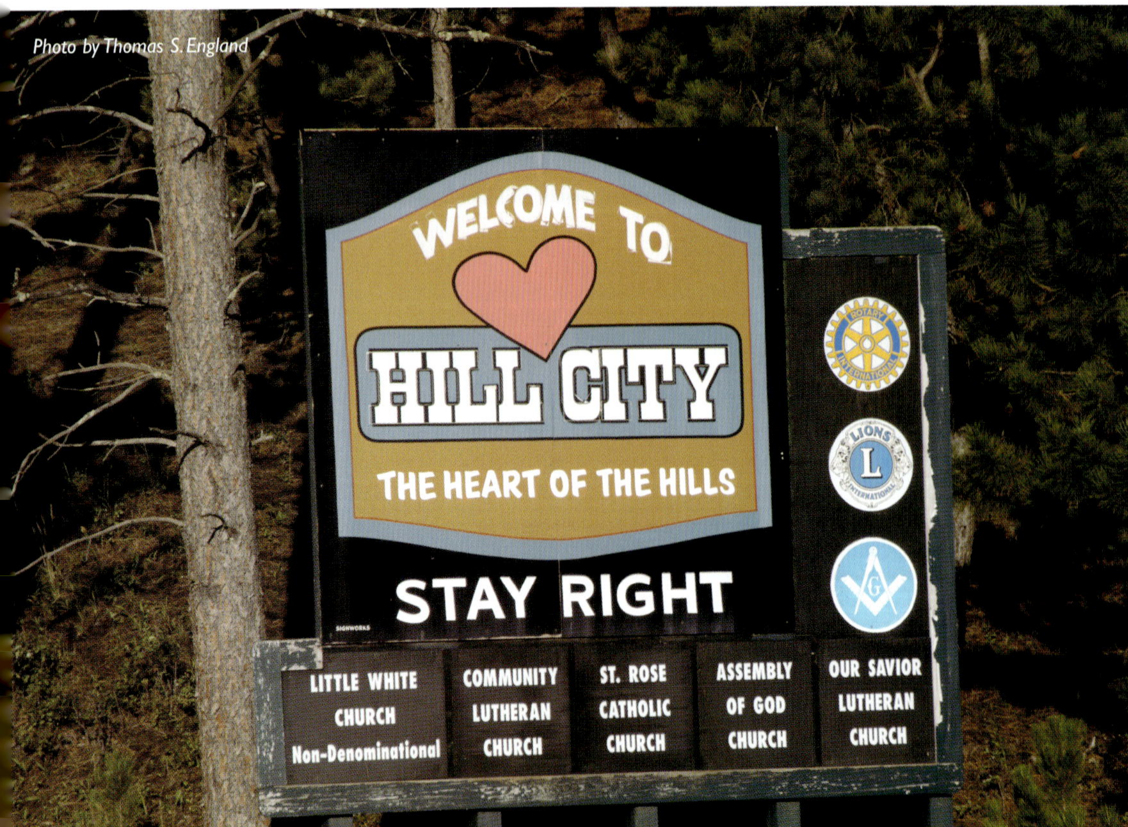

Photo by Thomas S. England

It's easy to "Stay Right" when a little town with a population of about eight hundred offers five choices for houses of worship. Hill City resides in a Black Hills mountain meadow along the banks of Spring Creek and offers old-town charm as well as easy access to the many activities of the area. ❖

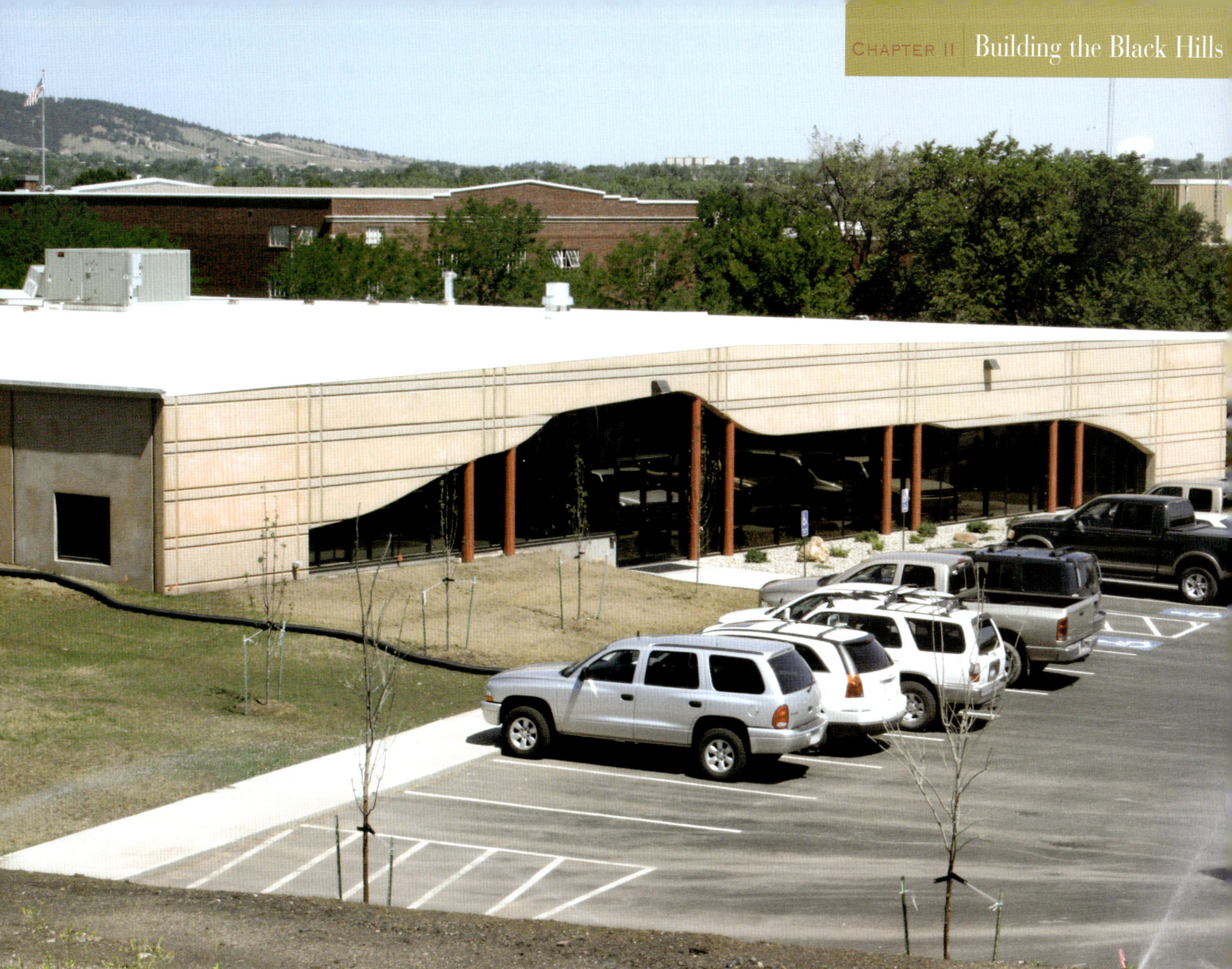

The Black Hills Business Development Center, an incubator project, promises to be a groundbreaking undertaking in every sense of the word. Located on the southeast corner of the School of Mines & Technology near O'Harra Field football stadium, the forty-thousand-square-foot building will provide an open area that can be modified to fit the needs of entrepreneurs who will rent space there. The $2.2 million structure was funded in part by grants from the governor and the West River Foundation. Black Hills Vision, which raised five hundred thousand dollars for operating expenses, is working in partnership with local economic development corporations in the Black Hills to create opportunities—primarily in technology research—for the region. The plan is to provide space for start-up companies to develop products, test prototypes, research markets, create promotional materials, and find venture capital. They can also consult with business development groups down the hall, such as West River Business Service Center, the Rapid City Economic Development Partnership, Service Corps of Retired Executives, and Genesis Equity Fund. ❖

Wells Fargo Rich in History and Community Service

The story of Wells Fargo Bank in Rapid City is actually two stories with two very distinctive beginnings. In 1852 Henry Wells and William Fargo founded Wells Fargo & Co. in San Francisco. Locations were concentrated in mining camps, and in addition to banking, the company provided reliable transportation of gold and goods. Equally important, it provided dependable mail delivery to western miners, merchants, and farmers.

Our other story begins in boomtown Deadwood. In 1878 the First National Bank came into being. According to historian Robert J. Chandler, "By 1880, the bank had ten thousand potential customers in the area, a fifth of them miners." At that time Rapid City was known as "The Gateway to the Black Hills."

From here the story gets a little complicated. In 1929, the First National Banks of Deadwood, Lead, Rapid City, and Sturgis became affiliated with Northwest Bancorporation, a holding company. The Bank of Spearfish joined Banco in 1930, followed by Belle Fourche in 1937. The FNB of Deadwood consolidated with the FNB of Lead in 1935, and in 1938 consolidated with FNB of Rapid City, setting up headquarters there. Subsequently all these banks became known as the FNB of the Black Hills. Finally, in 1983, the Banco banks all became Norwest Bank.

"Wherever you go across Wells Fargo territory, you'll see our team members rolling up their sleeves."

Photo by Dennis Keim

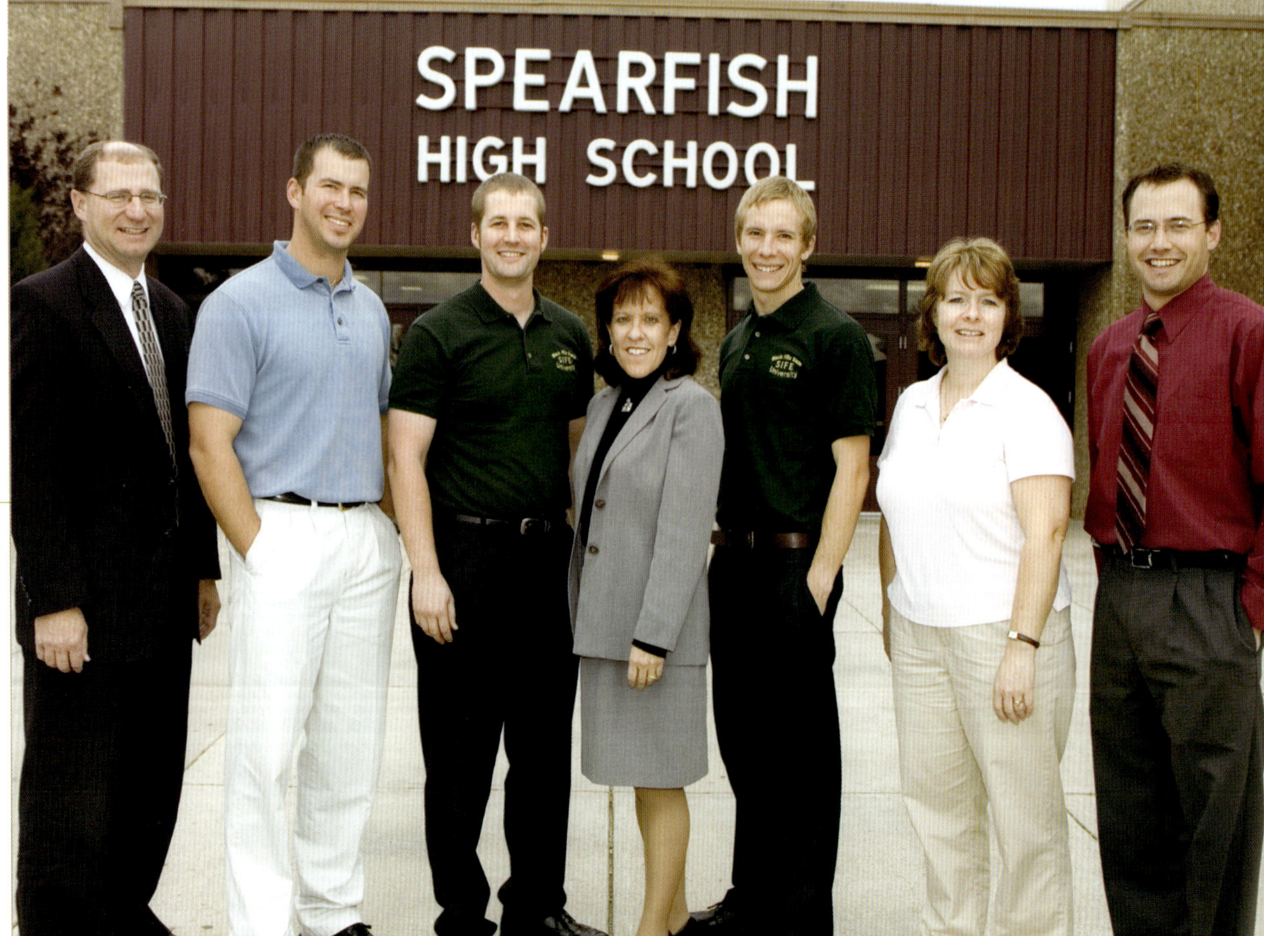

The Black Hills State University SIFE chapter works with Spearfish High School and Wells Fargo Bank, helping provide local students with needed financial education by combining the resources of a local business, college, and public school.

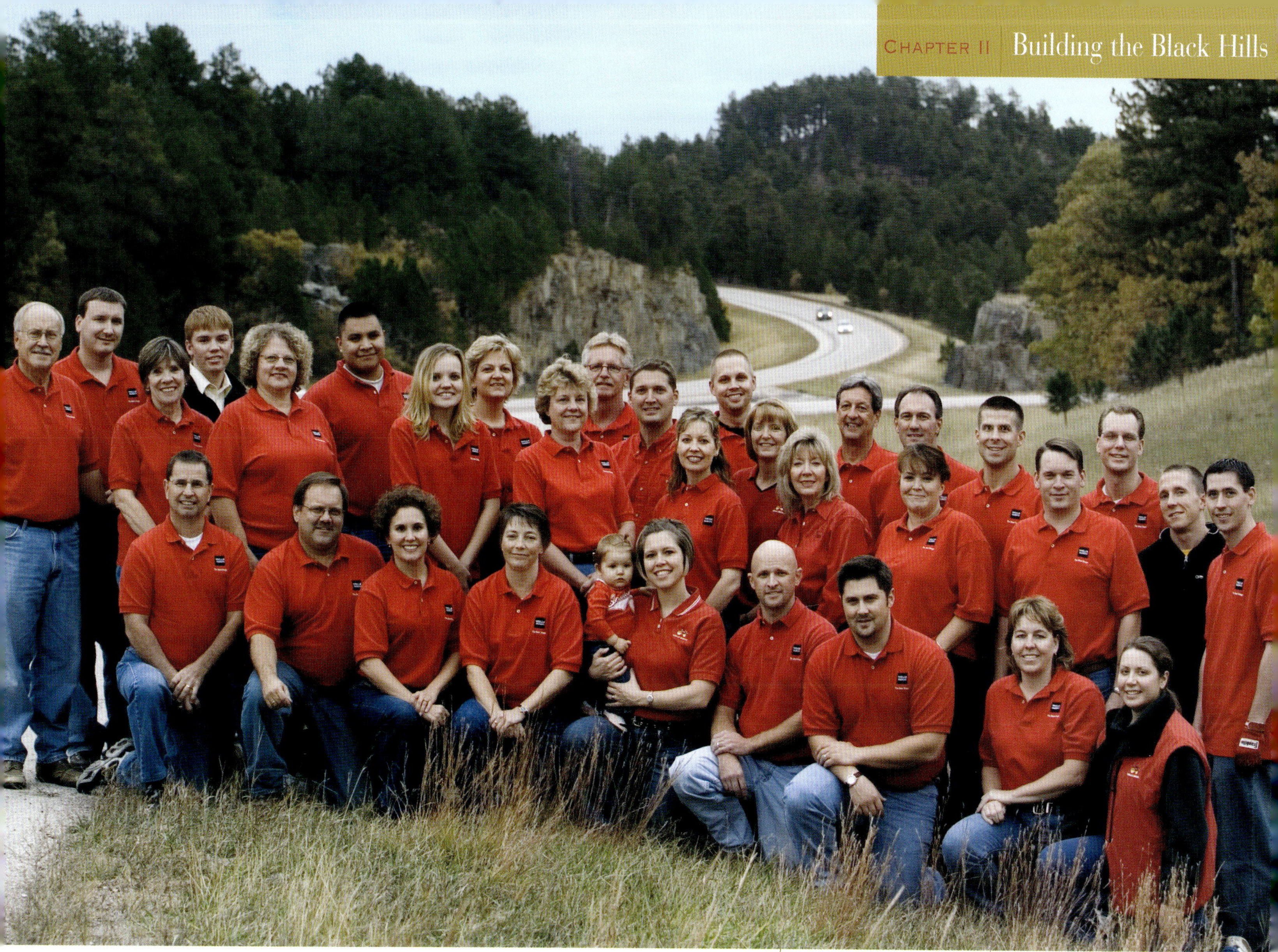

Photo by Dennis Keim

Twice a year all the employees from the Rapid City Wells Fargo stores—as they are referred to officially—get together to clean up their portion of Highway 16 as part of the Adopt-a-Highway program. "Our mile of highway is about ten miles from Mount Rushmore, and we've been taking part in this activity for about twenty years," said Pete Cappa, community banking president. After a job well done, volunteers get together to enjoy pizza.

Then in 1998 our two stories come together again, when Norwest announced a "merger of equals" with Wells Fargo. The resulting bank kept the historic Wells Fargo name and became the nation's seventh-largest bank.

"Even though we are the largest financial institution headquartered in the western United States, we realize that we have to provide a choice of services for all our customers' financial needs," said Pete Cappa, community banking president. "Historically Norwest was known for its personalized approach and customer service. Wells Fargo, on the other hand was known as a leader in online banking and technology, with a focus on efficiency. Putting the two together gave our customers the best of both worlds."

CEO Richard Kovacevich—former CEO of Norwest—would seem to agree. "We're known as active community leaders in services that promote economic self-sufficiency, education, social services, and the arts," he said. "Wherever you go across Wells Fargo territory, you'll see our team members rolling up their sleeves."

That involvement is certainly evident in the activities of the bank's employees in Rapid City. Cappa has served on the executive boards of Black Hills Vision, a regional economic development initiative focused on jobs and quality of life; the Black Hills Workshop, which helps people with disabilities and the Air Services, Military Affairs, and Ellsworth Task Forces, which foster ties between the air force base and neighboring communities.

Wells Fargo supplies office space for the local chapter of Junior Achievement and the Mount Rushmore Society. Team members from all areas of

Continued on page 138

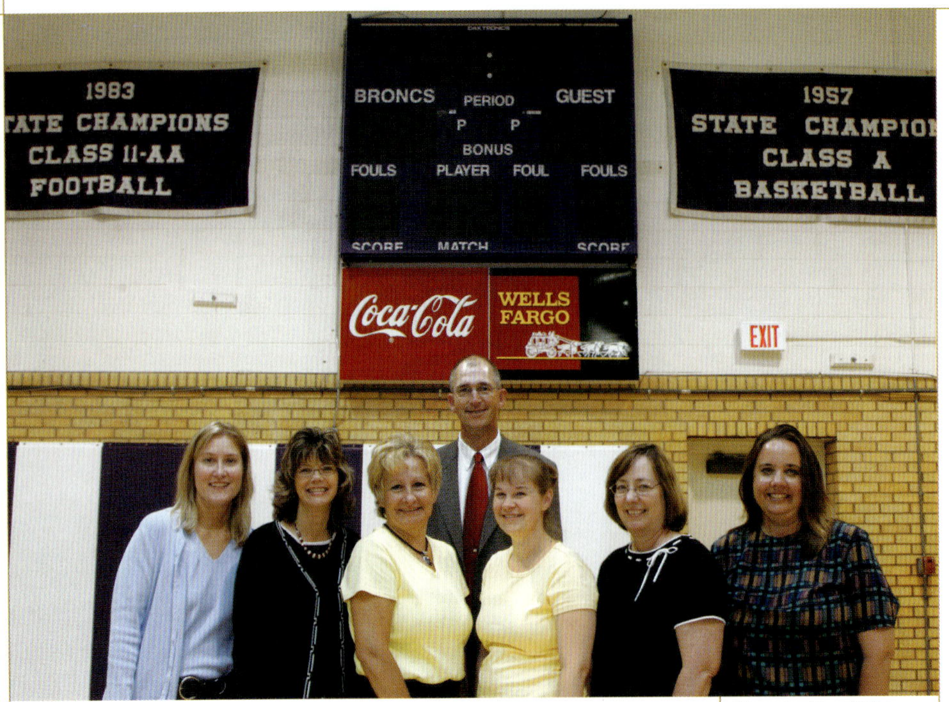

Photo by Alan S.Weiner

It's important to know the score, and students at Belle Fourche High School will find it easier to keep track since the installation of their new scoreboard. Wells Fargo was instrumental in funding the new board and the new gym floor. Wells Fargo employees (left to right) Melissa Kraft, Jeryl Bean, Dallerie Neff, Wade Pehl, Kelly Schmoker, Linda Stumpf, and Patty Miller are active in the area, and several served on the local school board. The school district and the community tend to work closely with each other. Several years ago, Belle Fouche High School students worked to get the town involved with the state's Guide to Opportunities for Local Development (GOLD) program.

Continued from page 137

the bank serve as volunteers for a long list of community programs and services. Wells Fargo is also among the top contributors to United Way and Rapid City YMCA.

Looking back, one of these stories developed in the gold fields on the far edge of the western frontier, the other in the gold fields of the western part of South Dakota. Two roads to success met to establish a company that now spans all of North America. "We plan to keep growing," said Cappa, "but no matter how big we get, we all share certain values that hold us together and will continue to make Wells Fargo one of America's great companies." ❖

Photo by Alan S.Weiner

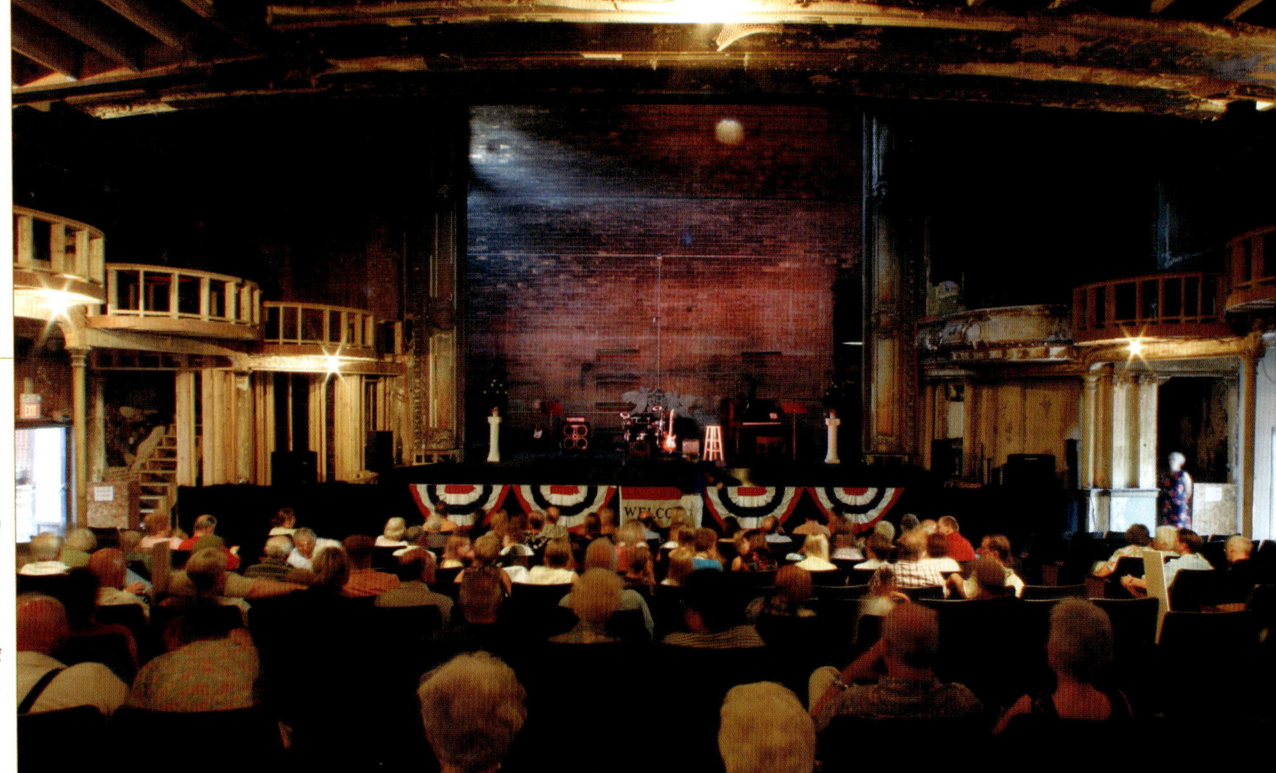

Known as the Jewel of the Black Hills, the Lead Opera House has been a local landmark for nearly a century. VaLinda Heinbaugh, an officer of the local branch of Wells Fargo Bank, sits on the opera's board of directors. Wells Fargo is an enthusiastic supporter of the current reconstruction project aimed at restoring the interior theatre and the Recreation Building to its former grandeur.

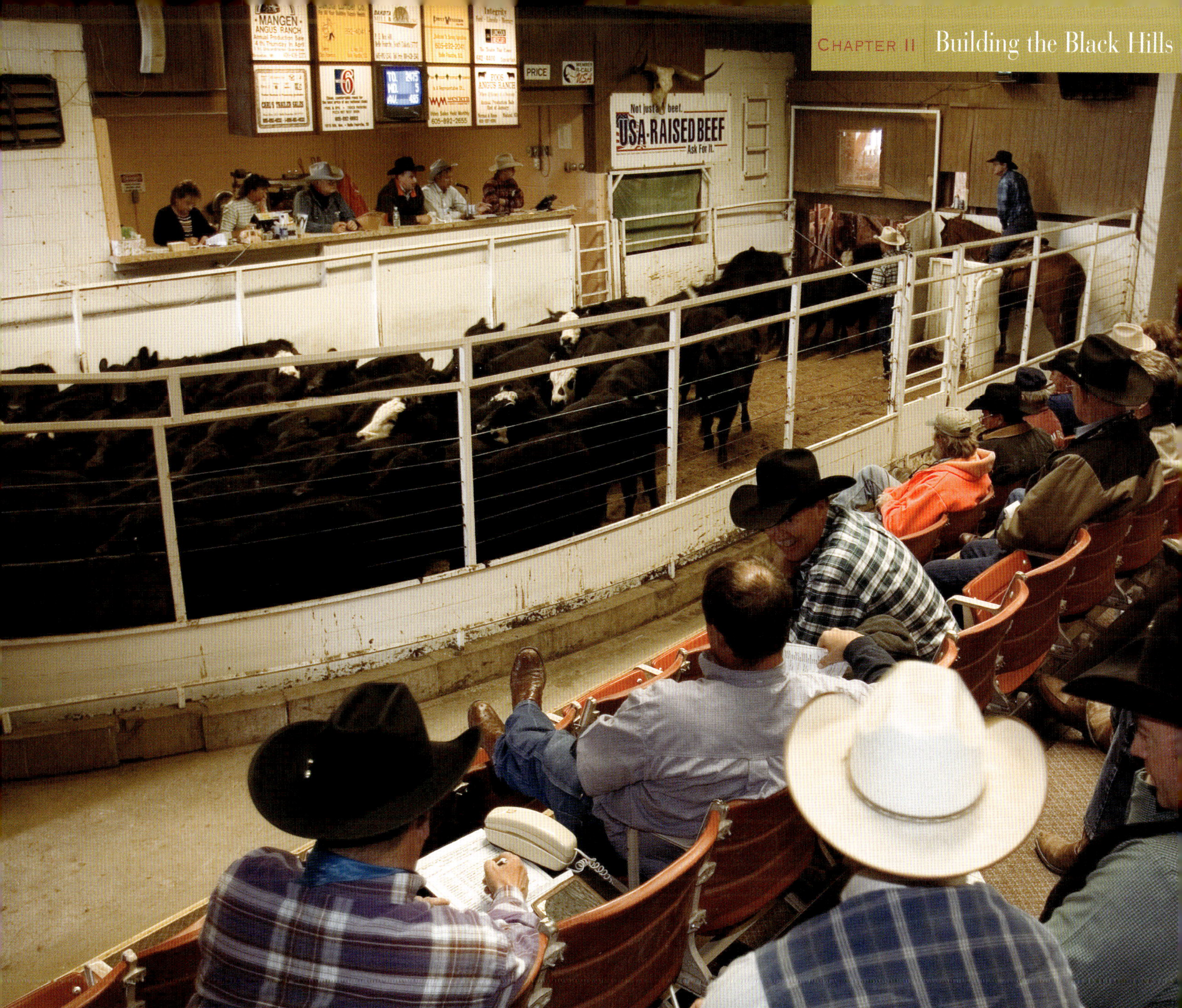

Photo by Dennis Keim

Belle Fourche Livestock Exchange

On Thursdays in the fall the trucks line up to participate in the Belle Fourche Livestock Exchange. Featuring spring calves, the auction is one of the few in the area and draws buyers and sellers from southeast Montana, Wyoming, and South Dakota. The city of Belle Fourche, considered the geographic center of the United States, means "beautiful fork," and lies near the junction of the Belle Fourche and Redwater rivers. ❖

Midcontinent Communications Bundles Telecommunication Needs

As the world of communications has evolved, so has Midcontinent Communications. With the roots of its family tree planted in the early years of the movie theatre business, Midcontinent's branches grew to include some of the Dakotas' first radio and television stations. More than a half-century later, Midcontinent Communications is a telecommunications leader, with technologically advanced operations in cable television, broadband Internet, telephone, and data network services.

"While we're proud that our expanding business interests have enabled us to serve more than two hundred communities in North and South Dakota, Minnesota, and northern Nebraska, we're particularly focused on the Dakotas," says Mark Niblick, Chief Executive Officer. "This is where we started, where we live, and where we choose to do business." Consequently, Midcontinent Communications makes significant capital investments in the network infrastructure such that nearly 98 percent of the South Dakota homes in the company's service area can access advanced broadband technology, thus enabling customers to choose from a suite of vital telecommunications services—all from one company.

Nearly 98 percent of the South Dakota homes in the company's service area can access advanced broadband technology.

Photo by Rodger Slott

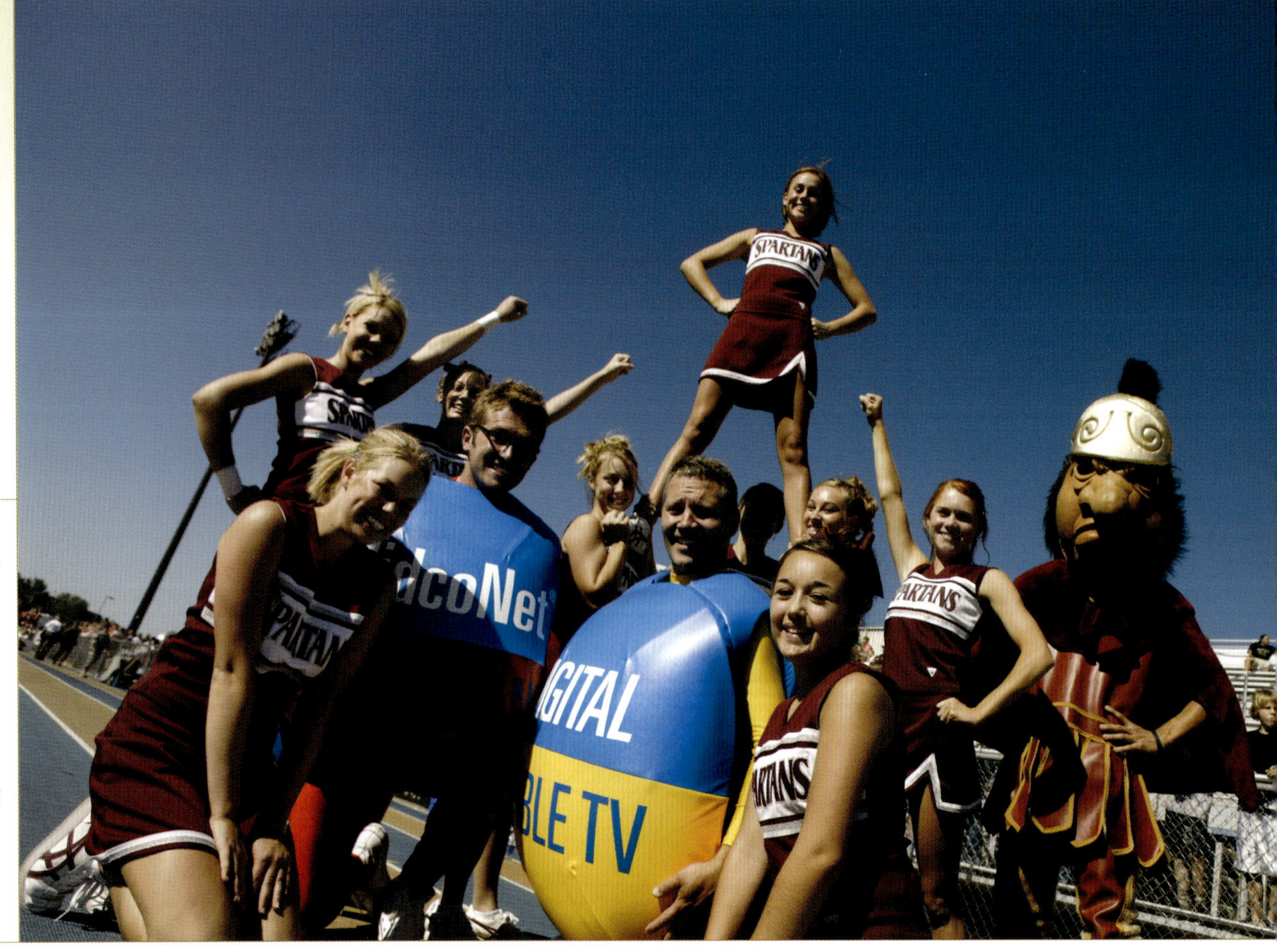

Midcontinent's "Bundle Guys" share their spirit with the Spearfish cheerleaders and mascot at the 2005 Rushmore Bowl. As a proud sponsor of this and other events, Midcontinent not only assists local causes financially, but also supports employee volunteers who enthusiastically lend a hand. Contributing to communities is a hallmark of Midcontinent Communications' mission.

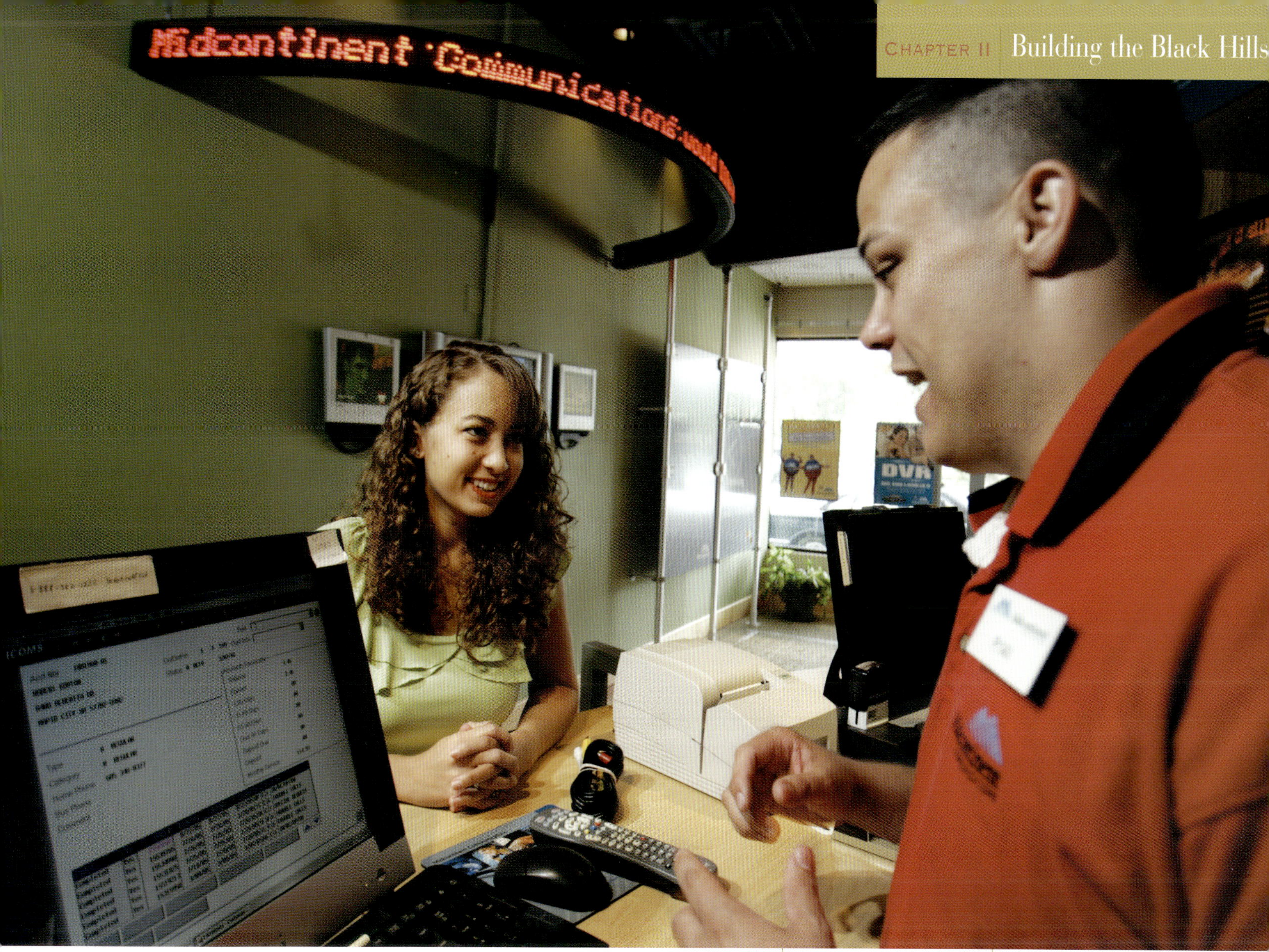

Photo by Eric Francis

Courteous, personal attention to each customer is the priority at Midcontinent's Customer Service Center location at 1301 West Omaha Street. Rapid City area customers can experience firsthand the clear pictures and great features of Digital, HD, and DVR video services and "test drive" the lightning-fast speeds of MidcoNet Broadband Service.

As the marketplaces of communications and entertainment services converge, customers prefer to do business with a single provider. By bundling telephone, Internet, and cable services together, customers receive a single discounted bill, along with the reliable service they come to count on from Midcontinent. In most communities, customers can enjoy faster, brighter, and clearer communications options: broadband cable modem Internet at blazing fast speeds, digital cable with the availability of digital video recorders, high-definition television, and telephone services all supported by well-trained and caring service representatives.

Being the region's pioneer in communications technology is just one of Midcontinent Communications' hallmarks. Community support is equally as important. Midcontinent sponsors a wide variety of local events, and the Midcontinent Media Foundation has granted over $1.8 million in financial assistance to nonprofit organizations in the communities it serves. In addition, Midcontinent provides assistance to schools and nonprofit organizations with public service messages and free access to cable and Internet for many schools. "Being part of this community is a privilege we take very seriously," says Niblick. "Lending our support is simply a part of our heritage." ❖

Photo by Doug Henderson

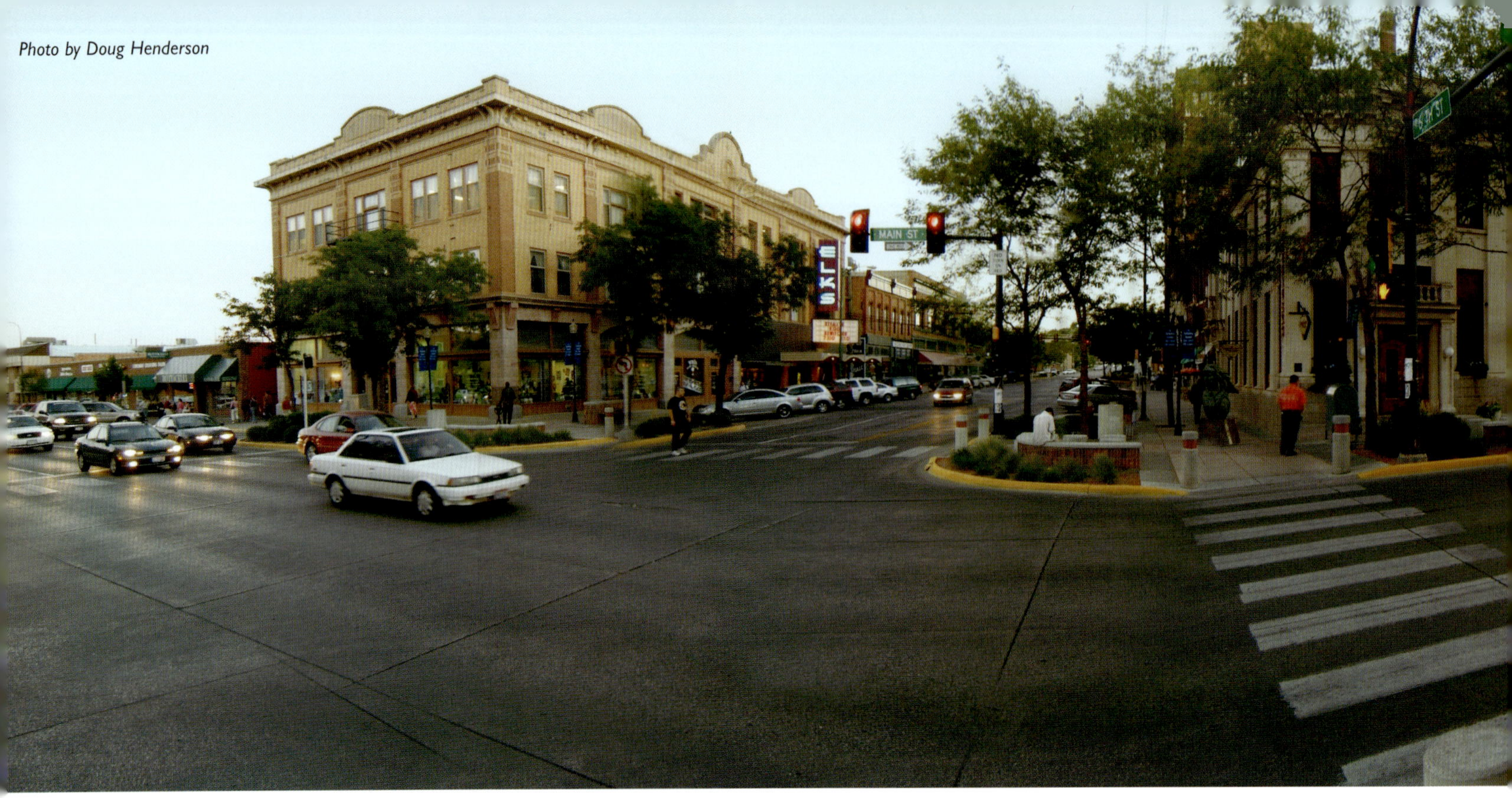

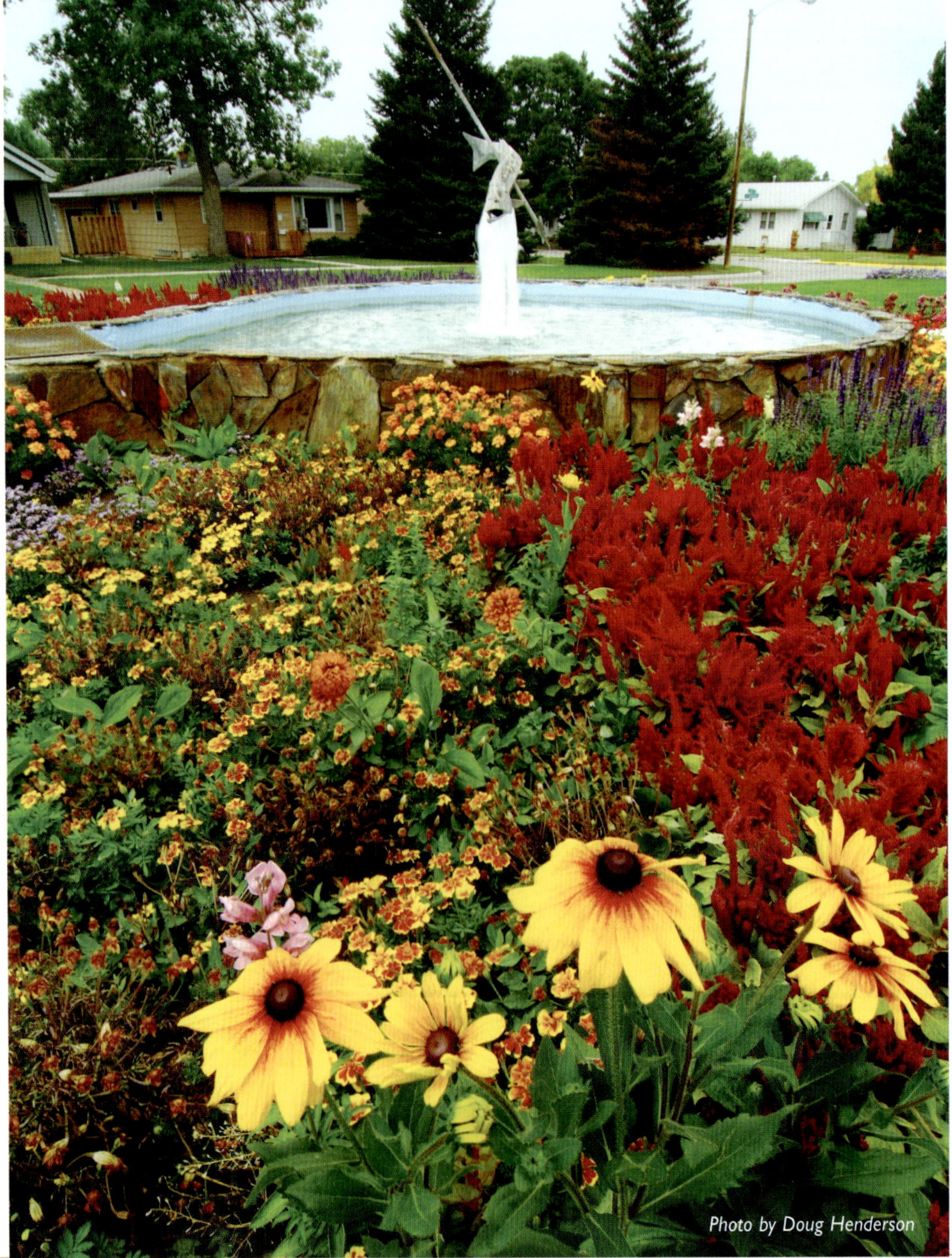
Photo by Doug Henderson

Each year in spring the RSVP Park in midtown Spearfish is replanted with a colorful blanket of flowers and plants. Named after the organization responsible for the upkeep, the city's Retired Senior Volunteer Program, RSVP Park also contains a beautiful iron sculpture of a leaping fish. Commissioned and funded by local rancher and philanthropist Gene Johnson, the sculpture pays tribute to the town's namesake, which is derived from reports by Native Americans and early settlers on the exceptional fishing conditions at a nearby stream. For his dedication to the community, in 2005 Johnson was the recipient of the Spearfish Chamber of Commerce's Spirit of Spearfish Award. Given each year, the award honors outstanding dedication to service in the community by people whose work otherwise goes unnoticed. ❖

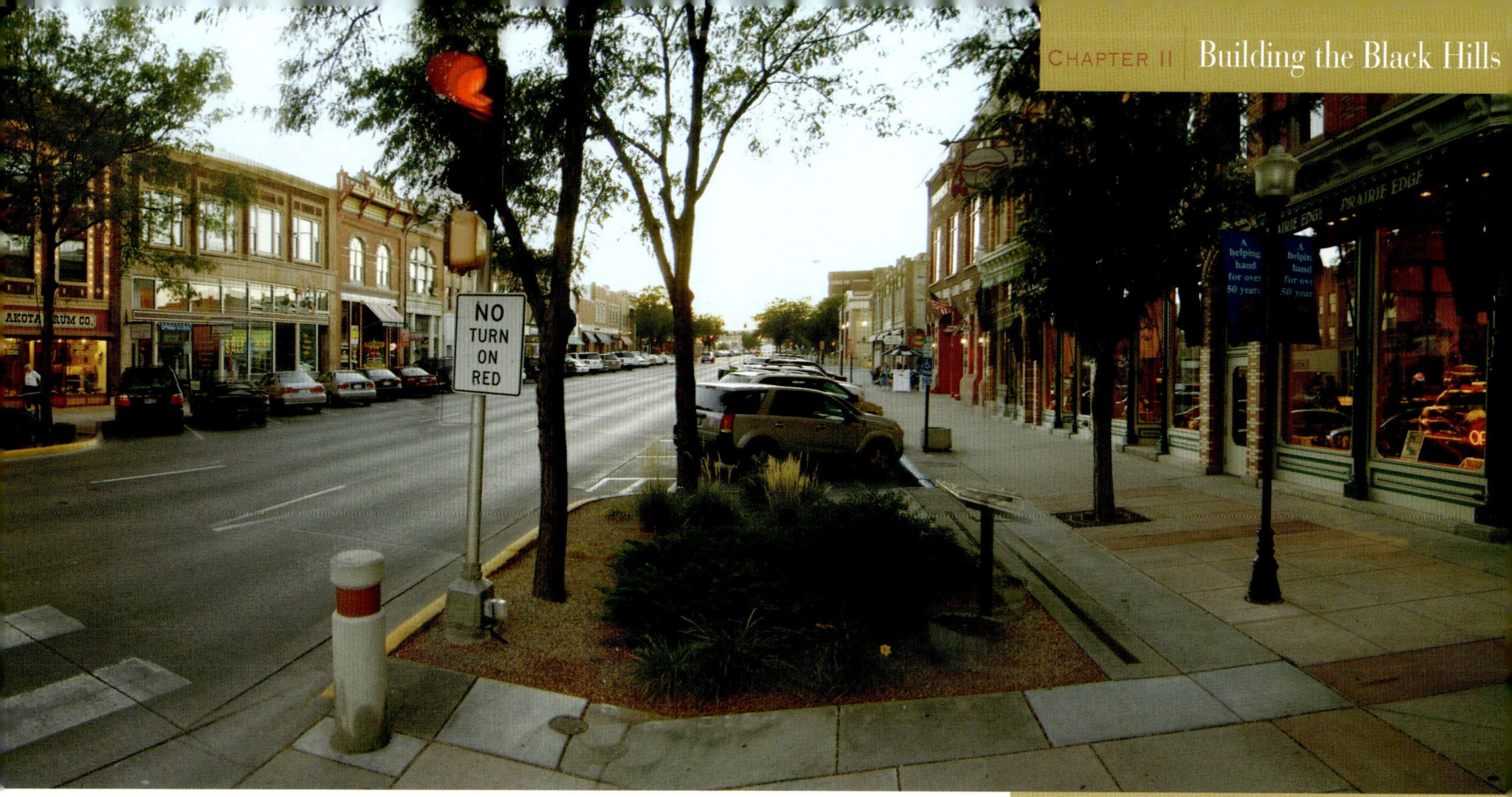

▲ *Old West meets New West* *in downtown Rapid City. Not only is it a bustling business center with many specialty shops, restaurants, and hotels, Rapid City is also an architecturally vibrant spot. A stroll through the area's commercial historic district, which includes St. Joseph and Main streets (shown here), reveals a wealth of beautifully preserved nineteenth- and early-twentieth-century buildings, reflecting Classical, Italianate, Victorian, and even Art Deco styles.* ❖

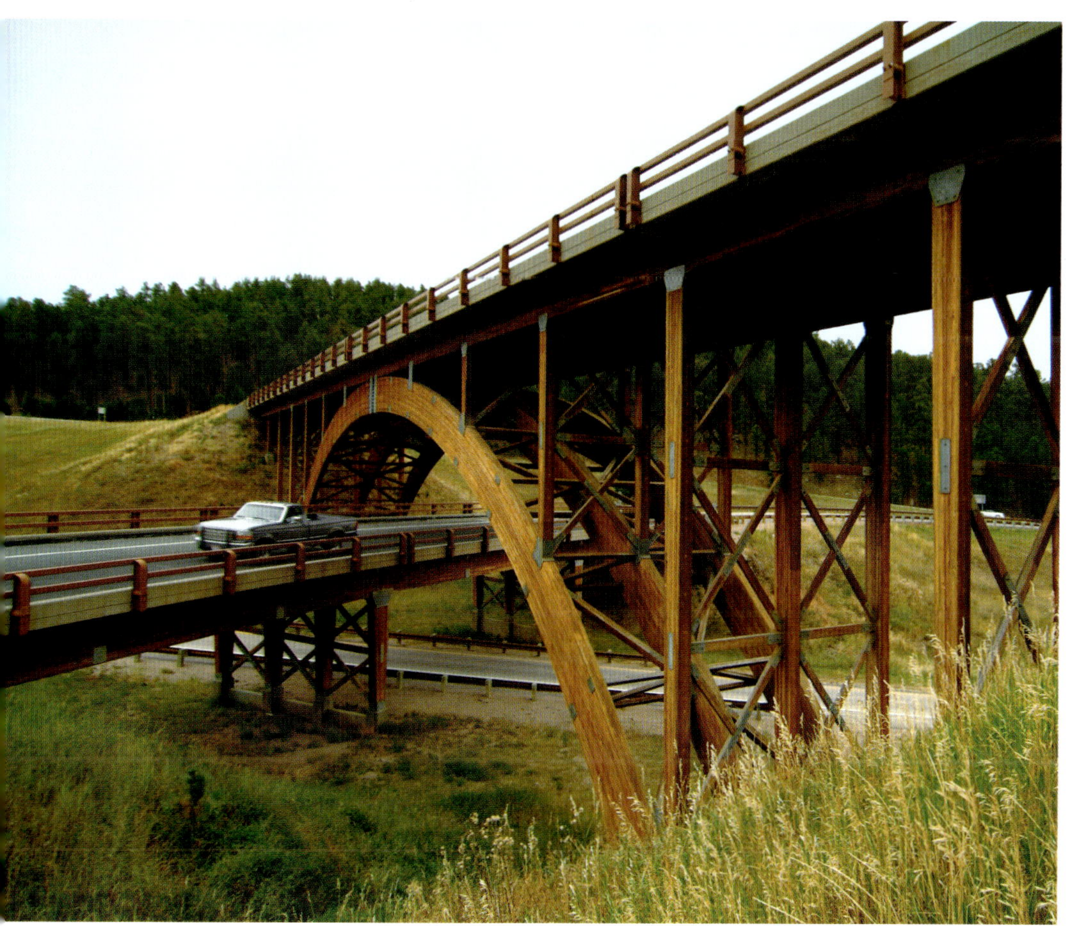

Photo by Doug Henderson

◄ *The Black Hills area is noted* *for its pristine beauty, and much is done to keep it that way. Even highway overpasses are as beautiful as they are functional. This all-wooden bridge marks the junction at Highway 16 and 385, from which motorists can access Hill City to the west and Keystone and Mount Rushmore to the east.* ❖

Black Hills Corporation Focused on the Future

The West is said to begin in Rapid City, corporate headquarters for Black Hills Corporation and home of our electric utility, Black Hills Power. A western entrepreneurial spirit founded this company in 1883, when its predecessors brought electricity to Deadwood, home of the legendary Wild Bill Hickok and Calamity Jane. Gold miners, bankers, cowboys, and a host of other lucky and unlucky settlers were its first customers. The historic company was called Black Hills Electric Light Company, and it powered the inter-urban railroad line between Deadwood and Lead.

Today Black Hills Corporation is a diversified energy company with operations focused in the West. Black Hills Energy, its wholesale nonregulated energy subsidiary, is located in Golden, Colorado, and consists of power generation, coal mining, natural gas and oil production, and energy marketing.

"In recent years we have built state-of-the-art power plants that are among the cleanest in the nation."

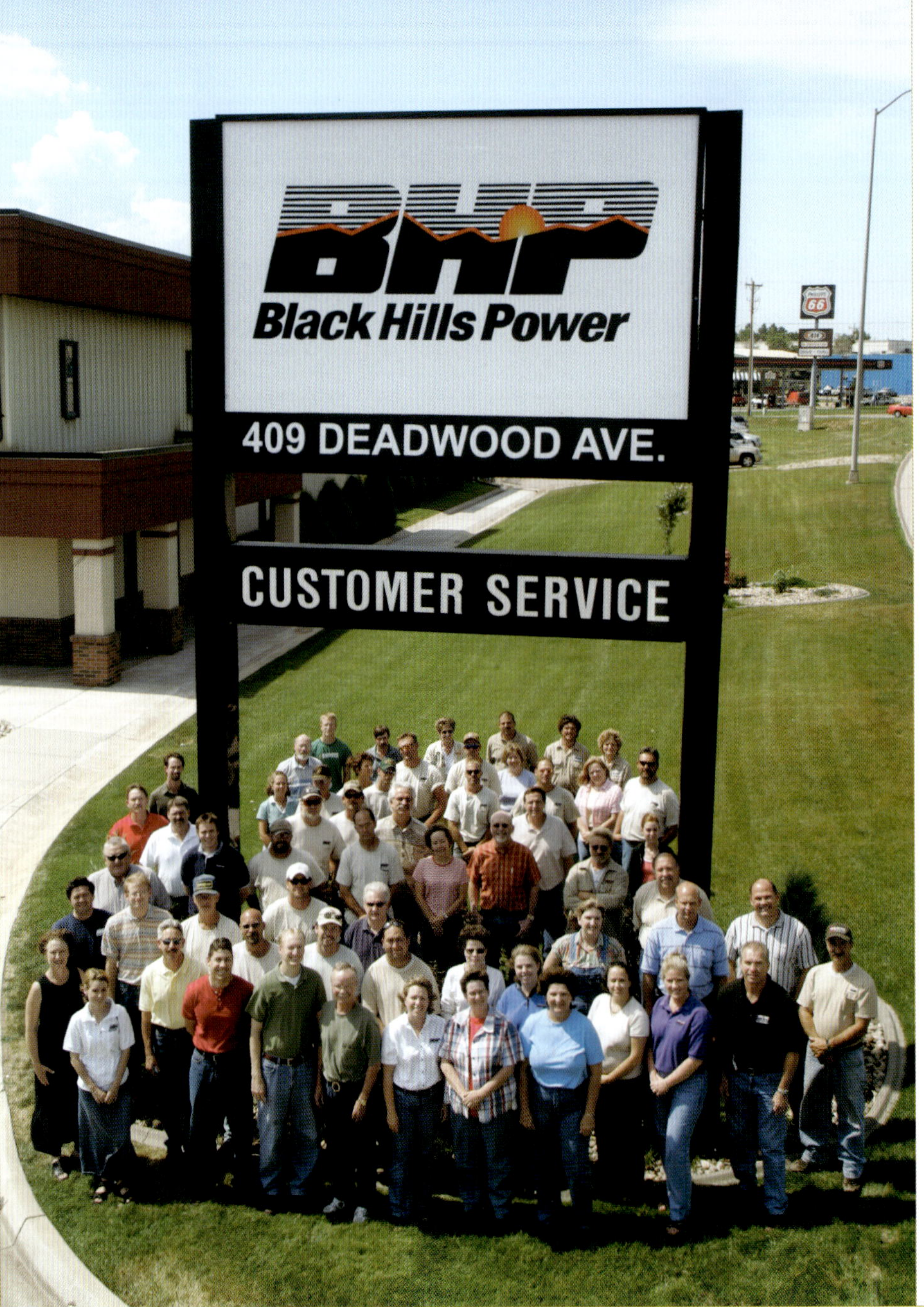

Black Hills Power's customer service team stands ready to serve at the Deadwood Avenue Rapid City hub.

Photo by Alan S.Weiner

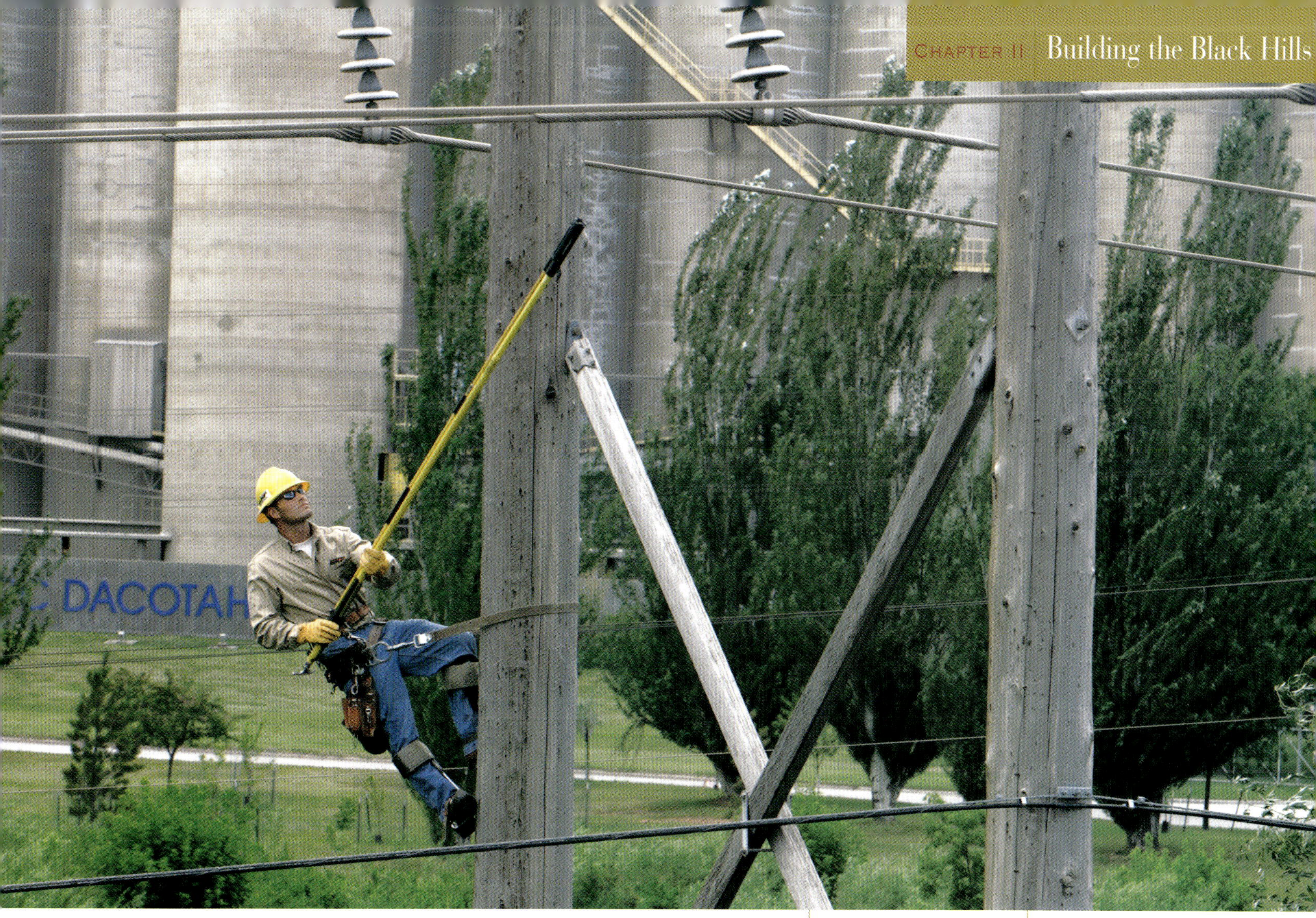

Photo by Alan S.Weiner

Black Hills Power's line crews keep the electricity flowing to communities throughout the region.The GCC Dacotah cement plant pictured here is BHP's largest customer.

Retail operations include Black Hills Power, serving electricity to over sixty-two thousand customers in South Dakota, Wyoming, and Montana; and Cheyenne Light, Fuel & Power, an electric and gas distribution utility serving thirty-eight thousand electric and thirty-one thousand gas customers in the Cheyenne, Wyoming, area. The companies' stable electric rates are below the national average, largely due to the use of efficient mine-mouth coal generation, thus avoiding expensive fuel transportation costs.

J. B. "Ben" French, the first president of Black Hills Power, consolidated smaller regional electric companies in 1941. In the 1942 Annual Report, he said of Black Hills Power's contribution to the war effort, "Approximately one-third of our 1941 employees are now in defense plants or in the armed service. This puts a much heavier burden on the employees still with us. They have accepted this additional burden with a splendid spirit of cooperation."

That spirit exists today. "We pledge responsible energy development for the West," said president, chief executive officer, and chairman David Emery. "We express our commitment through our relationships with customers, shareholders, and business partners, as well as through our respect for our land, water, and air.

"In developing and operating our facilities, we comply with the spirit as well as the letter of the law," said Emery. "In recent years we have built state-of-the-art power plants that are among the cleanest in the nation. Tribal taxes and fees from our gas and oil operations in the Southwest provide support for the Southern Ute and Jicarilla Apache nations."

Black Hills Corporation's 823 employees work for community betterment wherever they live. In Rapid City, they are the leading per-capita givers to United Way, and local employees volunteer over twenty thousand hours each year. Local sponsorships range from teaching children about the environment through "Wildlife Experiences" to helping people with emergency utility payments through "Energy Share."

"Though we've grown from a small electric utility to a $2 billion diversified energy company, we've never forgotten our roots deep in the Black Hills," concluded Emery. ❖

A friendly game of GOLF!

Held each year in early June, the Chamber Golf Challenge is one of the organization's most anticipated networking events. Originally held as a match between the Chamber and local military members, the Challenge switched to a corporate focus in 2005 as a result of an increase in deployments. At the first Battle of the Businesses, as it's now known, 148 golfers representing thirty-nine area businesses signed up for the one-day event, held at Rapid City's Golf Club at Red Rock. After a full day's worth of friendly competition, players meet up again at an evening social for dinner, cocktails, and an awards ceremony, which presents a trophy cup to winners in both the corporate and open divisions. ❖

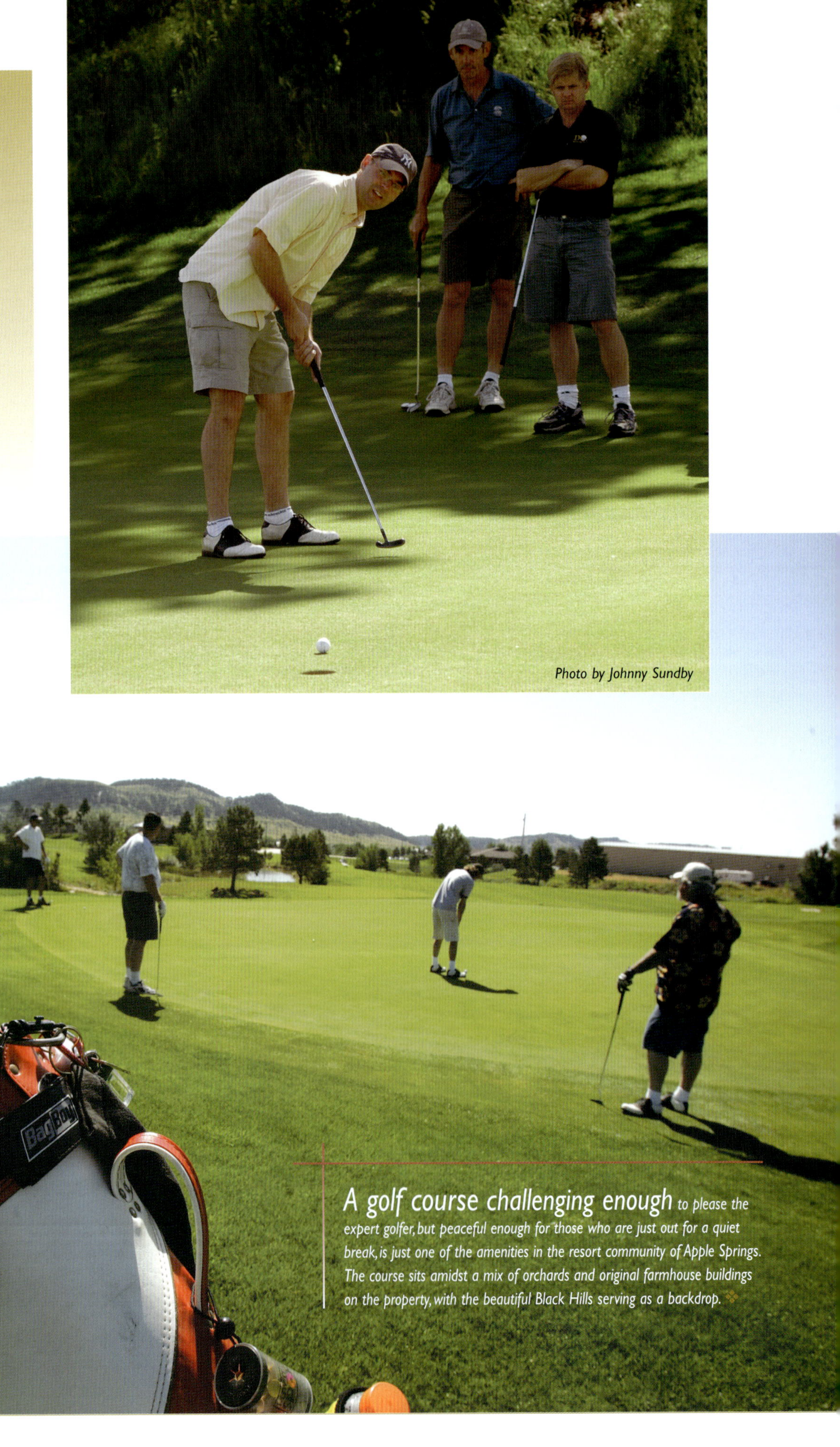

Photo by Johnny Sundby

A golf course challenging enough to please the expert golfer, but peaceful enough for those who are just out for a quiet break, is just one of the amenities in the resort community of Apple Springs. The course sits amidst a mix of orchards and original farmhouse buildings on the property, with the beautiful Black Hills serving as a backdrop. ❖

Photo by Eric Francis

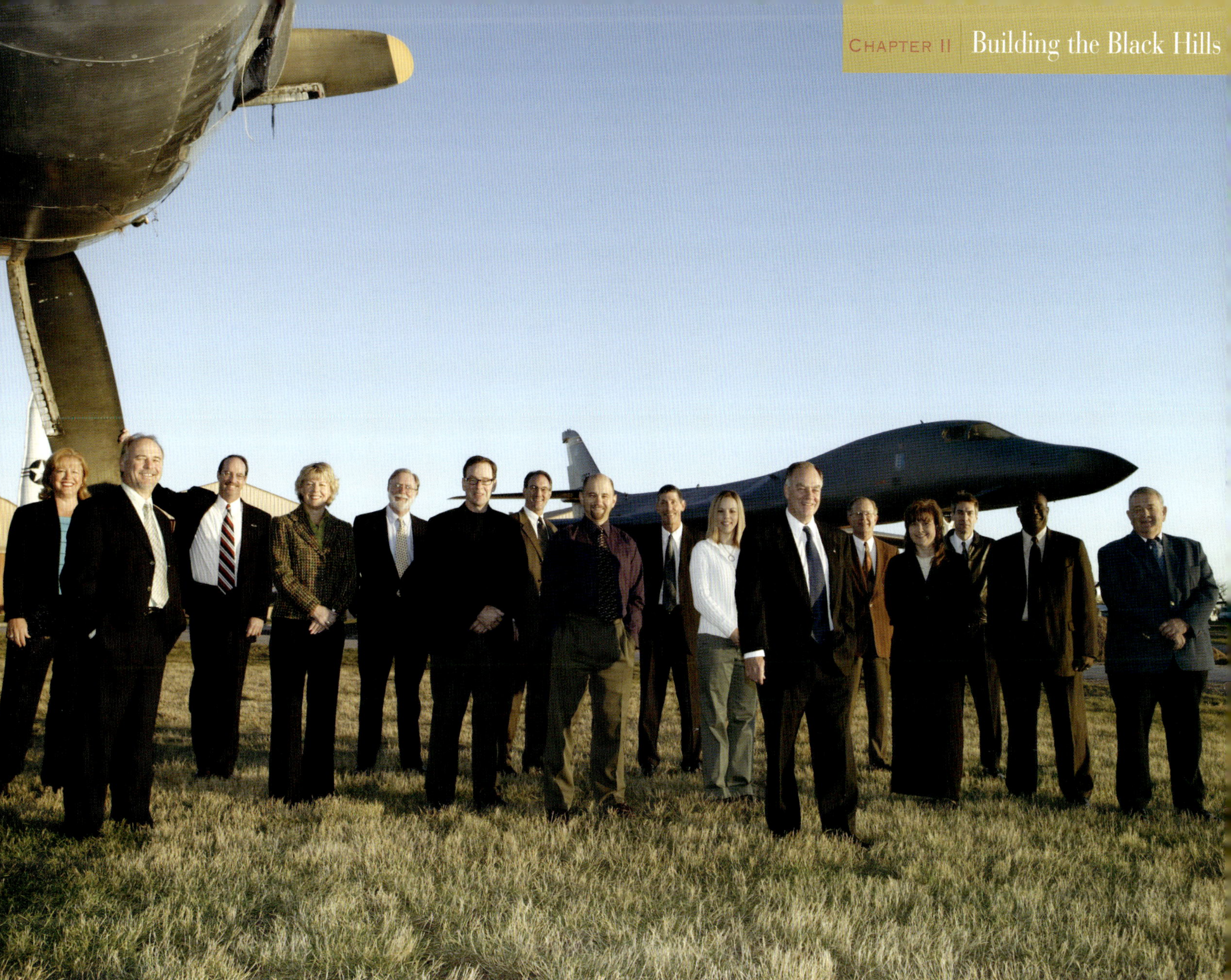

Photo by Rodger Slott

Rapid City Chamber leaders

are pictured with a B-1 bomber. Ellsworth Air Force Base is home to a fleet of 29 B-1 bombers and is South Dakota's second-largest employer, providing many military and civilian jobs and $278 million to the economy—so when the Pentagon proposed to close Ellsworth, the Chamber rallied its forces and thanks to the efforts of the Chamber's Ellsworth Task Force, which consisted of Chamber members, congressional delegates, local leaders, and private citizens, Ellsworth was successfully kept off the 2005 base closure list. In addition to supporting and protecting existing economies, the Chamber also focuses on promoting future economic initiatives, such as the Great Plains International Trade Corridor and Technology Corridor and the conversion of Homestake Gold Mine into the world's deepest underground science and engineering laboratory. ❖

Black Hills Vision Committed to Quality of Life and Economy

Black Hills Vision (BHV) is a regional economic development organization committed to preserving the region's quality of life and creating an economic development "opportunity environment."

BHV was conceived by three local and regional community groups: the Black Hills Community Economic Development Corporation, the Rapid City Area Chamber of Commerce, and the Rapid City Area Economic Development Partnership. BHV incorporated as a nonprofit organization in September 2004.

A BHV Steering Committee was formed in 2002 to determine priorities for fund-raising. A professional fund-raiser, NCDS, was retained to work with community volunteers to raise $3 million for six regional priorities:

$1,150,000	Marketing the Black Hills and a National Underground Laboratory
$300,000	Securing the Future of Ellsworth Air Force Base
$500,000	Air Service Task Force/New Market Initiatives
$500,000	Black Hills Business Development Incubator
$300,000	Affordable Housing Development

"No matter what the organizing principle may be, a sense of region is an essential starting point for any region looking to reinvent its economy."

The scope of Black Hills Vision encompasses the entire economic area. This unusual view of the Black Hills captures that spirit. The image is actually a high-resolution mosaic created from satellite imaging obtained by the Earth Resources Observation System (EROS) Data Center, which is a data management, systems development, and research field center for the United States Geological Survey (USGS). In this case, four satellite images were needed to cover the entire area. A number of these images were made on different days to obtain a cloud-free product. Once the mosaic was created, digital elevation was added to the model to create the 3-D effect.

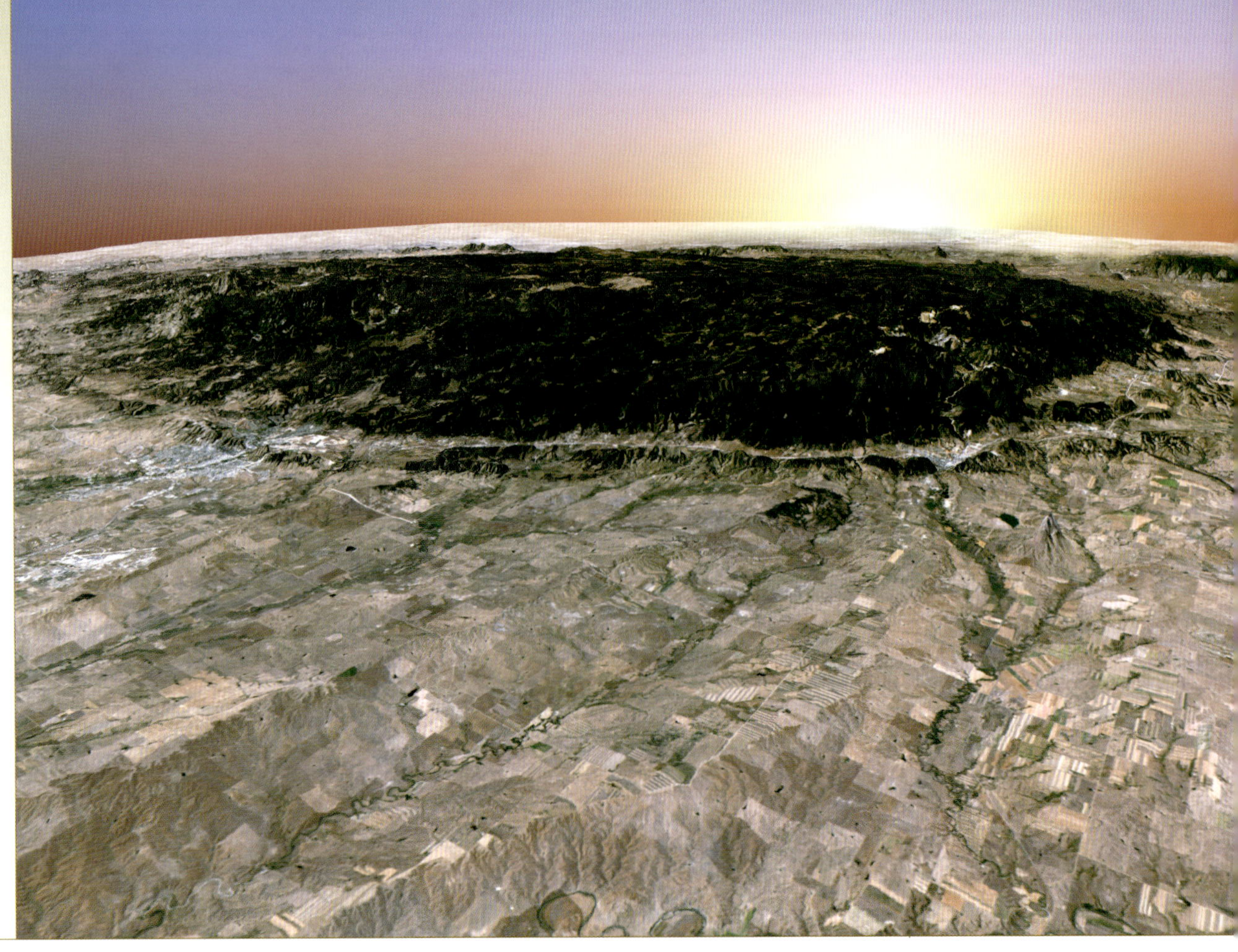

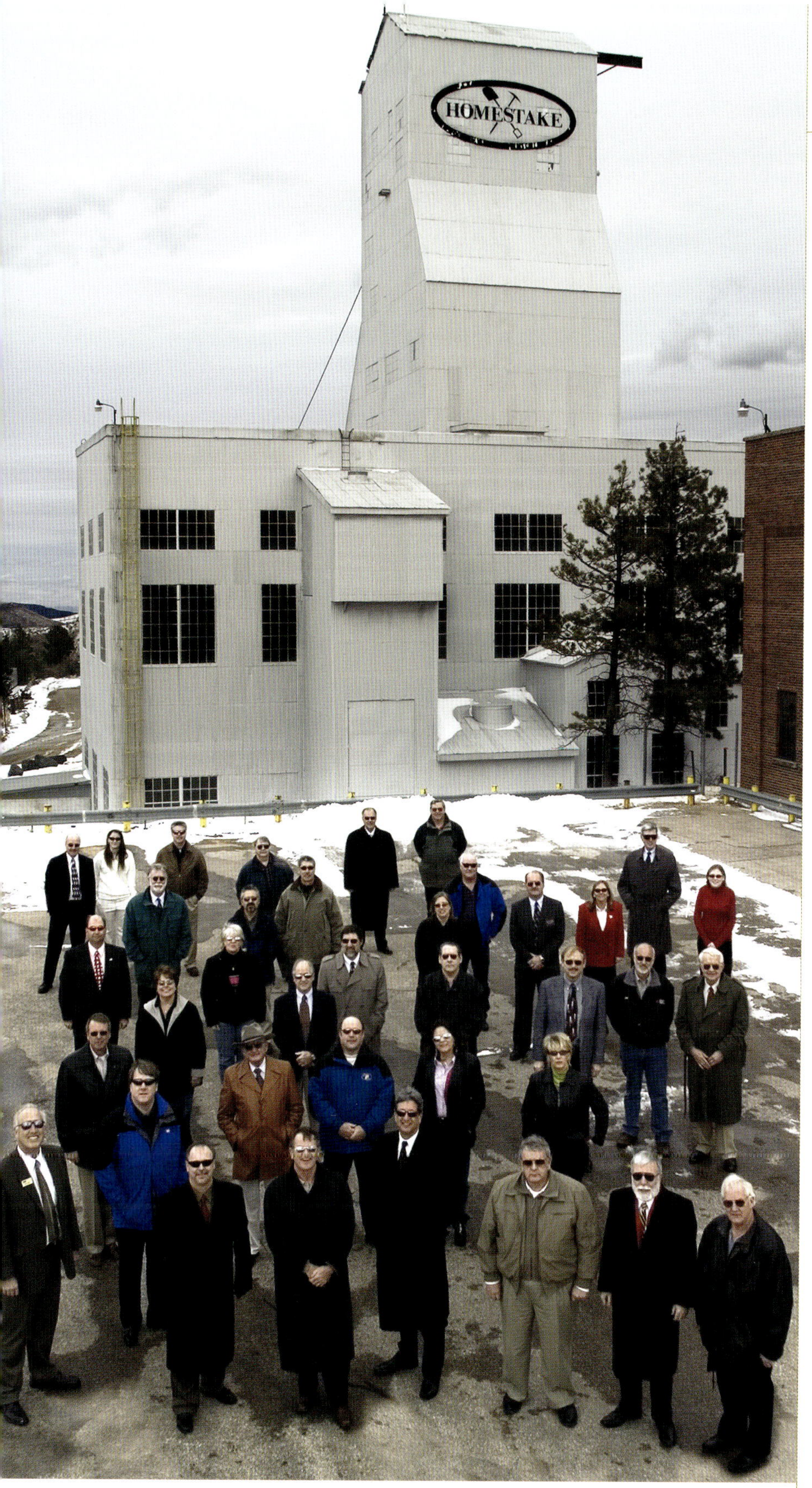

Representatives of over one hundred Black Hills Vision investors gathered at Homestake, a symbol representing a "future so bright they had to wear shades" after having raised $3 million to create an opportunity environment for the entire Black Hills region.

$250,000 Administration and Investor Relations Fundraising was completed in February 2005 with five-year pledges from over 114 investors. Thirty-six of these investors made commitments in excess of $50,000 and became members of the BHV Board of Directors, which included seven mayors, four county commissioners, and leaders from banking, utilities, publishing, health-care, business, chamber, and economic development organizations.

The possibility of a national underground laboratory at the former Homestake mine helped everyone realize what was good for one community could be good for everyone. BHV expanded this idea to include a technology corridor like the one that emerged around the National Laboratory in Oak Ridge, Tennessee. Battelle Memorial Institute was retained by BHV to develop a road map for the Technology Corridor Project. The mission statement for the Vision Technology Corridor Project is as follows:

"Future economies of states and regions will be determined by what our private- and public-sector leaders chart as a vision around knowledge assets and related areas such as workforce, technology infrastructure and business climate, the mobilization of resources around that vision, and a corresponding Roadmap and the commitment to its implementation over several years. The proposed Black Hills Technology Corridor Roadmap links these technology assets to new market opportunities, identifies the gaps that must be addressed, and the needed investments in near-, mid-, and long-term timeframes. The overall goal of such a plan, when implemented, is the creation of good, well-paying jobs and retention of an in-state workforce to sustain new and growing technology companies."

BHV is best characterized by the theme, "speaking with one voice." The Center for the Study of Rural America described regional economic development organizations like BHV this way: "Regions are becoming the policy framework for economic development in the twenty-first century. No matter what the organizing principle may be, a sense of region is an essential starting point for any region looking to reinvent its economy. Within any new institutional framework, an ongoing challenge is to make win/win the rule that governs all regional efforts. Reinventing the economy of a region is hard work that demands the best efforts of all players. Trust among the partners is essential to elicit the best contributions of all parties."

This description epitomizes BHV. ❖

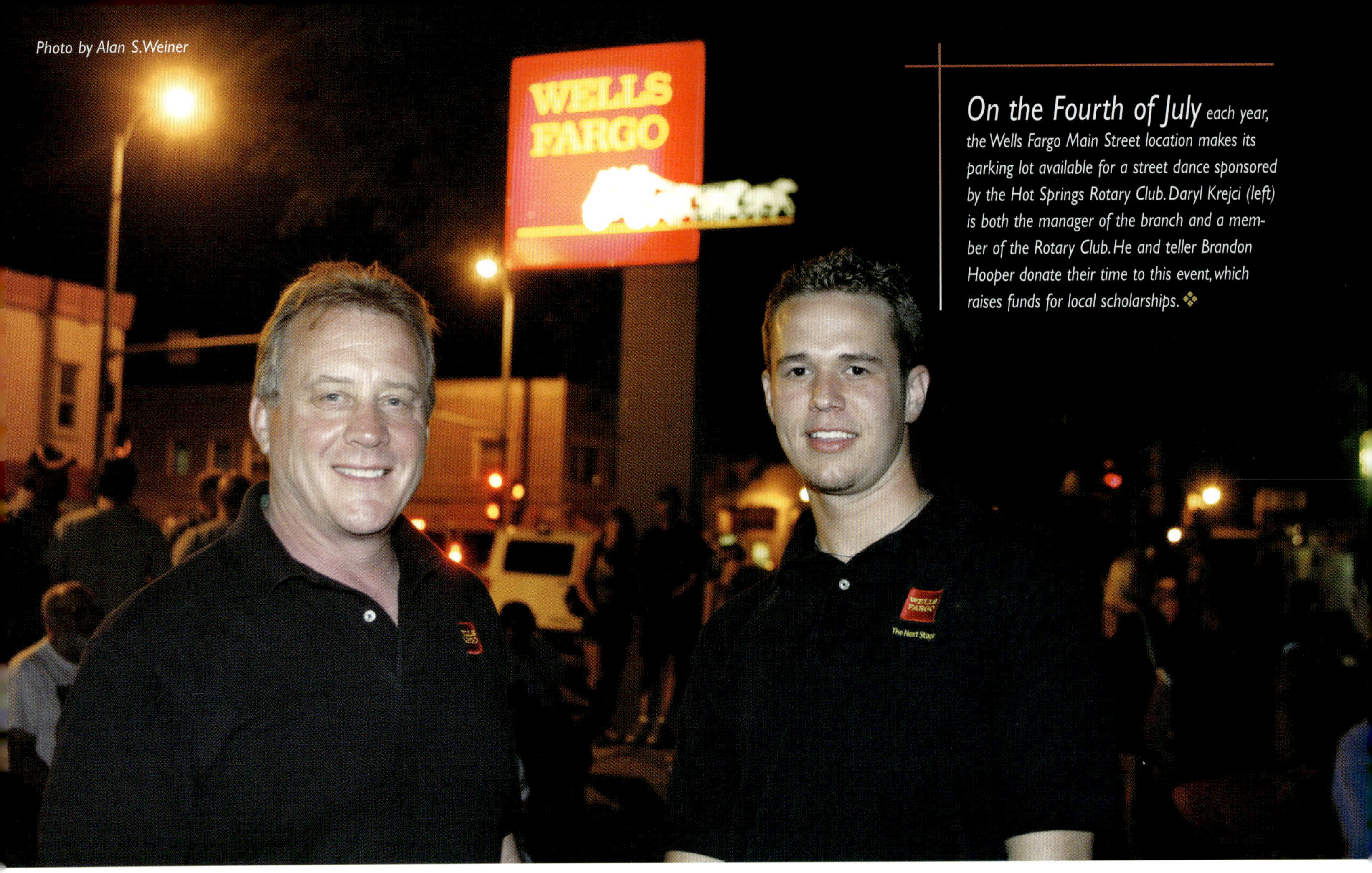

Photo by Alan S. Weiner

On the Fourth of July each year, the Wells Fargo Main Street location makes its parking lot available for a street dance sponsored by the Hot Springs Rotary Club. Daryl Krejci (left) is both the manager of the branch and a member of the Rotary Club. He and teller Brandon Hooper donate their time to this event, which raises funds for local scholarships. ❖

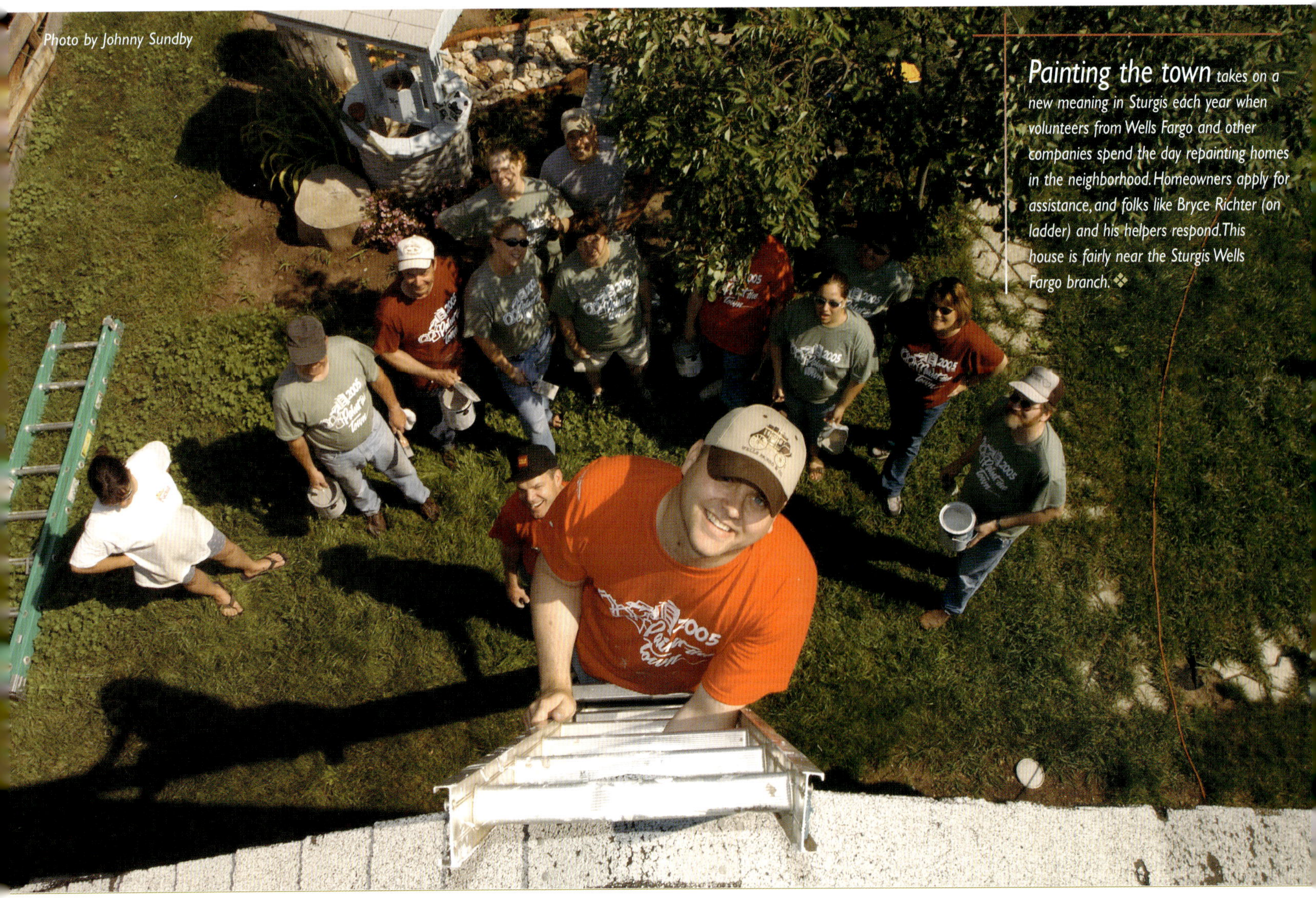

Photo by Johnny Sundby

Painting the town takes on a new meaning in Sturgis each year when volunteers from Wells Fargo and other companies spend the day repainting homes in the neighborhood. Homeowners apply for assistance, and folks like Bryce Richter (on ladder) and his helpers respond. This house is fairly near the Sturgis Wells Fargo branch. ❖

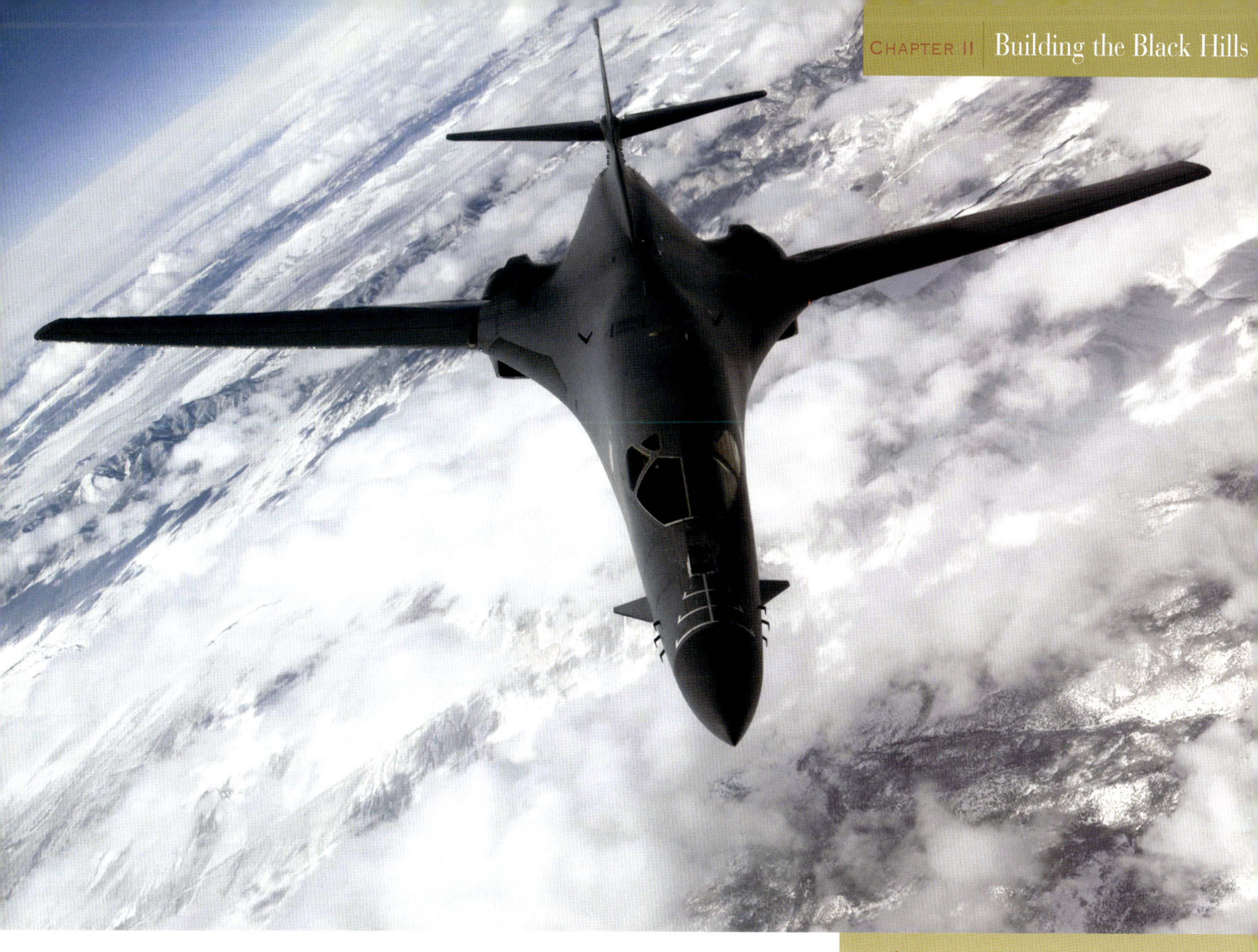

Since it opened in 1942, the Rapid City Army Air Base has changed both its name and its mission several times. However, today's Ellsworth Air Force Base has always been closely linked to the economy of the Rapid City area. In 2006, Black Hills Vision raised three hundred thousand dollars to support the Ellsworth Task Force, which was ultimately successful in getting the base removed from the list of military installations slated for closing. Home to the Twenty-eighth Bomb Wing, the base's mission is "to provide rapid, decisive, and sustainable combat air power; anytime, anywhere." Paramount in that mission is the B-1B Lancer, a multirole, long-range bomber capable of flying intercontinental missions without refueling. It carries the largest payload of both guided and unguided weapons in the Air Force inventory and is the backbone of America's long-range bomber force. Initially the B-1A was developed in the 1970s to replace the B-52. The B-1B is an improved version initiated by the Reagan administration in 1981. The statistics are impressive. The plane is 34 feet high, has a wingspan of 137 feet, weighs approximately 477,000 pounds when fully loaded, and has a thrust of 30,000-plus pounds with afterburner, per engine. ❖

Rapid City Chamber Offers Support and Protection to Local Businesses

As the cultural and economic heart of the Black Hills, Rapid City today is as rich in opportunity as it was when indigenous people and then American settlers first made their way into the area. Characterized by stunning natural beauty, a low cost of living, and a family-friendly environment, Rapid City and its surrounding communities have something to offer businesses of every kind and size.

Since 1886, the Rapid City Area Chamber of Commerce has fostered a healthy business environment as part of the high quality of life offered by the Black Hills region. With fourteen hundred member companies, almost double the national average for a community of its size, the Chamber focuses not only on supporting individual business members, but also on developing a managed economic growth plan for the entire Black Hills. Each year, twenty-five to thirty committees and task forces comprising hundreds of volunteers set about working on major goals that cover everything from transportation to environmental issues.

Supporting and protecting existing economies is a major part of the Chamber's mission. In 2005, the Ellsworth Air Force Base Task Force, consisting of Chamber members, congressional delegates, local leaders, and private citizens, successfully lobbied to keep Ellsworth off the Pentagon's 2005 base closure list. With the area growing in popularity as a tourism destination, the Chamber works to provide support for existing attraction and hospitality businesses, while partnering with the rest of the Black Hills and the state to develop new markets.

Rapid City and its surrounding communities have something to offer businesses of every kind and size.

Photo by Thomas S. England

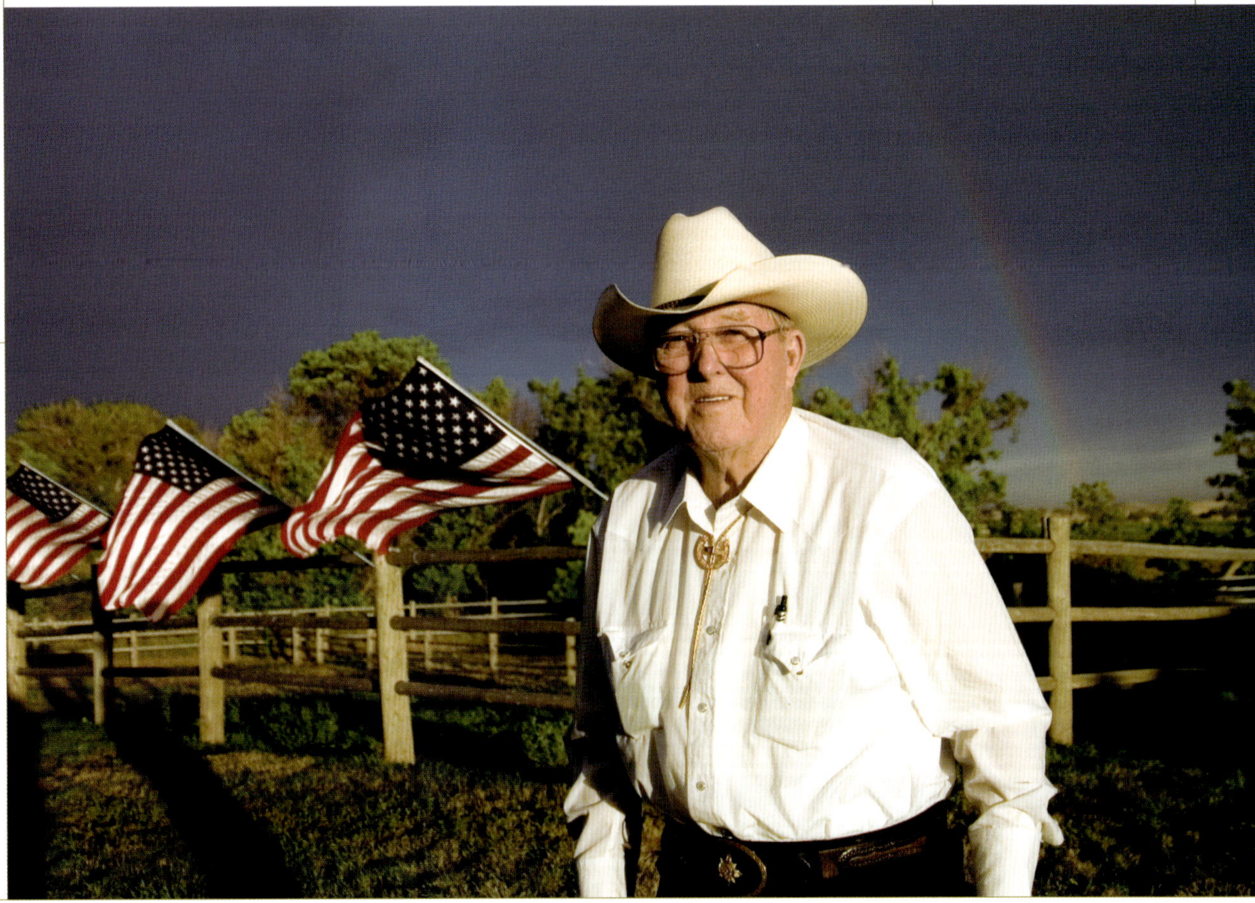

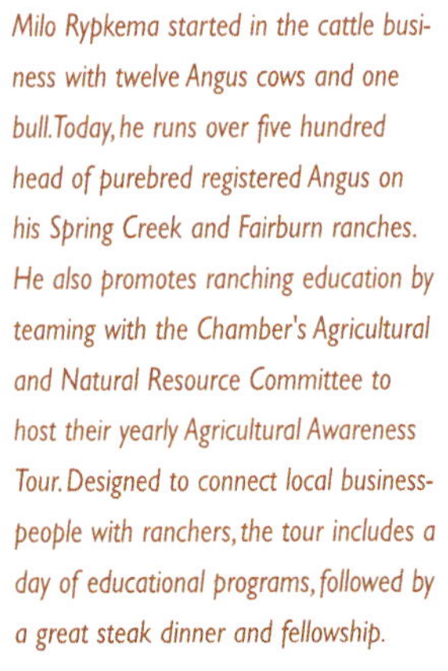

Milo Rypkema started in the cattle business with twelve Angus cows and one bull. Today, he runs over five hundred head of purebred registered Angus on his Spring Creek and Fairburn ranches. He also promotes ranching education by teaming with the Chamber's Agricultural and Natural Resource Committee to host their yearly Agricultural Awareness Tour. Designed to connect local businesspeople with ranchers, the tour includes a day of educational programs, followed by a great steak dinner and fellowship.

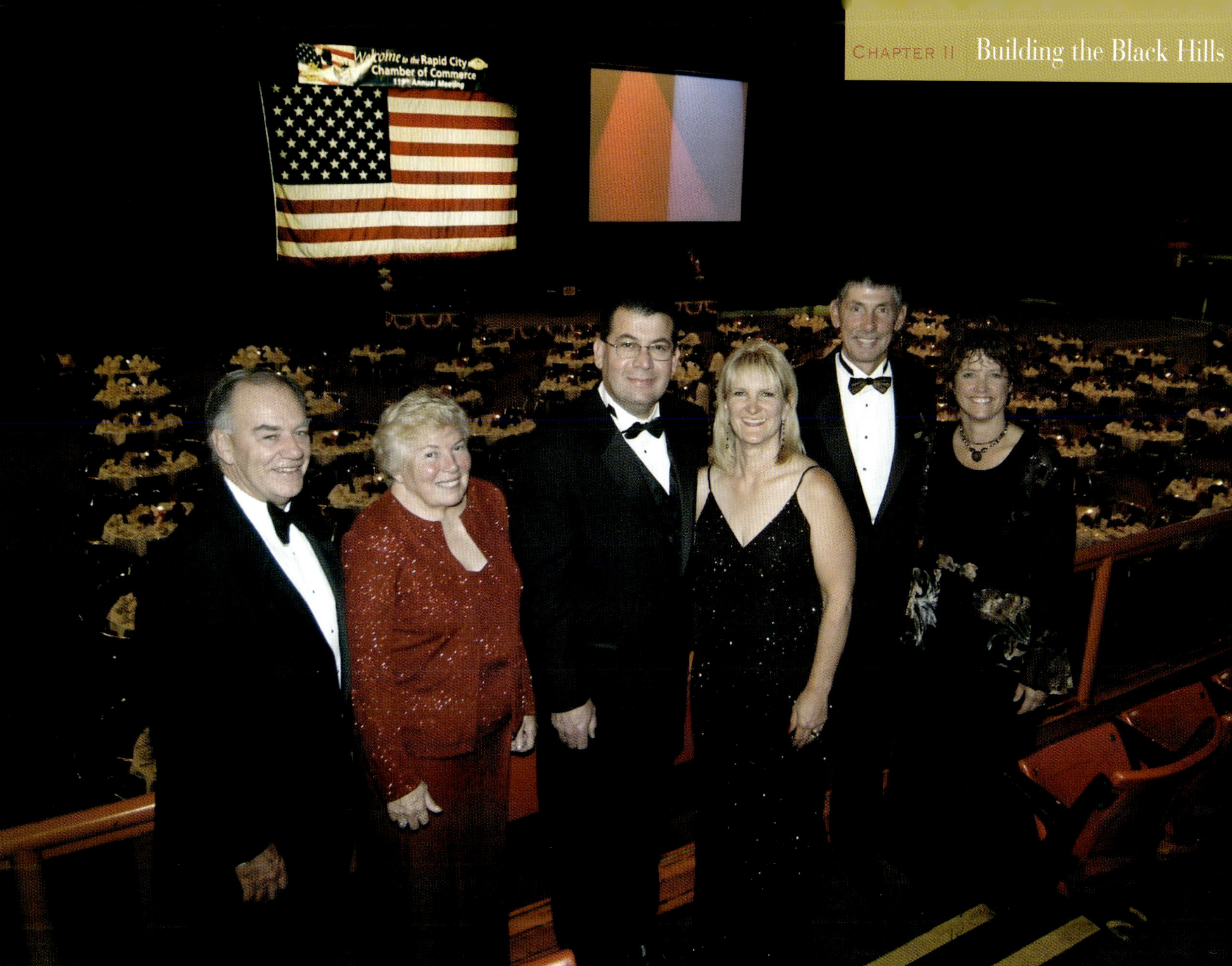

Photo by Doug Henderson

The purpose of the Chamber's annual meeting is to recognize the many volunteers within the community who make it possible for the Chamber to fulfill its mission, review the past year's accomplishments, and preview the upcoming year. Enjoying the festivities at the Chamber's 119th annual meeting are (left to right) president and CEO Jim McKeon and his wife Eileen; past chairman of the board Qusi Al-Haj with his wife Jamie; and chairman of the board Pat Wyss and his wife Jean. In honor of Ellsworth AFB being kept off the base closure list, the 2005 annual meeting featured a patriotic theme.

The Chamber also concentrates on attracting new business to the area. As a way to capitalize on the benefits created by interstate commerce traffic, its Transportation Task Force has successfully lobbied to fund South Dakota's section of the Heartland Expressway. As a section of the Great Plains Corridor, a four-lane north-south running artery that will connect cities and regional trade centers in the Great Plains from Canada to Mexico, the Heartland Expressway will provide remote locations throughout the Black Hills with revitalized economic opportunities.

Undoubtedly, a large part of Rapid City's attraction is its abundant surrounding natural beauty and outdoor recreational opportunities. Here, development and environmental protection are not mutually exclusive goals. By maintaining a proactive environmental policy, the Chamber works closely with local governments and business owners to most effectively allocate scarce resources for development. One plan currently in the works is a Chamber-supported regional transportation plan that will efficiently link area communities.

Likewise, the Black Hills National Forest serves as a valuable model for solving multiple use issues. The Chamber participates in the nation's first-of-its-kind National Forest Advisory Board that works with the forest supervisor to advise on the most sensible uses of the forest, from timber harvesting to recreational opportunities.

To be a member of the Rapid City Area Chamber of Commerce is to be a member of a close-knit family, one that offers members access to the events, ideas, and technologies that lead to success in today's business environment. A comprehensive Web site, seminars and expos, networking luncheons, and after-hours mixers provide invaluable exposure and

Continued on page 154

Continued from page 153

connections for members. Groups like the Chamber's Technology Committee provide new and existing businesses with a greater competitive edge, by helping them seek ways to use current and future technologies to improve business practices and increase profitability.

Membership in the Rapid City Area Chamber of Commerce also means inclusion in the greater community that is the Black Hills, a community in which business works to promote an exceptionally high quality of life enjoyed by all. ❖

Photo by Thomas S. England

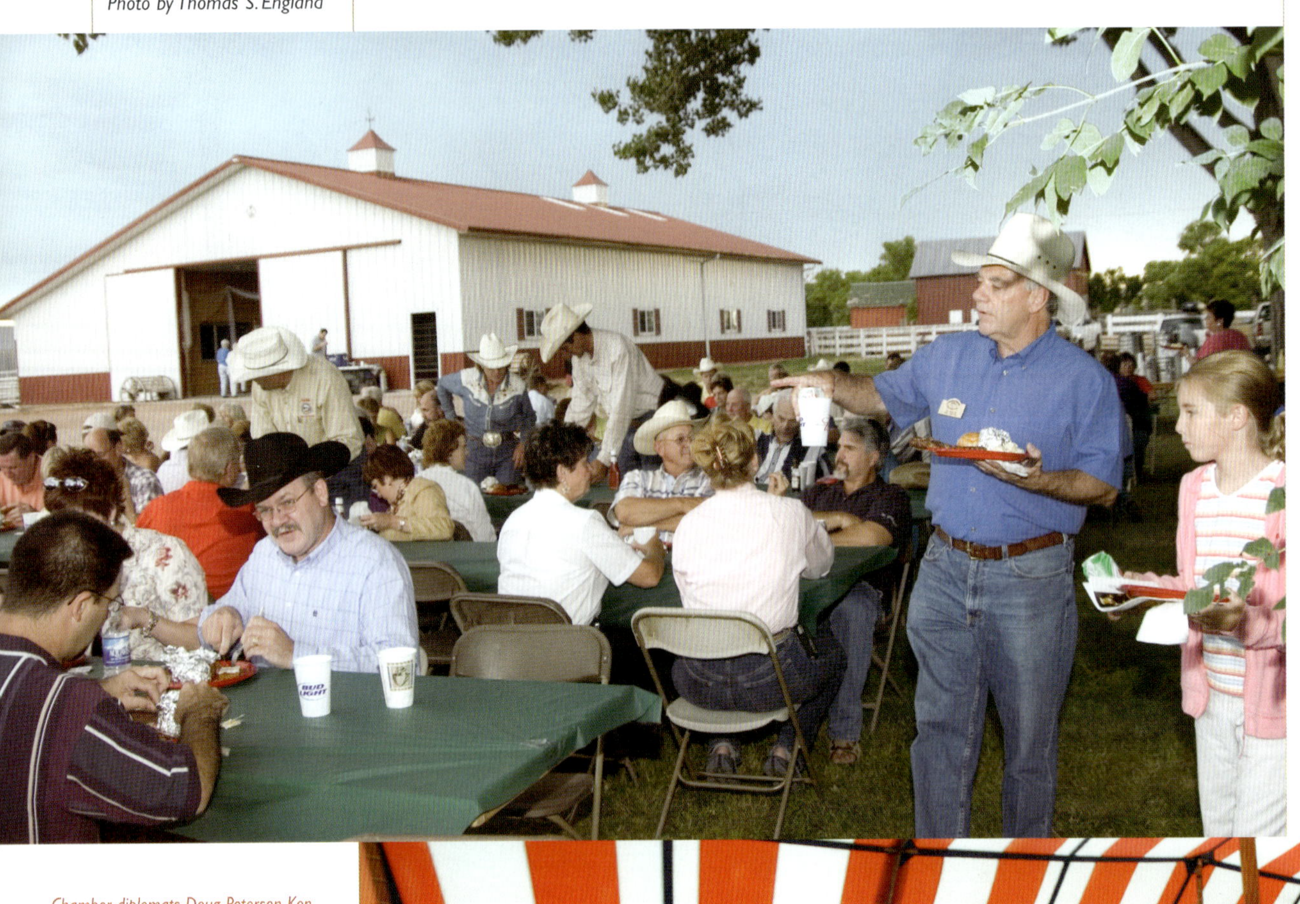

Photo by Eric Francis

Chamber diplomats Doug Peterson, Ken Kirkeby, and Ozzie Osheim (pictured left to right) take a break from their host duties of mixing, mingling, and welcoming new members at one of the Chamber's monthly mixers, which draw up to nine hundred people. Mixers provide great networking opportunities and are a tremendous resource for bringing members together. Chamber mixers are held all over the Black Hills. This mixer, held at the Central States Fair, had folks passing out at least ten business cards before enjoying the food and drink and proceeding on to the evening's concert. Above, Amanda McKeon listens as grandfather and Chamber president Jim McKeon points beyond the Ag & Natural Resources Committee and its guests enjoying a wonderful steak dinner to explain how the Mount Rushmore Angus Ranch (otherwise known as the Rypkema Ranch) works and the importance of agribusiness to the country.

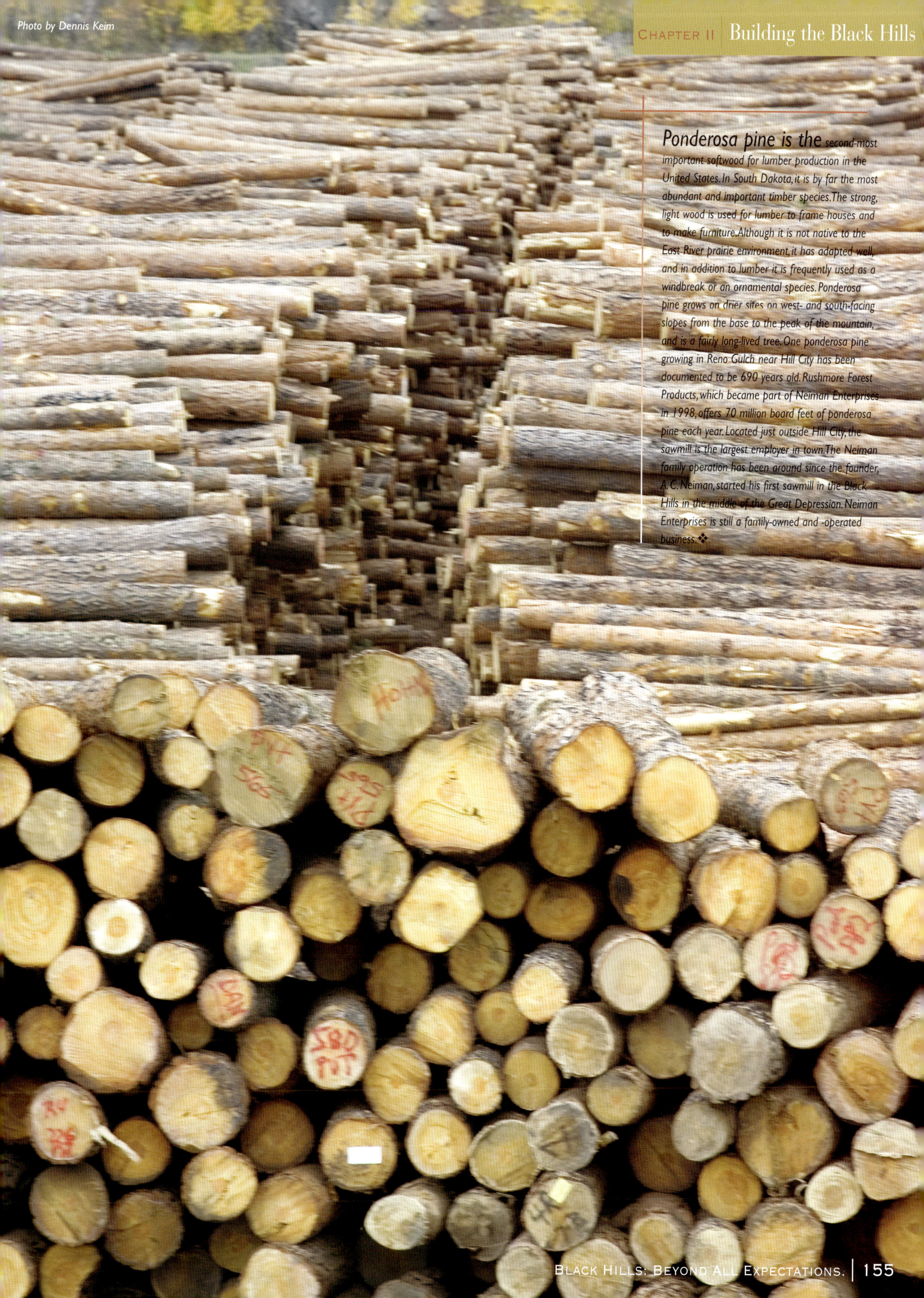

Photo by Dennis Keim

Ponderosa pine is the second-most important softwood for lumber production in the United States. In South Dakota, it is by far the most abundant and important timber species. The strong, light wood is used for lumber to frame houses and to make furniture. Although it is not native to the East River prairie environment, it has adapted well, and in addition to lumber it is frequently used as a windbreak or an ornamental species. Ponderosa pine grows on drier sites on west- and south-facing slopes from the base to the peak of the mountain, and is a fairly long-lived tree. One ponderosa pine growing in Reno Gulch near Hill City has been documented to be 690 years old. Rushmore Forest Products, which became part of Neiman Enterprises in 1998, offers 70 million board feet of ponderosa pine each year. Located just outside Hill City, the sawmill is the largest employer in town. The Neiman family operation has been ground since the founder, A. C. Neiman, started his first sawmill in the Black Hills in the middle of the Great Depression. Neiman Enterprises is still a family-owned and -operated business. ❖

Highmark Federal Credit Union: "We Can Make It Happen"

When it comes to money matters, there is a real sense of confidence and security that comes from working with Highmark Federal Credit Union. Originally chartered in 1940 to exclusively serve the needs of teachers, Highmark has grown to become one of the largest credit unions in the state, serving people from all walks of life in Pennington and surrounding counties with a main office and full-service branch in Rapid City and a full-service branch in downtown Custer.

Highmark has a dedicated and knowledgeable staff with the expertise to assist its members on their path to financial security.

Photo by Doug Henderson

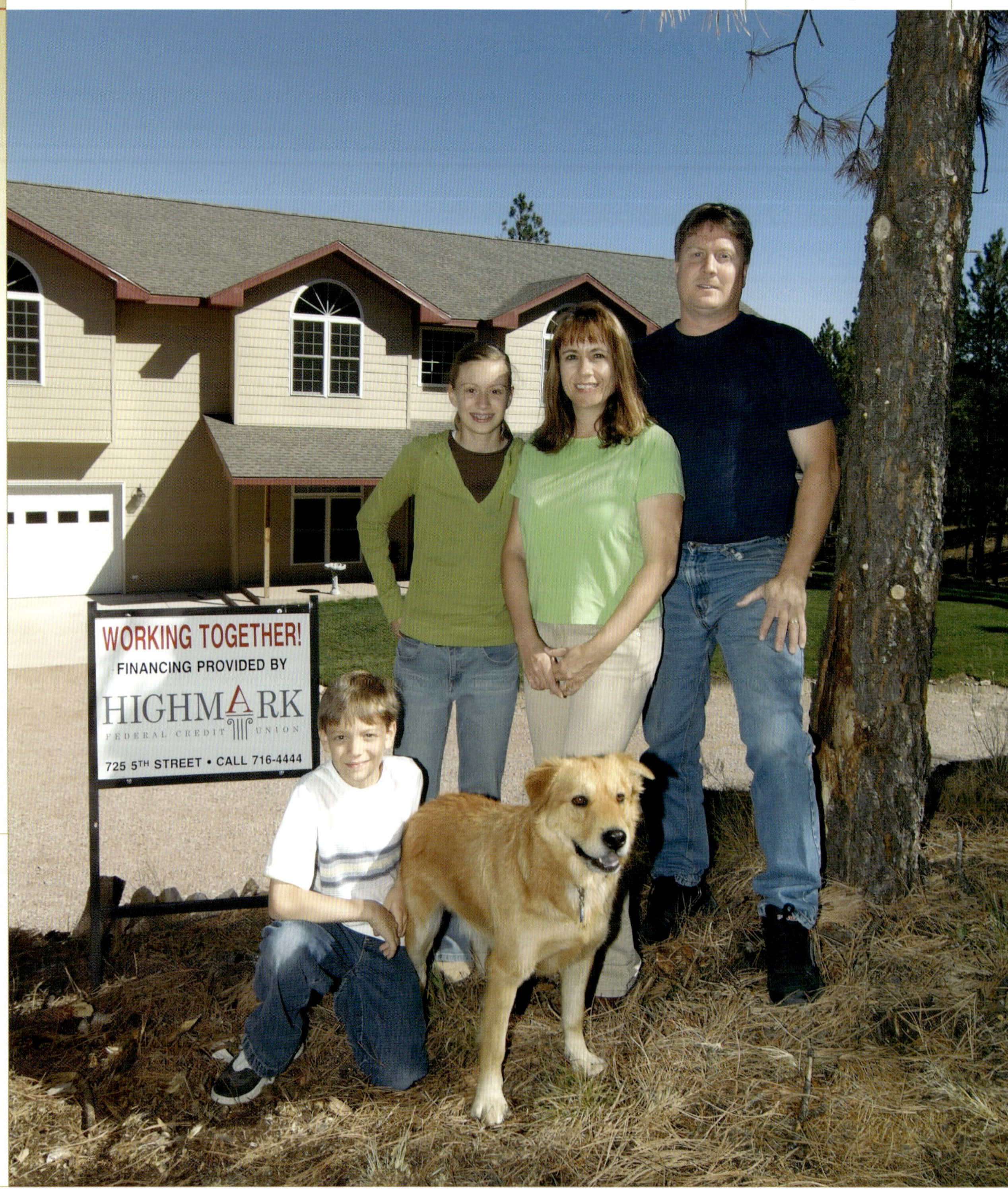

Highmark has gained the reputation as one of the area's premier home lenders providing financing for new home construction, home purchases, and refinancing.

Highmark's growth springs from its fundamental philosophy of truly delivering what people need. Their slogan, "We Can Make It Happen," is evident in everything that they do. Whether it's financing for a home, a college education, or a much-needed vacation, the entire staff is there to help its members reach their financial goals. As a full-service credit union, Highmark offers its members a number of traditional services including online banking, online bill pay, and twenty-four-hour telephone access, but Highmark goes above and beyond to offer its members even more. Free debt counseling, credit education, online mortgage services, more available home loan options, and unparalleled personal service make Highmark truly unique.

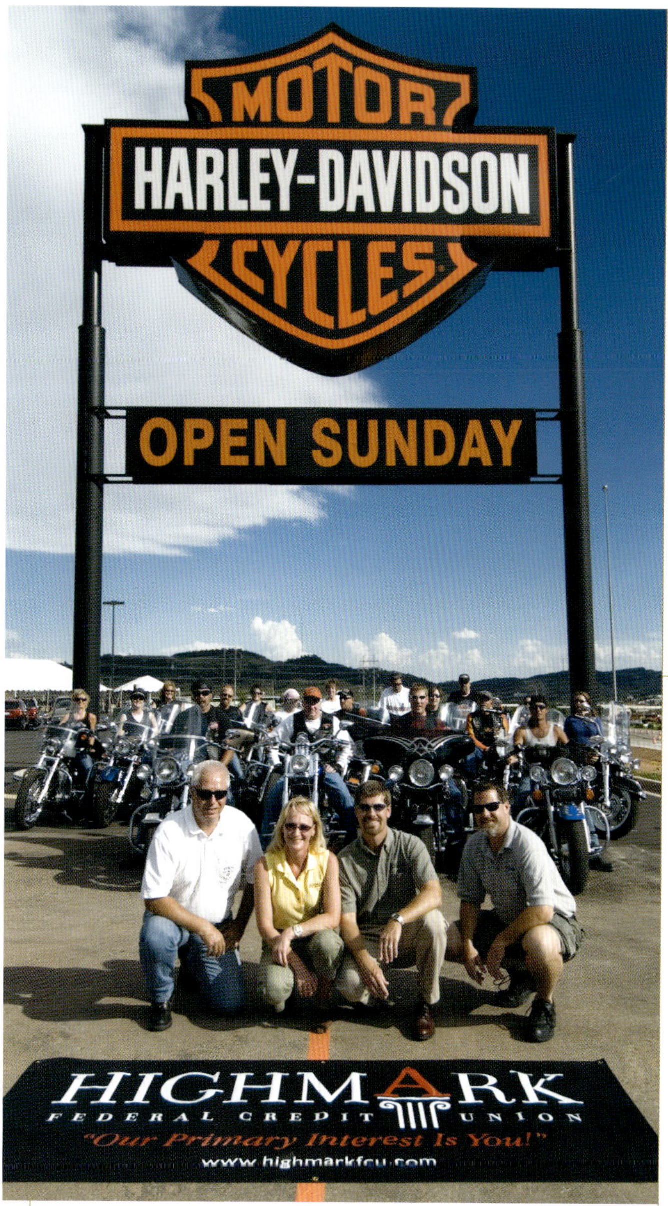

Photo by Thomas S. England

Highmark's indirect loan program offered at local dealerships, such as Black Hills Harley Davidson, has made it possible for thousands of people to finance their car, boat, motorcycle, or ATV with Highmark without ever having to visit the credit union.

On-the-spot financing is another convenient service made available through Highmark. Highmark's indirect loan program is designed to provide competitive financing through local car, motorcycle, and recreational vehicle dealerships. Thousands of area residents have chosen to finance their car, boat, motorcycle, or ATV through Highmark without ever having to visit the credit union. This indirect finance program saves Highmark members time and money.

Highmark also looks out for the future needs of its members with some of the most competitive rates on both short- and long-term savings options. From Share Certificates to IRAs, Highmark has a dedicated and knowledgeable staff with the expertise to assist its members on their path to financial security.

Pride in community is also evident at Highmark, as nearly every employee is involved in one community organization or another. Whether raising funds to help children with special needs or lending leadership talents to serve in areas of community development, the entire Highmark staff embodies the true spirit of "People Helping People!"

In 2006, Highmark marks its sixty-sixth anniversary and currently serves anyone who lives, works, worships, or attends school in Pennington, Meade, Lawrence, or Custer counties. Key to Highmark's continual growth is its long heritage of delivering personal service and, first and foremost, providing its members with individualized attention to their needs. ❖

Photo by Dennis Keim

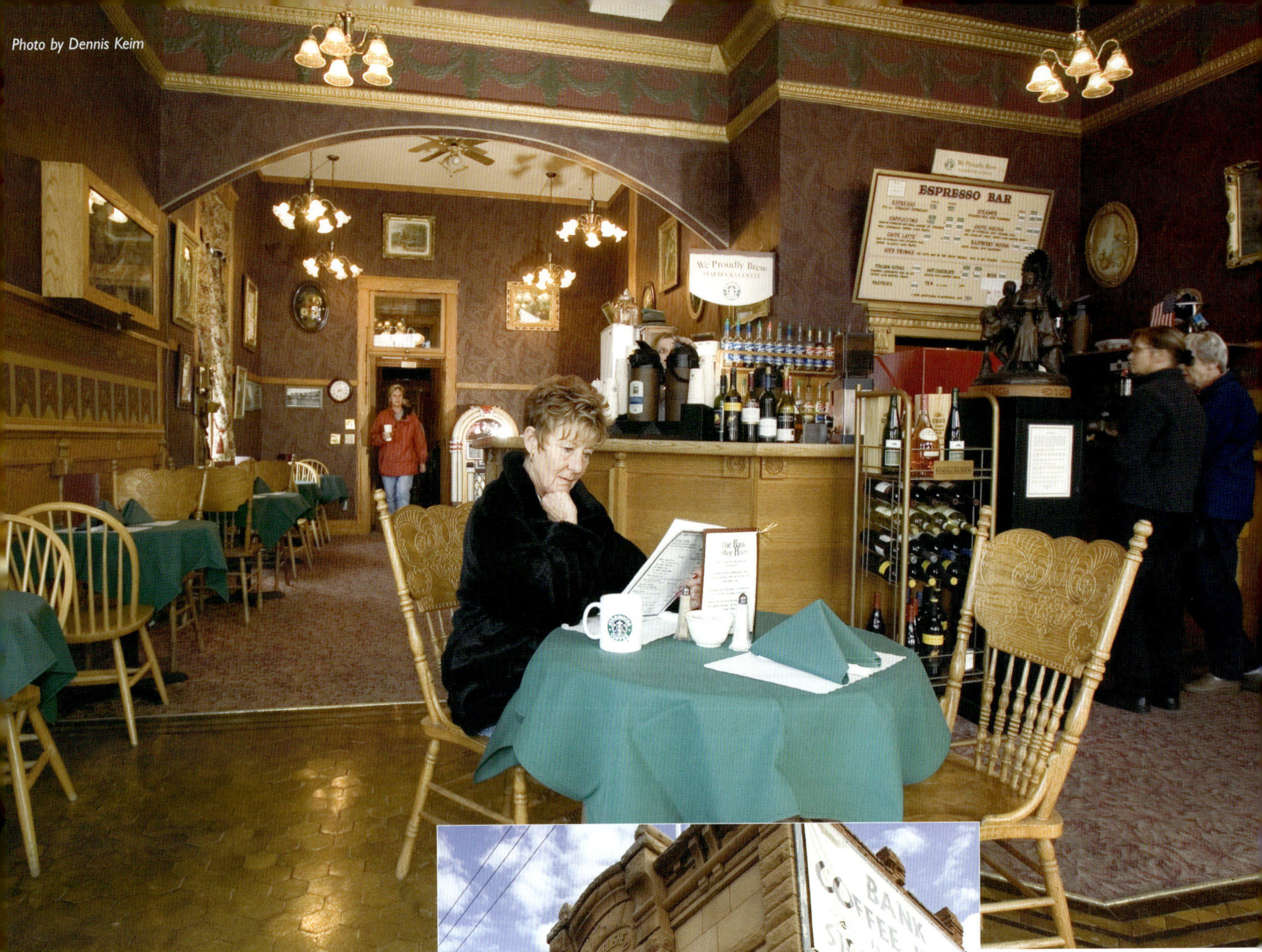

The Bank Coffee House

in Custer is unusual in a number of ways. This 1881 original brick building was a bank even before South Dakota was declared a state. Today, instead of greenbacks in the vault, you'll find a friendly staff preparing delicious sandwiches and serving java. Listed on the National Register of Historic Places, the Bank Coffee House, fomerly known as the First National Bank of Dakota Territory, still features original tile, windows, and wallboards. If you're lucky, Tim, the resident parrot, will let you know he'd like to see you back again one day. ❖

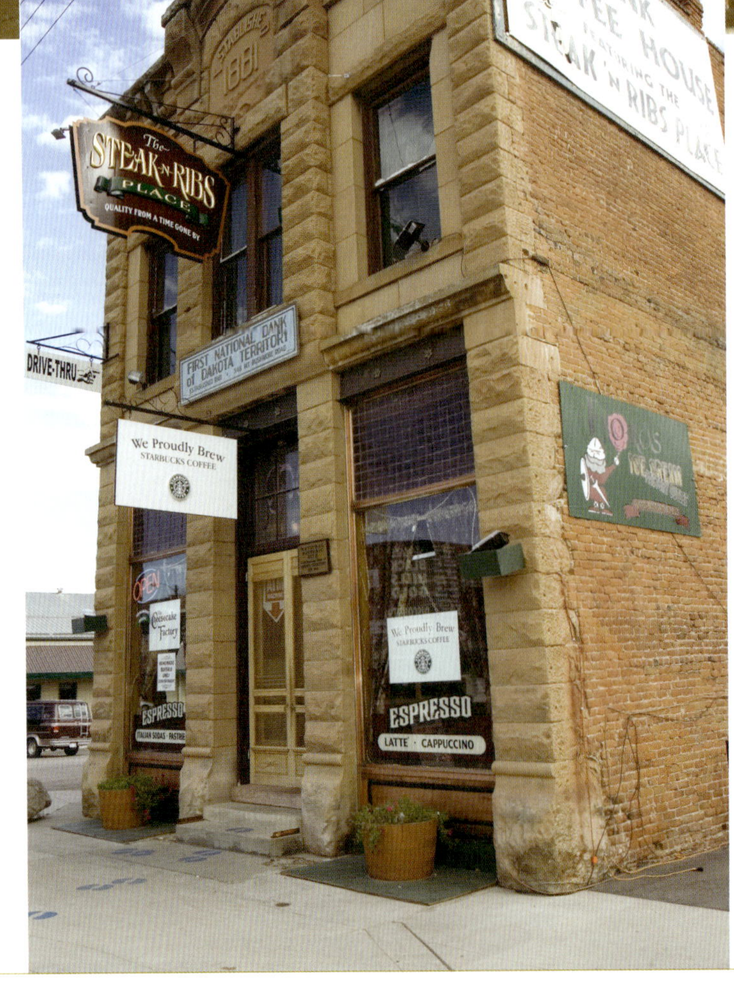

Photo by Dennis Keim

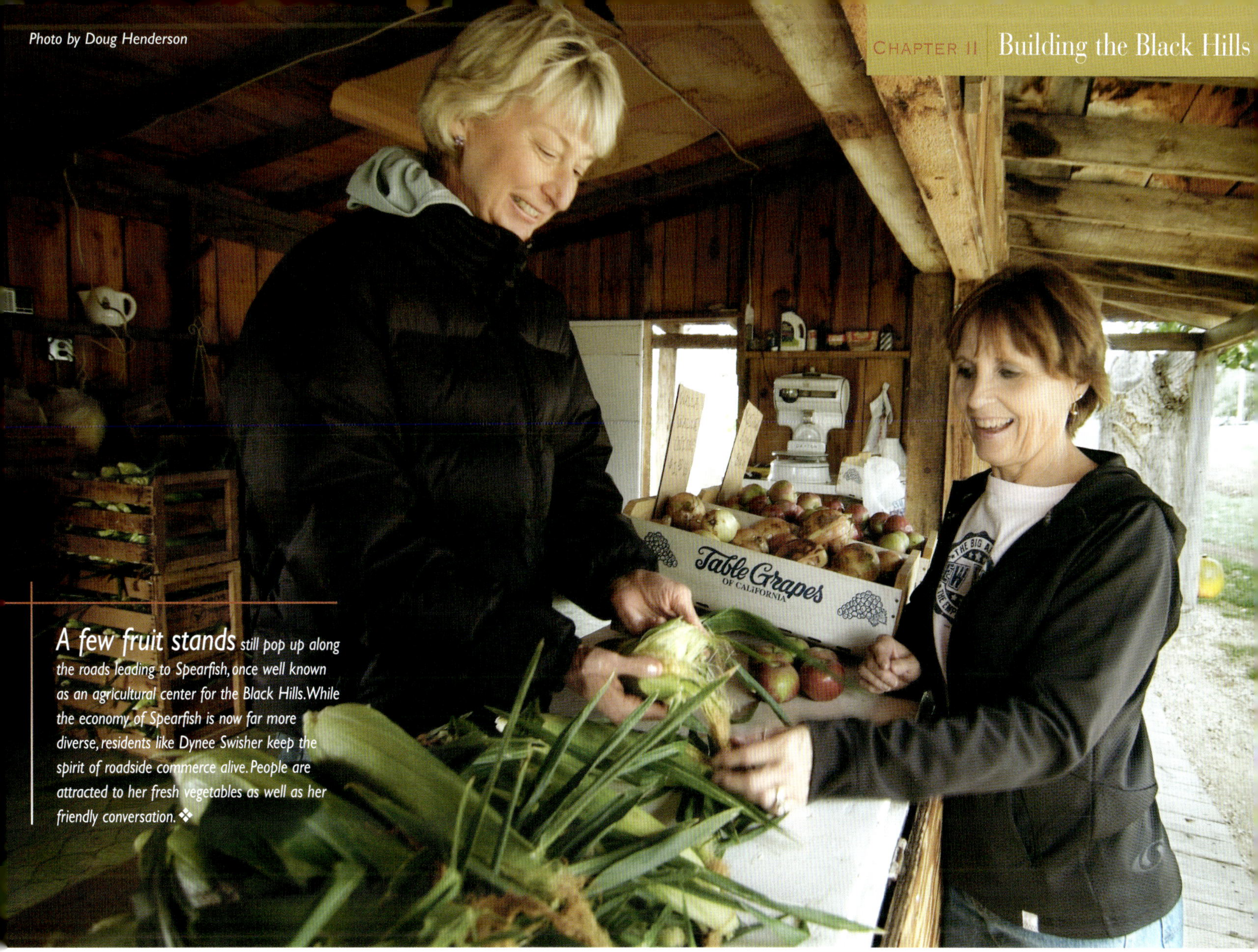

Photo by Doug Henderson

A few fruit stands still pop up along the roads leading to Spearfish, once well known as an agricultural center for the Black Hills. While the economy of Spearfish is now far more diverse, residents like Dynee Swisher keep the spirit of roadside commerce alive. People are attracted to her fresh vegetables as well as her friendly conversation. ❖

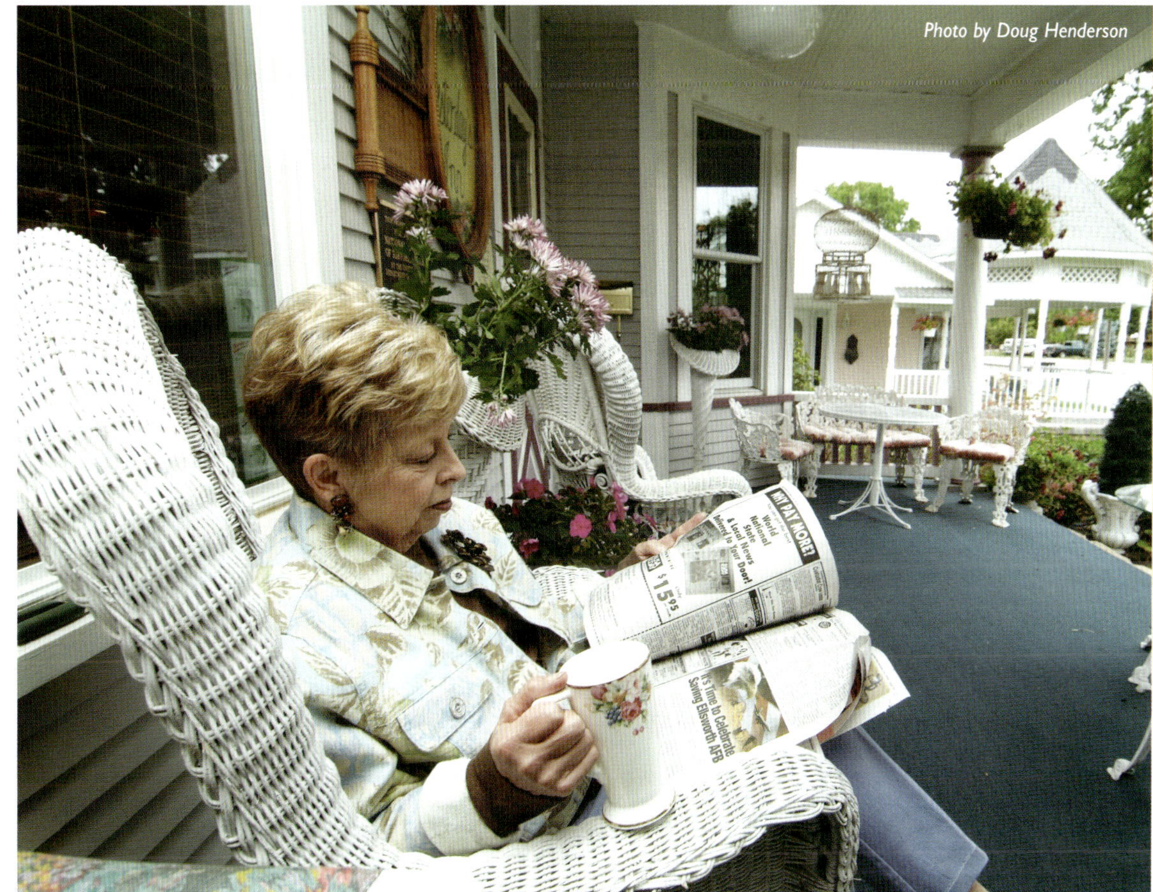

Photo by Doug Henderson

As the day gets under way, Norma Lee Ploog, proprietor of Yesterday's Inn in historic downtown Spearfish, relaxes on the wrap-around porch of the popular bed-and-breakfast while savoring a hot cup of coffee and a skim through the morning paper. The restored home, built in 1889 and now owned by Ploog and her husband Nathan, welcomes visitors year-round to enjoy an authentic Victorian-era experience with a modern sensibility. Three individual rooms, two suites, and a separate two-bedroom cottage have all been thoughtfully embellished with an array of elegant furnishings and trimmings, harkening back to bygone days when the house served as a private residence. Yesterday's Inn's sophisticated accommodations are accented by a large yard that boasts lush, colorful gardens, complete with gazebos and a delightful fishpond. The charming surroundings and intimate setting not only make the B&B an excellent lodging choice for visitors to the Black Hills region, who have convenient access to a wide variety of local tourist attractions, but also an ideal venue for weddings, reunions, and other special occasions. ❖

BankWest Puts Customers and Community First

At BankWest, helping customers achieve lifetime financial success and security is the driving force behind their products and hallmark customer-first service. BankWest has built a reputation for being not only a bank of choice but an employer of choice and a company that knows the power of reinvesting in the community.

BankWest's ability to provide customers with a foundation on which to succeed stems from over a century of serving South Dakotans. The bank was organized in 1889, two months before the territory obtained statehood, by a group of civic-minded entrepreneurs in the future capital city of Pierre. In the years that ensued, the bank became an integral part of the changing landscape, weathering the evolution of the community through both economic hardship and prosperity.

BankWest has the unique advantage of being able to respond quickly to customer needs.

Through the years, BankWest has remained on the leading edge of bank technology to support its personalized service. This formula has allowed the bank to pioneer such progressive ideas as car loans as early as the 1920s, federally backed home loans in the 1930s, and the first drive-up teller with an electronically controlled receiving drawer in the 1950s.

Today, BankWest provides customers unsurpassed conveniences, including free online banking, an extensive ATM network, and twenty-four-hour telephone banking.

In addition to its traditional bank products, BankWest provides financial planning, a full range of insurance products, trust services, and a full-service brokerage.

Photo by Alan S.Weiner

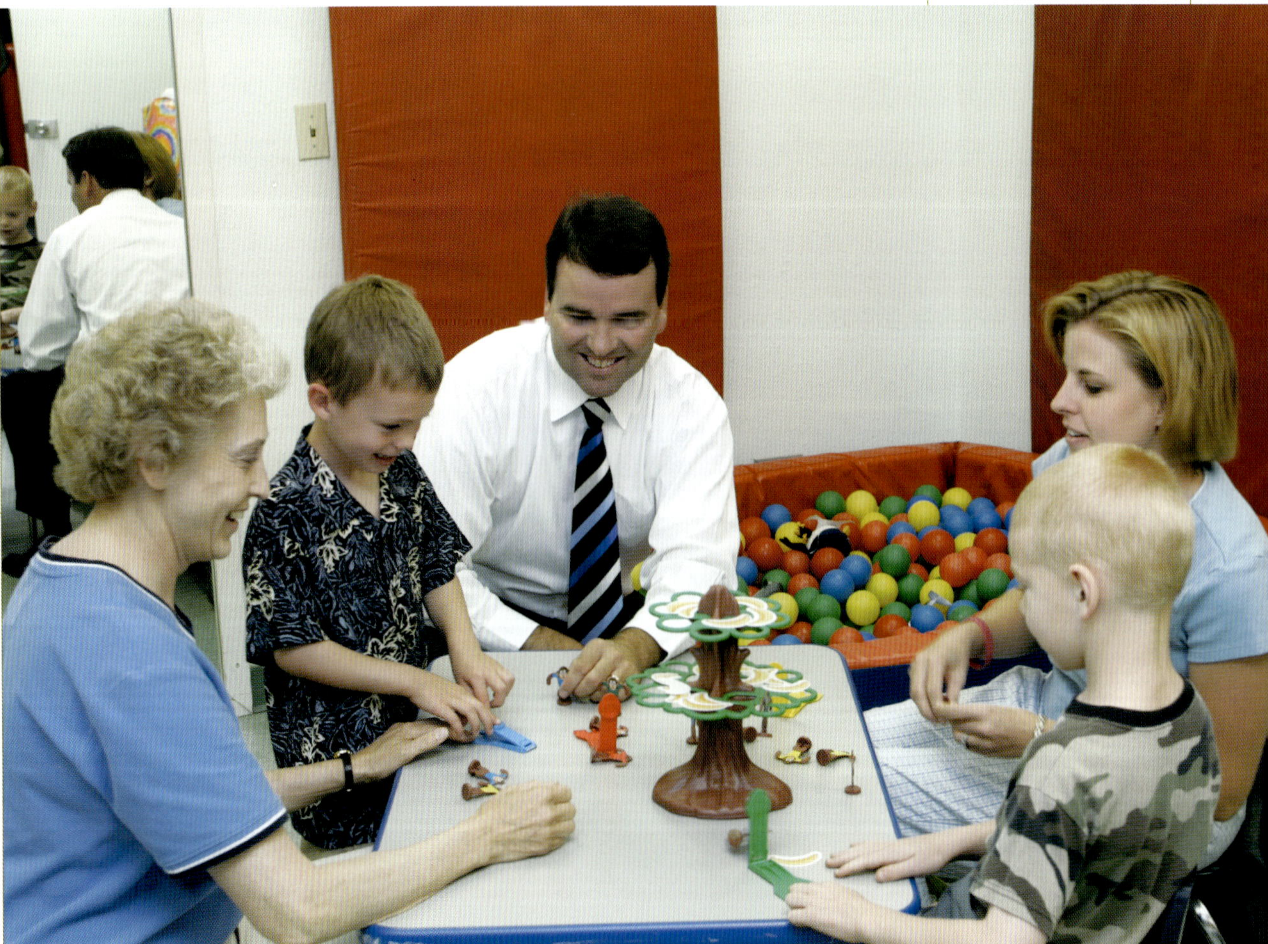

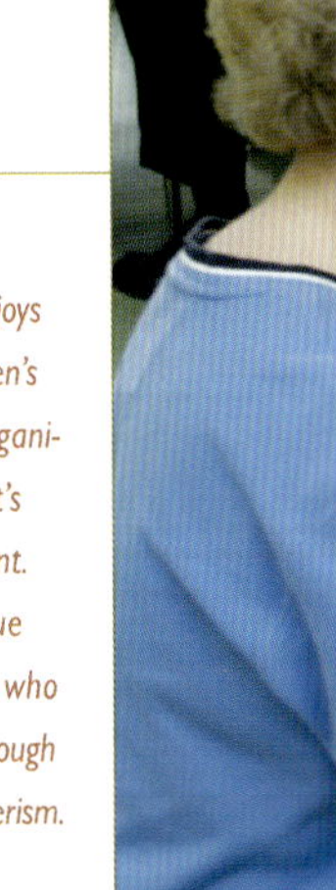

Regional president Jack Lynass enjoys interacting with patients at Children's Care Rehabilitation Center, an organization benefiting from BankWest's commitment to local reinvestment. Community involvement is a value shared by BankWest employees, who support numerous local causes through financial contributions and volunteerism.

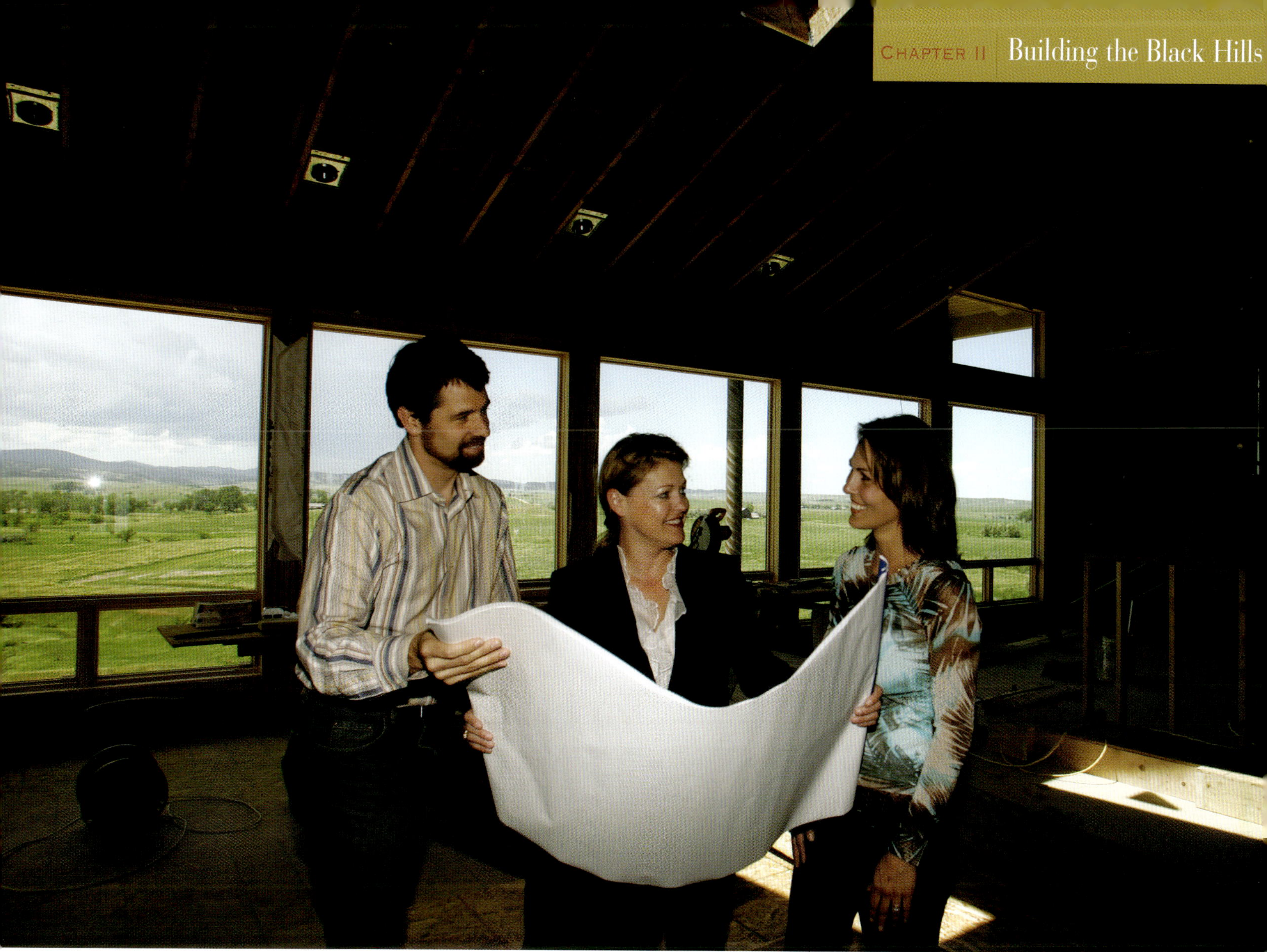

Photo by Alan S.Weiner

BankWest takes the bank to the customer. Here, a BankWest mortgage officer makes an on-site visit to review plans and share her customers' excitement as their dream home becomes a reality.

With more than a dozen offices in thirteen communities and over $500 million in assets, BankWest has the geographic scope and fiscal strength to be a leader in South Dakota. And, as a privately held community bank, BankWest has the unique advantage of being able to respond quickly to customer needs. Because BankWest associates and their families live and work in the communities they serve, they have a deep insight into both agricultural and business needs.

Such a close association, combined with a corporate philosophy that emphasizes putting customers and communities first, empowers BankWest bankers to consider each customer's personal circumstances, character, and history when making a decision about financial matters.

With their own roots firmly planted in South Dakota, the BankWest team is dedicated to ensuring the state is a place of broad-reaching opportunities. That is why the people of BankWest are found taking part in a host of community events, sitting on local boards, participating in school functions, donating to area charities, and influencing change through involvement in economic development initiatives.

As a good corporate citizen, BankWest in Rapid City also backs a number of reinvestment activities that benefit area residents. Among the major local organizations BankWest supports are Children's Home Society, Children's Care Rehab and Development Center, the Dahl Arts Center, Rapid City Club for Boys, Storybook Island, and Hospice of the Hills.

At BankWest, money matters are more than dollars and cents. They are relationships developed and dedicated to helping the people and communities of South Dakota succeed. ❖

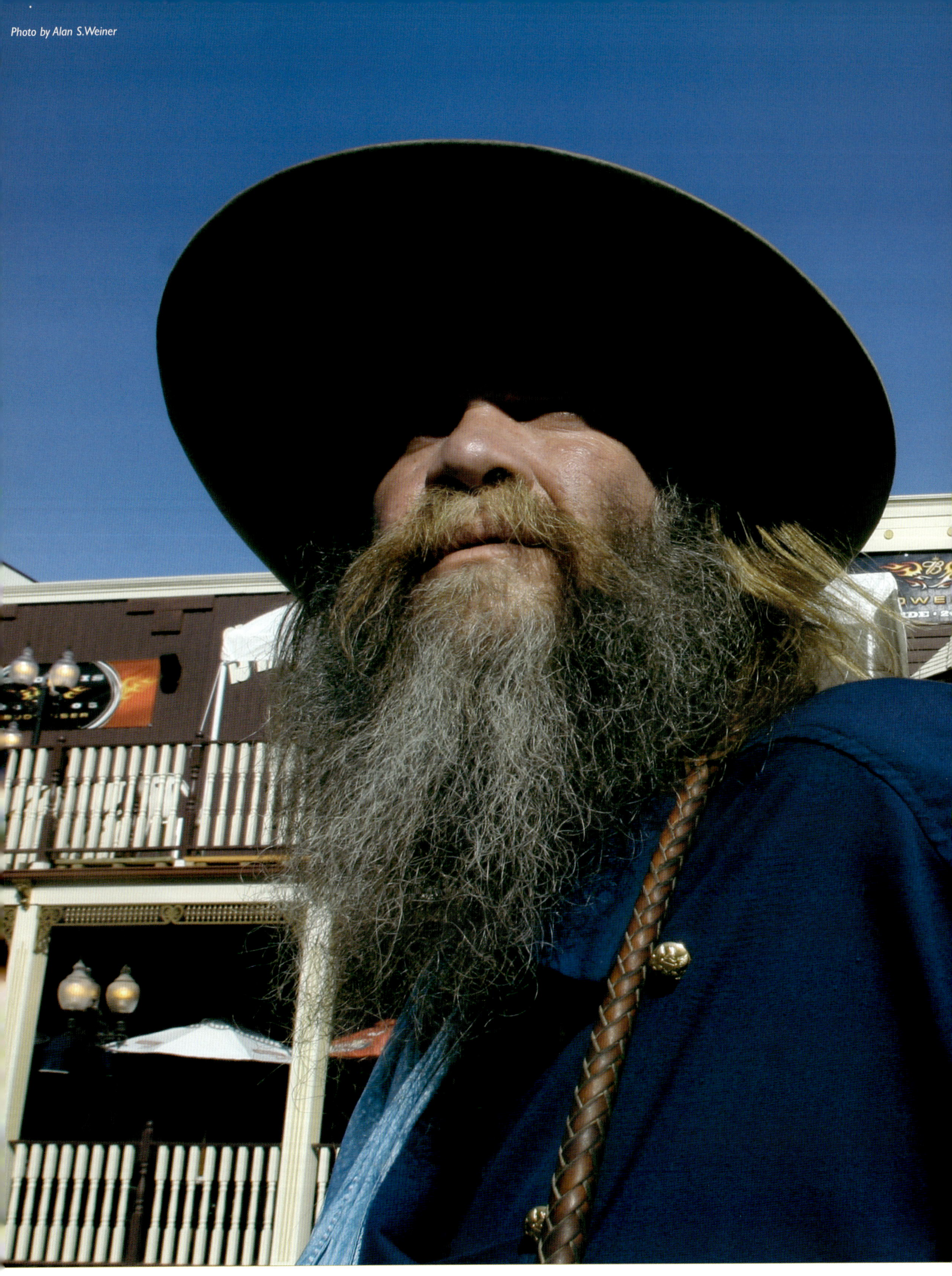

Photo by Alan S.Weiner

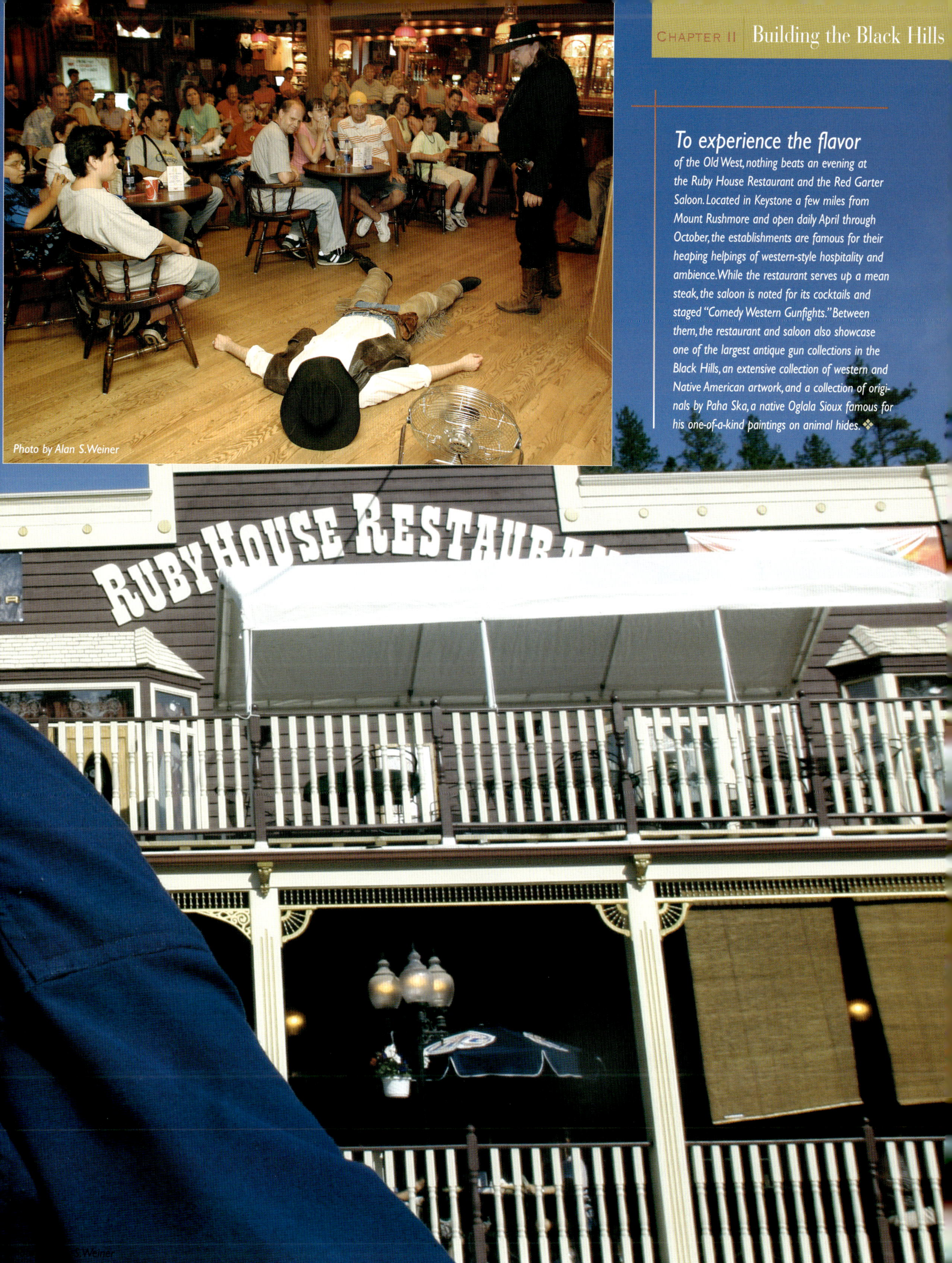

Photo by Alan S. Weiner

To experience the flavor of the Old West, nothing beats an evening at the Ruby House Restaurant and the Red Garter Saloon. Located in Keystone a few miles from Mount Rushmore and open daily April through October, the establishments are famous for their heaping helpings of western-style hospitality and ambience. While the restaurant serves up a mean steak, the saloon is noted for its cocktails and staged "Comedy Western Gunfights." Between them, the restaurant and saloon also showcase one of the largest antique gun collections in the Black Hills, an extensive collection of western and Native American artwork, and a collection of originals by Paha Ska, a native Oglala Sioux famous for his one-of-a-kind paintings on animal hides. ❖

Easy Access to the World

Located in the heart of one of the nation's most popular destinations, the Rapid City Regional Airport excels at providing visitors with safe, efficient, and accommodating air travel services.

Commercial air service to and from Rapid City was established in 1938, when the airport shared runways and space with the U.S. Army Air Corps at Ellsworth Air Force Base. In 1950, the airport moved to its present site, about eight miles southeast of the city. In 1989 the modern terminal building was completed.

As the primary commercial aviation facility serving western South Dakota and eastern Wyoming, Rapid City Regional Airport currently provides over forty daily arrivals and departures through Delta, Northwest, and United, with nonstop service to Minneapolis/St. Paul, Denver, Salt Lake City, and Chicago. In addition to daily service, Allegiant Air provides twice weekly service to Las Vegas. The airport also accommodates the air freight services of UPS, Federal Express, DHL, and Airborne Express.

A bright and comfortable two-story facility, the building contains a full-service restaurant and lounge, a coffee shop, gift shop and newsstand, baby care stations, and even an arcade. To better serve its growing number of business passengers, the airport offers free wireless Internet service on the second floor. On the second floor also, a full-service business center/conference room is available to anyone needing a conveniently located meeting facility.

For over half a century, the Rapid City Regional Airport has provided travelers with safe and efficient access in and out of the Black Hills.

Photo by Thomas S. England

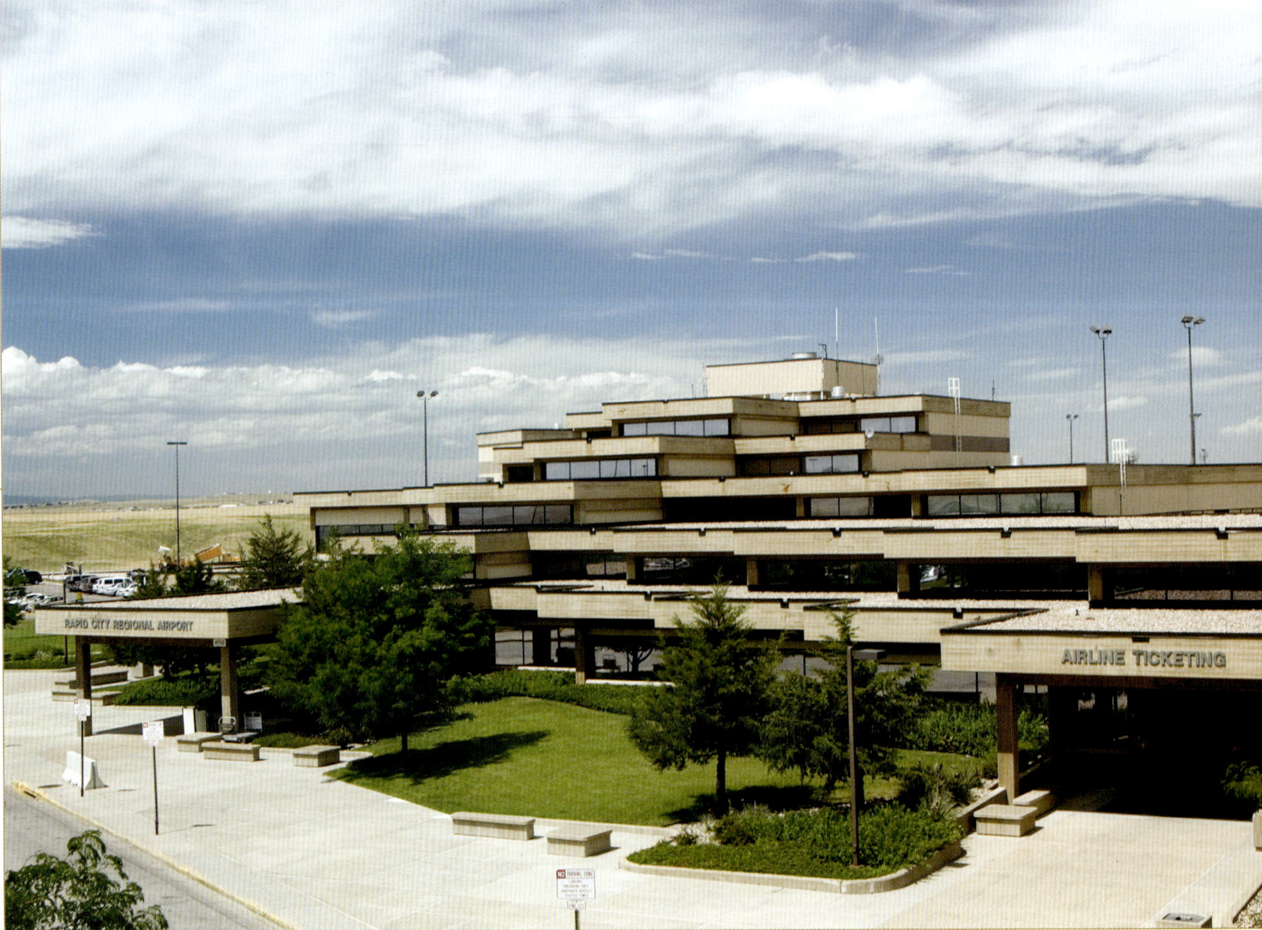

Although located in a community of around sixty-eight thousand people, the airport serves over five hundred thousand passengers each year, which means that Rapid City Regional Airport provides some of the best air service in terms of number of seats per capita of any airport in the country.

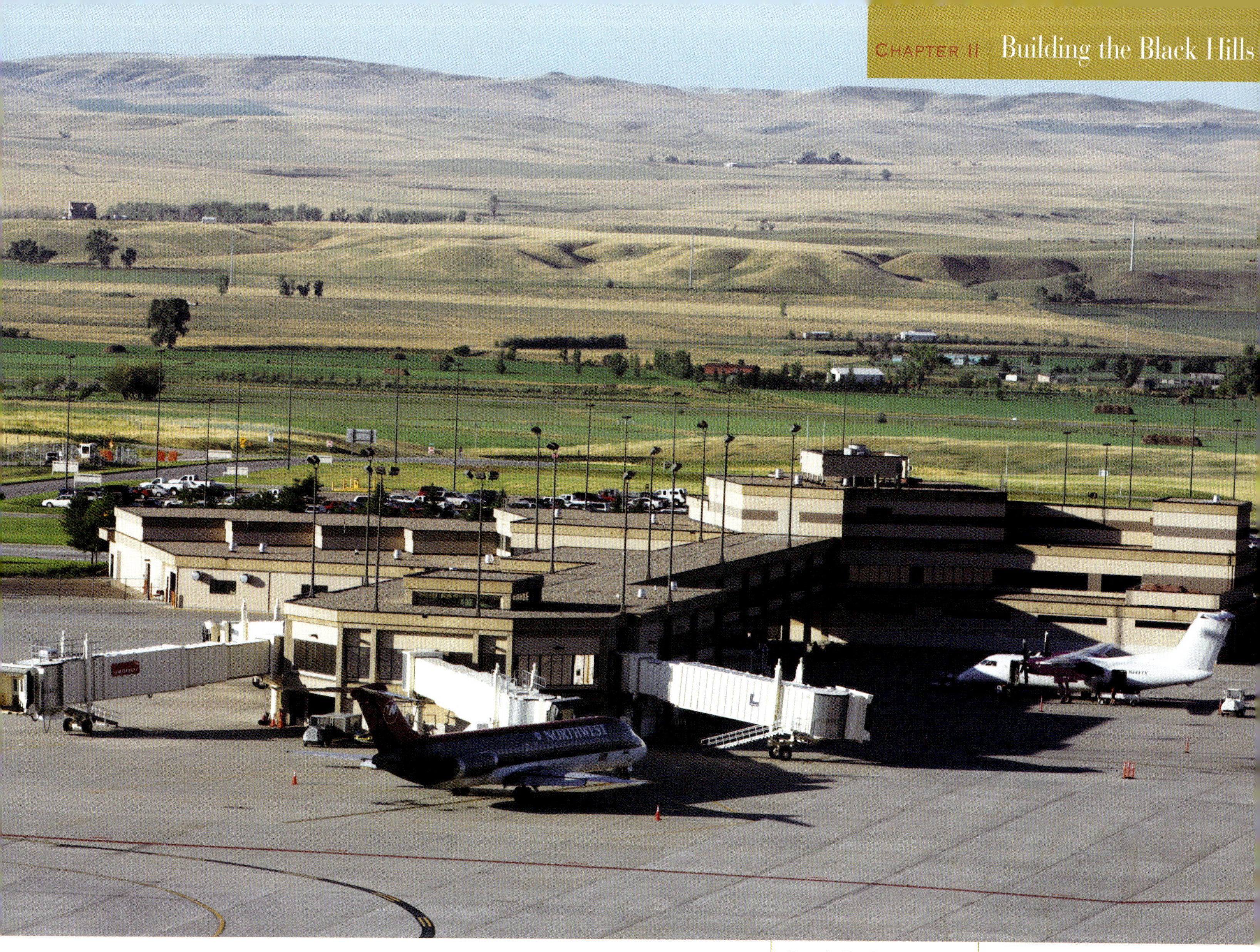

Photo by Eric Francis

In addition to its tourism traffic, the airport also accommodates an increasing number of business passengers. With over forty daily arrivals and departures, including six early-morning flights, the Rapid City Regional Airport makes it easy to do business in the Black Hills and throughout the country.

The Rapid City Regional Airport contributes significantly to the area's economic health. As home to fifteen businesses employing over three hundred personnel, the facility has an overall impact on Rapid City and its surrounding communities of over $100 million annually.

And that number is expected to grow. Spurred by a U.S. Department of Transportation Small Community Air Service Development grant, Rapid City Regional Airport is consolidating its short- and long-term goals, not only for the facility itself, but also for the Black Hills area.

"Our terminal building was constructed to eventually accommodate 1 million total passengers a year," says the airport's executive director, Mason Short. "This year we'll exceed five hundred thousand. So we're keeping a close eye on our growth, looking at eventually adding jet ways and a concourse to support additional aircraft. And we're continually speaking with airlines to bring in more nonstop flights to new hubs."

The airport is also partnering with neighboring communities like Spearfish, Custer, and Keystone to promote the Black Hills as a premier vacation destination. Says Short, "With our outdoor activities and high density of state and national parks and monuments, the Black Hills are able to favorably compete with such Rocky Mountain resort destinations as Jackson Hole, Santa Fe, and Park City."

For over half a century, the Rapid City Regional Airport has provided travelers with safe and efficient access in and out of the Black Hills. By helping to promote the area as a business and vacation destination, the facility is also expanding economic opportunities for those who call the area home. ❖

The Art of Glass Blowing

There's a lot of sweat and grime involved in the technique of glass blowing, as artist Pete Hopkins can attest. No wonder. With a furnace that must run twenty-four hours a day, seven days a week to maintain the proper temperature to melt glass, it's hot work. This highly intricate creative process, which dates back to the ancient Phoenicians, is fascinating to watch. Pete and partner Gail Damin, of Black Hills Glass Blowers, welcome visitors to their studio near scenic Keystone to watch them manipulate molten glass into beautiful bowls, vases, plates, and figurines. Pete, who first learned rudimentary techniques at the age of eighteen, has perfected his art over the years by attending industry classes, and of course by painstakingly creating pieces, each one unique. ❖

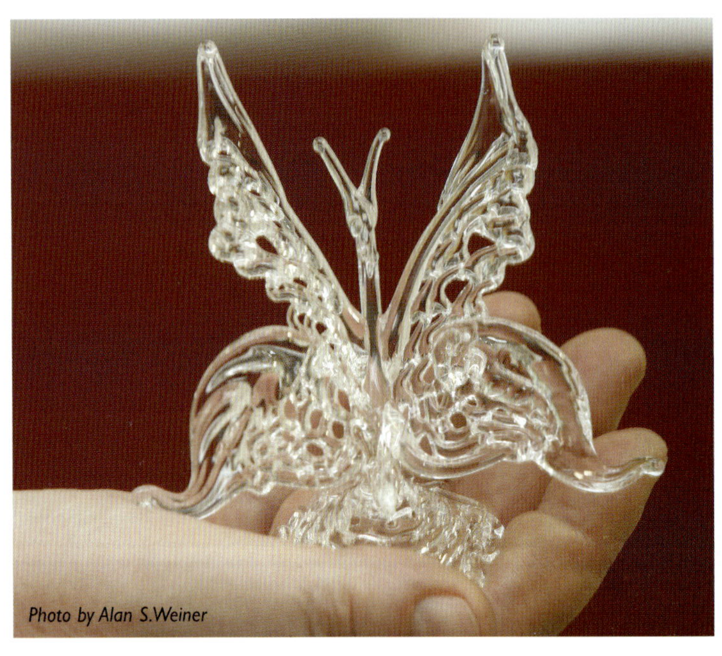

Photo by Alan S.Weiner

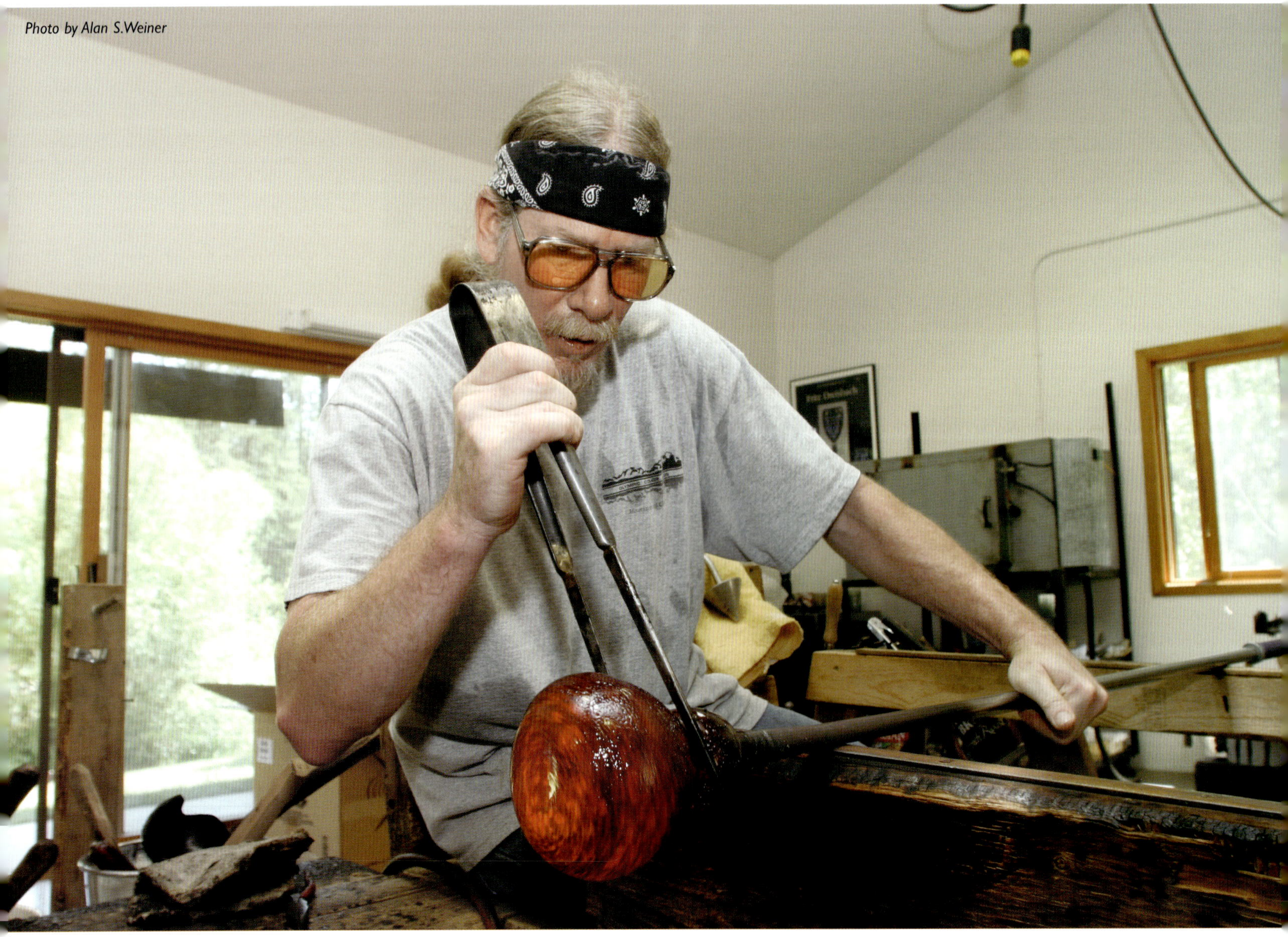

Photo by Alan S.Weiner

Photo by Thomas S. England

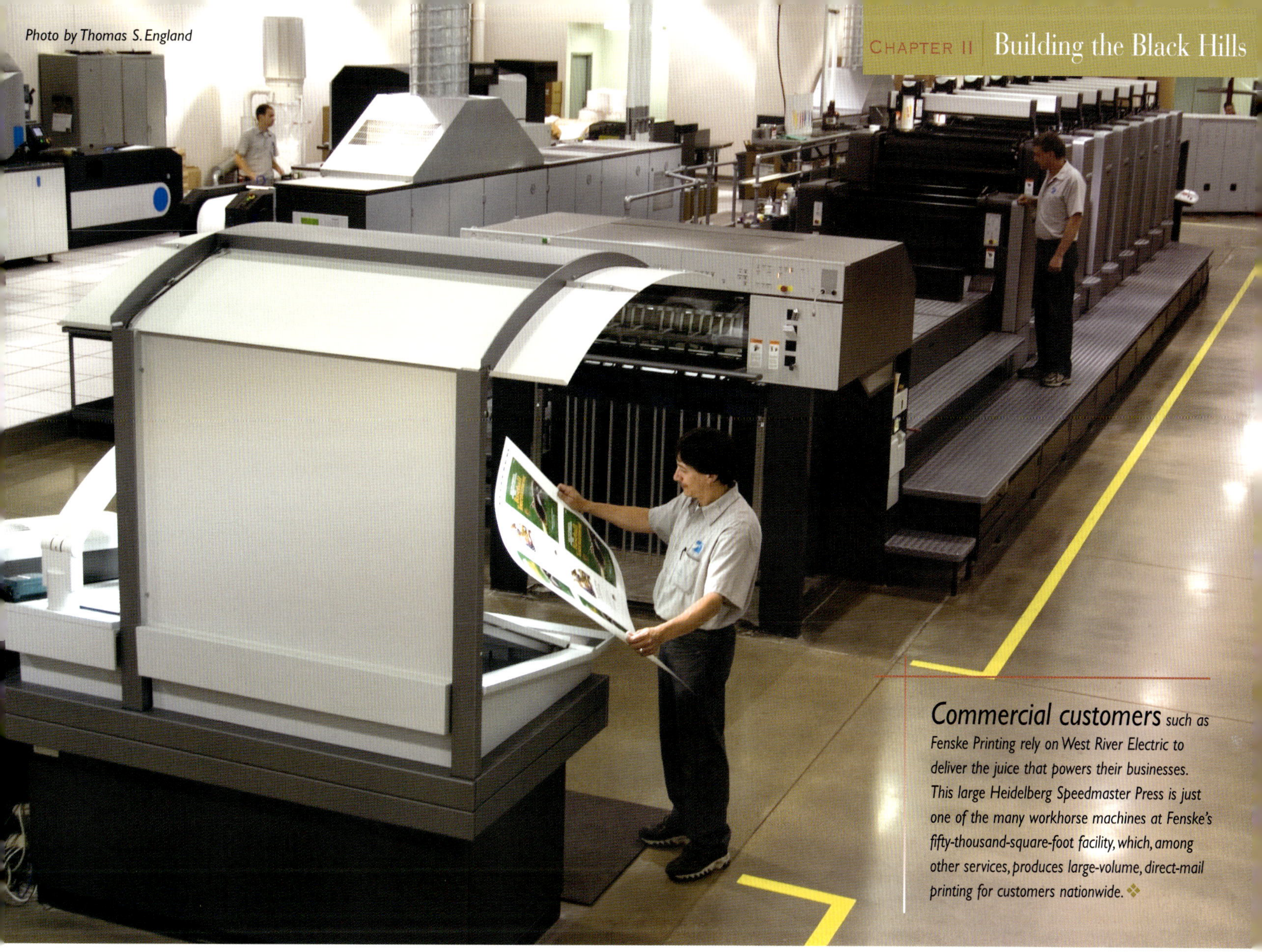

Commercial customers such as Fenske Printing rely on West River Electric to deliver the juice that powers their businesses. This large Heidelberg Speedmaster Press is just one of the many workhorse machines at Fenske's fifty-thousand-square-foot facility, which, among other services, produces large-volume, direct-mail printing for customers nationwide. ❖

Black Hills Children's Home Society is the oldest human services agency in South Dakota. It started as an orphanage in 1893 to provide a home and refuge for abused and unwanted children. Today it is still providing a home, school, and therapy for children from four to thirteen years old with emotional and behavioral problems. The Society also provides emergency shelter services and counseling for women and children who are victims of domestic abuse. The Black Hills Children's Home's facility is located sixteen miles southwest of Rapid City on eighty acres, and the Foster Care Facility is located in Rapid City. When new administration space was needed, they called on Dean Kurtz Construction, a third-generation, family-owned business. Kurtz Construction has been a longtime supporter of this charity, working with them for more than twenty years. It was the society's cofounders, William and Elizabeth Sherrard, who authored the first child protection laws for South Dakota. Today the Society continues to be a state leader in championing the welfare of children. ❖

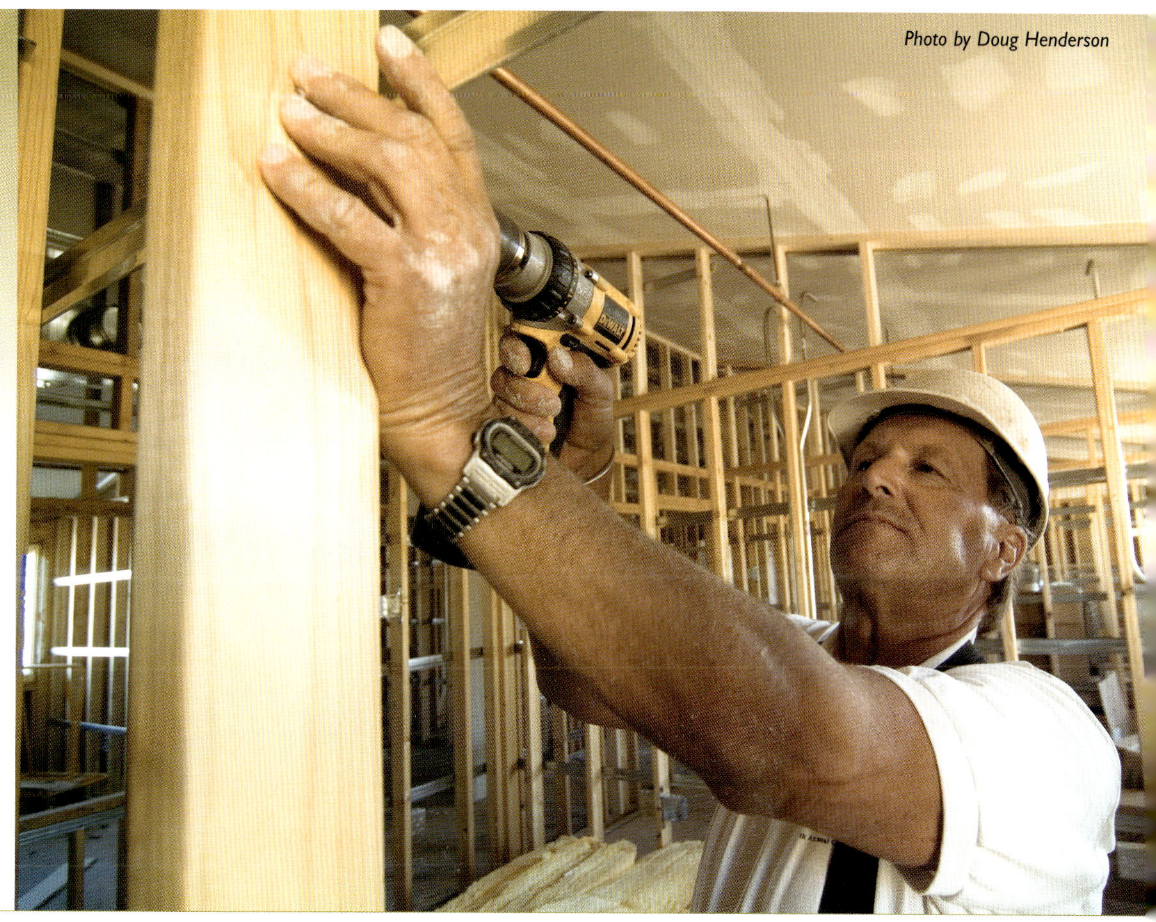

Photo by Doug Henderson

Westjet Air Center Provides Vital Service to Rapid City Area

After a stint in the army and twenty-seven years as a large-city banker, Westjet Air Center president Don Rydstrom became captivated by the Black Hills region.

"Rapid City is a tremendous community," he proclaims. "It is a wonderful place to raise a family, and the work ethic is alive and flourishing."

Westjet Air Center has been a welcome component of the Rapid City business landscape since 1978, when Don bought out the former Snedigar Flying Service. Today, Westjet provides a vital service to business professionals and vacationers attracted to the area. As Rapid City Regional Airport's premier fixed-base operator, Westjet specializes in fuel sales, hangar rentals, maintenance, and charter.

As an authorized Phillips 66 Company Aviation Performance Center, and supplier of refueling services for the airport's commercial flights, Westjet maintains rigid quality-control standards for its fuel product. Its efficient crew, operating eight fueling vehicles, can turn around aircraft in as little as ten minutes.

With two eleven-thousand-square-foot heated hangars, one twenty-thousand-square-foot heated hangar, sixteen T-hangars, and an eight-thousand-square-foot open-bay hangar, Westjet offers plenty of covered space for most any size aircraft. Fully trained personnel have the equipment and experience to safely prepare aircraft for arrival and departure, even in adverse weather conditions.

Fully trained personnel have the equipment and experience to safely prepare aircraft for arrival and departure, even in adverse weather conditions.

Photo by Alan S.Weiner

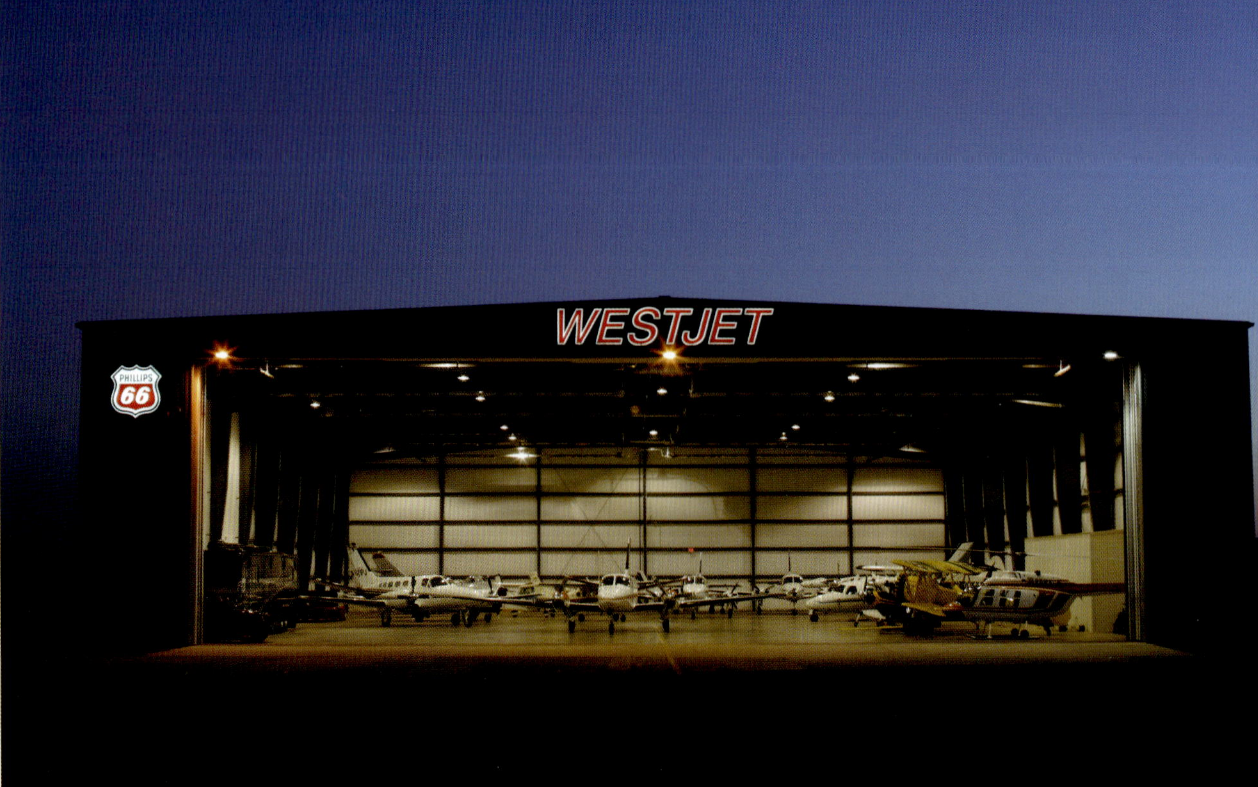

Westjet Air Center's largest hangar is twenty thousand square feet in size, big enough to park a DC-9 and Gulfstream jet. In addition to storage, maintenance, and fueling, Westjet also offers charter flight services. Equipped with three aircraft and eight Airline Transport Pilot–rated pilots, Westjet is licensed to fly anywhere in the United States and Canada.

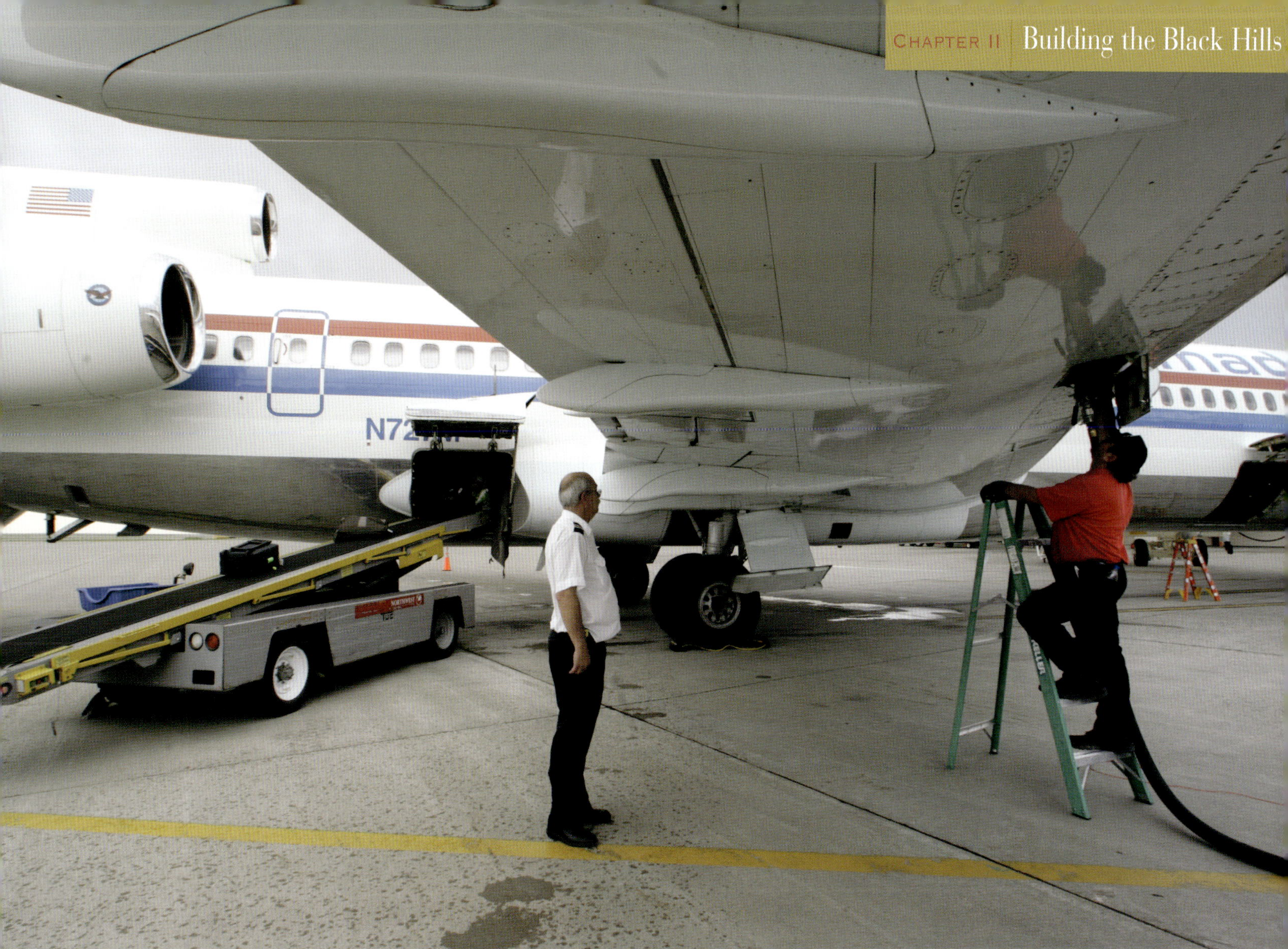

Photo by Alan S.Weiner

If you can fly it, they can fuel it. With seventeen fully trained and certified line personnel operating eight refuelers, the company refuels on average of up to twenty aircraft a day, from large commercial liners to small private planes. In winter, the department's two de-icing units and preheaters helps speed things along as well.

Three inspection-authorized aircraft mechanics render first-rate service in Westjet's maintenance facility, with its full airframe and power plant repair station. A staff of four airline-transport-rated pilots provide charter service throughout the United States, as well as tours over the scenic Black Hills.

Inside the twenty-four-hour facility, professionally trained staff handle arrangements for rental car transportation, catering, and overnight accommodations. The comfortable lounge, complete with satellite TV and video entertainment, offers passengers and crew a place for easy relaxation. A complete conference room facility is available for business gatherings, and a full weather reporting and flight planning facility features a WSI color weather computer, wall-sized map, and a complete selection of charts.

Pilot and aircraft supplies are available inside the company's lobby; for those interested in much larger purchases, Westjet's experienced aircraft sales department offers a world of buying connections in finding the perfect new or preowned aircraft to match business or personal needs.

In August, when the Sturgis Rally and Races are gearing up, it is not surprising to find a few Harley-Davidson motorcycles stored inside Westjet hangars. Today's "bikers" often ship their machines in advance and arrive for the event via commercial airlines, while others accompany their motorcycles on private jets.

Giving back to the community is second nature for Don, who lends his leadership abilities to several local organizations, such as the Rapid City Area Chamber of Commerce, the city's Planning Commission, the local Girls Club, and the Club for Boys.

Continued on page 170

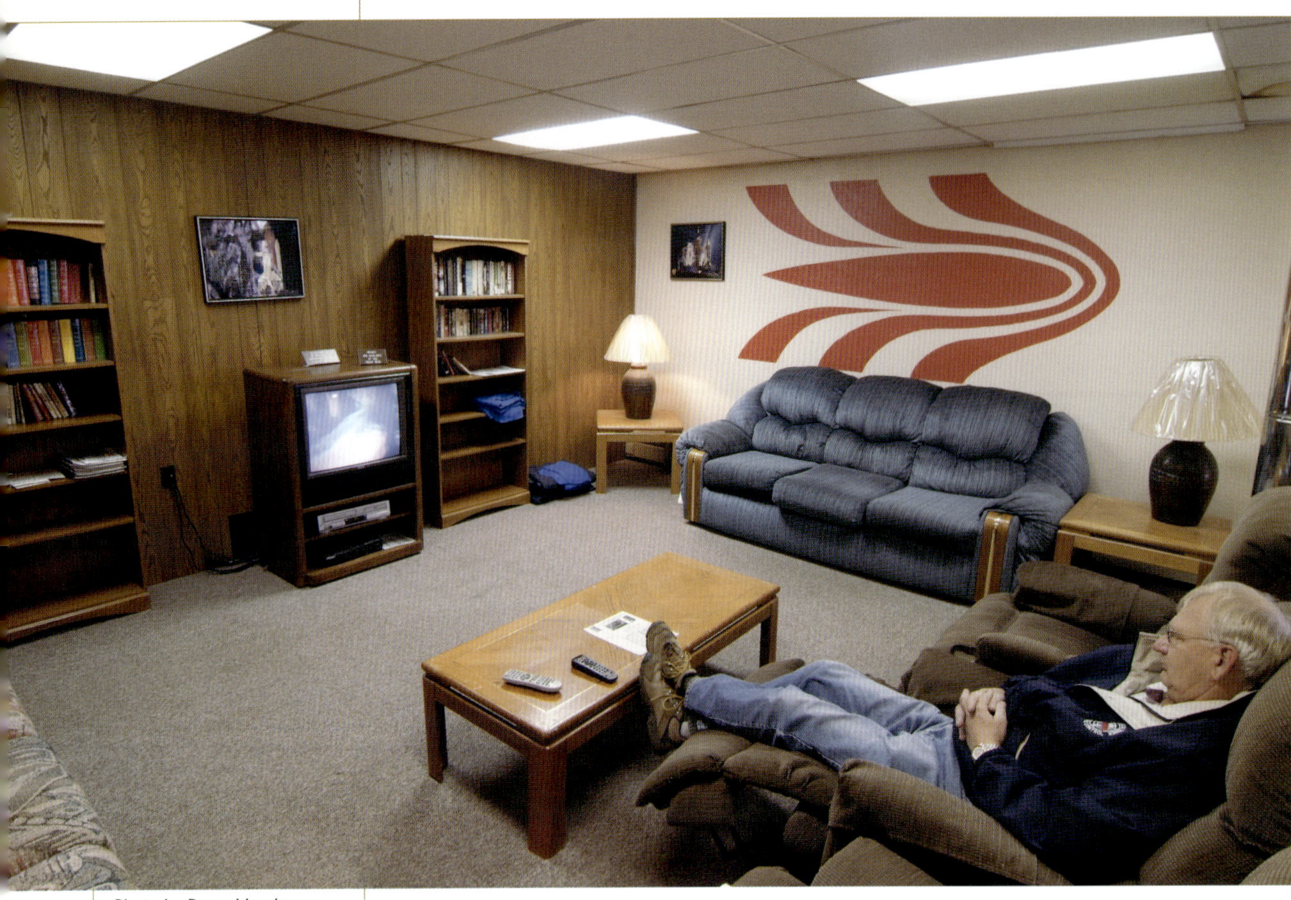

Customer service doesn't stop at fueling and maintenance. Equipped with comfy sofa and chairs, a television, books, magazines, and a vending station, Westjet's pilots' lounge is the perfect spot for pilots to relax, eat, or catch a couple winks.

Photo by Doug Henderson

Continued from page 169

"Flying is kind of an insidious disease. It gets in your blood, and it is very hard to get out," says Don. But when he talks about the beauty and vitality of Rapid City and the Black Hills, it is easy to see that aviation isn't the only reason for Don's high-flying spirits. ❖

Photo by Doug Henderson

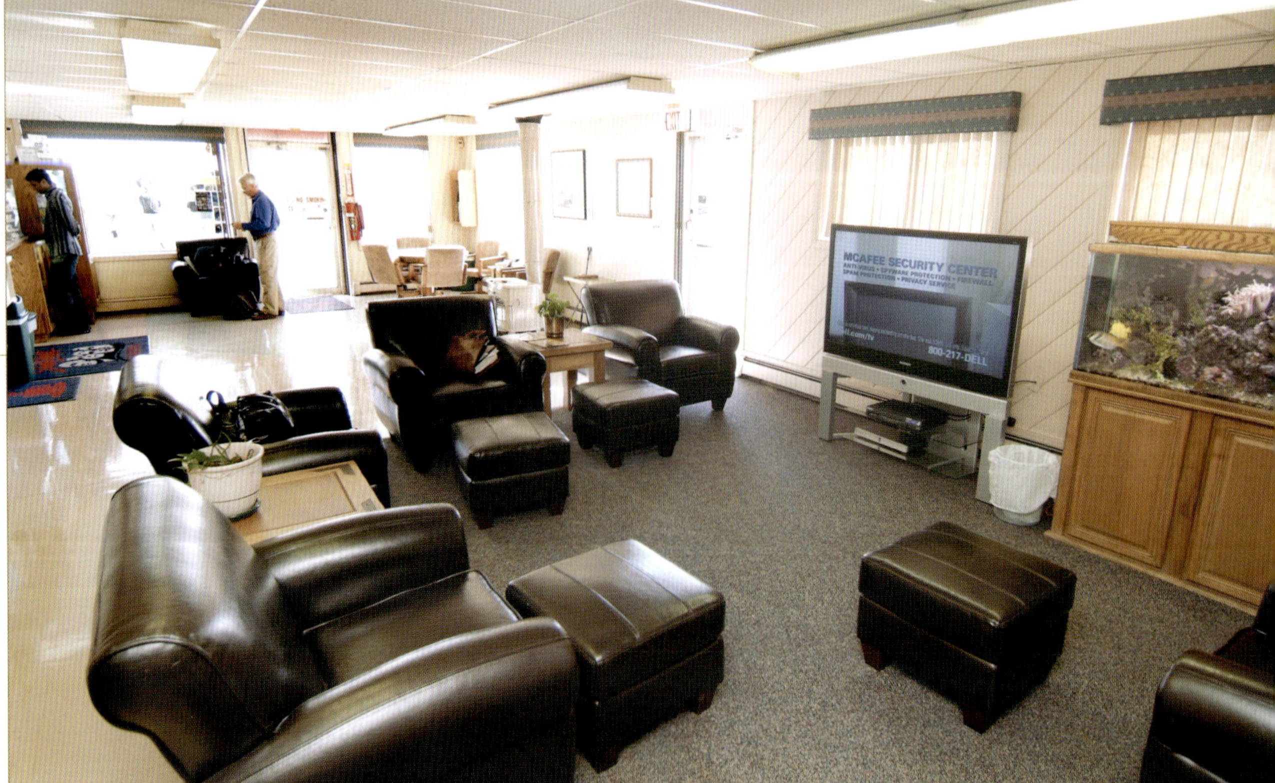

Between stops, passengers are invited to make themselves at home in Westjet's spacious lobby, with its comfortable chairs, big-screen television, and soothing two-hundred-gallon saltwater fish tank. Westjet also arranges between-flight and post-flight services, like passenger lunches, car rentals, and reservations at hotels with airport shuttle service. Even Sam, the company cat, loves to drop by and hang out in a lap or two.

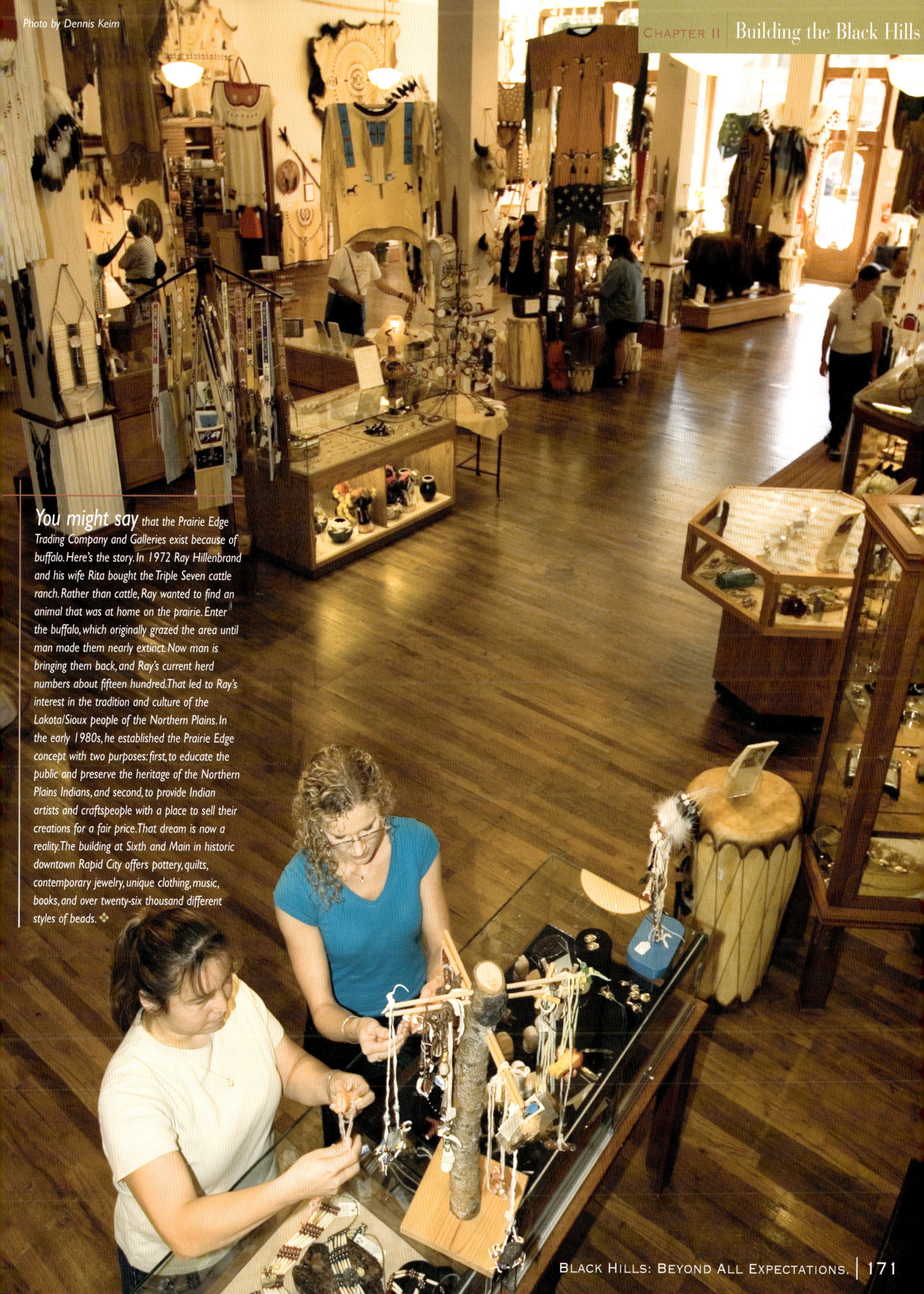

Photo by Dennis Keim

You might say that the Prairie Edge Trading Company and Galleries exist because of buffalo. Here's the story. In 1972 Ray Hillenbrand and his wife Rita bought the Triple Seven cattle ranch. Rather than cattle, Ray wanted to find an animal that was at home on the prairie. Enter the buffalo, which originally grazed the area until man made them nearly extinct. Now man is bringing them back, and Ray's current herd numbers about fifteen hundred. That led to Ray's interest in the tradition and culture of the Lakota/Sioux people of the Northern Plains. In the early 1980s, he established the Prairie Edge concept with two purposes: first, to educate the public and preserve the heritage of the Northern Plains Indians, and second, to provide Indian artists and craftspeople with a place to sell their creations for a fair price. That dream is now a reality. The building at Sixth and Main in historic downtown Rapid City offers pottery, quilts, contemporary jewelry, unique clothing, music, books, and over twenty-six thousand different styles of beads. ❖

Costello Porter Delivers Guidance for Your Future Growth

The pioneering law firm known today as Costello, Porter, Hill, Heisterkamp, Bushnell & Carpenter, LLP, was already providing quality legal services to its clients when South Dakota was still a part of the Dakota Territory. Today, this firm has one of the most respected law practices in the state. Its members serve with distinction in corporate, community, and nonprofit boardrooms; in local and state government; and in tribal, state, and federal courts. These professionals are independent thinkers, drawn to the lifestyle and challenges of practicing law in South Dakota.

Costello Porter's growing legal team of more than a dozen attorneys utilizes a group approach in offering its broad range and depth of expertise at two locations in the Black Hills. It is a full-service firm respected for its professional knowledge and skill in all of the tribal, state, and federal courts in South Dakota. Developers, businesses, contractors, architects, engineers, and homeowners frequently draw upon the firm's construction practice group and utilize its experience when working with governing bodies and their planning and zoning boards.

Banks, seasonal businesses, and individuals draw on the expertise of Costello Porter, as do plaintiffs and defendants in commercial and personal litigation, insurance, employment law, fire damage, premises, and product liability matters. The health-care

Costello Porter's growing legal team of more than a dozen attorneys utilizes a group approach in offering its broad range and depth of expertise.

Photo by Dennis Keim

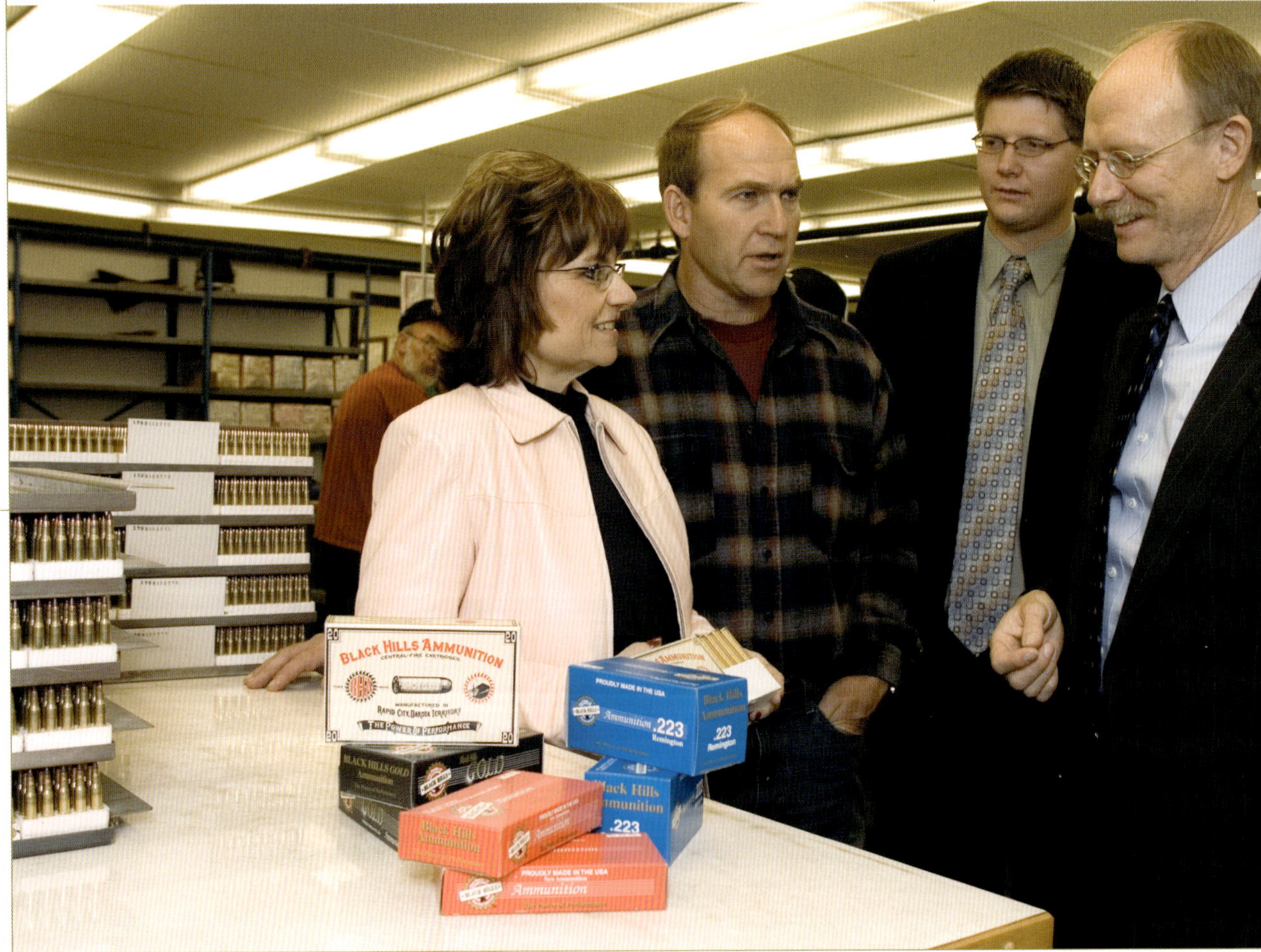

Kristi and Jeff Hoffman, the owners of Black Hills Ammunition, Inc., display a portion of their commercial product lines and discuss their ongoing commercial and military research and product developments with attorneys Jess Pekarski and Joe Lux.

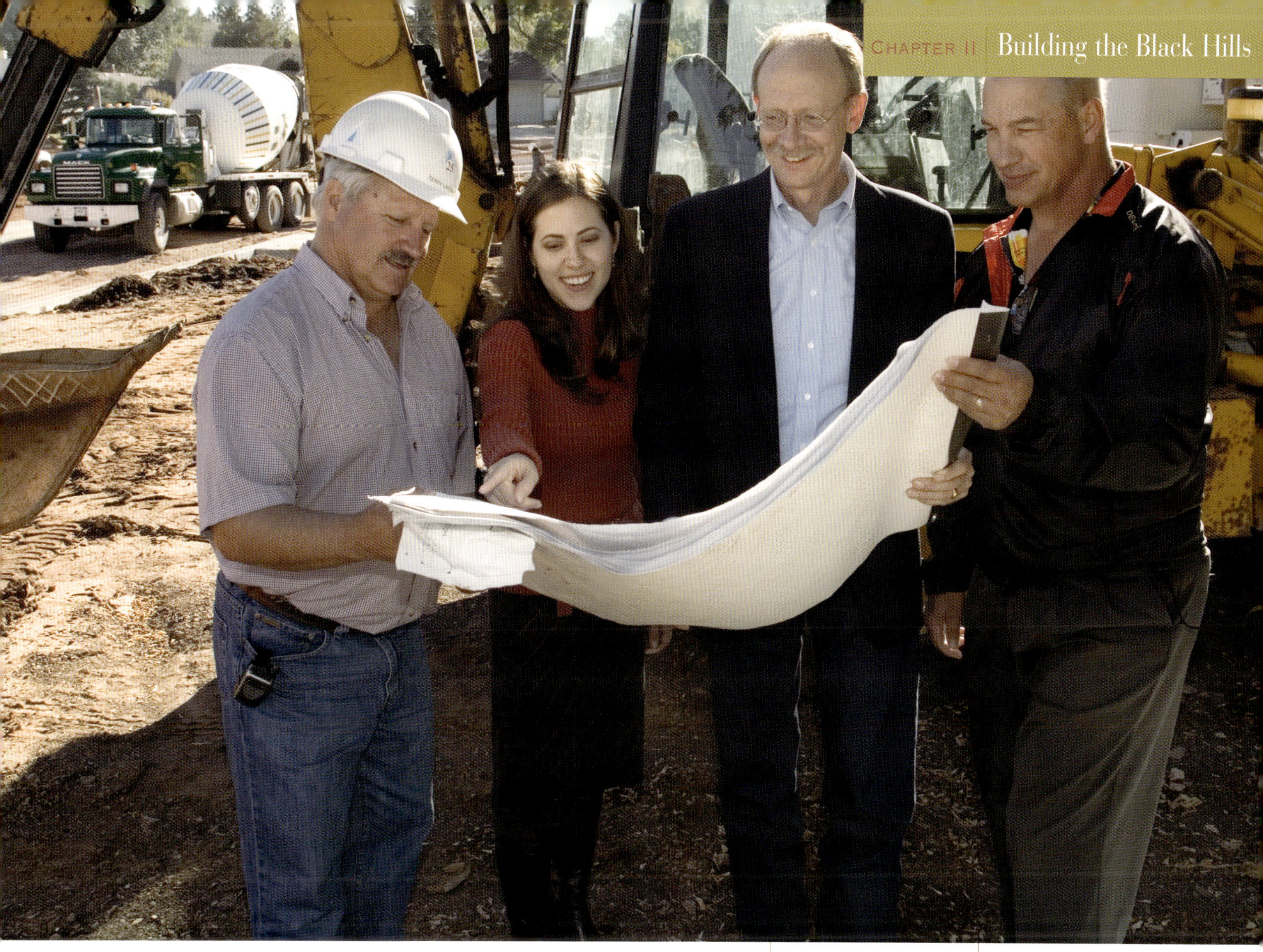

Photo by Dennis Keim

As Rapid City has grown, Costello Porter has provided guidance along the way. Here, Terry Larson, a principal in Heavy Constructors, Inc., reviews a major street reconstruction project with attorneys Becky Vogt and Joe Lux, and Joe Jagodzinski, P.E., of the Rapid City Public Works office.

community often looks to the firm's significant health law and regulatory practice. In offering advice on even such "basic" matters as how to structure a business venture, choose a form of business entity, and how to purchase, sell, or trade real estate, clients appreciate that Costello Porter recognizes that in addition to "mere" business considerations, there are often estate planning, trust, and probate implications to be addressed.

The firm's members and staff constantly hone their skills and expertise to stay on the cutting edge of the law and adhere to the highest standards of professionalism. In addition to state-of-the-art computer-assisted research capabilities, the firm maintains an extensive library of numerous specialty practice materials. Its attorneys and professional staff actively participate in continuing professional education seminars; professional secretary and paralegal associations; tribal, local, state, and American bar associations; American and South Dakota Trial Lawyers Associations; the Defense Research Institute; and the prestigious American Board of Trial Advocates. Clients benefit from the fact that many of the firm's attorneys and staff have practiced and worked together for years. "We're also proud of the fact that many of our attorneys previously served as judicial clerks for the justices of South Dakota's Supreme Court, and for the judges of the trial courts and the United States District Courts," states Joe Lux, a partner in the firm.

Steeped in tradition, prepared for the future, the legal team of Costello Porter continues to provide up-to-date legal services of the highest quality to its diverse clientele. ❖

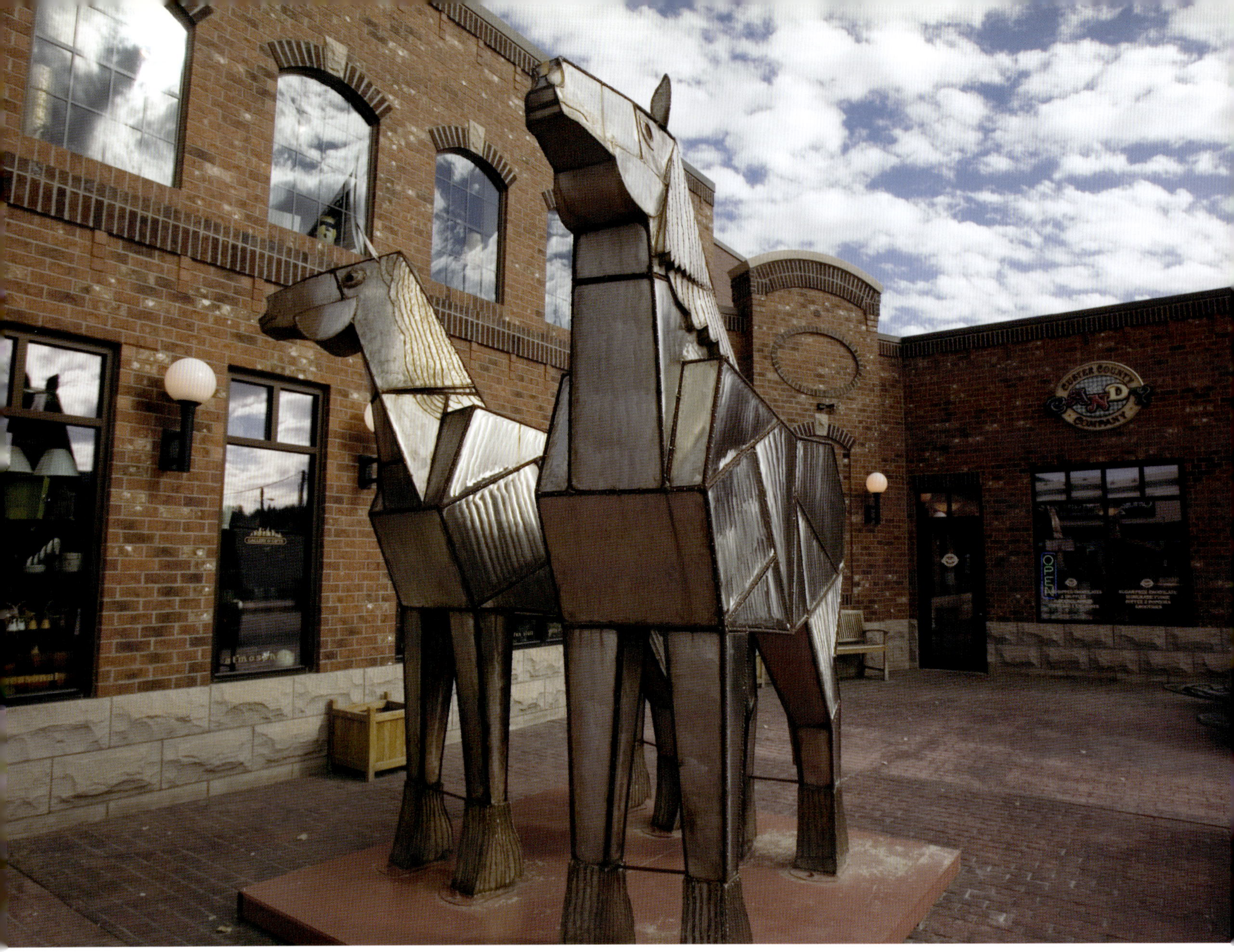

Photo by Dennis Keim

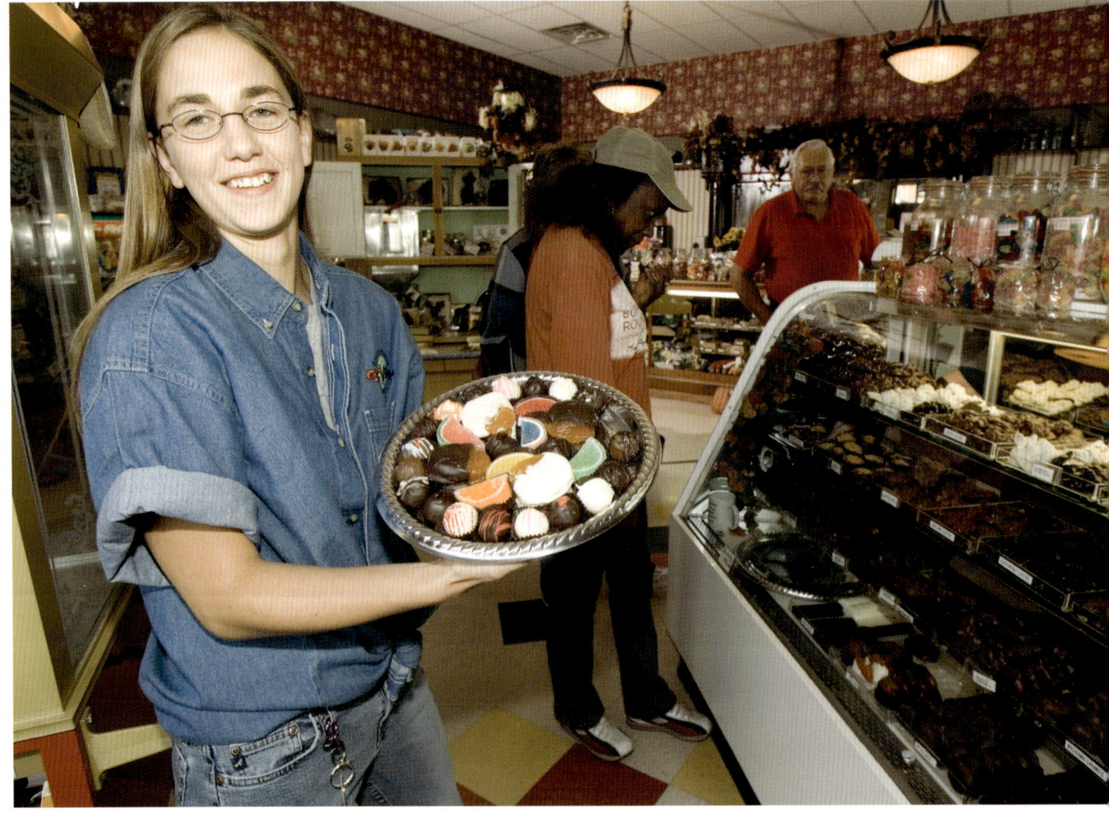

Photo by Dennis Keim

Standing in the courtyard

between the Custer County Candy Company and A Walk in the Woods, two popular shops located on Main Street in Custer County, is a sculpture that truly evokes the wild spirit of the Black Hills. These two majestic horses, crafted out of metal by renowned local artist Lloyd Kreitz, look like they are ready to take off into the surrounding hills to join the herds of wild buffalo, elk, and deer that call the area home. The chance to live in harmony with Mother Nature's creatures is one of the Black Hills' greatest characteristics. Even if someone only comes face-to-face with faux wild mustangs outside of the local sweet shop, he or she knows that real wildlife is all around, taking advantage of the region's outstanding natural wonders. ❖

Photo by Rich Gabrielson

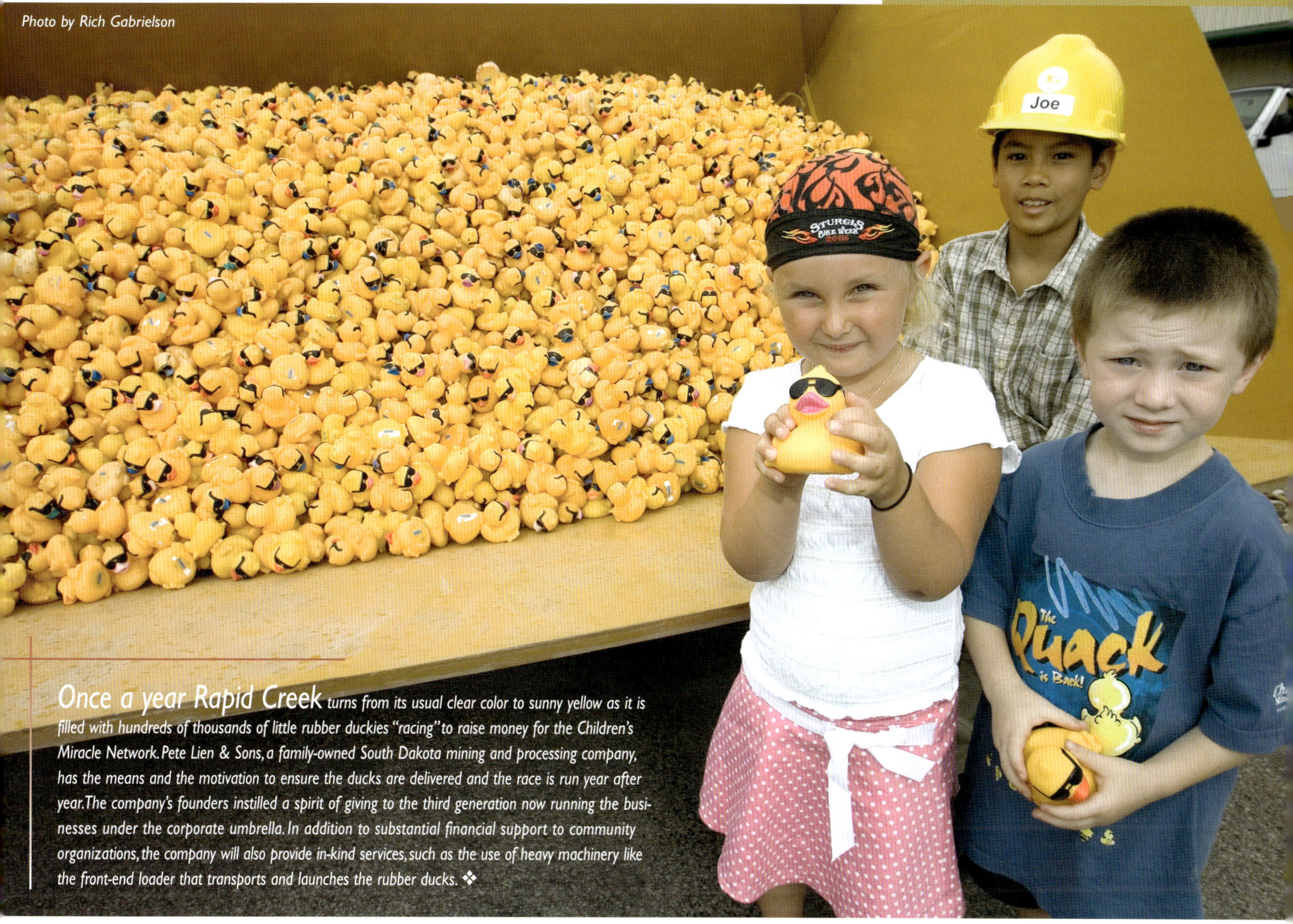

Once a year Rapid Creek turns from its usual clear color to sunny yellow as it is filled with hundreds of thousands of little rubber duckies "racing" to raise money for the Children's Miracle Network. Pete Lien & Sons, a family-owned South Dakota mining and processing company, has the means and the motivation to ensure the ducks are delivered and the race is run year after year. The company's founders instilled a spirit of giving to the third generation now running the businesses under the corporate umbrella. In addition to substantial financial support to community organizations, the company will also provide in-kind services, such as the use of heavy machinery like the front-end loader that transports and launches the rubber ducks. ❖

Family owned and operated

Pete Lien & Sons is the umbrella organization for many vital businesses, including Dakota Block, which manufactures more than ten thousand different sizes, shapes, and colors of masonry block. Since 1944, the related companies of Pete Lien & Sons have mined or manufactured key materials for everyday use in construction, the production of livestock feed, as well as the process of water and waste disposal. ❖

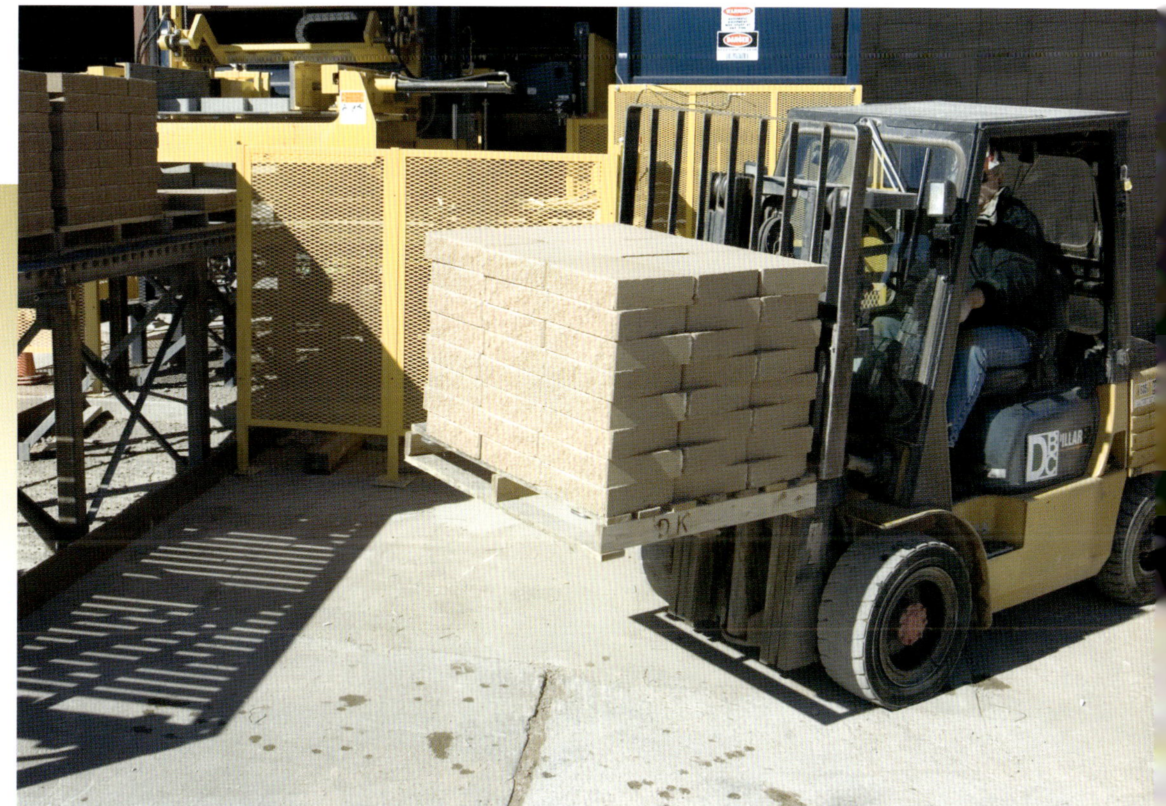

Photo by Rich Gabrielson

Dean Kurtz Construction: Generations of Expertise and Service

It may seem there are fewer family-owned businesses these days, but according to a recent study by the University of South Carolina, "More than 90 percent of all businesses in the United States are family owned." However, the article also said only 12 percent survive into the third generation. Dean Kurtz Construction has definitely beaten those odds. The company was started by Dean Kurtz in 1971. He served as president until 1985 when his son, Brad, took over the position. Presently Brad's two sons, Kelley and Kasey, are both part of the business. Recently Steve Burgess, a long-term, loyal employee became a part-owner.

"My two sons are learning the business from the ground up," said Brad, "just like I did. My first job was as a laborer on a project my father was building for the state-owned South Dakota Cement Plant. My oldest son, Kelley, is working as a cement finisher, and Kasey is working toward a construction management degree at South Dakota State University."

Perhaps one of the most familiar Dean Kurtz Construction projects is the Rapid City Regional Airport. At first glance, it appears that the structure's exterior is wood. In fact it is concrete.

Dean Kurtz Construction's team handles all the details of construction from design to move-in condition.

Photo by Doug Henderson

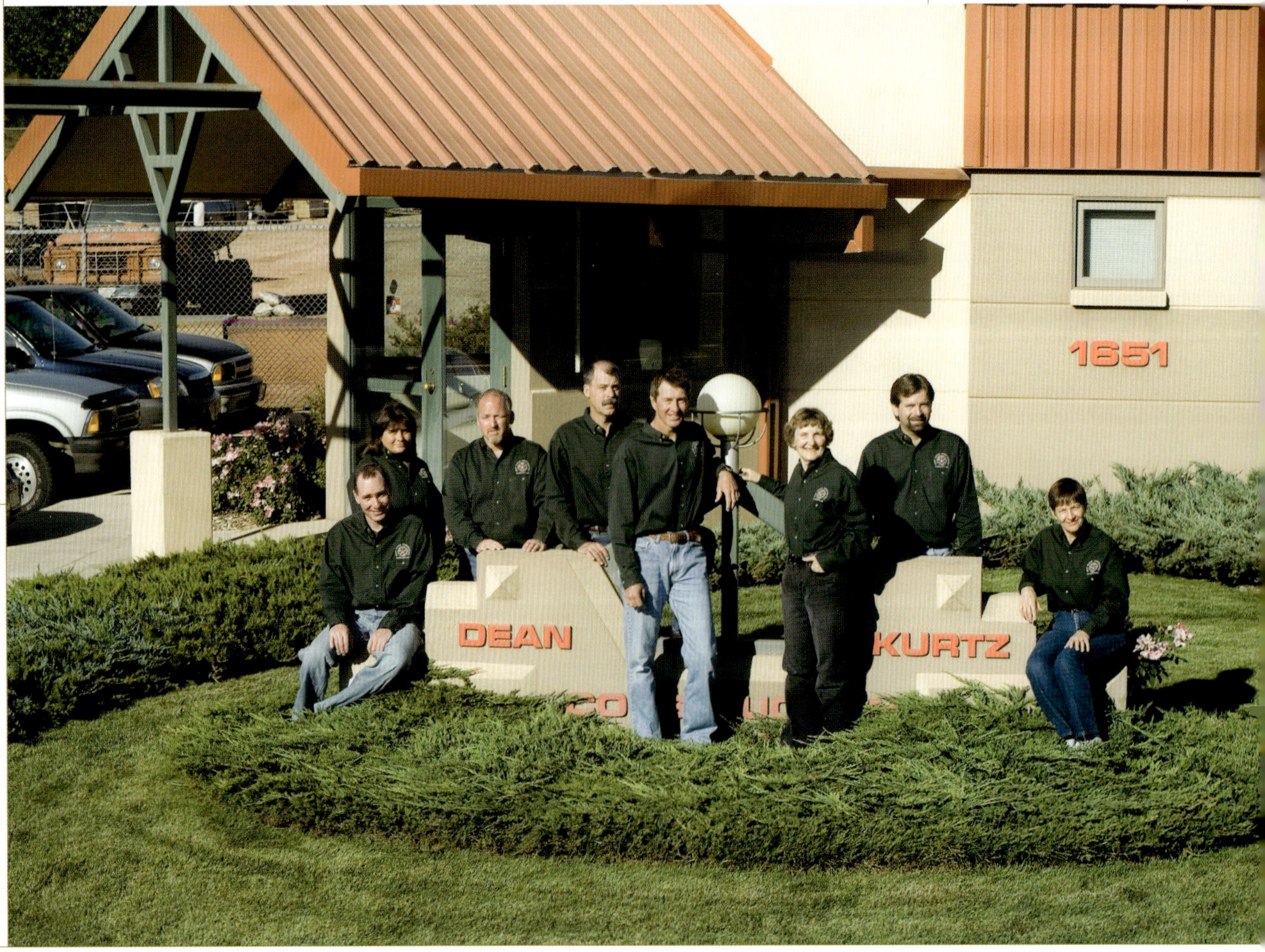

"Our staff has been the key to the successful operation of our business since the very beginning," said Brad Kurtz, current president of Dean Kurtz Construction, a family-owned business founded in 1971. The company is responsible for extensive construction in western South Dakota, "but our success isn't measured by steel and concrete. It's our people who meet the highest standards of skill, integrity, and responsibility."

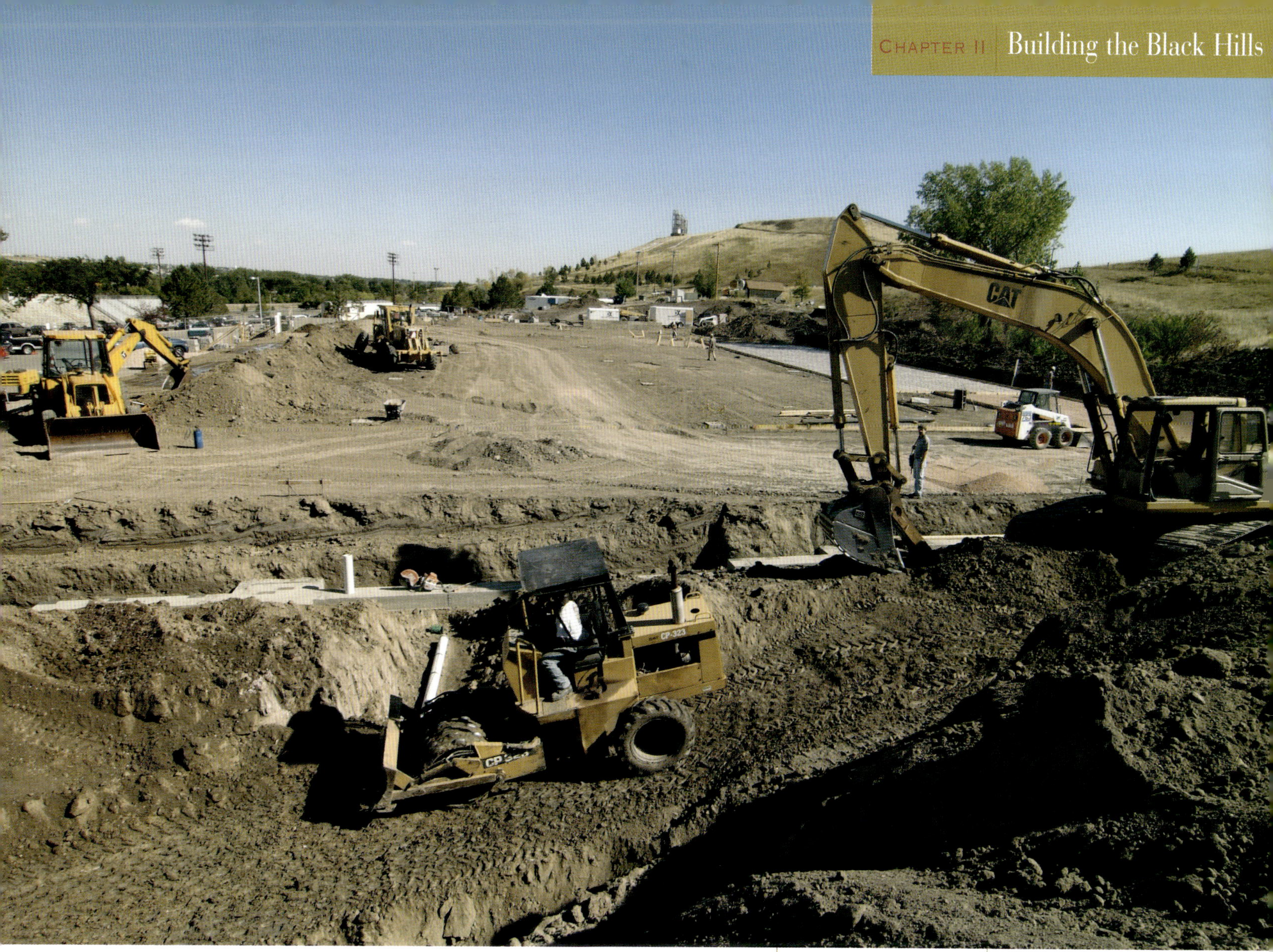

Photo by Doug Henderson

Every new Dean Kurtz Construction project begins at ground level, and the Black Hills Business Development Center on the South Dakota School of Mines and Technology Campus is no exception. When this forty-thousand-square-foot incubator facility is complete, it will provide for start-up companies and businesses with growth potential quality, affordable space for labs, light manufacturing, and offices.

A more recent, but equally challenging, project was the conversion of an old car dealership into a hotel/casino property in Deadwood. "In a move to revitalize the town, the state legalized limited gambling within the city limits. The taxes were used to fund renovation and preservation. Our client was Four Aces Hotel Corporation, and what we did was shore up the roof and rebuilt everything underneath."

Another series of projects that shows off Dean Kurtz Construction's expertise was the Mni Wiconi Rural water system works. Dean Kurtz Construction teamed with the Indian-owned firm of O'Bryan Construction to build the heart of the system. All together, in excess of $20 million in construction was put in place for the Oglala Sioux Tribe.

Dean Kurtz Construction's team handles all the details of construction from design to move-in condition, including finish carpentry work such as wood trim, crown molding, and built-in cabinetry.

The company also uses the latest building techniques to meet clients' budget and time requirements. Site-cast, tilt-up walls are a good example. "We pour the floor slabs first, next we pour the walls lying flat on the floor, and finally, we tilt them into place. This is a fairly new technique in this area," said Burgess.

Fast-track projects, another innovative option, involves starting construction before the final plans are complete. "Two things have to be in place to make this work. First we have to get the floor plan nailed down with the owners; then our project manager, site superintendent, and design professionals work very closely together. This can cut construction time 30 to 40 percent, and we are able to do this only because of

Continued on page 178

Continued from page 177

the experience of our project managers and supervisors. They're the ones who make this happen," Brad explained.

Still another example of the versatility of Dean Kurtz Construction is the Black Hills Business Development Center. This incubator facility will make quality, affordable space available for start-up companies. The challenge here was to create a building before knowing who the occupants would be. "We used solid tilt-up wall panels, because you can cut windows almost anywhere later to suit tenants without having to worry about studs. It is also very cost effective, and the owner had a very tight budget on this project."

Another notable project is the new Thirty-seventh B1-B Squadron Operations facility at Ellsworth Air Force Base. This massive, multimillion-dollar project, which included the complete design and construction of the operations facility, is just the latest in a long history of projects that Dean Kurtz Construction has completed for the military. The facility is

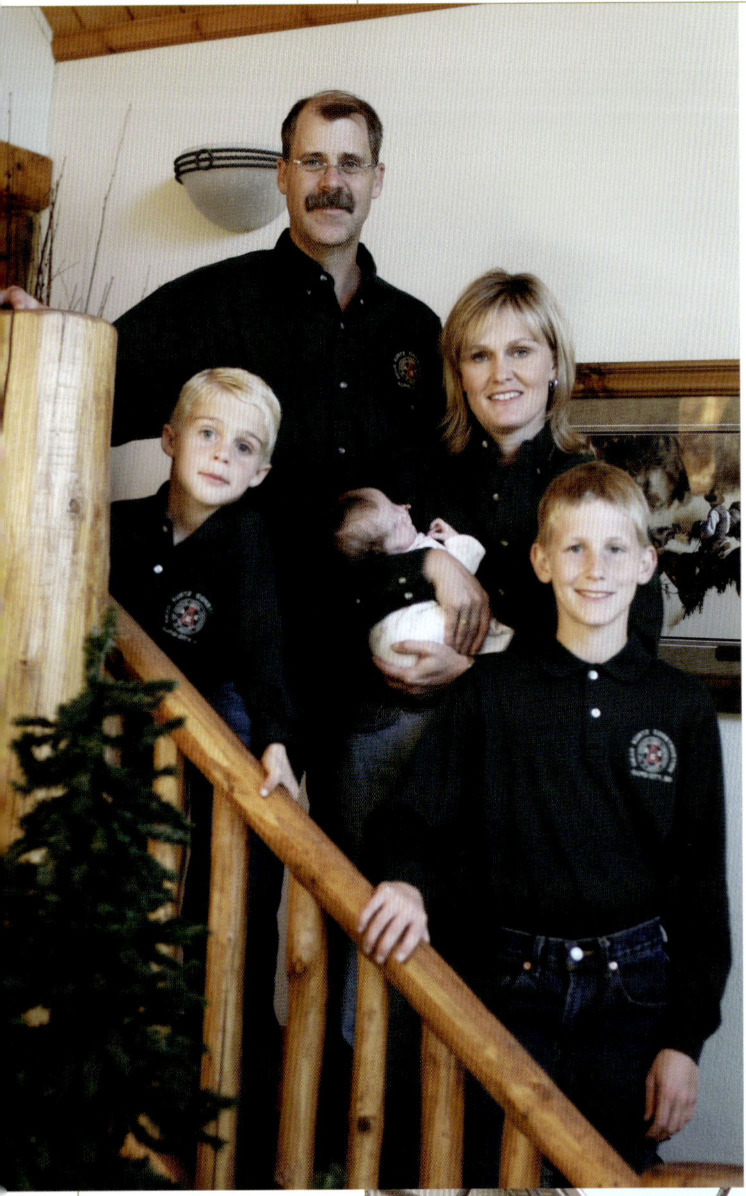

Photo by Doug Henderson

Crane booms are usually seen rising in the air hoisting heavy objects at one of Dean Kurtz Construction's work sites, rather than acting as a backdrop for a family portrait. Carrying on the proud tradition of this family business involves everyone, including son Kasey, who is studying construction management at college; Brad, the current president; his wife Colleen; son Kelley, who works as a field foreman; and daughter Kristin.

Steve Burgess, who is responsible for the operations side of Dean Kurtz Construction, is a long-term employee as well as a part owner of the business. In addition to his avid interest in hunting and fishing, his wife Gretchen, and his young family, Conner, Cadden, and baby Ashley, keep him busy.

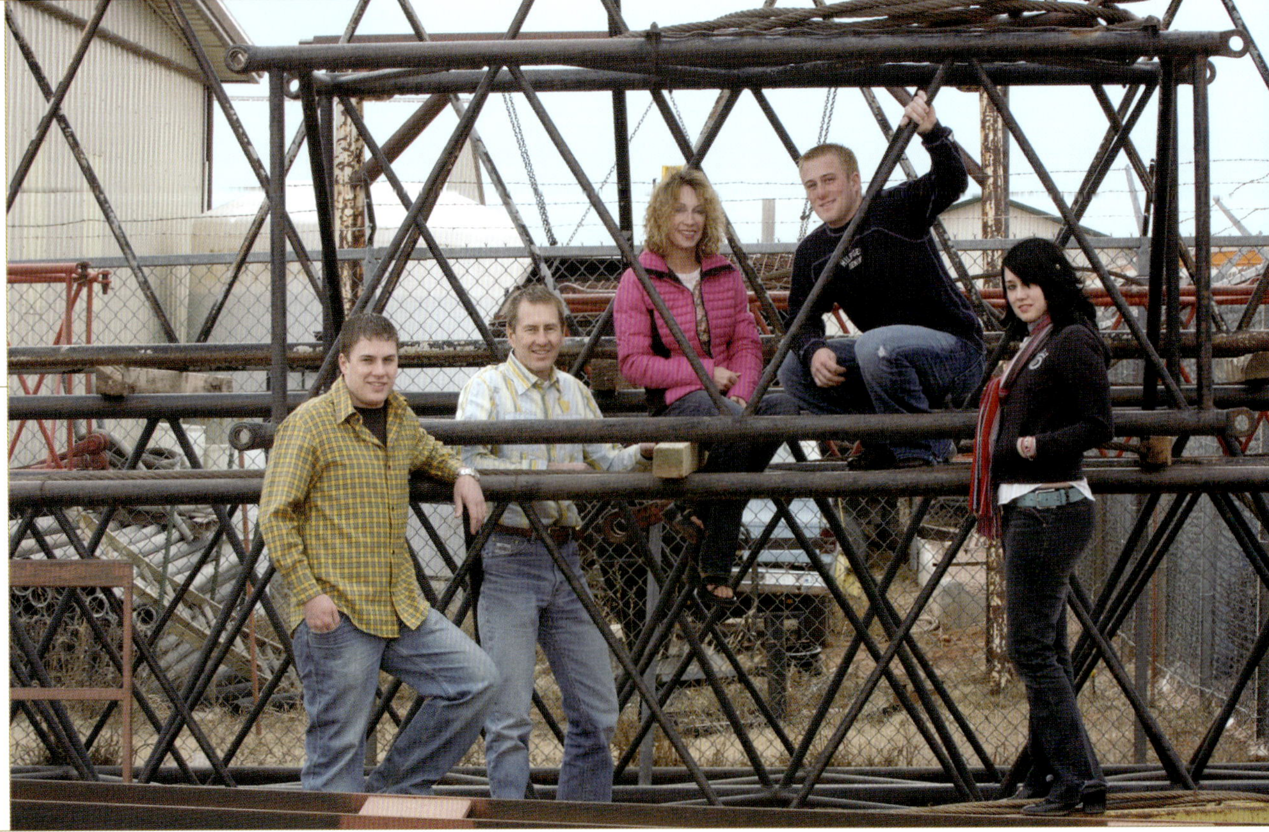

Photo by Joleen Zoller

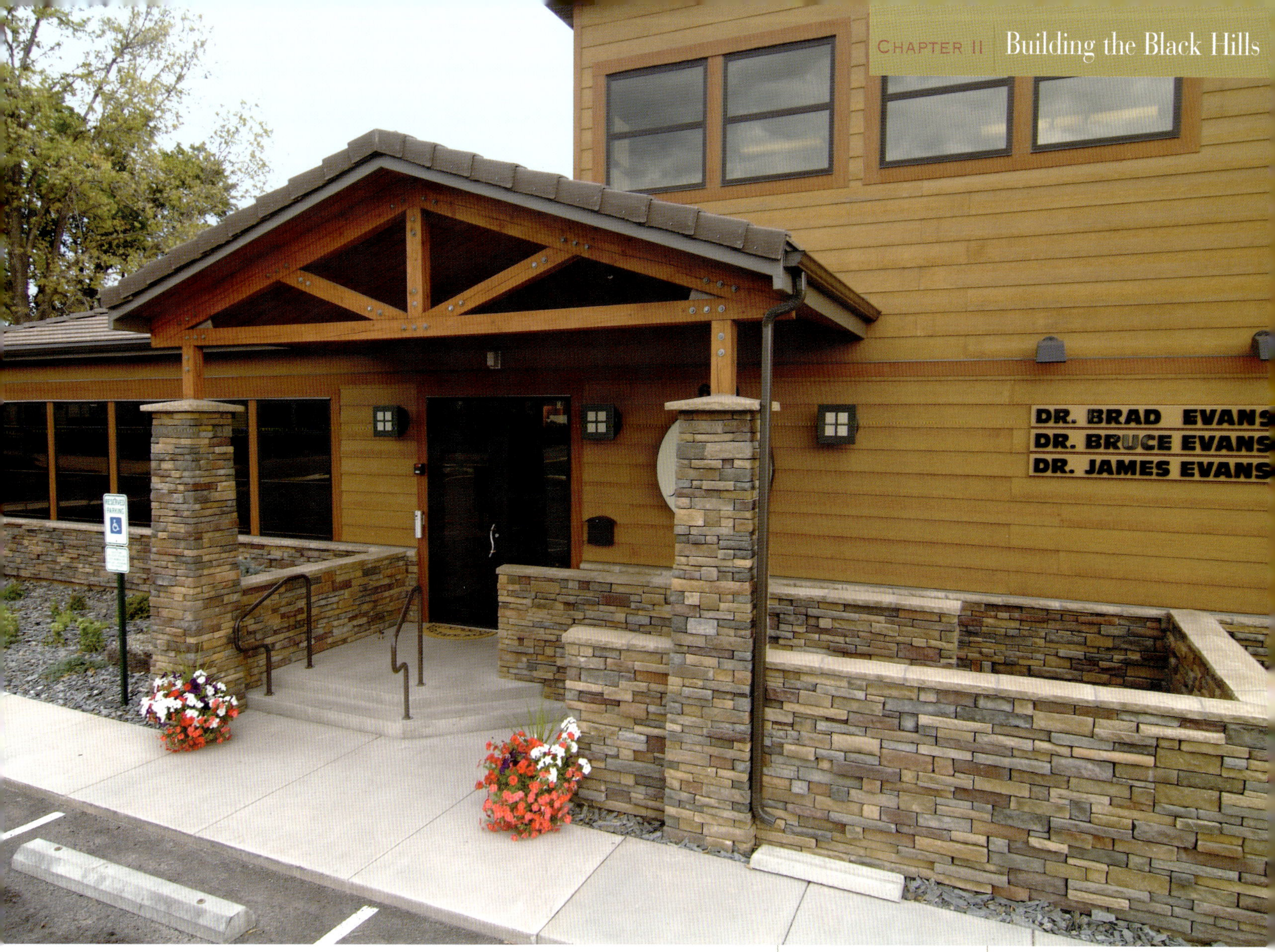

Photo by Doug Henderson

Dean Kurtz Construction has a long history of expertise in medical facility construction, from large projects like the Rapid City Regional Hospital Medical Office Building to the new three-doctor Evans Orthodontic Clinic. This facility is strategically located in a park setting, on a bike path that runs along the Greenway as it flows along through Rapid City, following the course of Rapid Creek.

state of the art, and Kurtz received an "Outstanding Contractor" award from the U.S. Army Corps of Engineers for its performance on the contract.

The list of accomplishments and projects of Dean Kurtz Construction could go on and on, but perhaps that is best left to the future generations of this family-owned business. ❖

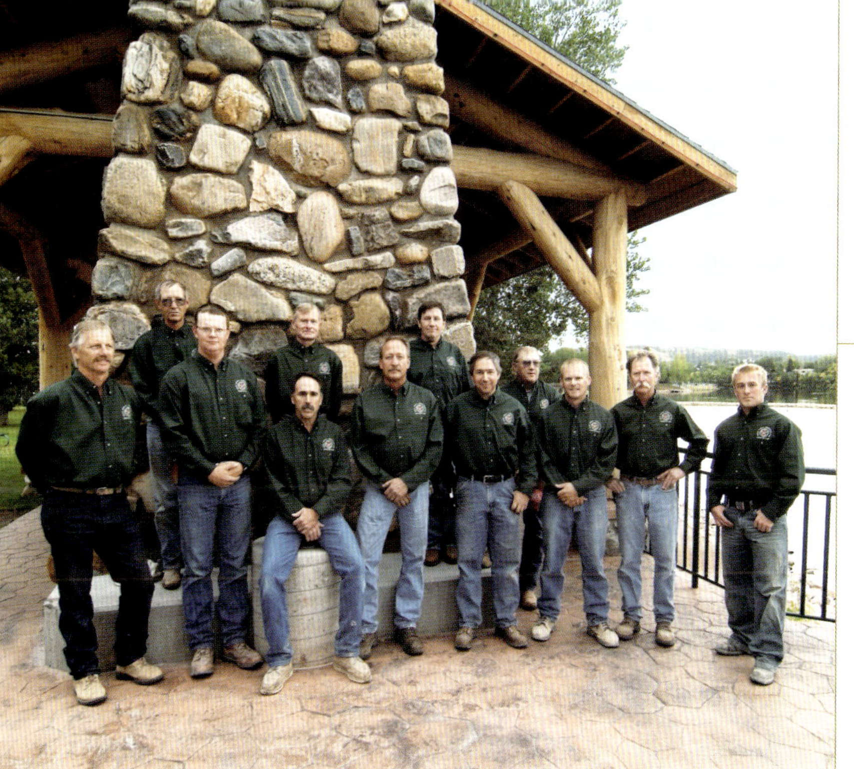

The design-build firm of Dean Kurtz Construction tackles a variety of jobs, including industrial construction, commercial building, structure renovation, and historical restoration. "No matter what the project is, it's this group of supervisors who are responsible for getting the jobs done out in the field. They're the ones who make it all come together and keep it moving," said Brad Kurtz, owner.

Photo by Doug Henderson

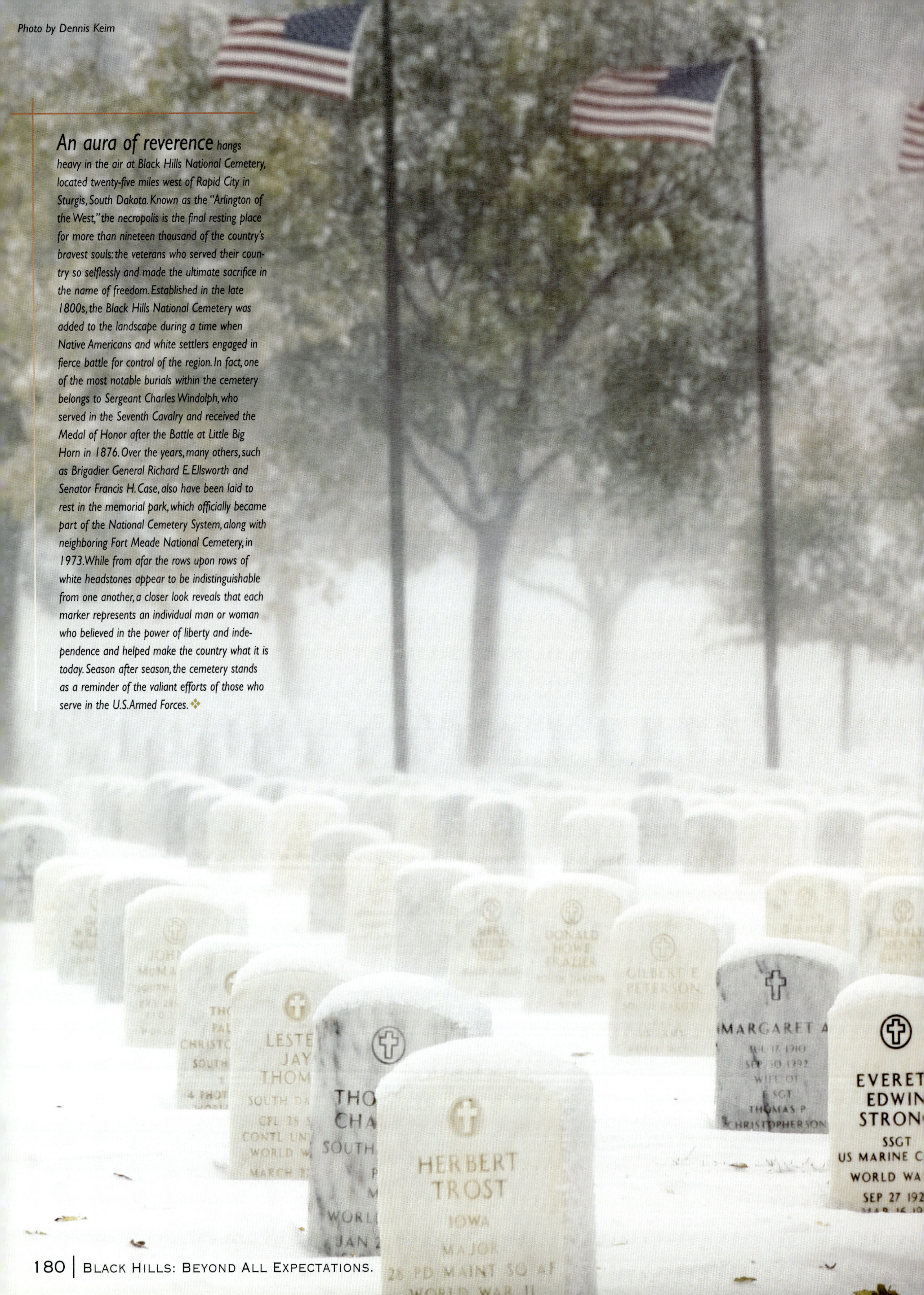

Photo by Dennis Keim

An aura of reverence hangs heavy in the air at Black Hills National Cemetery, located twenty-five miles west of Rapid City in Sturgis, South Dakota. Known as the "Arlington of the West," the necropolis is the final resting place for more than nineteen thousand of the country's bravest souls: the veterans who served their country so selflessly and made the ultimate sacrifice in the name of freedom. Established in the late 1800s, the Black Hills National Cemetery was added to the landscape during a time when Native Americans and white settlers engaged in fierce battle for control of the region. In fact, one of the most notable burials within the cemetery belongs to Sergeant Charles Windolph, who served in the Seventh Cavalry and received the Medal of Honor after the Battle at Little Big Horn in 1876. Over the years, many others, such as Brigadier General Richard E. Ellsworth and Senator Francis H. Case, also have been laid to rest in the memorial park, which officially became part of the National Cemetery System, along with neighboring Fort Meade National Cemetery, in 1973. While from afar the rows upon rows of white headstones appear to be indistinguishable from one another, a closer look reveals that each marker represents an individual man or woman who believed in the power of liberty and independence and helped make the country what it is today. Season after season, the cemetery stands as a reminder of the valiant efforts of those who serve in the U.S. Armed Forces. ❖

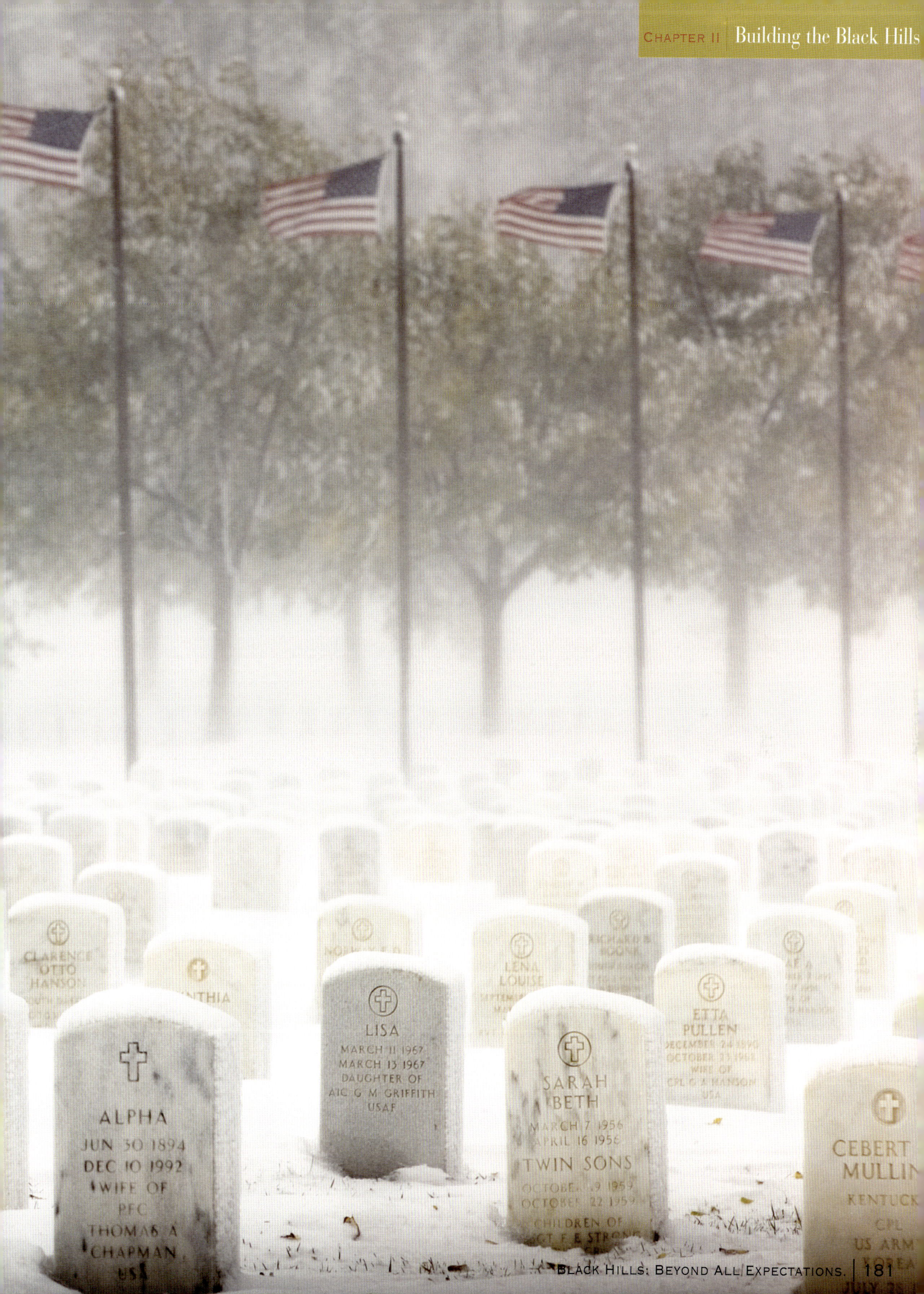
CLARENCE
OTTO
HANSON
LENA
LOUISE
ETTA
PULLEN
LISA
MARCH 11 1967
MARCH 13 1967
DAUGHTER OF
A1C G M GRIFFITH
USAF
ALPHA
JUN 30 1894
DEC 10 1992
WIFE OF
PFC
THOMAS A
CHAPMAN
SARAH
BETH
MARCH 7 1956
APRIL 16 1956
TWIN SONS

Talent and Determination Give Wyss Associates a Leading Edge

By far the most photographed site in South Dakota is Mount Rushmore National Memorial. The second most photographed feature is the Avenue of Flags, a 250-foot promenade of the flags of all fifty states and six territories. It connects the International Visitor Complex to the sculpture's Grand Terrace. Wyss Associates, Inc. has been involved as the landscape architect in several phases of the renovation work at Mount Rushmore and was the prime design consultant and lighting designer for the Avenue of Flags lighting project.

"This job presented some unique challenges," said Patrick Wyss, president. "There was a limited budget and limited amperage available, as well as a need for an inconspicuous solution consistent with the site's architecture, and it had to be low-maintenance and meet certain security requirements."

In addition to creative site lighting solutions, Wyss Associates provides services in landscape architecture, golf course architecture, park and recreation design, land planning, resort development, and historic preservation.

Wyss Associates has worked on numerous award-winning, high-profile projects throughout the Midwest.

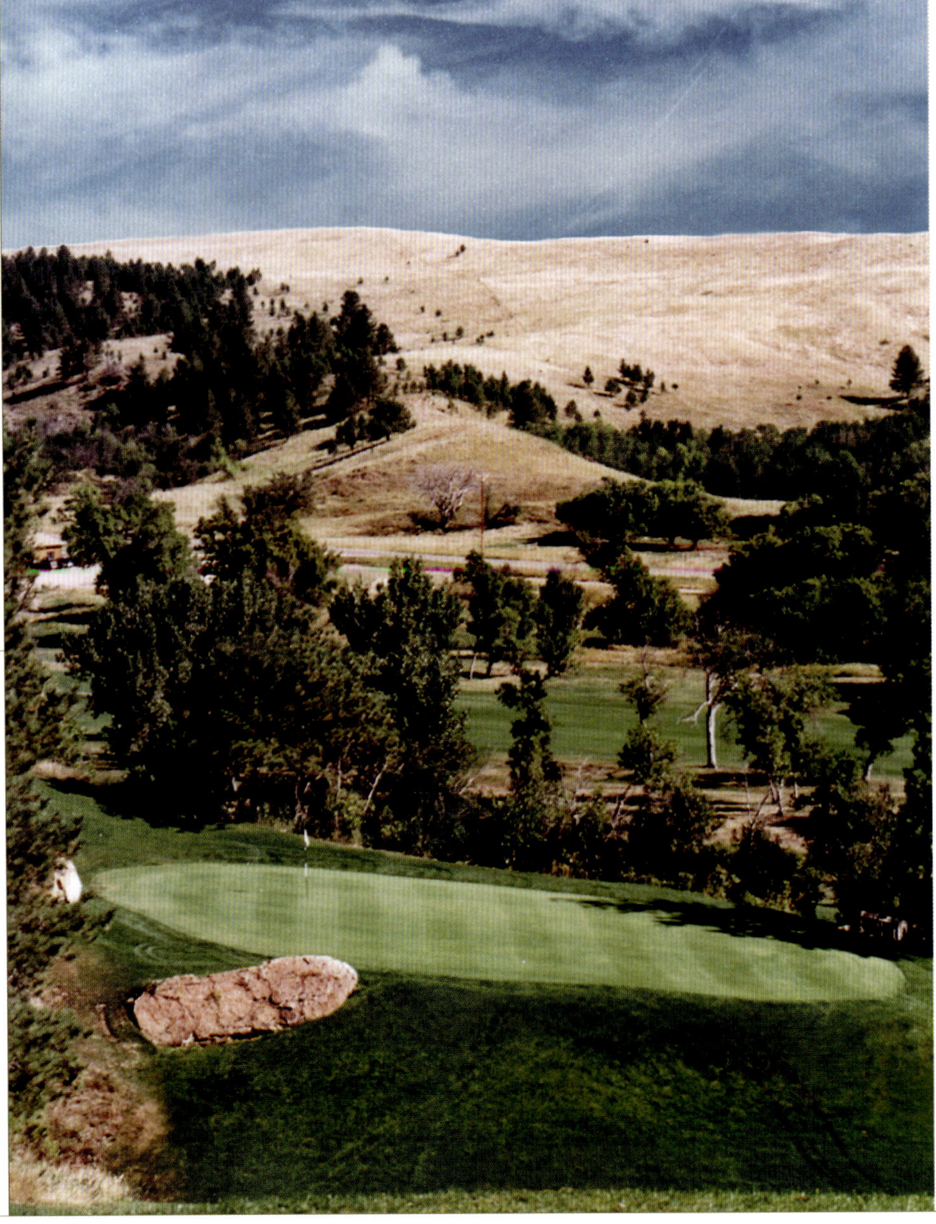

Wyss Associates, Inc. strives to have all their golf courses "lie gently on the land," as the Hart Ranch Resort Course does. This eighteen-hole course, which is nestled in a valley in the Black Hills of South Dakota, is a challenge as is evident in this shot of the sixteenth hole. It is a par three with a sixty-foot vertical drop from the tee to the green. Wyss Associates took advantage of the natural topography of the land in the design. Little earth was moved in the formation of the course, a feat that garnered recognition from the Great Plains Chapter of the American Society of Landscape Architects.

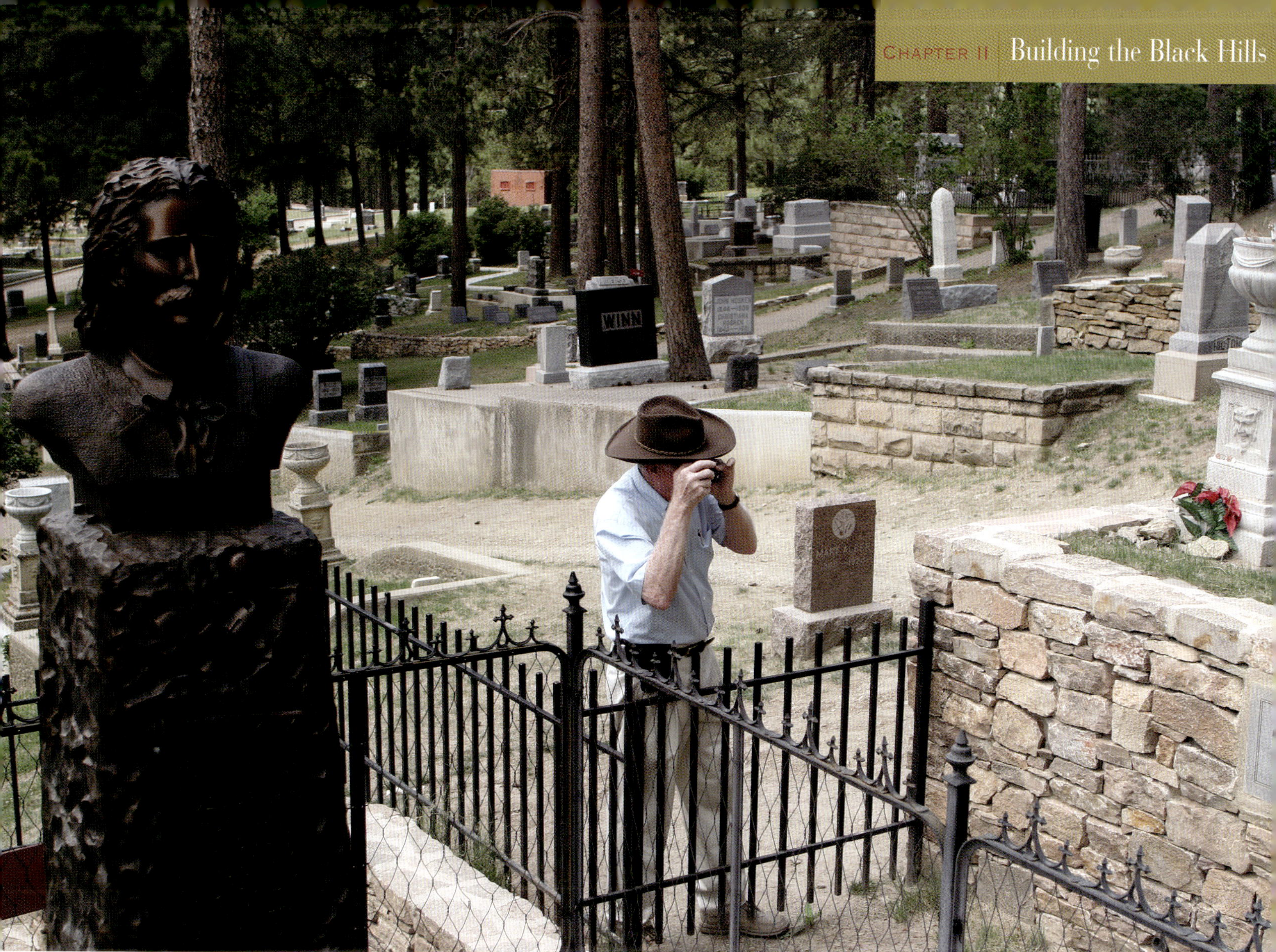

Photo by Alan S.Weiner

Mount Moriah Cemetery, the final resting place of Wild Bill Hickok and Calamity Jane, has a long and illustrious history. Originally the cemetery was on lower ground, but in 1878, the Deadwood Cemetery Association was established and decided to create a new cemetery on the hillside of Mount Moriah. When restoration was needed, Deadwood turned to Wyss Associates, Inc., which prepared a Historic Preservation Master Plan. Through this preservation effort, five hundred gravesites were restored, and several infrastructure improvements were completed.

Wyss Associates has worked on numerous award-winning, high-profile projects throughout the Midwest. They designed the Bluffs Golf Course in Vermilion, South Dakota, which is rated number-four in the state by *Golf Digest*. Their work on the Hart Ranch Resort Golf Course received merit awards from the Great Plains Chapter of the American Society of Landscape Architects. Wyss Associates is a leader in designing innovative and challenging golf courses for both the novice and the veteran golfer.

In the area of land planning, Wyss Associates strives to assure a proper fit between development and existing landscape characteristics by analyzing the existing site and understanding its opportunities and limitations. Their experience covers projects from small residential subdivisions to large plans such as the Elkhorn Ridge Land Plan on the historic Frawley Ranch near Spearfish, South Dakota.

When designing parks and recreation projects Wyss Associates has worked with the National Park Service; numerous state, county, and city governments; and private organizations to design water parks, athletic complexes, passive parks, linear greenway parks, nature parks, and trail systems.

Wyss Associates is recognized nationally for its knowledge and expertise with historic landscapes, specifically within historic cemeteries. "We conduct extensive research, prepare thoughtful preservation plans, and provide on-site coordination during the restoration," said Wyss. Wyss Associates has developed historic cemetery preservation plans in several states throughout the United States.

Wyss Associates comprises landscape architects, golf course architects, planners, graphic designers, technical staff, and administrative personnel, all of whom are active in their communities and professional societies. "This helps make our team stronger and more informed so our clients get a higher quality of design and a better overall product. It's that talent and determination that have kept us at the top of our game for over twenty years," Wyss said. ❖

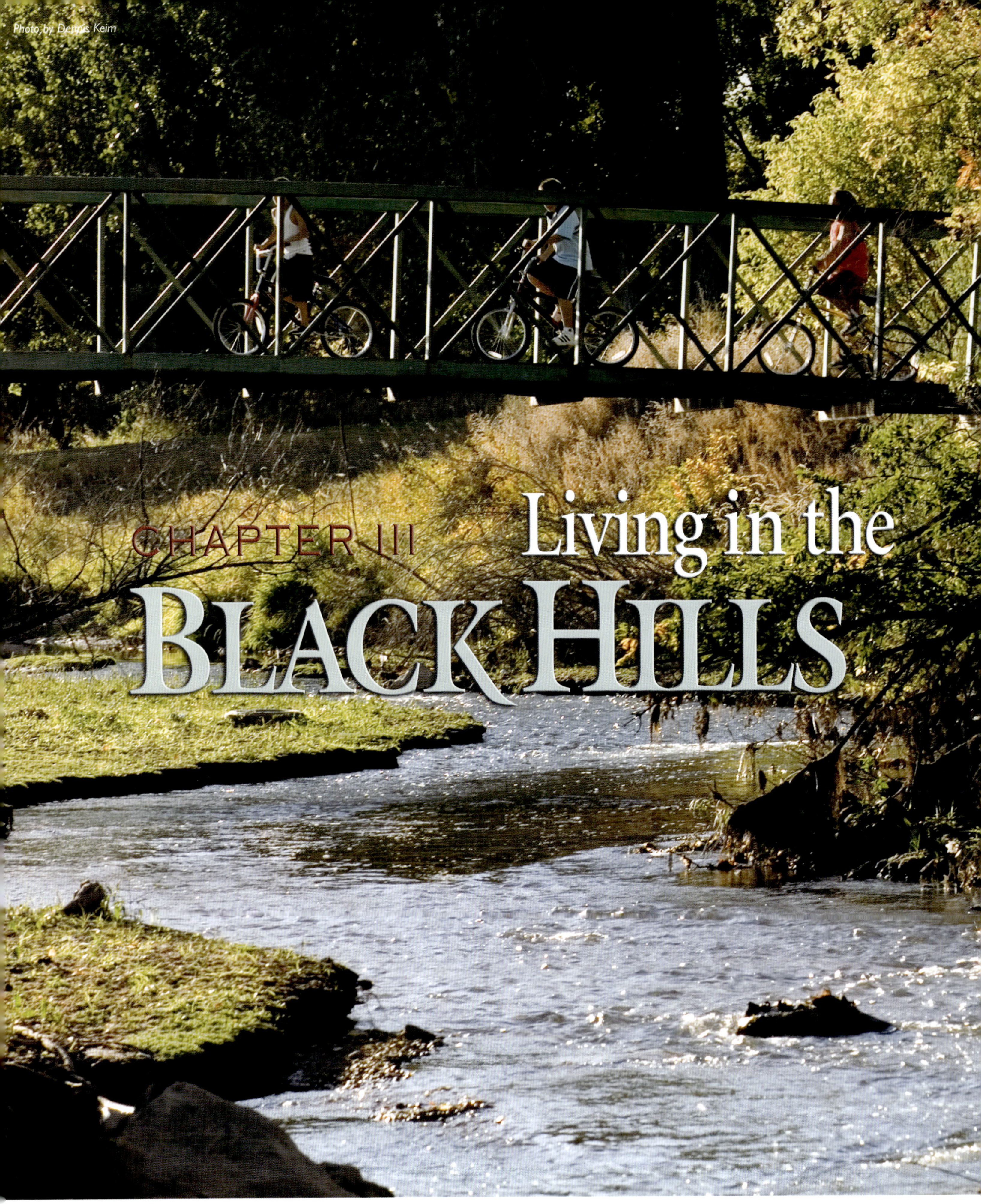

CHAPTER III

Living in the BLACK HILLS

With wide-open spaces underfoot and overhead, life in the Black Hills allows for a sense of life defined by limitless opportunities.

As the state's second-largest city, Rapid City is the region's metropolitan heart. A unique blend of Old West ambience, small-town charm, and urban savvy, it boasts a cost of living and median home prices that rank below the national average. With its historic downtown streets and picturesque tree-lined neighborhoods, it is also an attractive city, reflecting both civic and private pride of ownership.

To support the area's expanding opportunities in tourism, business, and high-tech-based industries, education is given top priority. Excellent public school systems prepare students for every step on the educational ladder, while higher-learning institutions offer the state-of-the-art instruction, facilities, and research usually found only in large urban areas.

An outdoors lover's paradise, the Black Hills is the perfect spot to get and stay active. To assist in maintaining a healthy lifestyle, the area supports a number of high-quality medical facilities. Additionally, programs and services like those offered at the VA Black Hills Health Care System in Hot Springs and Rapid City's Black Hills Center for American Indian Health ensure that no one gets left behind.

In many areas of the country, the qualities that once defined life in the West have long disappeared. But in the Black Hills those qualities still exist: room to dream, room to grow, room to live. ❖

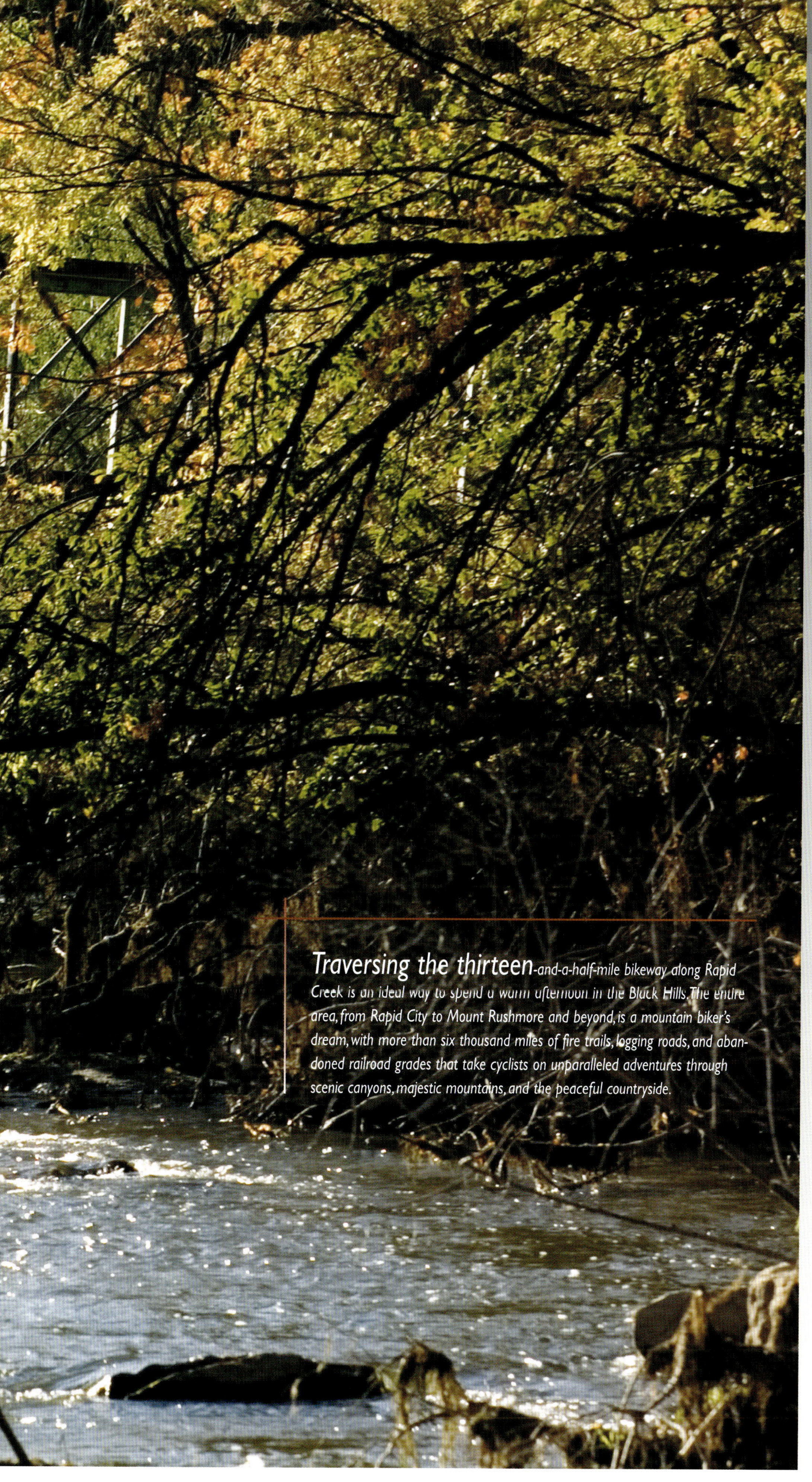

Traversing the thirteen-and-a-half-mile bikeway along Rapid Creek is an ideal way to spend a warm afternoon in the Black Hills. The entire area, from Rapid City to Mount Rushmore and beyond, is a mountain biker's dream, with more than six thousand miles of fire trails, logging roads, and abandoned railroad grades that take cyclists on unparalleled adventures through scenic canyons, majestic mountains, and the peaceful countryside.

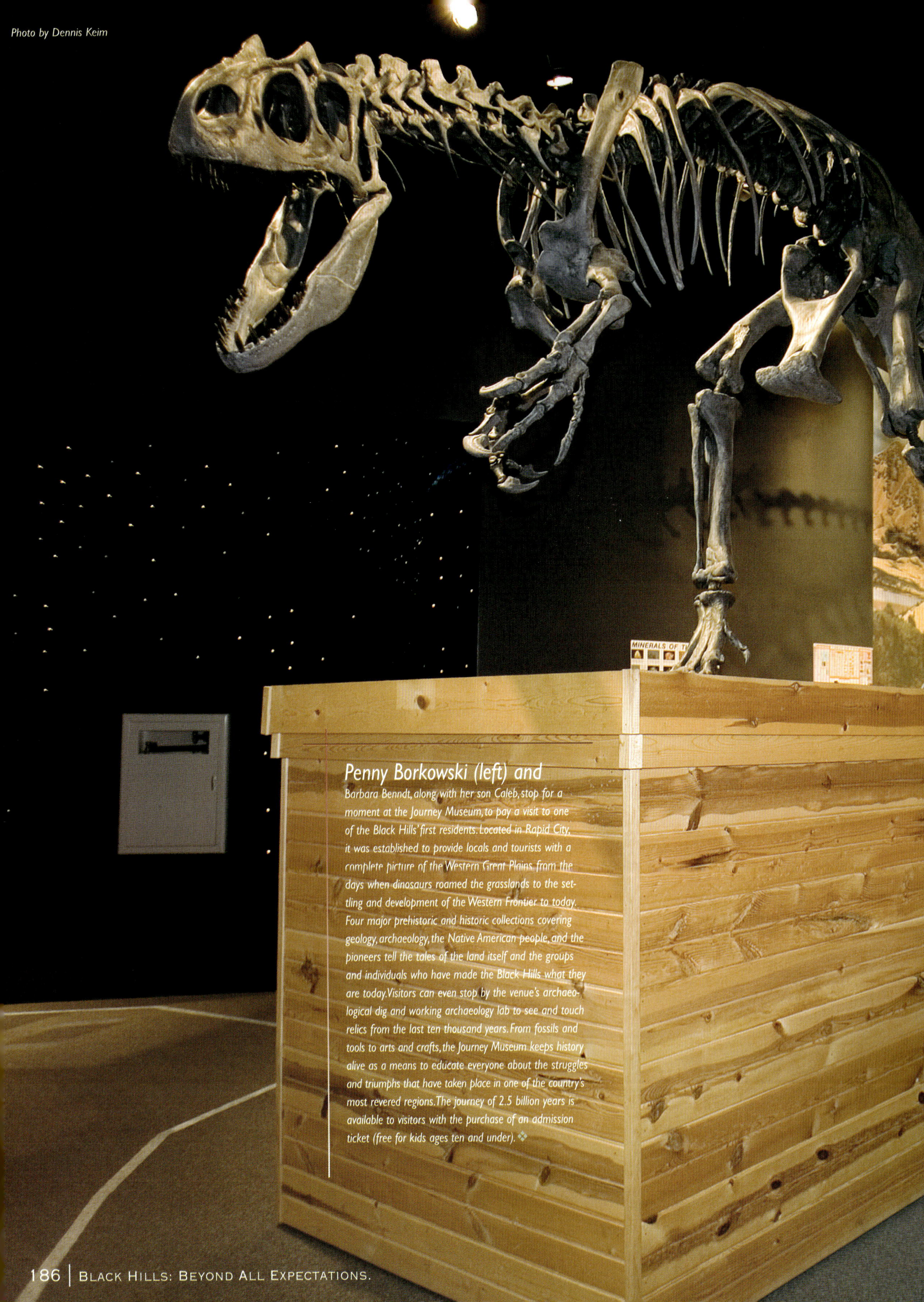

Photo by Dennis Keim

Penny Borkowski (left) and Barbara Benndt, along with her son Caleb, stop for a moment at the Journey Museum, to pay a visit to one of the Black Hills' first residents. Located in Rapid City, it was established to provide locals and tourists with a complete picture of the Western Great Plains, from the days when dinosaurs roamed the grasslands to the settling and development of the Western Frontier to today. Four major prehistoric and historic collections covering geology, archaeology, the Native American people, and the pioneers tell the tales of the land itself and the groups and individuals who have made the Black Hills what they are today. Visitors can even stop by the venue's archaeological dig and working archaeology lab to see and touch relics from the last ten thousand years. From fossils and tools to arts and crafts, the Journey Museum keeps history alive as a means to educate everyone about the struggles and triumphs that have taken place in one of the country's most revered regions. The journey of 2.5 billion years is available to visitors with the purchase of an admission ticket (free for kids ages ten and under).

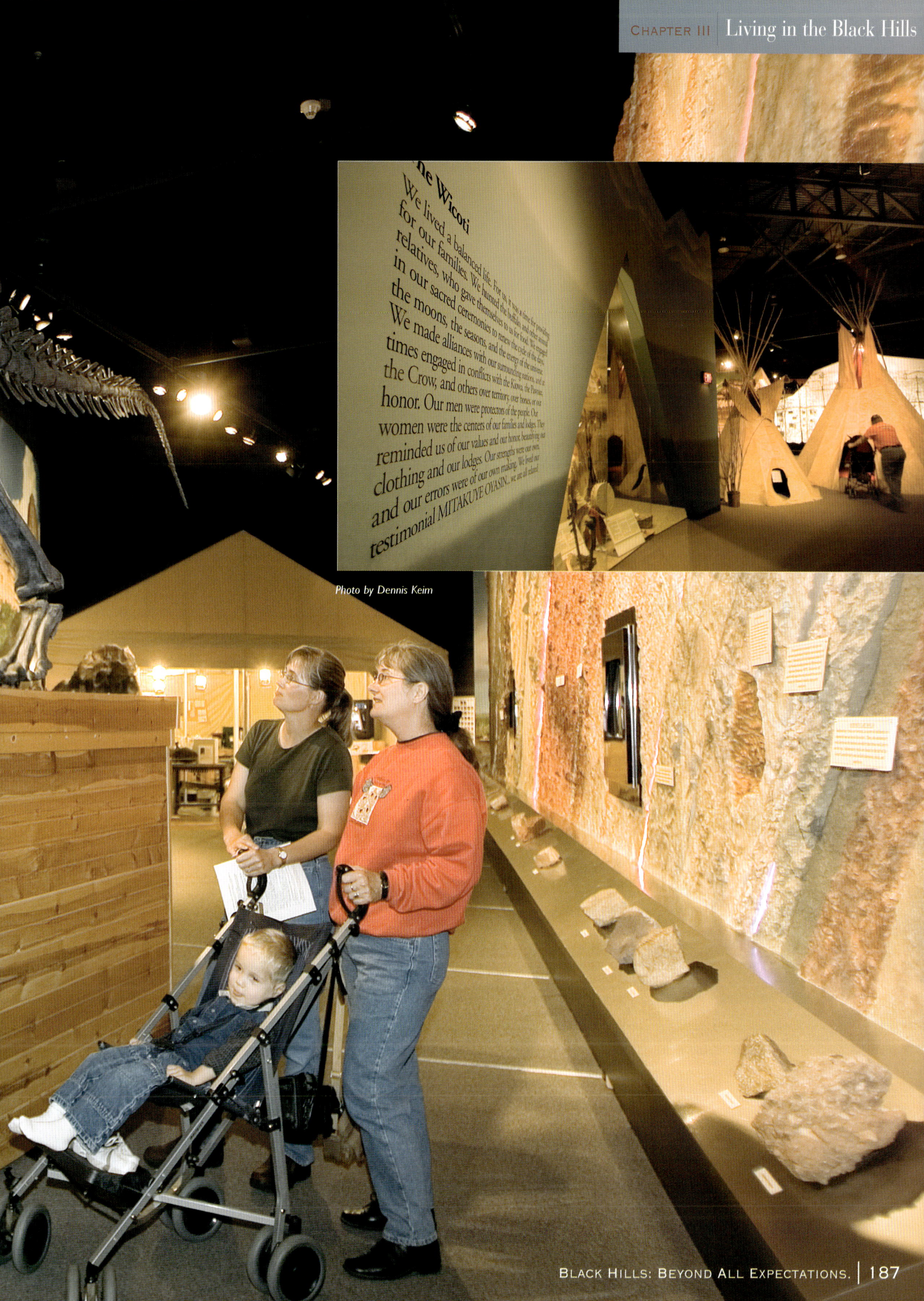

Photo by Dennis Keim

Regional Health—A Partnership with the Community

As a network of not-for-profit healthcare organizations, Regional Health is dedicated to providing health-care excellence in partnership with the communities it serves. Regional Health has more than forty facilities serving western South Dakota, eastern Wyoming, and the panhandle of Nebraska. Nearly forty-two hundred dedicated professionals work for Regional Health to bring about a positive impact on the health of each community.

Regional Health is committed to the region. As the only not-for-profit health system serving western South Dakota, Regional Health takes great pride in its primary mission, which is to provide care to everyone regardless of his or her ability to pay. In 2004, Regional Health facilities provided more than $28 million in uncompensated care to those who could not afford it. In addition, they reinvested profits in new equipment to offer new services and to improve facilities. No profits are paid to investors.

Regional Health is governed by community leaders who volunteer their time to the organizations' shared mission.

"Our board members are dedicated leaders," says Regional Health president and CEO Charles E. Hart, M.D., M.S. "They continually strive to provide the best care possible for everyone in the region."

"Our board members continually strive to offer everyone in the region the best care available."

As both a tertiary care hospital and a regional referral center, Rapid City Regional Hospital, the flagship hospital of the system, has distinguished itself as a leader in advanced, compassionate care in surgery, cancer care, behavioral health, orthopedics, cardiology, cardiac surgery, neurosurgery, diagnostic imaging, dialysis, adult intensive care, obstetrics, pediatrics, neonatal intensive care, rehabilitation, emergency care, pain

Photo by Thomas S. England

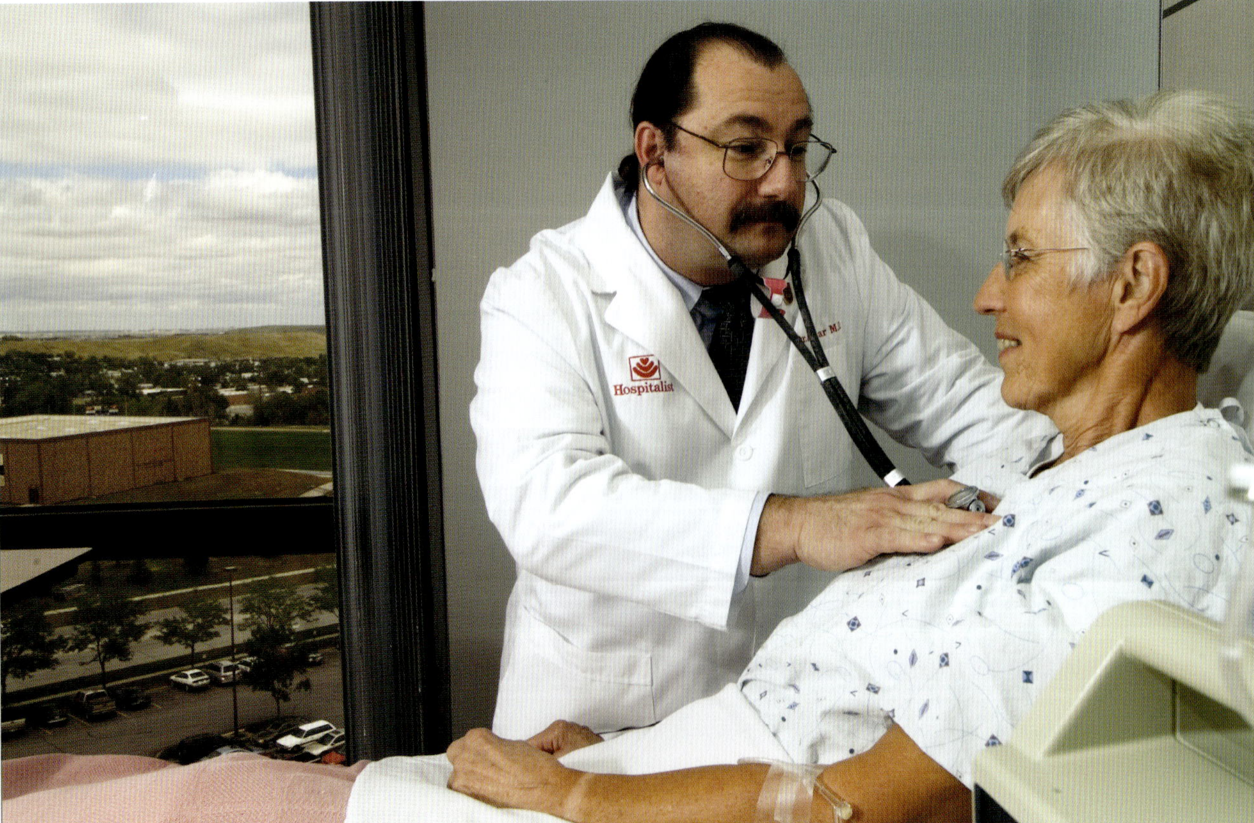

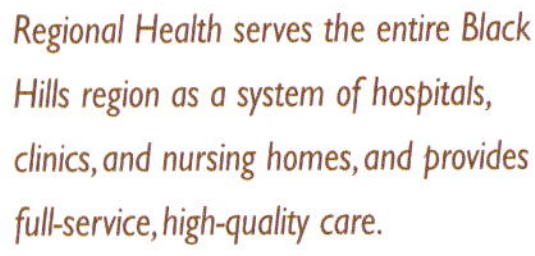

Regional Health serves the entire Black Hills region as a system of hospitals, clinics, and nursing homes, and provides full-service, high-quality care.

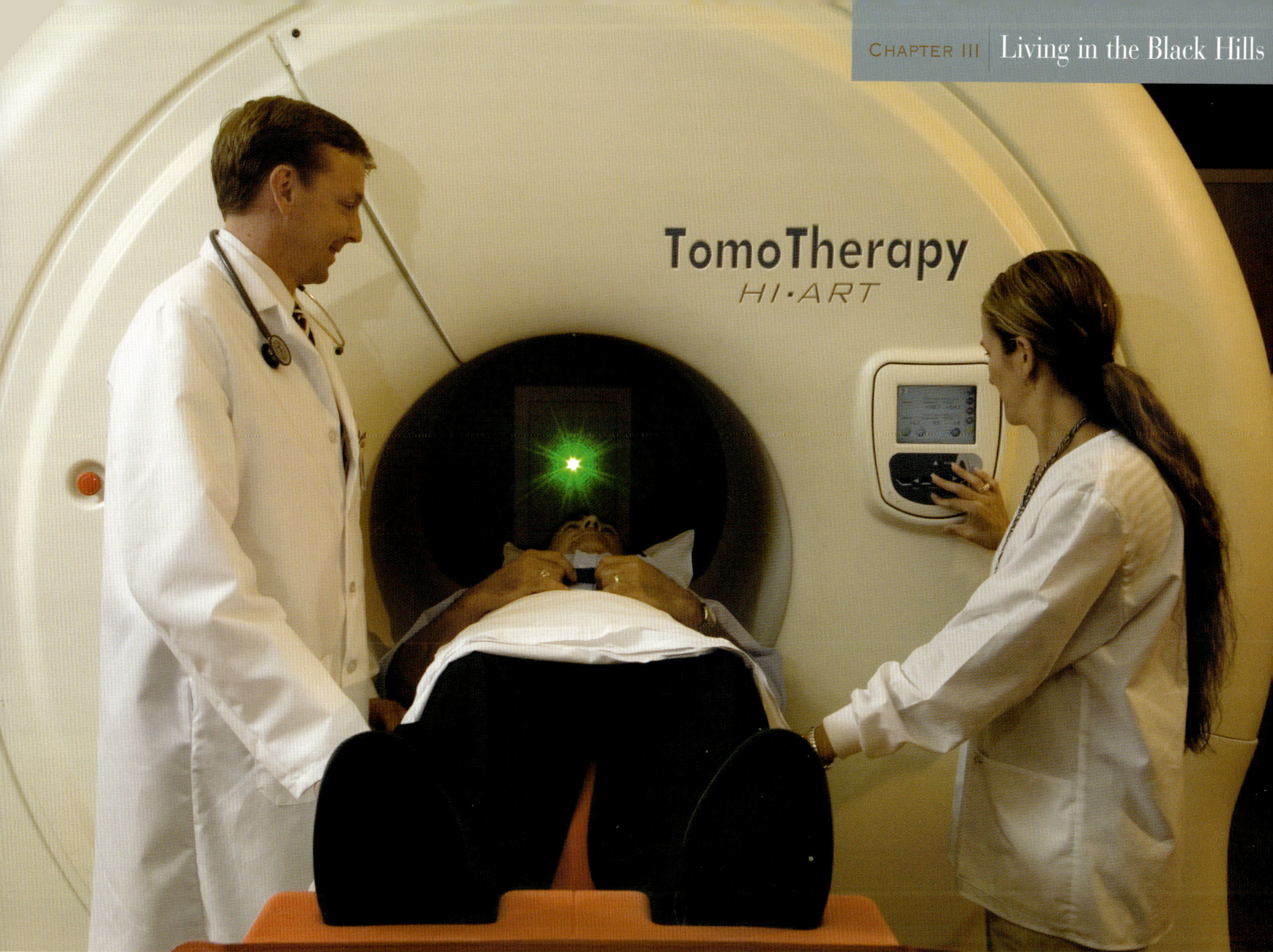

Photo by Thomas S. England

TomoTherapy, one of the most advanced cancer radiation treatments in the world, is available at the John T. Vucurevich Regional Cancer Care Institute, located in Rapid City Regional Hospital.

management, home health, and LifeFlight helicopter and fixed-wing transport services.

Regional Health Network operates all the system's hospitals located outside Rapid City as well as the Regional Senior Care facilities. The hospitals include Spearfish Regional Hospital, Sturgis Regional Hospital, Lead-Deadwood Regional Hospital, and Custer Regional Hospital. Regional Senior Care facilities are located in Rapid City, Spearfish, Sturgis, Lead-Deadwood, Belle Fourche, and Custer.

Regional Health Physicians operates all the system's Regional Medical Clinics, which are located in Rapid City, Spearfish, Sturgis, Lead-Deadwood, Belle Fourche, Newell, Custer, Hill City, and Edgemont.

Regional Health facilities have a strong tradition of providing high-quality care and have received many national awards. In 2005, HealthGrades named Rapid City Regional Hospital (RCRH) South Dakota's number-one hospital for orthopedics, and in the top 5 percent in the United States for joint replacements.

During the same period the Joint Commission on Accreditation of Healthcare Organizations accredited the hospital. Also in 2005, Medicare's Hospital Quality Incentive Demonstration Program awarded RCRH more than $130,000 for health-care quality outcomes in cardiac surgery and orthopedics.

In 2003, Press Ganey & Associates, the industry's premier customer satisfaction measurement firm, awarded RCRH its prestigious Compass Award, and in 2004 rated the Hospital's Emergency Department as one of the top in the country. Rapid City Regional Hospital was also listed in 1999 as a top 100 hospital for Cardiac Bypass Surgery by the Health Care Investment Group.

Western South Dakota is fortunate to have the level of healthcare experience, knowledge, and technology offered by Regional Health. The leadership of the boards and the dedication of the employees, medical staff, and volunteers have made Regional Health a true asset to the region.❖

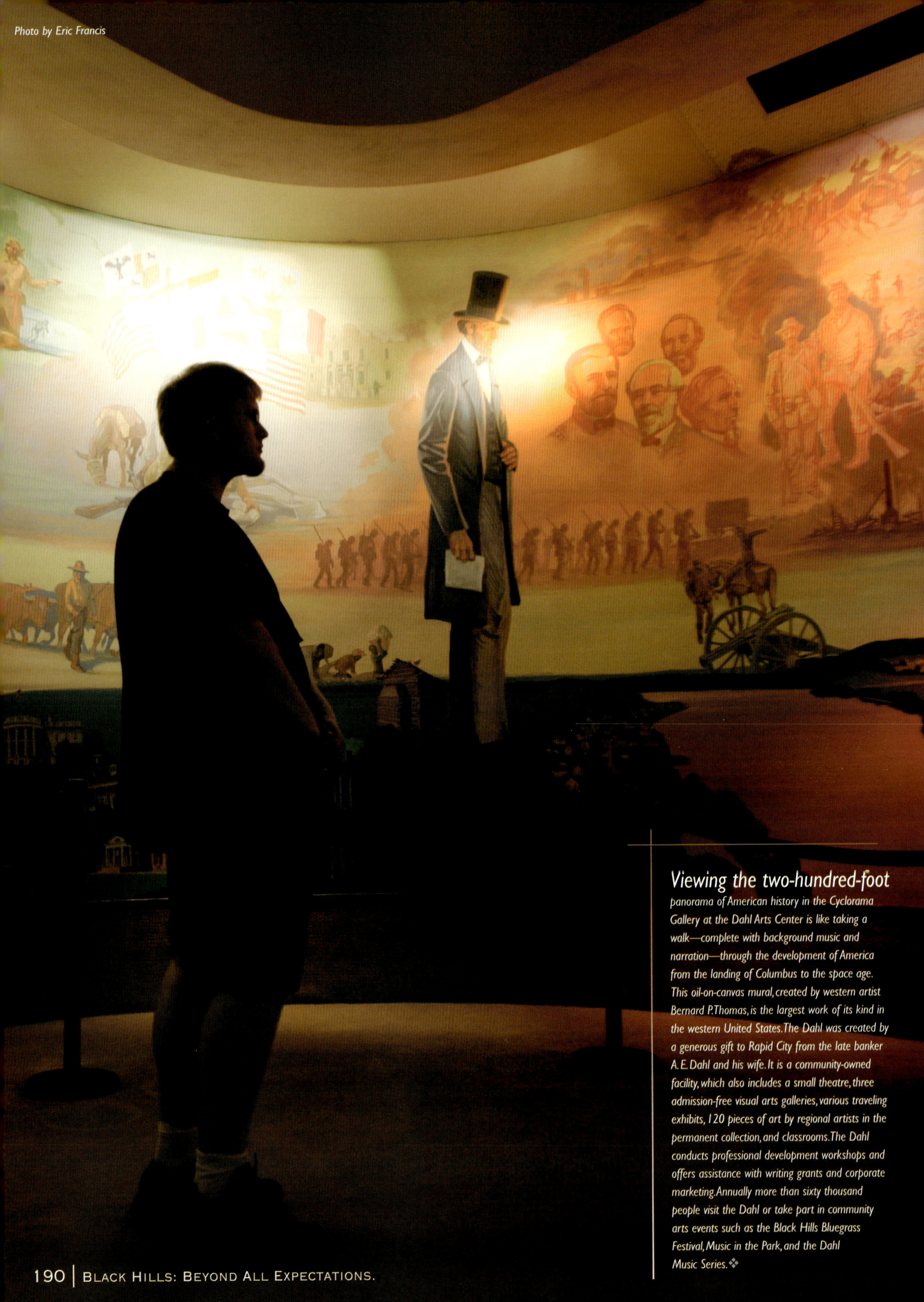

Photo by Eric Francis

Viewing the two-hundred-foot panorama of American history in the Cyclorama Gallery at the Dahl Arts Center is like taking a walk—complete with background music and narration—through the development of America from the landing of Columbus to the space age. This oil-on-canvas mural, created by western artist Bernard P. Thomas, is the largest work of its kind in the western United States. The Dahl was created by a generous gift to Rapid City from the late banker A. E. Dahl and his wife. It is a community-owned facility, which also includes a small theatre, three admission-free visual arts galleries, various traveling exhibits, 120 pieces of art by regional artists in the permanent collection, and classrooms. The Dahl conducts professional development workshops and offers assistance with writing grants and corporate marketing. Annually more than sixty thousand people visit the Dahl or take part in community arts events such as the Black Hills Bluegrass Festival, Music in the Park, and the Dahl Music Series.❖

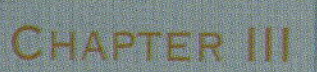

Photo by Alan S.Weiner

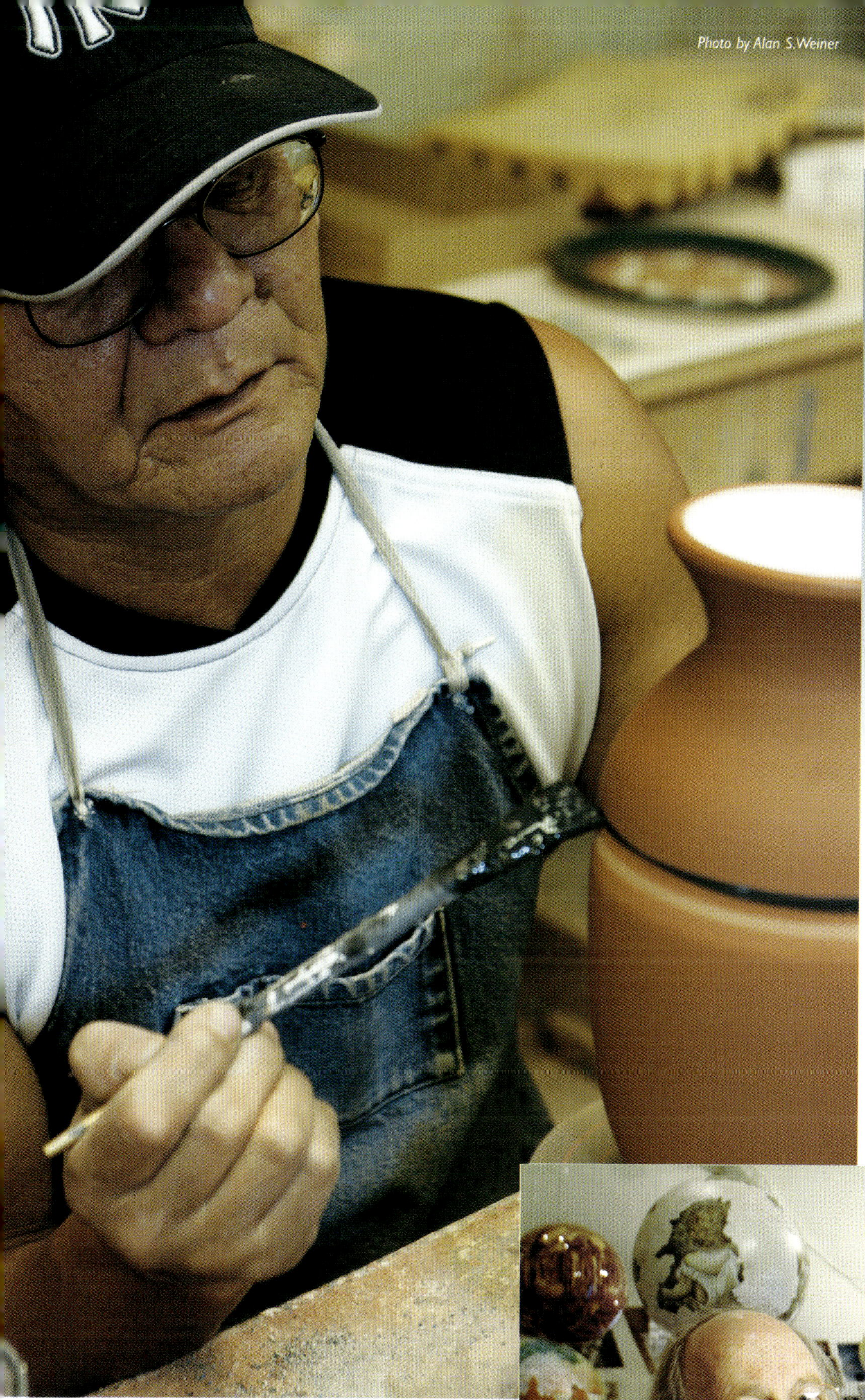

The Black Hills area supports

a thriving community of artists, from traditional to modern to out of this world. Artist Delbert Red Feather keeps alive the ancient designs and symbols of the Lakota Sioux culture with his finely crafted pottery, most of which is made from the red clay that is distinctive to the Black Hills and sacred to his people. Red Feather's work, along with a half dozen other noted Sioux artisans, is produced for and sold through Sioux Pottery, a Rapid City plant that has been producing and selling local American Indian art since 1958. Dick Termes, (Below) on the other hand, reproduces a world neither past nor present, but existing on another dimension altogether. Or, as he puts it, "What you'd see if you were inside a transparent ball, rolled into a cathedral, looked up, down, and in all four directions, and then painted what you saw." To explore this six-point perspective, Termes applies his paints to one-eighth-inch-thick polyethylene plastic balls of various sizes. The completed "Termespheres" are powered by electric motor to revolve around a central axis and depict subject matter ranging from historical places and events to fantastical universes to visual illustrations of scientific ideas. ❖

Photo by Doug Henderson

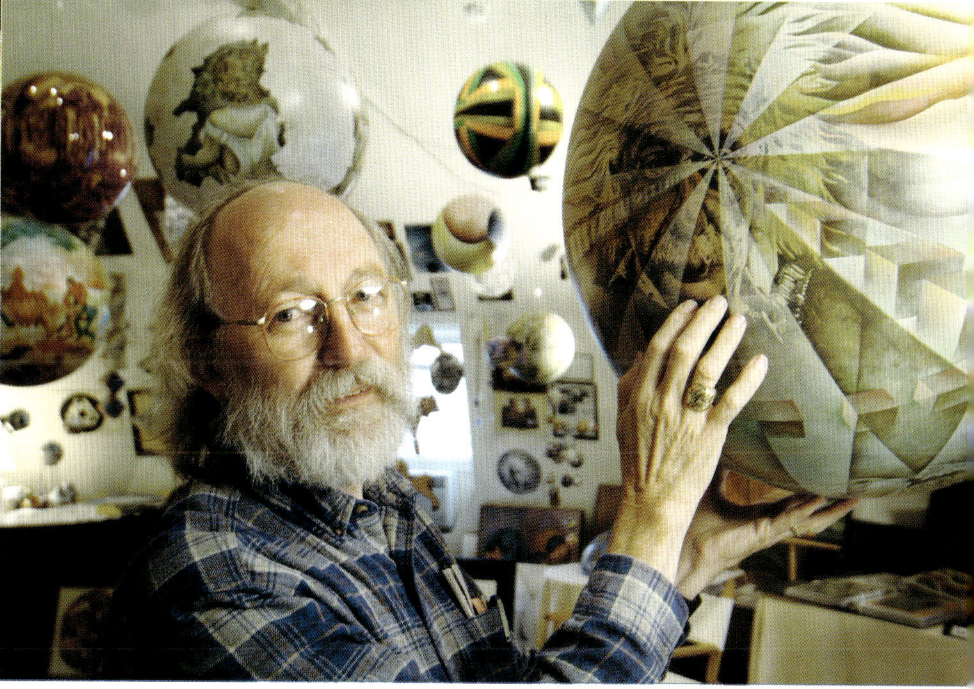

Eye Institute Offers Exceptional Services to Community

At the Black Hills Regional Eye Institute when asked, "Who cares about your vision?" the response is, "I care." Hundreds of doctors and patients count on the Eye Institute to provide the very best in diagnosis, treatment, consultation, surgery, research, and education. Eye Institute physicians and staff are honored to serve patients and are sincere when they say that the phrases "eye care" and "I care" have exactly the same meaning.

The Eye Institute is a forty-five-thousand-square-foot facility that houses a state-of-the-art ambulatory surgery center, laser/refractive center, and world-class retina center. In addition, a low-vision center helps patients with diminished vision maintain their independence, and Optical Works provides the latest options in prescription eyewear along with an ocularist to help patients with prosthetic eye needs.

The physicians at the Eye Institute are highly trained in a variety of subspecialties such as vitreoretinal disorders including macular degeneration and diabetic retinopathy, glaucoma, pediatrics, cataract surgery, eye muscle surgery, eye plastic surgery, neuro-ophthalmology, laser vision correction, and ocular inflammation. This comprehensive approach to eye care offers this rural region exceptional services that normally would only be found in major metropolitan areas.

"Visionary eye care. You'll see," is not just a slogan at the Black Hills Regional Eye Institute.

Photo by Rodger Slott

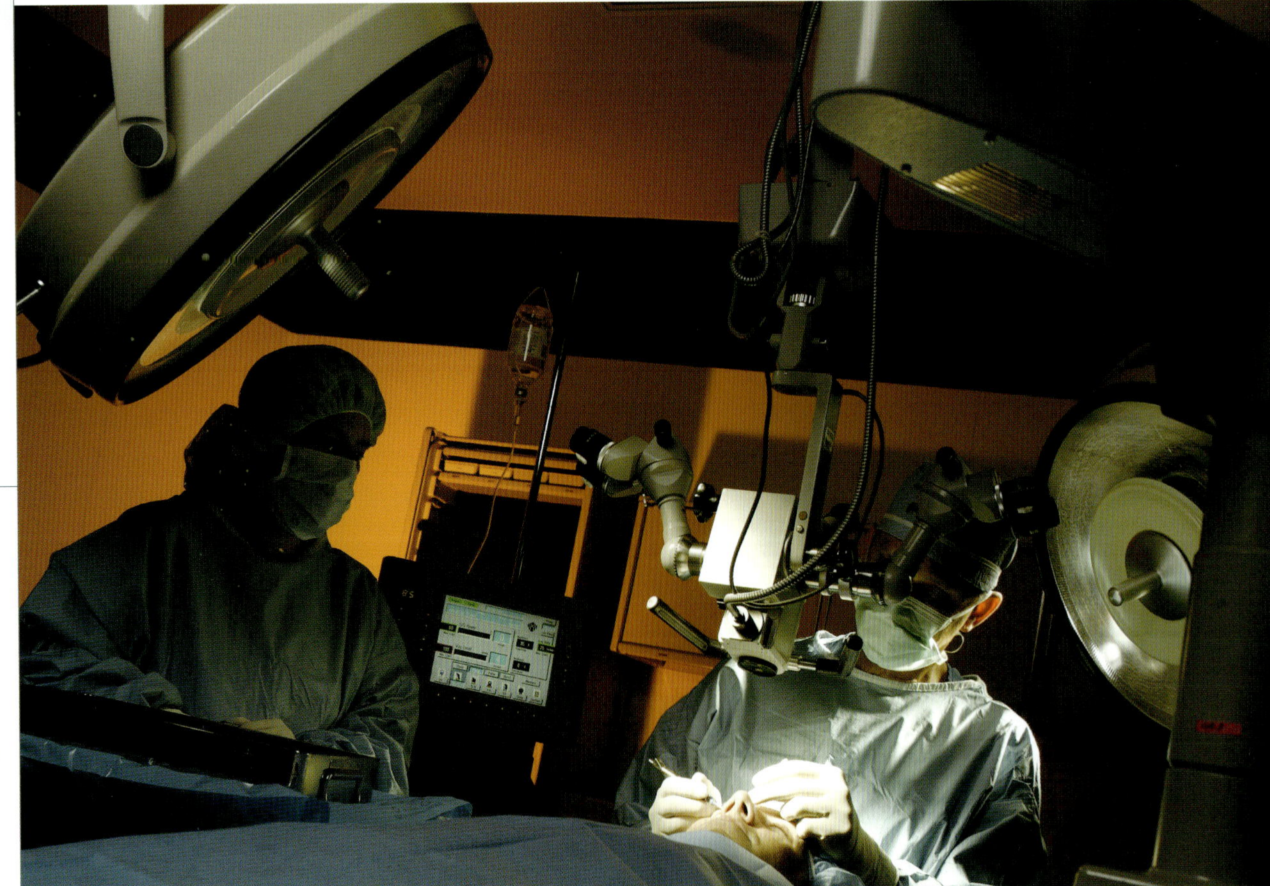

The Black Hills Regional Eye Surgery Center provides surgical services on an outpatient basis. Our operating suites are equipped with highly sophisticated equipment for the most complex eye surgery. Here Dr. Paul Zimmerman removes a cataract from a patient's eye.

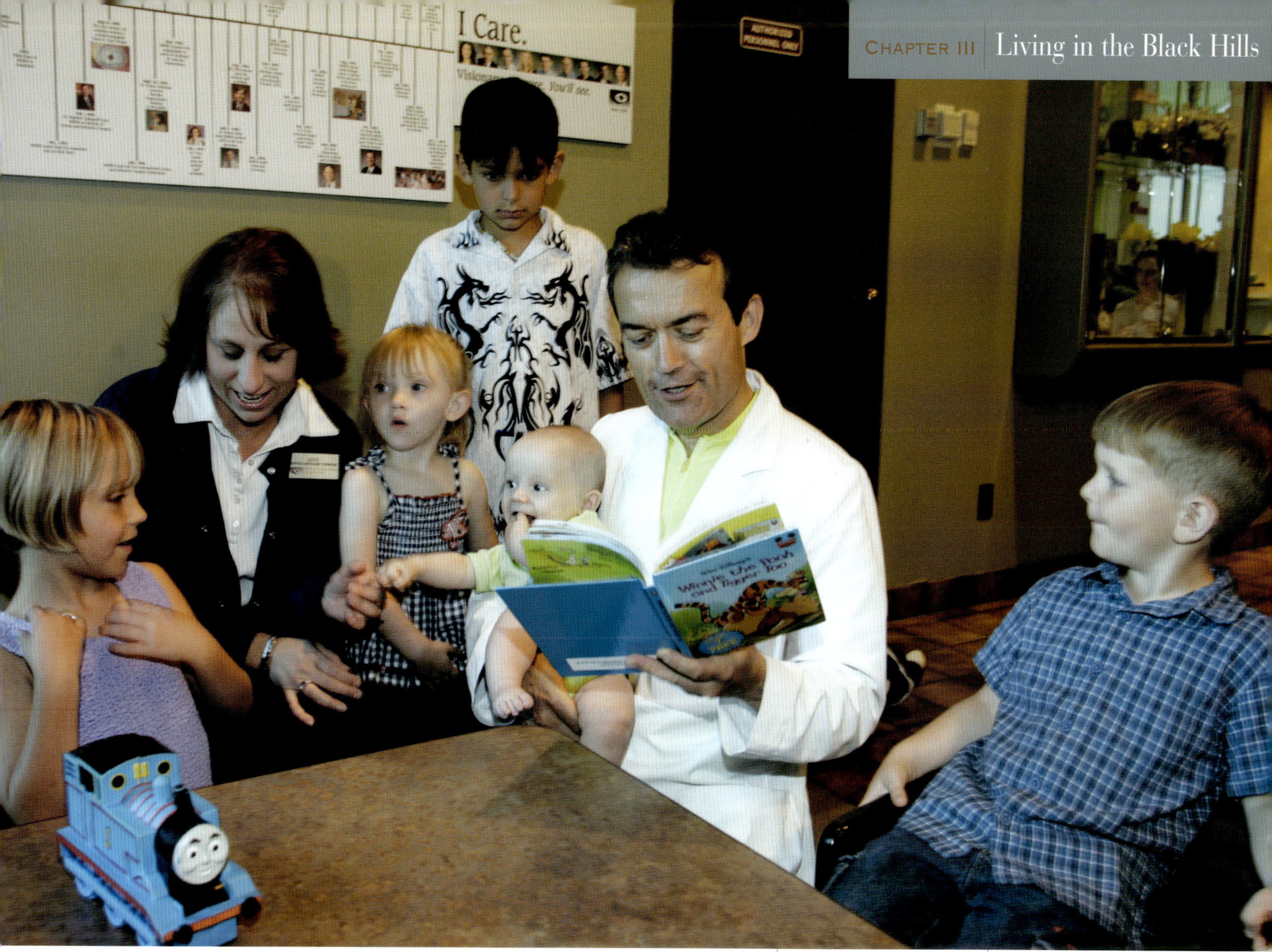

Photo by Alan S.Weiner

The Eye Institute provides a free children's eye screening yearly to detect any vision problems that might develop in a young child. Dr. Robert Nixon (above), who is fellowship trained in pediatric ophthalmology, interacts with several children during a screening.

For example, there was an Eye Institute patient who literally could not keep his eyes open, but he was not sleepy. He had to tape his eyelids open to be able to see. He went from doctor to doctor and finally saw the neuro-ophthalmologist at the Eye Institute, where he was diagnosed with ocular myasthenia/gravis, a nerve/muscle malfunction. Medical treatment and surgery corrected the problem for him, and now he can open and close his eyes at will. Difficult eye problems like this are what the physicians and staff at the Eye Institute do best.

The Eye Institute serves patients in a five-state area: North Dakota, South Dakota, Wyoming, Nebraska, and Montana. Black Hills Regional Eye Institute doctors work with local physicians and optometrists in twelve satellite locations that provide convenient eye care for patients near their homes. The Eye Institute also serves the large Native American population on the Pine Ridge, Rosebud, and Cheyenne River Sioux Tribe Indian Reservations.

Patients benefit from the Eye Institute's involvement in numerous Food and Drug Administration (FDA) national clinical research trials. Patients who qualify can take advantage of cutting-edge therapies at no cost. Providing access to these national studies keeps the community updated on the latest medical and surgical advances in eye care. Community education is provided through screenings for glaucoma, dry eye, and children's eye disease. Professional education is conducted for physicians, optometrists, and eye technicians.

"Visionary eye care. You'll see," is not just a slogan at the Black Hills Regional Eye Institute it is the basis of the Eye Institute's commitment to all patients. ❖

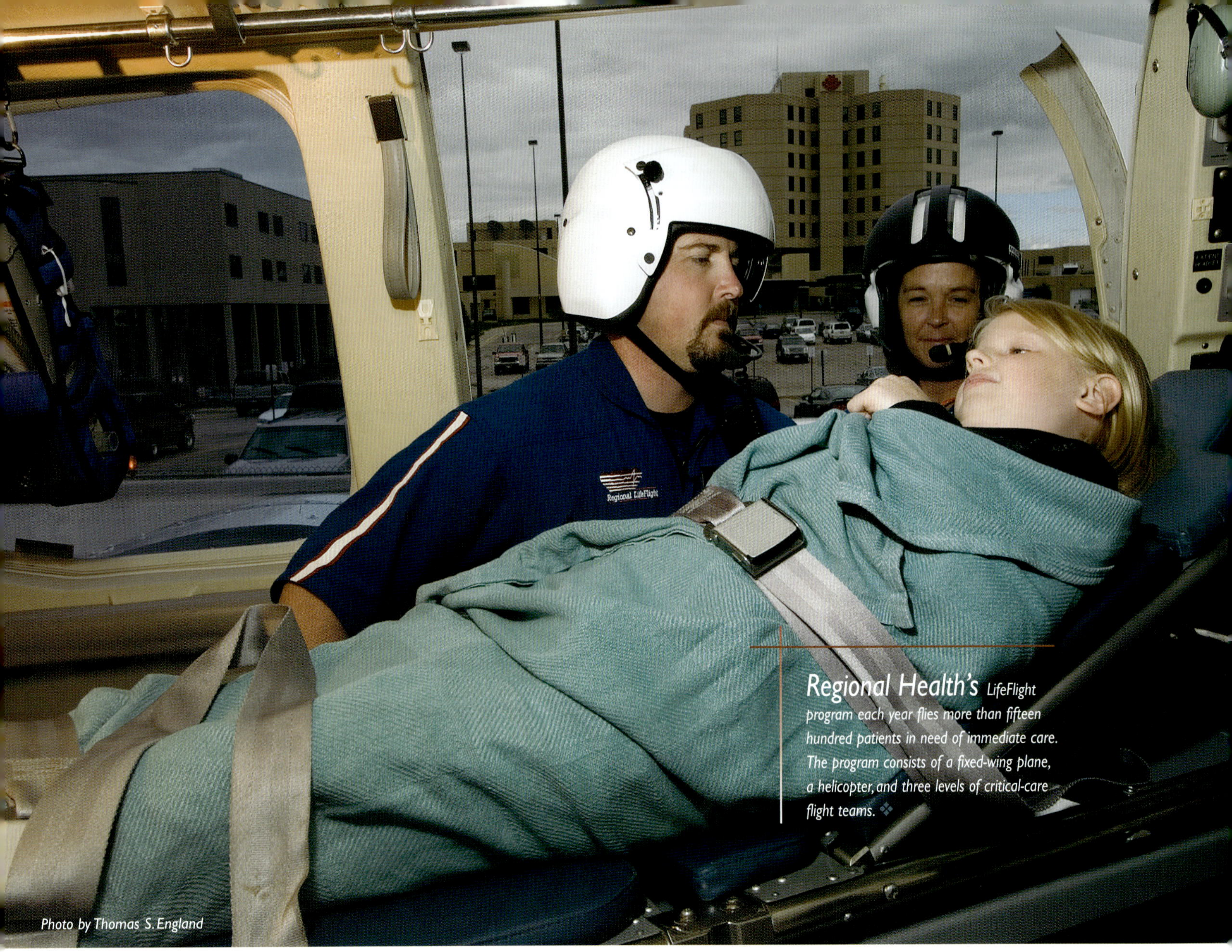

Regional Health's LifeFlight program each year flies more than fifteen hundred patients in need of immediate care. The program consists of a fixed-wing plane, a helicopter, and three levels of critical-care flight teams. ❖

Photo by Thomas S. England

By working with the American Legion Post 22 players, Clark Duchene, M.D. (left), orthopedic surgeon with fellowship training in sports medicine, and Paul Richter (right), certified athletic trainer, do their part to touch all the bases before the game begins. ❖

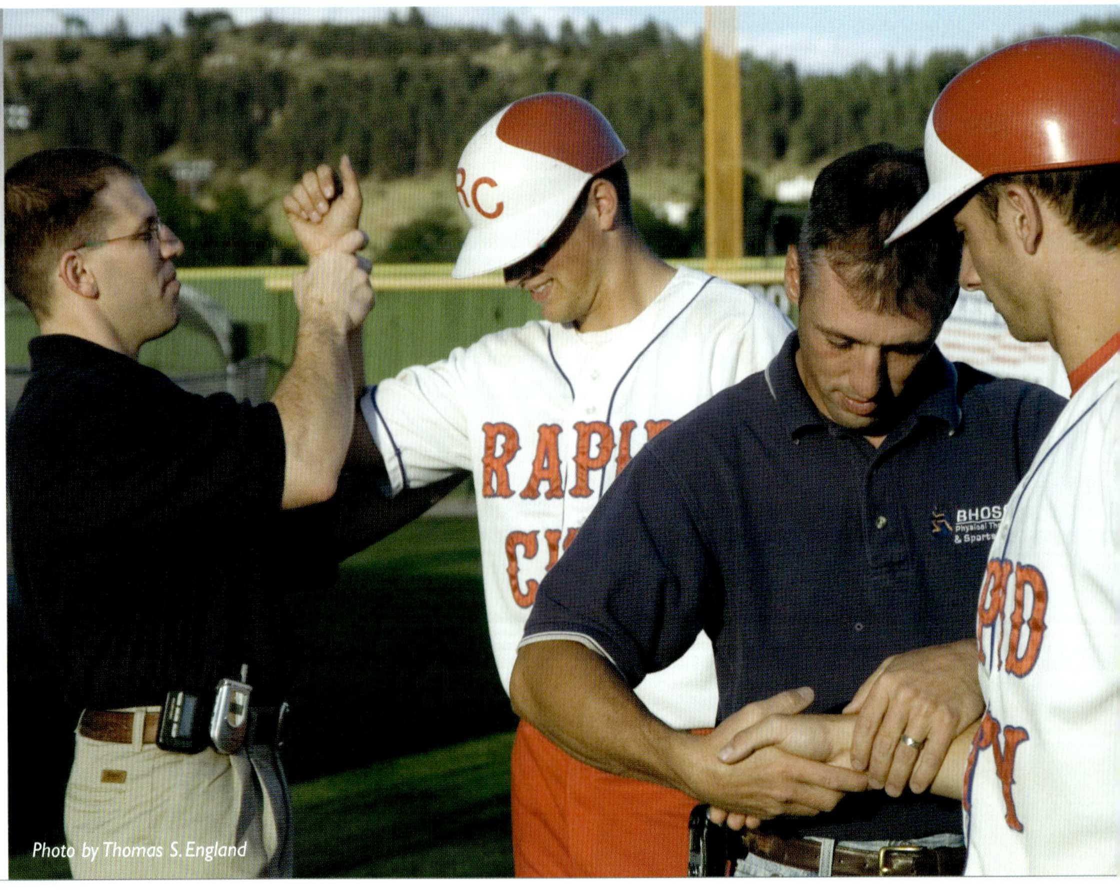

Photo by Thomas S. England

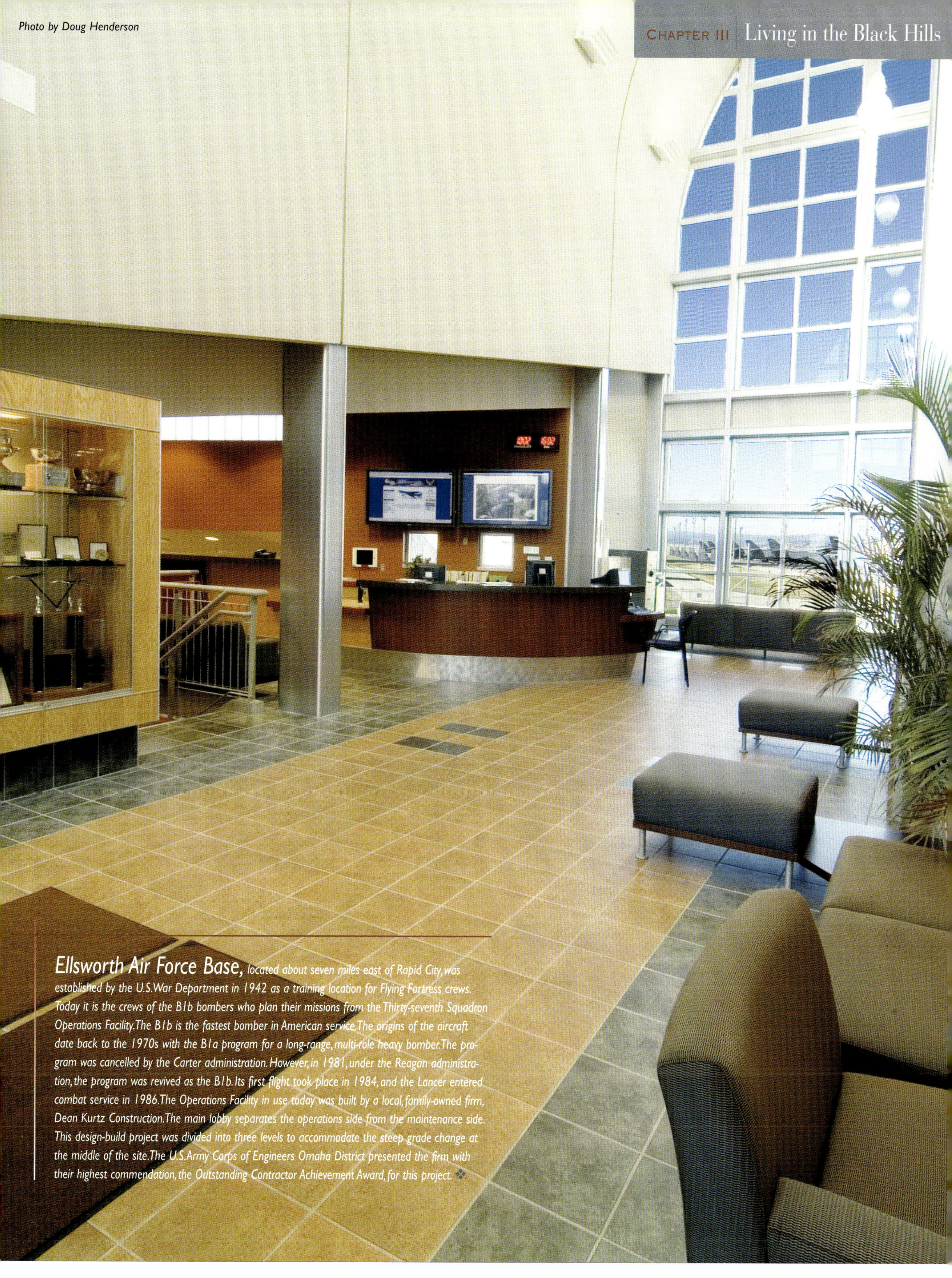

Photo by Doug Henderson

Ellsworth Air Force Base, *located about seven miles east of Rapid City, was established by the U.S. War Department in 1942 as a training location for Flying Fortress crews. Today it is the crews of the B1b bombers who plan their missions from the Thirty-seventh Squadron Operations Facility. The B1b is the fastest bomber in American service. The origins of the aircraft date back to the 1970s with the B1a program for a long-range, multi-role heavy bomber. The program was cancelled by the Carter administration. However, in 1981, under the Reagan administration, the program was revived as the B1b. Its first flight took place in 1984, and the Lancer entered combat service in 1986. The Operations Facility in use today was built by a local, family-owned firm, Dean Kurtz Construction. The main lobby separates the operations side from the maintenance side. This design-build project was divided into three levels to accommodate the steep grade change at the middle of the site. The U.S. Army Corps of Engineers Omaha District presented the firm with their highest commendation, the Outstanding Contractor Achievement Award, for this project.* ❖

Skin Care Is Serious Business in Black Hills

What would you say is the largest organ in your body? The lungs? Kidneys? Heart? None of the above. By far the largest organ is your skin, which covers and protects all other organs, thus serving a critical function for human beings.

By way of comparison, Black Hills Dermatology & Laser Surgery Centre and its SpaMeD division cover every aspect of skin care from laser surgery to manicures and pedicures, making it a convenient and efficient skin care center for the patients who come from four surrounding states. Perhaps the best way to grasp the range of services offered is to take a virtual tour of the facilities.

Let's begin on the medical side. Here you will find six surgical procedure rooms and six laser rooms. Unlike some practices that have to rent lasers, Black Hills Dermatology has nine of the most advanced lasers available on-site so they can provide immediate treatment for almost any skin condition.

"In putting this business together, our goal was to provide patients with dermatological, surgical, and laser surgery along with the latest treatments for skin disease," said founder and resident physician Vassilia D. Young. That includes MOHS surgical treatment of skin cancers, which has the highest reported cure rate. "We also offer laser ablation of birthmarks, broken blood vessels, wrinkles, tattoos, and age spots; laser treatment of psoriasis and warts; laser hair removal; and overall skin beautification with our photorejuvenating laser procedures," said Dr. Young.

"We have recently opened a satellite office in Spearfish in which we offer 80 percent of the services we provide here at the main office, making it easier for patients who live

"Our staff is very dedicated and always looking for ways to offer our services to more people more conveniently."

Photo by Eric Francis

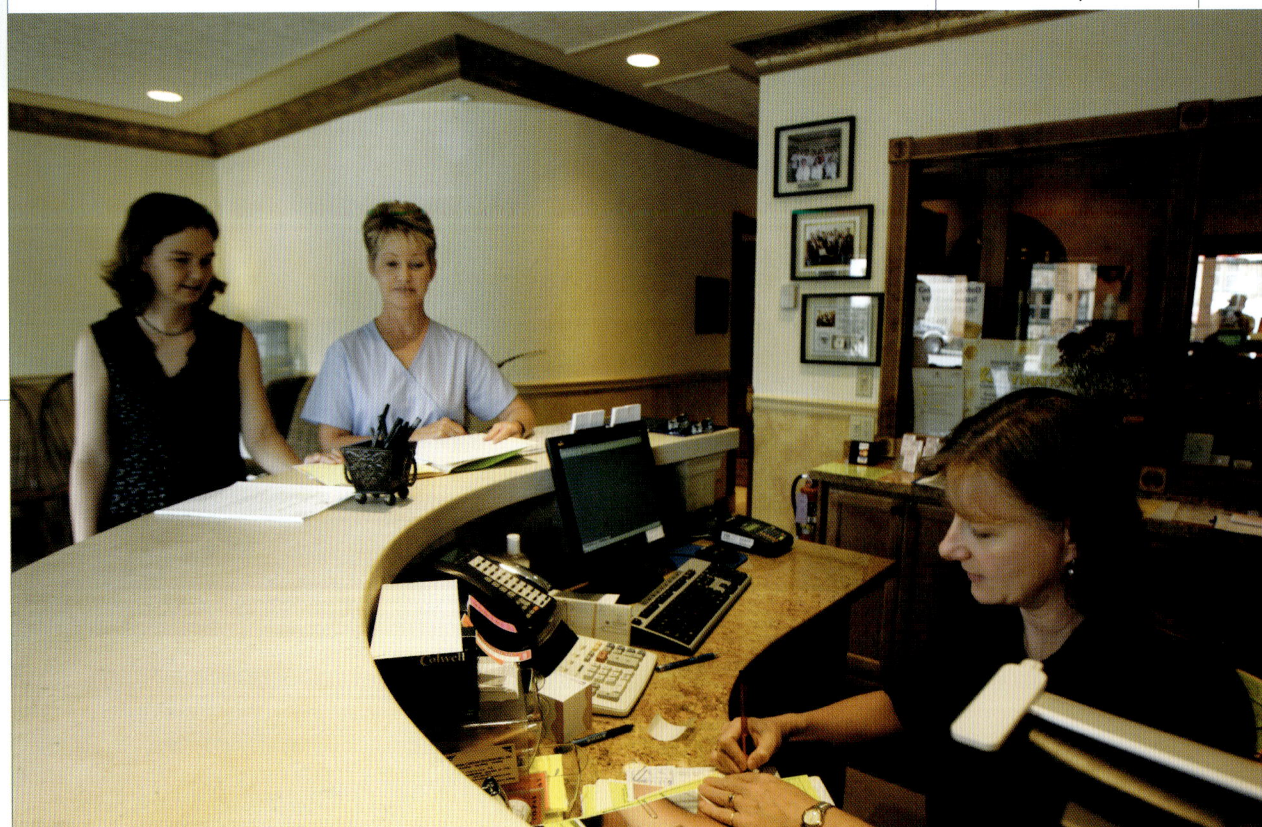

Julie Krein, a certified nurse practitioner; Seanna Linafelter, a licensed practical nurse; and receptionist Jude Warner are all part of the team at the recently opened Spearfish branch. Just like the main office, this clinic specializes in the evaluation and care of the skin, hair, and nails.

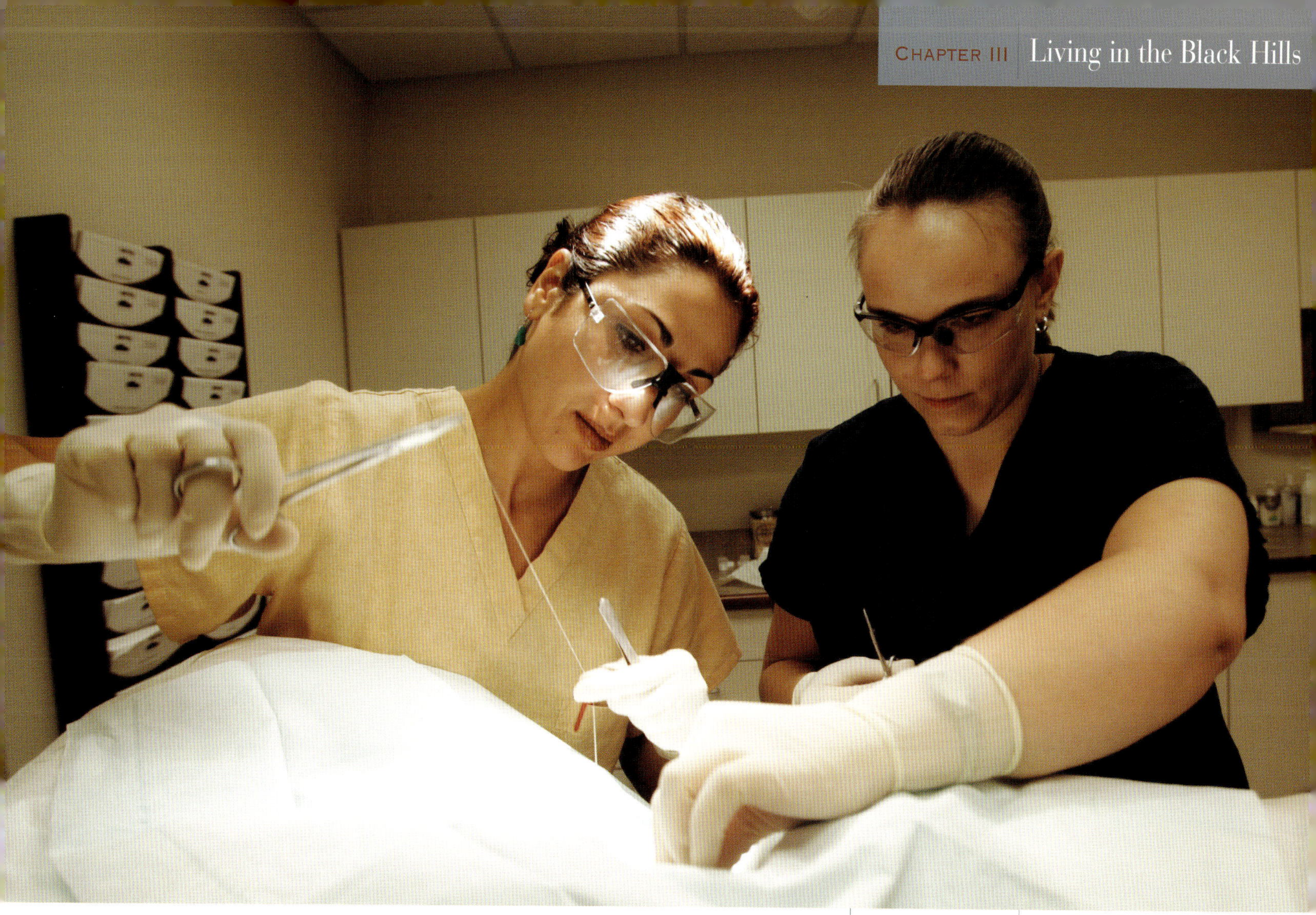

Photo by Eric Francis

The Black Hills Dermatology and Laser Surgery Centre was created to provide the region with dermatologic, surgical, and laser surgery services. Patients come from nine states for treatment by Dr. Vassilia D. Young and her team. She is being assisted here by medical assistant Tammy Bigley.

in northeastern Wyoming, southeastern Montana, and the northern Black Hills," said Jason Gorman, administrator. "Our staff is very dedicated and always looking for ways to offer our services to more people more conveniently."

The Black Hills Dermatology team is made up of the resident physician, two certified nurse practitioners, as well as the entire aesthetic department, which includes medical aestheticians and medical aesthetic specialists. Black Hills Dermatology also staffs and maintains its own skin care product retail center.

"Our nursing staff is there to answer patients' questions about their treatment plan, schedule surgical appointments, relay results, and coordinate patient care," said Tiffani Paez, nursing team leader. "It's one of the most important services we offer."

Now let's go through the French doors and into SpaMeD, the first medical spa in South Dakota. "It's similar to a day spa, but all the treatments are under the auspices of Dr. Young," said Mary Straub, team leader cosmetologist, who works on both the medical and the spa sides of the business.

Continued on page 198

Photo by Eric Francis

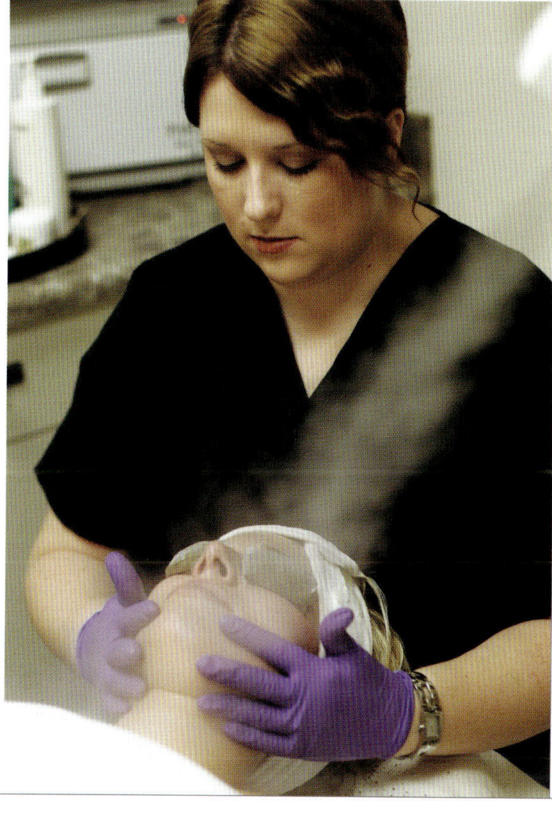

There is nothing like a customized spa facial to make a client feel pampered. Kendra Drane-Kellogg, a licensed cosmetologist at SpaMeD, a division of Black Hills Dermatology, knows how to work this relaxing magic.

Continued from page 197

"We use lasers not only for therapeutic services, but for cosmetic procedures as well. It's that combination of laser treatments and high-quality pharmaceutical skin care products that makes Black Hills Dermatology unique. For instance, there are three grades of skin care products: those you can buy in the drug store, those offered by department stores, and the pharmaceutical-grade products we offer. Although they don't require a prescription, they have a much higher percentage of active ingredients and far fewer additives," she explained.

Black Hills Dermatology also offers beautification packages developed by Dr. Young and her medical aestheticians. These packages include advanced laser technology and aesthetic treatments, combined with Dr. Young's custom-blended mineral makeup and dermatologist-researched skin care products. The most popular of these is the Silver Package, which can be specifically tailored for most skin types. Its aim is to improve the color and texture of skin and reduce aging changes without downtime.

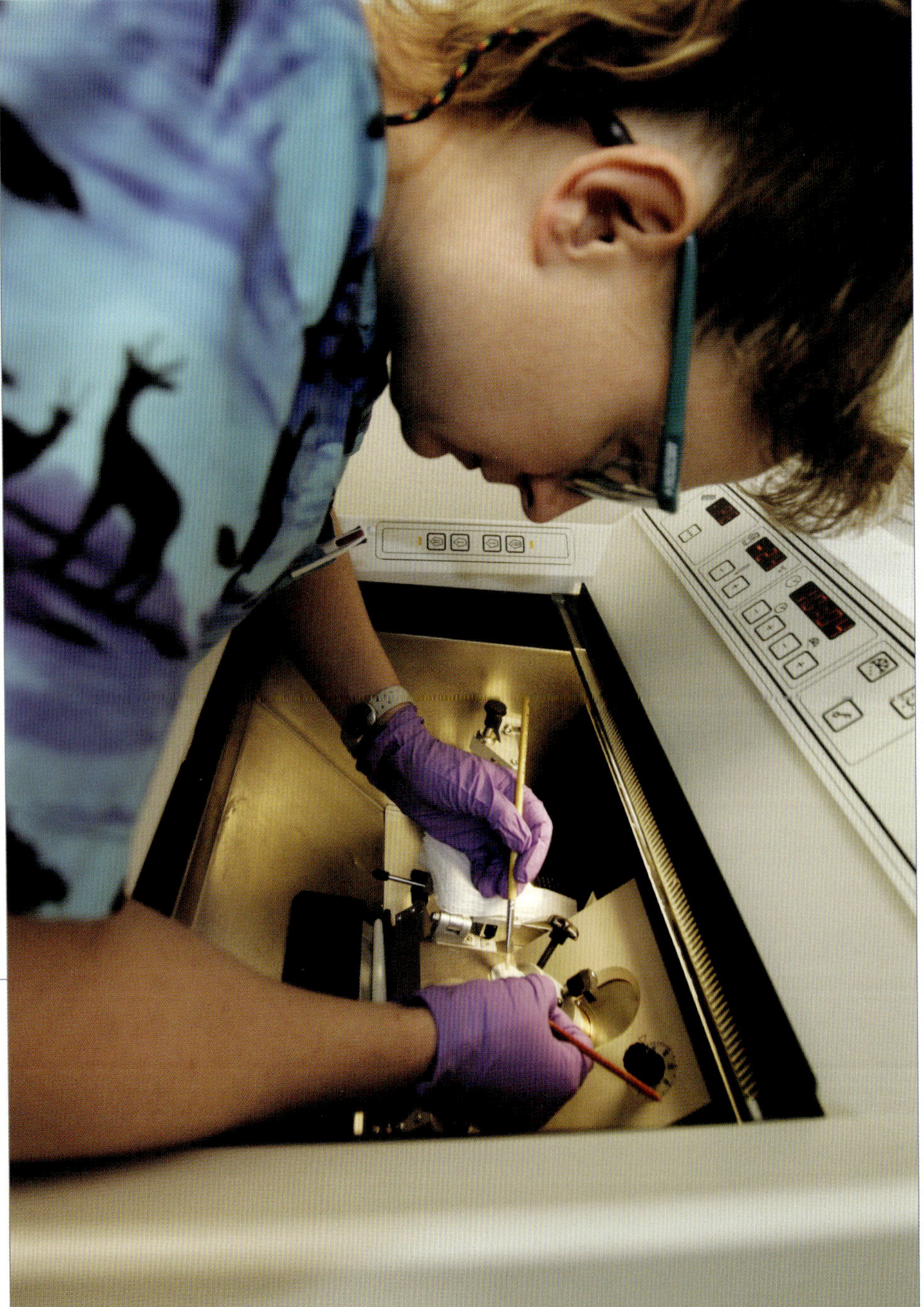

Tracy Lowry, an MOHS-certified technician, processes tissue to apply to slides for microscopic examination. This micrographic surgery is a specialized, highly effective technique for the removal of skin cancer.

Photo by Eric Francis

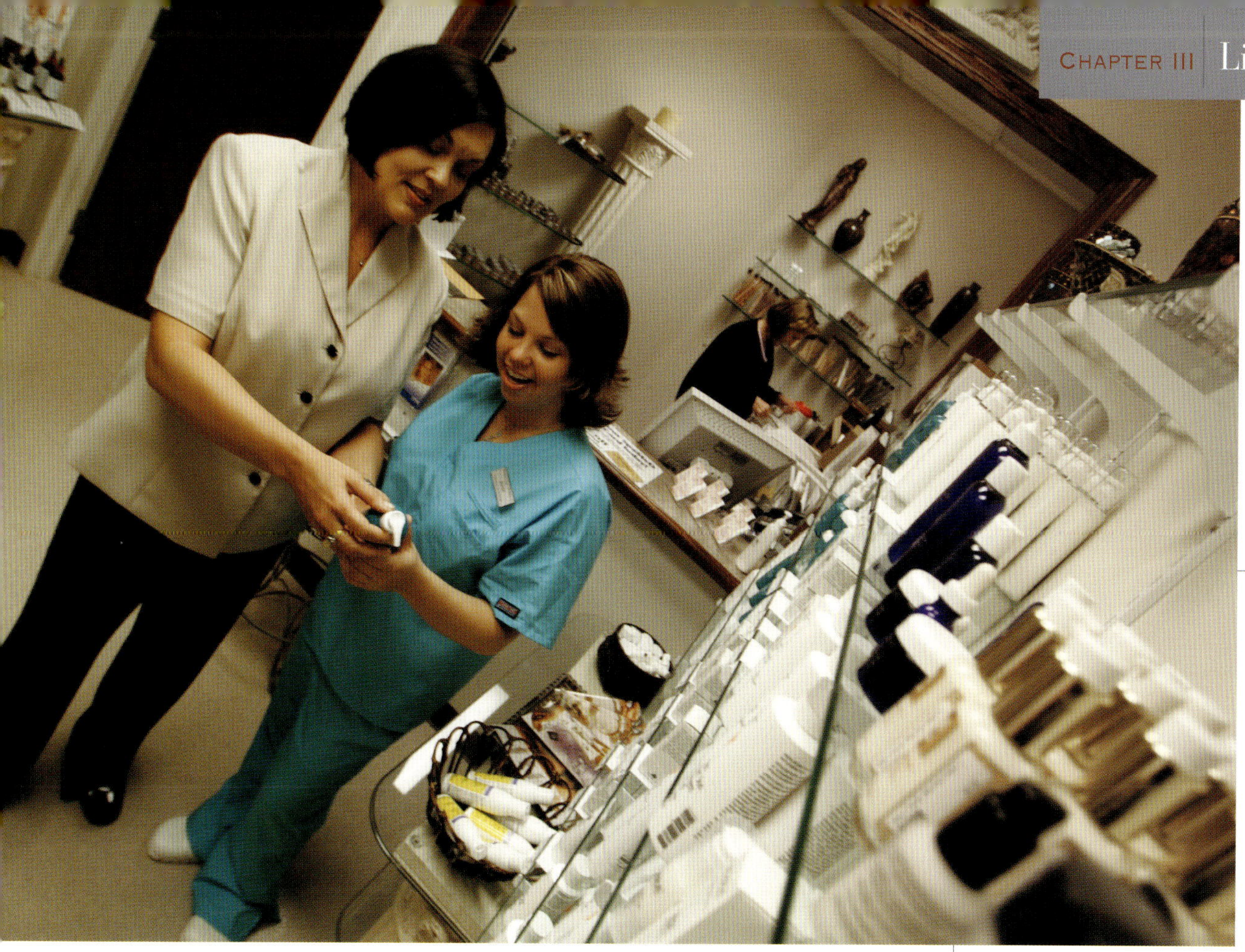

Following directions is important, and Jenna Lundquist, cosmeceutical pharmacy manager, makes sure patients understand the proper use of each product. Each treatment is formulated and researched by physicians, and Brenda Goetz, skin care specialist, makes sure all the skin care products are in order and easy to find.

Photo by Eric Francis

One of the latest advances in skin care across the nation is the use of topical vitamins as a way to fight the aging changes of skin. "Our specially formulated products are great on their own or used to complement our in-office laser and aesthetic treatments. They are equally effective for treating medical conditions, such as acne or rosacea, or for simply rejuvenating aging skin," Straub said.

Another exciting breakthrough is micropigmentation or permanent makeup. This offers relief and freedom for many women with allergies to makeup or for those who have problems seeing well enough to apply makeup. The procedure can also be used to camouflage scars, areola reconstruction, and to improve other skin irregularities.

Black Hills Dermatology & Laser Surgery offers its patients numerous benefits. After all, having smoother, more youthful, radiant skin does more than just make an individual look better—it makes them feel better too! ❖

Photo by Eric Francis

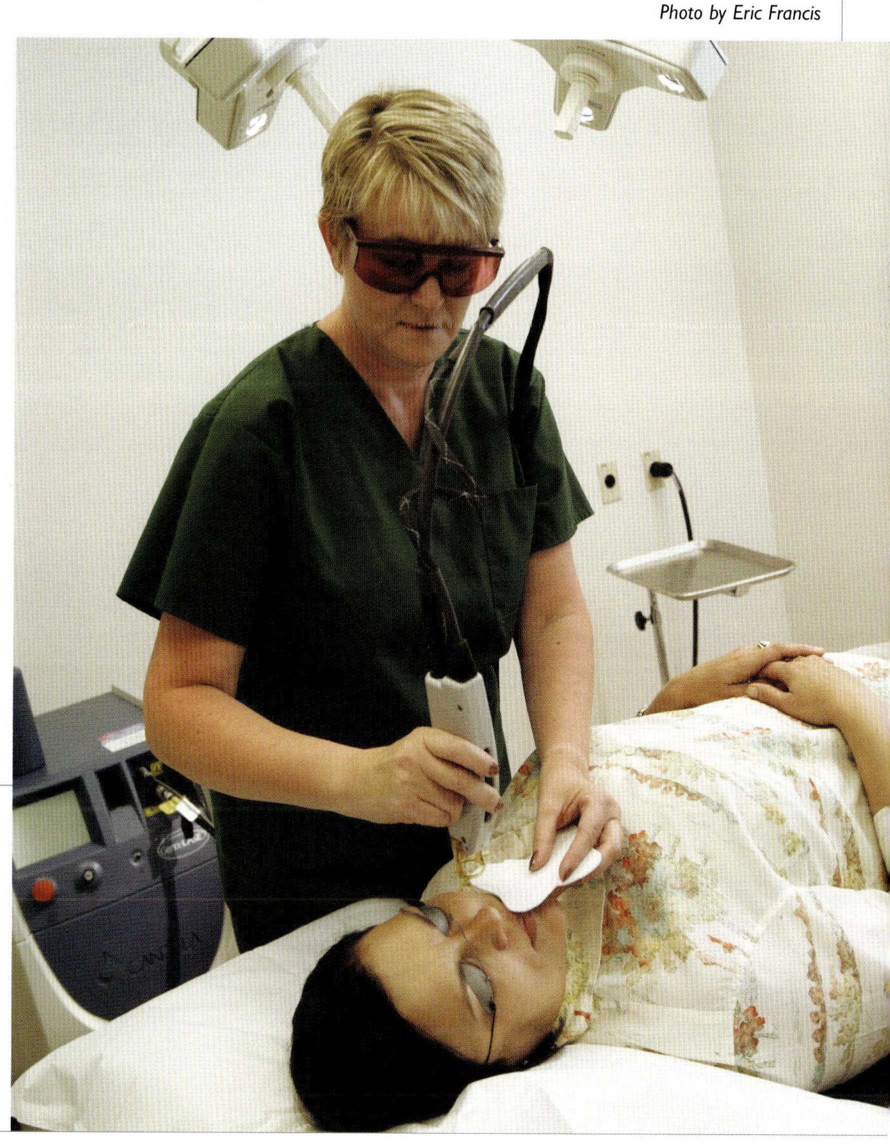

Laser hair removal is just one of the skin beautification techniques available at Black Hills Dermatology. Sue Matthew, a Certified Nurse Practitioner, uses a revolutionary, long-pulse, high-energy alexandrite laser which emits a gentle beam of light that absorbs the hair follicle.

Photo by Doug Henderson

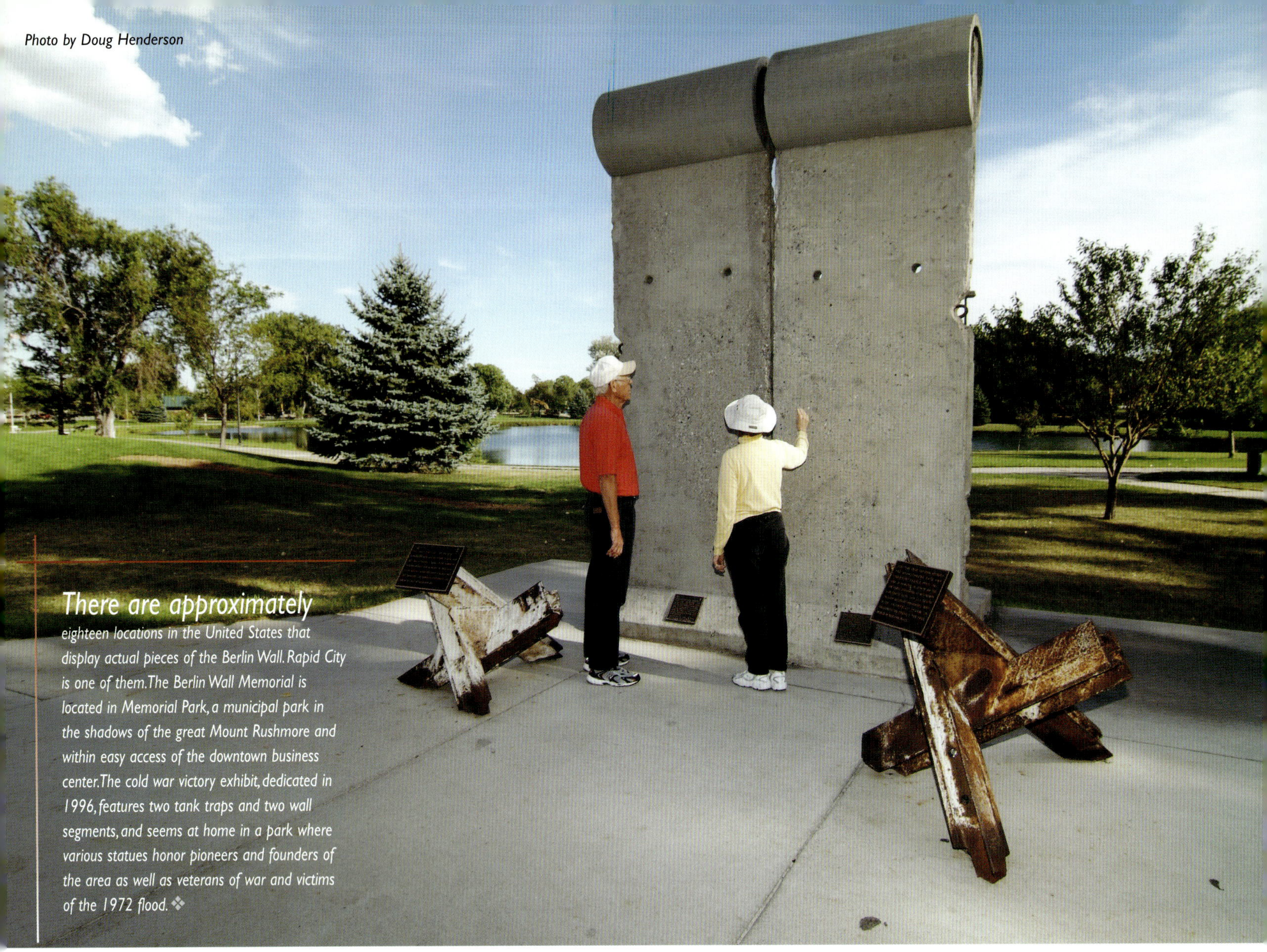

There are approximately eighteen locations in the United States that display actual pieces of the Berlin Wall. Rapid City is one of them. The Berlin Wall Memorial is located in Memorial Park, a municipal park in the shadows of the great Mount Rushmore and within easy access of the downtown business center. The cold war victory exhibit, dedicated in 1996, features two tank traps and two wall segments, and seems at home in a park where various statues honor pioneers and founders of the area as well as veterans of war and victims of the 1972 flood. ❖

From conception to design to construction, it takes about three months to create each life-sized figure featured at the National Presidential Wax Museum. But once completed, these presidential and other noted wax figures—artfully sculpted by the late Kathryn Stuberg-Keller and her protégé, Henry Alvaraz—provide visitors a firsthand glimpse into our nation's history. Founded in 1971 as the Parade of Presidents, the museum has become renowned for its interactive exhibits such as the signing of the Declaration of Independence and George W. Bush's dramatic visit to Ground Zero shortly after September 11, 2001. Open from April 1 to October 31 and located in the historic community of Keystone, the museum also houses a collection of presidential artifacts, a gift shop, a full-service restaurant, and a miniature golf course known as the Holy Terror. A popular spot for field trips and traveling groups, the museum offers guided tours and package rates for schools, bus and tour groups, company picnics, and family gatherings. ❖

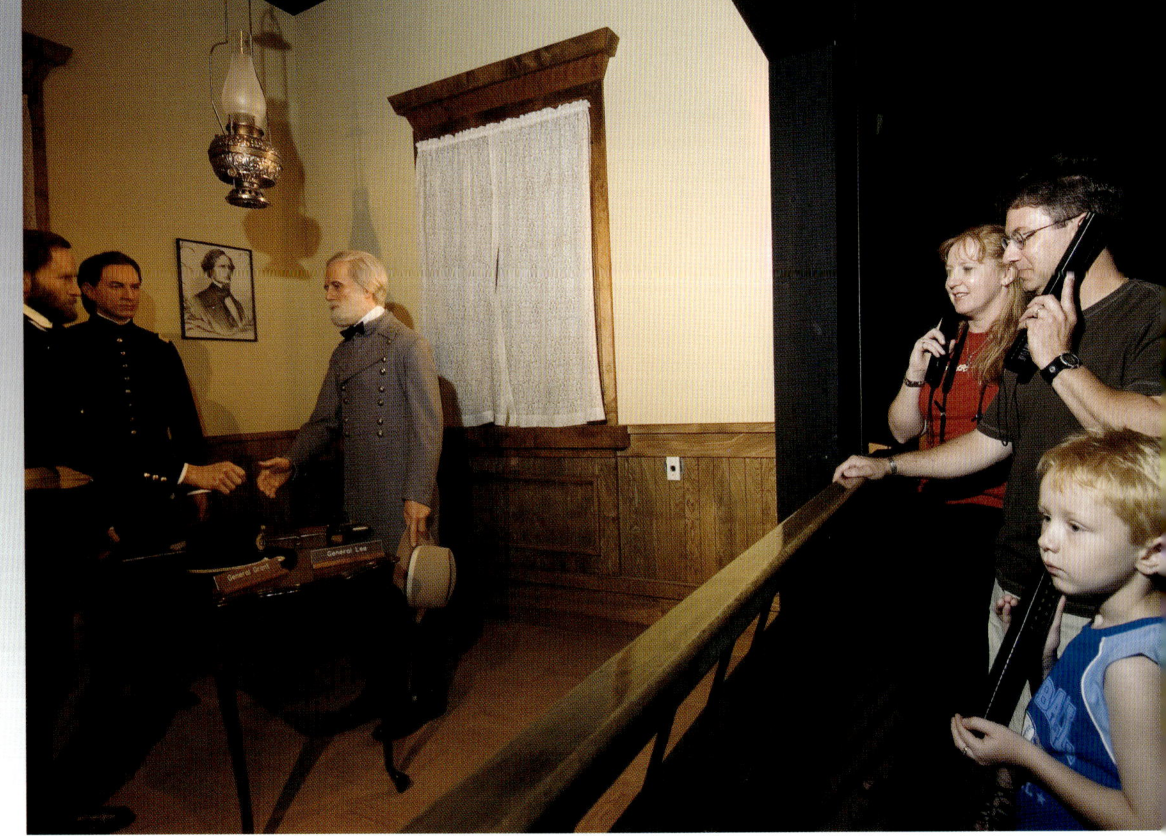

Photo by Thomas S. England

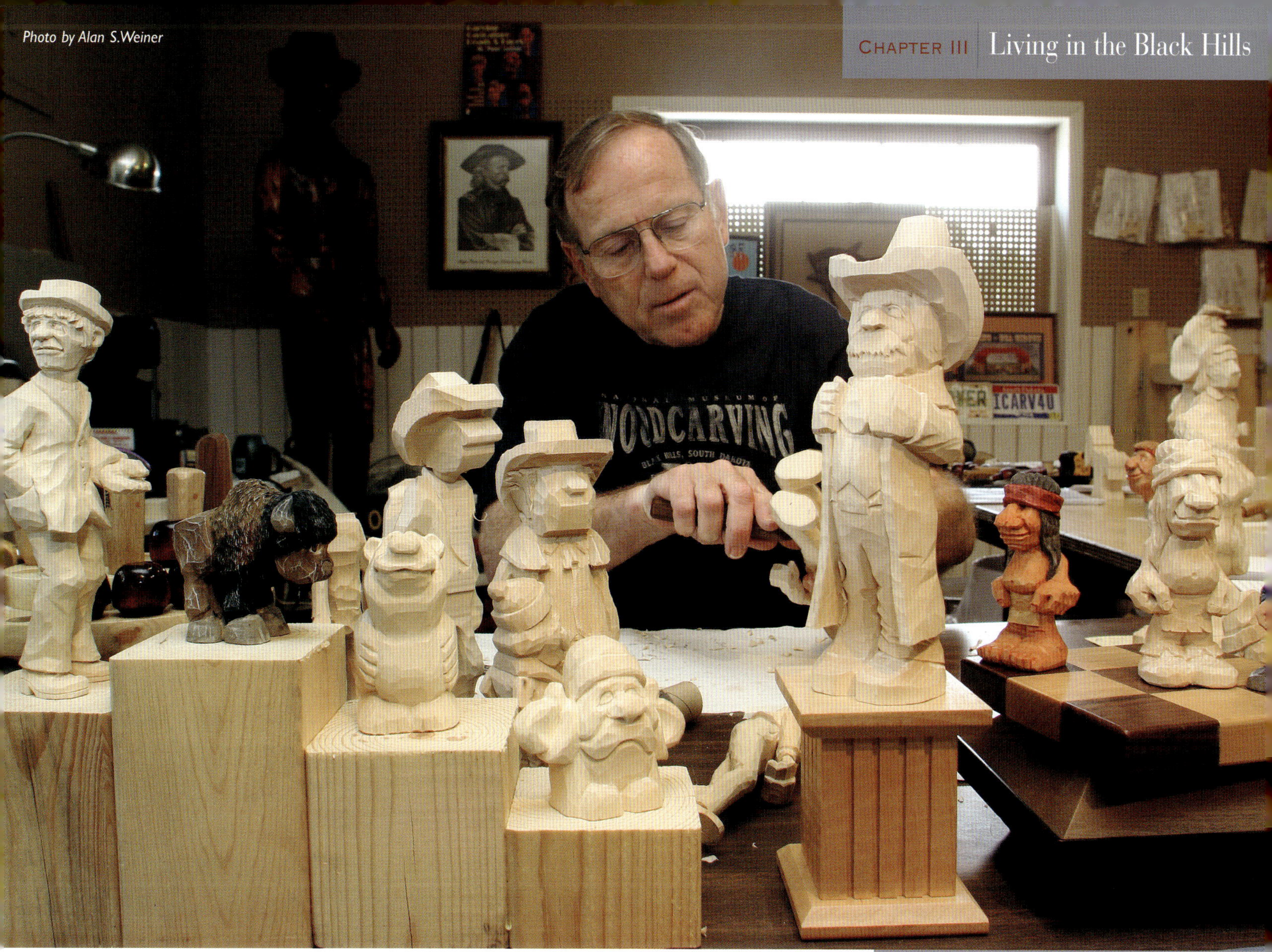

Photo by Alan S.Weiner

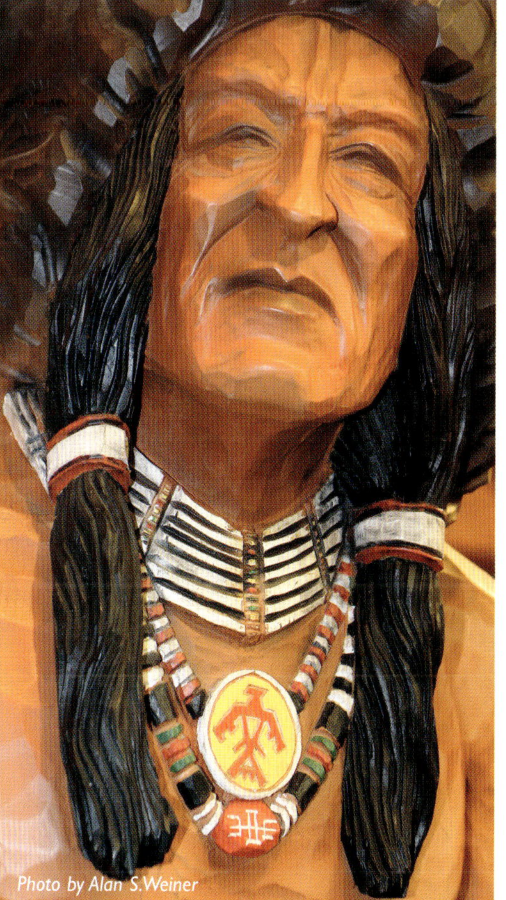

Photo by Alan S.Weiner

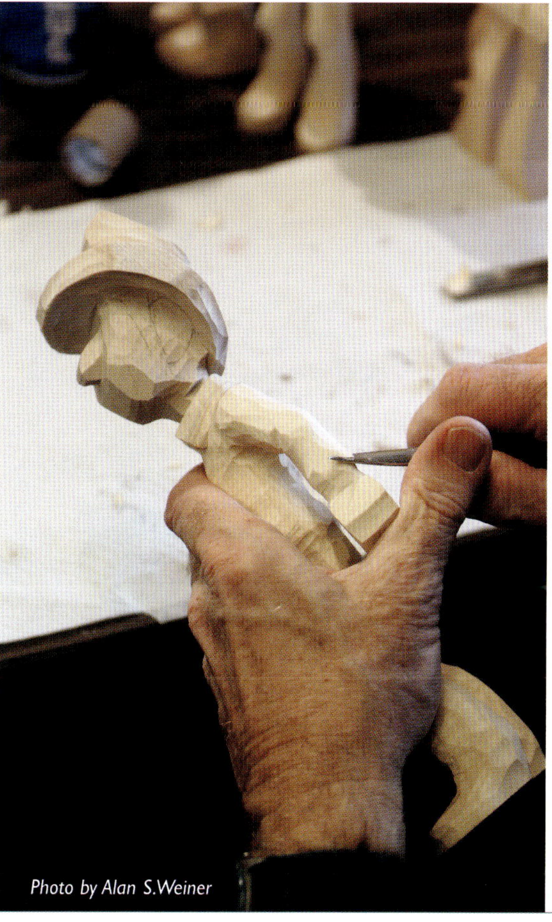

Photo by Alan S.Weiner

"I've always had an interest in carving, but back in the '60s when I started, there were only a handful of books and no way to locate other carvers. I finally found the National Woodcarvers Association, and when I joined my membership number was 531. Today there are over 120,000 members, hundreds of books and national magazines and, of course, a wealth of information on the Internet," said Keith Morrill, who is carver-in-residence at the National Museum of Wood Carving in Custer. Keith's main focus is caricatures inspired by the Old West. "I like to give my creations goofy names like Watts D. Matter, Brandon Irons, or Judge Notte. I watch people and make notes of interesting features. Folks are always taking pictures of me at the museum, and sometimes I ask to take pictures of them. I have three-ring binders filled with ideas. I'm about two hundred years behind on all the ideas I have for pieces." Keith works mainly with bass wood, which has a mild grain and is good for carving details without cracking. ❖

Foundations's Focus is Eye Health for People of the Northern Plains

The Northern Plains Eye Foundation (NPEF) is a nonprofit corporation whose mission is to optimize eye health through promotion and support of research, education, and service for the Northern Plains region. The Foundation, which began in 2002, is an offshoot of the original Black Hills Regional Eye Institute Foundation, founded in 1987. The NPEF office is centrally located in Rapid City, right across the street from the Public Library.

A major purpose of NPEF is to promote collaboration and networking among eye-care professionals and paraprofessionals. NPEF supports continuing education for eye-care providers by sponsoring workshops, seminars, and a local Journal Club. A rich history in promoting and facilitating cutting-edge research goes back to the original founders. NPEF continues this vision through research collaboration and dissemination benefiting both eye-care providers and patients. The Foundation also works with other service organizations to maximize services and resources in the region.

Educational programs focused on eye health are a high priority for the Foundation.

Educational programs focused on eye health are a high priority for the Foundation. Preschool and grade-school-aged children are taught about eye safety (firework safety, eye injuries, sun protection, etc.), preventative measures (eye protection), and optimal eye health through eye examinations. Middle school and high school students may have a local eye-care provider as a guest lecturer in a science or health class, and are encouraged to pursue Science Fair projects focused on the eye. The Foundation also sponsors a

Photo by Doug Henderson

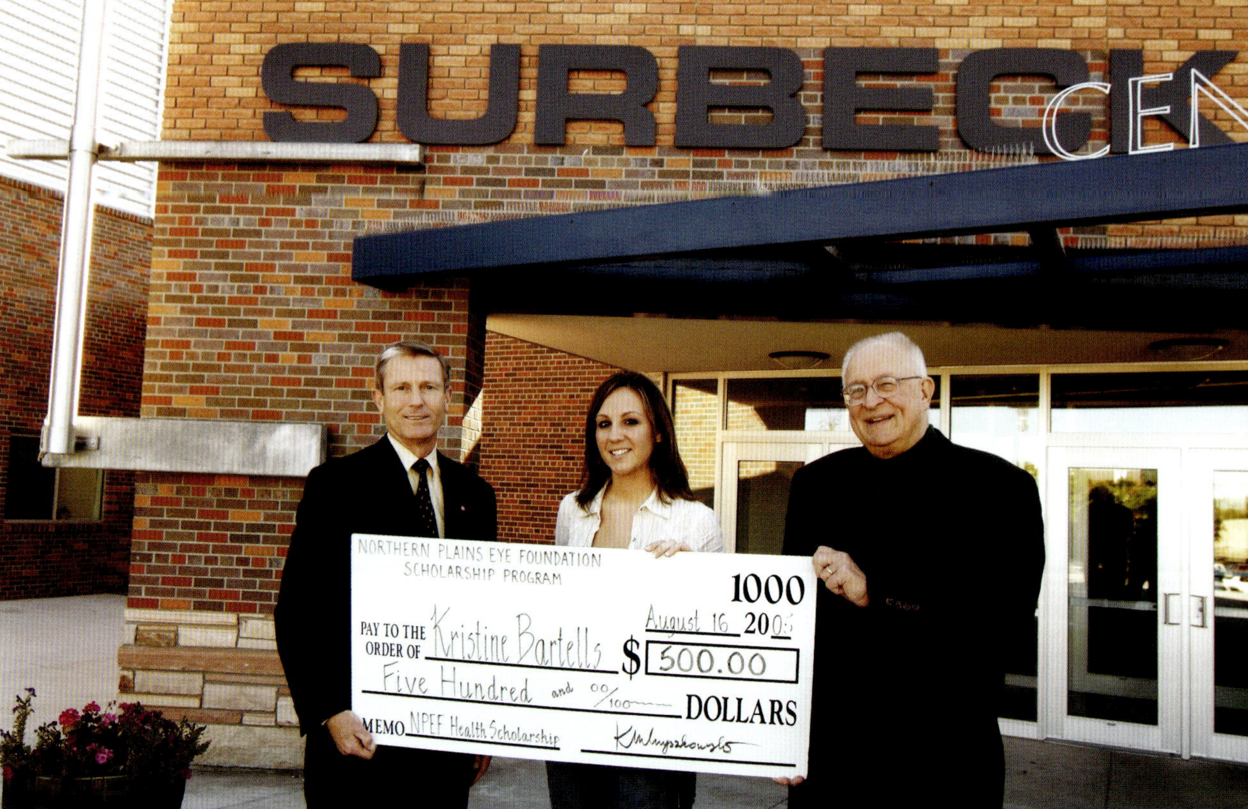

Kristine Bartells receives one of five scholarships awarded in the inaugural year of the Foundation's Scholarship Program, to be applied to her first-year studies at South Dakota School of Mines and Technology in a health-care field. Dr. John Barlow, board chairman (far right), and Chris Myszkowski (left), present the five-hundred-dollar check.

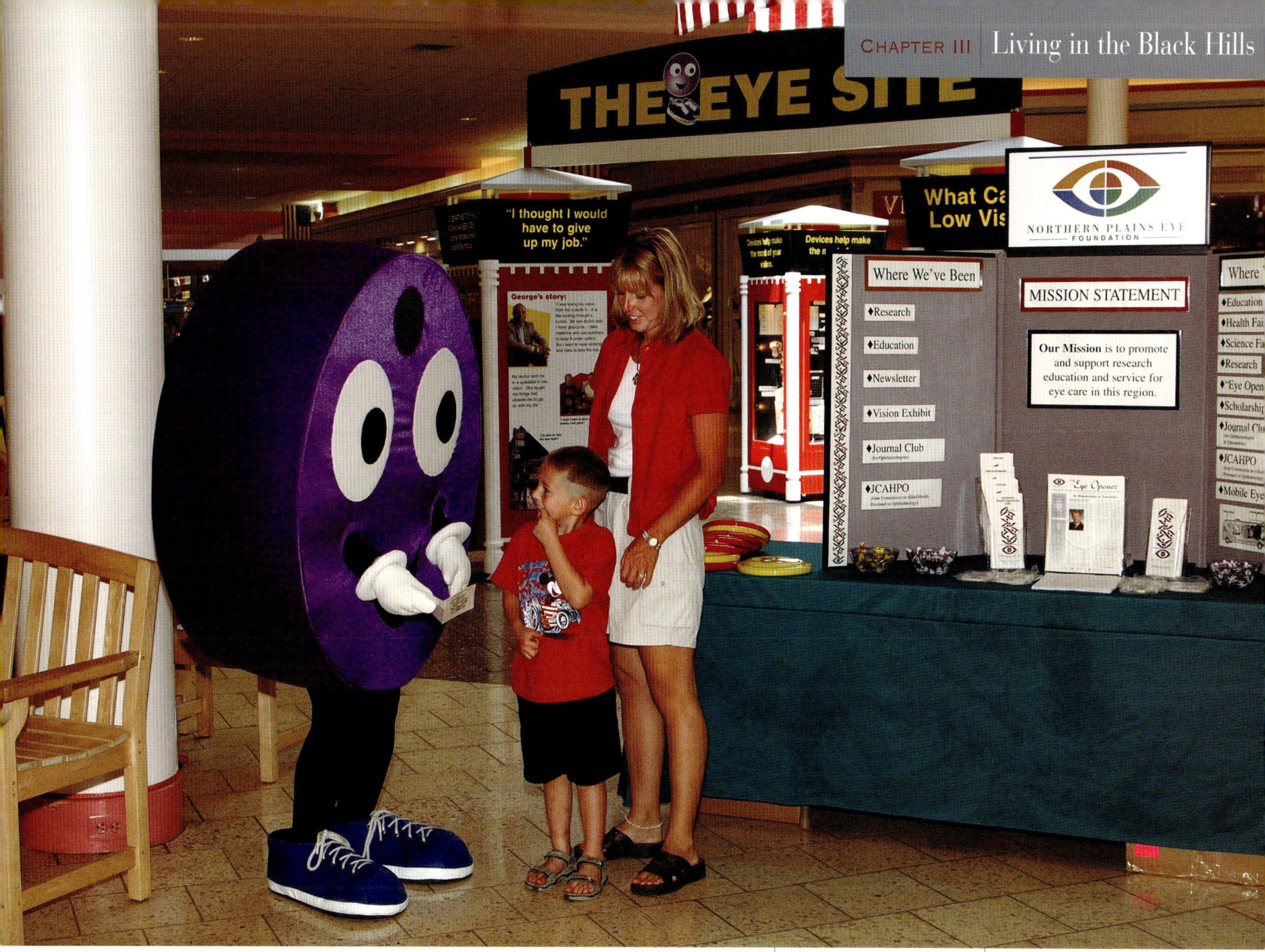

Photo by Joleen Zoller

Elvee, the National Eye Institute's mascot, attracts both young and old alike to the Eye Site exhibit cosponsored by the Northern Plains Eye Foundation at the Rushmore Mall. The exhibit featured a variety of eye-care information for shoppers at the Mall.

Health Scholarship program that awards multiple scholarships for high school seniors pursuing health-care-related studies, as well as Continuing Health Scholarships for former award-winners to continue pursuing their educational goals.

For the general public, the Foundation provides education and service in a variety of ways. NPEF has sponsored national-level exhibits commissioned by the National Eye Institute, such as the VISION exhibit (interactive and educational) and the Eye Site Exhibit (highlighting low-vision awareness). NPEF goes on the road with exhibits and programs from health fairs (covering all ends of the age spectrum), to health promotions events (such as Health and Safety Day at Storybook Island), to Optometric and Ophthalmologic Conferences. The Foundation also coordinates a speakers' bureau to make specialists available to teach in their area of expertise. NPEF serves as a regional resource center for eye health, and helps to link people to appropriate resources when they are facing limitations in their vision.

A dynamic Board of directors sets the vision for the Northern Plains Eye Foundation, which continues to expand. The Northern Plains Eye Foundation currently serves a broad region with Rapid City and the Black Hills at the hub, and with spokes extending out to northeast Wyoming, southwest North Dakota, southeast Montana, northwest Nebraska, and throughout South Dakota. With the help of supporters and contributors, a dedicated board, an enthusiastic staff, and a united community of eye-care providers, the Northern Plains Eye Foundation fulfills its motto, "Vision for a Lifetime," while serving the people of the Northern Plains by optimizing eye health. ❖

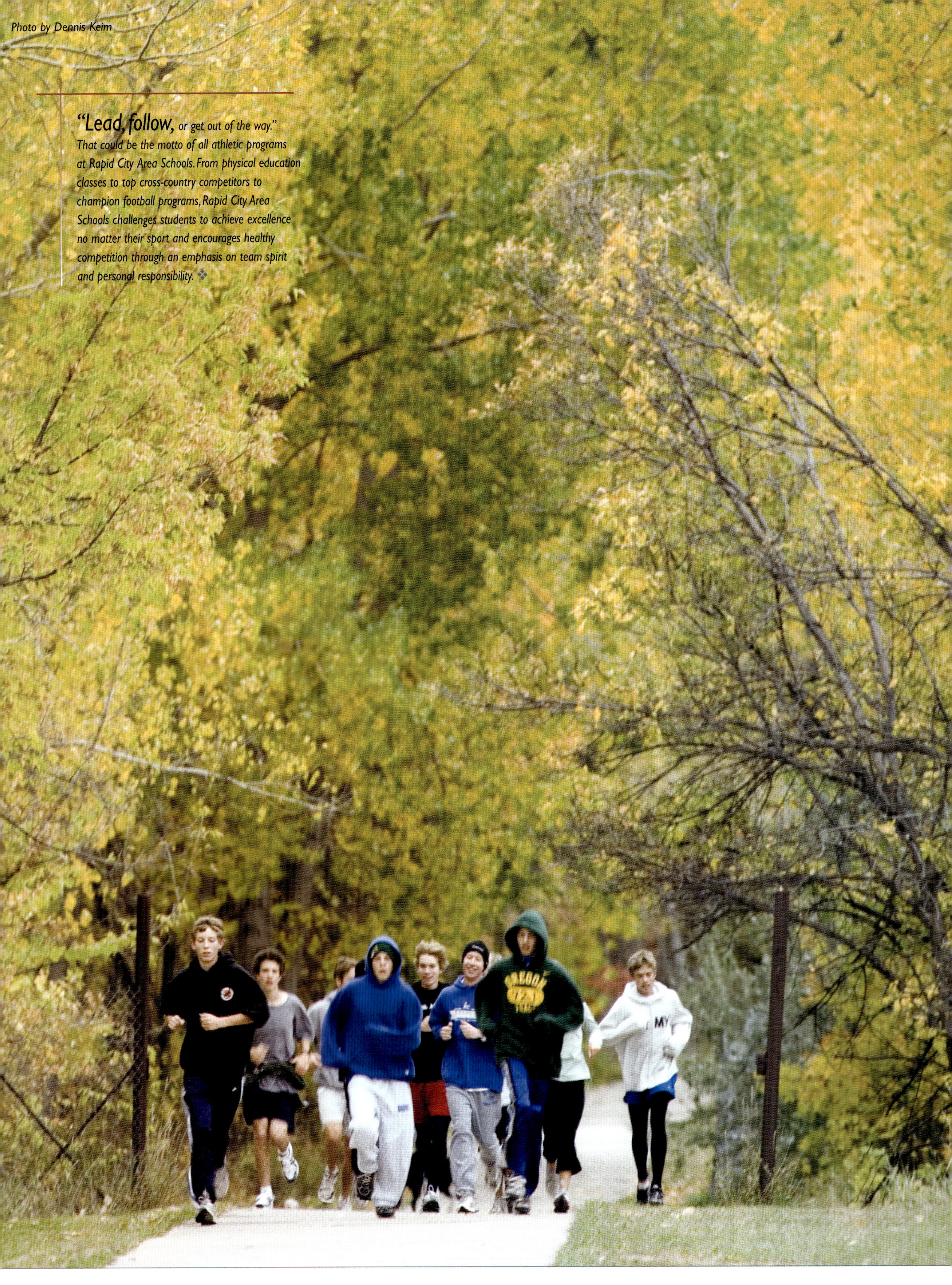

Photo by Dennis Keim

"Lead, follow, or get out of the way." That could be the motto of all athletic programs at Rapid City Area Schools. From physical education classes to top cross-country competitors to champion football programs, Rapid City Area Schools challenges students to achieve excellence no matter their sport and encourages healthy competition through an emphasis on team spirit and personal responsibility. ❖

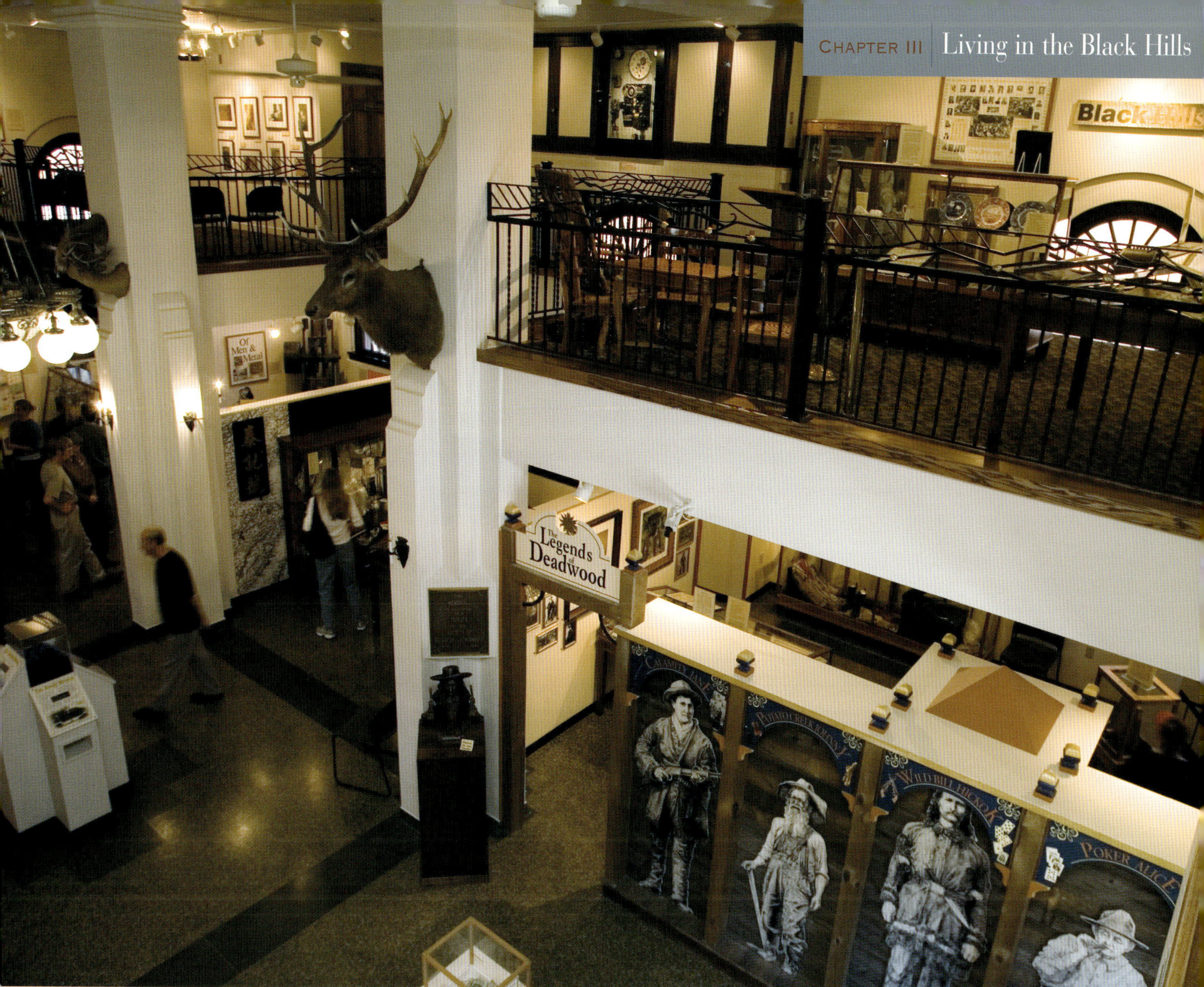

Photo by Dennis Keim

Considered the oldest history museum in the Black Hills, the Adams Museum in Deadwood was built by W. E. Adams in 1930 as a memorial to his family and to honor Black Hills pioneers. Covering the area's art, culture, and natural history, the museum's collection includes American Indian and folk art, antique guns, and artifacts belonging to Wild Bill, Calamity Jane, and Deadwood Dick. W. E. Adams also preserved a bit of Deadwood's more refined history. In 1920 he purchased an 1892 Queen Anne–style house that local press called the "grandest house west of the Mississippi." It remained in Adams's family until 1987 when his ailing widow sold the property to a couple who opened it as a bed-and-breakfast. In 1992 they sold the house to Deadwood's Historic Preservation Commission, which—under a costewardship agreement with the Adams Museum—restored the home and opened it as a museum devoted to the elegant lifestyles of its two Old West families. ❖

Behavior Management Systems Returns Quality of Life to Many

For people of all ages, the stresses of everyday life can sometimes present overwhelming challenges, many that lead to problems beyond one's control. When situations like these occur, it is good to have somewhere to turn like Behavior Management Systems.

Since 1948, Behavior Management Systems has been the largest behavioral health-care company in western South Dakota, providing the full scope of services to help people learn to cope with stress and lead productive lives.

Behavior Management Systems has become a place where over nine thousand people from a twenty-thousand-square-mile area turn for help. Today, Behavior Management Systems serves clients from offices in Rapid City, Hot Springs, and Spearfish.

While its physical facilities and services have grown, one thing that has remained constant is the company's steadfast vision: build positive change in the communities where we live, work, and play.

One of the primary ways Behavior Management Systems accomplishes its vision is through outpatient counseling with trained professionals who confront and deal with the emotional and behavioral issues that disrupt daily living. From concerns involving depression or anxiety to matters regarding marriage or relationships to intervention for violence or crisis situations, the counselors at Behavior Management Systems know how to return troubled individuals back to leading productive lives.

One thing that has remained constant is the company's steadfast vision: build positive change in the communities where we live, work, and play.

Photo by Thomas S. England

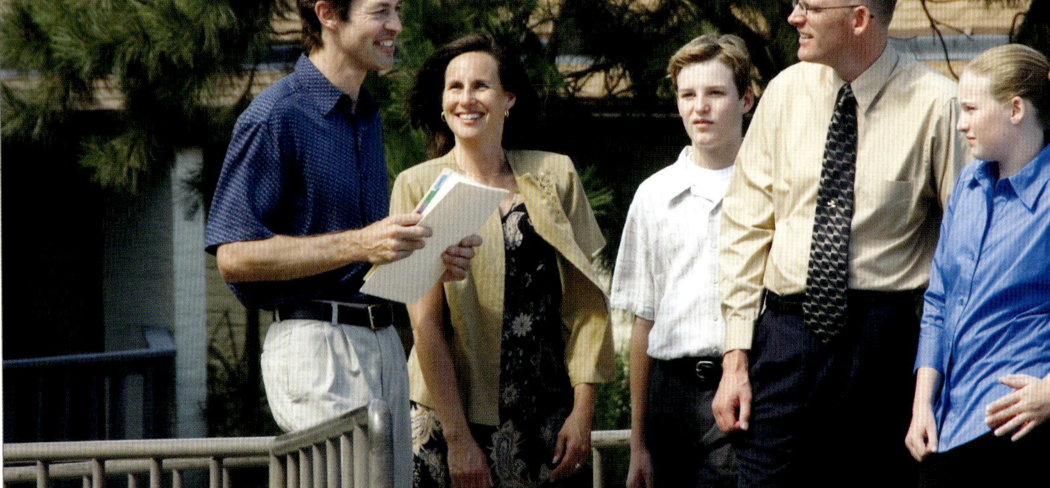

Families face a variety of issues when coping with the stresses of life. Mike Sprung is one of several professionals helping families deal with change.

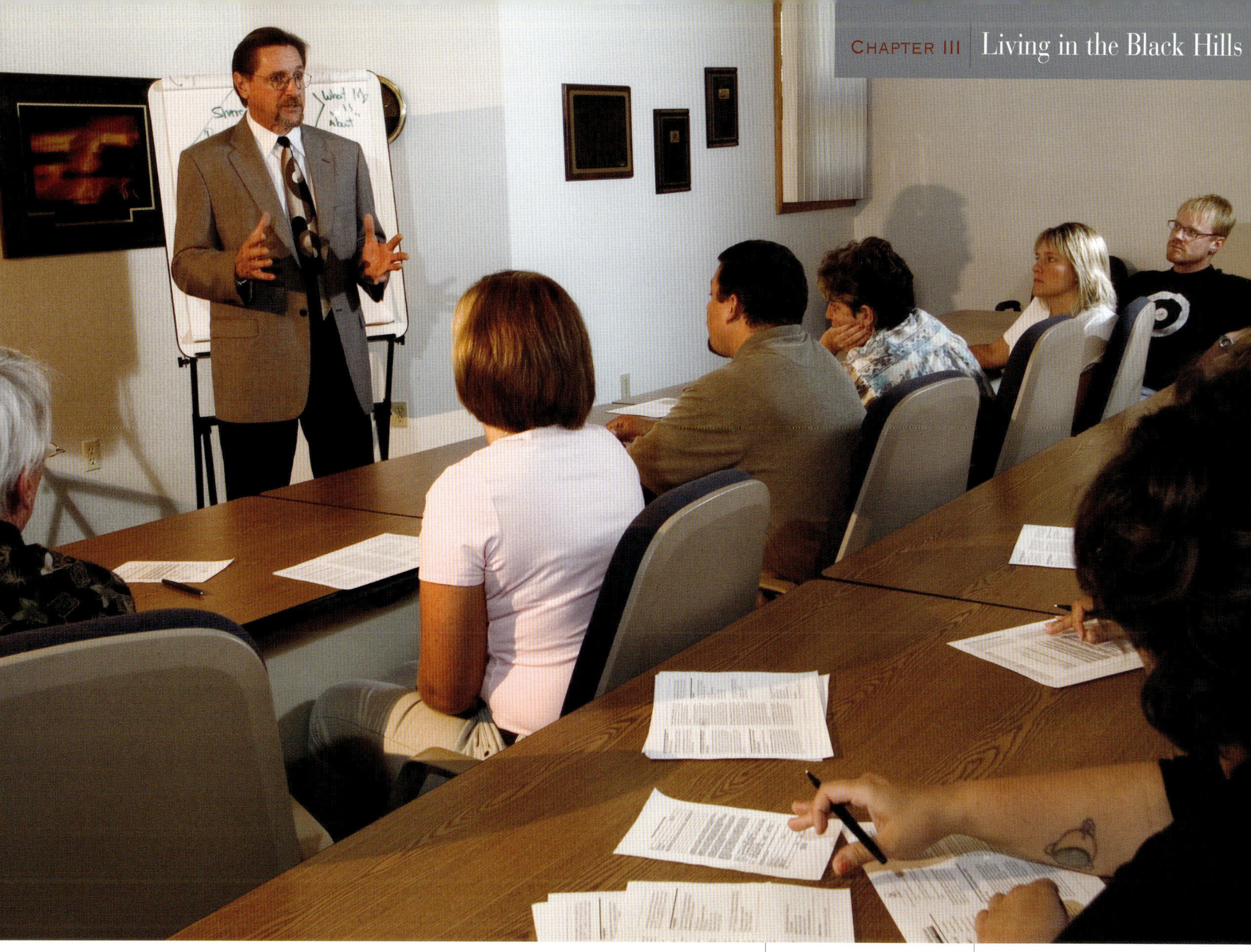

Photo by Thomas S. England

Bob Holmes, an outpatient counselor and workshop trainer at Behavior Management Systems, walks a group of businesspeople through a stress management seminar.

When younger members of society have a difficult time adjusting to the normal activities of living, Behavior Management Systems offers family outreach, or home-based, services. Going beyond outpatient counseling, family outreach deals with mental and behavioral health care for children and adolescents, their parents or guardians and siblings, and any other members of the household. Through in-home counseling, education, and support; school- or community-based services; case management and coordination with additional agencies and providers, Behavior Management Systems works to keep troubled families together.

Sometimes disturbing behavior stems from addiction. Whether that addiction centers on chemical dependency or compulsive gambling, Behavior Management Systems can help with services ranging from evaluation to minimally restrictive treatment. Behavior Management Systems also offers a unique addiction treatment program for pregnant women and women with young children.

Treatment for adults with serious, long-term mental illnesses like schizophrenia, bipolar disorder, or significant anxiety disorders can be difficult. For these individuals, Behavior Management Systems provides a program of continuous assistance, rehabilitation, and education as well as life skills training, social activities, vocational services, and residential housing.

Even in places like Rapid City, where beauty and tranquility reign, everyday stresses can impede the normalcy of daily life. But for those people who experience such serious concerns, there is comfort in knowing they can return to a quality of life, work, and play through the programs and services of Behavior Management Systems. ❖

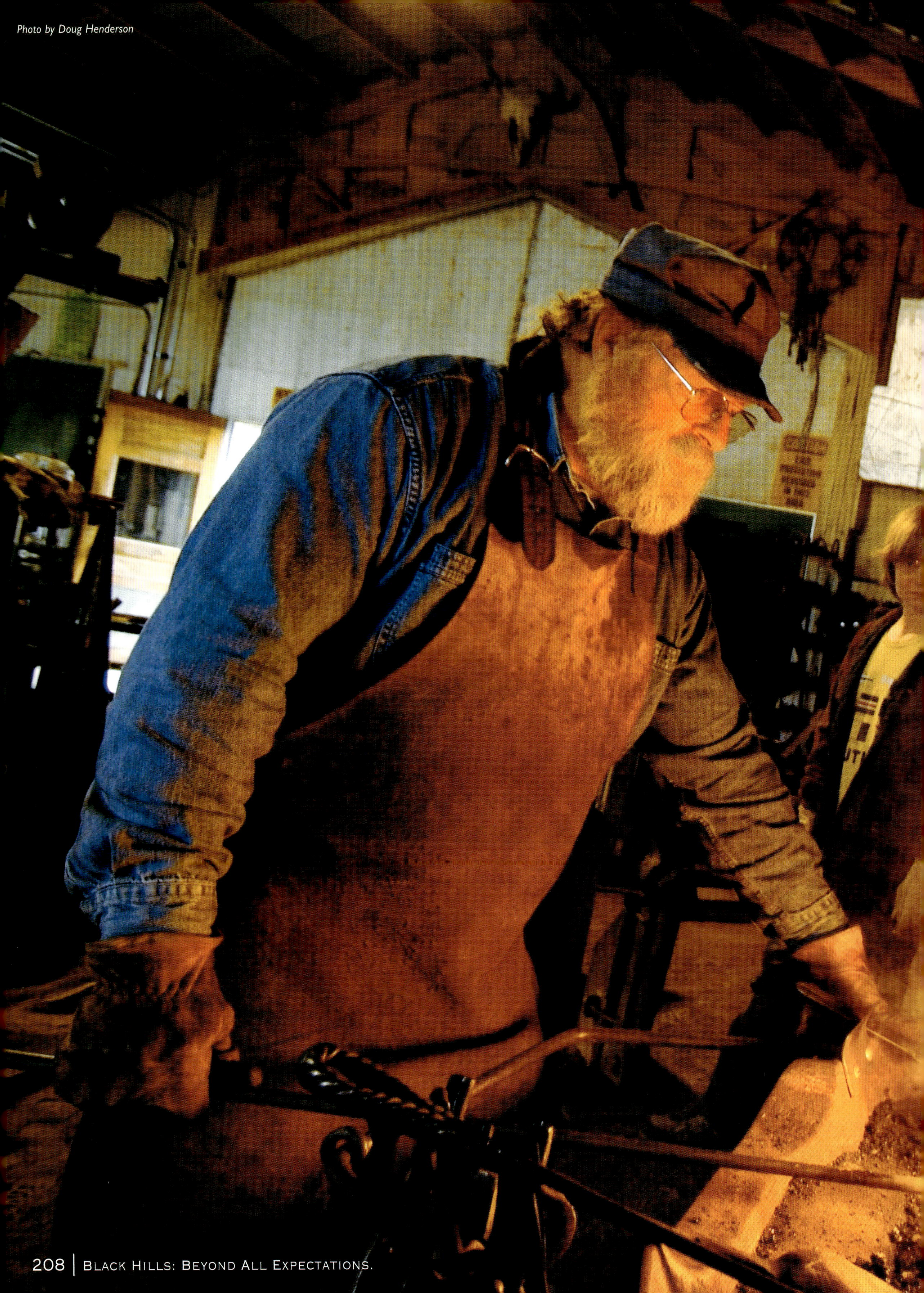

Photo by Doug Henderson

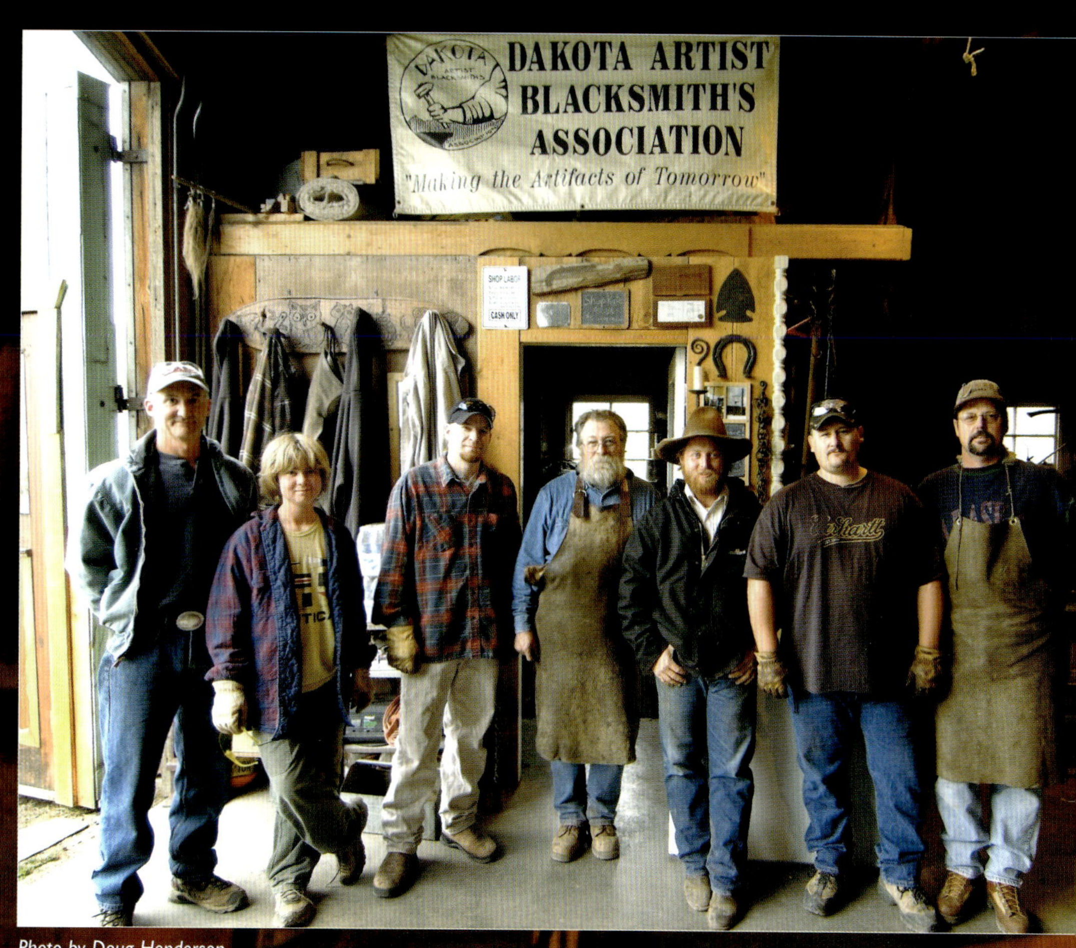

Photo by Doug Henderson

After the Civil War many blacksmiths migrated west because machine-made products were putting them out of business. They learned to shoe horses, fix wagons, fix carts, and fix and make wagon wheels. Now clubs like the Black Hills Blacksmith's Association are keeping the old skills alive, teaching and making items like stair railings, fireplace tools, cabinet hardware, tables, gates, and fences. Younger members like Jorgen Palm watch and learn from experienced craftsmen like Jack Parks. "We have about thirty members, and some of them drive as far as a hundred miles to get here," said Parks, who started blacksmithing as a hobby in the late '70s and opened a full-time business in 1988. The regulars (left to right)—Thomas Palm, his son Jorgen, Andy Roltgen, Parks, Kevin Willey, Chris "Romey" Bromwich, and Harold Fenhaus—meet the second Saturday of each month. They work from 9:30 to 4:00 and choose some project that can be completed in that length of time. The group is affiliated with the Artist Blacksmith's Association of North America, a nonprofit, educational association dedicated to promoting the art of blacksmithing. ❖

Black Hills Orthopedic & Spine Center—A Center of Excellence for Bone and Joint Care

From head to toe, when it comes to bone, muscle, or joint conditions, the physicians at Black Hills Orthopedic & Spine Center have dedicated themselves to restoring their patients' mobility. Through orthopedic and spine surgery, rheumatology, sports medicine, podiatry, and physical therapy, their goal is to return patients to the activities they love.

The healing starts when patients walk in the door. "We make every effort to make your visit with us a top-notch experience. That includes providing an outstanding group of doctors, the most advanced technological equipment, and a staff second to none," said Dr. David Boyer, who founded the clinic in 1976. Boyer is one of eleven orthopedic surgeons at the center. In addition, two fellowship-trained, board-certified rheumatologists and a podiatrist provide patients quality care.

> "We make every effort to make your visit with us a top-notch experience."

A quick look at the center's specialties underscores that quality care. The clinic's Wound Care program offers help for patients who have foot and ankle wounds that are not healing correctly or healing too slowly. Typically the wounds are diabetes related.

The Performance Plus Program, P3, is designed to help athletes in preseason training improve their skills. P3 instructors use a high-speed treadmill, core strengthening, plyometrics, and agility drills to produce measurable improvements. A companion program is Sports Medicine, which is designed to prevent and treat activity-related injuries. Three orthopedic physicians, fellowship trained in sports medicine, are teamed with certified physical therapists and athletic trainers to provide a workable program.

Photo by Eric Francis

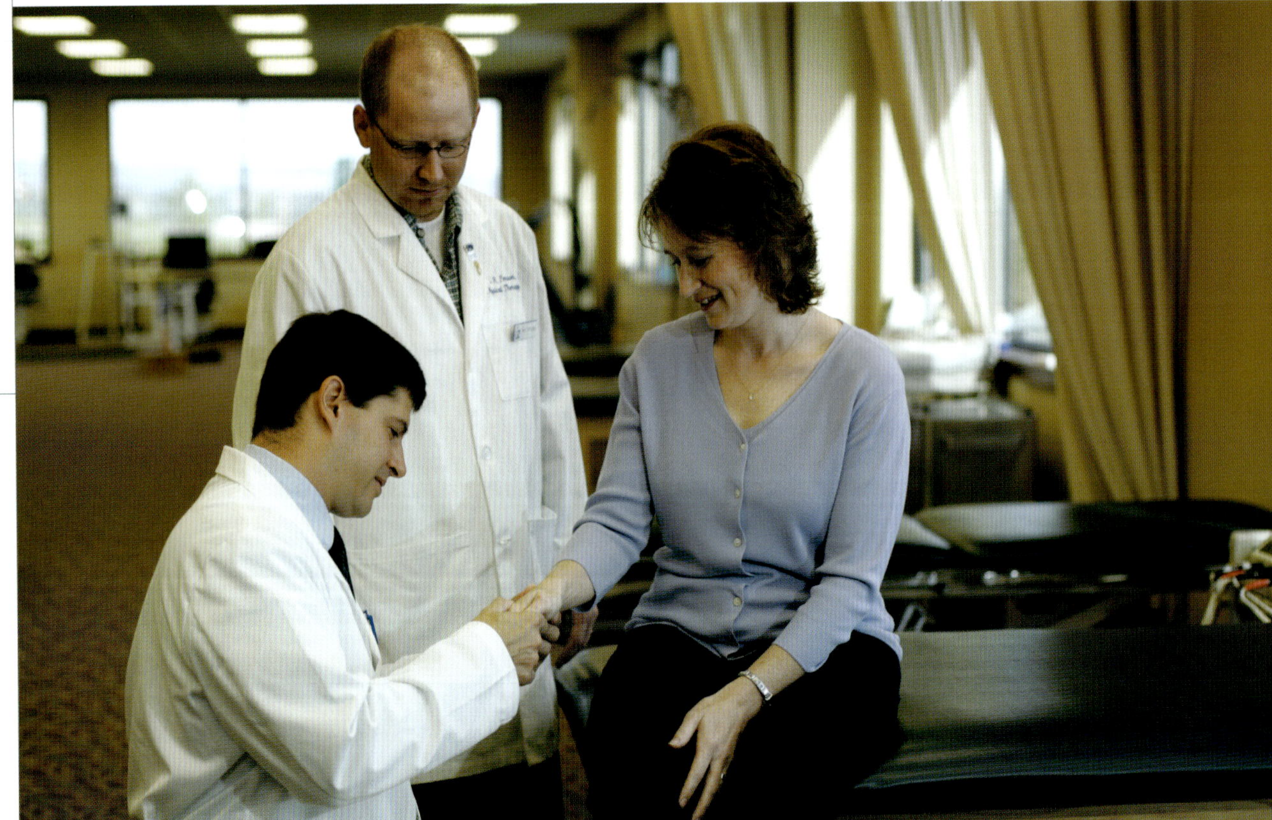

The hand is a complex structure of bone, ligaments, nerves, joints, and tendons. Orthopedic surgeon Michael Kadrmas, MD, and Pat Person, physical therapist, examine a patient's hand to make sure all these important parts are kept in good working order.

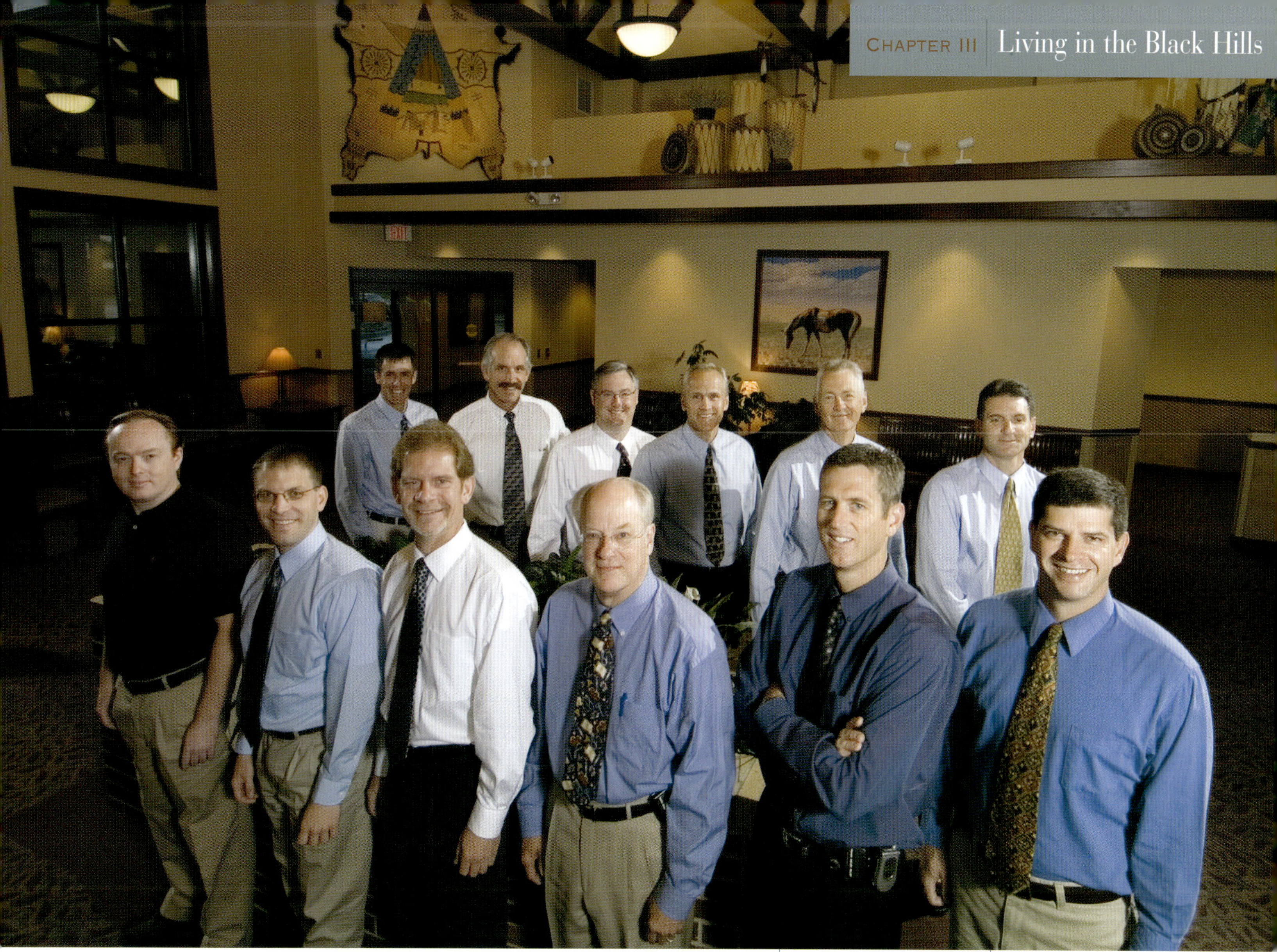

Photo by Thomas S. England

The physicians at BHOSC are dedicated to helping patients regain mobility so they can enjoy life. Back row, left to right: Kent Renaud, DPM; Rand Schleusener, M.D.; David Lang, M.D.; Bryan Den Hartog, M.D.; James Engelbrecht, M.D.; Mark Harlow, M.D. Front row, left to right: Jeff Marrs, M.D.; Clark Duchene, M.D.; Lew Papendick, M.D.; David Boyer, M.D.; Stuart Fromm, M.D.; and Michael Kadrmas, M.D.

Each of the orthopedic surgeons at the facility has subspecialty training and/or extensive experience. Surgical and nonsurgical treatment of foot and ankle injuries—such as heel pain, arthritis and diabetic foot problems, orthotics, and more—is available, as well as complete care for hand and wrist problems including carpal tunnel syndrome, fractures, and other conditions.

Using minimally invasive spine surgeries and the most advanced techniques, BHOSC also offers treatment for herniated disks, spinal stenosis, and scoliosis. The services are available to both children and adults. Deformity correction is another area of specialization at the center.

Knees and hips are the joints most commonly requiring replacement by orthopedic surgery. Again, BHOSC provides the region a Center of Excellence. Their skilled surgeons are experienced in the latest techniques for revisions and replacements of knees and hips. With all bone, muscle, and joint treatment, success depends in part on rehabilitative therapy. BHOSC has seven certified physical therapists who use a variety of approaches to restoring patients' range of motion, stabilizing functionality, and preventing re-injury.

For the convenience of patients in surrounding areas, BHOSC offers clinics in many communities in western South Dakota, eastern Wyoming, and northwestern Nebraska. "Our specialists maintain a regular schedule to area hospitals and clinics so patients are able to schedule appointments with our physicians in their home communities," said Boyer.

The physicians and staff of Black Hills Orthopedic & Spine Center are dedicated to helping patients regain active lifestyles. They are the regional Center of Excellence for surgical and nonsurgical treatment of bone, muscle, and joint conditions. ❖

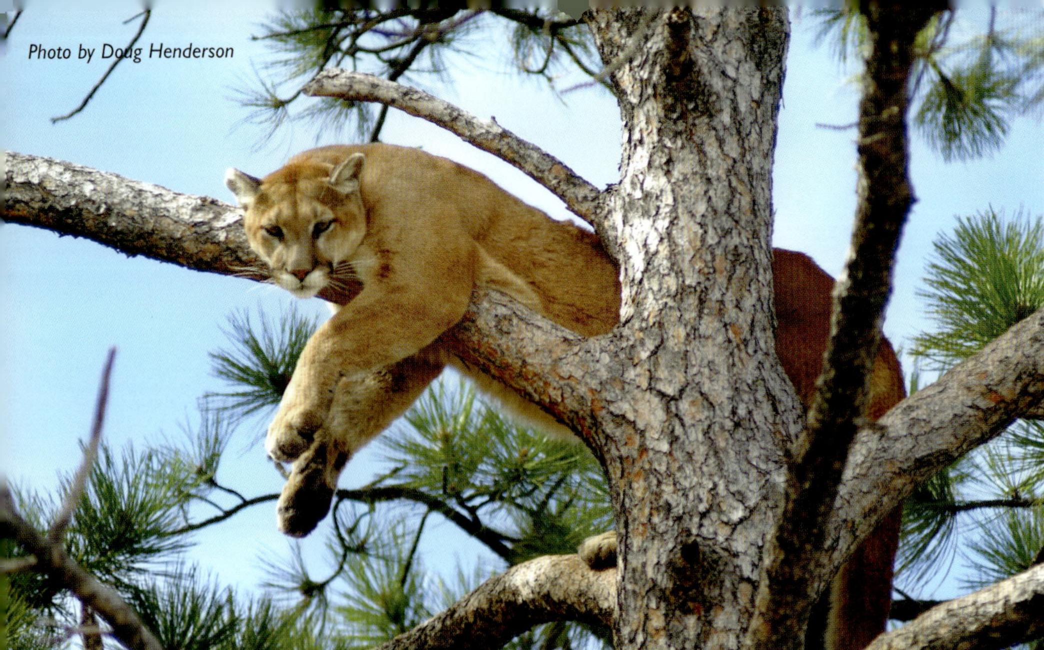

Photo by Doug Henderson

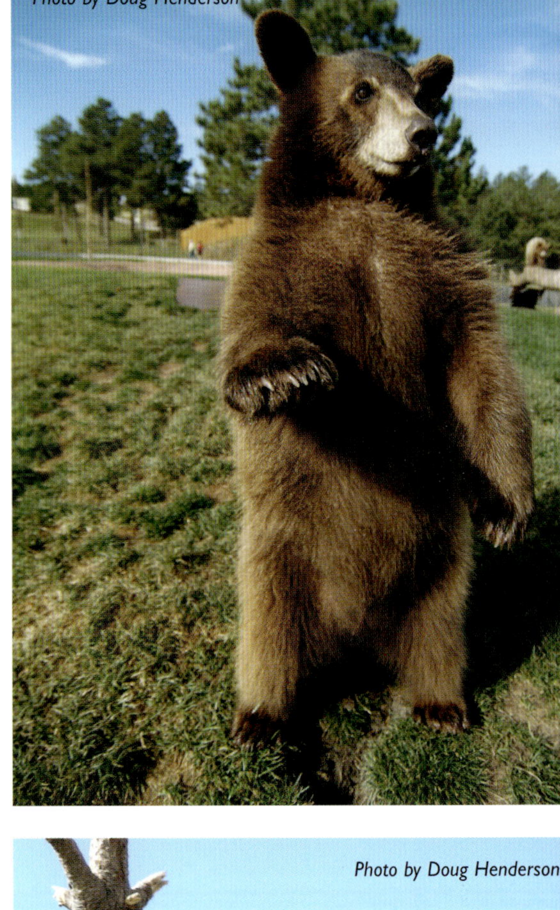

Photo by Doug Henderson

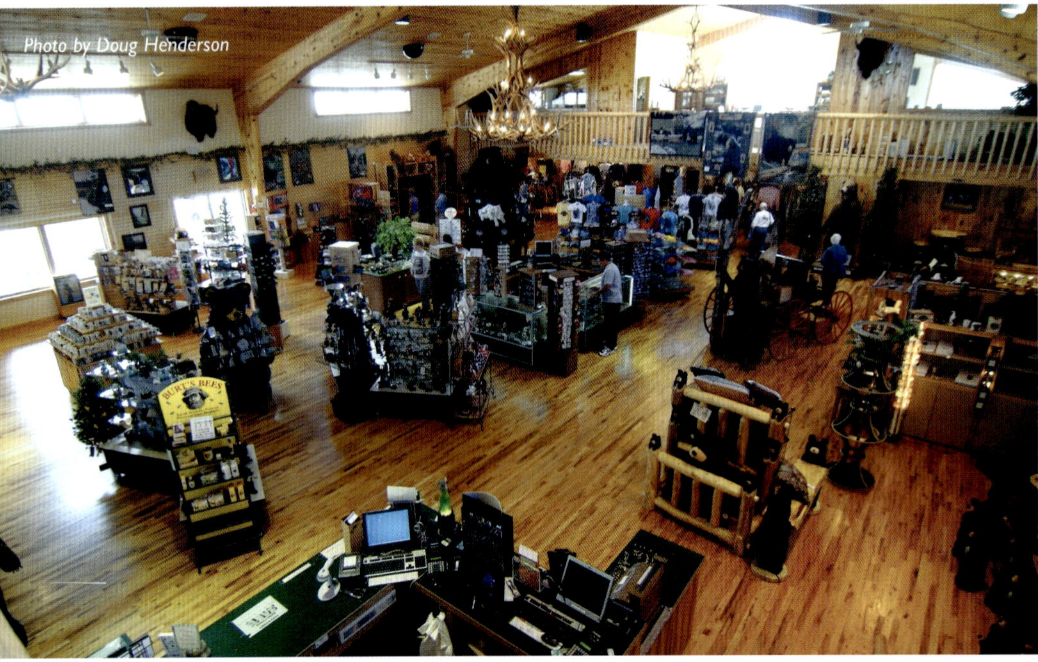

Photo by Doug Henderson

Wild animals have always

been an important part of the landscape and environment of the Black Hills, and even with diminishing habitats, there is a place where bears, elk, bobcats, reindeer, wolves, mountain lions, sheep, and buffalo still roam. At Bear Country, which opened in 1972, 250 acres of towering pines and rolling meadows give visitors a chance to see these wild creatures from the comfort and safety of their vehicles. Pauline Casey, wife of Doc Casey, the founder, and five of her seven children run Bear Country, "the largest collection of privately owned black bears in the world." The wildlife park started out with eleven black bears, one cougar, one wolf, three buffalo, and one bull elk. Today the bear population has grown to three hundred black bears. Most of the wildlife is born on the premises and hand-raised by the staff. This increases the survival rate, and aids in manageability and marketability. The park is continually improved to accommodate the growing number of animals. ❖

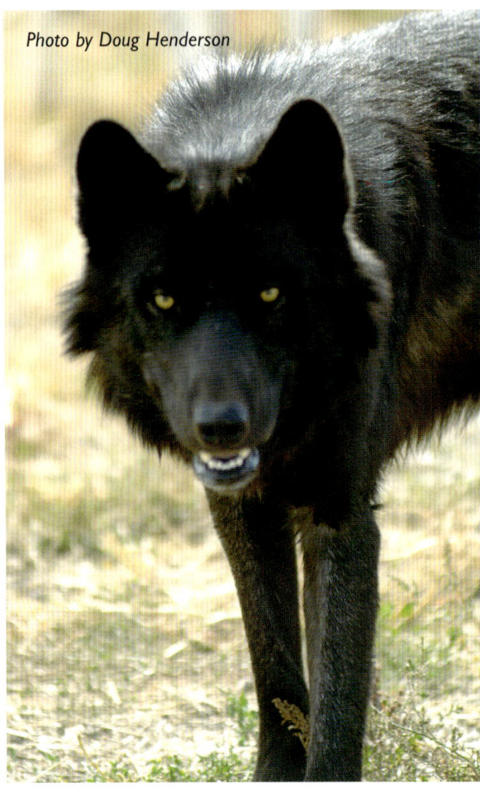

Photo by Doug Henderson

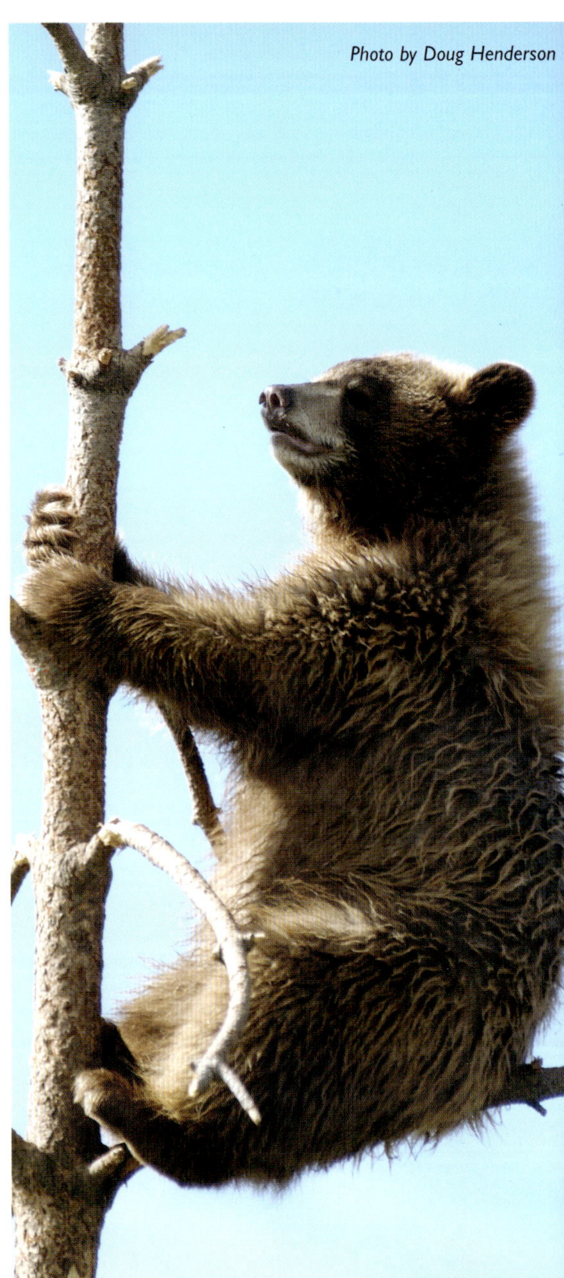

Photo by Doug Henderson

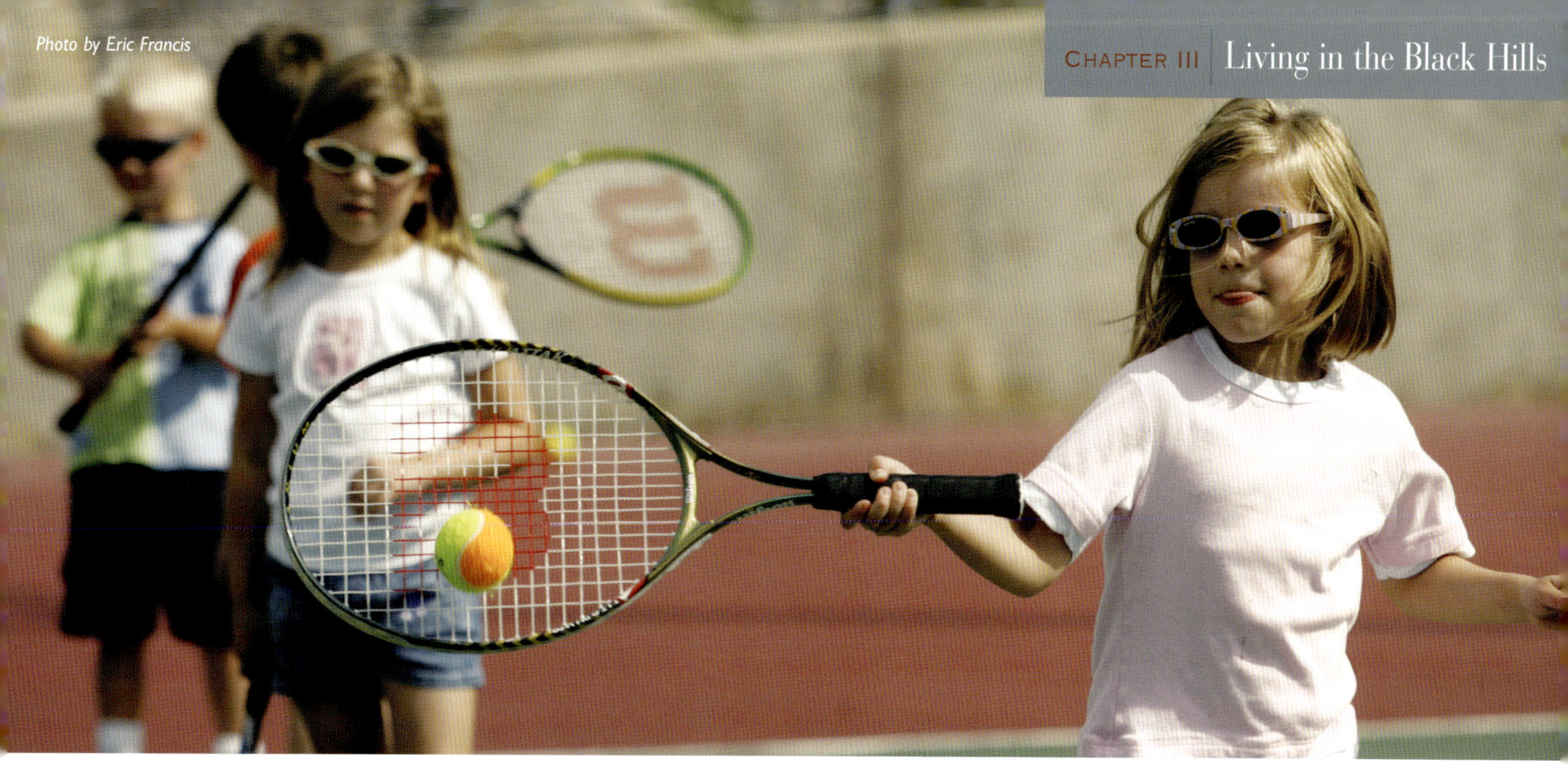

Photo by Eric Francis

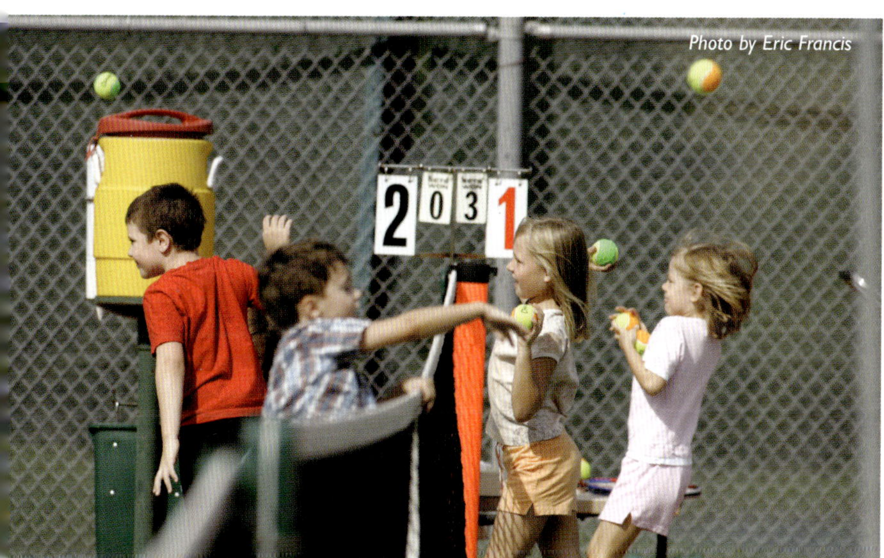

Photo by Eric Francis

Tennis, anyone?

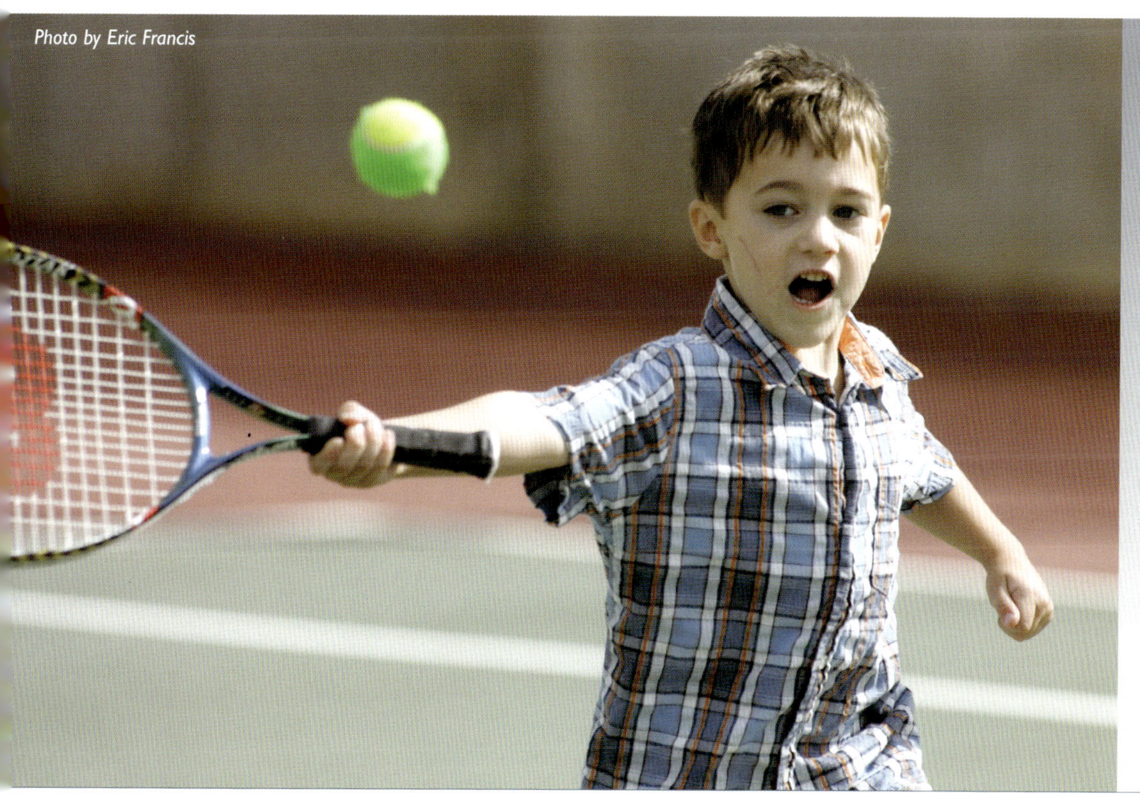

Photo by Eric Francis

On Mondays, Wednesdays, and Fridays, the young Andre Agassis and Venus Williamses of Rapid City head over to Arrowhead Tennis Center to participate in the facility's popular Pee Wee tennis class. Designed for four- and five-year-olds, the one-hour class helps little ones develop their sense of balance and coordination with a multitude of activities. According to Bryce Bernard, director of the tennis center, the children do everything from running around cones while balancing a tennis ball on a racket to executing simple bounce catches and bounce hits. These activities help the petite players, like Grady Dehler, get a feel for the court and what it's like to send a fuzzy yellow ball sailing over the net. And since Arrowhead Tennis Center also offers classes throughout the year for players of all ages and skill levels, it is the perfect location for some family-friendly fun. ❖

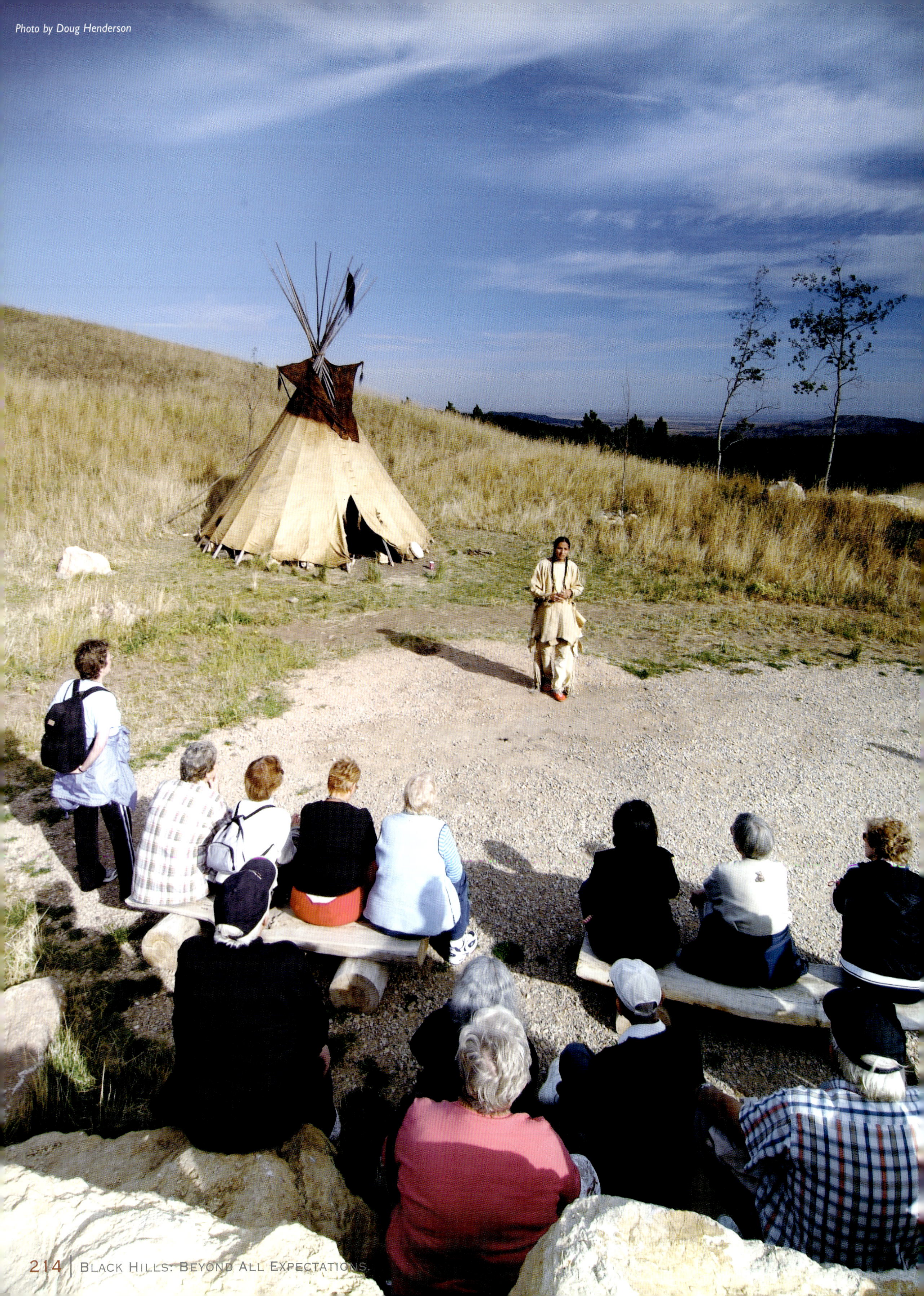

Photo by Doug Henderson

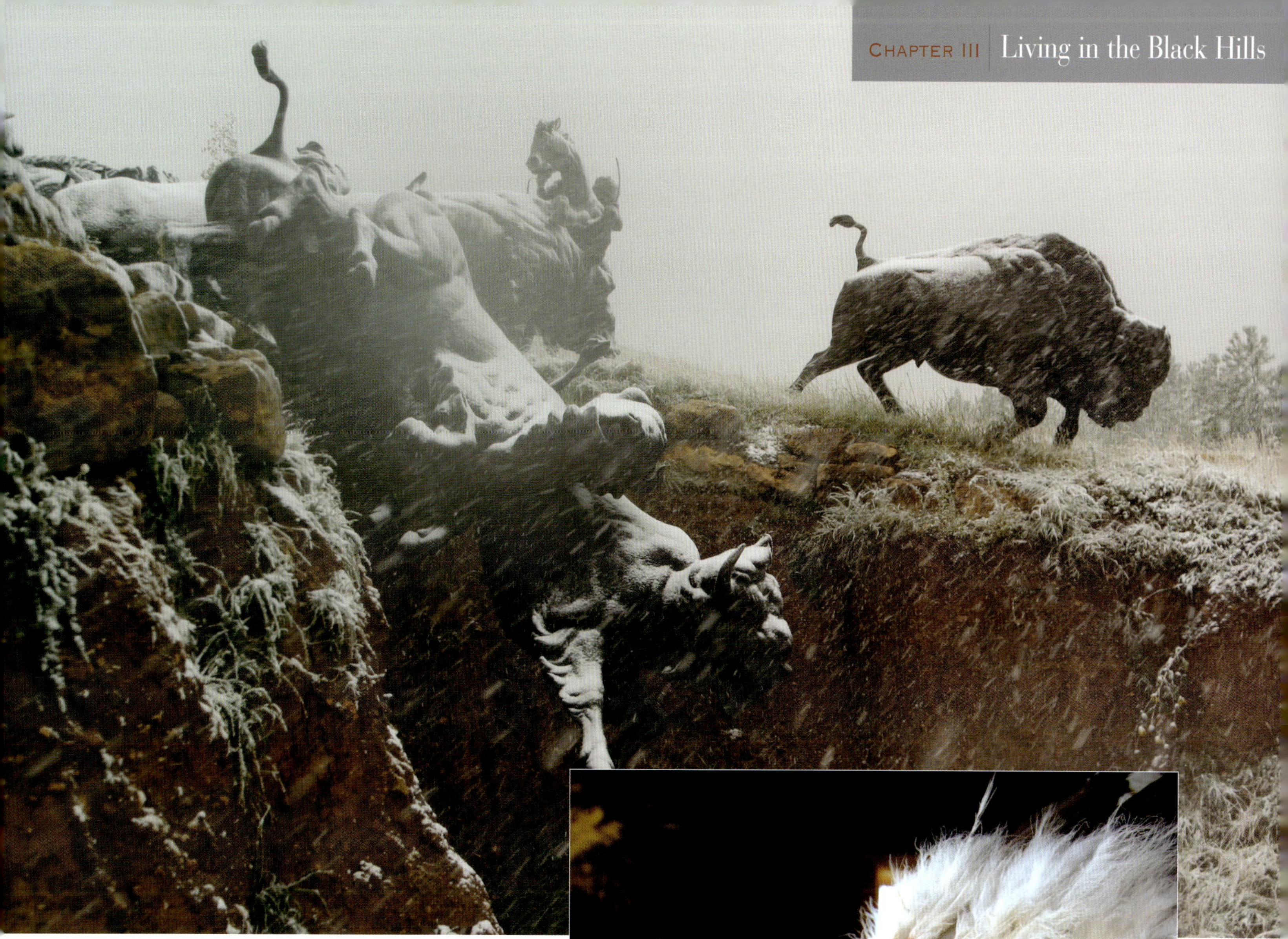

Millions of bison once roamed the American Plains, serving as a primary source of physical and spiritual sustenance for the people who lived there. By the late nineteenth century, however, it was estimated that less than one thousand bison survived. Thankfully, the majestic animal has made a comeback and continues to serve as a symbol of the American spirit. To honor that spirit, actor Kevin Costner conceived of and funded a unique attraction called Tatanka: Story of the Bison. Located about a mile north of Deadwood on U.S. Highway 85, the attraction features a larger-than-life bronze sculpture of fourteen bison pursued by three American Indian horseback riders. Also on-site is an educational center with interactive exhibits on both bison and the Lakota Indians, a gift shop, and an indoor-outdoor restaurant that serves grass-fed bison meat. ❖

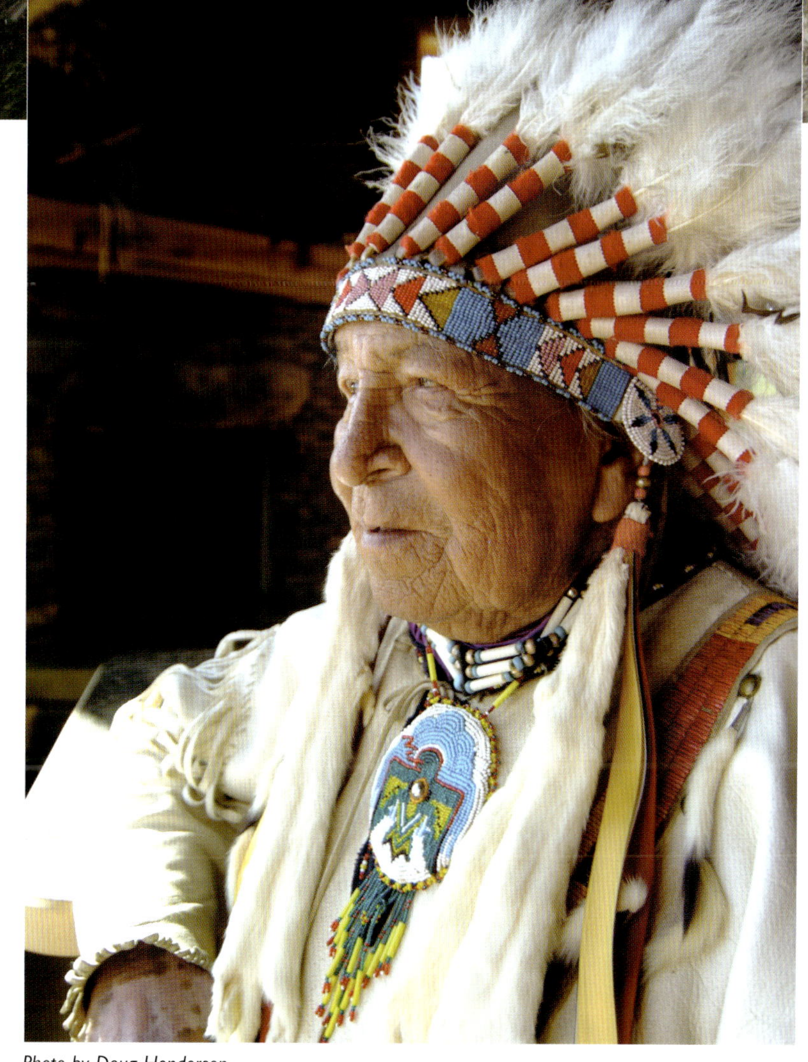

Photo by Doug Henderson

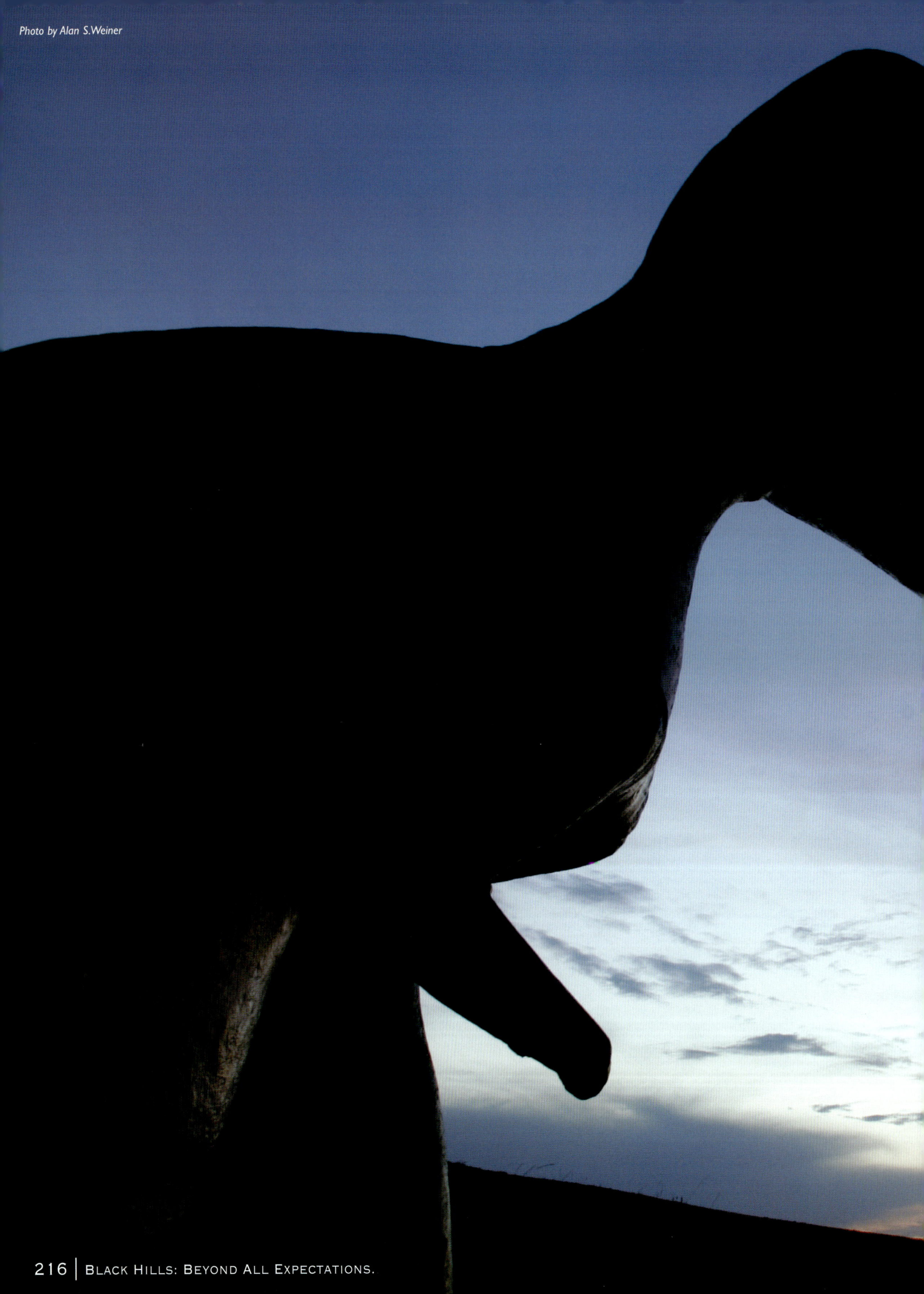

Photo by Alan S.Weiner

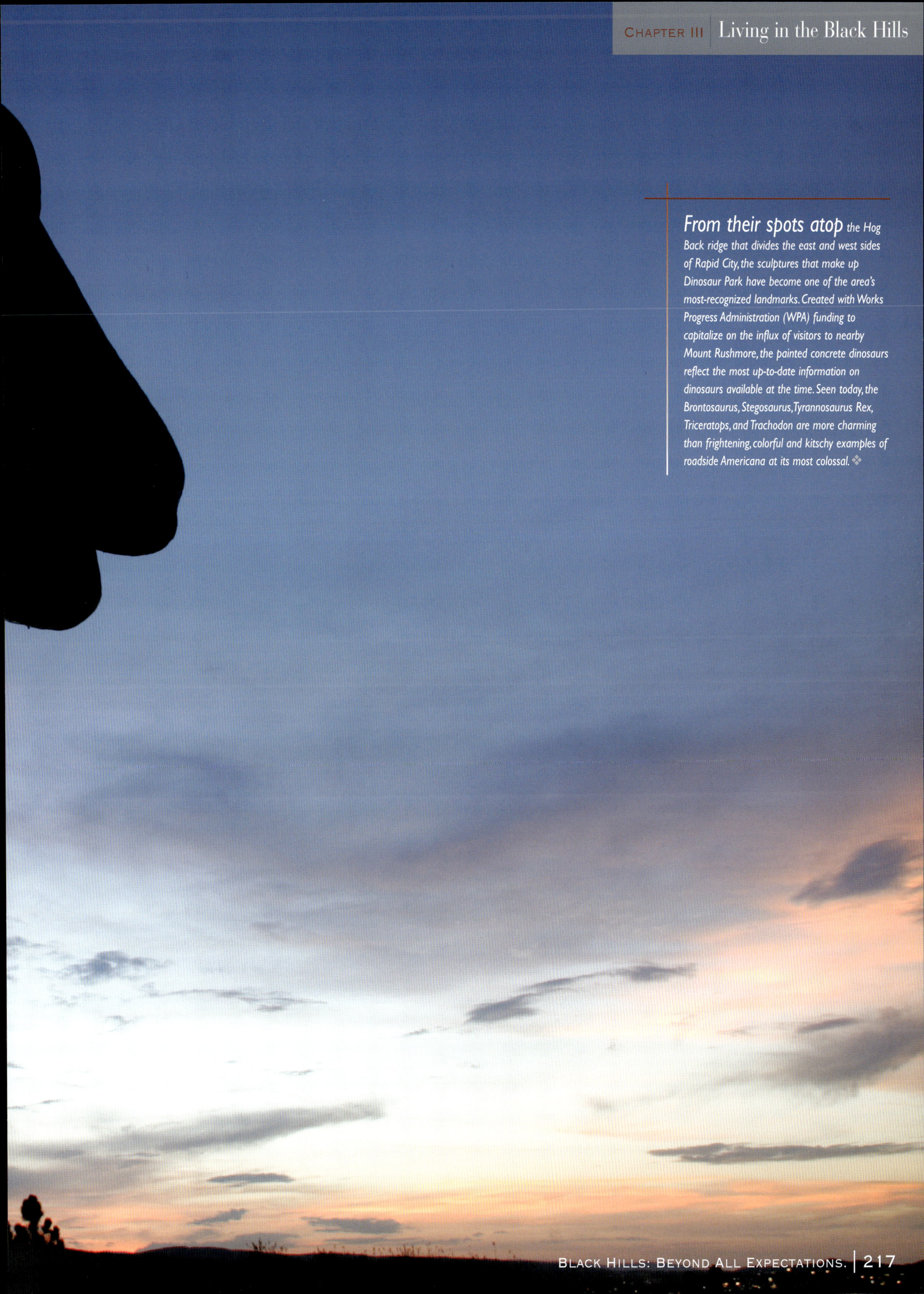

From their spots atop the Hog Back ridge that divides the east and west sides of Rapid City, the sculptures that make up Dinosaur Park have become one of the area's most-recognized landmarks. Created with Works Progress Administration (WPA) funding to capitalize on the influx of visitors to nearby Mount Rushmore, the painted concrete dinosaurs reflect the most up-to-date information on dinosaurs available at the time. Seen today, the Brontosaurus, Stegosaurus, Tyrannosaurus Rex, Triceratops, and Trachodon are more charming than frightening, colorful and kitschy examples of roadside Americana at its most colossal. ❖

BHCAIH Guides Patients Beyond Medical Needs

Some of the most pressing issues in health care today concern the rising rates of life-threatening diseases among American Indians. As a whole, Native populations on the Northern Plains suffer from diabetes, cancer, and heart disease at much higher rates than other Americans. Poverty, lack of education, and poor access to medical services compound these health disparities.

But here in the Black Hills, one organization is working to find solutions to these Indian health issues, while providing tribes throughout the region with the skills to implement effective health-care systems.

Led by founder Dr. Jeff Henderson and his wife, Dr. Patricia Nez Henderson, the nonprofit Black Hills Center for American Indian Health was established in Rapid City in 1998 to enhance the physical, mental, spiritual, and cultural health of American Indians and their communities.

As American Indian physicians with extensive backgrounds in both research and public health, the Hendersons are uniquely qualified to integrate traditional American

The Hendersons are uniquely qualified to integrate traditional American Indian beliefs with modern medical technologies.

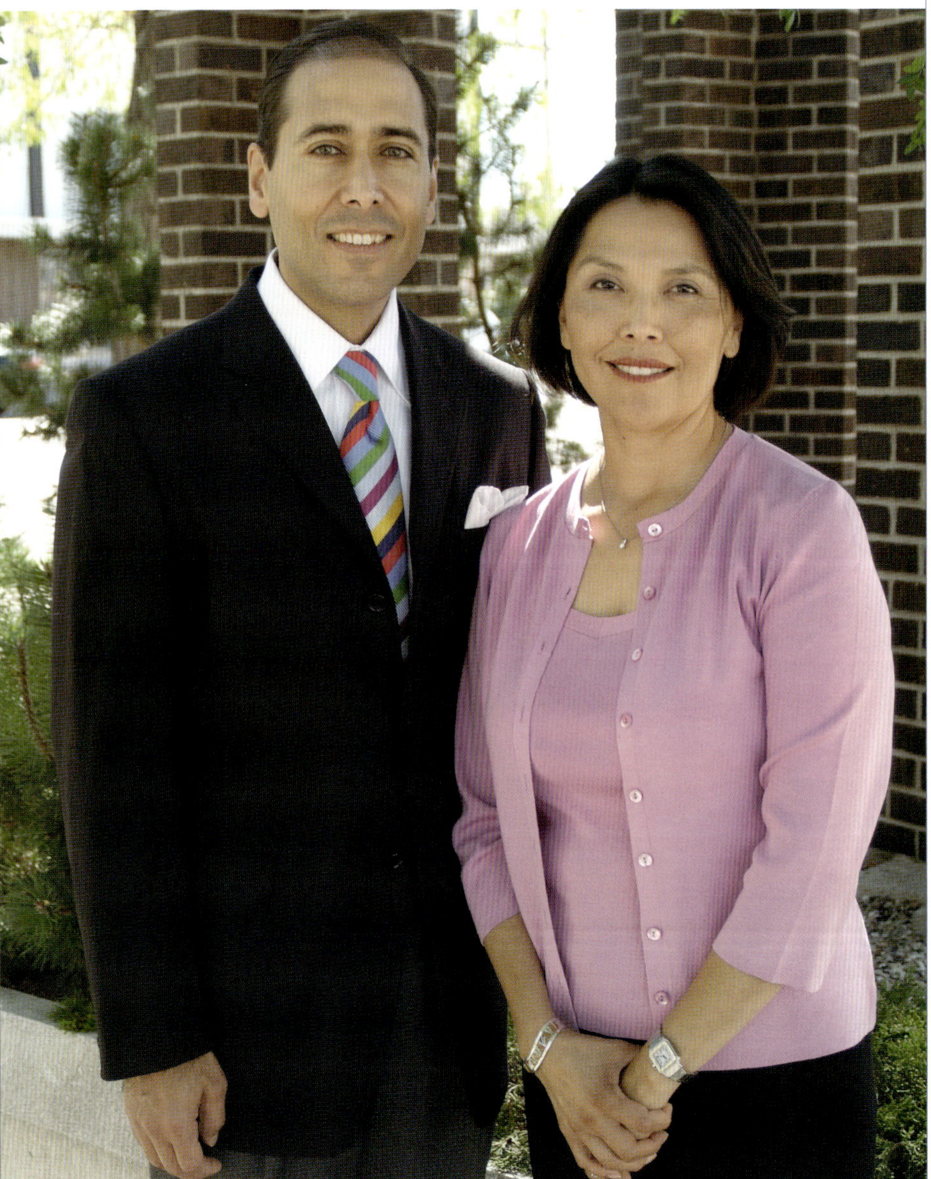

Drs. Jeff Henderson and Patricia Nez Henderson outside their offices in downtown Rapid City. After graduating medical school (he from the University of California–San Diego, she as the first-ever American Indian woman to graduate from Yale Medical School), the Hendersons dedicated themselves to public health work. In 2000, they joined together in marriage and entrepreneurial spirit.

Photo by Doug Henderson

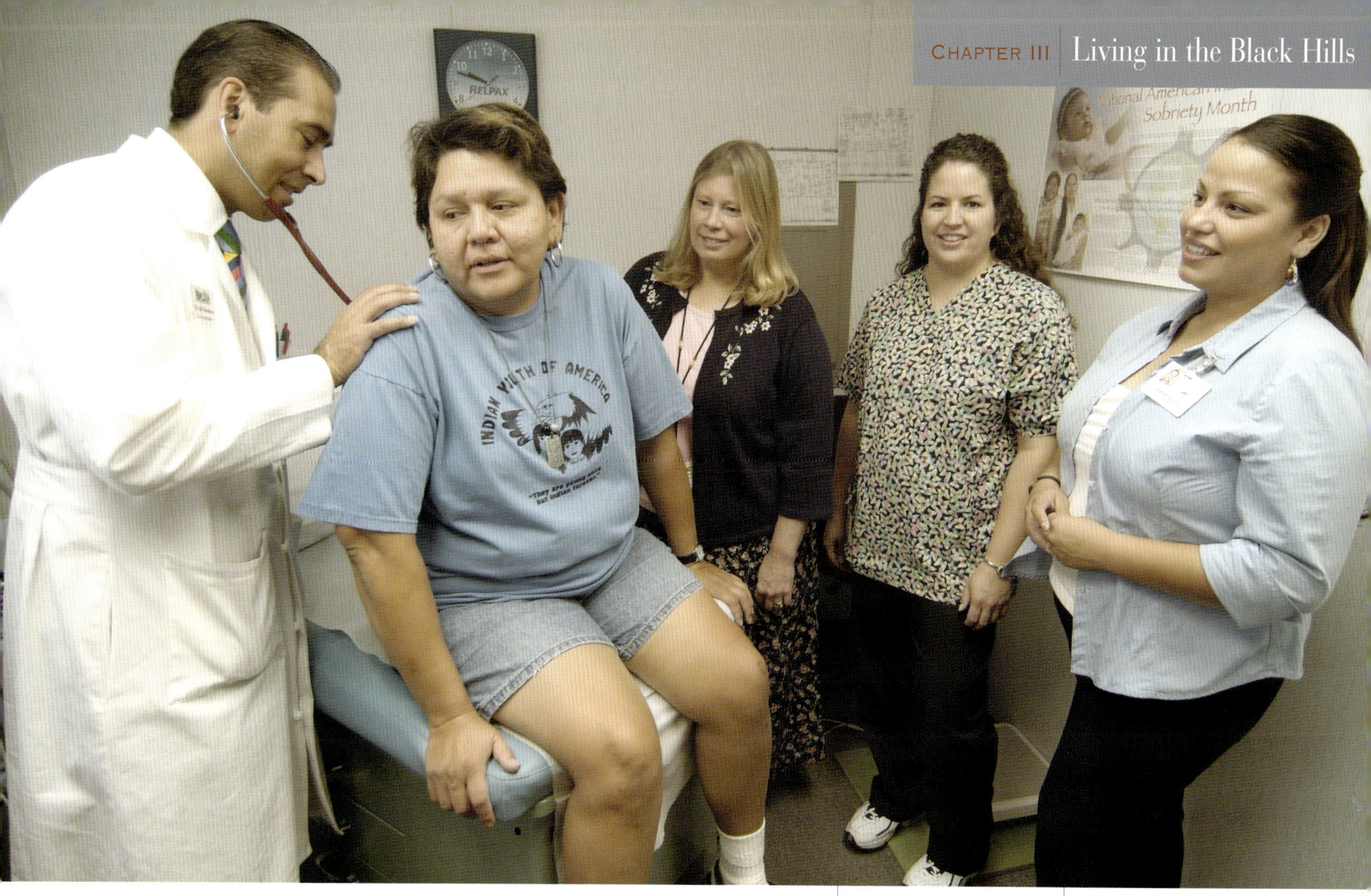

Photo by Doug Henderson

The BHCAIH Clinical Research Team examines a SANDS patient. Left to right: Dr. Jeff Henderson, patient Ida Fast Horse, PA Joanne Detwiler, RN Jackie Yotter, and research assistant Stephanie Big Crow. When completed, SANDS will provide medical professionals with invaluable information on lowering risk factors to prevent cardiovascular disease among persons with type 2 diabetes.

Indian beliefs with modern medical technologies. To date, their work has put BHCAIH on the ground in five reservations in three states, including South Dakota.

The Hendersons and their twelve-member staff currently conduct research through seven different grants, including one involving a study of Lakota Sioux attitudes toward participation in biomedical research. Another, funded by the Colorado State Tobacco Research Program, allows Dr. Nez Henderson to concentrate her efforts on a smoking cessation program on the Rosebud Sioux Reservation in south central South Dakota.

The Center also serves as the principal Northern Plains' investigator for two nationwide research studies designed to explore the biological, social, and cultural reasons for disease processes among American Indians. The Education and Research Towards Health (EARTH) study examines how lifestyle, diet, and physical activity contribute to the prevention of cancer, diabetes, and heart disease. The Stop Atherosclerosis in Native Diabetics Study (SANDS) is the first study of its kind to address the rise in heart disease among American Indians with type 2 diabetes. Among its various studies, BHCAIH is currently working with over five thousand American Indians, and anticipates the involvement of an additional three thousand before studies are complete.

Certainly, research into the causes of and solutions for American Indian health issues is a major part of the BHCAIH mission, but the Center also concentrates its efforts in education, service, and philanthropy. By partnering with Rapid City Area Public Schools, the South Dakota School of Mines and Technology, and Black Hills State University in Spearfish, the Center is augmenting science and health-care programs for the region while also encouraging increased American Indian participation in medical professions training. Likewise, BHCAIH plans to eventually serve as a training center in public health research methods for tribal health-care staff.

Finally, by offering educational and technical assistance to tribes throughout the region, much of it pro bono, BHCAIH is helping Native populations establish the personnel and infrastructure necessary for independent governance of their own health-care systems, including research, thus bridging the gap between traditions and modern medical science. ❖

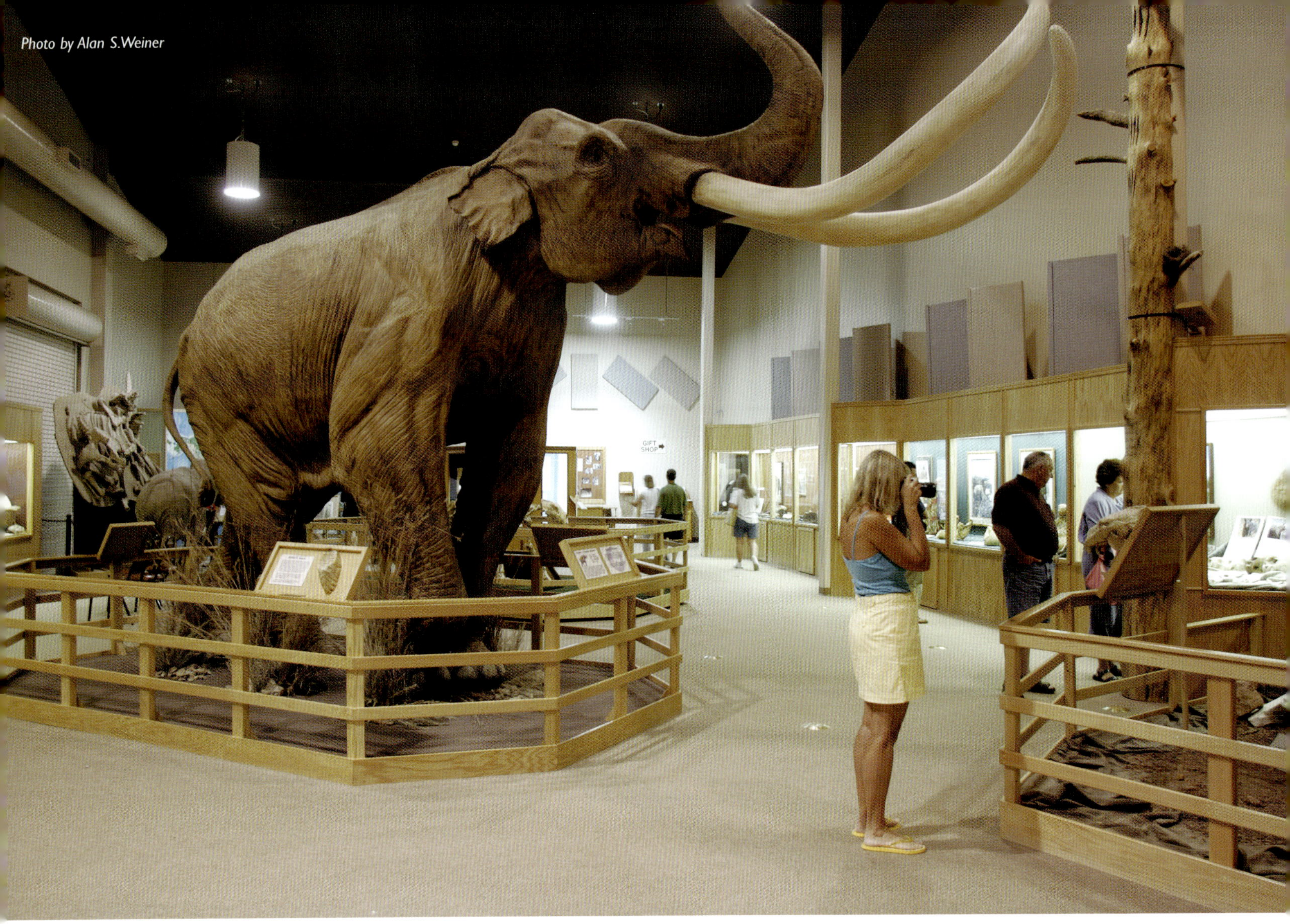

Photo by Alan S.Weiner

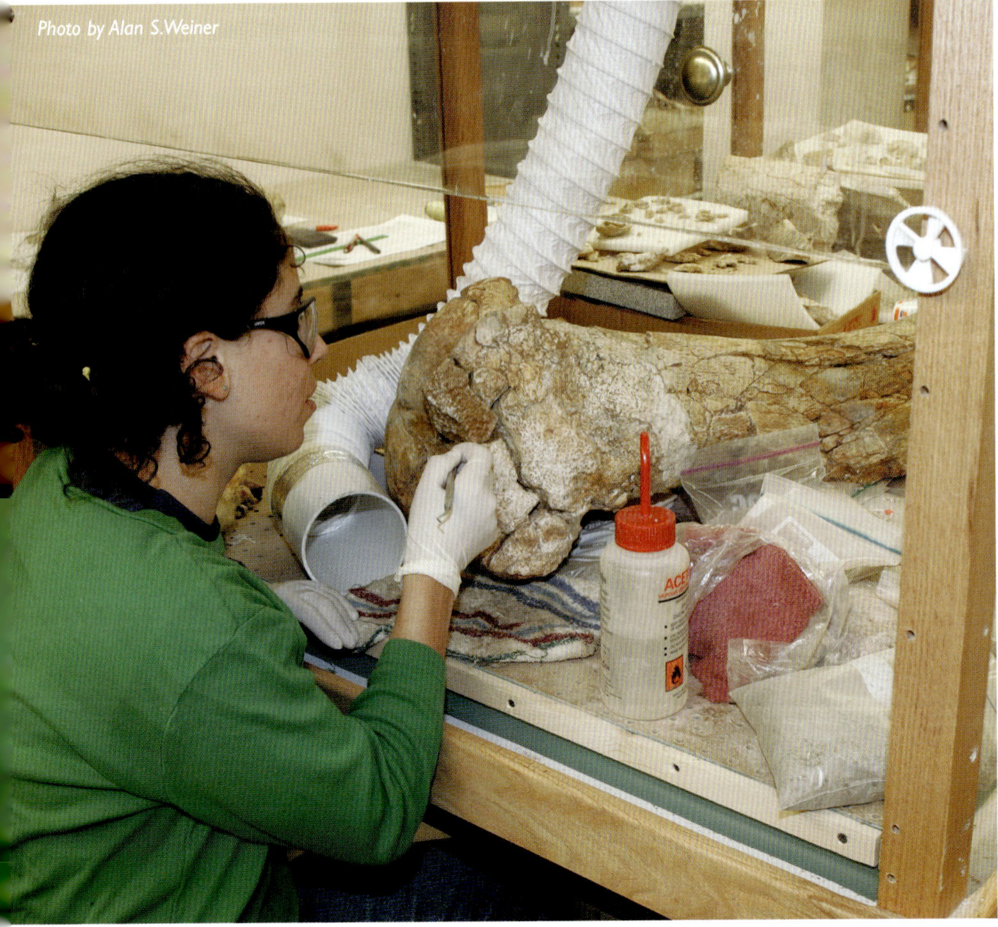
Photo by Alan S.Weiner

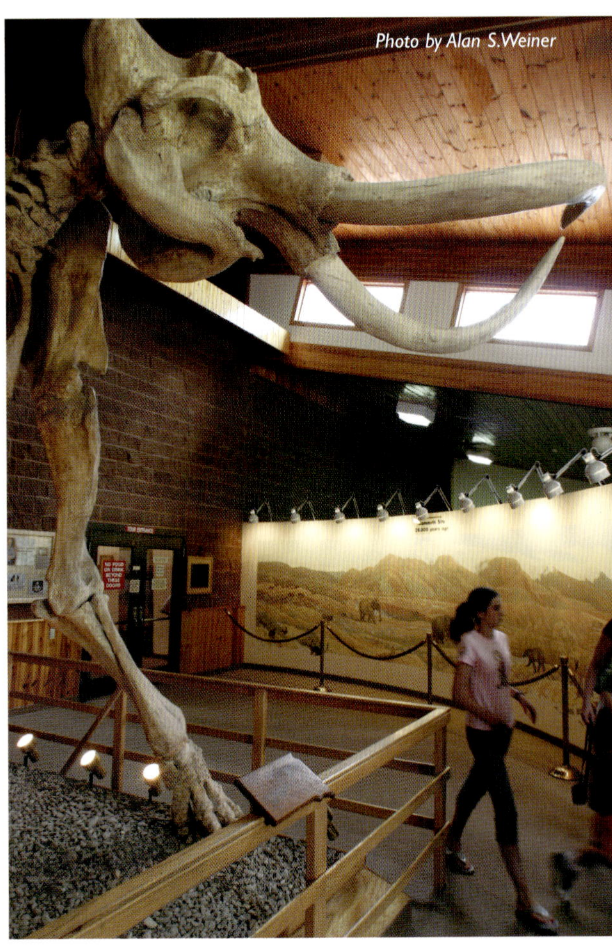
Photo by Alan S.Weiner

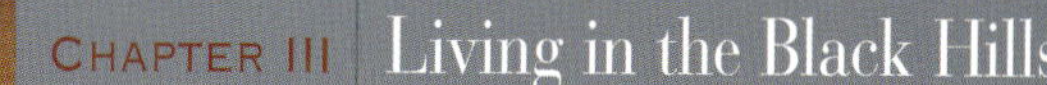

Photo by Alan S.Weiner

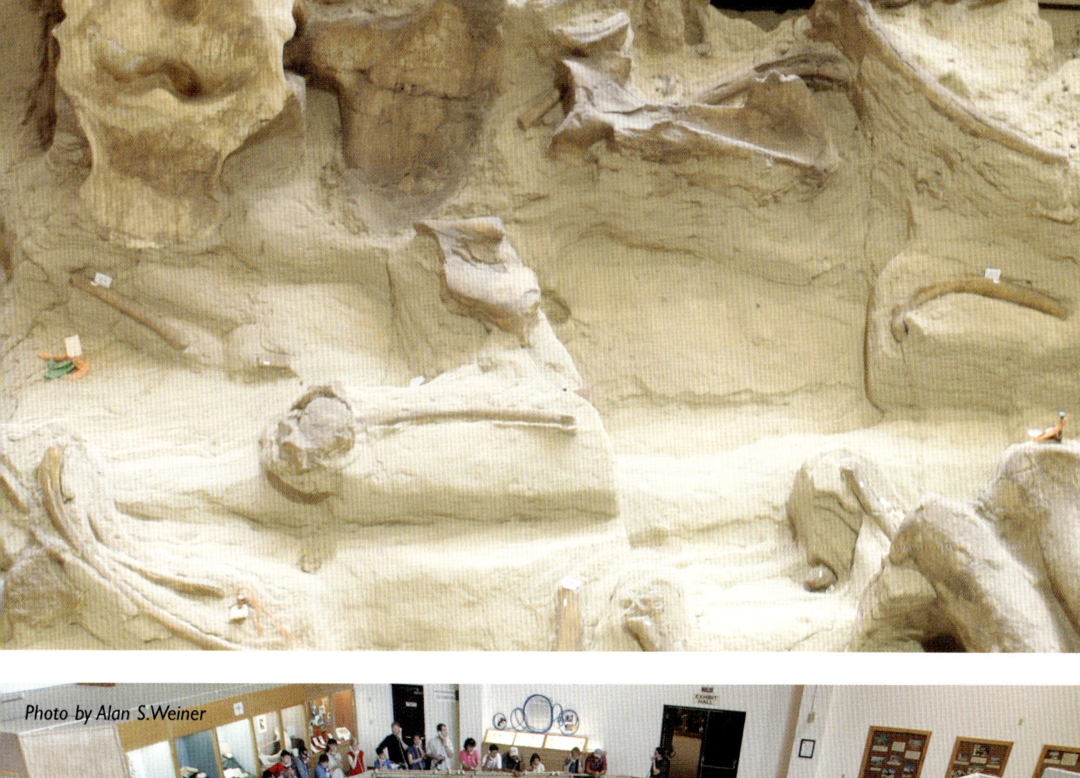

Photo by Alan S.Weiner

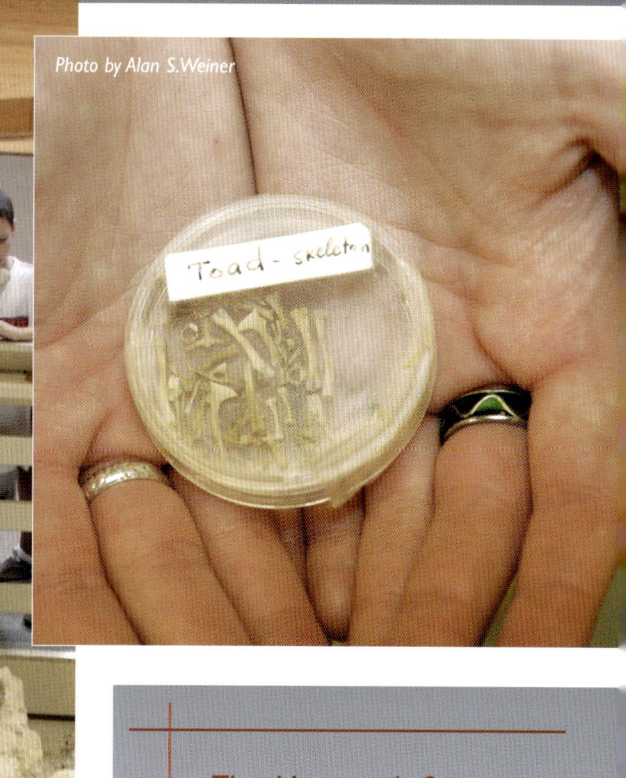

Photo by Alan S.Weiner

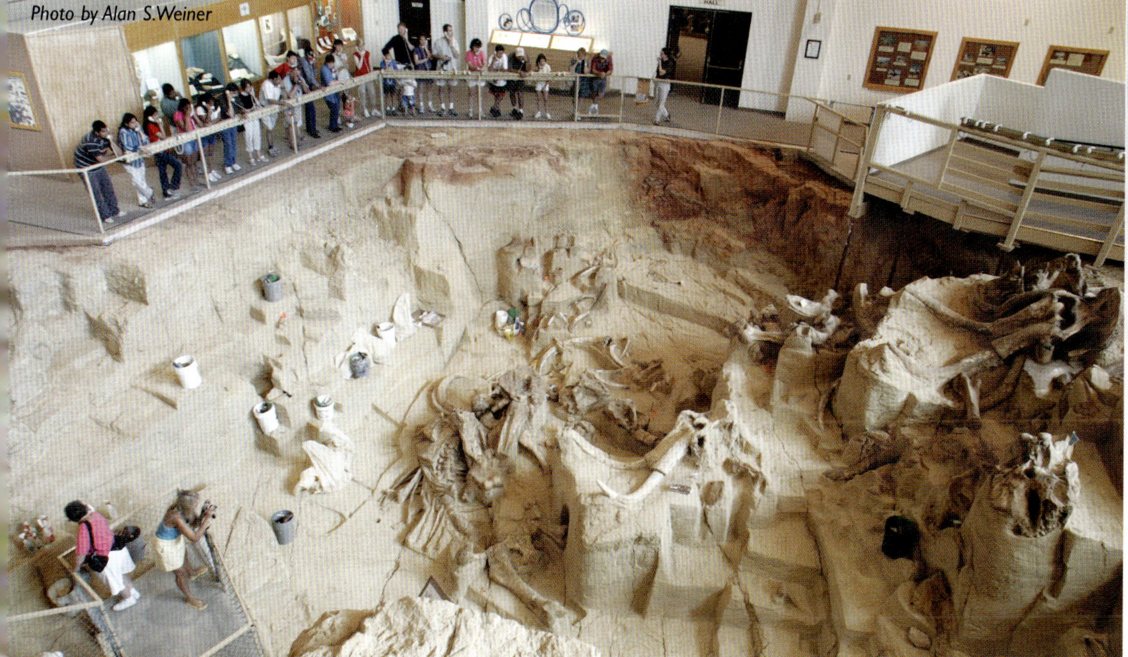

The Mammoth Site, located in Hot Springs, brings new meaning to the phrase "come play in the dirt again." Discovered in 1974 during a housing development initiative, the site is actually a sixty-foot karst sinkhole that produced a warm spring during the Ice Age more than twenty-six thousand years ago. The animals that visited that spring for drinking water, such as the North American Columbian mammoth and the giant short-faced bear, became trapped in the sinkhole, their bones fossilizing over the thousands of years they spent under the layers of silt and sediment that ultimately filled the pond. Today, under the direction of principal investigator Dr. Larry Agenbroad, the Mammoth Site is recognized as the world's largest Columbian mammoth exhibit and research center for Pleistocene studies. Fossils of both the Columbian mammoth and the woolly mammoth were uncovered in the in-situ exhibit, representing the first time in history the two species have been found together. Also, evidence of numerous other Ice Age animals, like the camel, llama, and wolf, are still being discovered during the daily excavations that go on at the site, which is now enclosed and protected by a climate-controlled building. In addition to the site's research staff, scientists from around the world are given the opportunity to dig and conduct their own research through the Visiting Scientist program, while aspiring paleontologists can participate in the Junior Paleontologists digs held each summer. And for those visitors who want to get a firsthand look at the fascinating work being done in the heart of America's Great Plains, the Mammoth Site offers thirty-minute guided tours of the dig area, as well as a trek through history in Muller Exhibit Hall, offering an array of exhibits, including a full-size replica of a Columbian mammoth. ❖

RCAS: Building a Community of Lifelong Learners

Serving over thirteen thousand students in twenty-four schools, the Rapid City Area Schools District (RCAS) is helping to build a community of lifelong learners, one student at a time. At all levels, RCAS provides for the needs of a diverse student body by maintaining a highly educated instructional staff, a supportive administration, and the latest in learning technologies. To ensure that all students reach their full potential, RCAS is committed to providing programs and services of the highest academic order, as well as enlisting resources and support among the public and private sectors.

RCAS is committed to providing programs and services of the highest academic order.

Student achievement remains a solid goal of the RCAS board of education. Attainment of that goal is reflected in some of the following key achievement data for 2005. Our schools exceeded "No Child Left Behind" (NCLB) Adequate Yearly Progress (AYP) goals in reading and math at each level (elementary, middle, and high school). RCAS students also exceeded state and national levels in ACT scores and the Stanford Achievement Test 10 (SAT 10). As a state, South Dakota students have consistently been among the top-ten states in the country in National Assessment of Educational Progress (NAEP) scores.

Student success begins within the system itself. Under the districtwide Building Leadership Teams (BLTs) Professional Development Program, each school forms a team made up of the school's principal and a minimum of six staff members. Teams receive intense training in data analysis, goal setting, learning theory, and instructional

Photo by Doug Henderson

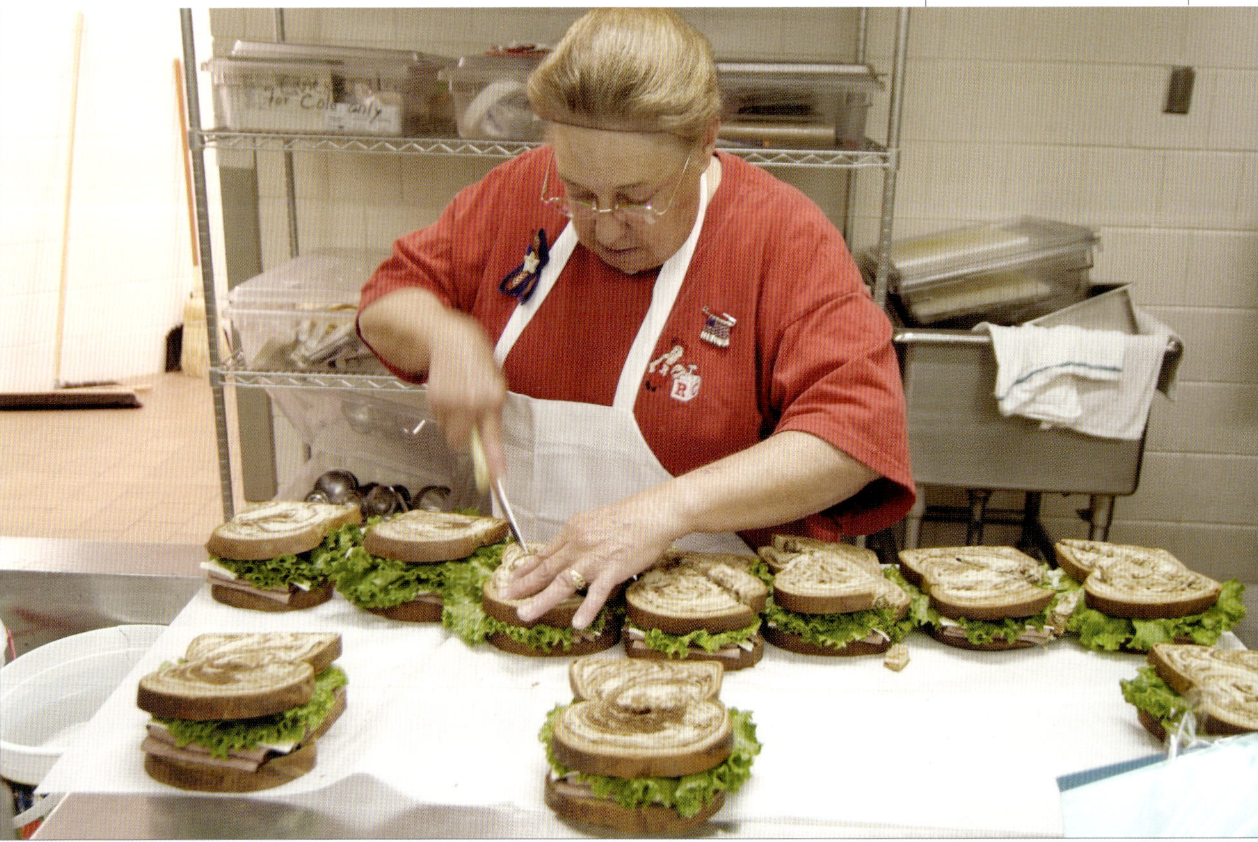

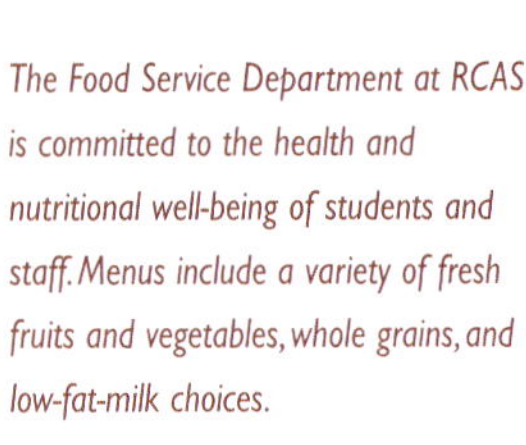

The Food Service Department at RCAS is committed to the health and nutritional well-being of students and staff. Menus include a variety of fresh fruits and vegetables, whole grains, and low-fat-milk choices.

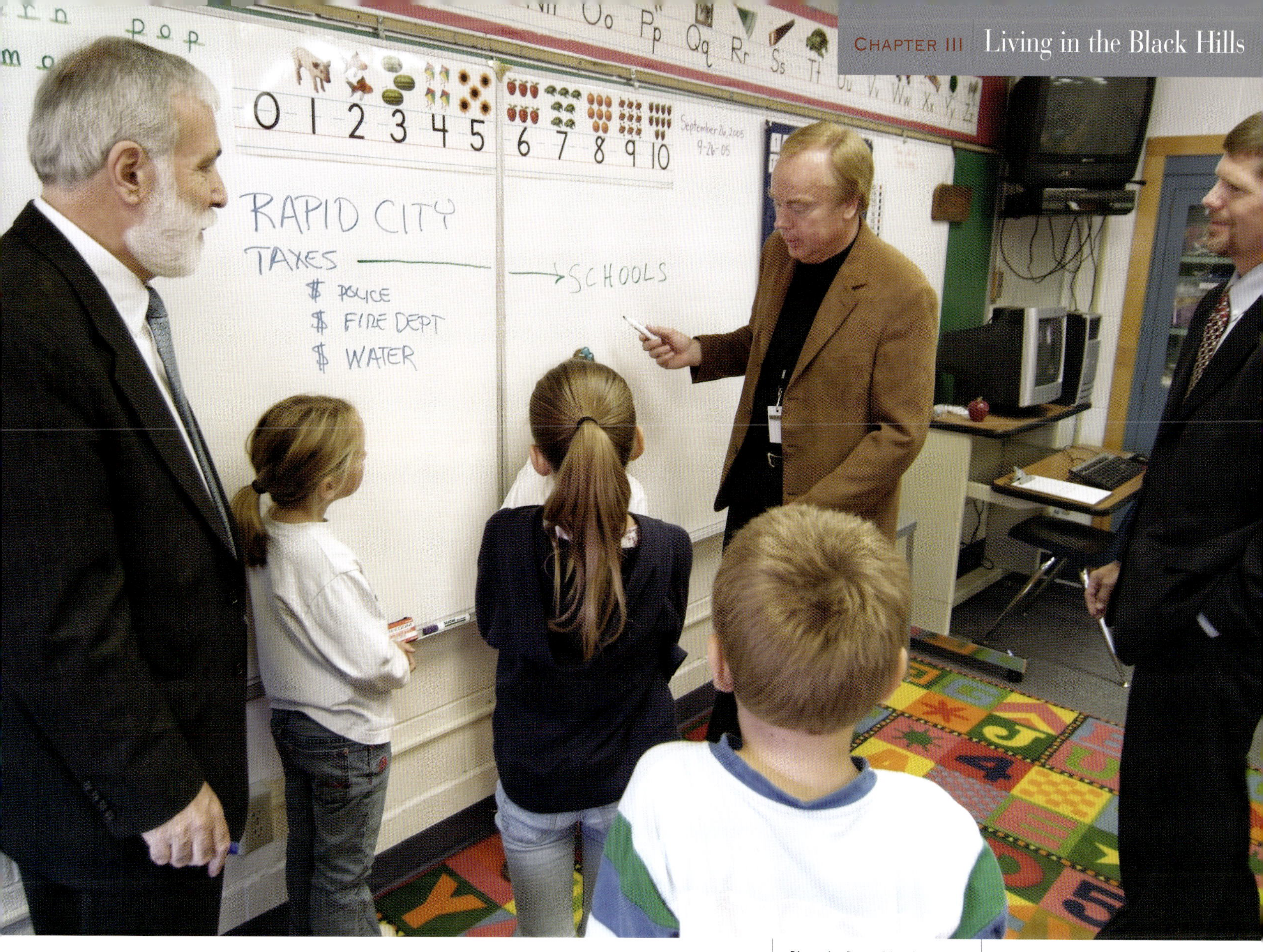

Photo by Doug Henderson

Partnering with RCAS, Junior Achievement sponsors business mentors in the classroom who teach and promote the "economics of real life" to students. Community leaders, including Mayor Jim Shaw (left), Superintendent Peter Wharton (center), and John Carlson, president of Highmark Federal Credit Union (right), are among the many volunteers.

strategies, and then extend that training to the rest of the staff via a collaborative work group structure.

Recognizing that a lifetime of learning is built upon a solid foundation of literacy and mathematics competence, the district has also implemented a K-12 literacy program featuring a Leadership for Literacy program at the elementary level. In each of the fifteen elementary schools, literacy teams develop a concise, effective literacy plan based on skills assessment, instructional and developmental processes, and ongoing teacher training. In tandem with the literacy emphasis, the district's focus on K-12 mathematics competence is supported by a National Science Foundation (NSF) grant.

The district also provides for the needs of non-traditional and at-risk students. Innovative programs at the Rapid City Academy provide students in grades 9 to 12 with trusting environments that build community, self-esteem, and academic success. At the Academy's Virtual Campus, students can earn high school credit through a flexible, accessible, fully accredited educational system available 24/7 online. Through Central High School's Lakolkiciyapi Room, incoming freshmen are provided with an alternative two-semester program designed to promote academic responsibility and commitment, and to encourage cultural understanding. The program prepares students for continued excellence upon reentering the traditional classroom setting in the sophomore year.

The district is also known for superlative athletic and extracurricular programs. Due in part to over ten years of consistent excellence in physical fitness and

Continued on page 224

Continued from page 223

athletics, in May 2005, *Sports Illustrated* magazine named Stevens High School the best athletic program in the state. The district's music program is one of the best in the nation. In 2004, Central High School's Chamber Orchestra was selected to perform at the prestigious fifty-eighth annual Midwest Clinic in Chicago, Illinois.

By promoting excellence in all programs, RCAS ensures the best possible opportunities for staff and students that allow them to reach their full potential. Rapid City Area Schools is proud to be "Educating Tomorrow's Leaders Today." ❖

Photo by Rodger Slott

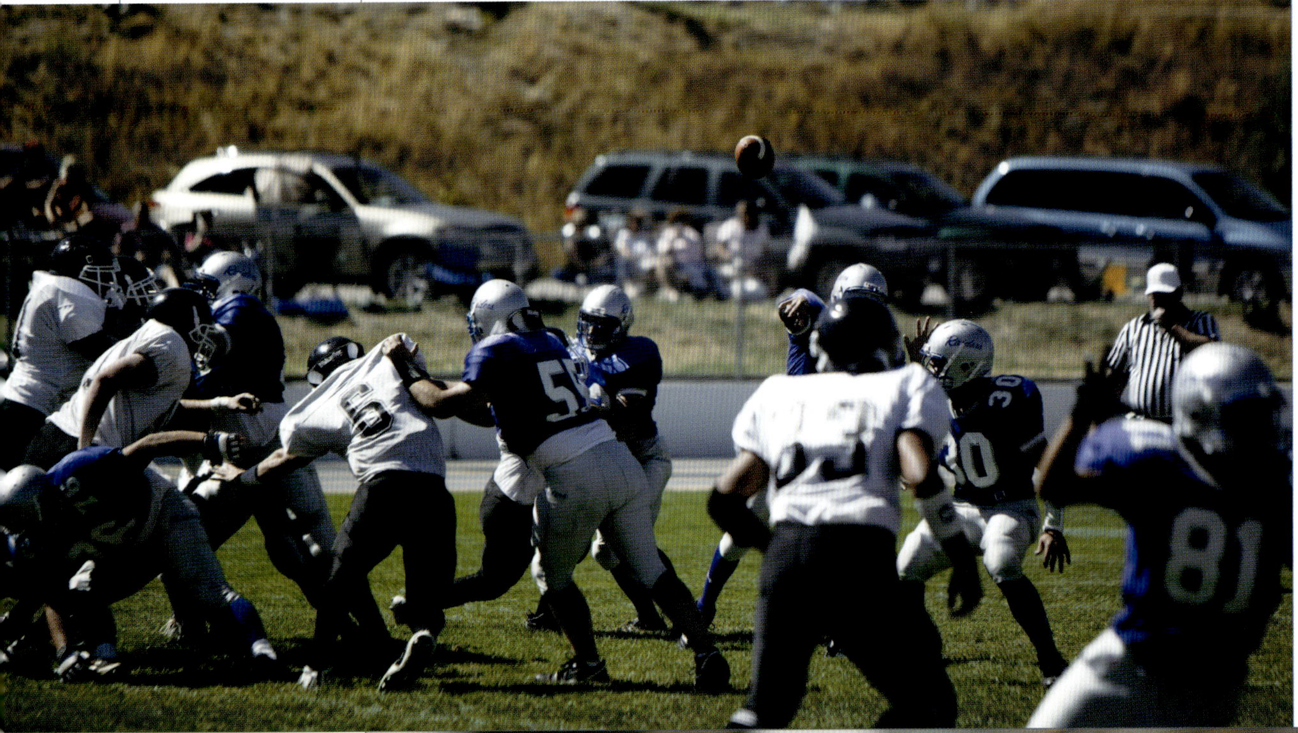

Photo by Rodger Slott

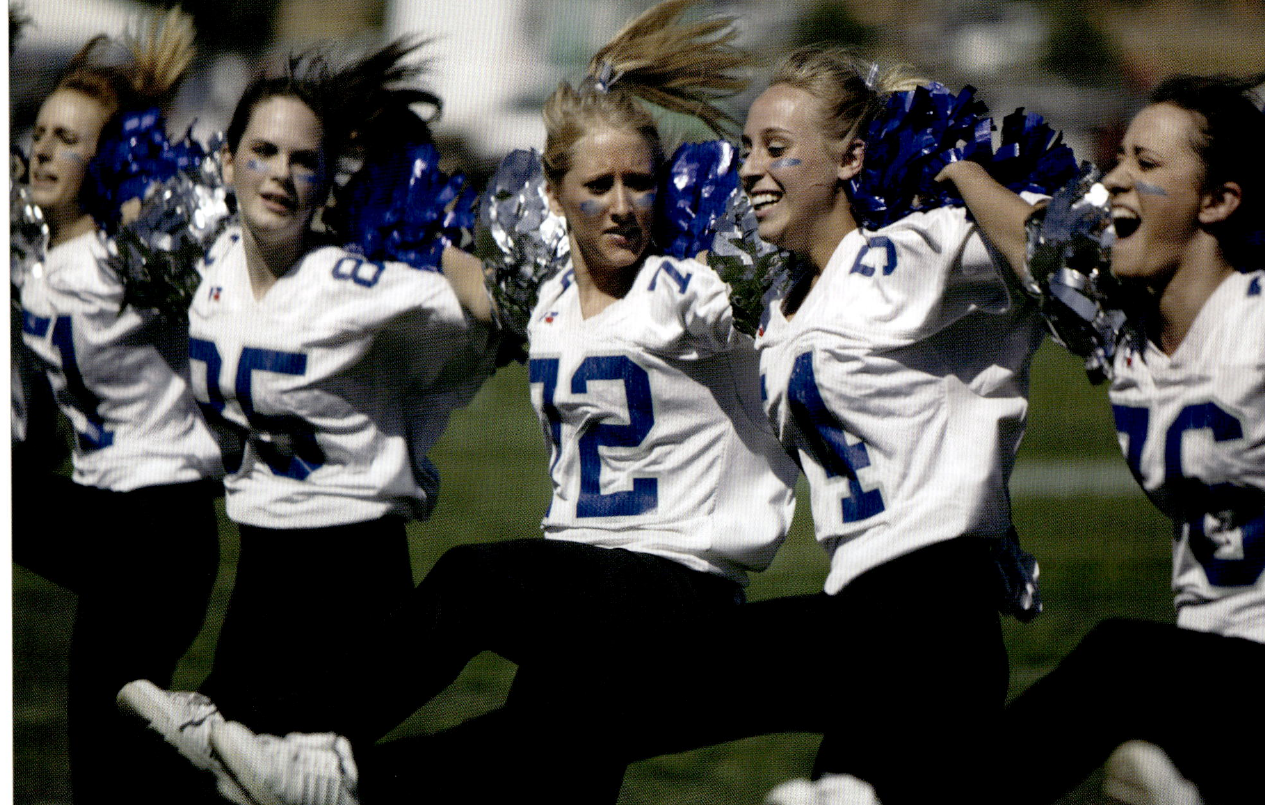

The Rushmore Bowl is an annual community fundraiser sponsored by the parent booster clubs at both high schools in Rapid City. Featuring fun, food, and football, revenue generated is used to supplement extracurricular activities at both high schools.

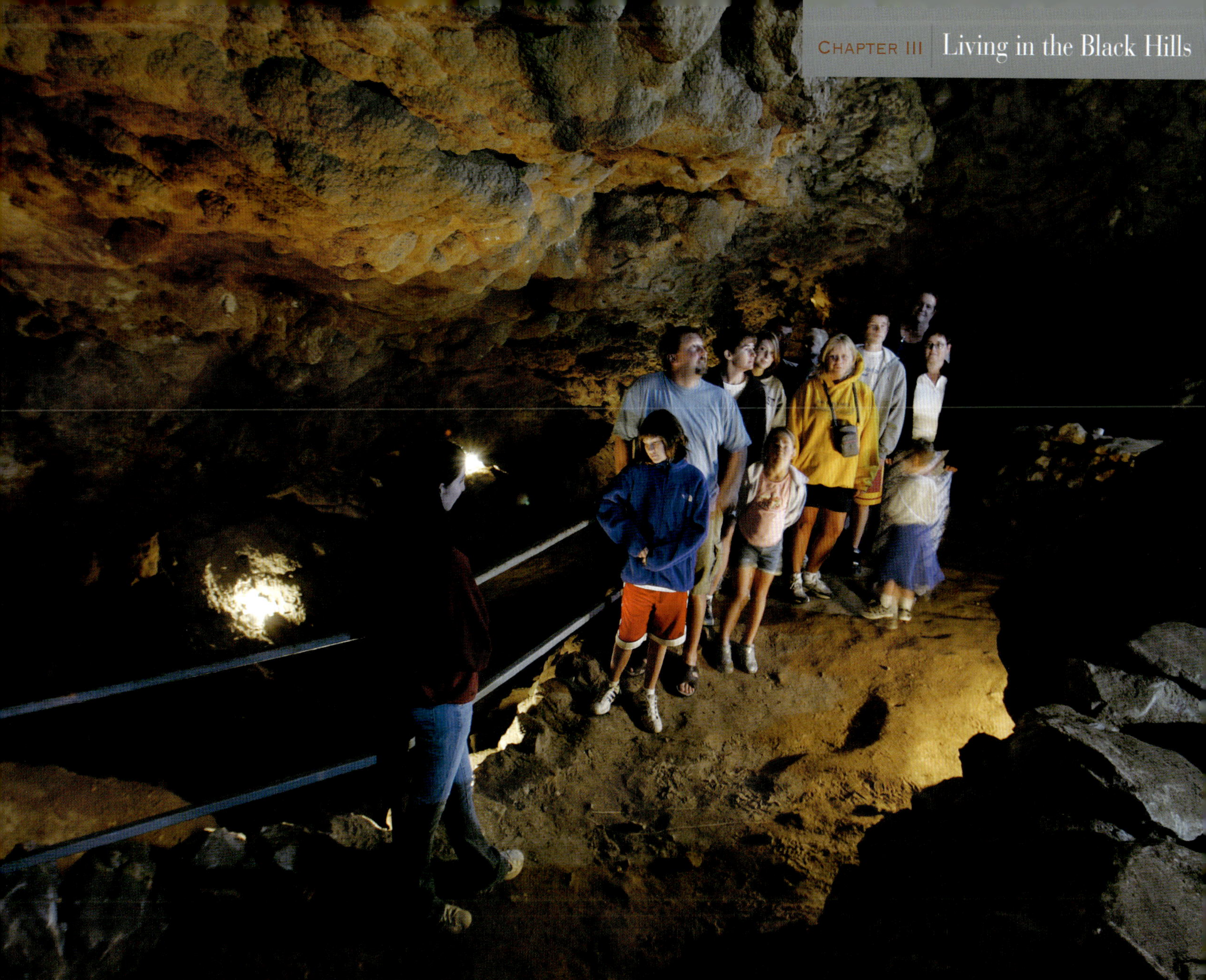

Photo by Eric Francis

Typically, a three-quarter-mile walk in forty-eight-degree temperatures doesn't sound very appealing. However, when that somewhat chilly journey takes place in the Black Hills Caverns, the trek becomes a true adventure. Located in a band of "paha sapa" limestone, the Lakota phrase meaning "hills that are black," the cavern actually comprises three levels of underground rooms that were created through different periods of the Earth's history. Within these rooms are a variety of fascinating formations that date back more than 6 million years, from sparkling stalagmites and stalactites to dazzling logomites, helictites, flowstone, columns, draperies, and rare frost crystal. In 1882, gold seekers discovered the multilevel cave, which is part of the second-longest cave system in the world. Guided tours of the caverns' rooms—including the "Hole in the Ceiling Room," the "Lions Den," and "The Pit"—are a popular tourist activity for people who want to literally step back in time to the earliest days of the celebrated Black Hills region. ❖

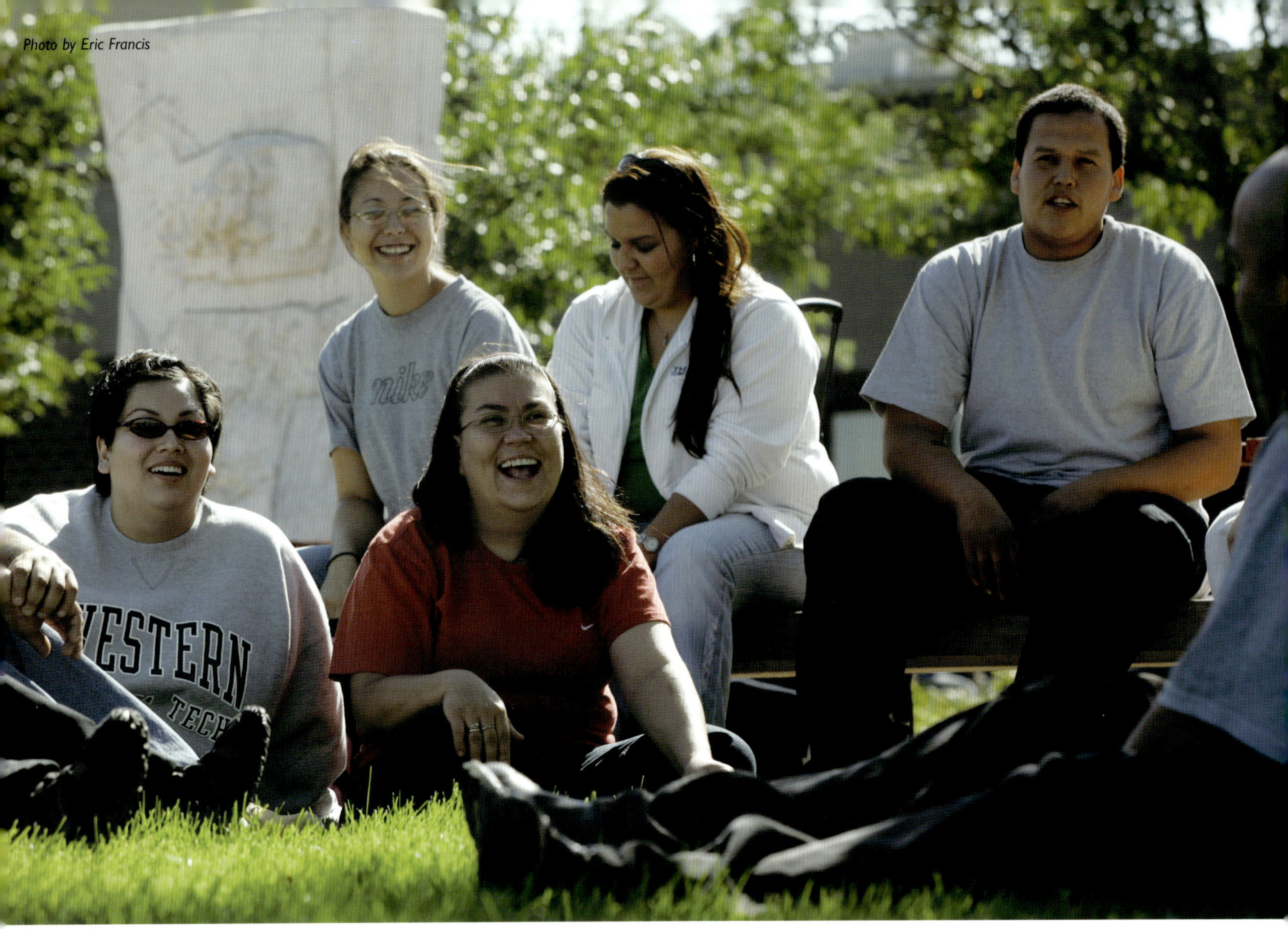

Photo by Eric Francis

▲ **An education at** Western Dakota Tech is a hands-on experience where students apply classroom theory to real-life projects. This type of study prepares students to enter the workforce upon graduation fully capable of completing the tasks at hand. As part of the school's welding manufacturing program, students learn a wide, and ever-evolving, variety of techniques and processes. Diplomas, associate degrees, and certifications are available in this area of study, and students may also opt to participate in internships with welding or machining companies. ❖

Western Dakota Tech serves a ▶ diverse group of students, equipping them with the communication, teamwork, and other core skills they need to succeed in their careers and in life. Individuals participating in any one of a number of student groups, such as the Student Government Association or the Eagle Feather Society, learn hands-on what it means to make a real impact on other students and members of the community through their activities on campus and in the local area. ❖

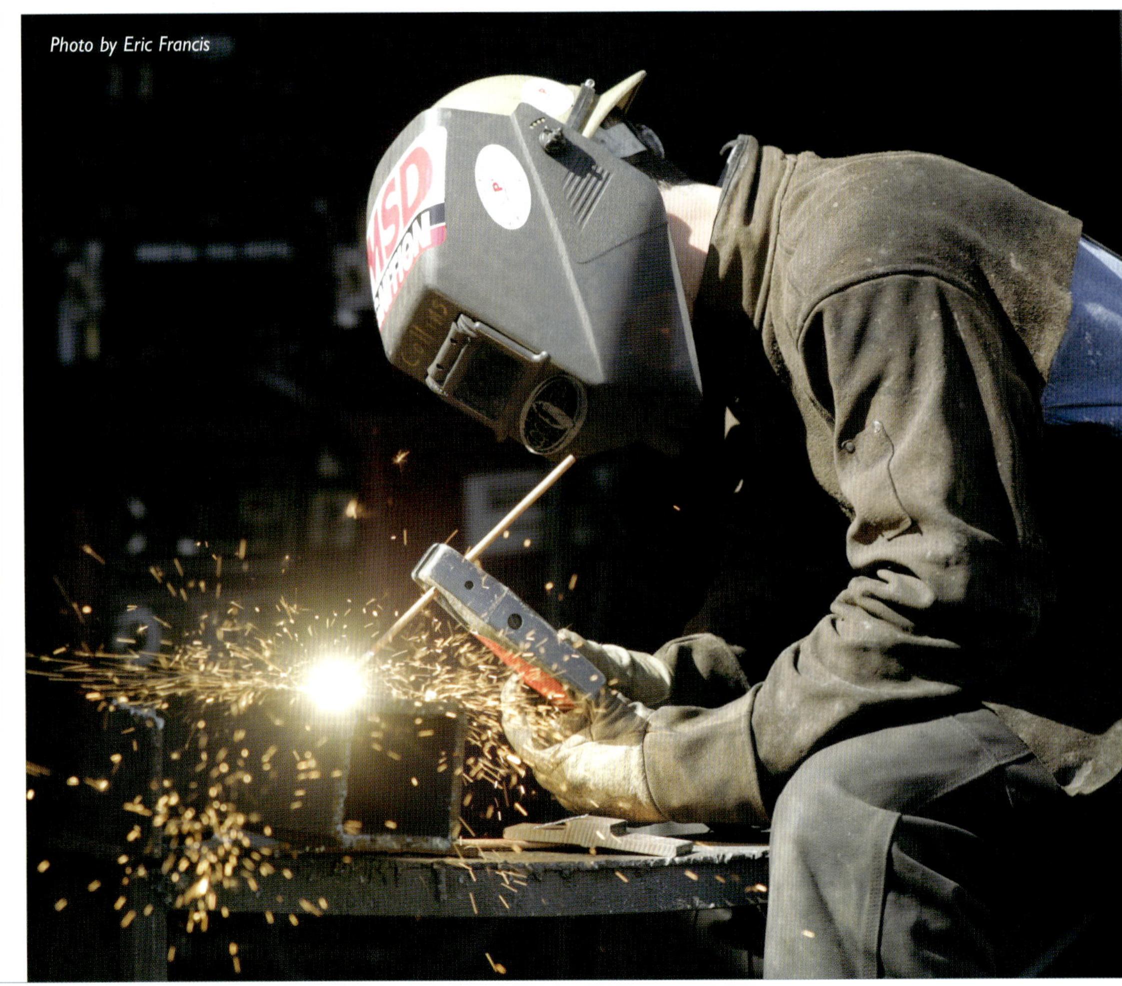

Photo by Eric Francis

Photo by Eric Francis

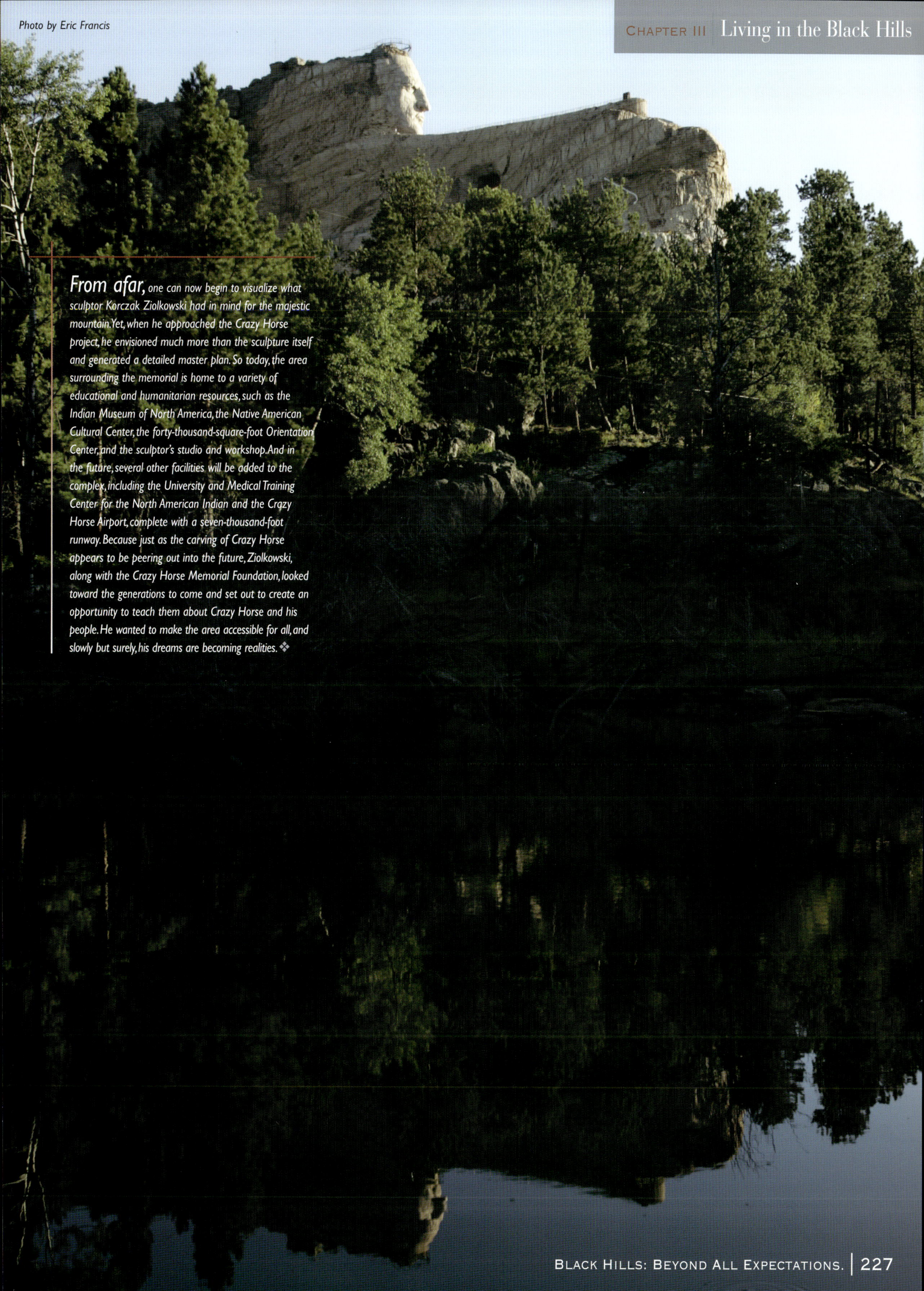

From afar, one can now begin to visualize what sculptor Korczak Ziolkowski had in mind for the majestic mountain. Yet, when he approached the Crazy Horse project, he envisioned much more than the sculpture itself and generated a detailed master plan. So today, the area surrounding the memorial is home to a variety of educational and humanitarian resources, such as the Indian Museum of North America, the Native American Cultural Center, the forty-thousand-square-foot Orientation Center, and the sculptor's studio and workshop. And in the future, several other facilities will be added to the complex, including the University and Medical Training Center for the North American Indian and the Crazy Horse Airport, complete with a seven-thousand-foot runway. Because just as the carving of Crazy Horse appears to be peering out into the future, Ziolkowski, along with the Crazy Horse Memorial Foundation, looked toward the generations to come and set out to create an opportunity to teach them about Crazy Horse and his people. He wanted to make the area accessible for all, and slowly but surely, his dreams are becoming realities. ❖

Fountain Springs Health Care Redefines Long-Term Care

When generations can come together, everyone benefits. That's the guiding philosophy of the Fountain Springs Community in Rapid City. "By partnering with families, we can honor the ones we love," says Dave Simpson, founder and managing partner of the community, which includes a long-term and rehabilitation health-care facility, a child-care center, an apartment complex for low-income seniors, a retirement condominium complex, and a nine-hole public golf course.

The multigenerational dimension of the Fountain Springs Community is just one of its distinguishing aspects. Creating the most homelike atmosphere of Fountain Springs Health Care Center, the cornerstone of the overall community, is another. As one of the newest health-care facilities in the state, the nursing home is anything but the typical nursing home. In fact, Fountain Springs Health Care redefines long-term and rehabilitative care, starting with the architecture. Instead of the traditional nondescript nurses' station and administrative offices, a turn-of-the-century Main Street welcomes guests and brings a bit of nostalgia to the residents. The town square also serves as a social gathering spot

"It's our hope that by honoring the lives of our residents through remembering the era in which they lived, families will be brought closer together."

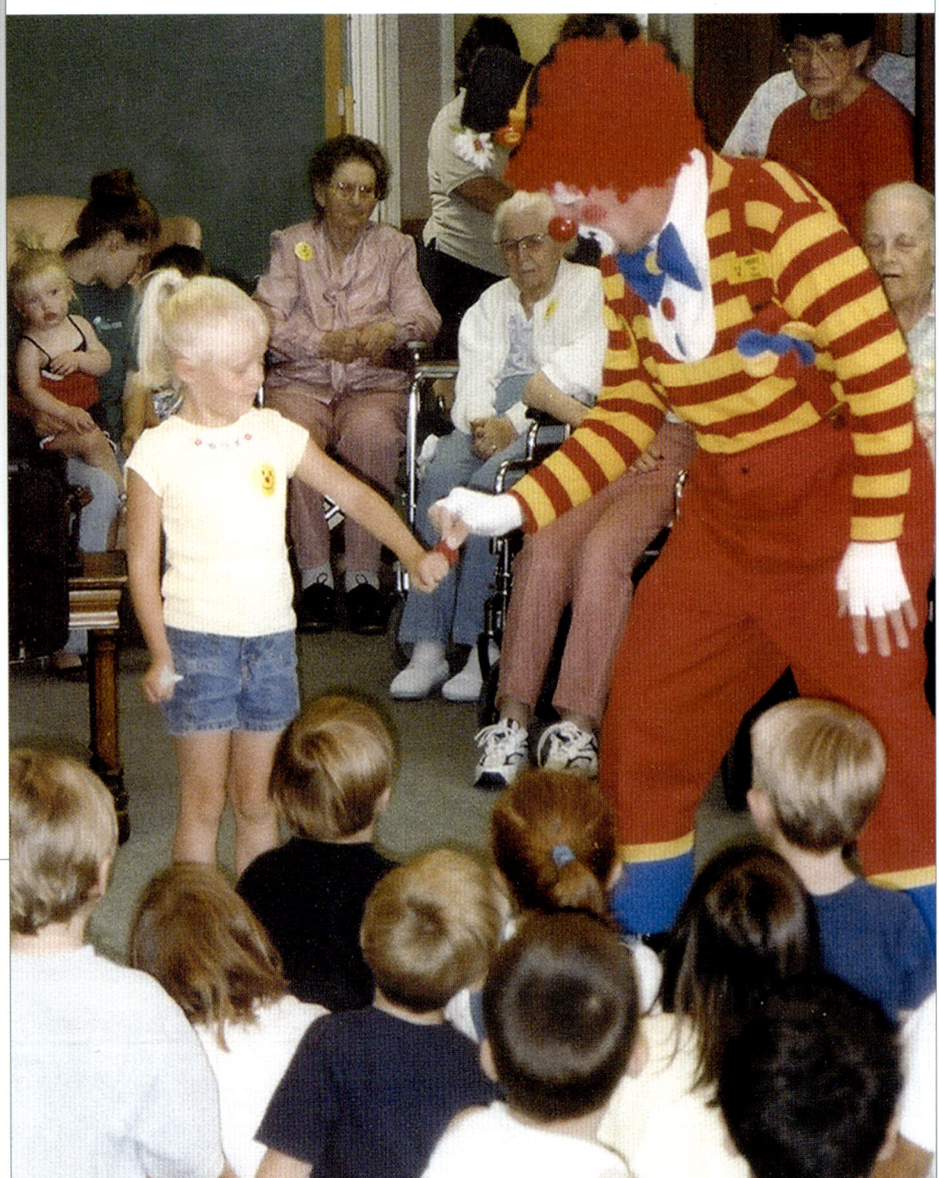

Laughter is ageless at Fountain Springs, and Bobo the clown enjoys bringing generations together.

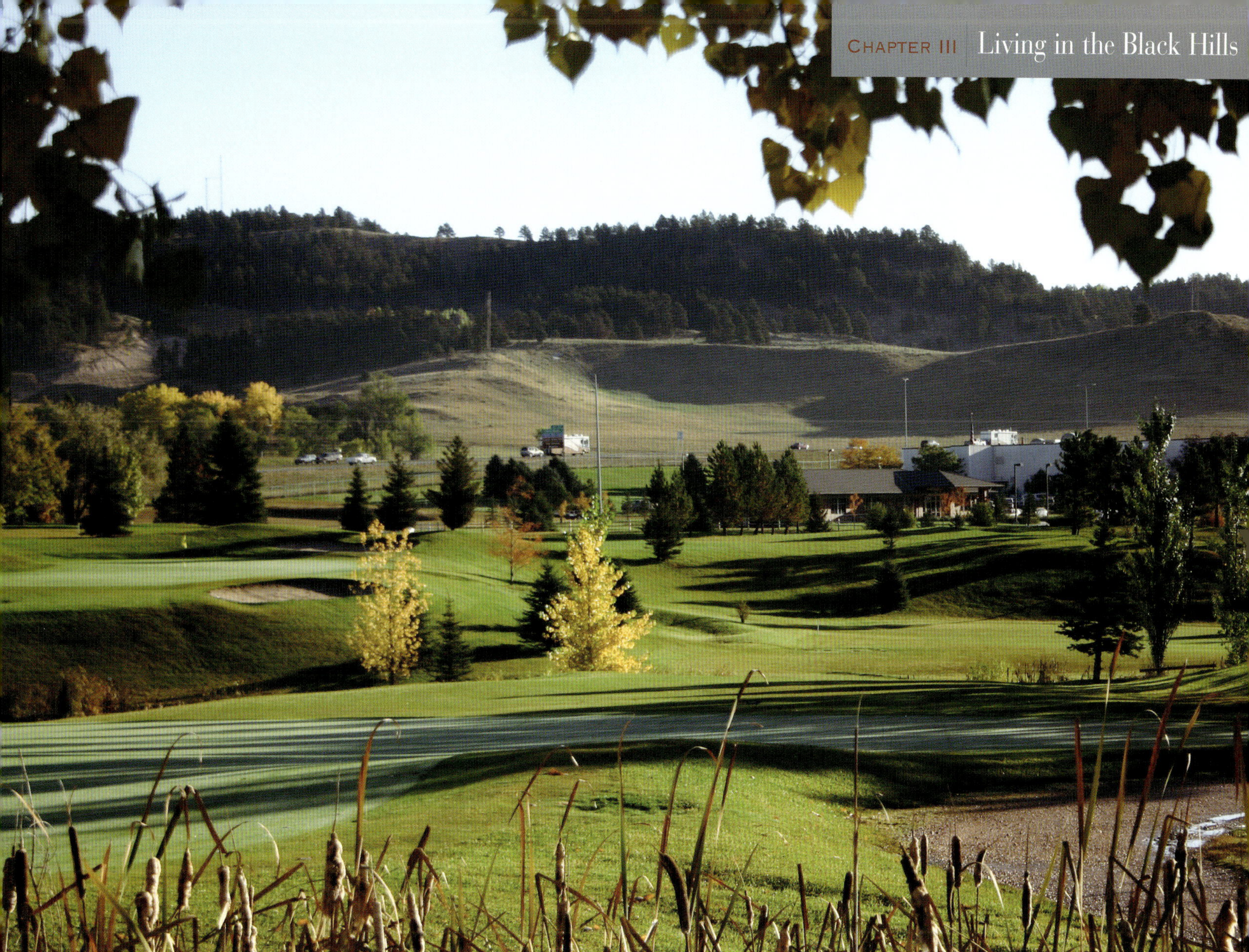

Golfers might be distracted by the view at the fifth hole of Fountain Springs Golf Course.

for residents and their visitors. There's a one-room country school where visiting children can enjoy their grandparents, a mercantile storefront that displays historical photographs from the Journey Museum, and even an old-fashioned ice cream shop where residents and visitors can help themselves to a tasty treat. "It's our hope that by honoring the lives of our residents through remembering the era in which they lived, families will be brought closer together," says Simpson. "People can feel like they're living in a caring facility, not just a medical facility."

Behind the thoughtful and cheerful ambience of the locally owned and operated Fountain Springs Health Care Center is a facility providing superior care to its ninety residents. Individualized attention is given to each resident by a competent staff of licensed nurses, certified nursing assistants, and dietary and other support staff. In addition, physical therapy, occupational therapy, and speech therapy are available to each individual, as directed by each resident's physician. Additional medical services, such as dental care, podiatry, and eye care, are arranged through the staff.

Fountain Springs Health Care's accommodations also differentiate the facility from others. In addition to having an ample number of private rooms, the facility offers the option of a "combination room," where a married couple can remain together even when only one requires the specialized services of a skilled nursing facility. In addition, a special-care wing is dedicated to those with advanced Alzheimer's and dementia. While there truly is "no place like home," when a long-term care facility becomes necessary, shouldn't it be the most homelike setting available? Fountain Springs Health Care thinks so.

"Through our commitment to compassion and quality, Fountain Springs Health Care continually strives to advance the care of our residents," says Simpson. ❖

The Black Hills are an oasis of pine-clad mountains on the Great Plains. Every year thousands of visitors come to enjoy national parks, scenic drives, waterfalls, wildlife, recreational trails, and trout fishing. Residents may take all of this for granted. One thing they don't take for granted is the outstanding level of health care offered in the Black Hills region. Hospitals and specialty clinics abound. Pictured left to right are Prema Abraham, MD; Robert Nixon, MD; Monte Dirks, MD; Paul Zimmerman, MD; Timothy Minton, MD; and Daniel Hafner, MD. These Black Hills Regional Eye Institute owners and surgeons are part of the greater medical community serving the area. They began providing eye care to the Black Hills in 1982. ❖

Photo by Rodger Slott

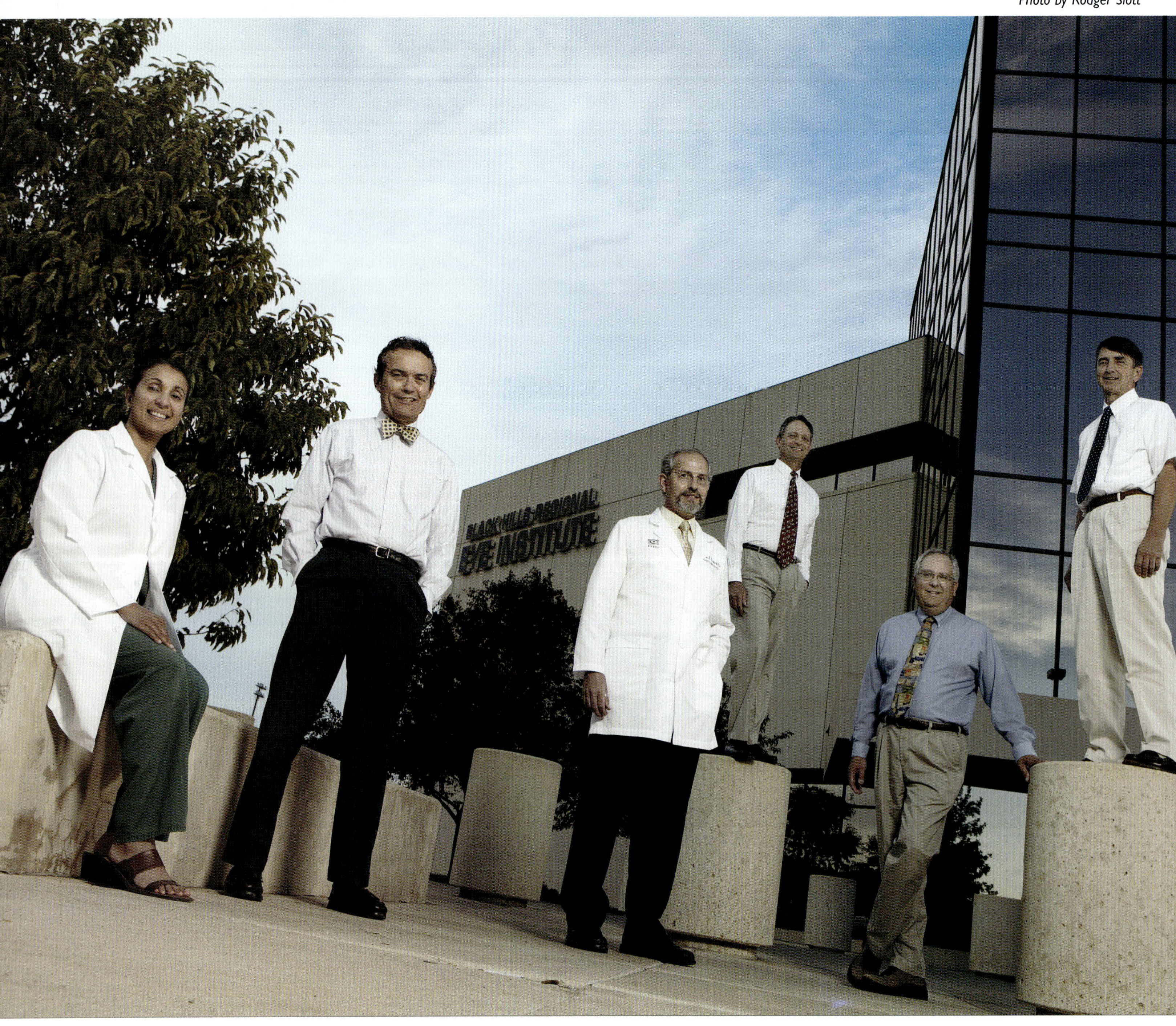

Photo by Thomas S. England

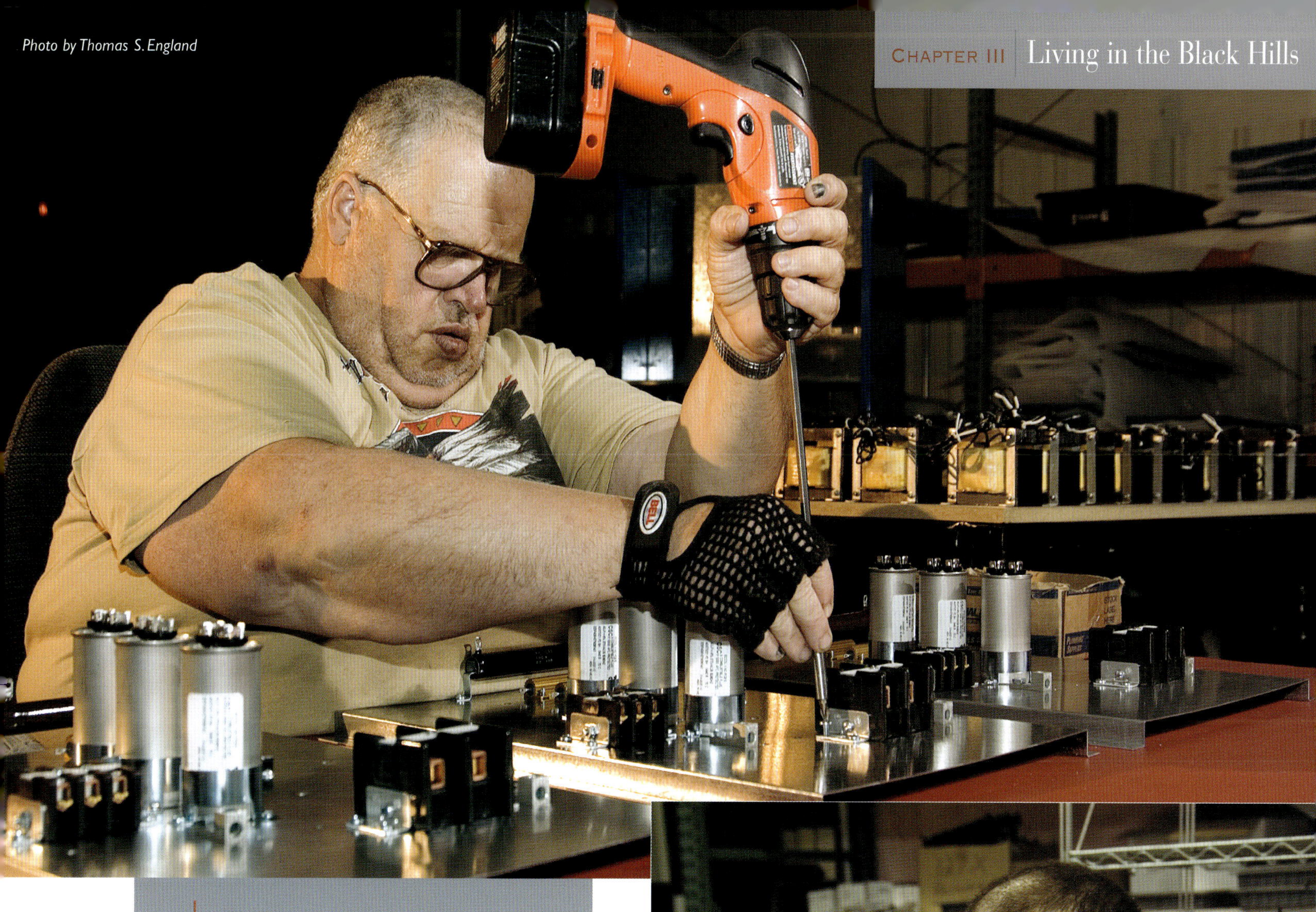

The Employment Resources Division of the Black Hills Workshop helps people find jobs in the community. Clients receive individualized instruction at the job site as well as continuing support for employers such as Phase Technologies. In addition to light manufacturing and electronics, BHW provides vocational training for a number of other jobs including food service, housekeeping, janitorial services, maintenance, and packaging. Other employers include the U.S. Department of Defense, Rapid City Regional Hospital, South Dakota Department of Tourism, SymCom Inc. (electronic controls), and the South Dakota Department of Game, Fish and Parks. ❖

Everybody likes killing two birds with one stone, but sometimes you can do even better than that. The next time you need a toner cartridge for your ink jet or laser printer, if you order it from Dakota Laser Tech, you will be saving yourself some money, supporting the work of the Black Hills Workshop, and giving someone a chance at independence they might not have otherwise. The Black Hills Workshop's mission is to provide quality services and supports to people with disabilities so they can explore opportunities and make choices. This community rehabilitation program for adults with disabilities was established in 1958 and has provided employment for hundreds of individuals with special needs. ❖

Photo by Thomas S. England

NAU Combines Quality Education with Practical Experience

National American University is in the career enhancement business. Beyond the obvious—educating its diverse student body—this affordable private university is all about getting people jobs, or getting people better jobs. It's about developing marketable skills. Enhancing careers. Meeting the needs of today's employers. Most of all, it's about preparing students for tomorrow's world today.

"We're career focused. That's what drives us," says Richard Buckles, JD, CPA, vice president of the Rapid City campus. Since 1941, this campus has turned out students who find a job in their field quickly and can hit the ground running. "As a private career

This timely and comprehensive real-world approach to education means the students learn with a purpose and are work-ready upon graduation.

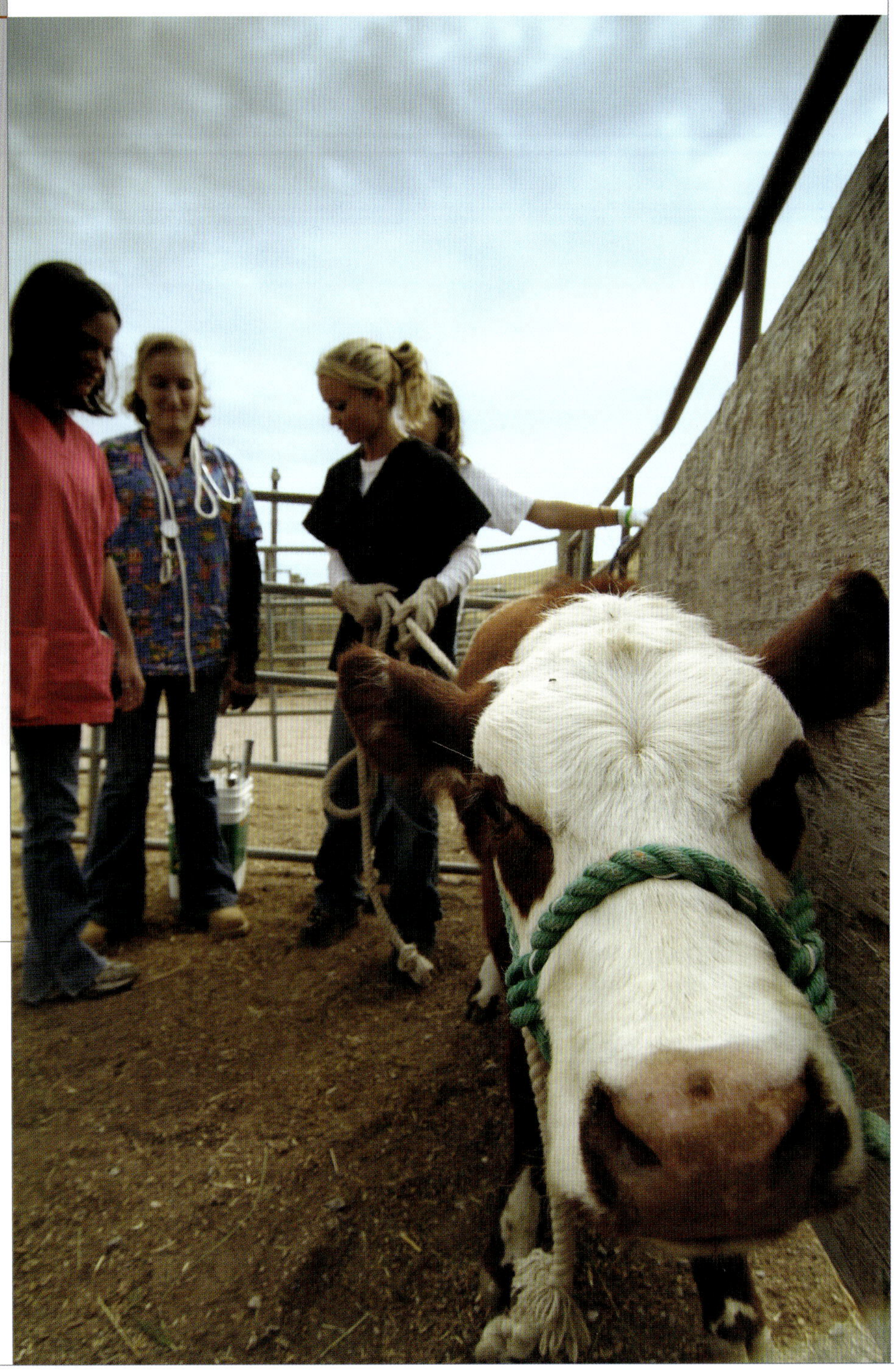

Veterinary technology students practice the approved methods they learned in Dr. Rabe's Animal Restraint class at National American University.

Photo by Doug Henderson

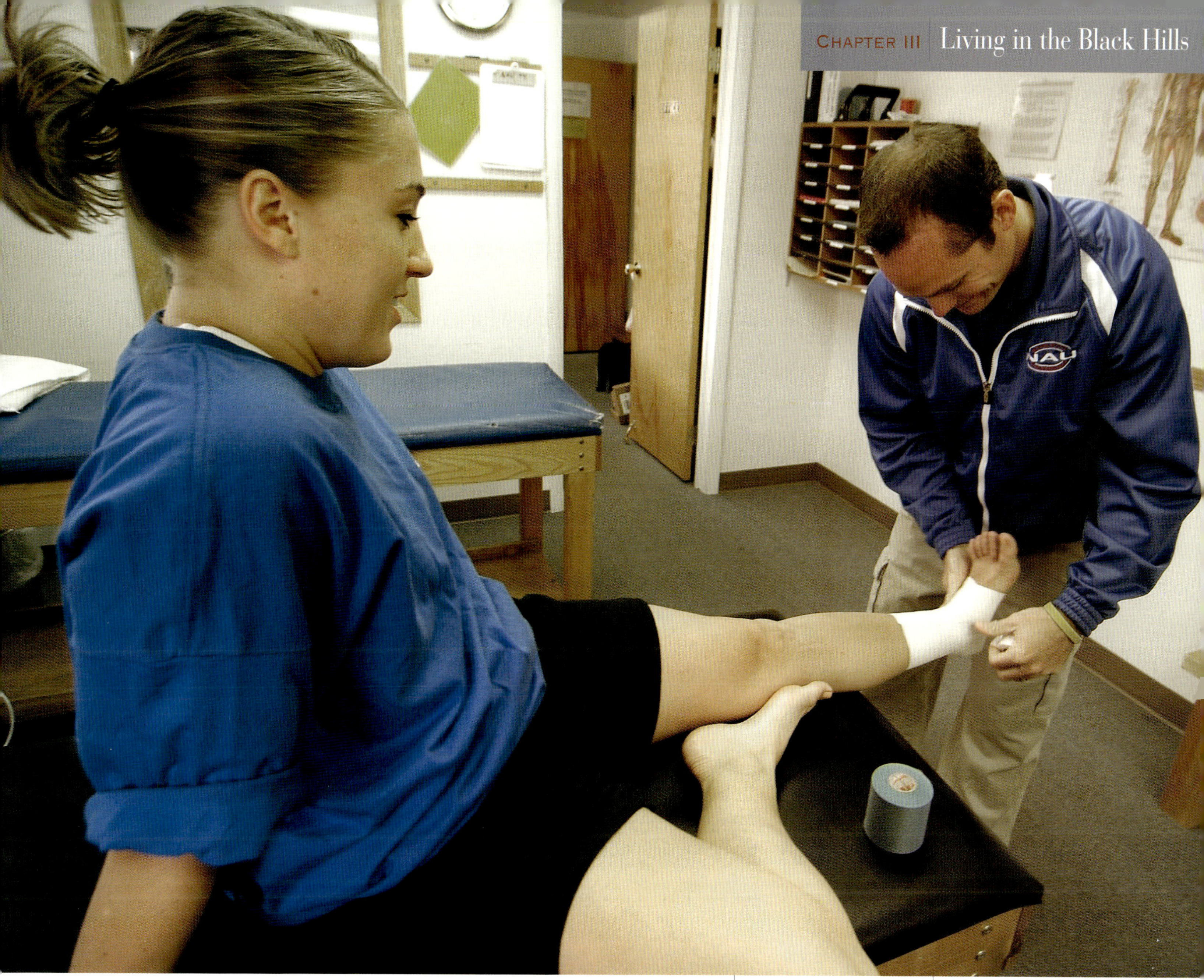

Photo by Doug Henderson

Josh Ellis, athletic training clinical coordinator, demonstrates a taping technique to Kodi Marker of Wheatland, Wyoming. NAU's athletic training program moved into its new facility in 2006.

university, NAU has the infrastructure that allows us to respond rapidly to the shifting needs of the workplace," explains Buckles. Practicing professionals serve on industry advisory groups in every instructional program to provide meaningful input into the curriculum design and review process. A highly qualified faculty features instructors holding master's degrees or higher with significant experience in their field. This timely and comprehensive real-world approach to education means the students learn with a purpose and are work-ready upon graduation.

NAU only offers programs culminating in associate's, bachelor's, or master's degrees or diplomas that are in high demand in the marketplace, thus ensuring that each graduate has a degree they can use. From business administration and information technology programs such as accounting, marketing, network administration, international business, and pre-law, to health-care management, athletic training, veterinary technology, equine management, and paralegal studies, NAU provides a strong foundation to excel in a range of traditional and emerging careers.

Most programs are structured so that students begin field coursework in the first year. "For example, in the equine management program, each student is assigned a horse to start training on day one," explains Buckles. "In other schools, you may exercise the horse that someone else is working with, but you will not be involved in actual training until your second year." Additionally, every instructional

Continued on page 234

Continued from page 233

program has a strong business core so that all completing students have developed quantitative and communication skills; a foundation in technology, accounting, economics, management, and marketing; and breadth and depth in their chosen field. "The IT students, for example, are learning systems design, programming, and networking, but also receiving a management degree and can be a businessperson in their field," says Lois Facer, academic dean. "Our veterinary technology program graduates have a 98 percent licensing pass rate. We're training people to walk into a position and impress their employers with their practical experience."

NAU's commitment to student success is also evident in other ways. "In addition to high-quality programs, NAU's small size and family culture are strengths," says Peggy Schlechter, dean of student success, whose title says it all. Student services are provided through personnel, programs, and procedures to stimulate student development, as well as personal and social growth. An academic advisor works with every student each and every quarter. Free tutoring and organized study groups are readily available. All students are required to take a career management class. In addition, through the career services department, students and staff work together to identify career objectives and seek out employment opportunities that fit the individual's needs. "We make a real connection with every student," says Schlechter. "The reward is the enjoyment of hearing good news from our students about their accomplishments long after they've graduated." ❖

Photo by Doug Henderson

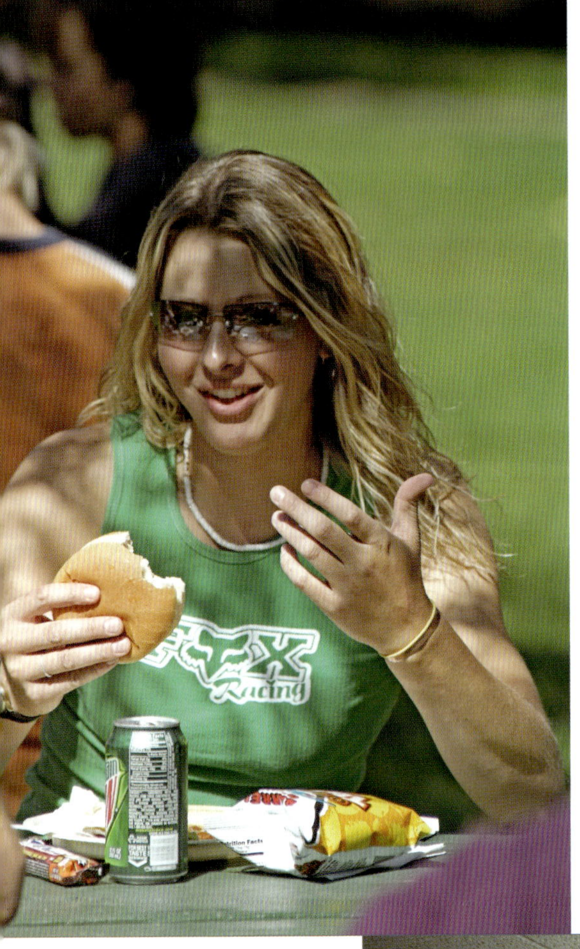

Carrie Ostrander, an equine management major from Rushville, Nebraska, catches some shade at NAU's autumn picnic. As a student senator, Carrie helps plan activities for the Rapid City campus students.

After a day of classes and volleyball at NAU, Heather Cox channel surfs in her dorm room. Heather is a senior business administration major from Colorado Springs, Colorado.

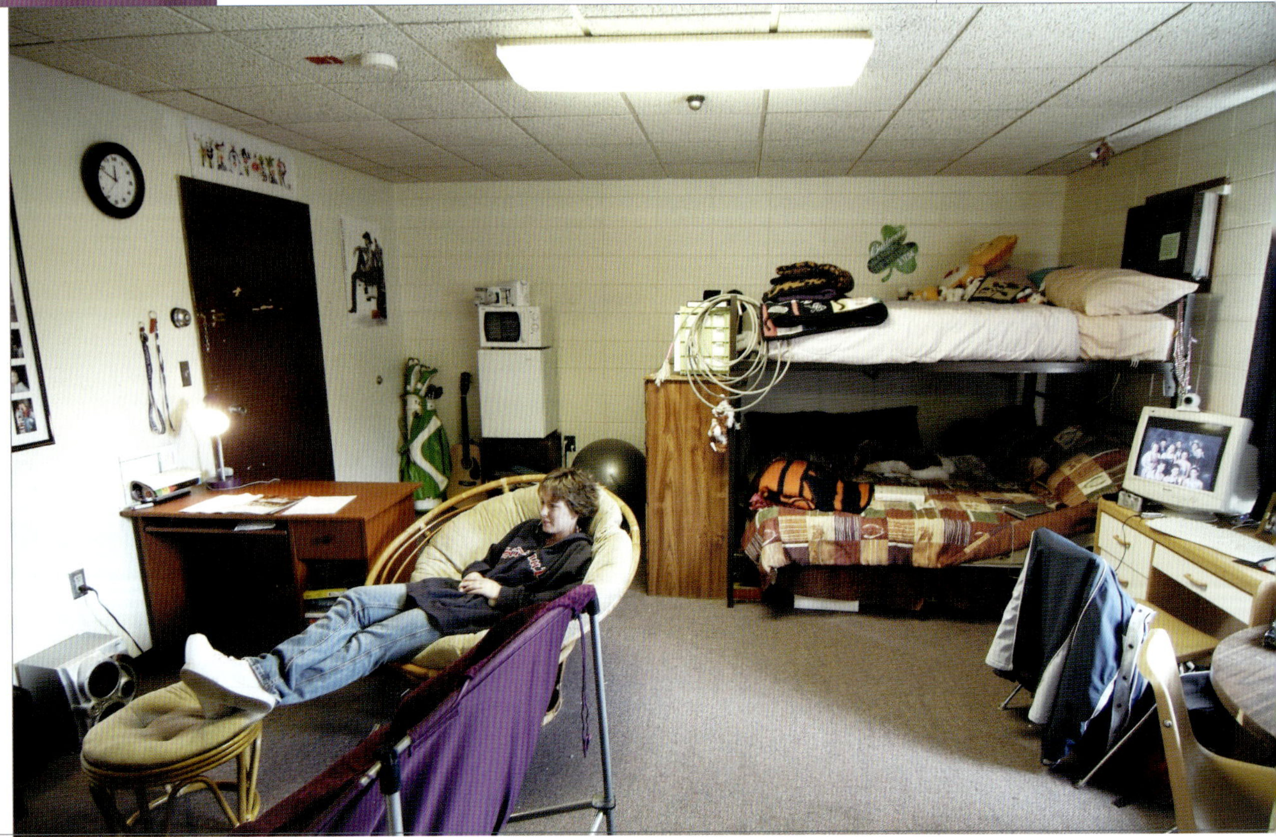

Photo by Doug Henderson

relax and enjoy

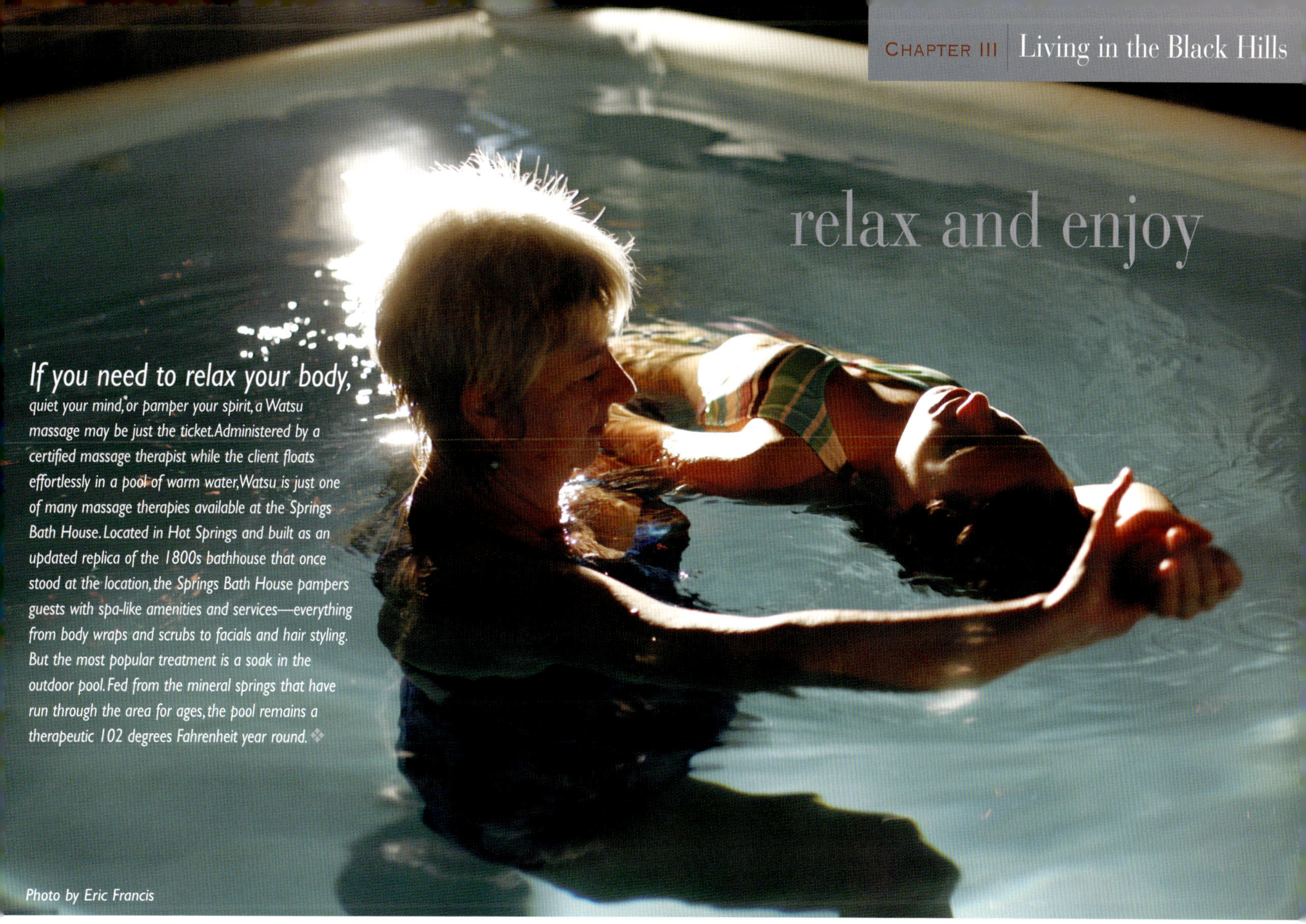

If you need to relax your body, quiet your mind, or pamper your spirit, a Watsu massage may be just the ticket. Administered by a certified massage therapist while the client floats effortlessly in a pool of warm water, Watsu is just one of many massage therapies available at the Springs Bath House. Located in Hot Springs and built as an updated replica of the 1800s bathhouse that once stood at the location, the Springs Bath House pampers guests with spa-like amenities and services—everything from body wraps and scrubs to facials and hair styling. But the most popular treatment is a soak in the outdoor pool. Fed from the mineral springs that have run through the area for ages, the pool remains a therapeutic 102 degrees Fahrenheit year round. ❖

Photo by Eric Francis

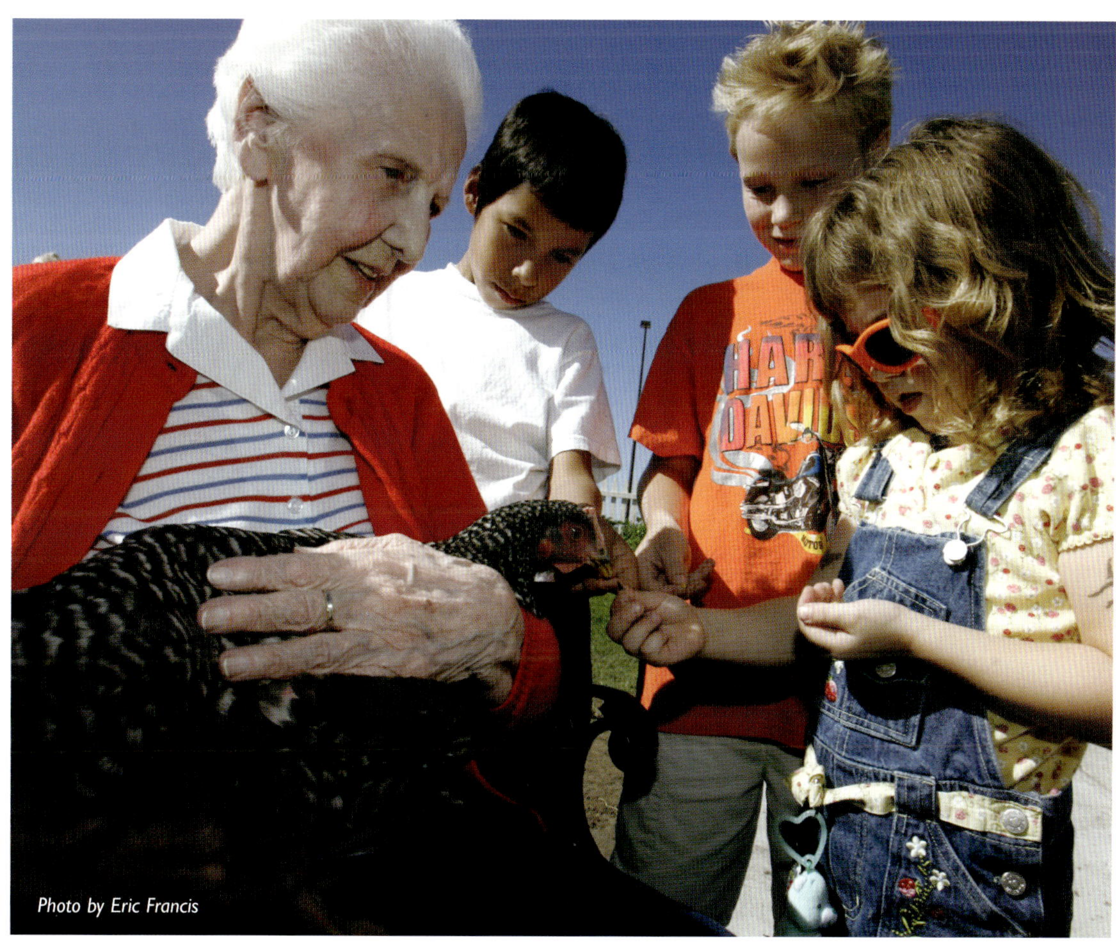

Photo by Eric Francis

Nothing brings about smiles quite like children and animals. Add in a friendly and wise grandmotherly elder, and the smiles are sure to turn to rich conversation. Here, residents from Fountain Springs, a unique long-term care facility with an on-site child-care center, bridge the generation gap by sharing a farm experience together. These activities are everyday events at Fountain Springs, which is known for its multi-generational philosophy. ❖

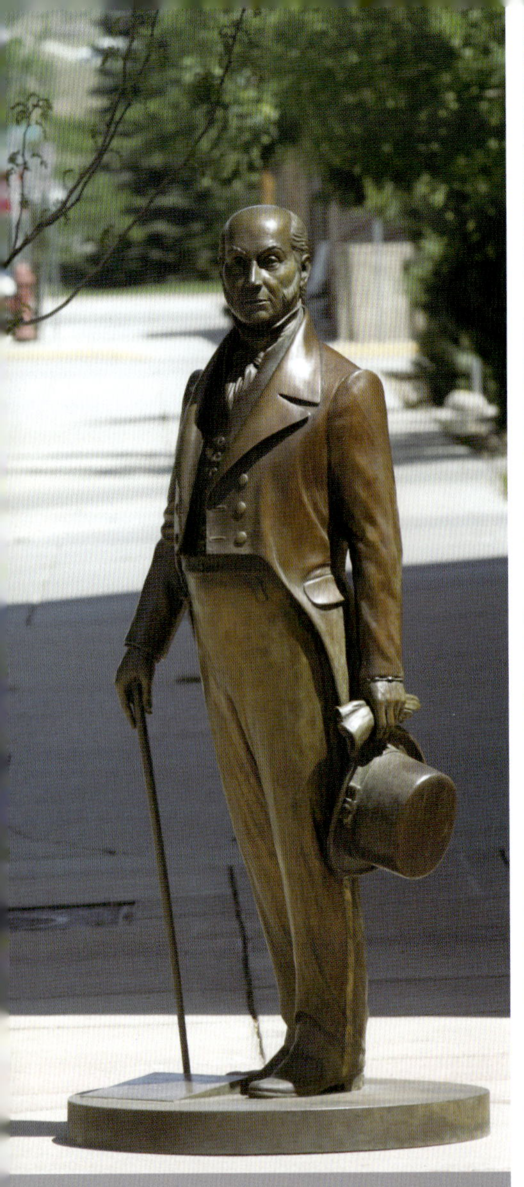

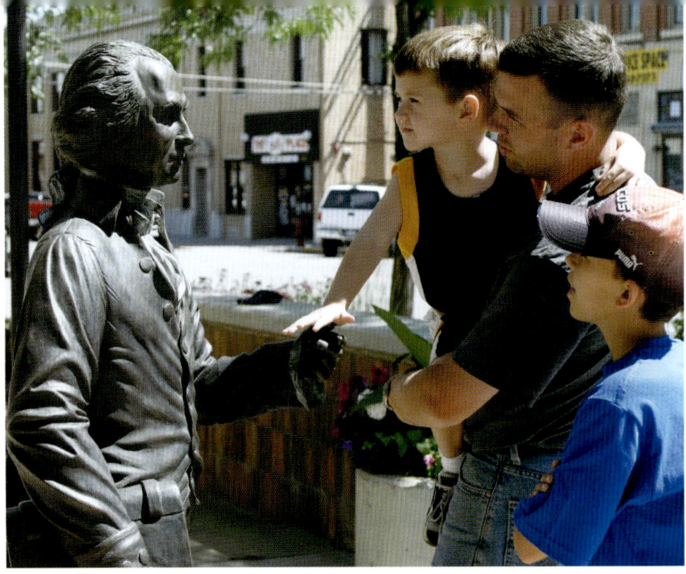

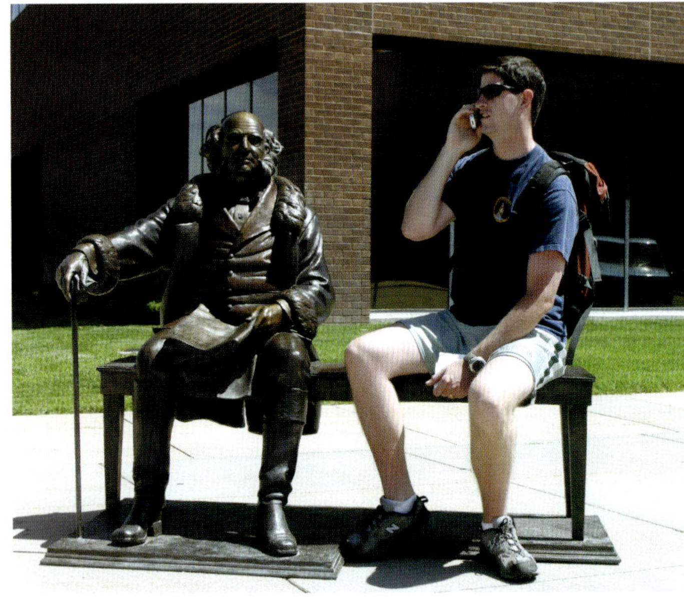

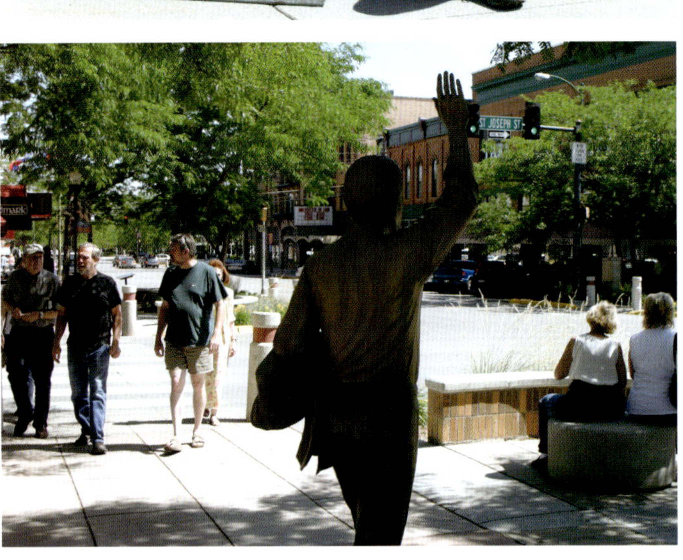

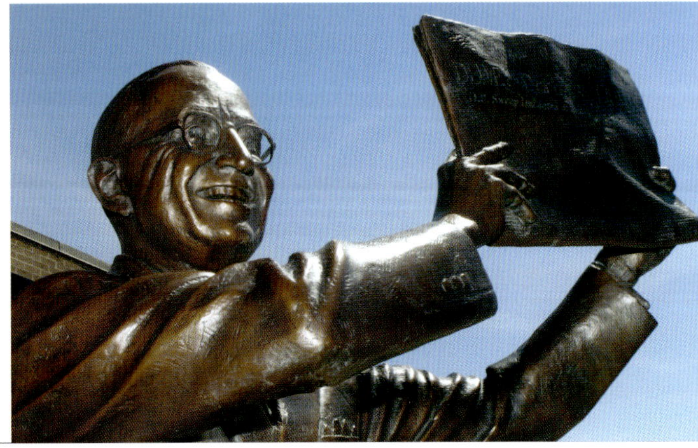

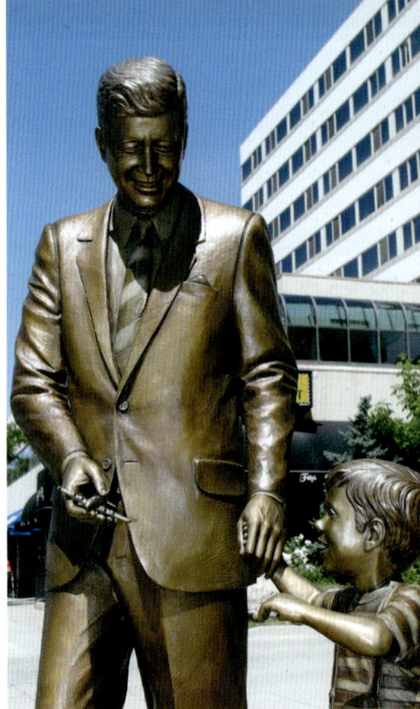

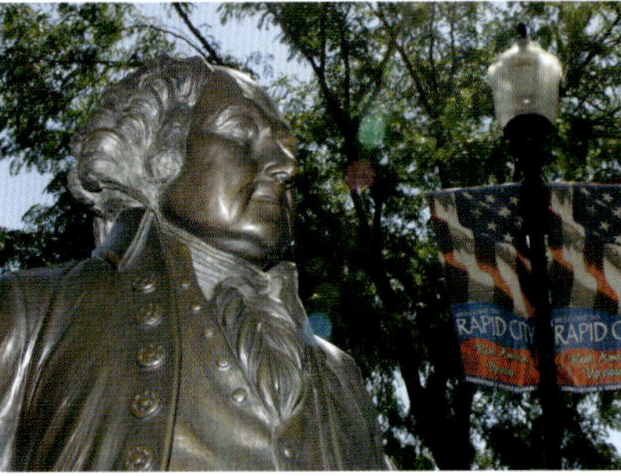

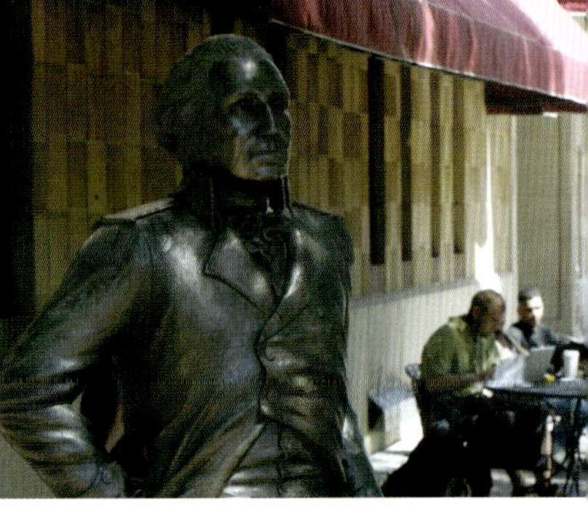

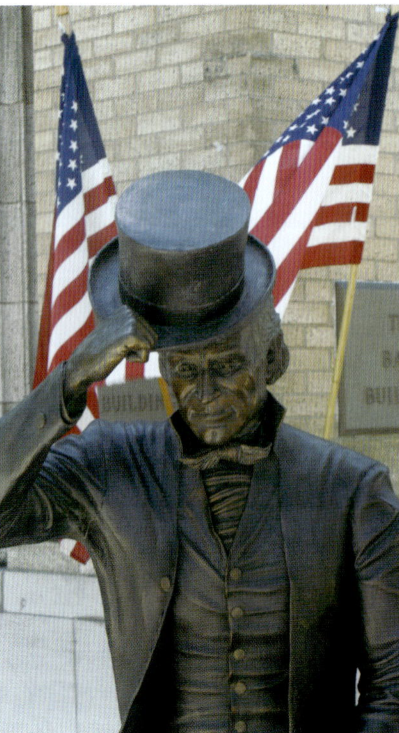

When people think about

U.S. presidents and Rapid City, they automatically envision George Washington, Thomas Jefferson, Theodore Roosevelt, and Abraham Lincoln—the distinguished faces that look down from high atop Mount Rushmore. However, in 2000, more commanders-in-chief began making appearances in the city's historic downtown area, thanks to the City of Presidents project. In fact, on strategic street corners along Main Street and St. Joseph Street, residents and visitors now come face-to-face with life-size bronze sculptures of the nation's most notable leaders, from George Washington and John Adams to John F. Kennedy and Ronald Reagan. Ultimately, by 2011, the first forty presidents will be represented with statues created by some of South Dakota's most renowned sculptors, who plan to add four presidents each year—two from the country's earliest days and two from more recent times—for the duration of the ten-year project. The sculptures feature the chief executives wearing period clothing and include inscriptions that describe each man's character and greatest accomplishments. ❖

Photos by Alan S. Weiner

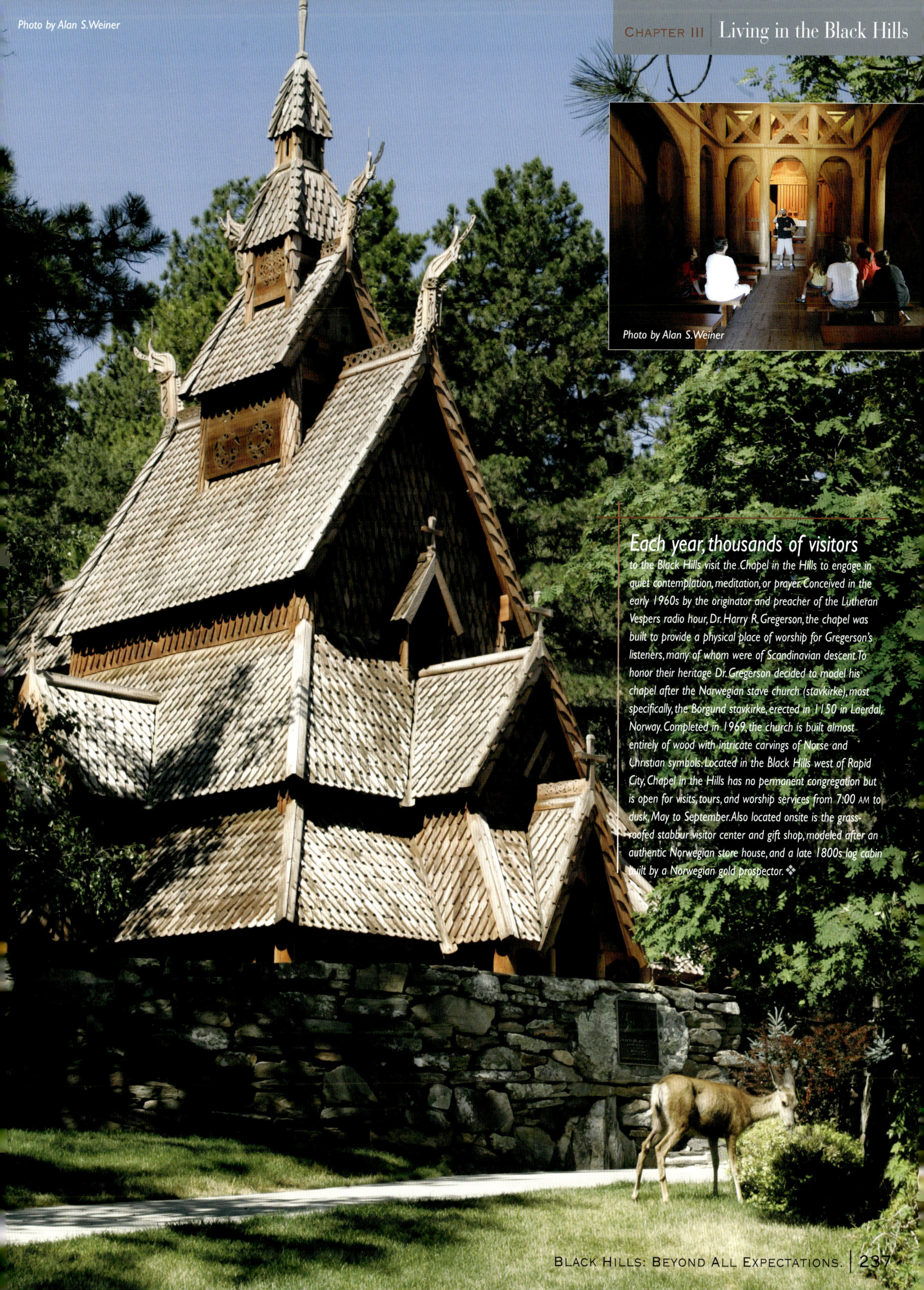

Photo by Alan S.Weiner

Photo by Alan S.Weiner

Each year, thousands of visitors to the Black Hills visit the Chapel in the Hills to engage in quiet contemplation, meditation, or prayer. Conceived in the early 1960s by the originator and preacher of the Lutheran Vespers radio hour, Dr. Harry R. Gregerson, the chapel was built to provide a physical place of worship for Gregerson's listeners, many of whom were of Scandinavian descent. To honor their heritage Dr. Gregerson decided to model his chapel after the Norwegian stave church (stavkirke), most specifically, the Borgund stavkirke, erected in 1150 in Laerdal, Norway. Completed in 1969, the church is built almost entirely of wood with intricate carvings of Norse and Christian symbols. Located in the Black Hills west of Rapid City, Chapel in the Hills has no permanent congregation but is open for visits, tours, and worship services from 7:00 AM to dusk, May to September. Also located onsite is the grass-roofed stabbur visitor center and gift shop, modeled after an authentic Norwegian store house, and a late 1800s log cabin built by a Norwegian gold prospector. ❖

Black Hills Surgery Center Pampers Patients with Individual Care

Fresh flowers waiting in your room. Warm, rich colors throughout the facility. Laptops available upon request. A choice of gourmet meals. It sounds like a five-star hotel, but it is just standard operating procedure at Black Hills Surgery Center, a specialty hospital.

Why this departure from the hospital food, noisy tile floors, and medicinal odors? "Quality," says BHSC's chief operating officer Bill May. "When patients are more comfortable and receive more individual care, they get better faster. Additionally, at Black Hills Surgery Center, patients have shorter stays and less risk of infection."

"When patients are more comfortable and receive more individual care, they get better faster."

The key is to reduce the disruption to a patient's personal routine. Unlike a hospital that may view a visitor or family member as an intrusion on the hospital's routine and policies, Black Hills Surgery Center understands that friends and family are crucial to patients' emotional support and recovery.

"We know that patients feel more secure having a loved one with them during their hospital stay, so we look after their needs. Each of our rooms has a Murphy bed and amenities to accommodate a friend or family member," May said.

Photo by Alan S.Weiner

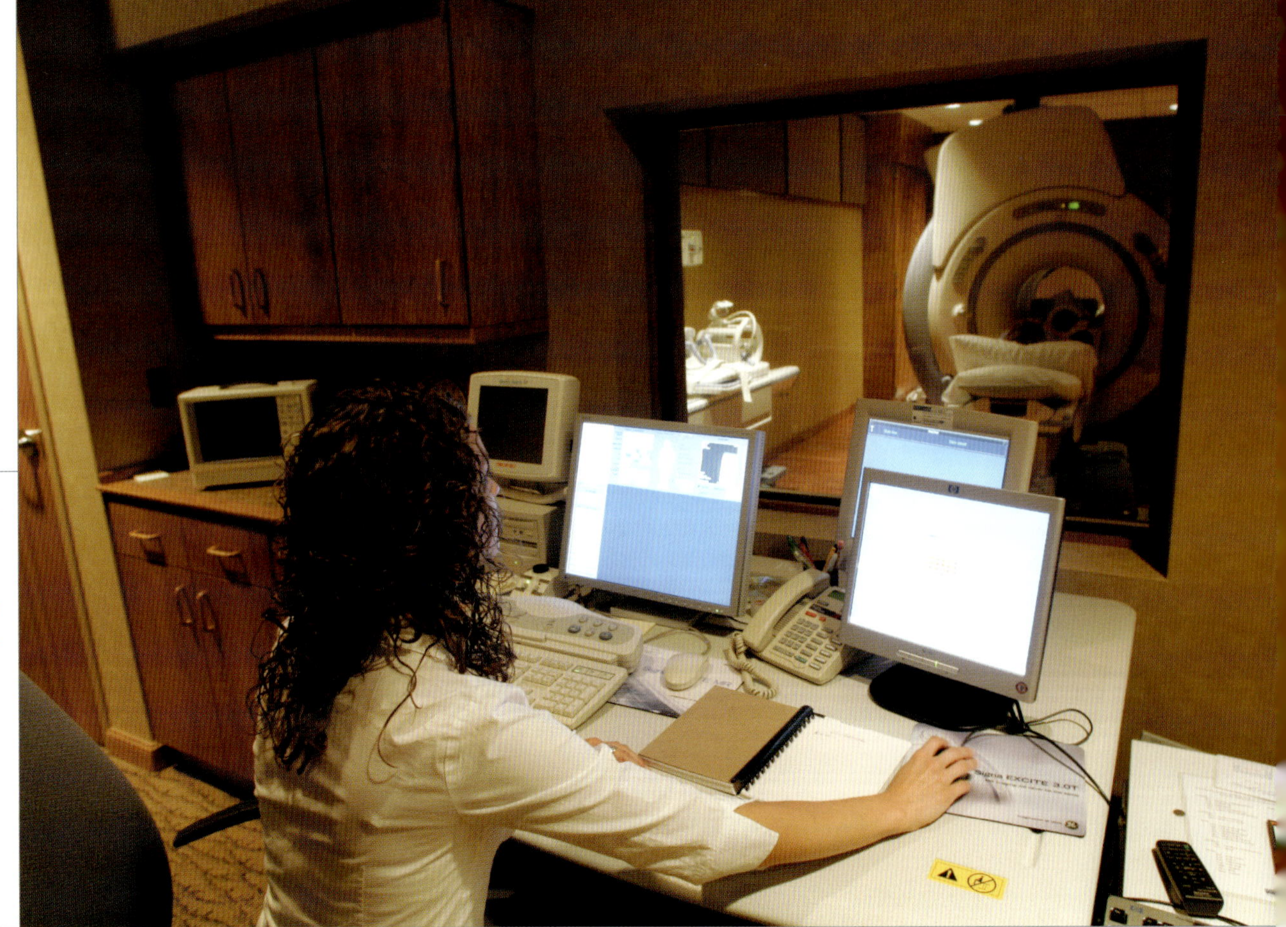

Medical experts predict modern specialty hospitals like Black Hills Surgery Center are the wave of the future. By their very nature they specialize in select areas, and research has shown that clinical quality is directly correlated to the volume and frequency of procedures performed. They can also provide the most modern technology—like this high-tech MRI machine—at a lower cost than the older hospital models that must spread their budgets and personnel over dozens of departments.

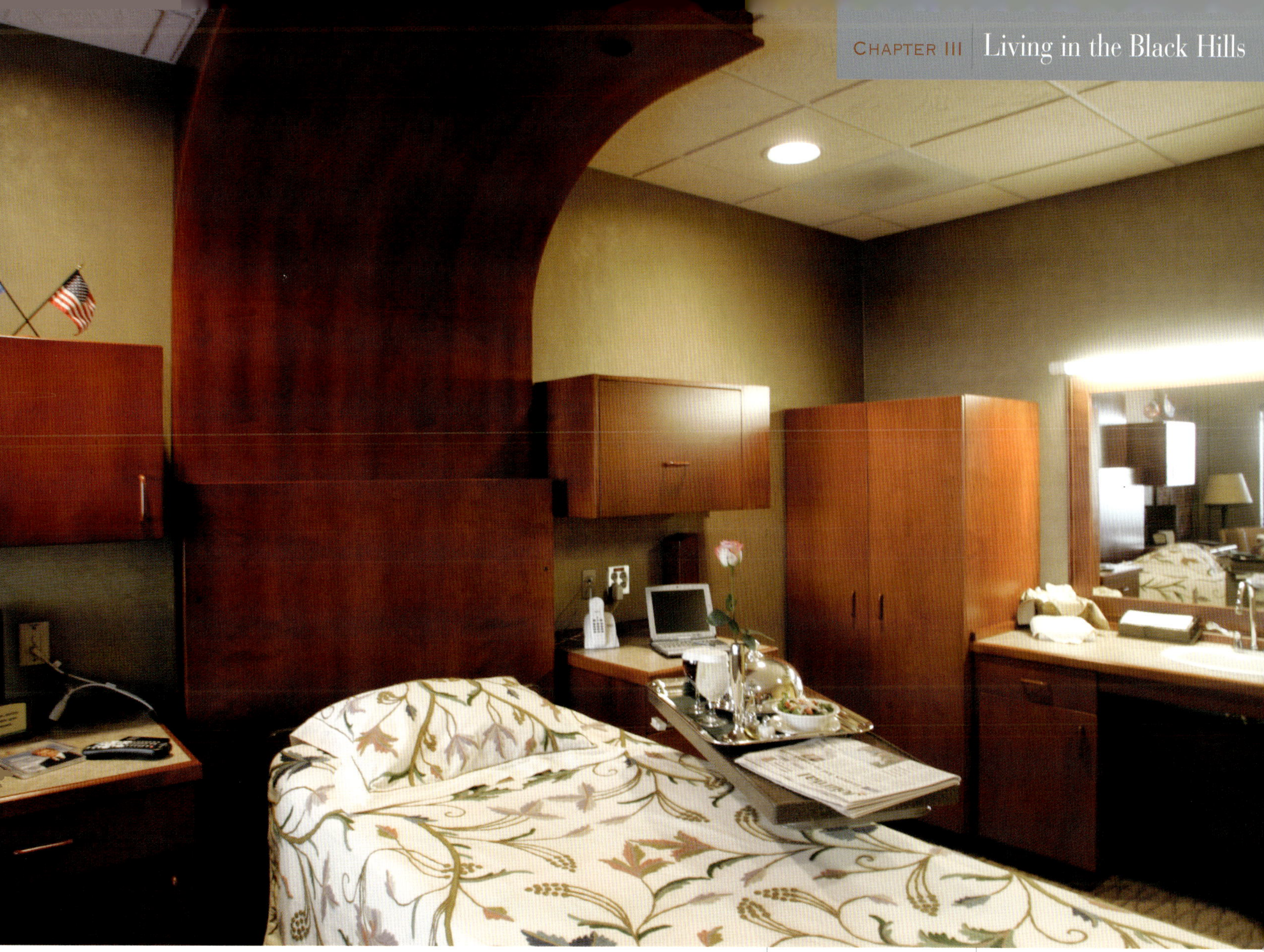

Photo by Alan S.Weiner

Black Hills Surgery Center turns patients' expectations about a hospital upside down. The clinical feel of tiled rooms, drab colors, and hospital food is a thing of the past here. The goal is to put patients at ease, to make them feel comfortable in a room that resembles a luxury hotel. Some of the patient amenities include fresh flowers, aromatherapy, luxurious robes, refreshing bath products, a DVD player and an extensive DVD library, and even a wireless laptop computer and Internet access. The whole idea is to hasten recovery by catering to a patient's need for comfort and relaxation.

Perhaps most astonishing is that this level of quality care comes at a competitive cost. "We've streamlined operations at Black Hills Surgery Center. We specialize in orthopedics; neurosurgery; ear, nose, and throat; general surgery; urology; and gynecology. Each of our surgical teams is a well-oiled unit with expertise in these specialties to assure the best possible outcome for our patients," May continued.

"Another thing that adds to the quality care provided here is the ratio of one nurse to every three patients," said director of nursing Taphne Blue. Many hospitals staff one nurse to five patients, and it is not unusual to have hospitals with one nurse to cover seven patients. "At Black Hills Surgery Center, each person is assigned a nurse who is available to them throughout their time here. From check-in to check-out, that person is always there. Nurses love working here because they have time to spend with patients and their loved ones to give them an extraordinary level of care."

Black Hills Surgery Center is a relatively new facility that opened in 1997. It has seven operating rooms and twenty-three recovery care suites, and it is still growing. Black Hills Surgery Center also has a state-of-the-art imaging center that includes a new high-definition 3T MRI. "This 3T MRI gives the highest image quality in the world to allow physicians to better diagnose disease. In fact, we are the only hospital in South Dakota that has the 3T MRI," said May, "and we're very proud of the quality of care it allows us to offer our patients."

Whether talking about surgical teams, nurse-to-patient ratios, or 3T MRIs, high-quality care for patients is the utmost priority at BHSC.❖

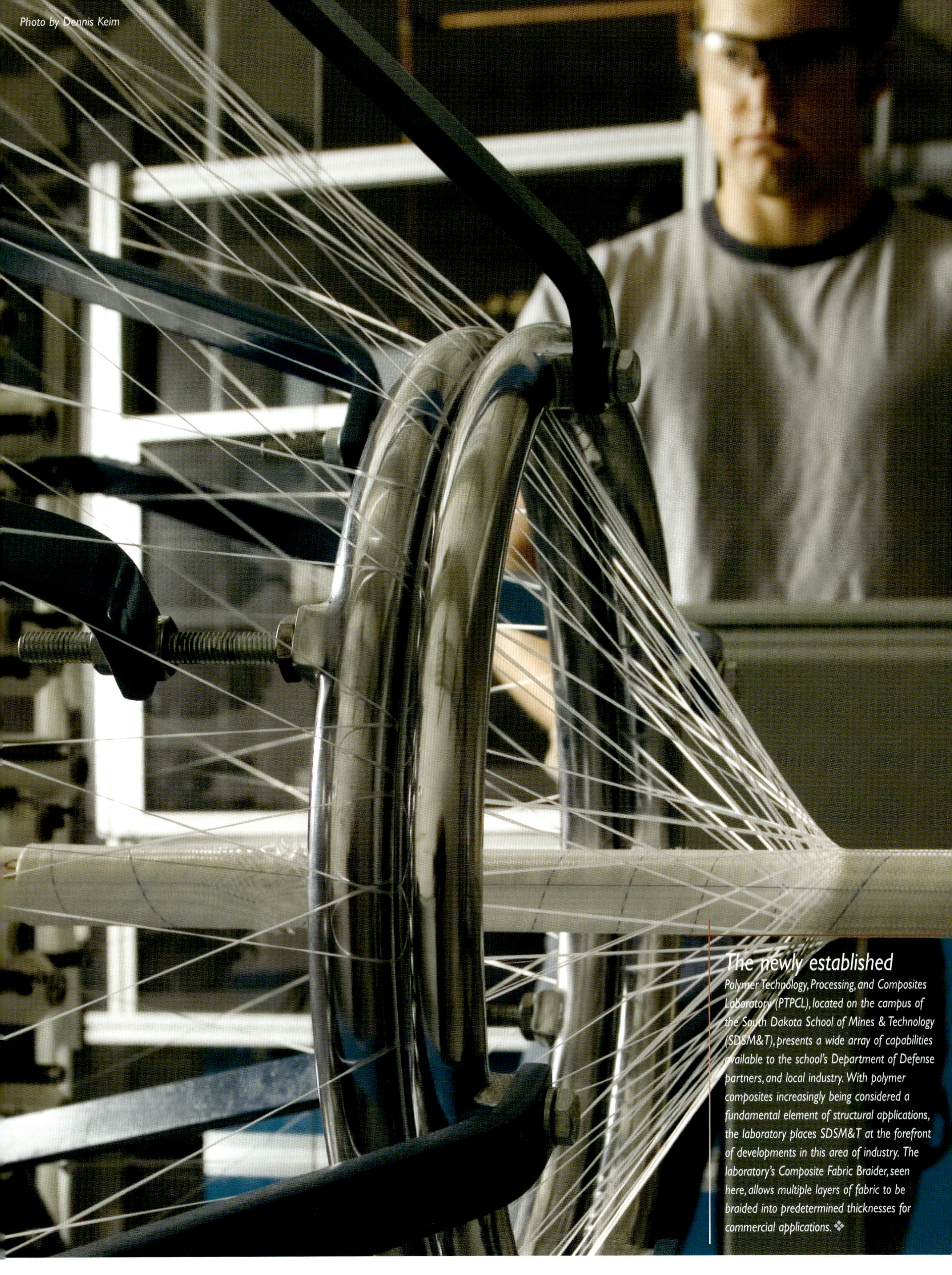
Photo by Dennis Keim

The newly established Polymer Technology, Processing, and Composites Laboratory (PTPCL), located on the campus of the South Dakota School of Mines & Technology (SDSM&T), presents a wide array of capabilities available to the school's Department of Defense partners, and local industry. With polymer composites increasingly being considered a fundamental element of structural applications, the laboratory places SDSM&T at the forefront of developments in this area of industry. The laboratory's Composite Fabric Braider, seen here, allows multiple layers of fabric to be braided into predetermined thicknesses for commercial applications. ❖

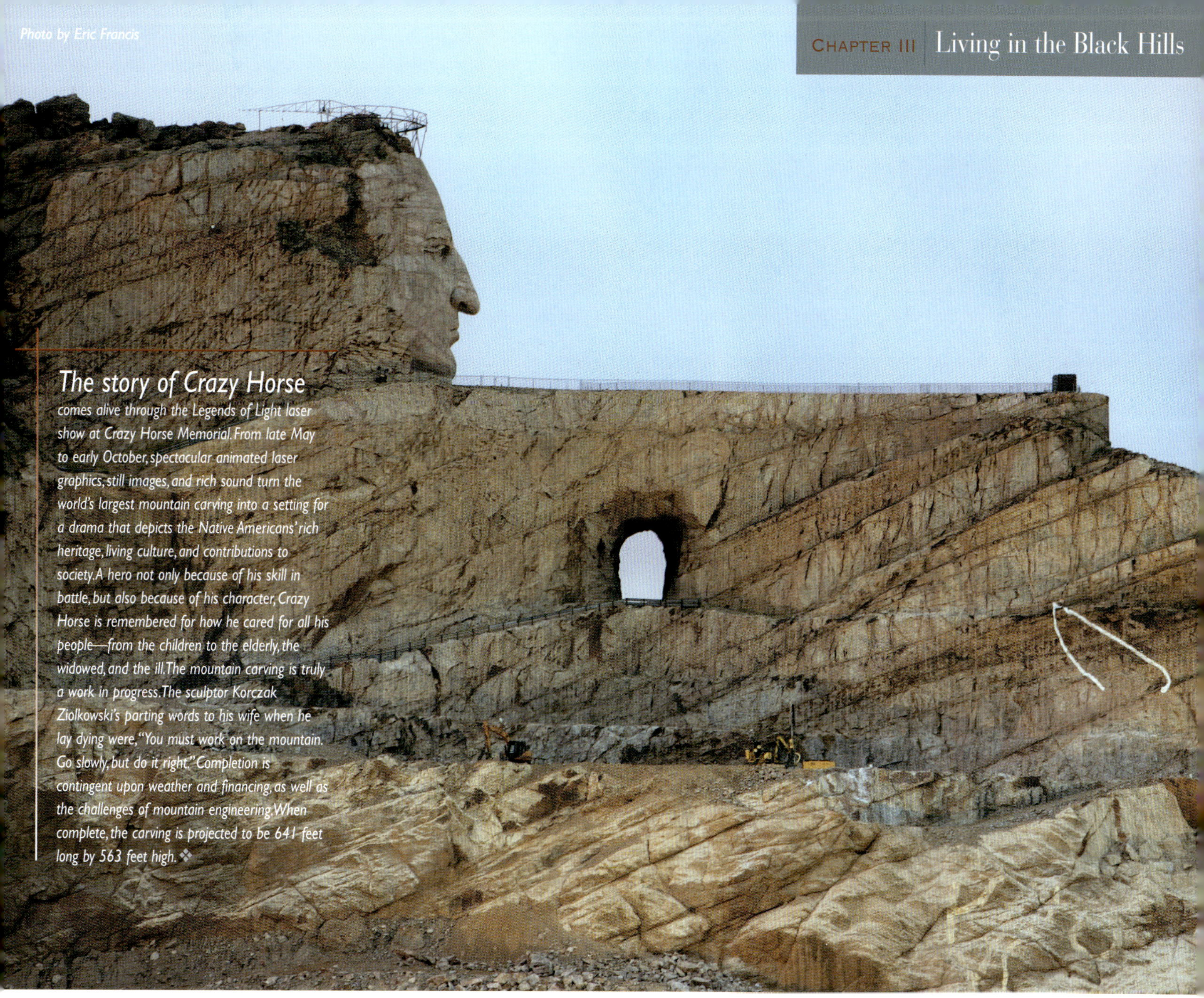

Photo by Eric Francis

The story of Crazy Horse

comes alive through the Legends of Light laser show at Crazy Horse Memorial. From late May to early October, spectacular animated laser graphics, still images, and rich sound turn the world's largest mountain carving into a setting for a drama that depicts the Native Americans' rich heritage, living culture, and contributions to society. A hero not only because of his skill in battle, but also because of his character, Crazy Horse is remembered for how he cared for all his people—from the children to the elderly, the widowed, and the ill. The mountain carving is truly a work in progress. The sculptor Korczak Ziolkowski's parting words to his wife when he lay dying were, "You must work on the mountain. Go slowly, but do it right." Completion is contingent upon weather and financing, as well as the challenges of mountain engineering. When complete, the carving is projected to be 641 feet long by 563 feet high. ❖

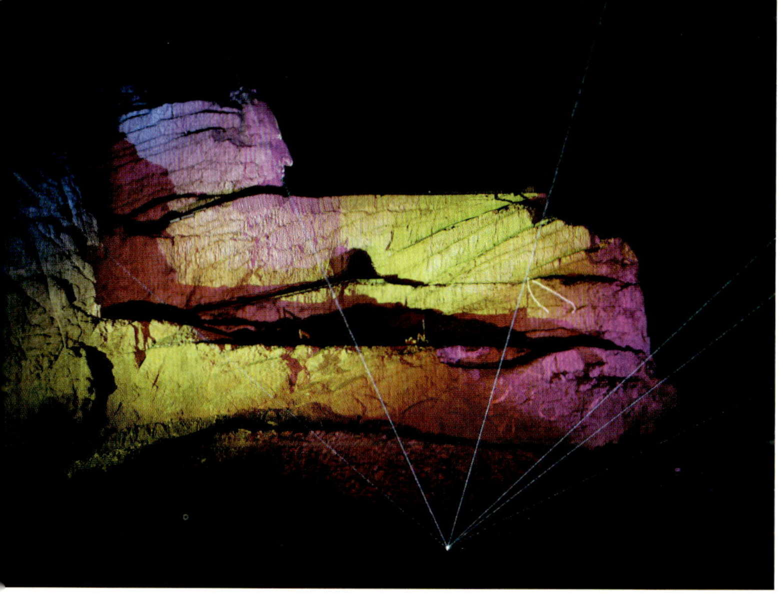

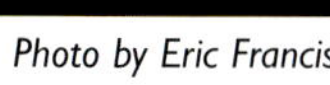

Photo by Eric Francis

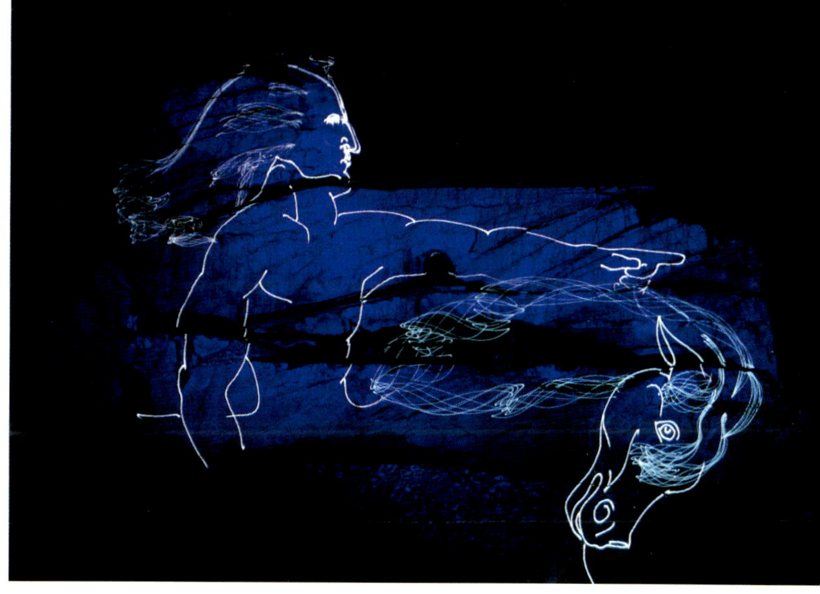

Photo by Eric Francis

Radiology Associates Offers Exceptional Care with Latest Technology

Fifty years is a long time for a medical practice to be together, but Radiology Associates, Professional LLC has accomplished just that. The group has been in business since 1955 at the same location—just one indication that Radiology Associates is exceptional in many other ways as well.

The practice of radiology has come a long way since the mid-1950s when founder Dr. George F. Wood opened his radiology office. In those days, X-rays had to be developed on film, and then hand delivered for viewing. Today Radiology Associates' twelve board-certified radiologists use state-of-the-art equipment and computer systems to provide diagnostic and interventional radiology services at the speed of light.

"I would say that computer digitalization has been the single most important development in our field in the last fifty years," said Tom Kushman, practice administrator. "Currently our Radiologists can reconstruct the inside of the human body in three dimensions so that they can better see what's going on. Digital images can be stored in databases such as Picture Archive Communication System (PACS) and a Radiology Information System (RIS), and transferred with amazing speed and efficiency. However, we never let technology cloud the fact that excellence in patient care is the constant in our practice."

> "I would say that computer digitalization has been the single most important development in our field in the last fifty years."

Photo by Doug Henderson

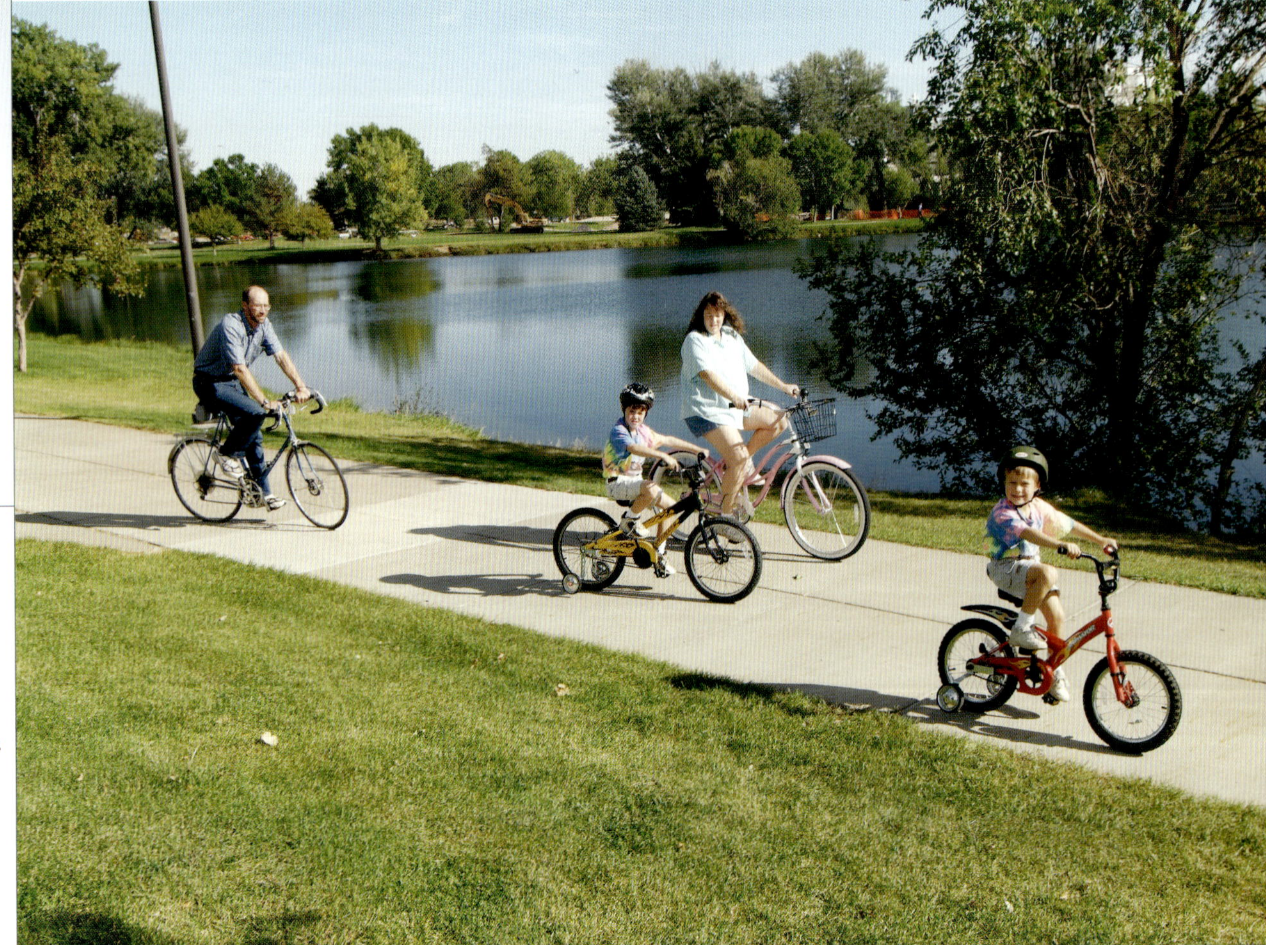

Dr. Brian, a partner in Radiology Associates, enjoys bicycling with his family in Memorial Park. Youngest son Isaiah, four, leads the way, followed by mother Tammie and Joshua, six. Rapid Creek meanders through the park, which includes bike paths, a rose garden, a band shell, and monuments dedicated to veterans and to the 238 people who lost their lives in the 1972 flood.

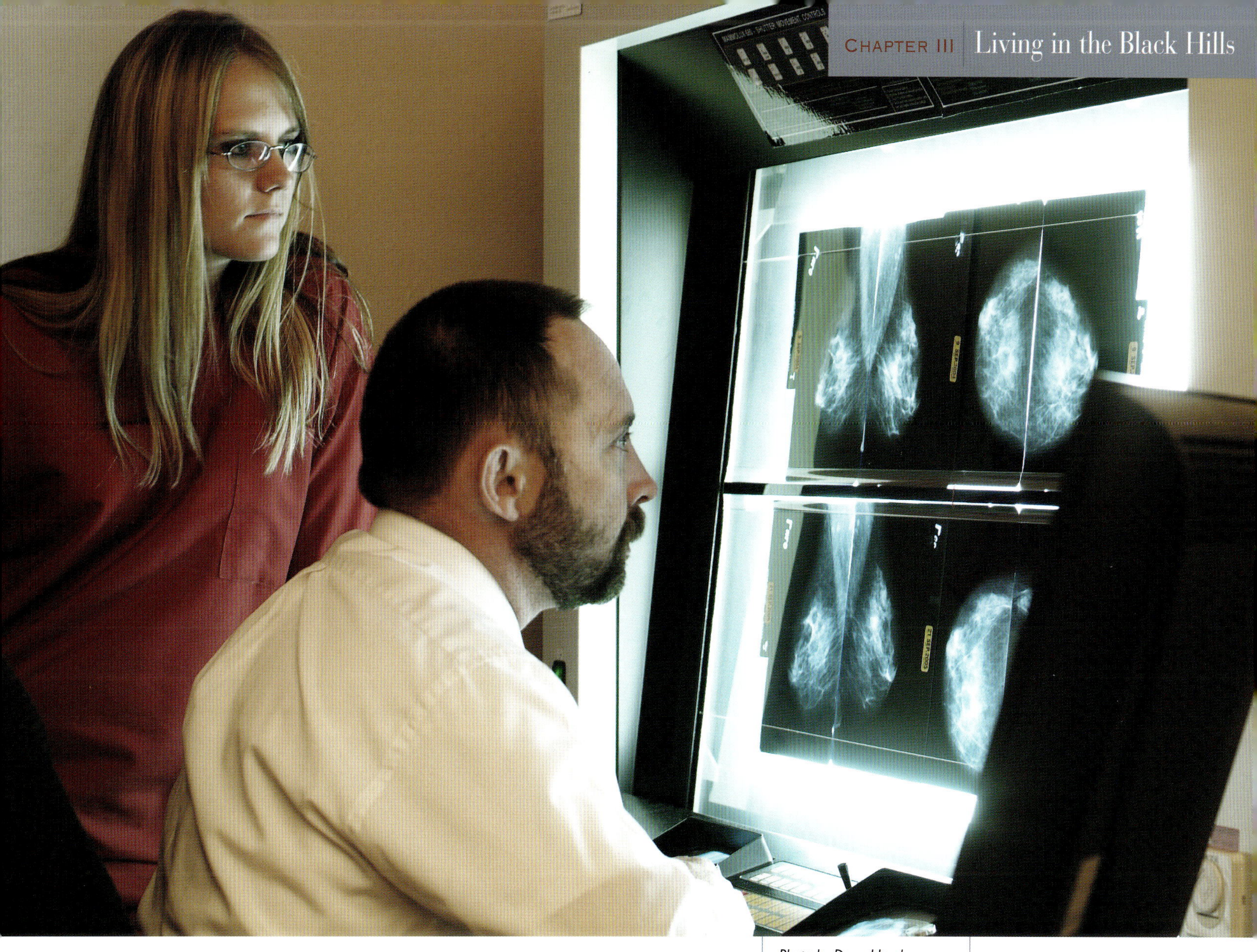

Photo by Doug Henderson

Dr. Gregory Saffell, one of the twelve partners at Radiology Associates, and Jessie Muir, a technology assistant, take time to study a mammogram. In addition to the services offered at their main location, Radiology Associates operates a mobile van which delivers mammography services to rural communities in South Dakota, Montana, Nebraska, and Wyoming. Other outpatient services include general radiology, fluoroscopy, and ultrasound.

Today, X-rays make up only a small portion of the practice of radiology. Now the doctors at Radiology Associates use MRIs, CTs, ultrasound, nuclear medicine, intervention radiology, and mammography. These services are all provided at Rapid City Regional Hospital and twenty teleradiology sites in Wyoming, Montana, Nebraska, and outlying areas of South Dakota. Radiology Associates owns and operates the Mammography Referral Center, and they dispatch a mobile van to rural areas across a three-state area.

Radiology Associates' interventional radiologists have the expertise, experience, and technology to offer patients a wide variety of treatment alternatives that were not available until recently. Two exciting procedures are vertebroplasty and kyphoplasty, which treat intense back pain. Both procedures involve the injection of acrylic cement under local anesthesia to repair vertebral fractures associated with osteoporosis, tumors, and trauma. The procedures require approximately forty minutes per level treated, and pain reduction or elimination is immediate.

Radiology Associates is proud of the continuous service it has provided throughout its history, and the practice is looking to the next fifty years with anticipation. The doctors have personally committed themselves to investing their time and resources to ensure quality radiology services are available in this area. Serving Rapid City and the greater Black Hills area extends beyond the office, too. The staff is involved in numerous civic and community projects, and fund-raising efforts.

There will be extraordinary advancements in this field of medicine, and Radiology Associates will be on the cutting edge of this new technology while continuing to provide the personal care to its patients for which the doctors and staff are known. ❖

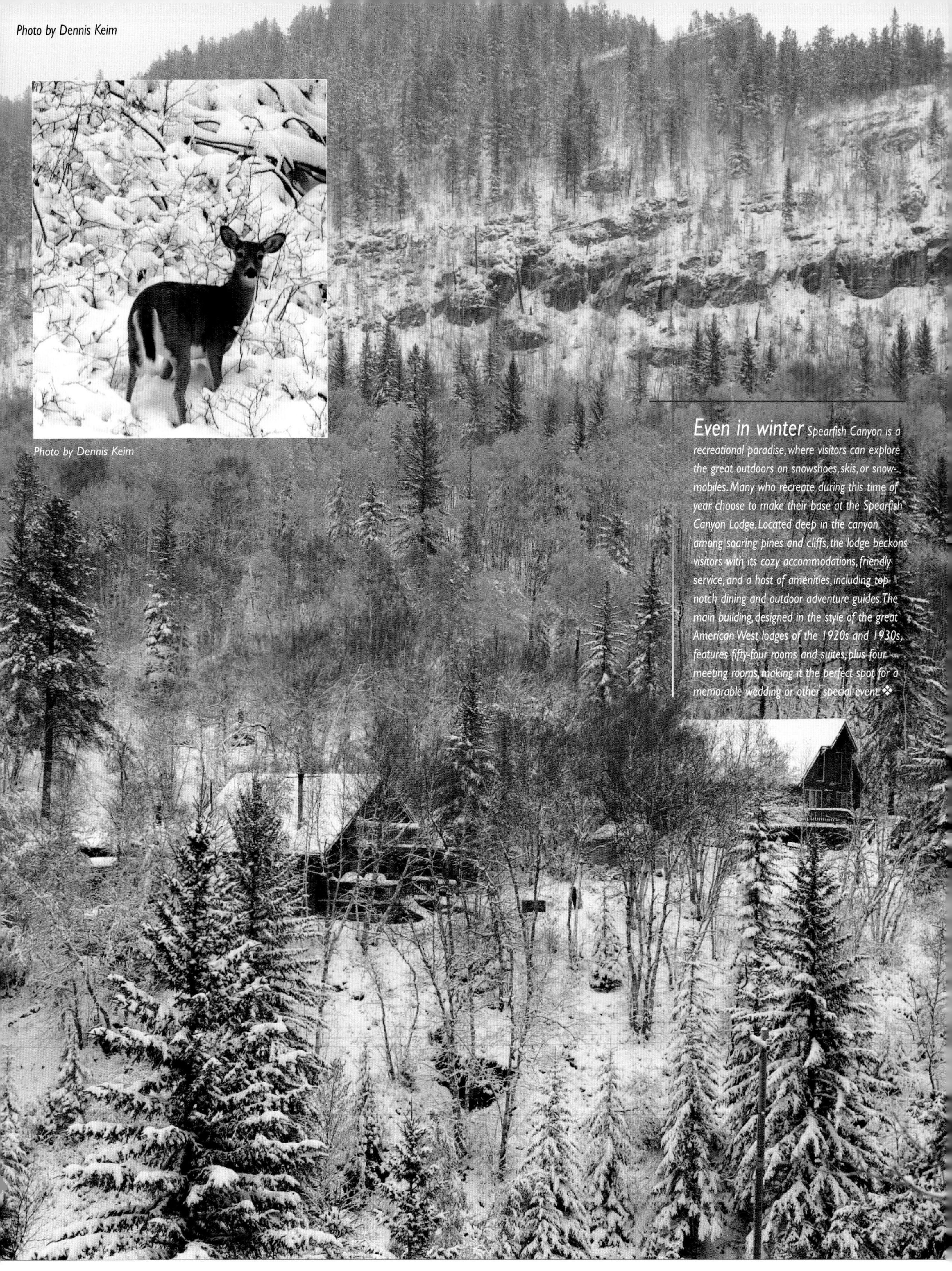

Photo by Dennis Keim

Photo by Dennis Keim

Even in winter Spearfish Canyon is a recreational paradise, where visitors can explore the great outdoors on snowshoes, skis, or snowmobiles. Many who recreate during this time of year choose to make their base at the Spearfish Canyon Lodge. Located deep in the canyon, among soaring pines and cliffs, the lodge beckons visitors with its cozy accommodations, friendly service, and a host of amenities, including top-notch dining and outdoor adventure guides. The main building, designed in the style of the great American West lodges of the 1920s and 1930s, features fifty-four rooms and suites, plus four meeting rooms, making it the perfect spot for a memorable wedding or other special event ❖

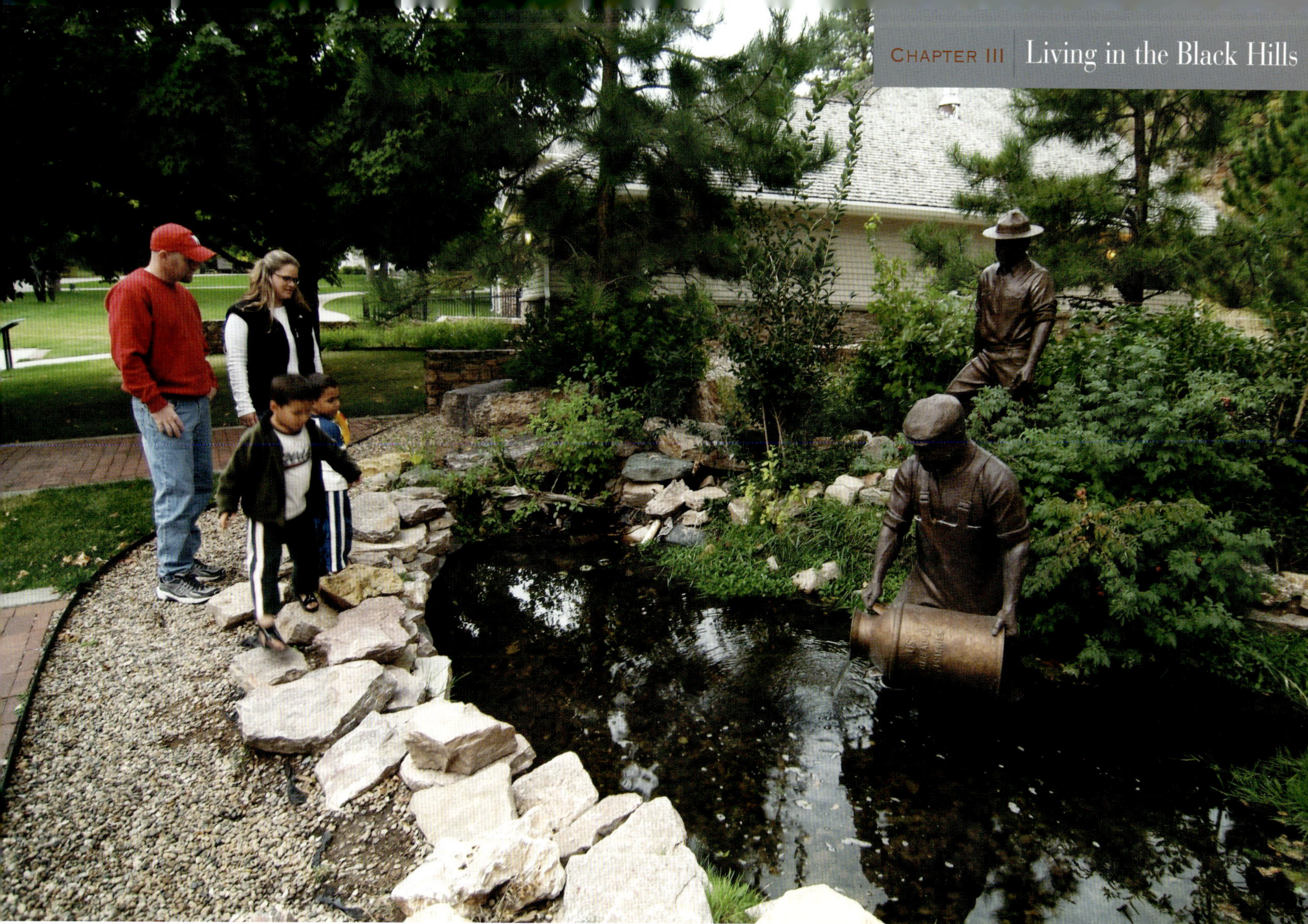

Photo by Doug Henderson

Established in 1896, the D.C. Booth Historic National Fish Hatchery is not only one of the oldest hatcheries in the United States, it is also one of the most comprehensive living fishery museums. Through a cooperative effort with the South Dakota Department of Game, Fish and Parks, the hatchery still maintains its original mission to propagate and stock trout populations in the Black Hills of South Dakota and Wyoming. D. C. Booth also maintains two on-site museums that preserve and protect fishery records, artifacts, equipment, and publications for educational, research, and historic purposes. An active volunteer program allows participants aged eleven years and up the unique opportunity to help out with hatchery operations, education, and outreach. ❖

Prepare for the Future

Western Dakota Technical Institute trains the people who are the foundation of economic development. This is a place where people learn to manufacture and maintain engineers' emerging technologies, provide patient care in area hospitals and clinics, keep busy networks up and running, ensure that the community's lights stay on, build businesses and homes, and protect people from harm.

Because our graduates are such an integral part of the economic generator, Western Dakota Tech is driven to be a leader in quality educational programs and to develop practices that continually improve the quality of life for our graduates and communities.

Based on these tenets, Western Dakota Tech has become a leading resource for training and education in the Black Hills region. From a first-year enrollment of twenty students in 1968, we have grown. We now award some three hundred certificates, diplomas, and associate of applied science degrees each year.

Of these graduates, more than 98 percent are employed upon completion of their programs, with some 85 percent placed in a degree-related position within one year of finishing their studies. This means that we are preparing hundreds of people each year to work in the fields of business, construction trades, health services, human services, and mechanical and manufacturing trades. Some 87 percent of our graduates stay in South Dakota, many earning up to fifty-six thousand dollars within only one year of graduation.

Western Dakota Tech ensures everyone departing this school's halls is equipped to excel in the modern world.

Photo by Eric Francis

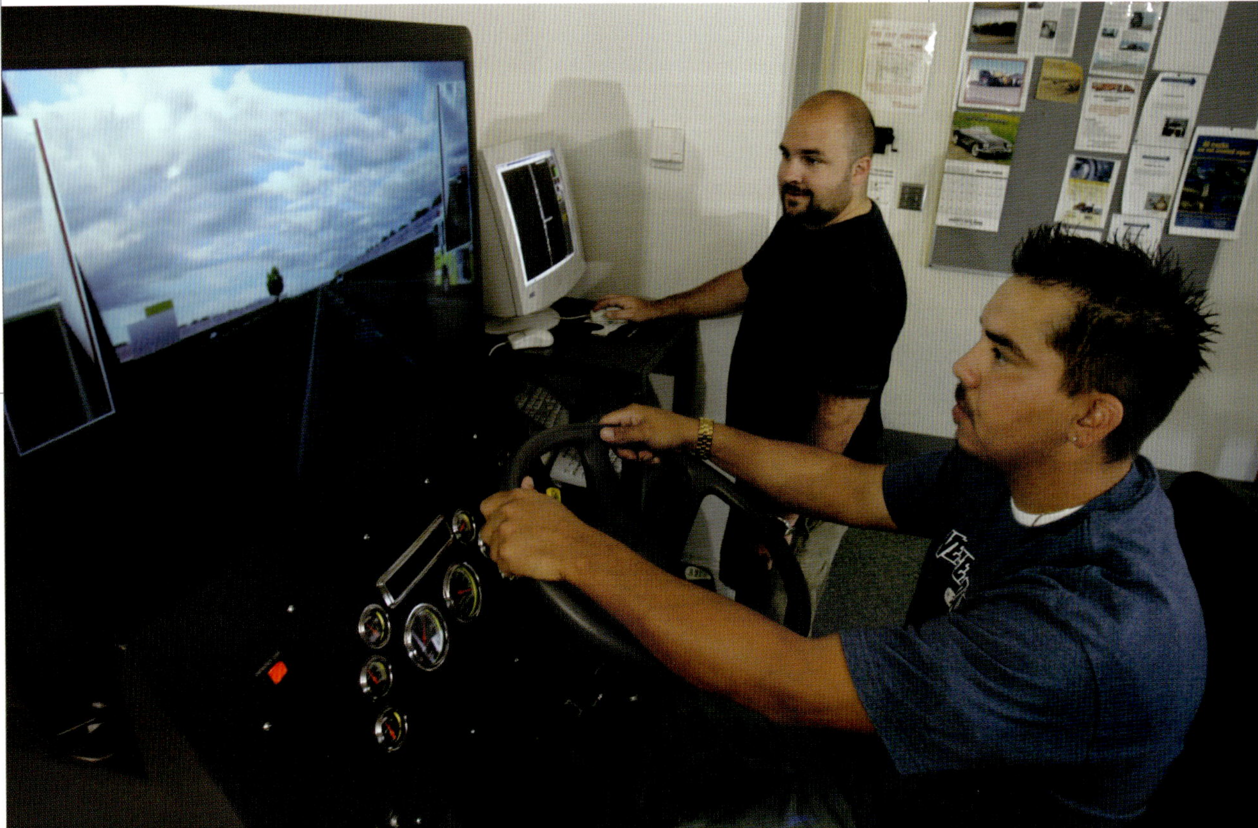

WDT's Business & Industry Training Center offers short-term training that builds the skills of more than three thousand members of the region's workforce every year.The Professional Truck Driving program uses simulator technology to train student drivers.

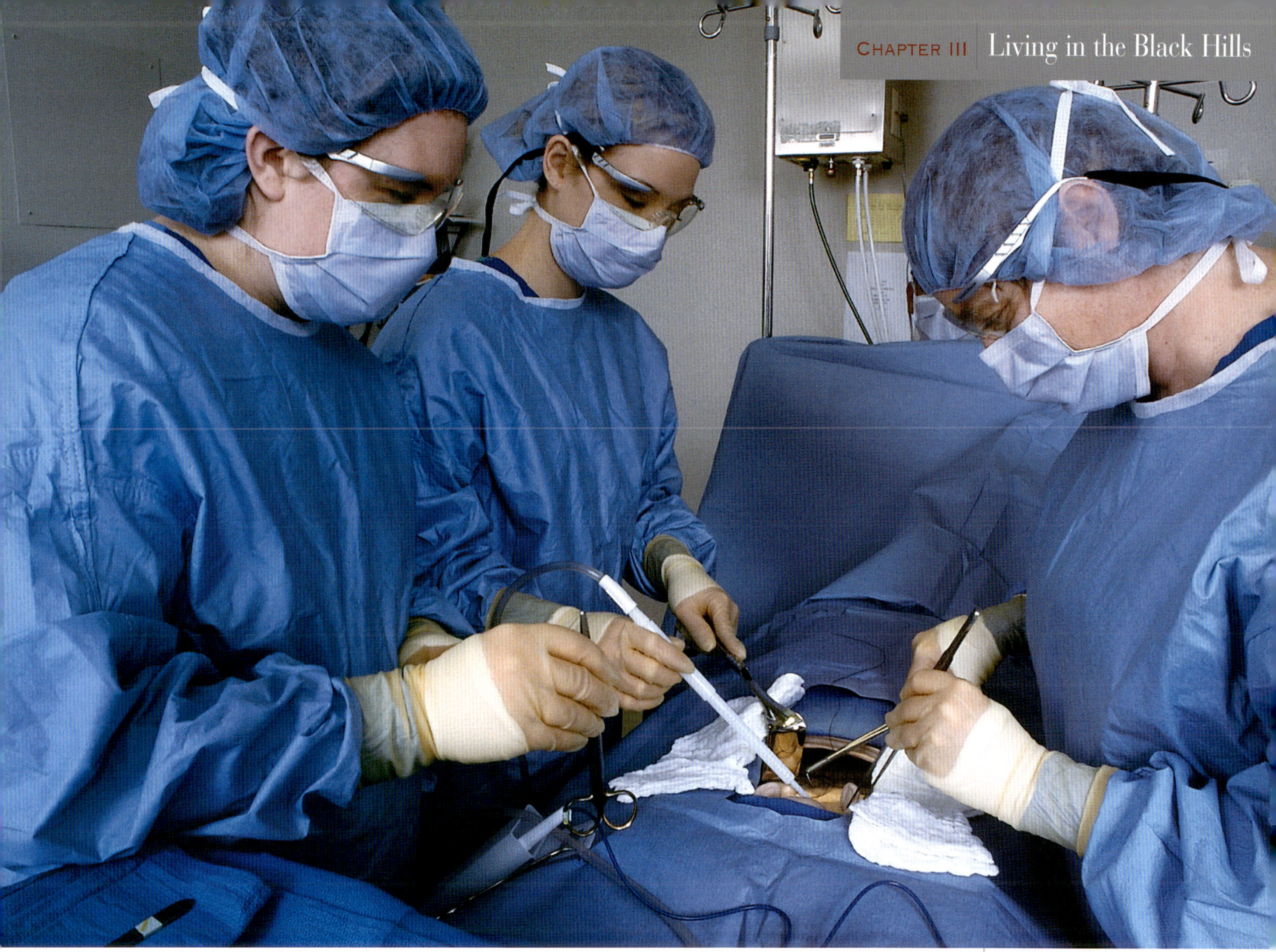

Western Dakota Tech graduates play critical roles in the health-care industry in the Black Hills region, including assisting surgeons as surgical technologists.

While our student body has grown over time, our mission has remained centered on preparing people for successful employment. In the early years, that meant teaching people the vocational and technical trades needed to work in an evolving, hands-on world.

Today, career success relies on proficiency in basic computer skills, something every student of Western Dakota Tech has upon graduation. Whether they are nurses using computerized monitors and records, carpenters who understand computer-aided design programs, accountants well-versed in bookkeeping software, or welders programming robotic welding machines, Western Dakota Tech ensures everyone departing this school's halls is equipped to excel in the modern world.

There are more than twenty-five programs to choose from at Western Dakota Tech, each offering a more personalized education through real-world environments and through smaller class sizes that allow for individual attention from instructors.

For our graduates who choose to continue their education, Western Dakota Tech has also secured articulation agreements with state universities governed by the Board of Regents.

In our growing region, where a well-trained workforce is so vitally important, businesses know they can rely on Western Dakota Tech to produce knowledgeable graduates and ongoing educational opportunities. In fact, we have become known as a partner in the region's growth through resources like our Business and Industry Training Center (BIT). Every year, some three thousand individuals use BIT to update their skills in everything from customer service to computerized software. BIT even takes training to the business site and can customize its

Continued on page 248

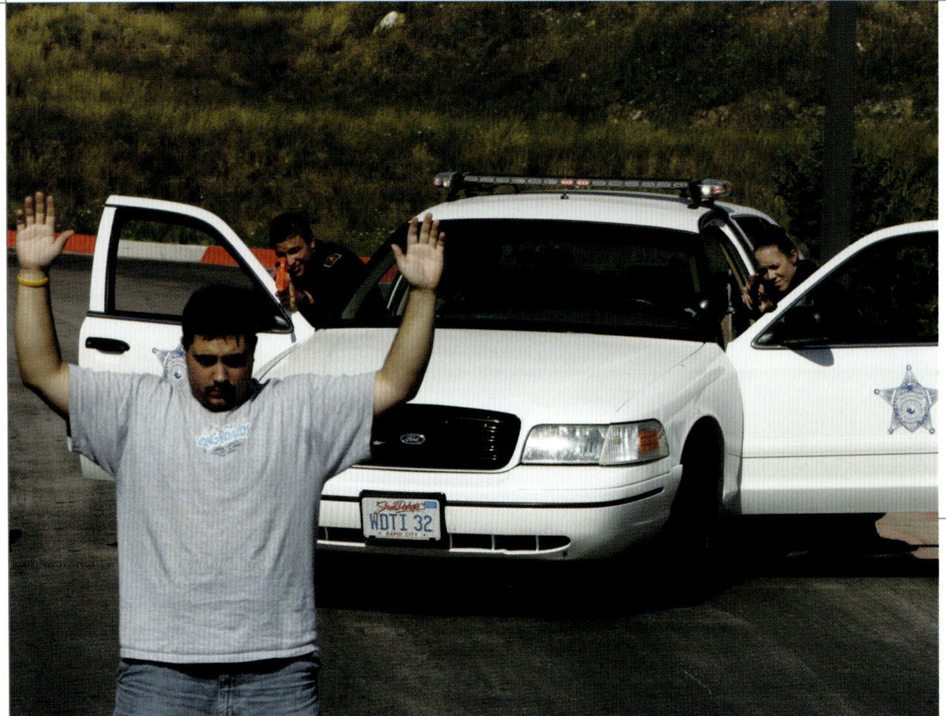

Photo by Eric Francis

Real-life experiences equal career preparation. At Western Dakota Tech, students practice what instructors teach throughout the various aspects of each of the school's twenty-five programs.

Continued from page 247

courses to meet a company's needs. We also make more than two hundred technology and business courses available online and help local entrepreneurs hone their skills at their choice of time and place.

To enroll in Western Dakota Tech is to embark on a journey of change. Whether just graduating from high school, needing to upgrade some skills, or looking for a new career, Western Dakota Tech will provide solid footing on the path to future success. ❖

Photo by Eric Francis

In Fire Science, one of Western Dakota Tech's newest programs, students learn the technical, tactical, medical, and behavioral skills they need to become effective wildland and municipal firefighters protecting our communities.

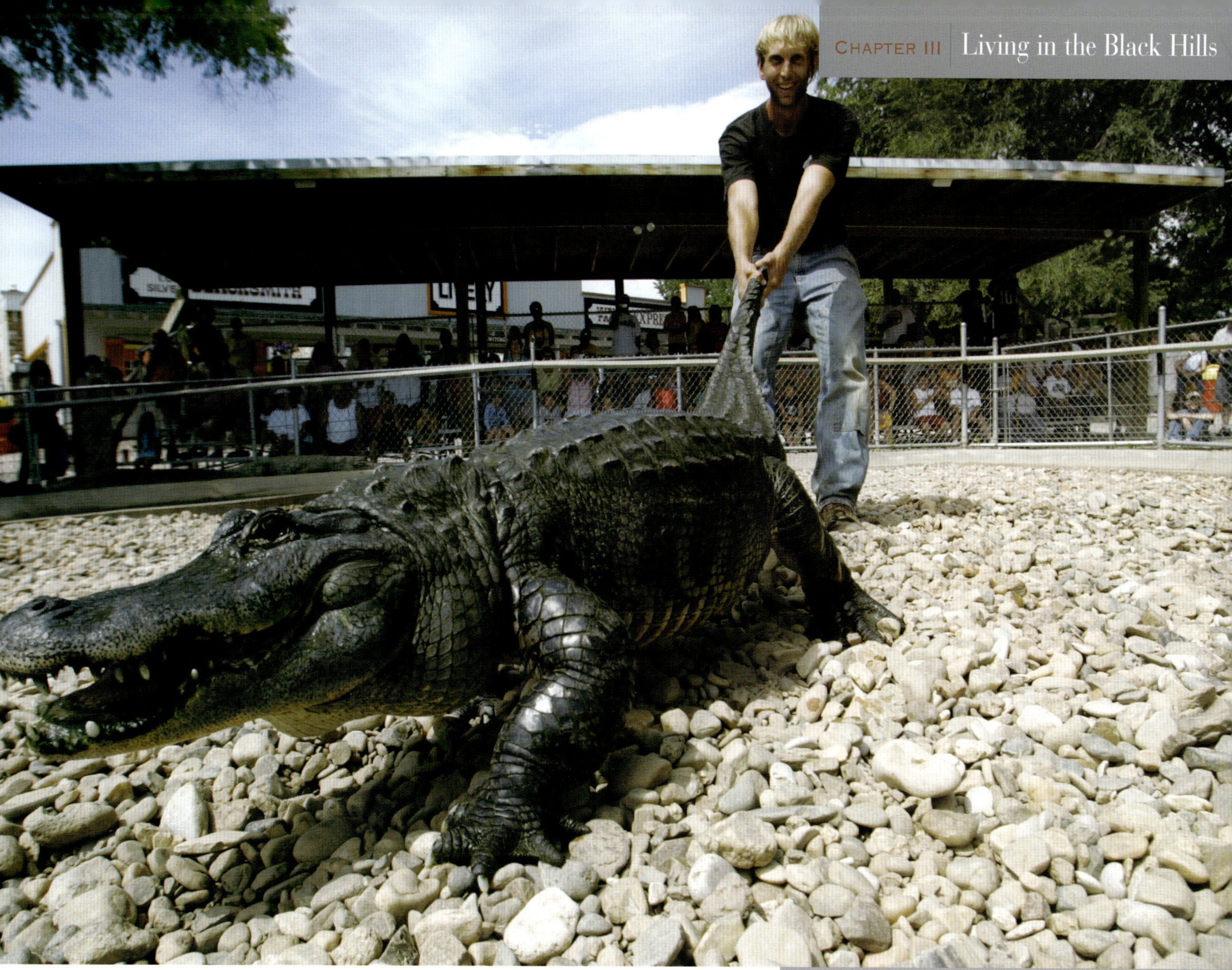

Photo by Eric Francis

The Black Hills may be known for their buffalo, deer, and antelope, but those quintessential midwestern animals aren't the only creatures that inhabit the area. Just ask visitors who have had the chance to take a tour of Black Hills Reptile Gardens, home to one of the largest reptile and amphibian collections in the world. In fact, the well-visited tourist attraction features more reptile species than any other zoo or park anywhere. Founded in 1937 by reptile enthusiast Earl Brockelsby, Reptile Gardens has grown from a tiny building located three miles south of Rapid City into a sprawling compound, complete with a Sky Dome and the world's first walk-through jungle. On exhibit at the gardens is everything from tiger salamanders, marine toads, and green tree frogs to snapping turtles, American alligators, and rhino iguanas. Two Komodo dragons, named Awas and Naga, have also taken up residence here. And, of course, there are plenty of snakes, including some of the deadliest snakes known to man, such as the Australian brown snake and the coral snake. But the most well-known local at Reptile Gardens is Methuselah, the giant six-hundred-pound tortoise who was born in 1881 and is recognized as South Dakota's oldest resident. With so much to see and do, it's no wonder that USA Today *ranked Reptile Gardens as one of the "Top 10 Places to Stop the Car and Take a Look."* ❖

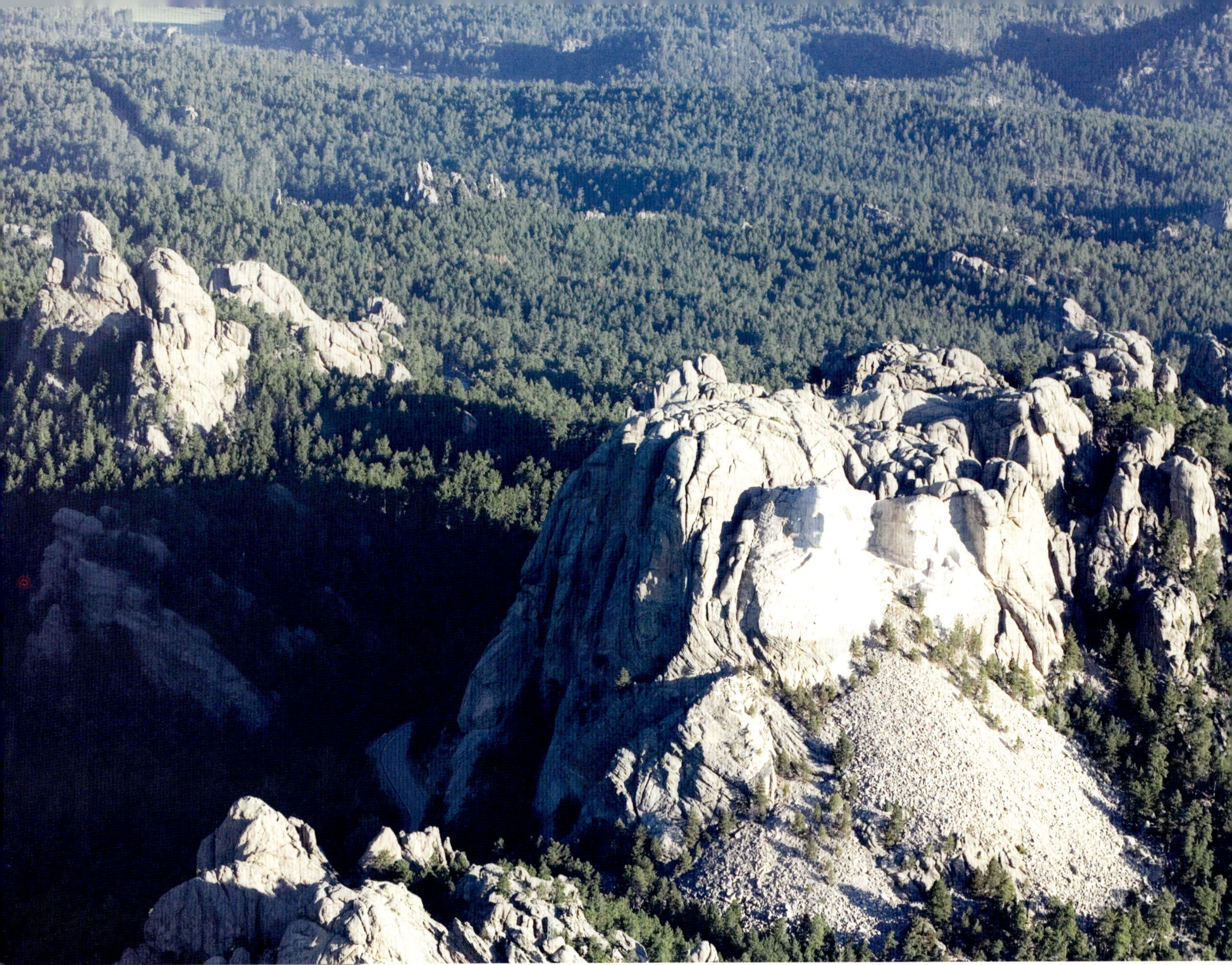

Photo by Eric Francis

Up close or far away,

Mount Rushmore is awesome no matter where you are. And the views are really great from the air. As owner of Black Hills Aerial Adventures in Rapid City and Custer, Mike Jacob regularly thrills his customers with helicopter rides over the monument. "You'll see things you'll never experience from the ground," he says. "It's a whole new perspective." In addition to Mount Rushmore, Jacob runs tours over Crazy Horse, Sylvan Lake, Custer State Park, and Harney Peak. ❖

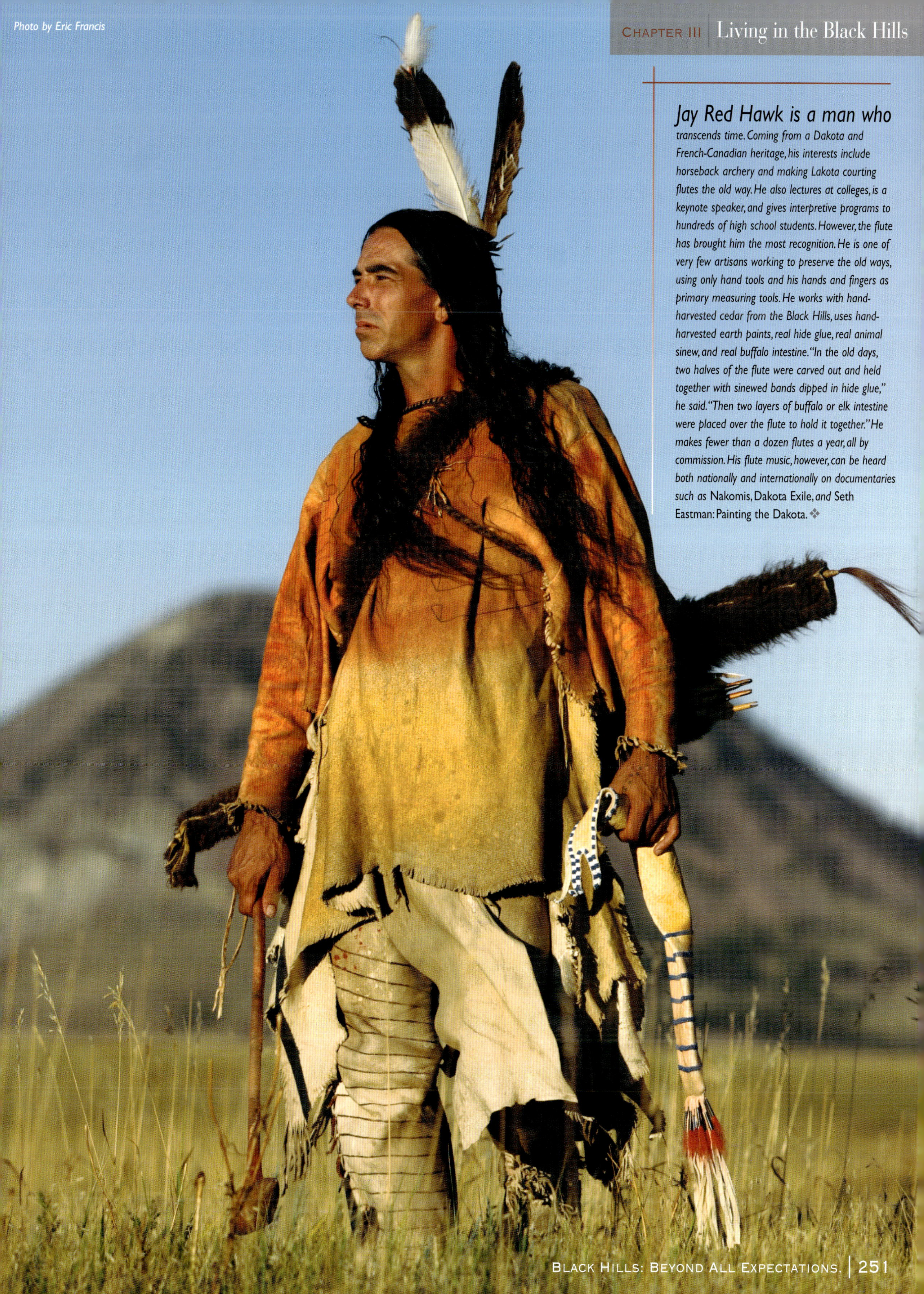

Photo by Eric Francis

Jay Red Hawk is a man who transcends time. Coming from a Dakota and French-Canadian heritage, his interests include horseback archery and making Lakota courting flutes the old way. He also lectures at colleges, is a keynote speaker, and gives interpretive programs to hundreds of high school students. However, the flute has brought him the most recognition. He is one of very few artisans working to preserve the old ways, using only hand tools and his hands and fingers as primary measuring tools. He works with hand-harvested cedar from the Black Hills, uses hand-harvested earth paints, real hide glue, real animal sinew, and real buffalo intestine. "In the old days, two halves of the flute were carved out and held together with sinewed bands dipped in hide glue," he said. "Then two layers of buffalo or elk intestine were placed over the flute to hold it together." He makes fewer than a dozen flutes a year, all by commission. His flute music, however, can be heard both nationally and internationally on documentaries such as Nakomis, Dakota Exile, *and* Seth Eastman: Painting the Dakota. ❖

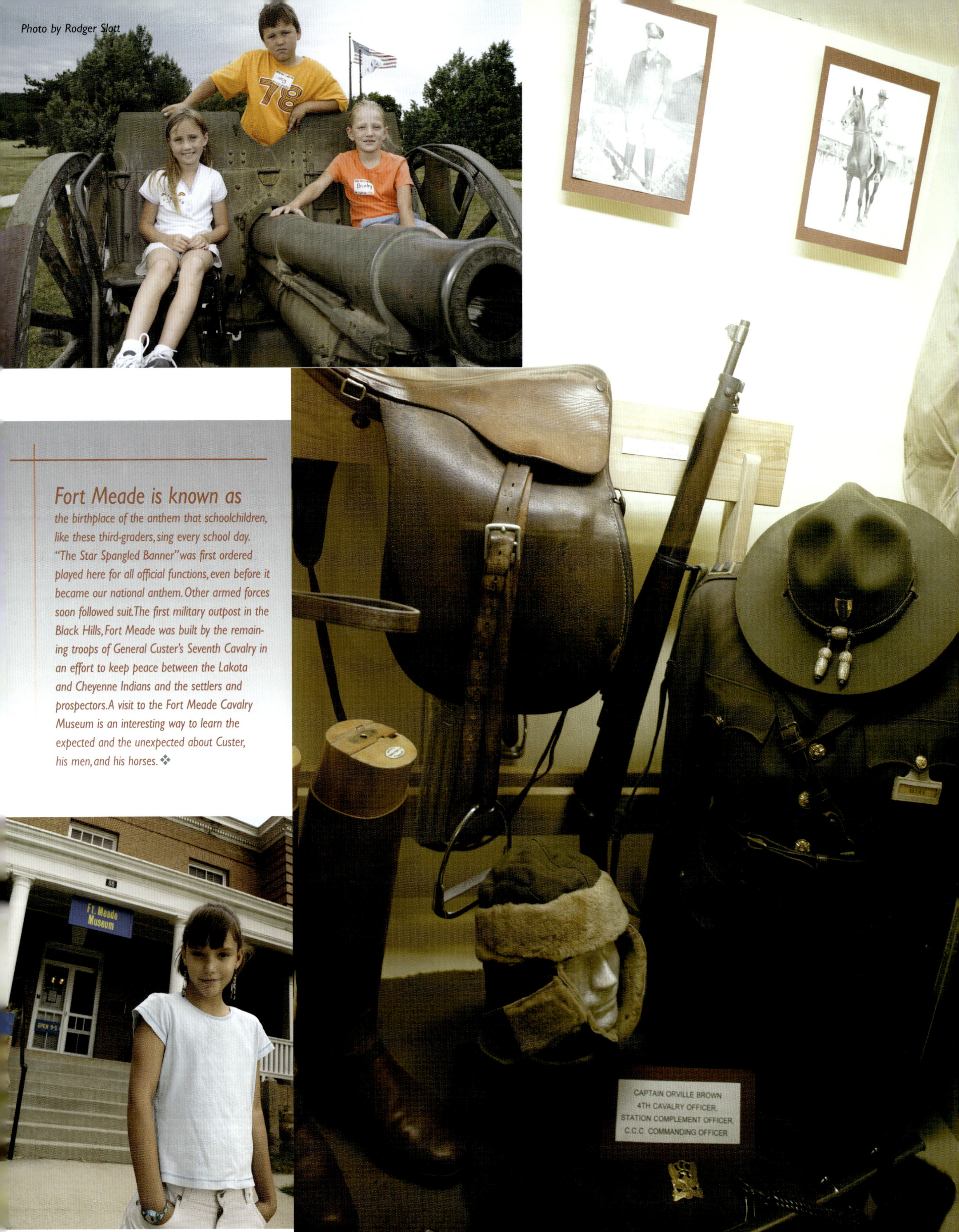

Photo by Rodger Slott

Fort Meade is known as *the birthplace of the anthem that schoolchildren, like these third-graders, sing every school day. "The Star Spangled Banner" was first ordered played here for all official functions, even before it became our national anthem. Other armed forces soon followed suit. The first military outpost in the Black Hills, Fort Meade was built by the remaining troops of General Custer's Seventh Cavalry in an effort to keep peace between the Lakota and Cheyenne Indians and the settlers and prospectors. A visit to the Fort Meade Cavalry Museum is an interesting way to learn the expected and the unexpected about Custer, his men, and his horses.* ❖

Photo by Rodger Slott

Photo by Rodger Slott

Photo by Dennis Keim

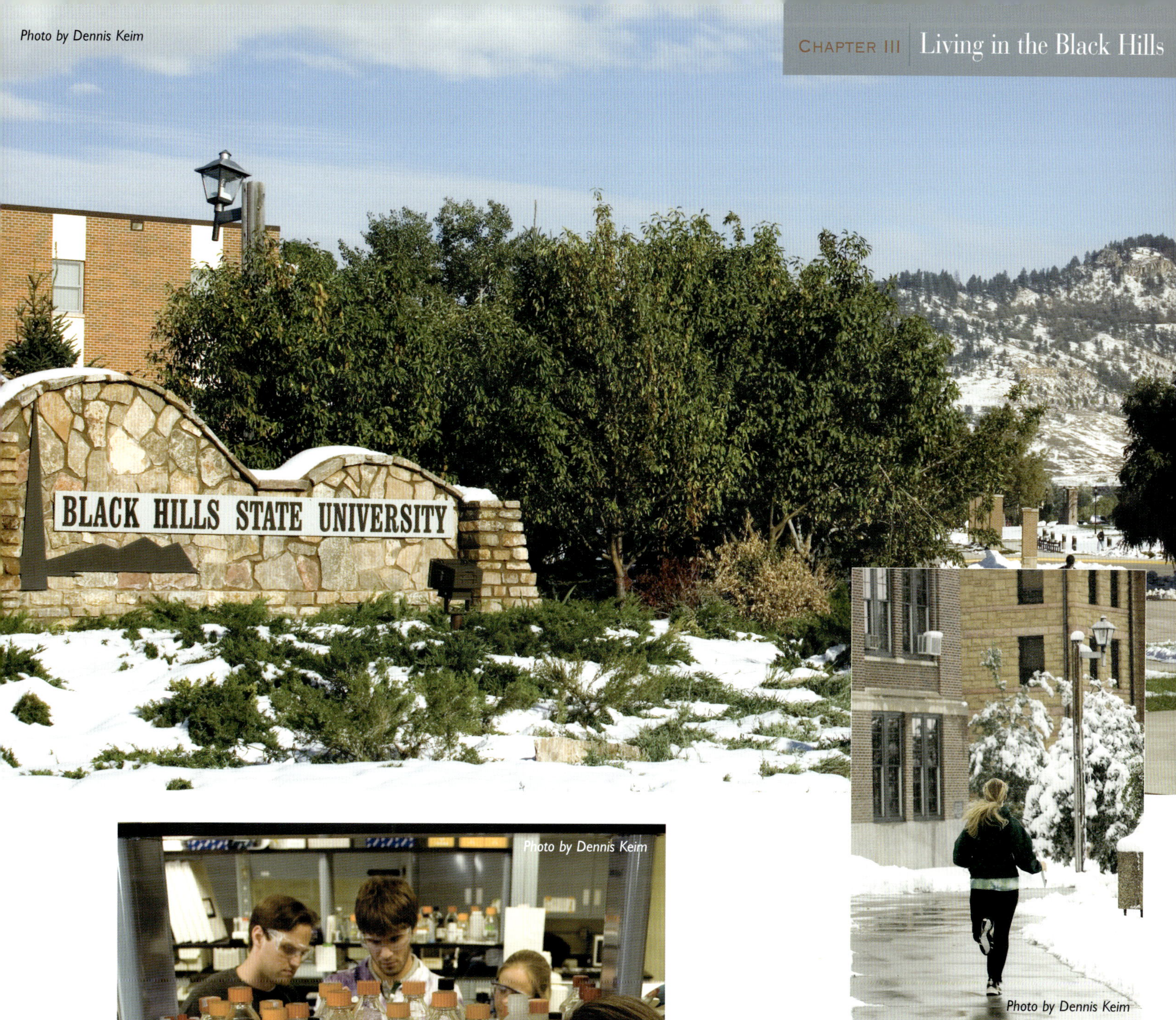

Photo by Dennis Keim

Photo by Dennis Keim

Known for combining outstanding academics with plentiful recreation, Black Hills State University in Spearfish also offers unique research opportunities to its undergraduates. Many of them regularly work side-by-side with their professors on important projects, a privilege usually reserved for those seeking graduate-level degrees. Here, at the university's Center for Conservation Biology, undergraduate students Alexia Steffes and Shane Ziogenbein test buffalo DNA to determine what percentage of a certain population contains domestic versus wild DNA. Established through a federal grant, the Center is the only facility in the region for DNA sequencing and genotyping. The university itself was founded in 1883 in Spearfish, and is the only multipurpose four-year liberal arts university in western South Dakota. ❖

SDSM&T Rooted in Research and Development

Amid the rustic beauty of the Black Hills is a place where education, research, and technology are changing the face of industry.

For more than a century, the South Dakota School of Mines and Technology (SDSM&T) has prepared graduates to serve as leaders in the fields of engineering and science. Today, SDSM&T is rooted in a world of research and development focused on advancing scientific knowledge and its application for regional and national benefit. Every year, some twenty-five hundred students from around the world attend SDSM&T, participating in more than thirty graduate and undergraduate degree programs.

Every year, the emphasis on research builds at SDSM&T, drawing the world's attention.

Already home to several research institutions and centers, SDSM&T has plans under way to expand the number of graduate degrees and to enhance the technology transfer process.

Among its activities already in place are the Center for Integrated Research in Bioprocessing, where scientists work to produce products in energy and environmentally friendly manners; the Maskless Mesoscale Materials Deposition (M3D), bridging the research areas between nanoparticles and nanosensors and the Institute of Atmospheric Sciences, emphasizing weather research and prediction, simulation, and sensors.

In addition, the SDSM&T campus houses the Advanced Materials Processing and Joining Center, where research and development are advancing materials joining and parts fabrication technology. This center houses three-dimensional friction stir processing equipment that is a key component in SDSM&T's partnership with eighteen industry

Photo by Dennis Keim

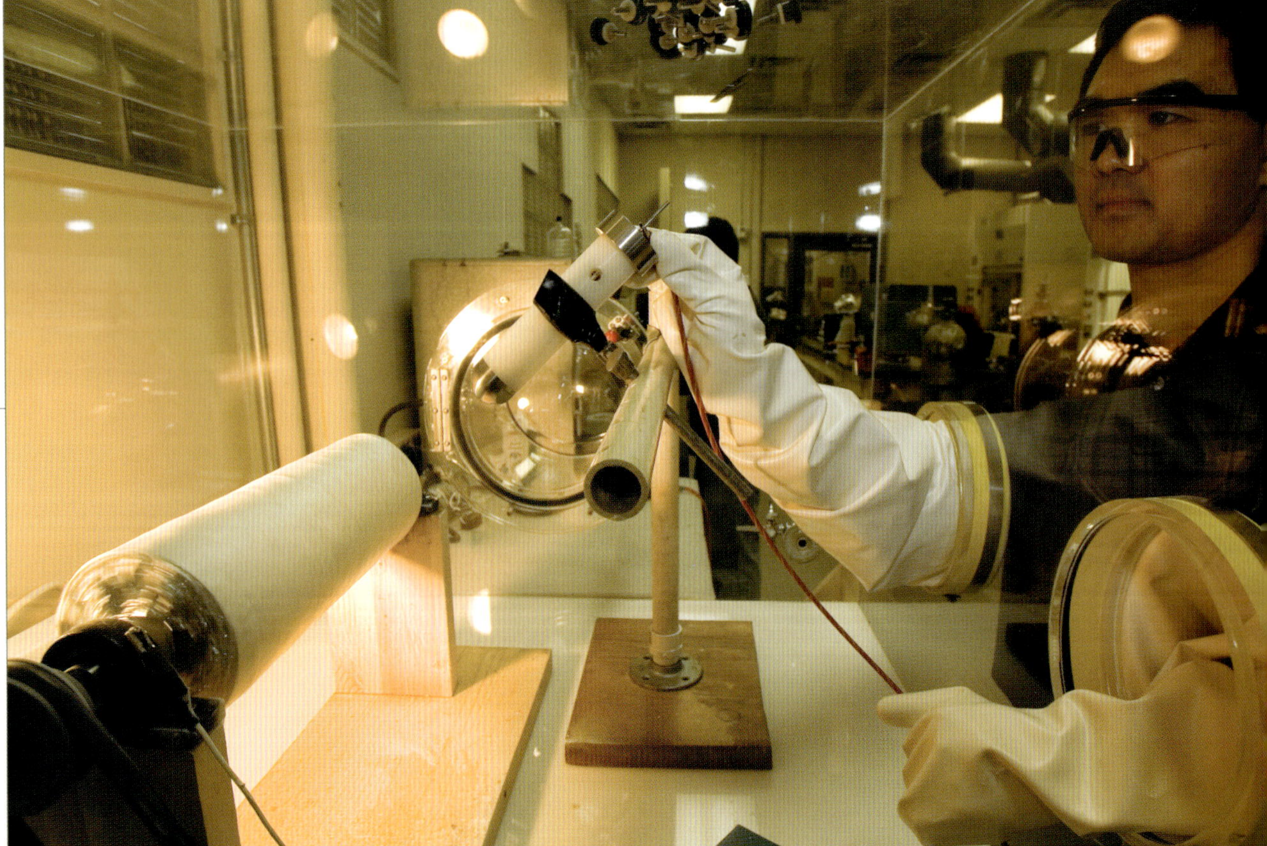

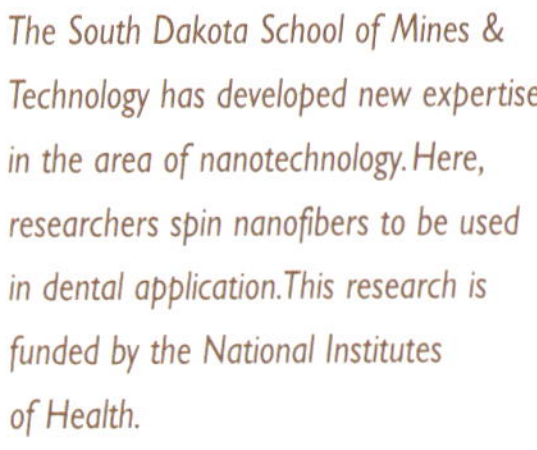

The South Dakota School of Mines & Technology has developed new expertise in the area of nanotechnology. Here, researchers spin nanofibers to be used in dental application. This research is funded by the National Institutes of Health.

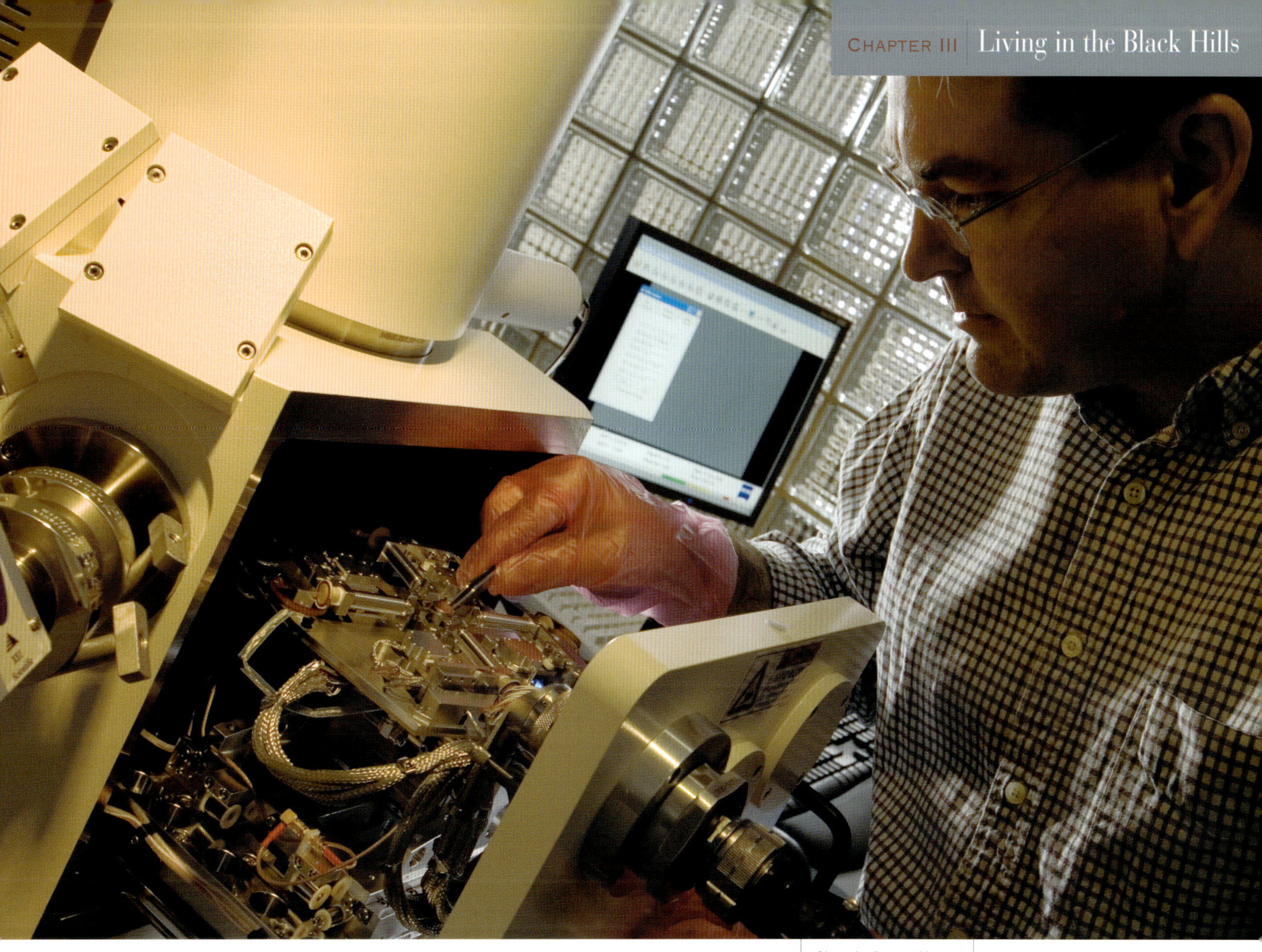

Photo by Dennis Keim

The Center for Accelerated Applications at the Nanoscale (CAAN), a Governor's 2010 Center, has partnered with Zyvex Corp., a leading nanomanufacturer, to be the exclusive provider of integrated circuit failure analysis services to the semiconductor industry.

partners that formed the National Science Foundation Friction Stir Processing Industry/ University Cooperative Research Center. As lead institution of this center, SDSM&T will help to change the way industry builds the products people use every day.

A fundamental component of many of SDSM&T's research and development programs is active collaboration with local and national industrial partners.

For instance, an exciting partnership formed by the school is between the campus-based Center for Accelerated Applications at the Nanoscale and Zyvex Corp., a leading supplier of nanotechnology tools, products, and services. Through this partnership, SDSM&T will be at the forefront of developments in the field of nanotechnology, conducting materials development activities that impact everything from flooring to pharmaceuticals.

The school's business relationships also provide students with valuable experience through internships and cooperative education opportunities. These hands-on activities take place at such prestigious organizations as the Smithsonian Institution's National Museum of Natural History, the Air Force Research Laboratory, Bobcat, Rockwell Collins, Archer Daniels Midland, Caterpillar, Cargill, the U.S. Forest Service, and more.

Every year, the emphasis on research builds at SDSM&T, drawing the world's attention and, in turn, significant funding. For instance, in a single fiscal year, the school's researchers and professors received over $12.7 million, used for studies ranging from national defense projects to the role of wetlands in climate change. These awards, nearly one hundred in all, came from competitive peer-reviewed grants from state and federal agencies and congressional appropriations: entities that recognize SDSM&T's place on the changing industrial landscape. ❖

Photo by Doug Henderson

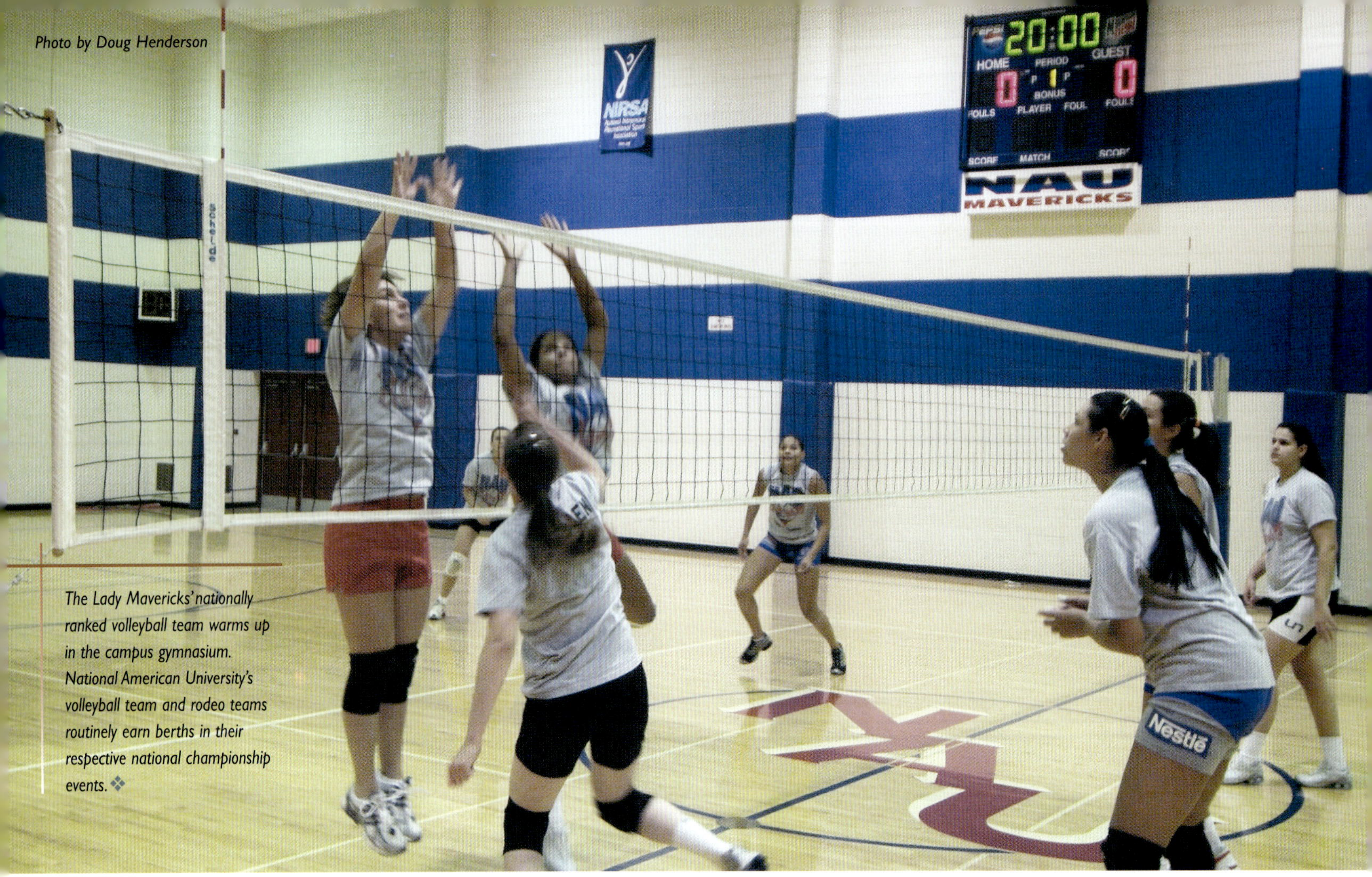

The Lady Mavericks' nationally ranked volleyball team warms up in the campus gymnasium. National American University's volleyball team and rodeo teams routinely earn berths in their respective national championship events. ❖

Photo by Doug Henderson

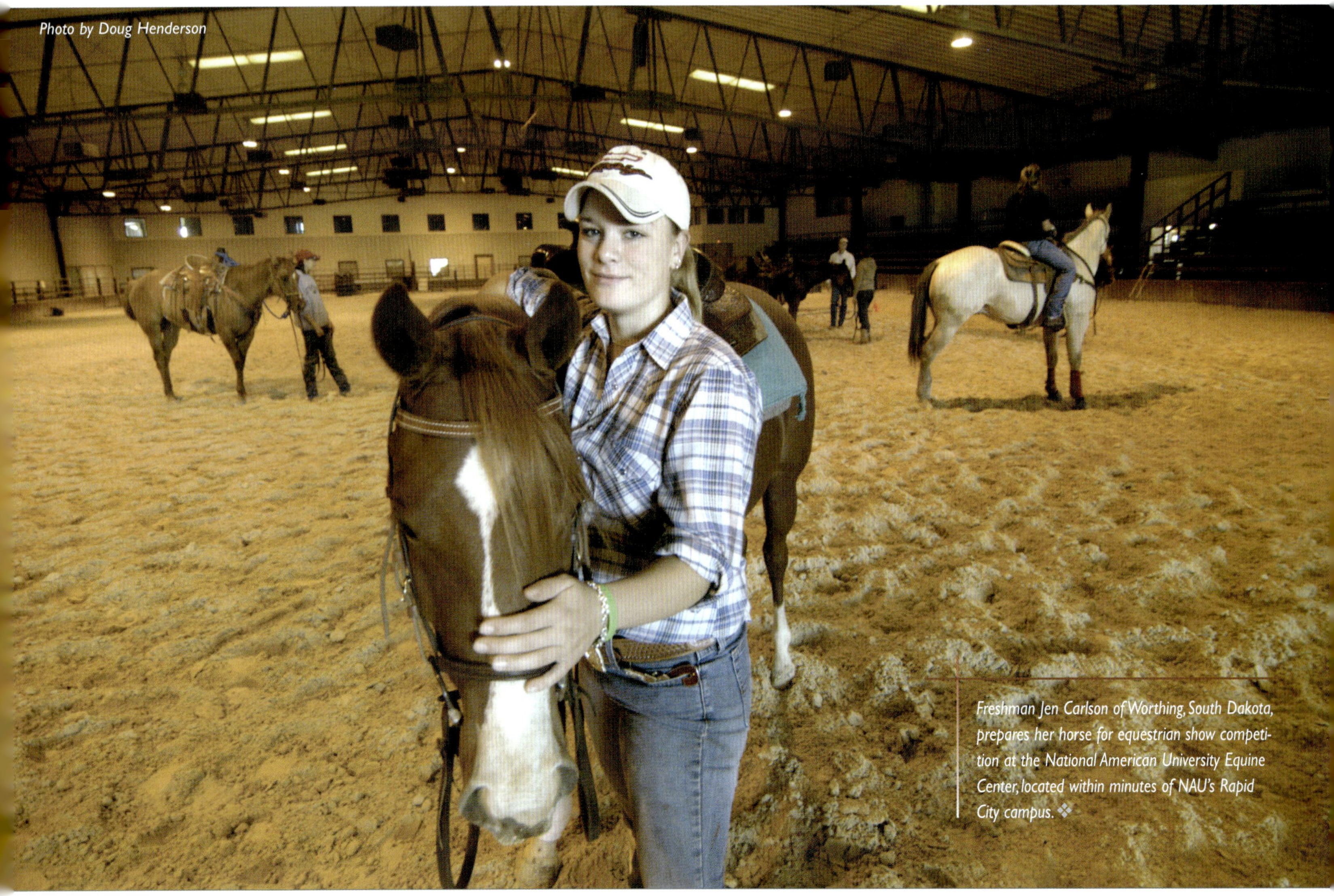

Freshman Jen Carlson of Worthing, South Dakota, prepares her horse for equestrian show competition at the National American University Equine Center, located within minutes of NAU's Rapid City campus. ❖

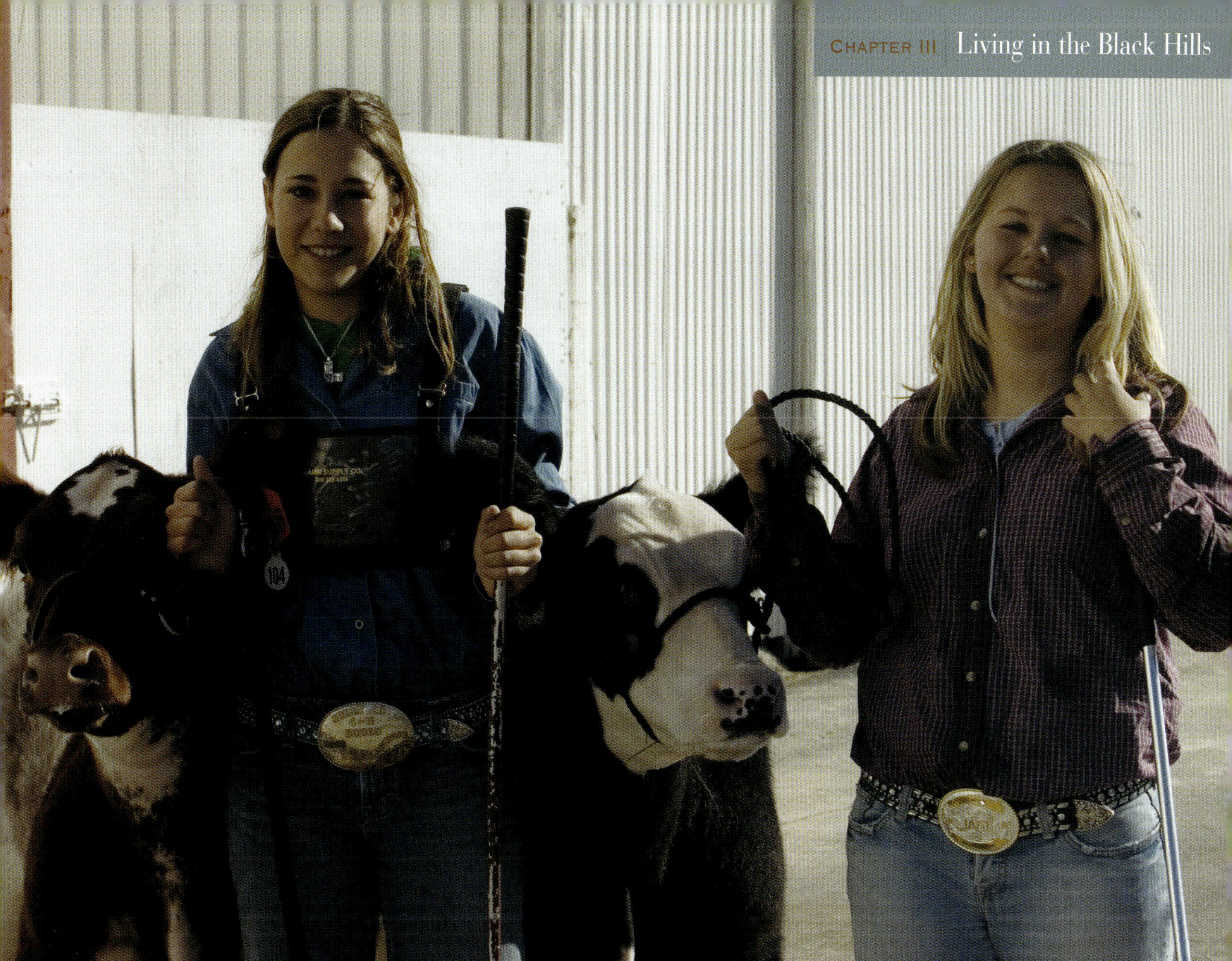

Photo by Dennis Keim

Since 1937, young people like Cally Thomas and Shelby Kroupa (pictured left to right) have participated in the Western Junior Livestock Show (WJLS), a volunteer-based 4-H youth organization dedicated to helping its participants forge successful careers in the agricultural industry by teaching them how to become self-reliant and productive. The group's annual four-day event, held at Rapid City's Central States Fairgrounds in October, allows participants from counties throughout South Dakota and the surrounding states to enter projects in a wide variety of categories relating to livestock production, including sheep, swine, cattle, and dairy, among many others. Exhibitors have the chance to win a number of prizes for their impressive and dedicated efforts, from ribbons and buckles to plaques and trophies. And participants who are senior 4-H members and meet specific qualifications can enter to compete for an all-expenses-paid trip to the National Western Stock Show held each January in Denver. ❖

Assurant Preneed Offers Peace of Mind during Difficult Time

Just for a moment, imagine the unimaginable. . . . Someone you love dearly has passed away. In the midst of your grief, you must also select a funeral home, a casket, music, flowers, pallbearers, even clothes for your loved one. Then, you have to decide how all this will be paid for!

Now imagine having those difficult decisions made by your loved one before he is gone. The services, music, flowers, and casket are just as he wanted. Instead, you are able to spend time with your family and friends remembering your loved one and celebrating his life through pictures, stories, and being together.

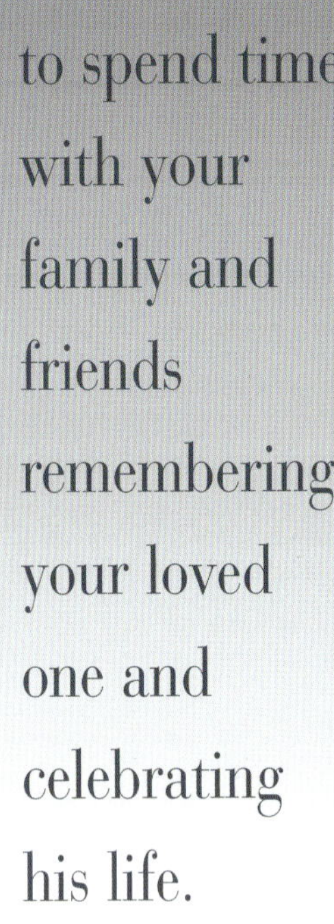

Funeral preplanning or prearranging is the process of making plans for your own funeral—or that of a loved one—well in advance of need, in a nonstressful environment. By providing insurance products and services that help people plan and fund funerals in advance, Assurant Preneed helps to offer peace of mind to the individual and allow his or her family and friends to cope with the passing of a life with the greatest amount of dignity and the least amount of burden.

Assurant Preneed in Rapid City began writing new insurance business in 1959 as Prairie States Life Insurance Company. Over the years, the organization grew and focused its business on the funeral services industry and changed its name to American

Photo by Johnny Sundby

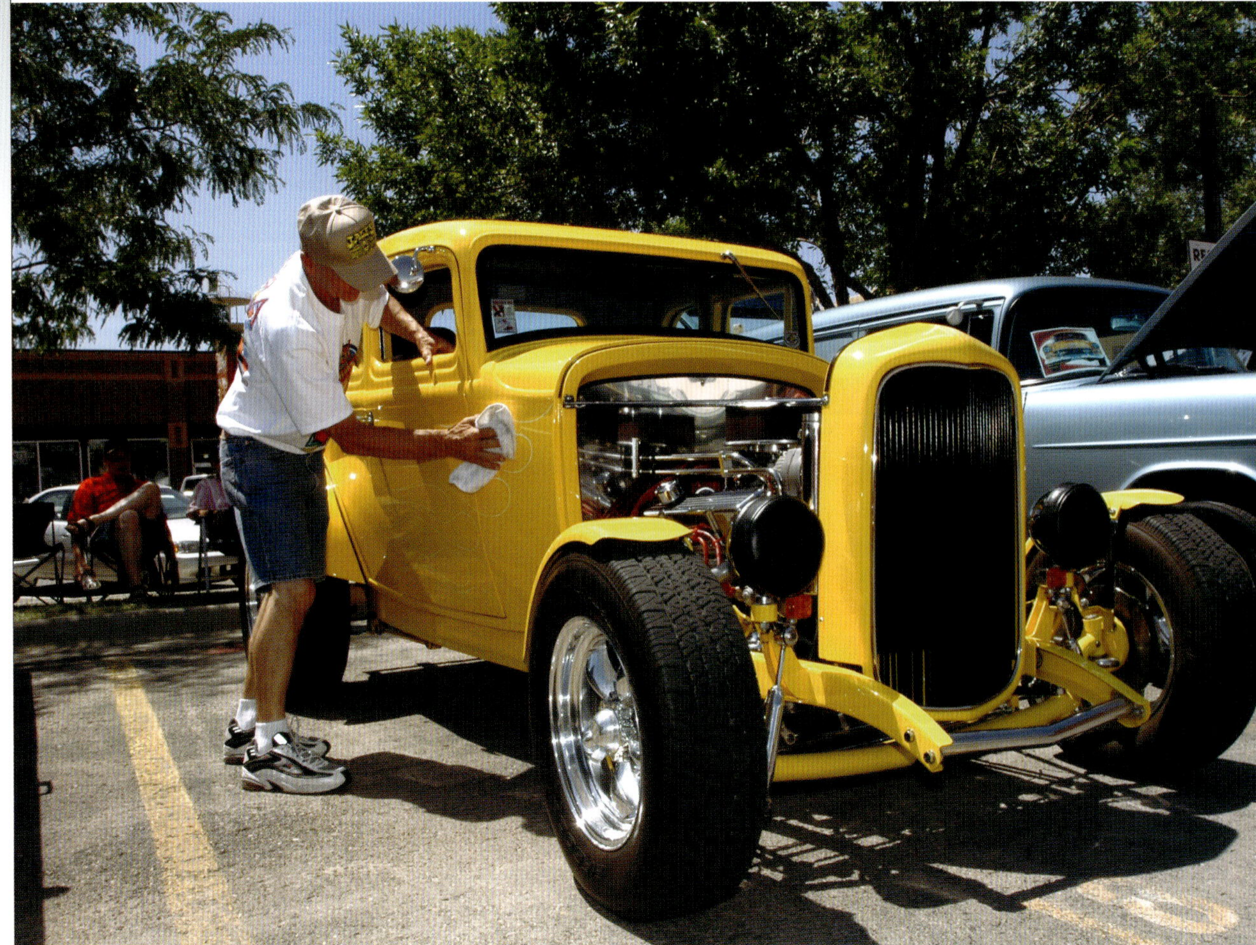

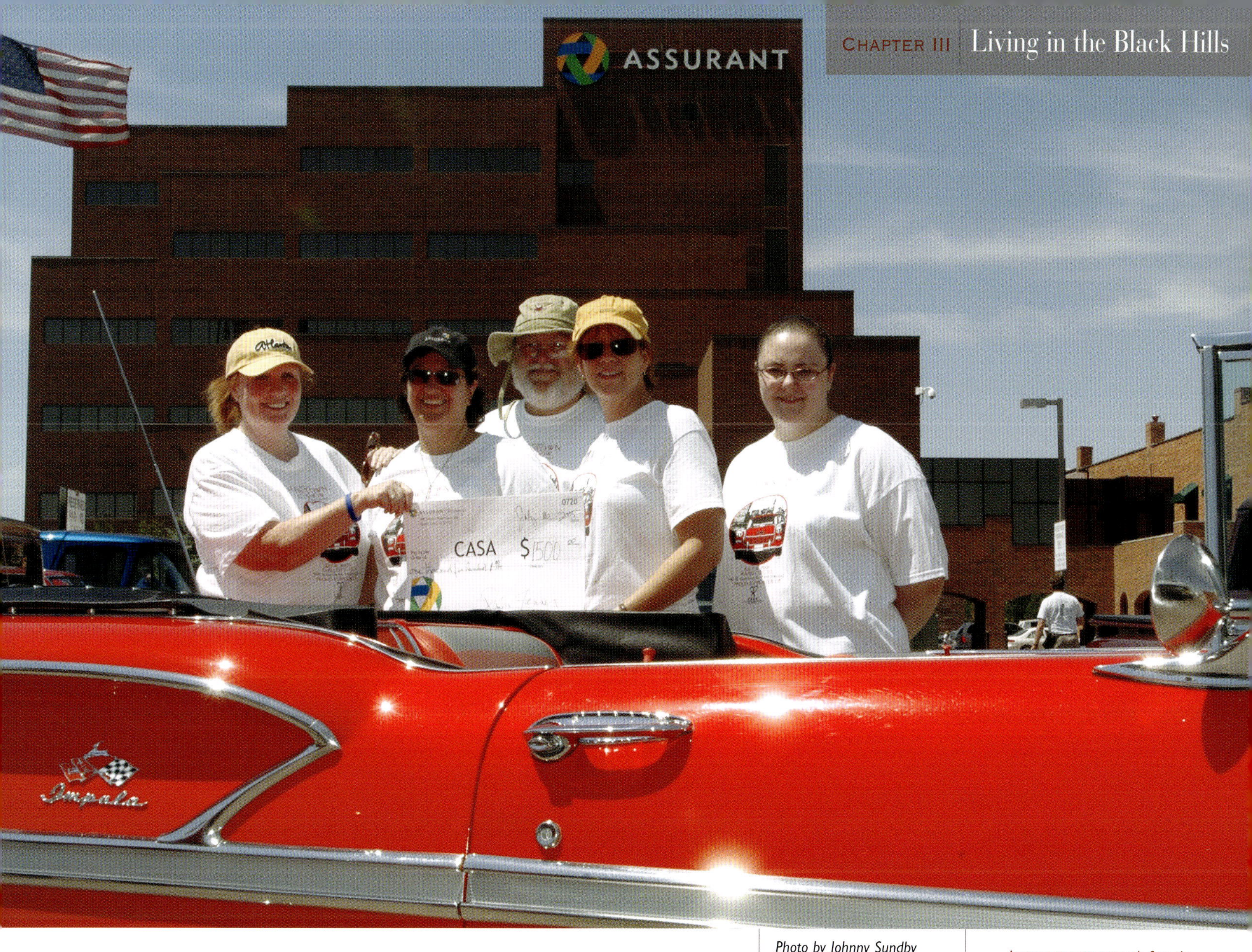

Photo by Johnny Sundby

Assurant presents proceeds from the 2005 Downtown Car Show to representatives from Seventh Circuit CASA, the Court Appointed Special Advocates.

Memorial Life Insurance Company to reflect a nationwide market scope. In 2000, American Memorial Life joined forces with United Family Life Insurance Company of Atlanta, Georgia, and, subsequently, has become known as Assurant Preneed. With more than $4.4 billion in assets and over 1.7 million policies in force, Assurant Preneed is a leader in its industry.

The 155 professionals of Assurant Preneed in the Rapid City office have a clear mission ". . . to simplify the lives of the people we serve." They accomplish this mission by providing expert support to the funeral directors, funeral service associations, marketing organizations, and general insurance agencies that distribute their products and through superior customer service for the families they serve.

Assurant Preneed is probably best known locally for the landmark Christmas tree that is perched atop its six-story building each holiday season in downtown Rapid City. Less known, but more importantly, Assurant Preneed is committed to making a difference in the community. Through its support for community organizations like the United Way, Assurant Preneed and its employees reach out to those who can use a hand and offer dignity, respect, and support when it is needed most.

Assurant Preneed is a part of Assurant, a premier provider of specialized insurance products and related services in North America and selected other markets. Assurant, which is traded on the New York Stock Exchange under the symbol AIZ, has over $24 billion in assets and $7 billion in annual revenue. Assurant has approximately twelve thousand employees, primarily in North America, and is headquartered in New York's financial district. ❖

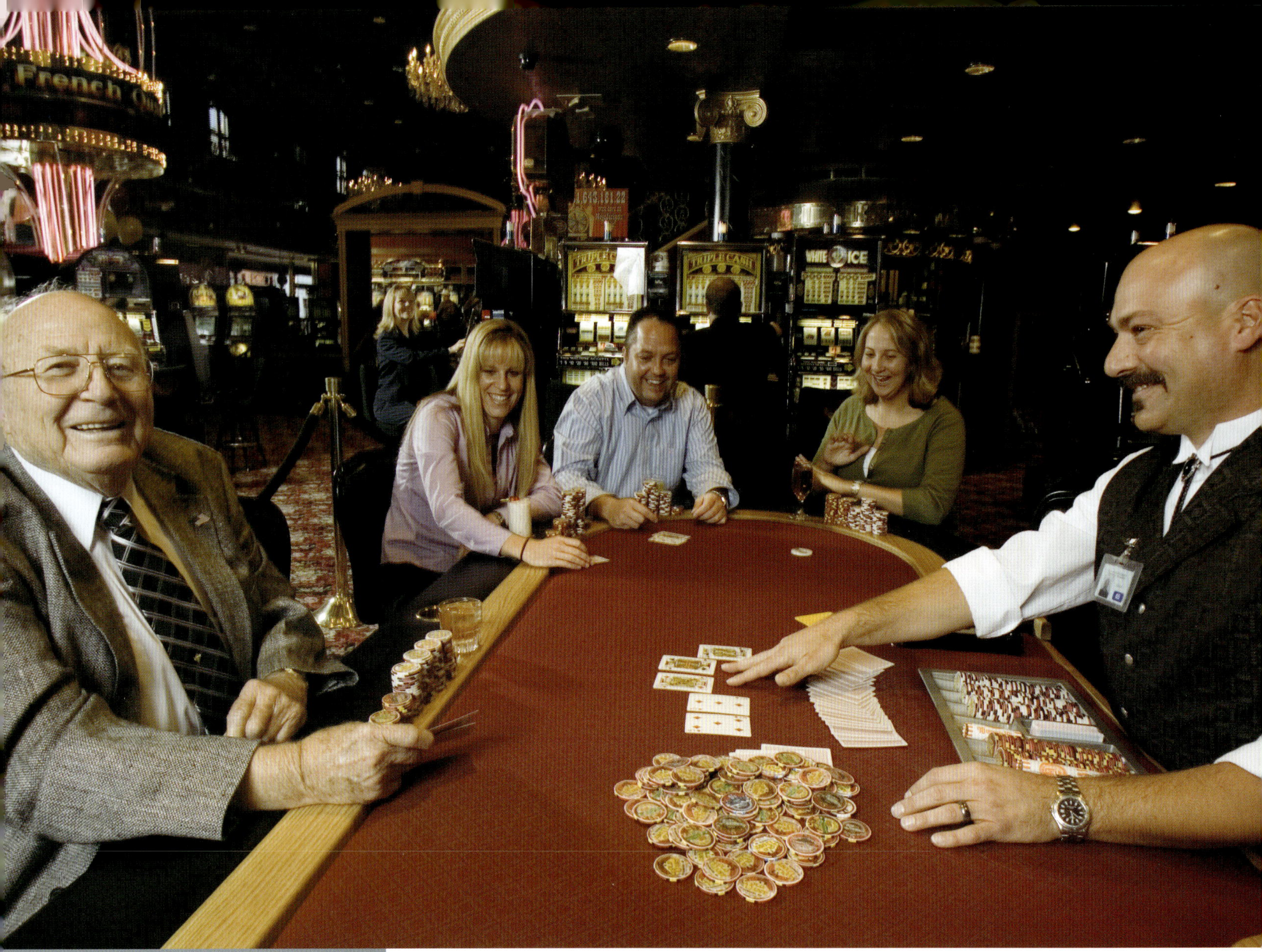

Photo by Dennis Keim

Bob Regan, Cari Geuke, Tony Miles, and Kelli Kammerer (pictured left to right) go all-in during a rousing game of Texas Hold'em at Gold Dust Gaming in Deadwood. Handling the shuffle-up-and-deal duties is Keith Rice, poker room manager for the casino, the largest gaming establishment on historic Main Street and one of the city's most popular tourist attractions, thanks to the eleven gaming halls that welcome players twenty-four hours a day. From poker to blackjack to slots, there's truly something for everyone at Gold Dust. Even novice players can get in on the action, thanks to the facility's highly trained and engaging dealers, who are happy to provide lessons upon request in all versions of low-limit poker and blackjack. And when the chips are down, there's always the Gold Dust Buffet, where those who have parted ways with their cash can raise their spirits with a delicious meal. Then they can retire to their well-appointed rooms at the casino's conveniently located Holiday Inn Express Hotel to prepare for their next encounter with Lady Luck. ❖

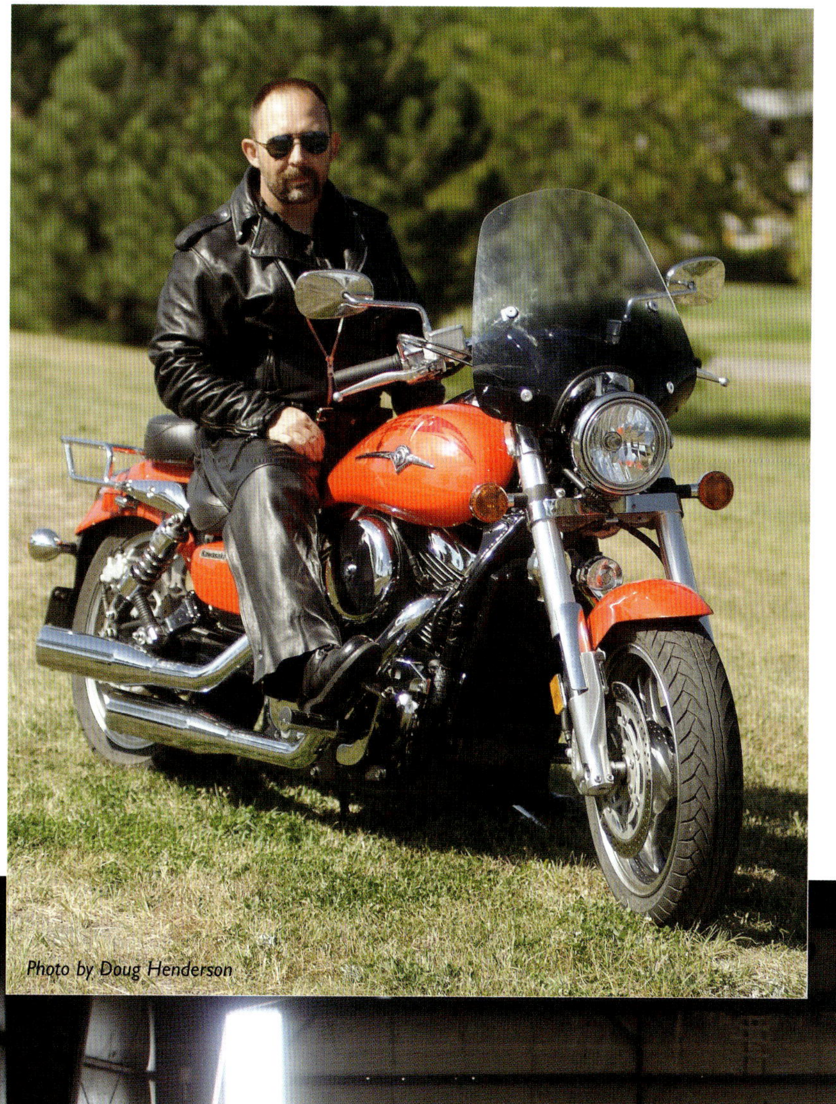
Photo by Doug Henderson

Like thousands of visitors and residents each year, Dr. Gregory Saffell, of Radiology Associates, takes to the open road to enjoy the beauty of the Black Hills. East-west Interstate 90 covers a lot of territory, but the smaller roads offer unexpected treasures. Needles Highway in Custer State Park is a fourteen-mile ride featuring granite spires, narrow tunnels, hairpin curves, and gorgeous views of Sylvan Lake. Iron Mountain Road is slightly longer at seventeen miles, with pigtail bridges and perfectly framed views of Mount Rushmore in the distance. The Wildlife Loop road offers everything from forests to prairie grass lands and bison, deer, elk, burros, and prairie dogs. Spearfish Canyon National Scenic Byway takes you through an ancient narrow canyon, especially beautiful when dressed in fall colors. All these rides are under twenty-five miles. For something longer, try the Peter Norbeck Scenic Byway. This seventy-mile loop is well worth the time, and you can camp out along the way if you want to extend your adventure. ❖

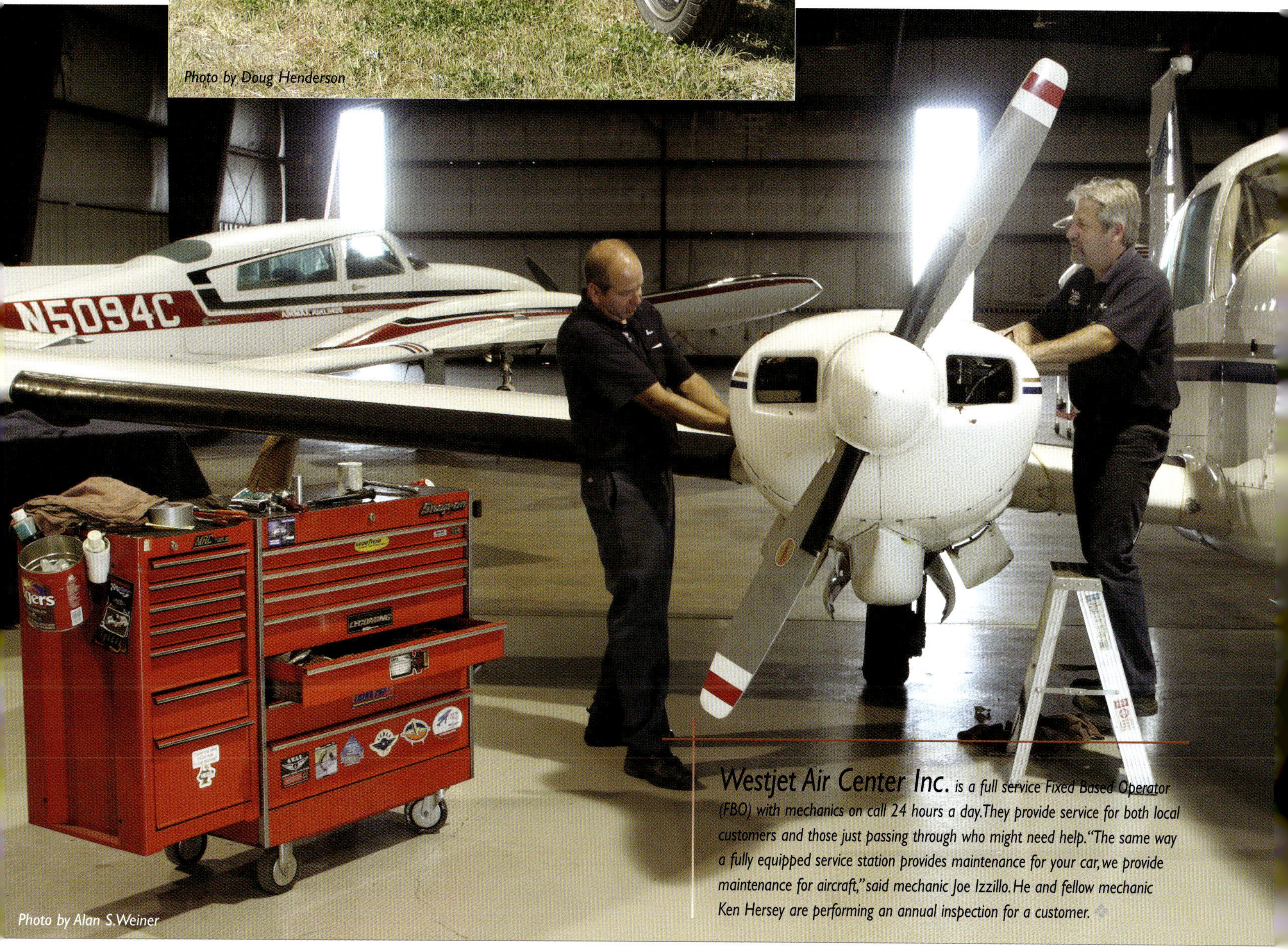

Photo by Alan S. Weiner

Westjet Air Center Inc. is a full service Fixed Based Operator (FBO) with mechanics on call 24 hours a day. They provide service for both local customers and those just passing through who might need help. "The same way a fully equipped service station provides maintenance for your car, we provide maintenance for aircraft," said mechanic Joe Izzillo. He and fellow mechanic Ken Hersey are performing an annual inspection for a customer. ❖

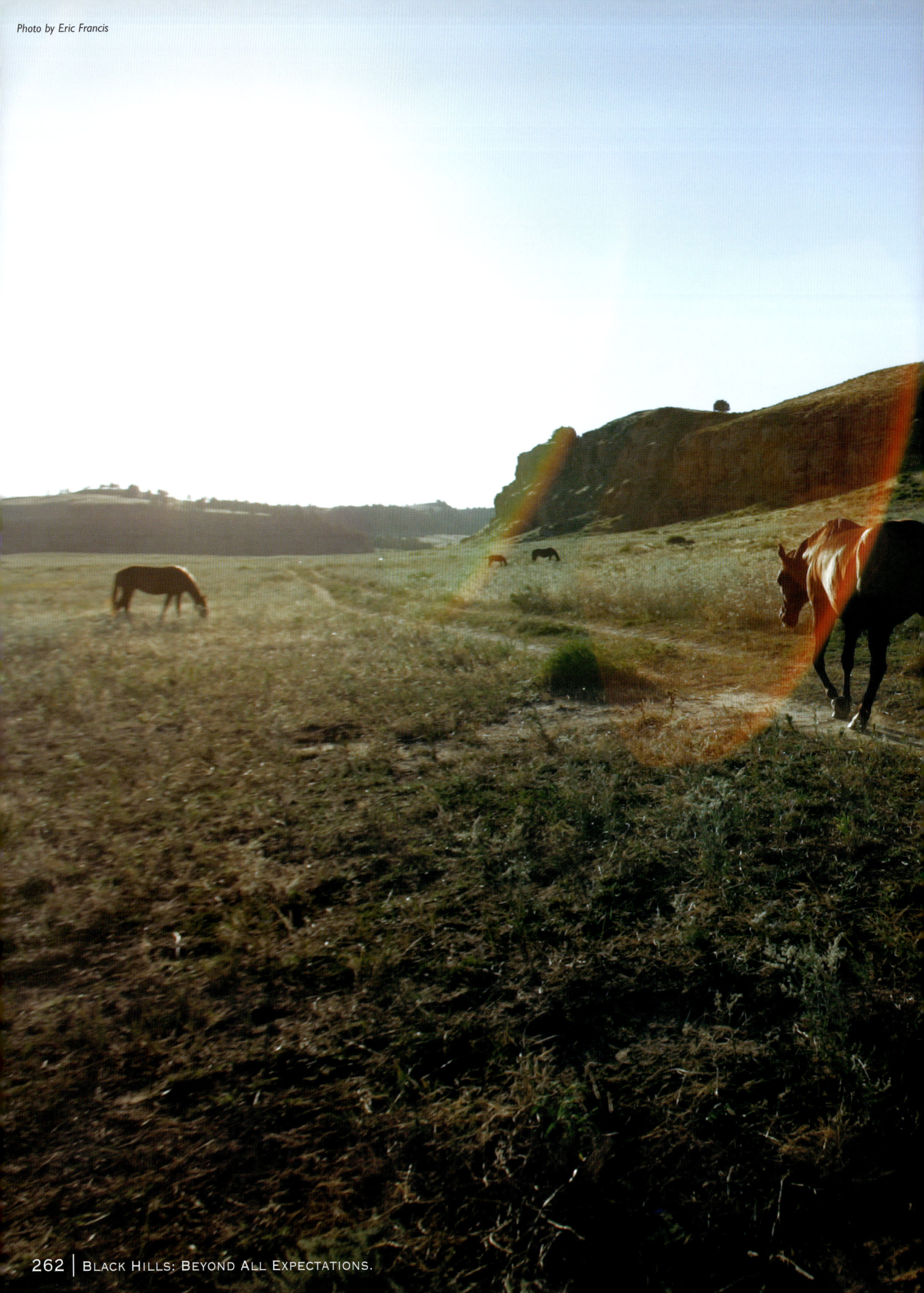
Photo by Eric Francis

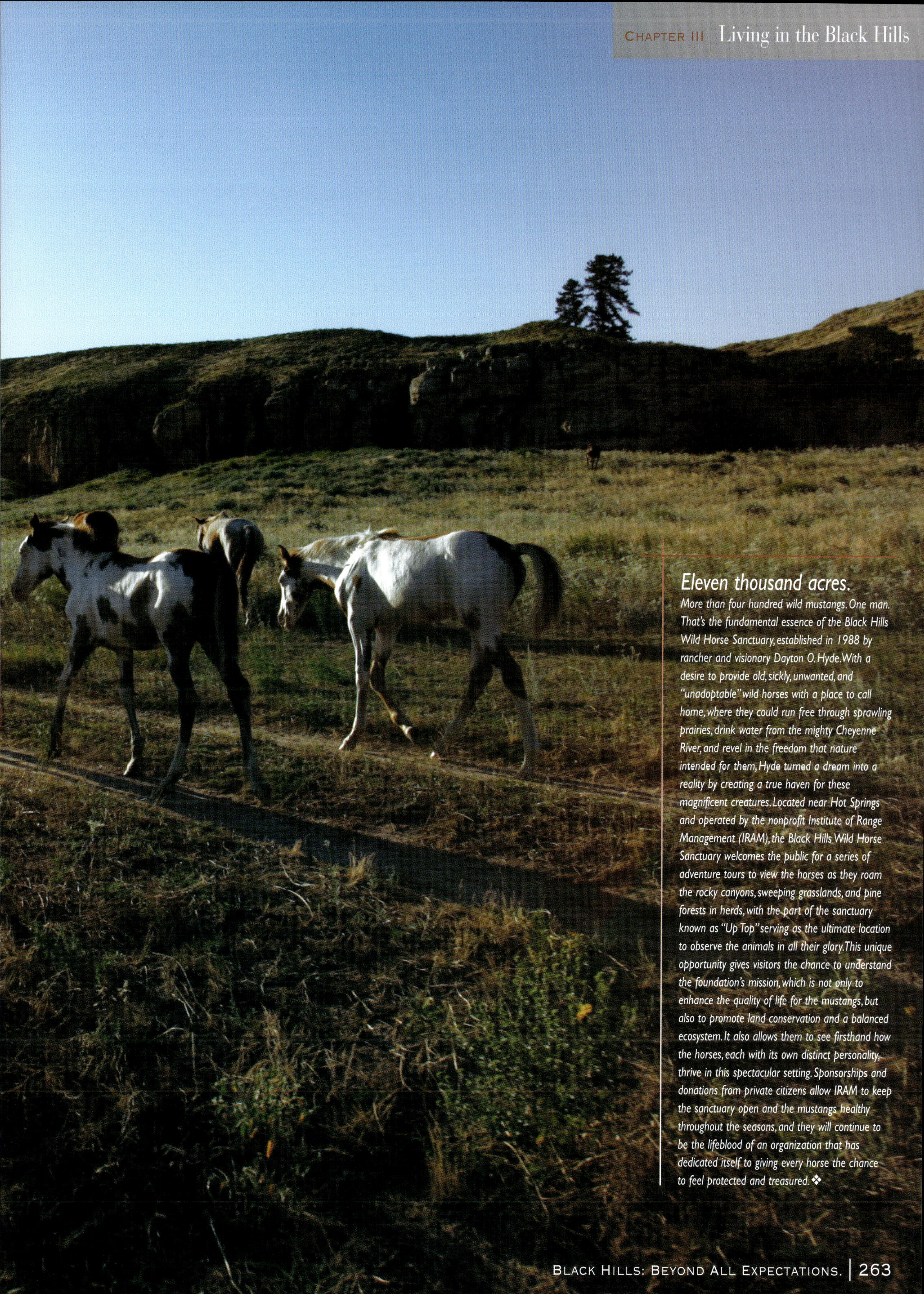

Eleven thousand acres.

More than four hundred wild mustangs. One man. That's the fundamental essence of the Black Hills Wild Horse Sanctuary, established in 1988 by rancher and visionary Dayton O. Hyde. With a desire to provide old, sickly, unwanted, and "unadoptable" wild horses with a place to call home, where they could run free through sprawling prairies, drink water from the mighty Cheyenne River, and revel in the freedom that nature intended for them, Hyde turned a dream into a reality by creating a true haven for these magnificent creatures. Located near Hot Springs and operated by the nonprofit Institute of Range Management (IRAM), the Black Hills Wild Horse Sanctuary welcomes the public for a series of adventure tours to view the horses as they roam the rocky canyons, sweeping grasslands, and pine forests in herds, with the part of the sanctuary known as "Up Top" serving as the ultimate location to observe the animals in all their glory. This unique opportunity gives visitors the chance to understand the foundation's mission, which is not only to enhance the quality of life for the mustangs, but also to promote land conservation and a balanced ecosystem. It also allows them to see firsthand how the horses, each with its own distinct personality, thrive in this spectacular setting. Sponsorships and donations from private citizens allow IRAM to keep the sanctuary open and the mustangs healthy throughout the seasons, and they will continue to be the lifeblood of an organization that has dedicated itself to giving every horse the chance to feel protected and treasured. ❖

BLACK HILLS Featured Companies

Apple Springs Resort
2000 Wesleyan Boulevard
Rapid City, South Dakota 57702
605.343.3555
www.applespringsresort.com

Real Estate - Developer (p.60)
Apple Springs Development is a unique resort and housing project situated on 370 acres in Boulder Canyon. When complete, the development will include single-family homes, town-homes, and resort accommodations.

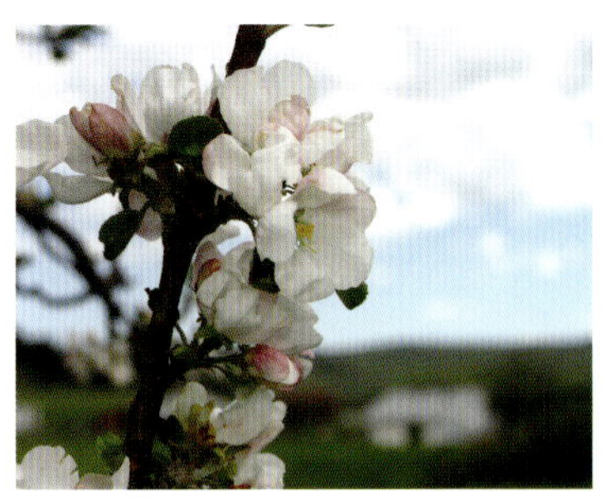

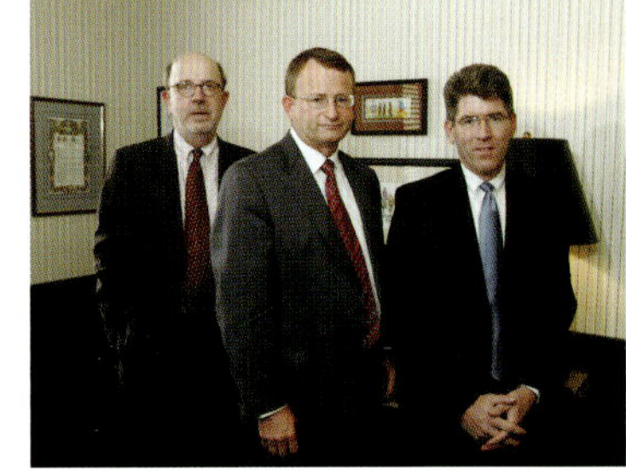

Assurant Preneed
440 Mt. Rushmore Road
Rapid City, South Dakota 57701
605.719.0999
www.assurantpreneed.com

Burial Insurance and Planning (p.258-259)
The prearrangement and prefunding services provided by this multibillion-dollar division of Assurant help enable families to mourn the passing of their loved ones with dignity and security.

Bangs, McCullen, Butler, Foye & Simmons, LLP
333 West Boulevard
Suite 400
Rapid City, South Dakota 57701
605.343.1040
www.bangsmccullen.com

Law Firm (p.126-127)
Bangs McCullen has a long and proud history of providing authoritative legal counsel for individuals and businesses throughout South Dakota, Wyoming, Nebraska, North Dakota, Minnesota, and Iowa. What began as a one-person firm in the 1800s has grown into one of the most recognized and respected law firms in the area.

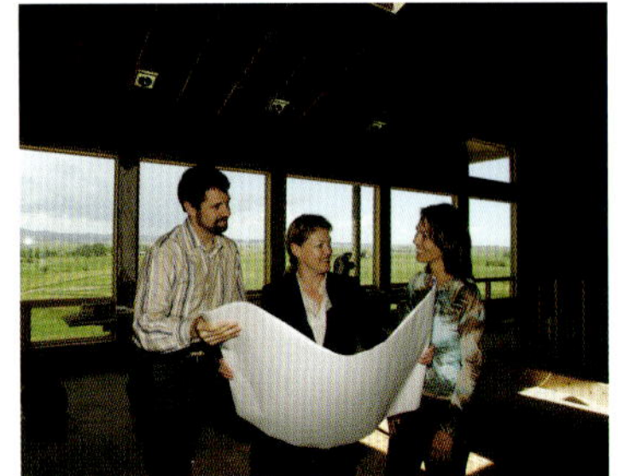

BankWest
709 Main Street
Rapid City, South Dakota 57701
605.399.2265
www.bankwest-sd.com

Financial Institution—Bank (p.160-161)
BankWest is a privately owned community bank that helps customers achieve lifetime financial success and security. The bank has more than a dozen area branches and offices offering a complete range of banking and financial services.

Behavior Management Systems
350 Elk Street
Rapid City, South Dakota 57701
605.343.7262
www.behaviormanagement.org

HealthCare (p.206-207)
Behavior Management Systems is the largest behavioral health-care company in western South Dakota, providing the full scope of services to help people learn to cope with stress and lead productive lives.

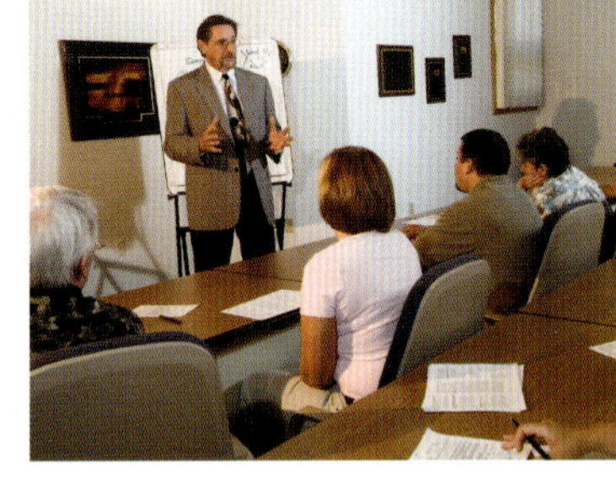

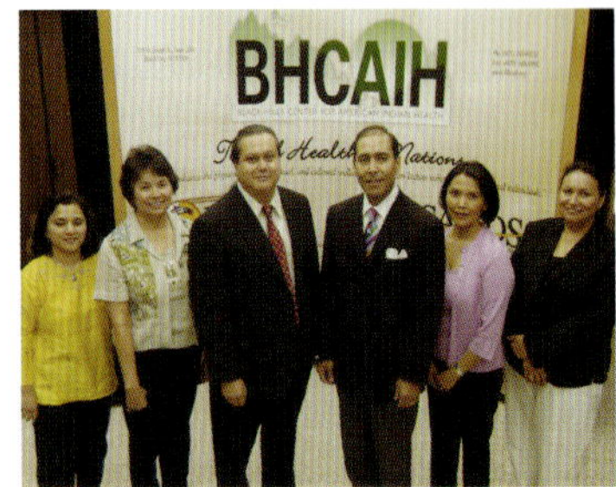

Black Hills Center for American Indian Health
701 Saint Joseph Street
Suite 204
Rapid City, South Dakota 57701
605.348.6100
www.bhcaih.org

Nonprofit health-care research center (p.218-219)
By partnering with universities, national health-care organizations, and regional tribes, this nonprofit organization researches the causes of and solutions to the most pressing American Indian health-care issues.

Black Hills Corporation
625 9th Street
Rapid City, South Dakota 57701
605.721.1700
www.blackhillscorp.com

Utility (p 144-145)
Black Hills Corporation is a diversified energy company with operations focused in the West. Black Hills Energy, its wholesale nonregulated energy subsidiary, is located in Golden, Colorado, and consists of power generation, coal mining, natural gas and oil production, and energy marketing.

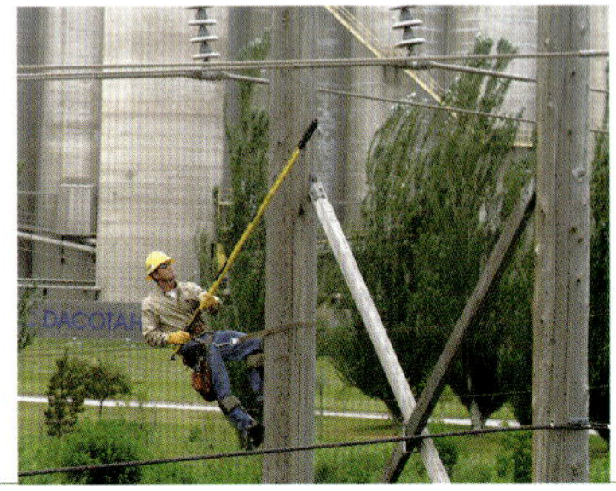

Black Hills Dermatology & Laser Surgery Centre
7236 Jordan Drive
Rapid City, South Dakota 57701
605.341.5565
www.bhdermatology.com

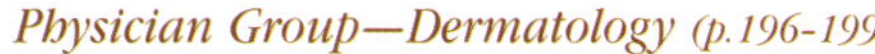

Physician Group—Dermatology (p.196-199)

Black Hills Dermatology & Laser Surgery Centre and its SpaMeD division cover every aspect of skin care from laser surgery to manicures and pedicures, making it a convenient and efficient skin care center for the patients who come from four surrounding states.

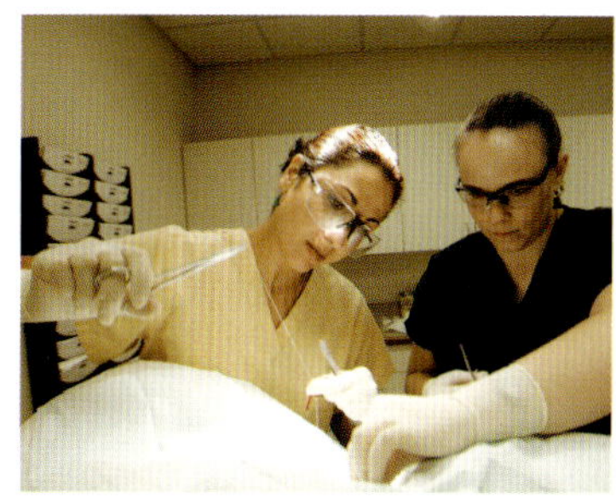

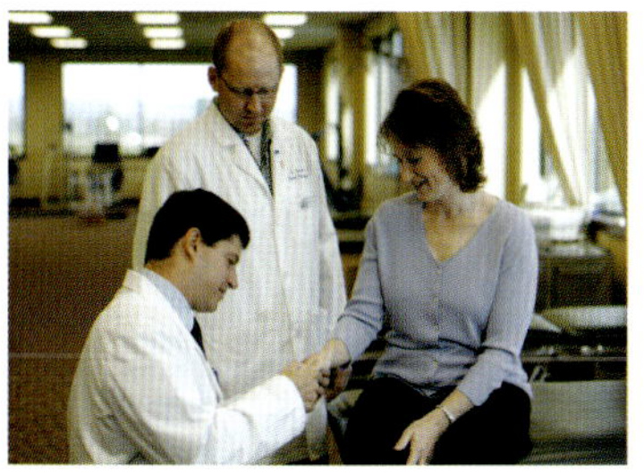

Black Hills Orthopedic & Spine Center, P.C.
P.O. Box 6850
Rapid City, South Dakota 57709
605.341.1414
www.bhosc.com

Physician Group (p.210-211)

The physicians at Black Hills Orthopedic & Spine Center have dedicated themselves to restoring their patients' mobility. Through orthopedic and spine surgery, rheumatology, sports medicine, podiatry, and physical therapy, their goal is to return patients to the activities they love.

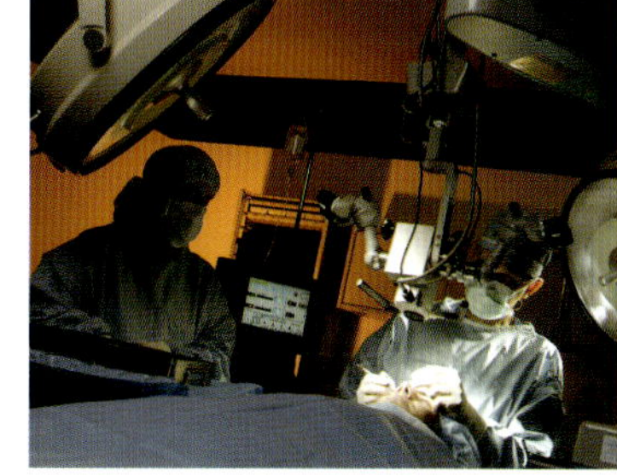

Black Hills Regional Eye Institute
2800 3rd Street
Rapid City, South Dakota 57701
605.341.2000
www.blackhillseyes.com

Physician Group (p.192-193)

The Black Hills Regional Eye Institute serves patients in a five-state area: North Dakota, South Dakota, Wyoming, Nebraska, and Montana. Black Hills Regional Eye Institute doctors work with local physicians and optometrists in twelve satellite locations that provide convenient eye care for patients near their homes.

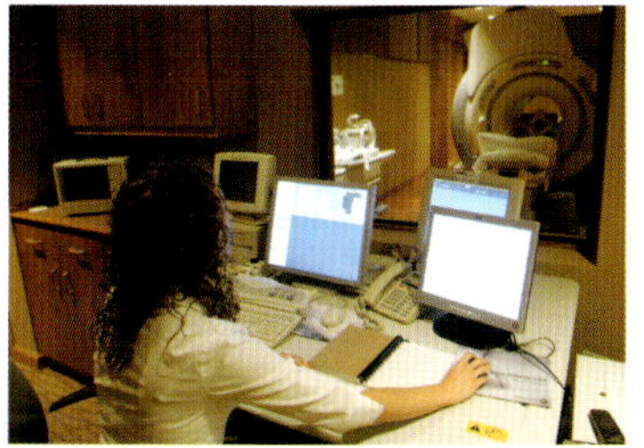

Black Hills Surgery Center
1868 Lombardy Drive
Rapid City, South Dakota 57701
605.721.4700
www.bhsc.com

Hospital—Medical Center (p.238-239)

Black Hills Surgery Center specializes in orthopedics, neurosurgery, ear, nose and throat, general surgery, urology, and gynecology. Each of their surgical teams is a well-oiled unit with expertise in these specialities to assure the best possible outcome for their patients.

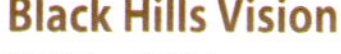

Black Hills Vision
P.O. Box 8028
Rapid City, South Dakota 57702
605.718.6001
www.blackhillsvision.org

Strategic Planning Organization (p.148-149)

Black Hills Vision (BHV) is a regional economic development organization committed to preserving the region's quality of life and creating an economic development "opportunity environment."

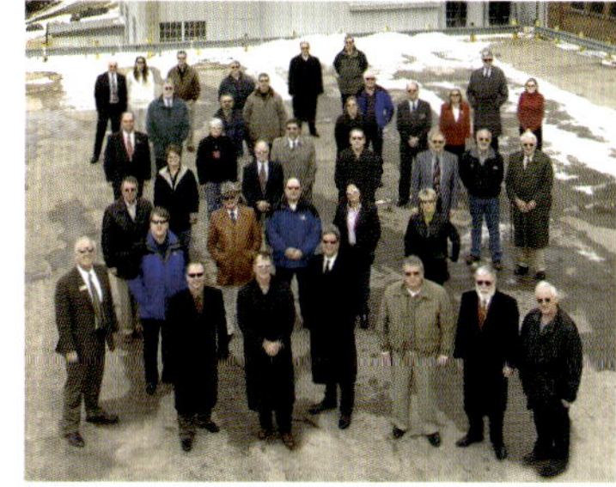

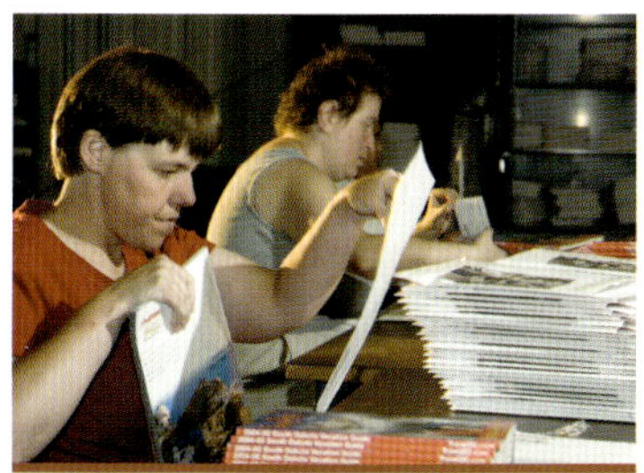

Black Hills Workshop
P.O. Box 2104
Rapid City, South Dakota 57709
605.343.4550
www.bhws.com

Rehabilitation Facility (p.106)

The Black Hills Workshop and Training Center is a community rehabilitation program for adults with disabilities. Employment allows them to explore opportunities and make choices. Since the workshop was established in 1958, it has provided employment for hundreds of individuals with disabilities.

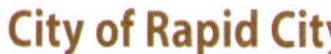

City of Rapid City
300 6th Street
Rapid City, South Dakota 57701
605.394.4110
www.rcgov.org

Government—City (p.94-96)

For over one hundred years, Rapid City relied on natural resources such as gold mining, timber, farming, and ranching along with more recent additions of the military and tourism. Now the city is making a concerted effort to take control of its destiny by focusing on building a high-tech corridor throughout the Black Hills.

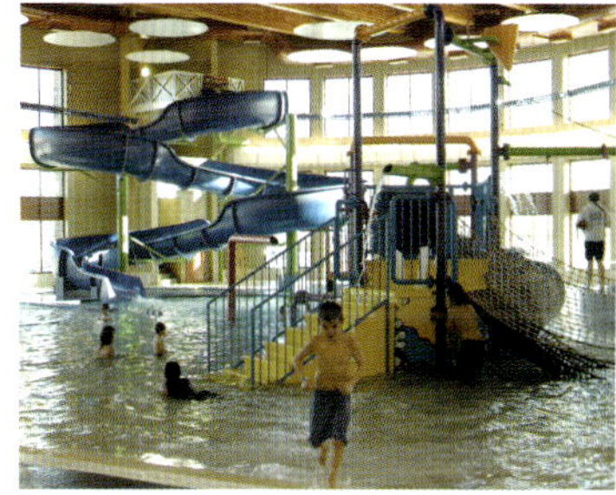

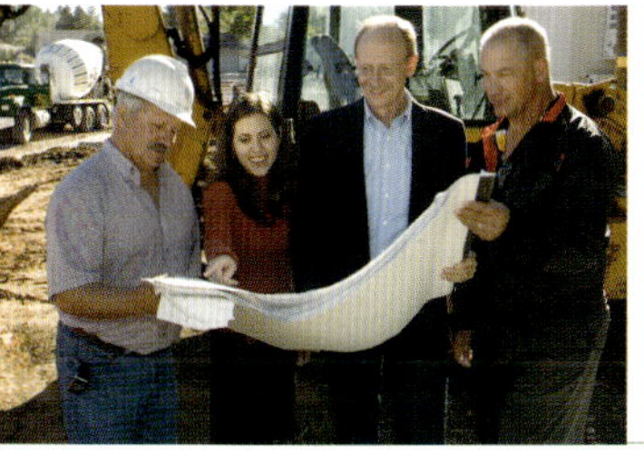

Costello, Porter, Hill, Heisterkamp, Bushnell & Carpenter, LLP
704 Saint Joseph Street
Rapid City, South Dakota 57701
605.343.2410
www.costelloporter.com

Law Firm (p.172-173)

With the distinction as one of the oldest law firms in South Dakota, Costello, Porter, Hill, Heisterkamp, Bushnell & Carpenter, LLP represents a diverse clientele, including individuals, corporations, medical clinics, professionals, banks, insurance and bonding companies, and major employers and their employees in South Dakota.

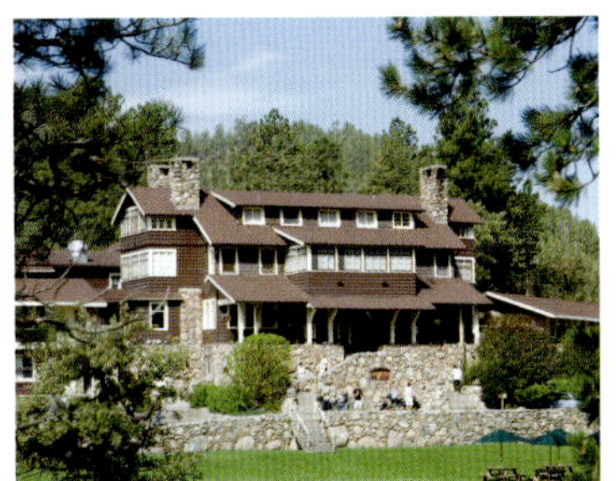

Custer Resort Company
13389 US Highway 16A
Custer, South Dakota 57730
605.255.4772
www.custerresorts.com

Government—City (p.66-67)
As operators of four different resorts located in Custer State Park, this privately owned and operated company provides guests with top-notch lodging, dining, and recreational experiences among the natural splendor of the Black Hills.

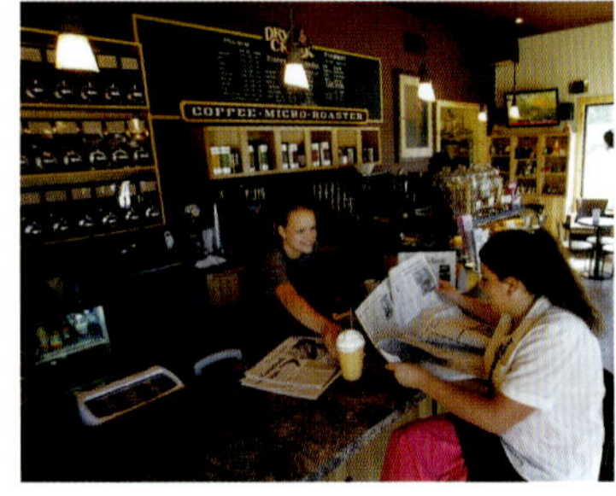

Dakota's Best
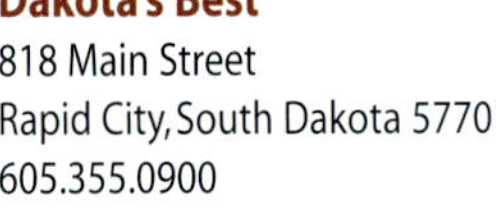
818 Main Street
Rapid City, South Dakota 57701
605.355.0900

Coffee Shop (p.28-29)
Located inside the Radisson Hotel, this unique gift shop features an array of South Dakota arts and crafts, foodstuffs, gifts, and mementos. It's also a great place to stop for a quick sandwich and an aromatic cup of locally produced coffee or tea.

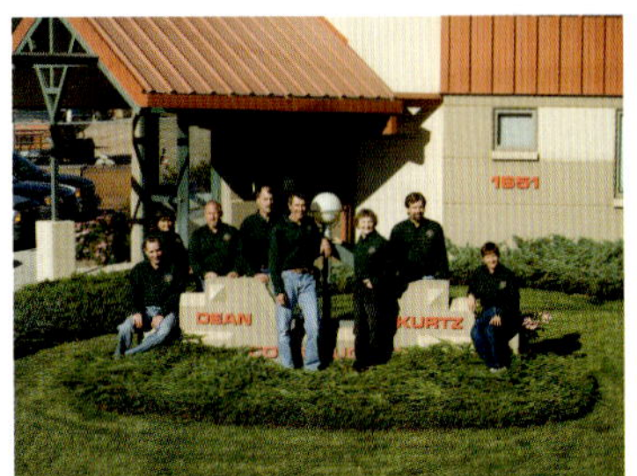

Dean Kurtz Construction
1651 Rand Road
Rapid City, South Dakota 57702
605.343.6665
www.deankurtzconstruction.com

Construction Company (p.176-179)
During the past quarter-century, a significant part of construction in western South Dakota has come from Dean Kurtz Construction Company. They have a track record of successes in industrial projects, commercial buildings, structure renovation, and housing projects.

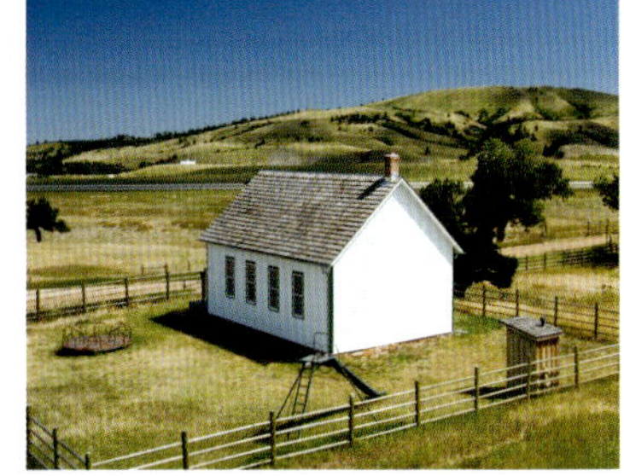

Elkhorn Ridge at Frawley Ranches, LLC
20189 U.S. Highway 85
Spearfish, SD 57783
605.722.1800
www.frawleyranches.com

Planned Community (p.54-57)
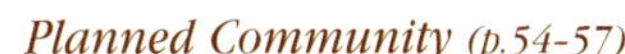
A unique master planned community, Elkhorn Ridge at Frawley Ranches provides a wealth of economic opportunity in the Black Hills region while also helping to preserve the beautiful Frawley Ranch and its many historic structures.

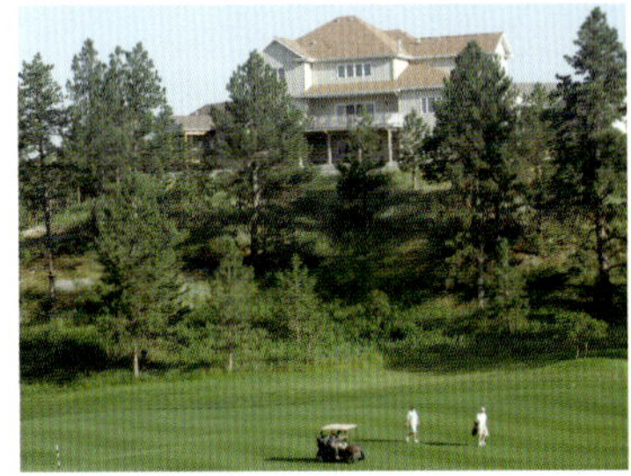

Estates and Golf Club at Red Rock, The
6520 Birkdale Drive
Rapid City, South Dakota 57702
605.718.4717
www.estatesatredrock.com or
www.golfatredrock.com

Golf Club (p.40-41)
The Estates and Golf Club at Red Rock offers some of the most luxurious living and recreational fun in the Black Hills region.

Fort Welikit Family Campground
24992 Sylvan Lake Road
Custer, South Dakota 57730
605.673.3600
www.blackhillsrv.com

Campground and RV Park (p.18)
Fort Welikit Family Campground is a full-service facility surrounded by the splendor of the Black Hills. From there visitors can ride horses, take a tour, visit area attractions, and go hiking, rock climbing, or jump in nearby Sylvan Lake. Motor homes, campers, trailers, bikes, and mopeds are also available for rent.

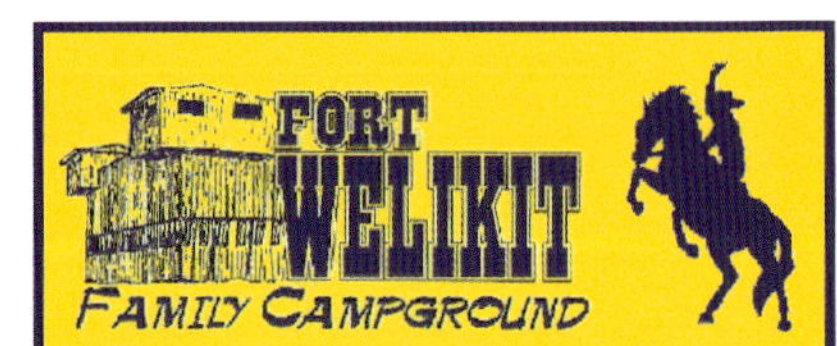

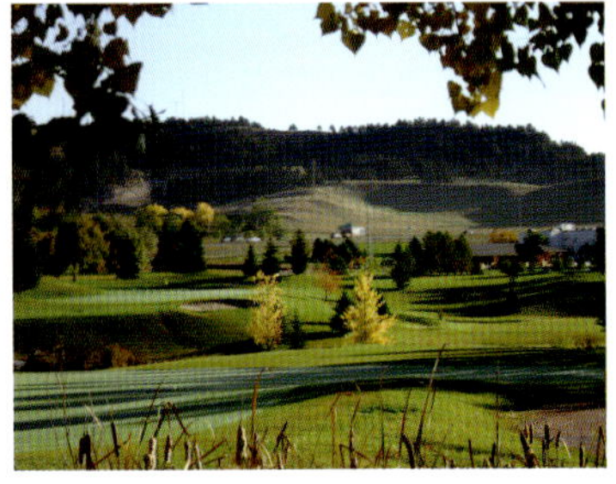

Fountain Springs Health Care
2000 Wesleyan Boulevard
Rapid City, South Dakota 57702
605.343.3555
www.fountainsprings.net

Real Estate—Developer (p.228-229)
Fountain Springs Health Care is dedicated to bringing generations together. The community includes a long-term care and rehabilitation center, an apartment complex for low-income seniors, a retirement condominium, a child-care center, and a nine-hole public golf course.

GCC Dacotah, Inc.
501 North Saint Onge
Rapid City, South Dakota 57702
605.721.7100
www.gcc.com

Manufacturing—Cement (p.118)
GCC Dacotah, Inc. is a cement manufacturing company and a subsidiary of GCC.

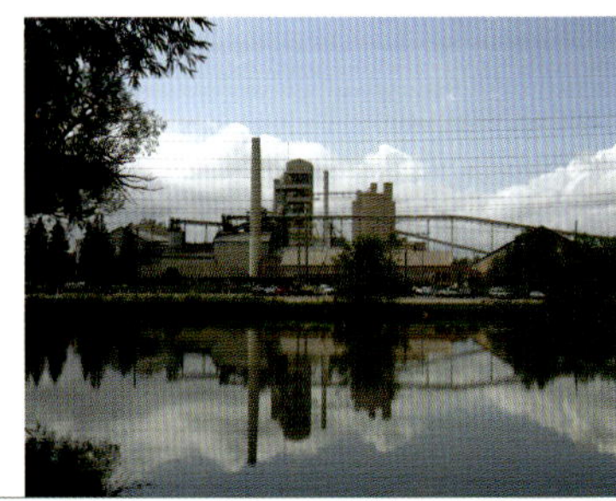

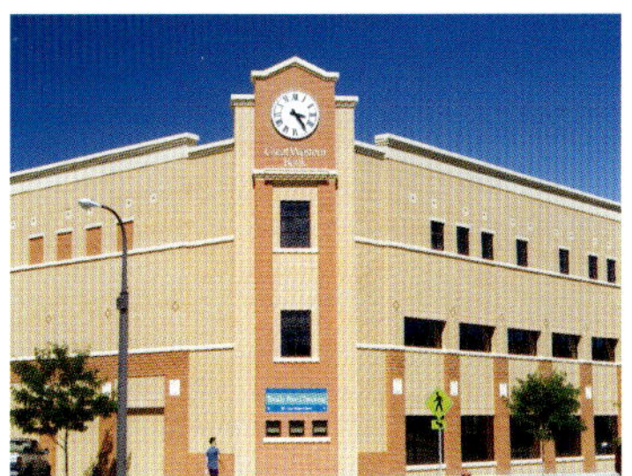

Great Western Bank
14 Saint Joseph Street
Rapid City, South Dakota 57701
605.343.9230
www.greatwesternbanksd.com

Bank (p.108-110)
Great Western Bank opened its doors in 1935, and today they have twenty-seven locations throughout South Dakota and northeastern Nebraska, including seven in the Black Hills. Their combined assets have grown to over $1 billion. What has not changed is the independent-minded way they do business.

Gunderson, Palmer, Goodsell & Nelson, LLP
Assurant Building
440 Mt. Rushmore Road
Rapid City, South Dakota 57701
605.342.1078
www.gundersonpalmer.com

Legal Services (p 120-121)
Teamwork, client-focus, and extensive experience in a wide range of legal services distinguishes Gunderson, Palmer, Goodsell & Nelson as one of the top law firms serving Rapid City and the Black Hills region.

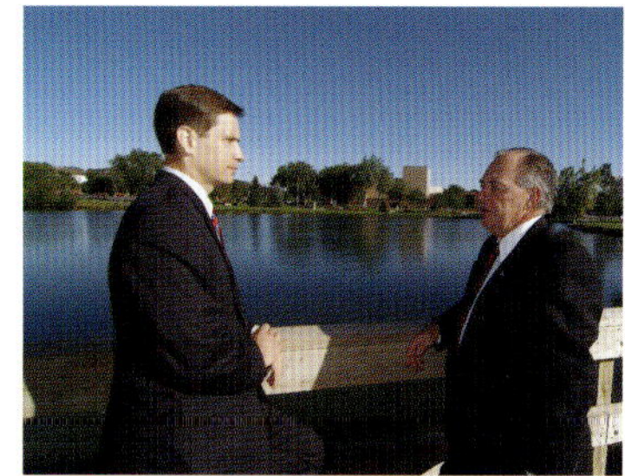

Highmark Federal Credit Union
725 5th Street
Rapid City, South Dakota 57701
605.716.4444
www.highmarkfcu.com

Financial—Credit Union (p.156-157)
Highmark is one of the state's largest credit unions, serving anyone who lives, works, worships, or attends school in Pennington, Meade, Lawrence, or Custer counties.

Hill City Area Chamber of Commerce
555 East Main Street
Hill City, South Dakota 57745
605.574.2368
www.hillcitysd.com

Chamber of Commerce (p.76)
Hill City, South Dakota, is a unique mountain community situated in the heart of the Black Hills. The city offers visitors an array of unique shops and restaurants, as well as easy access to area attractions.

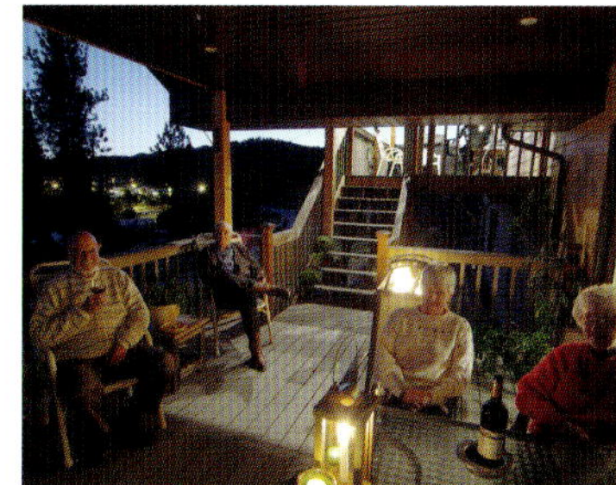

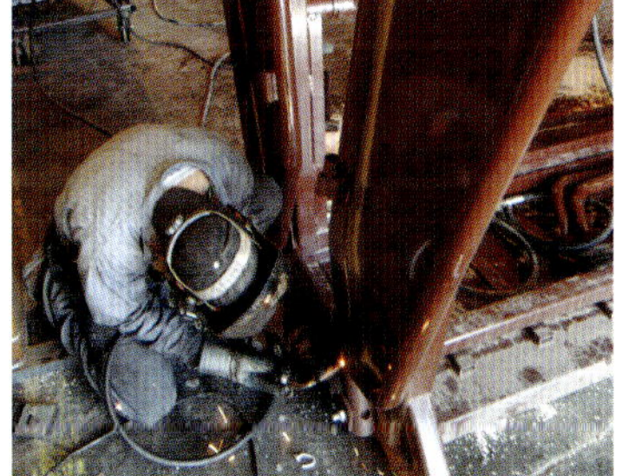

HiQual Manufacturing
3139 Creek Drive
Rapid City, South Dakota 57703-4153
605.343.1234
www.hi-qual.com

Manufacturing—horse and cattle products (p.130)
HiQual Manufacturing is an industry leader in livestock equipment, servicing more than 350 qualified dealerships across the country.

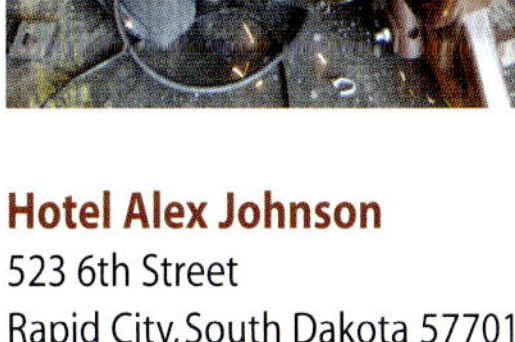

Hotel Alex Johnson
523 6th Street
Rapid City, South Dakota 57701
605.342.1210
www.alexjohnson.com

Hotel (p.70-71)
Hotel Alex Johnson combines classic luxury, western ambiance, and tradition for an extraordinary lodging experience. The grand hotel, built in 1928, is listed on the National Register of Historic Places, and features 143 comfortable rooms, an award-winning restaurant, banquet/reception facilities, and a unique art gallery and gift shop.

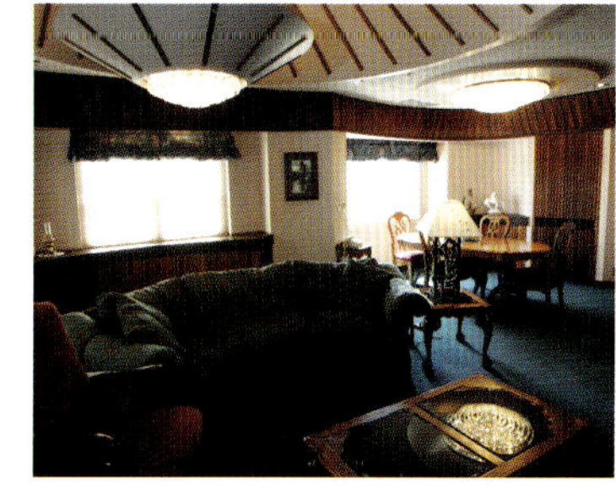

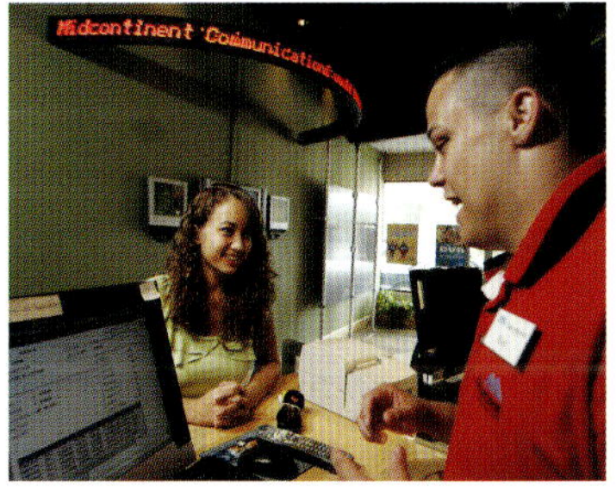

Midcontinent Communications
1624 Concourse Court
Rapid City, South Dakota 57703
800.888.1300
www.midcocomm.com

Telecommunications (p.140-141)
Midcontinent Communications, a partnership of Midcontinent Media, Inc., and Comcast Corporation, is a premier provider of cable television, local and long-distance telephone service, high-speed Internet access, cable advertising, and data network services. The company serves more than two hundred communities in North and South Dakota, northern Nebraska, and Minnesota.

National American University
321 Kansas City Street
Rapid City, South Dakota 57701
605.394.4800
www.national.edu

College—University (p.232-234)
National American University is a private career college committed to high-quality instructional programs and services, as well as technical and professional career orientation. The Rapid City campus, established in 1941, is one of thirteen campus locations through the central United States. NAU is accredited by the Higher Learning Commission, and is a member of the North Central Association.

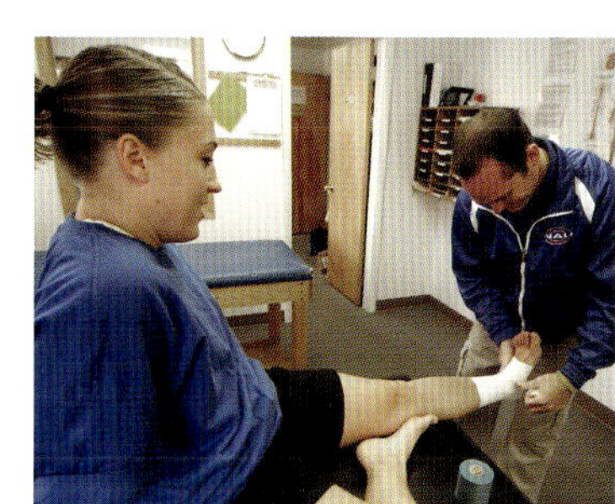

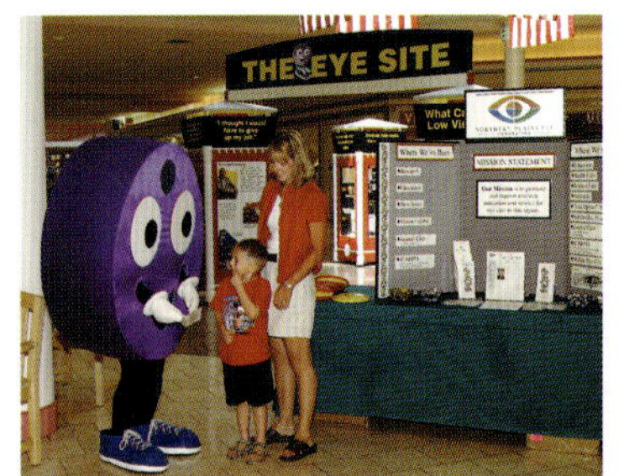

Northern Plains Eye Foundation
623 Quincy Street, Suite 101
Rapid City, South Dakota 57701
605.716.6733
www.npef.org

Non-Profit (p.202-203)
The Northern Plains Eye Foundation is a not-for-profit 501(c)(3) corporation chartered for charitable, educational, and scientific purposes related to eye care.

Pete Lien & Sons, Inc.
P.O. Box 440
Rapid City, South Dakota 57709
605.342.7224
www.petelien.com

Mining and Processing (p.112-115)
Pete Lien & Sons, Inc., is a private, family-owned mining and processing company. Founded in 1944, the umbrella company now has more than thirty facility and mineral sites in South Dakota, Wyoming, Colorado, and Montana. The company is diversified in mining, lime, pulverized limestone, sand and gravel, ready-mix concrete, concrete block manufacturing, and steel fabrication.

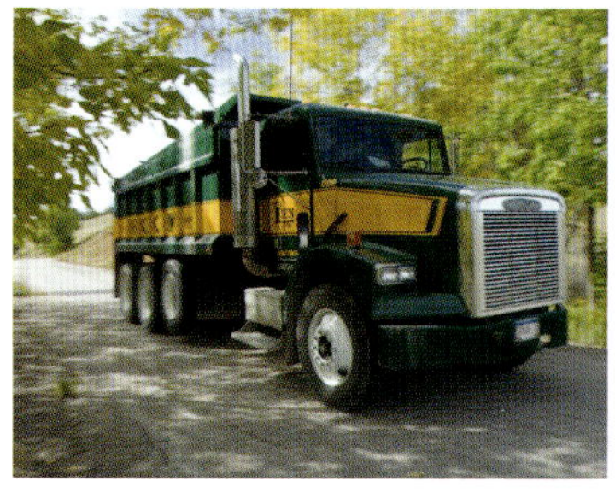

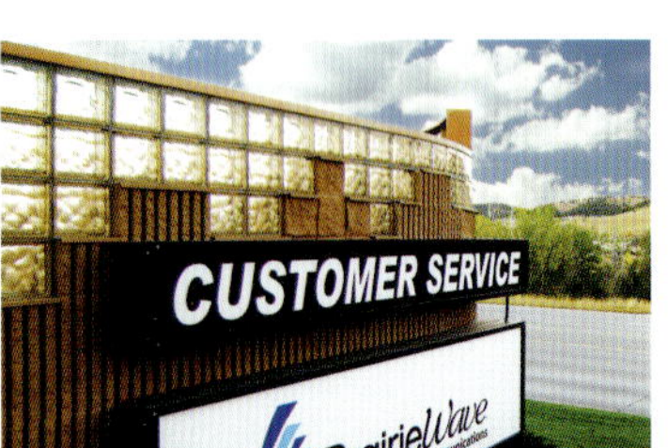

PrairieWave Communications
5100 South Broadband Lane
Sioux Falls, South Dakota 57108
877.633.4567
www.prairiewave.com

Telecommunications (p.124)
PrairieWave Communications is a leader in advanced telephone, cable TV, and Internet services throughout South Dakota, southwest Minnesota, and northwest Iowa.

Radiology Associates, Professional LLC
716 Quincy Street
Rapid City, South Dakota 57701
605.342.2852

Physician Group (p.242-243)
The twelve board-certified radiologists at Radiology Associates, Professional LLC use state-of-the-art equipment and computer systems to provide diagnostic and interventional radiology services at the speed of light. These services are all provided at Rapid City Regional Hospital and twenty teleradiology sites in Wyoming, Montana, Nebraska, and outlying areas of South Dakota.

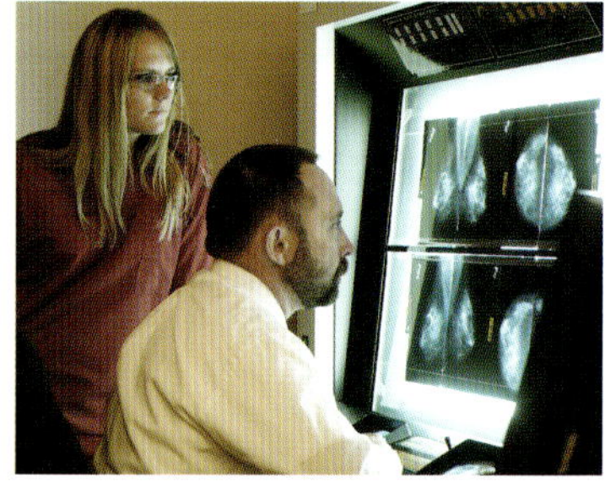

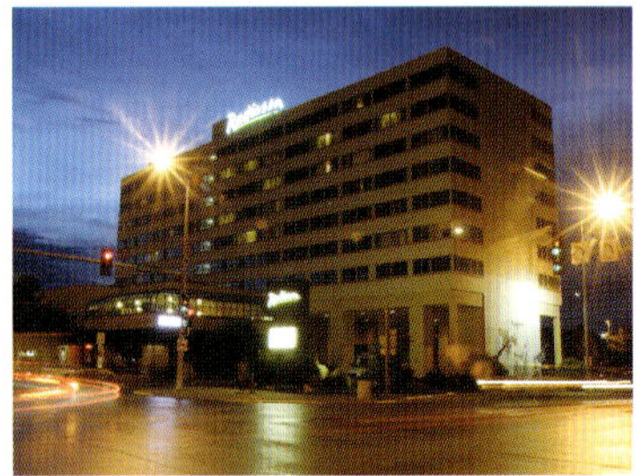

Radisson Hotel Rapid City/ Mt. Rushmore
444 Mt. Rushmore Road
Rapid City, South Dakota 57701
605.348.8300
www.radissonrapidcity.com

Hotel (p.22-25)
Located in the heart of downtown, the Radisson Hotel Rapid City/Mt. Rushmore offers the finest in service and amenities while reflecting the area's unique identity and surrounding natural beauty.

Rapid City Area Chamber of Commerce
444 Mt. Rushmore Road North
Rapid City, South Dakota 57701
605.343.1744
www.rapidcitychamber.com

Chamber of Commerce (p.152-154)
Since 1886, the Rapid City Area Chamber of Commerce has fostered a healthy business environment as part of the high quality of life offered by the Black Hills region.

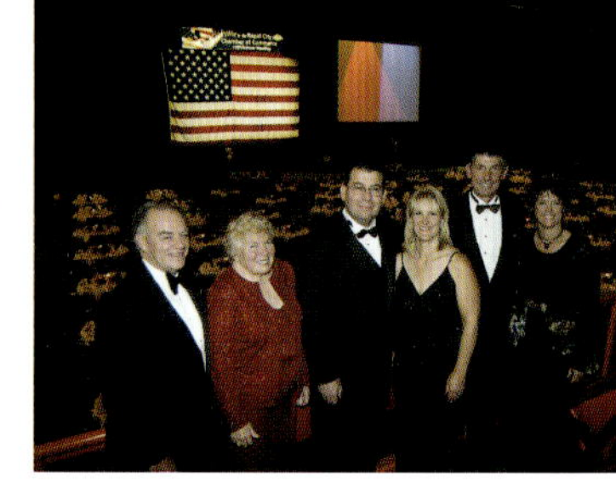

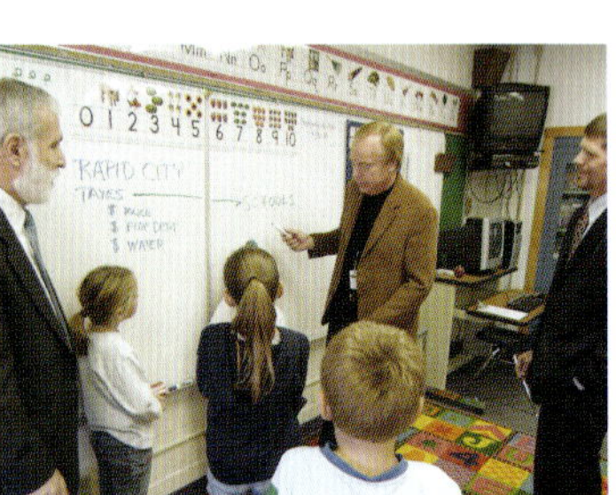

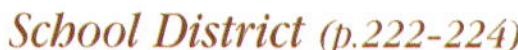

Rapid City Area Schools District
300 6th Street, 3rd Floor
Rapid City, South Dakota 57701
605.394.4031
www.rcas.org

School District (p.222-224)
By promoting excellence among its staff and educators and teaming up with community leaders, Rapid City Area Schools ensures that each student in the district has the best possible chance to reach his or her full academic potential.

Rapid City Regional Airport
4550 Terminal Road
Suite 102
Rapid City, South Dakota 57703
605.394.4195
www.rcgov.org/Airport/pages/

Airport (p.164-165)
Rapid City Regional Airport accommodates the needs of both business and pleasure travelers with a host of on-site amenities and dozens of nonstop flights to six major hubs daily.

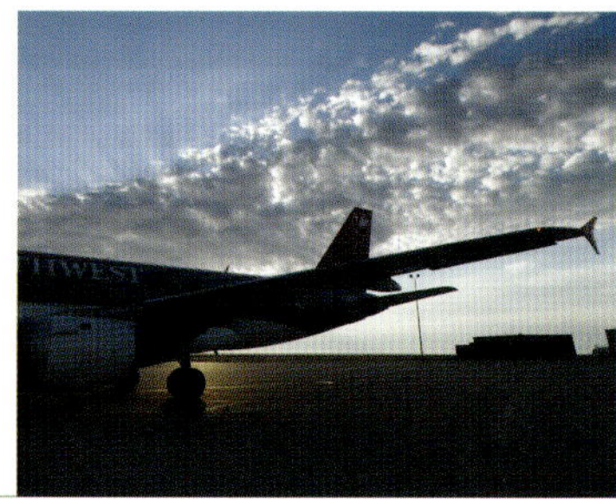

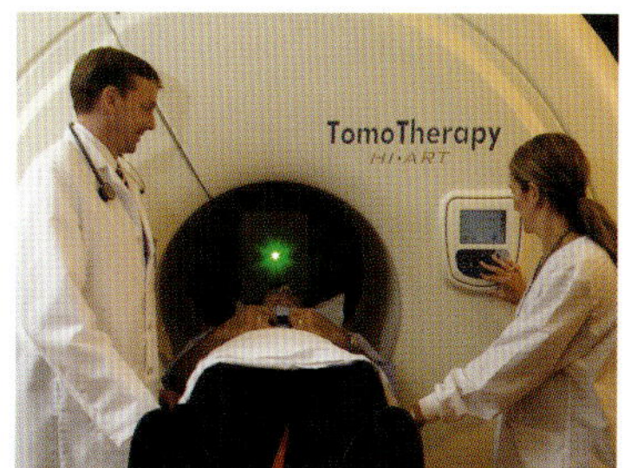

Regional Health
353 Fairmont Boulevard
Rapid City, South Dakota 57701
605.719.1000
www.rcrh.org

Health Care *(p.188-189)*
Working to provide and support health-care excellence in partnership with the communities it serves, Regional Health oversees the performance of more than forty facilities serving western South Dakota, eastern Wyoming, and the panhandle of Nebraska.

Rushmore Plaza Civic Center
444 Mt. Rushmore Road North
Rapid City, South Dakota 57701
605.394.4115
www.rushmore.com

Convention Center *(p.84)*
Rushmore Plaza Civic Center serves a local market of more than three hundred thousand people, as well as a tourist market of more than 3 million visitors a year. As the area's premier entertainment venue, the Civic Center offers events as versatile and dynamic as the Black Hills.

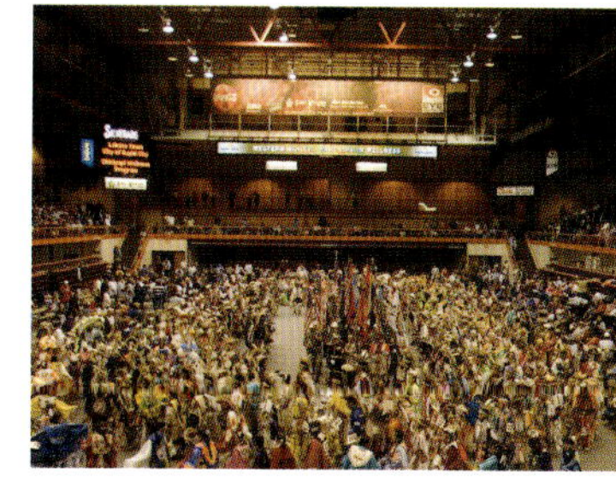

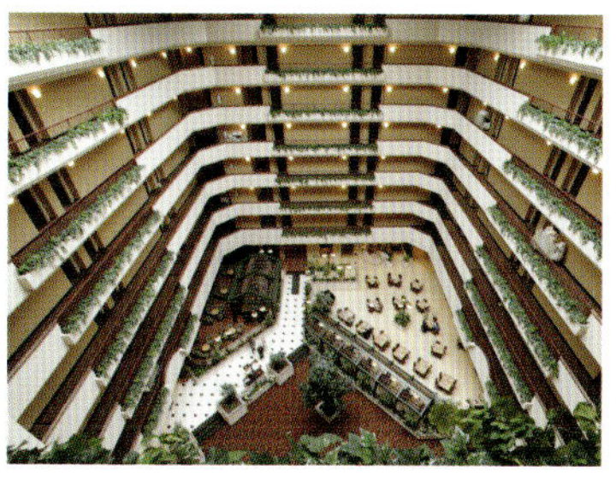

Rushmore Plaza Holiday Inn Hotel & Conference Center
505 North 5th Street
Rapid City, South Dakota 57701
605.348.4000
www.rushmoreplaza.com

Hotel *(p.32-34)*
The 205-room Rushmore Plaza Holiday Inn Hotel and Conference Center sets the standard in the area for superior service and accommodations. Its unique eight-story open-atrium style features cascading waterfalls, lounge, restaurant, and fourteen-thousand-square-foot conference center. The hotel is also located convenient to all the area attractions.

South Dakota School of Mines and Technology
501 East Saint Joseph Street
Rapid City, South Dakota 57701
605.394.2511
www.sdsmt.edu

College *(p.254-255)*
The South Dakota School of Mines and Technology prepares graduates to serve as leaders in the fields of engineering and science. SDSM&T faculty and students also conduct applied research and technology development programs for the benefit of the state and the nation.

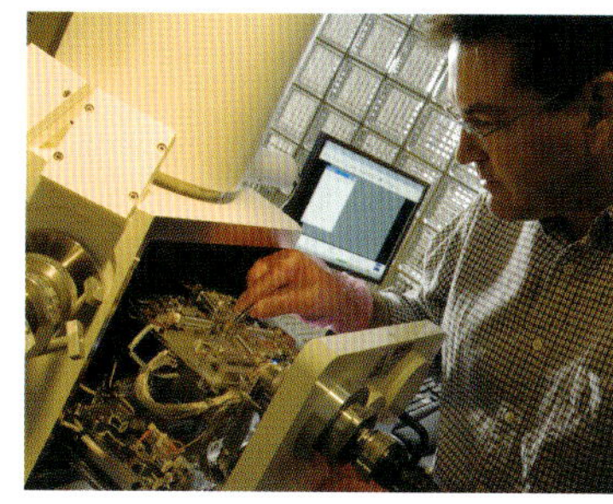

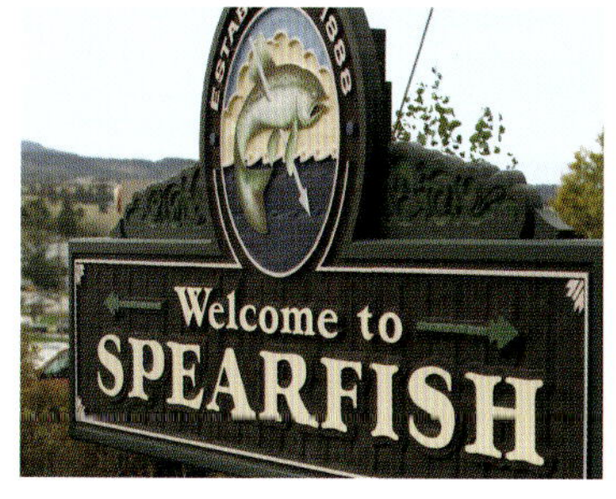

Spearfish Area Chamber of Commerce
106 West Kansas Street
Spearfish, South Dakota 57783
605.642.2626
www.spearfishchamber.org

Chamber of Commerce *(p.46-48)*
The mission of the Spearfish Area Chamber of Commerce is to advance a positive business climate and provide leadership in promotion and managed growth of the community. The chamber provides services to members, as well as information to visitors, community members, and businesses outside the area.

Wells Fargo Bank
825 Saint Joseph Street
Rapid City, South Dakota 57701
605.394.3882
www.wellsfargo.com

Bank *(p.136-138)*
In 1998, Norwest Bank announced a "merger of equals" with Wells Fargo, kept the historic Wells Fargo name, and became the nation's seventh-largest bank and the largest financial institution headquartered in the western United States. Wells Fargo is a financial services company, providing a diversified range of options to serve their customers' financial needs.

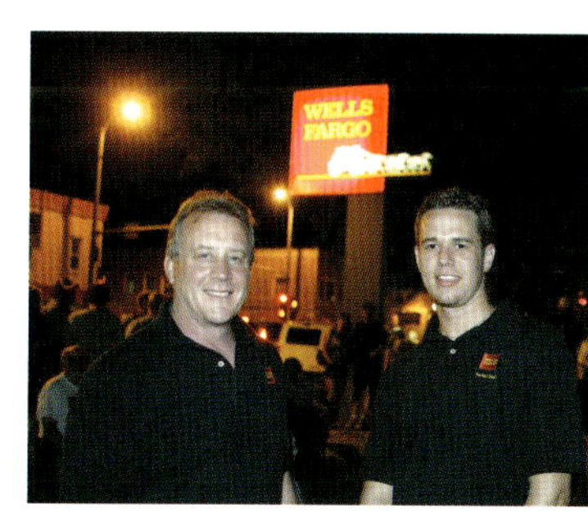

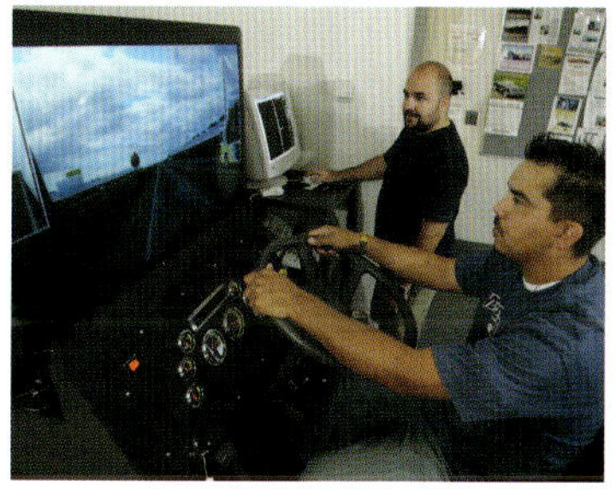

Western Dakota Technical Institute
800 Mickelson Drive
Rapid City, South Dakota 57703
605.394.4034
www.westerndakotatech.org

College—Technical *(p.246-248)*
Western Dakota Technical Institute offers more than twenty-five diploma, certificate, and associate of applied science degree programs in the areas of business, construction trades, health services, human services, and mechanical and manufacturing trades.

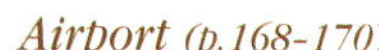

Westjet Air Center
4160 Fire Station Road
Rapid City, South Dakota 57703
605.393.2500
www.westjetair.com

Airport *(p.168-170)*
With over fifty thousand square feet of covered hangar space, Westjet is Rapid City Regional Airport's premier fixed-base operator, specializing in fuel sales, hangar rentals, maintenance, and charter.

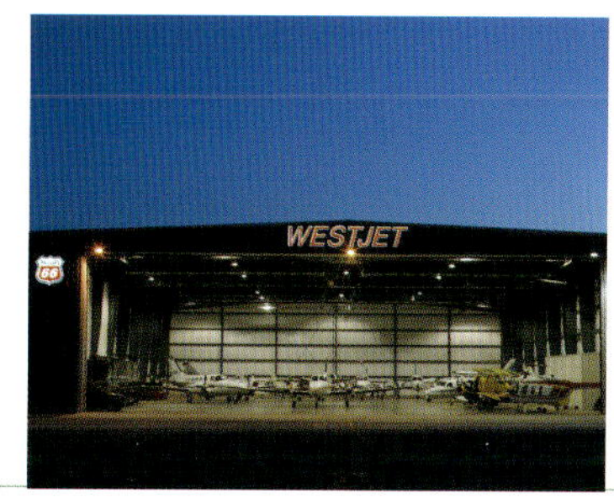

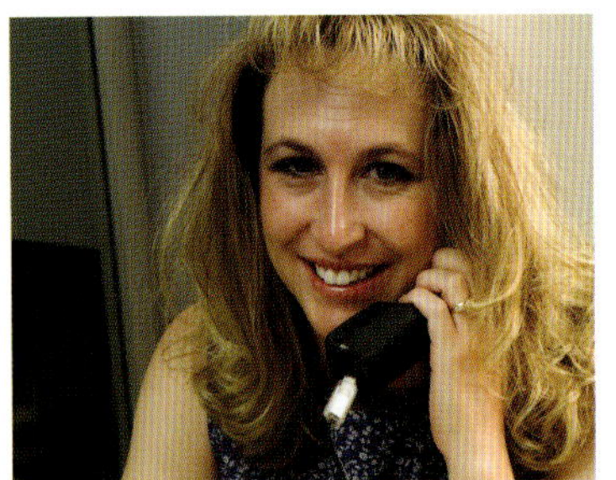

West River Electric
3250 East Highway 44
Rapid City, South Dakota 57703
605.393.1500
www.westriver.com

Utility—Electric (p.132-133)
As the fastest-growing electrical cooperative in South Dakota, West River Electric provides over eleven thousand customers throughout six Black Hills counties with efficient, low-cost electric power and a host of safety and educational services.

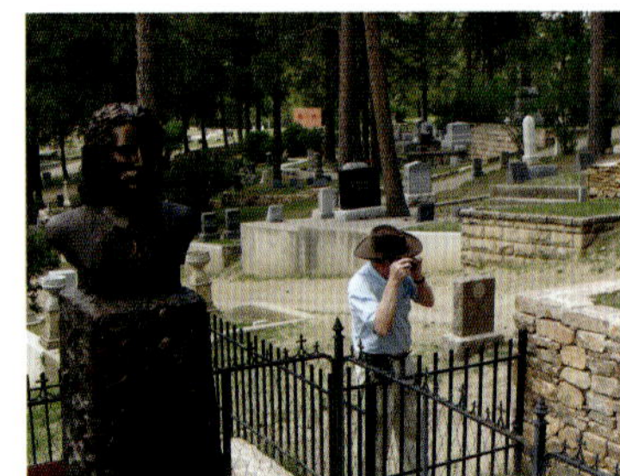

Wyss Associates, Inc.
728 6th Street
Rapid City, South Dakota 57701
605.348.2268
www.wyssassociates.com

Landscape Architect (p.182-183)
Wyss Associates provides services in landscape architecture, golf course architecture, park and recreation design, land planning, resort development, and historic preservation. The firm includes landscape architects, golf course architects, planners, graphic designers, technical staff, and administrative personnel.

About the Publisher

BLACK HILLS: *Beyond All Expectations* was published by Bookhouse Group, Inc., under its imprint of Riverbend Books. What many people don't realize is that in addition to picture books on American communities, we also develop and publish institutional histories, commemorative books of all types, contemporary books, and others for clients across the country.

Bookhouse has developed various types of books for prep schools from Utah to Florida, colleges and universities, country clubs, a phone company in Vermont, a church in Atlanta, hospitals, banks, and many other entities. We've also published a catalog for an art collection for a gallery in Texas, a picture book for a worldwide Christian ministry, and a book on a priceless collection of art and antiques for the Atlanta History Center.

These beautiful and treasured tabletop books are developed by our staff as turnkey projects, thus making life easier for the client. If your company has an interest in our publishing services, do not hesitate to contact us.

Founded in 1989, Bookhouse Group is headquartered in a renovated 1920s tobacco warehouse in downtown Atlanta. If you're ever in town, we'd be delighted if you looked us up. Thank you for making possible the publication of BLACK HILLS: *Beyond All Expectations*. ❖

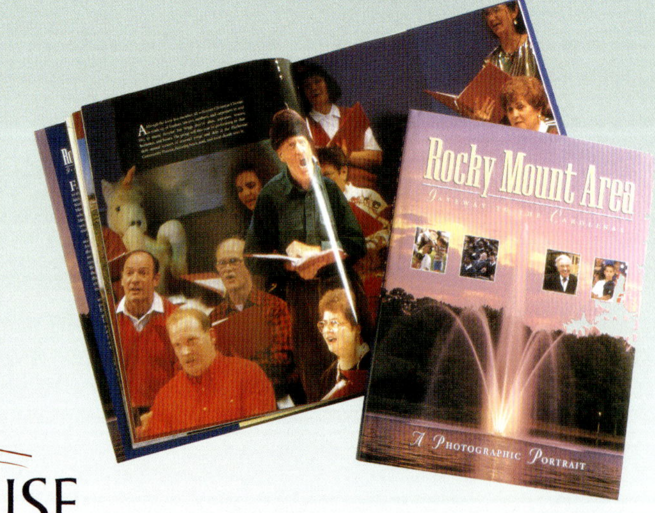

BOOKHOUSE
GROUP, INC.

Banks ❖ Prep Schools ❖ Hospitals ❖ Insurance Companies ❖ Art Galleries ❖ Museums ❖ Utilities ❖ Country Clubs ❖ Colleges ❖ Churches ❖ Military Academies ❖ Associations

Black Hills Editorial Team

Rena Distasio, Writer, Tijeras, New Mexico. Freelance writer Rena Distasio contributes articles and reviews on a variety of subjects to regional and national publications. In her spare time she and her husband and three dogs enjoy the great outdoors from their home in the mountains east of Albuquerque.

Kimberly Fox DeMeza, Writer, Roswell, Georgia. Combining business insight with creative flair, DeMeza writes to engage the audience as well as communicate the nuances of the subject matter. While officially beginning her career in public relations in 1980 with a degree in journalism, and following in 1990 with a master's in health management, writing has always been central to her professional experience. From speechwriting to corporate brochures to business magazine feature writing, DeMeza enjoys the process of crafting the message. Delving into the topic is simply one of the benefits, as she believes every writing opportunity is an opportunity to continue to learn.

Grace Hawthorne, Writer, Atlanta, Georgia. Starting as a reporter, she has written everything from advertising for septic tanks to the libretto for an opera. While in New York, she worked for Time-Life Books and wrote for *Sesame Street*. As a performer, she has appeared at the Carter Presidential Center, Callanwolde Fine Arts Center, and at various corporate functions. Her latest project is a two-woman show called *Pushy Broads and Proper Southern Ladies*.

Regina Roths, Writer, Andover, Kansas. Roths has written extensively about business since launching her journalism career in the early 1990s. Her prose can be found in corporate coffee-table books nationwide as well as on regionally produced Web sites, and in print and online magazines, newspapers, and publications. Her love of industry, history, and research gives her a keen insight into writing and communicating a message.

Thomas S. England, Photographer, Decatur, Georgia. England grew up internationally, graduated from Northwestern University, and began photography as a newspaper photographer in the Chicago area. He began freelancing for *People* magazine in 1974. Since then he has taken assignments from national magazines and corporations, specializing in photographing people on location. He lives in Decatur, Georgia, with Nancy Foster, a home renovator, and their little dog Chessey. More of his photographs may be viewed online at www. england-photo.com.

Eric Francis, Photographer, Omaha, Nebraska. Francis was born and raised in Nebraska. Early on, he honed his skills freelancing for local newspapers, magazines, and commercial clients. Francis now also works regularly for some of the nation's largest and best-known magazines, newspapers, and wire services, covering news, features, and sports. He continues to make his home in Omaha with his son Mitch, his girlfriend Michelle, and her children.

Douglas Henderson, Photographer, Tulsa, Oklahoma. Doug is a commercial photographer and graphic designer. As a professional photographer his work has appeared in *The New York Times*, *Newsweek*, *Newsweek Japan*, *The National Enquirer*, and others. He has worked in the United States, Mexico, South Africa, Ghana, and Côte D'Ivoire. He is the author of several textbooks on digital photography and Adobe Photoshop. See more of his work online at www.douglashenderson.com.

Dennis Keim, Photographer, Huntsville, Alabama. Keim is a local photographer with over twenty-five years of experience producing creative imagery for the editorial, advertising, and corporate communities. His editorial work has been featured in regional, national, and international publications. Notable in his professional career was his employment as an Aerospace Photojournalist by NASA (National Aeronautics and Space Administration) from 1976 to 2000 at the Marshall Space Flight Center. Dennis is a member of ASMP and currently maintains a commercial studio specializing in corporate, editorial, and stock photography. In addition he is an exhibited and published fine arts photographer. You can view more of his work at www.dk-studio.com.

Rodger Slott, Photographer, Rapid City, South Dakota. After graduating Black Hills State University, Slott moved to Dallas, Texas, and began working with Fortune 500 companies through the media group CCG. After five years of extensive training, Slott became a freelancer, shooting for such companies as JC Penney, Dillards, Kimberly-Clark, 7-Up, and many more. Returning home, Slott quickly established himself as a go-to guy for commercial work. Slott now enjoys friends and clients in fields as far ranging as energy, health care, manufacturing, and architecture. For more information call 605.341.2429, and soon at flashbox.biz.

Johnny Sundby, Photographer, Rapid City, South Dakota. Sundby grew up in the Black Hills of South Dakota photographing the varied landscape with his father. After graduating from Augustana College in 1990, Sundby spent seven years as a photojournalist, mostly with the *Rapid City* (SD) *Journal*, before turning to a full-time stock image and portrait career. He has authored three regional coffeetable books and has photographed for over thirty national magazines and newspapers. Sundby's studio and gallery can be found in Rapid City, South Dakota, where he lives with his wife, son, and daughter. More about Sundby and his images can be found at www.johnnysundby.com.

Alan S. Weiner, Photographer, Portland, Oregon. Weiner travels extensively both in the United States and abroad. Over the last twenty-three years his work has appeared regularly in *The New York Times*. In addition, his pictures have been published in USA *Today* and in *Time*, *Newsweek*, *Life*, and *People* magazines. He has shot corporate work for IBM, Pepsi, UPS, and other companies large and small. He is also the cofounder of The Wedding Bureau (www.weddingbureau.com). Alan has worked throughout the Pacific Northwest and the Carolinas on books. His strengths are in photojournalism.

Joleen Zoller, Photographer, Rapid City, South Dakota. Joleen began working in photo labs at the age of seventeen. She graduated from Colorado State University with a bachelor's degree in psychology, and began working with the Larimer County Sheriff's Department in Fort Collins, Colorado, doing crime scene photography and evidence analysis, while also shooting as a freelance wedding photographer. In 1996 she had an opportunity to buy the family award business in Rapid City. She immediately opened her own photography business called Lasting Memories Studio. To see more of her photographs go to www.lastingmemoriesstudio.com.

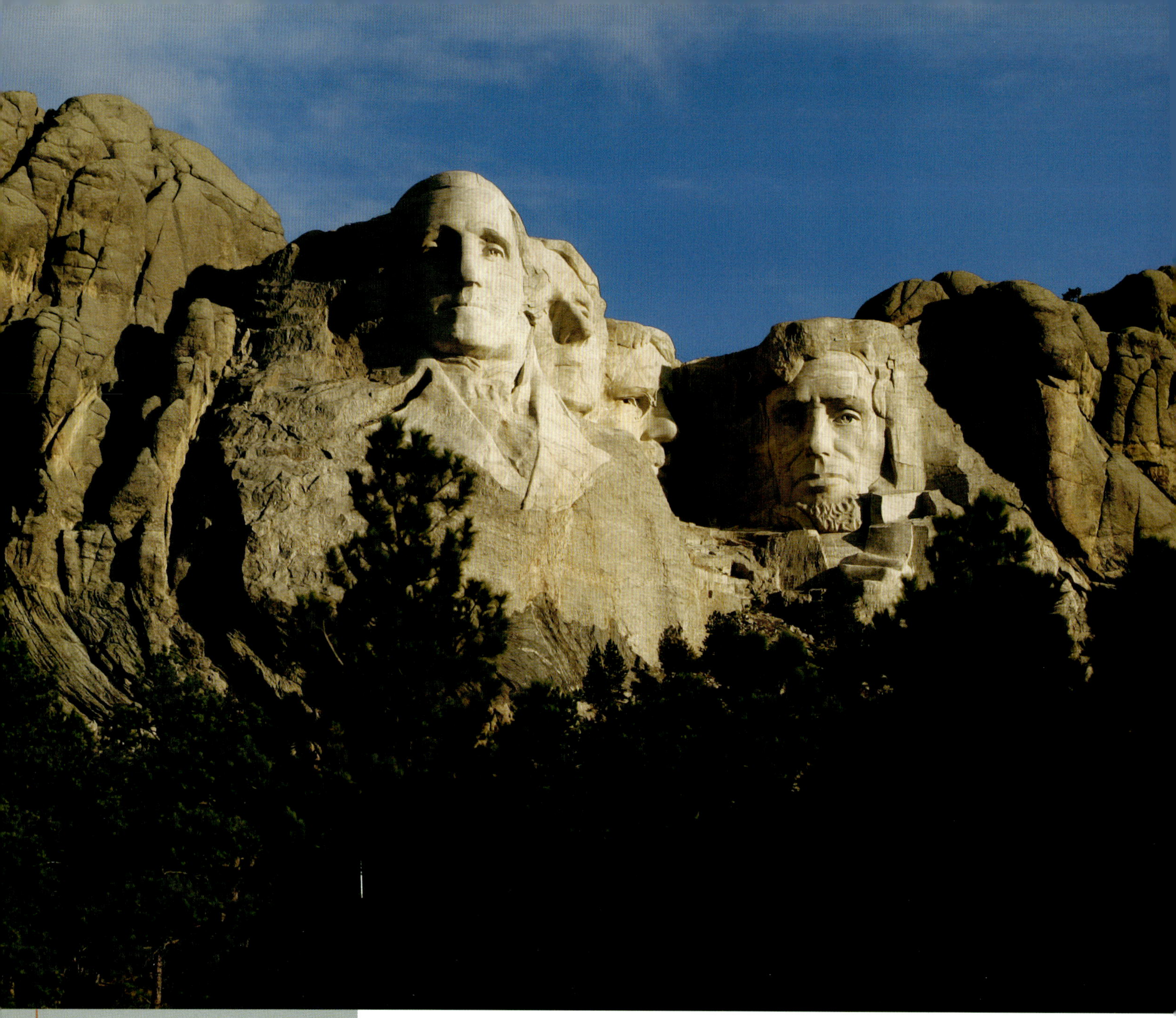

Photo by Eric Francis

In choosing the subject of his monumental carving at Mount Rushmore, sculptor Gutzon Borglum sought to honor America's democratic spirit as revealed in its first 150 years of history. George Washington represents the birth of our nation; Thomas Jefferson, its greatest proponent of a government by and for the people; Abraham Lincoln, its fearless champion of equality and unity; and Theodore Roosevelt, the leader who would guide us in our new role as world power. Work began on the monument in 1927 and continued until Borglum's death in 1941. No carving has been done since, and the monument was finally dedicated in 1991. Although unfinished, Mount Rushmore remains a powerful commemoration of America's highest ideals. ❖